A NEXTEXT ANTHOLOGY

MODERN
WORLD
LITERATURE

nextext

Printed in the United States of America.

ISBN 0-618-00376-2

2 3 4 5 6 7 — QKT — 06 05 04 03 02 01

Modern World Literature

CHAPTER 1: AFRICA

CHAPTER 3: EAST ASIA

CHAPTER 4: SOUTHEAST ASIA AND AUSTRALIA

CHAPTER 5: CANADA AND THE CARIBBEAN

CHAPTER 6: LATIN AMERICA

CHAPTER 7: EUROPE

Throughout the anthology, vocabulary words appear in boldface type and are footnoted. Specialized or technical words and phrases appear in lightface type and are footnoted.

Africa

Have and Have Nots

In Search of Justice

Old Roles in a Changing World

◀ Done in 1991, Tilly Willis's painting captures a characteristic landscape of the Sahel, a semiarid region south of the Sahara Desert in north central Africa.

[handwritten annotations:] Innocence + trust / guide - headthen / gradma - Begs tekeewho Need / guide grandpa

The Ultimate Safari

NADINE GORDIMER

Nadine Gordimer (1923–   ) was the first South African and the first woman from Africa to win the Nobel Prize in literature. "The Ultimate Safari" is from Gordimer's 1991 collection Jump and deals with an attempt to escape the horrors of a civil war. After World War II, it was clear that the European domination of Africa was drawing to a close. Africans were clamoring for self-government, and the European powers were so weakened by the war that maintaining their empires was impossible. The four colonial powers—Britain, France, Portugal, and Belgium—took very different attitudes to decolonization, and many of the colonies were fiercely divided along ethnic lines. Between 1957 and 1975 all the countries of Africa gained their independence; however, in many colonies high hopes dissolved into disaster and civil war. Tribal divisions, dictators, and army coups took a great toll. One of the last countries to gain its independence was Mozambique. It had been engaged in a long struggle for independence from Portugal, and various factions opposed the new government, leading to civil wars that have continued right to the present day. The civilian casualties over the years have been horrific, and vast numbers of refugees have fled the country. "The Ultimate Safari" describes the refugee experience of one family who flee Mozambique for South Africa, a country they are tied to by ancient tribal bonds that predate the national borders. While the story is about Mozambique, Gordimer meant it to be a universal portrayal of the tragedy wrought by civil war.

The African Adventure Lives On . . .
You can do it!
The ultimate safari or expedition
with leaders who <u>know</u> Africa.

—TRAVEL ADVERTISEMENT,
Observer, London, 27/11/88

That night our mother went to the shop and she didn't come back. Ever. What happened? I don't know. My father also had gone away one day and never come back; but he was fighting in the war. We were in the war, too, but we were children, we were like our grandmother and grandfather, we didn't have guns. The people my father was fighting—the bandits, they are called by our government—ran all over the place and we ran away from them like chickens chased by dogs. We didn't know where to go. Our mother went to the shop because someone said you could get some oil for cooking. We were happy because we hadn't tasted oil for a long time; perhaps she got the oil and someone knocked her down in the dark and took that oil from her. Perhaps she met the bandits. If you meet them, they will kill you. Twice they came to our village and we ran and hid in the bush[1] and when they'd gone we came back and found they had taken everything; but the third time they came back there was nothing to take, no oil, no food, so they burned the thatch and the roofs of our houses fell in. My mother found some pieces of tin and we put those up over part of the house. We were waiting there for her that night she never came back.

We were frightened to go out, even to do our business, because the bandits did come. Not into our house—without a roof it must have looked as if there was no one in it, everything gone—but all through the village. We heard people screaming and running. We were afraid even to run, without our mother to tell us where. I am the middle one, the girl, and my little brother clung against my stomach with his arms round my neck and his legs round my waist like a baby monkey to its mother. All night my first-born brother kept in his hand a broken piece of wood from one of our burnt house-poles. It was to save himself if the bandits found him.

We stayed there all day. Waiting for her. I don't know what day it was; there was no school, no church any more in our village, so you didn't know whether it was a Sunday or a Monday.

When the sun was going down, our grandmother and grandfather came. Someone from our village had told them we children were alone, our mother had not come back. I say "grandmother" before "grandfather" because it's like that: our grandmother is big and strong, not yet old, and our grandfather is small, you don't know where he is, in his loose trousers, he smiles but he hasn't heard what you're saying, and his hair looks as if he's left it full of soap suds. Our grandmother took us—me, the baby, my first-born brother, our grandfather—back to her house and we were all afraid (except the baby, asleep on our grandmother's back) of meeting the bandits on the way. We waited a long time at our grandmother's place. Perhaps it was a month. We were hungry. Our mother never came. While we were waiting for her to fetch us our grandmother had no food for us, no food for our grandfather and herself. A woman with milk in her breasts gave us some for my little brother, although at our house he used to eat porridge, same as we did. Our grandmother took us to look for wild spinach but everyone else in her village did the same and there wasn't a leaf left.

Our grandfather, walking a little behind some young men, went to look for our mother but didn't find her. Our grandmother cried with other women and I sang the hymns with them. They brought a little food—some beans—but after two days there was nothing again. Our grandfather

---

[1] bush—a large, sparsely populated, uncleared area.

used to have three sheep and a cow and a vegetable garden but the bandits had long ago taken the sheep and the cow, because they were hungry, too; and when planting time came our grandfather had no seed to plant.

So they decided—our grandmother did; our grandfather made little noises and rocked from side to side, but she took no notice—we would go away. We children were pleased. We wanted to go away from where our mother wasn't and where we were hungry. We wanted to go where there were no bandits and there was food. We were glad to think there must be such a place; away.

> **We wanted to go away from where our mother wasn't and where we were hungry.**

Our grandmother gave her church clothes to someone in exchange for some dried mealies[2] and she boiled them and tied them in a rag. We took them with us when we went and she thought we would get water from the rivers but we didn't come to any river and we got so thirsty we had to turn back. Not all the way to our grandparents' place but to a village where there was a pump. She opened the basket where she carried some clothes and the mealies and she sold her shoes to buy a big plastic container for water. I said, *Gogo*, how will you go to church now even without shoes, but she said we had a long journey and too much to carry. At that village we met other people who were also going away. We

joined them because they seemed to know where that was better than we did.

To get there we had to go through the Kruger Park. We knew about the Kruger Park. A kind of whole country of animals—elephants, lions, jackals, hyenas, hippos, crocodiles, all kinds of animals. We had some of them in our own country, before the war (our grandfather remembers; we children weren't born yet) but the bandits kill the elephants and sell their tusks, and the bandits and our soldiers have eaten all the buck. There was a man in our village without legs—a crocodile took them off, in our river; but all the same our country is a country of people, not animals. We knew about the Kruger Park because some of our men used to leave home to work there in the places where white people come to stay and look at the animals.

So we started to go away again. There were women and other children like me who had to carry the small ones on their backs when the women got tired. A man led us into the Kruger Park; are we there yet, are we there yet, I kept asking our grandmother. Not yet, the man said, when she asked him for me. He told us we had to take a long way to get round the fence, which he explained would kill you, roast off your skin the moment you touched it, like the wires high up on poles that give electric light in our towns. I've seen that sign of a head without eyes or skin or hair on an iron box at the mission hospital we used to have before it was blown up.

---

[2] mealies—word used for ears of corn in South Africa.

When I asked the next time, they said we'd been walking in the Kruger Park for an hour. But it looked just like the bush we'd been walking through all day, and we hadn't seen any animals except the monkeys and birds which live around us at home, and a tortoise that, of course, couldn't get away from us. My first-born brother and the other boys brought it to the man so it could be killed and we could cook and eat it. He let it go because he told us we could not make a fire; all the time we were in the Park we must not make a fire because the smoke would show we were there. Police, wardens, would come and send us back where we came from. He said we must move like animals among the animals, away from the roads, away from the white people's camps. And at that moment I heard—I'm sure I was the first to hear—cracking branches and the sound of something parting grasses and I almost squealed because I thought it was the police, wardens —the people he was telling us to look out for—who had found us already. And it was an elephant, and another elephant, and more elephants, big blots of dark moved wherever you looked between the trees. They were curling their trunks round the red leaves of the Mopane trees and stuffing them into their mouths. The babies leant against their mothers. The almost grown-up ones wrestled like my first-born brother with his friends— only they used trunks instead of arms. I was so interested I forgot to be afraid. The man said we should just stand still and be quiet while the elephants passed. They passed very slowly because elephants are too big to need to run from anyone.

The buck ran from us. They jumped so high they seemed to fly. The warthogs stopped dead, when they heard us, and swerved off the way a boy in our village used to zigzag on the bicycle his father had brought back from the mines. We followed the animals to where they drank. When they had gone, we went to their water-holes. We were never thirsty without finding water, but the animals ate, ate all the time. Whenever you saw them they were eating, grass, trees, roots. And there was nothing for us. The mealies were finished. The only food we could eat was what the baboons ate, dry little figs full of ants that grow along the branches of the trees at the rivers. It was hard to be like the animals.

When it was very hot during the day we would find lions lying asleep. They were the color of the grass and we didn't see them at first but the man did, and he led us back and a long way round where they slept. I wanted to lie down like the lions. My little brother was getting thin but he was very heavy. When our grandmother looked for me, to put him on my back, I tried not to see. My first-born brother stopped talking; and when we rested he had to be shaken to get up again, as if he was just like our grandfather, he couldn't hear. I saw flies crawling on our grandmother's face and she didn't brush them off; I was frightened. I picked a palm leaf and chased them.

We walked at night as well as by day. We could see the fires where the white people were cooking in the camps and we could smell the smoke and the meat. We watched the hyenas with their backs that slope as if they're ashamed, slipping through the bush after the smell. If one turned its head, you saw it had big brown shining eyes like our own, when we looked at each other in the dark. The wind brought voices in our own language from the compounds where the people who work in the camps live. A woman among us wanted to go to them at night and ask them to help us. They can give us the food from the dustbins, she said, she started wailing and our grandmother had to grab her and put a hand over her mouth. The man who led us had told us that we must keep out of the way of our people who worked at the Kruger Park; if they helped us they would lose their work. If they saw us, all they could do was pretend we were not there; they had seen only animals.

Sometimes we stopped to sleep for a little while at night. We slept close together. I don't know which night it was, because— we were walking, walking, any time, all the time—we heard the lions very near. Not groaning loudly the way they did far off. Panting, like we do when we run, but it's a different kind of panting: you can hear they're not running, they're waiting, somewhere near. We all rolled closer together, on top of each other, the ones on the edge fighting to get into the middle. I was squashed against a woman who smelled bad because she was afraid but I was glad to hold tight on to her. I prayed to God to make the lions take someone on the edge and go. I shut my eyes not to see the tree from which a lion might jump right into the middle of us, where I was.

The man who led us jumped up instead, and beat on the tree with a dead branch. He had taught us never to make a sound but he shouted. He shouted at the lions like a drunk man shouting at nobody, in our village. The lions went away. We heard them groaning, shouting back at him from far off.

We were tired, so tired. My first-born brother and the man had to lift our grandfather from stone to stone where we found places to cross the rivers. Our grandmother is strong but her feet were bleeding. We could not carry the basket on our heads any longer, we couldn't carry anything except my little brother. We left our things under a bush. As long as our bodies get there, our grandmother said. Then we ate some wild fruit we didn't know from home and our stomachs ran. We were in the grass called elephant grass because it is nearly as tall as an elephant, that day we had those pains, and our grandfather couldn't just get down in front of people like my little brother, he went off into the grass to be on his own. We had to keep up, the man who led us always kept telling us, we must catch up, but we asked him to wait for our grandfather.

So everyone waited for our grandfather to catch up. But he didn't. It was the middle of the day; insects were singing in our ears and we couldn't hear him moving through the grass. We couldn't see him because the grass was so high and he was so small. But he must have been some- where there inside his loose trousers and his shirt that was torn and our grandmother couldn't sew because she had no cotton. We knew he couldn't have gone far because he was weak and slow. We all went to look for him, but in groups, so we too wouldn't be hidden from each other in that grass. It got into our eyes and noses; we called him softly but the noise of the insects must have filled the little space left for hearing in his ears. We looked and looked but we couldn't find him. We stayed in that long grass all night. In my sleep I found him curled round in a place he had tramped down for himself, like the places we'd seen where the buck hide their babies.

When I woke up he still wasn't any-where. So we looked again, and by now there were paths we'd made by going through the grass many times, it would be easy for him to find us if we couldn't find him. All that day we just sat and waited. Everything is very quiet when the sun is on your head, inside your head, even if you lie, like the animals, under the trees. I lay on my back and saw those ugly birds with hooked beaks and **plucked**[3] necks flying round and round above us. We had passed them often where they were feeding on the bones of dead animals, nothing was ever left there for us to eat. Round and round, high up and then lower down and then high again. I saw their necks poking to this side and that. Flying round and round. I saw our grandmother, who sat up all the time with my little brother on her lap, was seeing them, too.

In the afternoon the man who led us came to our grandmother and told her the other people must move on. He said, If their children don't eat soon they will die.

Our grandmother said nothing.

I'll bring you water before we go, he told her.

Our grandmother looked at us, me, my first-born brother, and my little brother on her lap. We watched the other people getting up to leave. I didn't believe the grass would be empty, all around us, where they had been. That we would be alone in this place, the Kruger Park, the police or the animals would find us. Tears came out of my eyes and nose onto my hands but our grandmother took no notice. She got up, with her feet apart the way she puts them when she is going to lift firewood, at home in our village, she swung my little brother onto her back, tied him in her cloth—the top of her dress was torn and her big breasts were showing but there was nothing in them for him. She said, Come.

So we left the place with the long grass. Left behind. We went with the others and the man who led us. We started to go away, again.

There's a very big tent, bigger than a church or a school, tied down to the ground. I didn't understand that was what it would be, when we got there, away. I saw a thing like that the time our mother took us to the town because she heard our soldiers were there and she wanted to ask them if they knew where our father was. In that tent, people were praying and singing.

---

[3] **plucked**—featherless.

This one is blue and white like that one but it's not for praying and singing, we live in it with other people who've come from our country. Sister from the clinic says we're two hundred without counting the babies, and we have new babies, some were born on the way through the Kruger Park.

Inside, even when the sun is bright it's dark and there's a kind of whole village in there. Instead of houses each family has a little place closed off with sacks or cardboard from boxes—whatever we can find—to show the other families it's yours and they shouldn't come in even though there's no door and no windows and no thatch,[4] so that if you're standing up and you're not a small child you can see into everybody's house. Some people have even made paint from ground rocks and drawn designs on the sacks.

Of course, there really is a roof—the tent is the roof, far, high up. It's like a sky. It's like a mountain and we're inside it; through the cracks paths of dust lead down, so thick you think you could climb them. The tent keeps off the rain overhead but the water comes in at the sides and in the little streets between our places—you can only move along them one person at a time—the small kids like my little brother play in the mud. You have to step over them. My little brother doesn't play. Our grandmother takes him to the clinic when the doctor comes on Mondays. Sister says there's something wrong with his head, she thinks it's because we didn't have enough food at home. Because of the war. Because our father wasn't there. And then

because he was so hungry in the Kruger Park. He likes just to lie about on our grandmother all day, on her lap or against her somewhere, and he looks at us and looks at us. He wants to ask something but you can see he can't. If I tickle him he may just smile. The clinic gives us special powder to make into porridge for him and perhaps one day he'll be all right.

When we arrived we were like him— my first-born brother and I. I can hardly remember. The people who live in the village near the tent took us to the clinic, it's where you have to sign that you've come—away, through the Kruger Park. We sat on the grass and everything was muddled.[5] One Sister was pretty with her hair straightened and beautiful high-heeled shoes and she brought us the special powder. She said we must mix it with water and drink it slowly. We tore the packets open with our teeth and licked it all up, it stuck round my mouth and I sucked it from my lips and fingers. Some other children who had walked with us vomited. But I only felt everything in my belly moving, the stuff going down and around like a snake, and hiccups hurt me. Another Sister called us to stand in line on the verandah[6] of the clinic but we couldn't. We sat all over the place there, falling against each other; the Sisters helped each of us up

---

[4] **thatch**—roof covering, usually made of a material such as straw or leaves.

[5] **muddled**—confused.

[6] **verandah**—a porch, usually roofed and partially enclosed.

by the arm and then stuck a needle in it. Other needles drew our blood into tiny bottles. This was against sickness, but I didn't understand, every time my eyes dropped closed I thought I was walking, the grass was long, I saw the elephants, I didn't know we were away.

But our grandmother was still strong, she could still stand up, she knows how to write and she signed for us. Our grandmother got us this place in the tent against one of the sides, it's the best kind of place there because although the rain comes in, we can lift the flap when the weather is good and then the sun shines on us, the smells in the tent go out. Our grandmother knows a woman here who showed her where there is good grass for sleeping mats, and our grandmother made some for us. Once every month the food truck comes to the clinic. Our grandmother takes along one of the cards she signed and when it has been punched we get a sack of mealie meal. There are wheelbarrows to take it back to the tent; my first-born brother does this for her and then he and the other boys have races, steering the empty wheelbarrows back to the clinic. Sometimes he's lucky and a man who's bought beer in the village gives him money to deliver it—though that's not allowed, you're supposed to take that wheelbarrow straight back to the Sisters. He buys a cold drink and shares it with me if I catch him. On another day, every month, the church leaves a pile of old clothes in the clinic yard. Our grandmother has another card to get punched, and then we can choose

something: I have two dresses, two pants and a jersey, so I can go to school.

The people in the village have let us join their school. I was surprised to find they speak our language; our grandmother told me, That's why they allow us to stay on their land. Long ago, in the time of our fathers, there was no fence that kills you, there was no Kruger Park between them and us, we were the same people under our own king, right from our village we left to this place we've come to.

Now that we've been in the tent so long—I have turned eleven and my little brother is nearly three although he is so small, only his head is big, he's not come right in it yet—some people have dug up the bare ground around the tent and planted beans and mealies and cabbage. The old men weave branches to put up fences round their gardens. No one is allowed to look for work in the towns but some of the women have found work in the village and can buy things. Our grandmother, because she's still strong, finds work where people are building houses—in this village the people build nice houses with bricks and cement, not mud like we used to have at our home. Our grandmother carries bricks for these people and fetches baskets of stones on her head. And so she has money to buy sugar and tea and milk and soap. The store gave her a calendar she has hung up on our flap of the tent. I am clever at school and she collected advertising paper people throw away outside the store and covered my schoolbooks with it. She makes my first-born brother and me do our homework every afternoon before it gets dark because there is no room except to lie down, close together, just as we did in the Kruger Park, in our place in the tent, and candles are expensive. Our grandmother hasn't been able to buy herself a pair of shoes for church yet, but she has bought black school shoes and polish to clean them with for my first-born brother and me. Every morning, when people are getting up in the tent, the babies are crying, people are pushing each other at the taps outside and some children are already pulling the crusts of porridge off the pots we ate from last night, my first-born brother and I clean our shoes. Our grandmother makes us sit on our mats with our legs straight out so she can look carefully at our shoes to make sure we have done it properly. No other children in the tent have real school shoes. When we three look at them it's as if we are in a real house again, with no war, no away.

Some white people came to take photographs of our people living in the tent—they said they were making a film, I've never seen what that is though I know about it. A white woman squeezed into our space and asked our grandmother questions which were told to us in our language by someone who understands the white woman's.

How long have you been living like this?
She means here? our grandmother said. In this tent, two years and one month.
And what do you hope for the future?
Nothing. I'm here.
But for your children?
I want them to learn so that they can get good jobs and money.

Do you hope to go back to Mozambique—to your own country?
I will not go back.
But when the war is over—you won't be allowed to stay here? Don't you want to go home?
I didn't think our grandmother wanted to speak again. I didn't think she was going to answer the white woman. The white woman put her head on one side and smiled at us.
Our grandmother looked away from her and spoke—There is nothing. No home.
Why does our grandmother say that? Why? I'll go back. I'll go back through that Kruger Park. After the war, if there are no bandits any more, our mother may be waiting for us. And maybe when we left our grandfather, he was only left behind, he found his way somehow, slowly, through the Kruger Park, and he'll be there. They'll be home, and I'll remember them.

QUESTIONS TO CONSIDER

1. Why does the family make the safari referred to in the title?

2. How does the young narrator's understanding of the situation differ from what you can infer about what was actually occurring?

3. How would you describe the tone of "The Ultimate Safari?" What is its message? What does Gordimer hope her Western audience will understand?

The Prisoner Who Wore Glasses

BESSIE HEAD

Bessie Head (1937–1986) was born into tragedy in South Africa. Her father was a black stable hand; her mother was the daughter of white immigrants from England. When they learned of the pregnancy and the father's identity, they placed Head's mother in an asylum for the insane. Bessie Head was assigned the racial status "colored" by the South African government, and her mother committed suicide when Head was one year old. She was raised by a poor family in Capetown, eventually becoming a teacher and journalist. The South Africa that Head knew was dominated by apartheid. In 1948, the Afrikaner Nationalists came to power and passed a series of laws designed to ensure the continued rule of whites. Called apartheid (the Afrikaans word for "separate"), the laws ruthlessly prevented all nonwhites from participating in political life, living in all but certain areas, traveling freely, owning land, or working at most nonmenial jobs. Black South Africans were defined as belonging to one tribe or another and ruthlessly kept in designated homelands where it was often impossible to grow food or make a living. Due to political pressure, Head eventually emigrated to Botswana. She considered herself an exile, both spiritually and physically. Head's racial status divided her from both the white and black communities. Her writing became a search for identity and a testament to the absolute horrors of racism. "The Prisoner Who Wore Glasses" is from her collection of short stories The Collector of Treasures *(1977) and is based on a real event.*

Scarcely a breath of wind disturbed the stillness of the day, and the long rows of cabbages were bright green in the sunlight. Large white clouds drifted slowly across the deep blue sky. Now and then they obscured the sun and caused a chill on the backs of the prisoners who had to work all day long in the cabbage field.

This trick the clouds were playing with the sun eventually caused one of the prisoners who wore glasses to stop work, straighten up and peer short-sightedly at them. He was a thin little fellow with a hollowed-out chest and comic knobbly knees. He also had a lot of fanciful ideas because he smiled at the clouds.

"Perhaps they want me to send a message to the children," he thought tenderly, noting that the clouds were drifting in the direction of his home some hundred miles away. But before he could frame the message, the **warder**[1] in charge of his work span[2] shouted:

---

[1] **warder**—official.

[2] work span—a group of workers in the prison.

"Hey, what you tink you're doing, Brille?"

The prisoner swung round, blinking rapidly, yet at the same time sizing up the enemy. He was a new warder, named Jacobus Stephanus Hannetjie. His eyes were the color of the sky but they were frightening. A simple, primitive, brutal soul gazed out of them. The prisoner bent down quickly and a message was quietly passed down the line:

> As political prisoners they were unlike the other prisoners in the sense that they felt no guilt nor were they outcasts of society.

"We're in for trouble this time, comrades."

"Why?" rippled back up the line.

"Because he's not human," the reply rippled down, and yet only the crunching of the spades[3] as they turned over the earth disturbed the stillness.

This particular work span was known as Span One. It was composed of ten men, and they were all political prisoners. They were grouped together for convenience, as it was one of the prison regulations that no black warder should be in charge of a political prisoner lest[4] this prisoner convert him to his views. It never seemed to occur to the authorities that this very reasoning was the strength of Span One and a clue to the strange terror they aroused in the warders. As political prisoners they were unlike the other prisoners in the sense that they felt no guilt nor were they outcasts[5] of society. All guilty men instinctively cower,[6] which was why it was the kind of prison where men got knocked out cold with a blow at the back of the head from an iron bar. Up until the arrival of Warder Hannetjie, no warder had dared beat any member of Span One and no warder had lasted more than a week with them. The battle was entirely psychological. Span One was assertive and it was beyond the scope[7] of white warders to handle assertive black men. Thus, Span One had got out of control. They were the best thieves and liars in the camp. They lived all day on raw cabbages. They chatted and smoked tobacco. And since they moved, thought and acted as one, they had perfected every technique of group concealment.

Trouble began that very day between Span One and Warder Hannetjie. It was because of the shortsightedness of Brille. That was the nickname he was given in prison and is the Afrikaans word for someone who wears glasses. Brille could never judge the approach of the prison gates, and on several previous occasions he had munched on cabbages and dropped them almost at the feet of the warder, and all previous warders had overlooked this. Not so Warder Hannetjie.

---

[3] **spades**—shovels, tools for digging.

[4] **lest**—for fear that.

[5] **outcasts**—people who are thrown out of or ignored by a group.

[6] **cower**—crouch or shrink from fear.

[7] **scope**—abilities.

"Who dropped that cabbage?" he thundered.

Brille stepped out of line. "I did," he said **meekly**.[8]

"All right," said Hannetjie. "The whole span goes three meals off."

"But I told you I did it," Brille protested.

The blood rushed to Warder Hannetjie's face, "Look 'ere," he said.

"I don't take orders from a kaffir.[9] I don't know what kind of kaffir you tink you are. Why don't you say Baas.[10] I'm your Baas. Why don't you say Baas, hey?"

Brille blinked his eyes rapidly but by contrast his voice was strangely calm.

"I'm twenty years older than you," he said. It was the first thing that came to mind, but the comrades seemed to think it a huge joke. A **titter**[11] swept up the line. The next thing Warder Hannetjie whipped out a knobkerrie[12] and gave Brille several blows about the head. What surprised his comrades was the speed with which Brille had removed his glasses or else they would have been smashed to pieces on the ground.

That evening in the cell Brille was very apologetic.

"I'm sorry, comrades," he said. "I've put you into a hell of a mess."

"Never mind, brother," they said. "What happens to one of us, happens to all."

"I'll try to make up for it, comrades," he said. "I'll steal something so that you don't go hungry."

Privately, Brille was very philosophical about his head wounds. It was the first time an act of violence had been **perpetrated**[13] against him, but he had long been a witness of extreme, almost unbelievable human brutality. He had twelve children and his mind traveled back that evening through the sixteen years of **bedlam**[14] in which he had lived. It had all happened in a small drab little three-bedroomed house in a small drab little street in the Eastern Cape, and the children kept coming year after year because neither he nor Martha managed the contraceptives the right way and a teacher's salary never allowed moving to a bigger house and he was always taking exams to improve this salary only to have it all eaten up by hungry mouths. Everything was pretty horrible, especially the way the children fought. They'd get hold of each other's heads and give them a good bashing against the wall. Martha gave up somewhere along the line, so they worked out a thing between them. The bashings, biting and blood were to operate in full swing until he came home. He was to be the bogeyman,[15] and when it worked he never failed to have a sense of godhead[16] at the way in which his presence could change savages into fairly reasonable human beings.

---

[8] **meekly**—submissively and without spirit.

[9] kaffir—insulting term for a black in South Africa.

[10] Baas—Afrikaans word for "master."

[11] **titter**—giggle.

[12] knobkerrie—a short club.

[13] **perpetrated**—committed.

[14] **bedlam**—scene of violent disturbance.

[15] bogeyman—a person who causes fear or difficulty.

[16] godhead—the state of being a god.

Yet somehow it was this **chaos**[17] and mismanagement at the center of his life that drove him into politics. It was really an ordered beautiful world with just a few basic slogans to learn along with the rights of mankind. At one stage, before things became very bad, there were conferences to attend, all very far away from home.

"Let's face it," he thought **ruefully**.[18] "I'm only learning right now what it means to be a politician. All this while I've been running away from Martha and the kids."

And the pain in his head brought a hard lump to his throat. That was what the children did to each other daily and Martha wasn't managing, and if Warder Hannetjie had not interrupted him that morning, he would have sent the following message:

"Be good comrades, my children. Cooperate, then life will run smoothly."

The next day Warder Hannetjie caught this old man with twelve children stealing grapes from the farm shed. They were an enormous quantity of grapes in a ten-gallon tin, and for this **misdeed**[19] the old man spent a week in the isolation cell. In fact, Span One as a whole was in constant trouble. Warder Hannetjie seemed to have eyes at the back of his head. He uncovered the trick about the cabbages; how they were split in two with the spade and immediately covered with earth and then unearthed again and eaten with split-second timing. He found out how tobacco smoke was beaten into the ground, and he found out how conversations were whispered down the wind.

For about two weeks Span One lived in **acute**[20] misery. The cabbages, tobacco and conversations had been the **pivot**[21] of jail life to them. Then one evening they noticed that their good old comrade who wore the glasses was looking rather pleased with himself. He pulled out a four-ounce packet of tobacco by way of explanation, and the comrades fell upon it with great greed. Brille merely smiled. After all, he was the father of many children. But when the last shred had disappeared, it occurred to the comrades that they ought to be puzzled. Someone said:

"I say, brother. We're watched like hawks these days. Where did you get the tobacco?"

"Hannetjie gave it to me," said Brille.

There was a long silence. Into it dropped a quiet bombshell.

"I saw Hannetjie in the shed today," and the failing eyesight blinked rapidly. "I caught him in the act of stealing five bags of fertilizer, and he bribed me to keep my mouth shut."

There was another long silence.

"Prison is an evil life," Brille continued, apparently discussing some **irrelevant**[22] matter. "It makes a man contemplate all kinds of evil deeds."

He held out his hand and closed it.

---

[17] **chaos**—confusion.

[18] **ruefully**—with great sadness.

[19] **misdeed**—crime, wrong action.

[20] **acute**—severe or sharp.

[21] **pivot**—most important part.

[22] **irrelevant**—having nothing to do with a topic or concern.

"You know, comrades," he said. "I've got Hannetjie. I'll betray him tomorrow."

Everyone began talking at once.

"Forget it, brother. You'll get shot." Brille laughed.

"I won't," he said. "That is what I mean about evil. I am a father of children, and I saw today that Hannetjie is just a child and stupidly truthful. I'm going to punish him severely because we need a good warder."

The following day, with Brille as witness, Hannetjie confessed to the theft of the fertilizer and was fined a large sum of money. From then on Span One did very much as they pleased while Warder Hannetjie stood by and said nothing. But it was Brille who carried this to extremes. One day, at the close of work Warder Hannetjie said:

"Brille, pick up my jacket and carry it back to the camp."

"But nothing in the regulations says I'm your servant, Hannetjie," Brille replied coolly.

"I've told you not to call me Hannetjie. You must say Baas," but Warder Hannetjie's voice lacked **conviction**.[23] In turn, Brille squinted up at him.

"I'll tell you something about this Baas business, Hannetjie," he said. "One of these days we are going to run the country. You are going to clean my car. Now, I have a fifteen-year-old son, and I'd die of shame if you had to tell him that I ever called you Baas."

Warder Hannetjie went red in the face and picked up his coat.

On another occasion Brille was seen to be walking about the prison yard, openly smoking tobacco. On being taken before the prison commander he claimed to have received the tobacco from Warder Hannetjie. All throughout the **tirade**[24] from his chief, Warder Hannetjie failed to defend himself, but his nerve broke completely. He called Brille to one side.

> *"One of these days we are going to run the country. You are going to clean my car."*

"Brille," he said. "This thing between you and me must end. You may not know it, but I have a wife and children, and you're driving me to suicide."

"Why don't you like your own medicine, Hannetjie?" Brille asked quietly.

"I can give you anything you want," Warder Hannetjie said in desperation.

"It's not only me but the whole of Span One," said Brille cunningly. "The whole of Span One wants something from you."

Warder Hannetjie brightened with relief.

"I tink I can manage if it's tobacco you want," he said.

Brille looked at him, for the first time struck with pity and guilt. He wondered if he had carried the whole business too far. The man was really a child.

---

[23] **conviction**—a strong belief or opinion.

[24] **tirade**—a long passionate speech, often a criticism or condemnation.

"It's not tobacco we want, but you," he said. "We want you on our side. We want a good warder because without a good warder we won't be able to manage the long stretch ahead."

Warder Hannetjie interpreted this request in his own fashion, and his interpretation of what was good and human often left the prisoners of Span One speechless with surprise. He had a way of slipping off his revolver and picking up a spade and digging alongside Span One. He had a way of producing unheard-of luxuries like boiled eggs from his farm nearby and things like cigarettes, and Span One responded nobly and got the reputation of being the best work span in the camp. And it wasn't only taken from their side. They were awfully good at stealing commodities[25] like fertilizer which were needed on the farm of Warder Hannetjie.

---

[25] **commodities**—things of value.

QUESTIONS TO CONSIDER

1. Why have the men in Span One been imprisoned?

2. What does politics mean to Brille? How do his actions in prison reflect his beliefs?

3. Does the story end on an optimistic or a pessimistic note concerning the future of South Africa? Explain your answer.

Two Poems

GABRIEL OKARA

Gabriel Okara (1921–   ) was born in what is now the western part of Nigeria while it was still a British colony. A member of the Ijaw people, one of Nigeria's smaller tribes, Okara has done much to perpetuate Ijaw culture and make it accessible to the world. His poetry is an eloquent testament to the independence and artistic merit of Nigeria's many cultures and to the development of a truly African literature. The following two poems both testify to Okara's deep belief in the spirit of Africa and Africans.

The Snow Flakes Sail Gently Down

The snow flakes sail gently
down from the misty eye of the sky
and fall lightly lightly on the
winter-weary elms. And the branches,
winter-stripped and nude, slowly
with the weight of the weightless snow
bow like grief-stricken mourners
as white funeral cloth is slowly
unrolled over deathless earth.
And dead sleep stealthily from the
heater rose and closed my eyes with
the touch of silk cotton on water falling.

Then I dreamed a dream
in my dead sleep. But I dreamed
not of earth dying and elms a vigil
keeping. I dreamed of birds, black
birds flying in my inside, nesting
and hatching on oil palms bearing suns
for fruits and with roots denting the
uprooters' spades. And I dreamed the
uprooters tired and limp, leaning on my roots—
their abandoned roots—
and the oil palms gave them each a sun.

But on their palms
they balanced the blinding orbs
and frowned with schisms[1] on their
brows—for the suns reached not
the brightness of gold!
Then I awoke. I awoke
to the silently falling snow
and bent-backed elms bowing and
swaying to the winter wind like
white-robed Moslems salaaming[2] at evening
prayer, and the earth lying **inscrutable**[3]
like the face of a god in a **shrine.**[4]

---

[1] schisms—furrows or grooves.

[2] salaaming—bowing low, often with the palm of the right hand placed against the forehead.

[3] **inscrutable**—not capable of being investigated or analyzed, mysterious.

[4] **shrine**—a structure or place devoted to a god or holy person as a place of worship.

You Laughed and Laughed and Laughed

In your ears my song
is motor car misfiring
stopping with a choking cough;
and you laughed and laughed and laughed.

In your eyes my ante-
natal[5] walk was inhuman passing
your "omnivorous understanding"
and you laughed and laughed and laughed.

You laughed at my song
You laughed at my walk.

Then I danced my magic dance
to the rhythm of talking-
drums pleading, but you shut your
eyes and laughed and laughed and laughed.

And then I opened my mystic
inside wide like
the sky, instead you entered your
car and laughed and laughed and laughed.

You laughed at my dance
You laughed at my inside.

You laughed and laughed and laughed.

But your laughter was ice-block
laughter and it froze your inside froze
your voice froze your ears
froze your eyes and froze your tongue.

---

[5] **natal**—related to a person's birth.

And now it's my turn to laugh;

but my laughter is not ice-block
ice-block laughter. For I
know not cars, know not ice-blocks.

My laughter is the fire

of the eye of the sky, the fire
of the earth, the fire of the air
the fire of the seas and the
rivers fishes animals trees
and it thawed your inside,
thawed your voice, thawed your
ears, thawed your eyes, and
thawed your tongue.

So a **meek**[6] wonder held
your shadow and you whispered:
"Why so?"
And I answered:
"Because my fathers and I
are owned by the living
warmth of the earth
through our naked feet."

---

[6] **meek**—gentle, kind.

QUESTIONS TO CONSIDER

1. In "The Snow Flakes Sail Gently Down," what does the memory of Africa mean to Okara?

2. To whom is "You Laughed and Laughed and Laughed" addressed?

3. What sort of things about Africa is Okara celebrating in these two poems? What does he think is the spirit of Africans?

The Voter

CHINUA ACHEBE

Chinua Achebe (1930–   ) is one of Africa's most famous writers. His first novel, Things Fall Apart, *is the best-known African novel in English. Achebe was born into the Ibo tribe of eastern Nigeria, and his novels depict the traditional world of the Ibo and how this world clashed with modernity. Achebe has also satirized the corruption and strongman tactics of Nigeria's governments since independence in 1964. He has used his writing to point out that the Nigerians who replaced the British colonial officers quickly became corrupt, undermining every process of government. Due to the military coups, Achebe has spent most of the last three decades in exile in the United States.*

Rufus Okeke—Roof, for short—was a very popular man in his village. Although the villagers did not explain it in so many words Roof's popularity was a measure of their gratitude to an energetic young man who, unlike most of his fellows nowadays, had not abandoned the village in order to seek work—any work—in the towns. And Roof was not a village **lout**[1] either. Everyone knew how he had spent two years as a bicycle repairer's apprentice in Port Harcourt and had given up of his own free will a bright future to return to his people and guide them in these political times. Not that Umuofia needed a lot of guidance. The village already belonged en masse to the People's Alliance Party, and its most illustrious son—Chief the Honorable Marcus Ibe—was Minister of Culture in the out-going government (which was pretty certain to be the in-coming one as well). Nobody doubted that the Honorable Minister would be re-elected in his constituency. Opposition to him was like the proverbial fly trying to move a dunghill. It would have been ridiculous enough without coming, as it did now, from a complete nonentity.[2]

As was to be expected Roof was in the service of the Honorable Minister for the coming elections. He had become a real expert in election campaigning at all levels —village, local government or national.

[1] **lout**—a clumsy, crude person.
[2] complete nonentity—entirely unimportant person.

He could tell the mood and temper of the electorate at any given time. For instance he had warned the Minister months ago about the radical change that had come into the thinking of Umuofia since the last national election.

The villagers had had five years in which to see how quickly and plentifully politics brought wealth, chieftaincy titles, doctorate degrees and other honors, some of which like the last had still to be explained satisfactorily to them; for they expected a doctor to heal the sick. Anyhow, these honors had come so readily to the man they had given their votes to free of charge five years ago that they were now ready to think again.

Their point was that only the other day Marcus Ibe was a not too successful Mission-school teacher. Then politics had come to their village and he had wisely joined up, some say just in time to avoid imminent dismissal arising from a female teacher's pregnancy. Today he was Chief the Honorable; he had two long cars and had just built himself the biggest house anyone had seen in those parts. But let it be said that none of these successes had gone to Marcus's head—as they well might. He remained a man of the people. Whenever he could he left the good things of the capital and returned to his village which had neither running water nor electricity. He knew the source of his good fortune, unlike the little bird who ate and drank and went out to challenge his personal spirit. Marcus had **christened**[3] his new house "Umuofia Mansions" in honor

of his village and slaughtered five bulls and countless goats to entertain the people on the day it was opened by the Archbishop.

Everyone was full of praise for him. One old man said: "Our son is a good man; he is not like the mortar which as soon as food comes its way turns its back on the ground." But when the feasting was over the villagers told themselves that they had under-rated the power of the ballot-paper before and should not do so again. Chief the Honorable Marcus Ibe was not unprepared. He had drawn five months' salary in advance, changed a few hundred pounds into shining shillings and armed his campaign boys with eloquent little jute bags. In the day he made his speeches; at night his stalwarts conducted their whispering campaign. Roof was the most trusted of these campaigners.

"We have a Minister from our village, one of our own sons," he said to a group of elders in the house of Ogbuefi Ezenwá, a man of high traditional title. "What greater honor can a village have? Do you ever stop to ask yourselves why we should be singled out for this honor? I will tell you: it is because we are favored by the leaders of PAP. Whether we cast our paper for Marcus or not PAP will continue to rule. Think of the pipe-borne water they have promised us . . ."

Besides Roof and his assistant there were five elders in the room. An old hurricane lamp with a cracked, sooty, glass

---

[3] **christened**—named.

chimney gave out yellowish light in their midst. The elders sat on very low stools. On the floor, directly in front of each of them, lay two shilling pieces. Outside the moon kept a straight face.

"We believe every word you say to be true," said Ezenwa. "We shall every one of us drop his paper for Marcus. Who would leave an *ozo* feast and go to a poor ritual meal? Tell Marcus he has our papers, and our wives' papers too. But what we do say is that two shillings is shameful." He brought the lamp close and tilted it at the money before him as if to make sure he had not mistaken its value. "Yes, two shillings; it is too shameful. If Marcus were a poor man—which our ancestors forbid—I should be the first to give him my paper free, as I did before. But today Marcus is a great man and does his things like a great man. We did not ask him for money yesterday; we shall not ask him tomorrow. But today is our day; we have climbed the *iroko* tree today and would be foolish not to take down all the fire-wood we need."

Roof had to agree. He had lately been taking down a lot of fire-wood himself. Only yesterday he had asked Marcus for one of his many rich robes—and had got it. Last Sunday Marcus's wife (the teacher that nearly got him in trouble) had objected (like the woman she was) when Roof pulled out his fifth bottle of beer from the kerosene refrigerator, and was roundly and publicly rebuked by her husband. To cap it all Roof had won a land case recently because, among other things, he had been

chauffeur-driven to the disputed site. So he understood the elders about the fire-wood.

"Alright," he said in English and then reverted to Ibo. "Let us not quarrel about small things." He stood up and adjusted his robes. Then he bent down like a priest distributing the host[4] and gave one shilling more to every man: only he did not put it into their palms but on the floor in front of them. The men, who had so far not **deigned**[5] to touch the things, looked at the floor and shook their heads. Roof got up again and gave each man another shilling.

"I am through," he said with a defiance that was no less effective for being transparently faked. The elders too knew how far to go without losing decorum. So when Roof added: "Go cast your paper for the enemy if you like!" they quickly calmed him down with a suitable speech from each of them. By the time the last man had spoken it was possible—without great loss of dignity—to pick up the things from the floor.

The enemy Roof had referred to was the Progressive Organization Party (POP) which had been formed by the tribes down the coast to save themselves, as the founders of the party proclaimed—from "total political, cultural, social and religious annihilation." Although it was clear the party had no chance here it had plunged—with typical foolishness—into a

---

[4] host—bread or wafer made sacred and used in the Catholic ritual of Holy Communion.

[5] **deigned**—agreed to do something that is not appropriate or self-respecting.

straight fight with PAP, providing cars and loudspeakers to a few local rascals and thugs to go around and make a lot of noise. No one knew for certain how much money POP had let loose in Umuofia but it was said to be very considerable. Their local campaigners would end up very rich, no doubt.

Up to last night everything had been "moving according to plan"—as Roof would have put it. Then he had received a strange visit from the leader of the POP campaign team. Although he and Roof were well known to each other and might even be called friends his visit was cold and business-like. No words were wasted. He placed five pounds on the floor before Roof and said, "We want your vote." Roof got up from his chair, went to the outside door, closed it carefully and returned to his chair. The brief exercise gave him enough time to weigh the proposition. As he spoke his eyes never left the red notes on the floor.

"You know I work for Marcus," he said feebly. "It will be very bad. . ."

"Marcus will not be there when you put in your paper. We have plenty of work to do tonight; are you taking this or not?"

"It will not be heard outside this room?" asked Roof.

"We are after votes not gossip."

"Alright," said Roof in English.

The man nudged his companion and he brought forward an object covered with red cloth and proceeded to remove the cover. It was a fearsome little affair contained in a clay pot with feathers stuck into it.

"This *iyi*[6] comes from Mbanta. You know what that means. Swear that you will vote for Maduka. If you fail to do so, this *iyi* is to note."

Roof's heart had nearly flown out of his mouth when he saw the *iyi*; and indeed he knew the fame of Mbanta in these things. But he was a man of quick decision. What could a single vote cast in secret for Maduka take away from Marcus's certain victory? Nothing.

"I will cast my paper for Maduka; if not, this *iyi* take note."

"Das all," said the man as he rose with his companion, who had covered up the object again and was taking it back to their car.

"You know he has no chance against Marcus," said Roof at the door.

"It is enough that he gets a few votes now; next time he will get more. People will hear that he gives out pounds, not shillings, and they will listen."

Election morning. The great day every five years when the people exercised power—or thought they did. Weather-beaten posters on walls of houses, tree trunks and telegraph poles. The few that were still whole called out their message to those who could read. Vote for the People's

---

[6] *iyi*—a tribal god.

Alliance Party! Vote for the Progressive Organization Party! Vote for PAP! Vote for POP! The posters that were torn called out as much of the message as they could.

As usual Chief the Honorable Marcus Ibe was doing things in grand style. He had hired a highlife band from Umuru and stationed it at such a distance from the voting booths as just managed to be lawful. Many villagers danced to the music, their ballot papers held aloft, before proceeding to the booths. Chief the Honorable Marcus Ibe sat in the "owner's corner"[7] of his enormous green car and smiled and nodded. One enlightened villager came up to the car, shook hands with the great man and said in advance: "Congrats!" This immediately set the pattern. Hundreds of admirers shook Marcus's hand and said "Corngrass!"

Roof and the other organizers were prancing up and down, giving last minute advice to the voters and pouring with sweat.

"Do not forget," he said again to a group of **illiterate**[8] women who seemed ready to burst with enthusiasm and good humor, "our sign is the motor-car. . ."

"Like the one Marcus is sitting inside."

"Thank you, mother," said Roof. "It is the same car. The box with the car shown on its body is the box for you. Don't look at the other with the man's head: it is for those whose heads are not correct."

This was greeted with loud laughter. Roof cast a quick and busy-like glance towards the Minister and received a smile of appreciation.

"Vote for the car," he shouted, all the veins in his neck standing out. "Vote for the car and you will ride in it!"

"Or if we don't our children will," piped the same sharp old girl.

The band struck up a new number: "Why walk when you can ride?"

In spite of his apparent calm and confidence Chief the Honorable Marcus was a relentless **stickler**[9] for detail. He knew he would win what the newspapers called "a landslide victory" but he did not wish even so to throw away a single vote. So as soon as the first rush of voters was over he promptly asked his campaign boys to go one at a time and put in their ballot-papers.

"Roof, you had better go first," he said.

Roof's spirits fell; but he let no one see it. All morning he had masked his deep worry with a surface exertion which was unusual even for him. Now he dashed off in his springy fashion towards the booths. A policeman at the entrance searched him for illegal ballot papers and passed him. Then the electoral officer explained to him about the two boxes. By this time the spring had gone clean out of his walk. He **sidled**[10] in and was confronted by the car and the head. He brought out his ballot paper from his pocket and looked at it. How could he betray Marcus even in

---

[7] owner's corner—the owner of the car rides in the back seat diagonally behind the driver as a mark of his wealth and the respect due to him.

[8] **illiterate**—unable to read and write.

[9] **stickler**—a person who absolutely insists on something.

[10] **sidled**—edged along in a secretive manner.

secret? He resolved to go back to the other man and return his five pounds . . . FIVE POUNDS! He knew at once it was impossible. He had sworn on that *iyi*.

At this point he heard the **muffled**[11] voice of the policeman asking the electoral officer what the man was doing inside. "Abi na pickin im de born?"[12]

Quick as lightning a thought leapt into Roof's mind. He folded the paper, tore it in two along the crease and put one half in each box. He took the precaution of putting the first half into Maduka's box and confirming the action verbally: "I vote for Maduka."

They marked his thumb with **indelible**[13] purple ink to prevent his return, and he went out of the booth as jauntily as he had gone in.

---

[11] **muffled**—deadened or supressed.

[12] Abi na pickin im de born—pidgin English for "Is he giving birth to a child in there," which suggests "Why is he taking so long?"

[13] **indelible**—permanent.

QUESTIONS TO CONSIDER

1. Why does Roof work for Marcus? Why does he take the money from Maduka?

2. Does Roof's decision in the voting booth seem a satisfactory answer to his quandary? Why or why not?

3. How do you think Achebe feels about Nigeria's experience as a democracy? Point to details in the story that support your answer.

Your Logic Frightens Me, Mandela

WOLE SOYINKA

Wole Soyinka (1935–   ) was the first African writer to win the Nobel Prize in literature. Born in western Nigeria, Soyinka is a member of the Yoruba people. Soyinka was educated in Nigeria and then in England, where he began to write poems and plays. When he returned to Nigeria in 1960, he devoted himself to mastering the traditional African forms of drama. In 1967, Soyinka was imprisoned by the military government that had taken over. After his release in 1970, Soyinka went into exile abroad. Though he has been able to return to Nigeria from time to time, Soyinka has spent much of the last three decades in exile in Europe and America. His outspoken opposition to the various military dictators who have held power in Nigeria has made him a target of the government. "Your Logic Frightens Me, Mandela" is about the South African leader who was imprisoned by the government for almost thirty years. In 1994, Mandela became the first freely elected president of South Africa and is one of the world's most admired leaders.

Your logic frightens me, Mandela
Your logic frightens me. Those years
Of dreams, of time accelerated in
Visionary hopes, of savoring the task anew,
The call, the tempo **primed**[1]
To burst in supernovae round a "brave new world"!
Then stillness. Silence. The world closes round
Your sole reality; the rest is . . . dreams?

Your logic frightens me.
How coldly you disdain legerdemains![2]
"Open Sesame" and—two decades' rust on hinges

---

[1] **primed**—made ready.

[2] legerdemains—tricks.

Peels at the touch of a conjurer's wand?
White magic, ivory-topped black magic wand,
One moment wand, one moment riot club
Electric cattle prod and whip or *sjambok* [3]
Tearing flesh and spilling blood and brain?

This bag of tricks, whose silk streamers
Turn knotted cords to crush dark temples?
A rabbit punch sneaked beneath the rabbit?
Doves metamorphosed in milk-white **talons?**[4]
Not for you the olive branch that sprouts
Gun muzzles, barbed-wire garlands, tangled thorns
To wreathe the brows of black, unwilling Christs.
Your patience grows inhuman, Mandela.
Do you grow food? Do you make friends
Of mice and lizards? Measure the growth of grass
For time's unhurried pace?
Are you now the crossword puzzle expert?
Chess? Ah, no! Subversion lurks among
Chess pieces. Structured clash of black and white,
Equal ranged and paced? An equal board? No!
Not on Robben Island.[5] Checkers? Bad to worse.
That game has no respect for class or king-**serf**[6]
Ordered universe. So, scrabble?

Monopoly? Now, that . . . ! You know
The game's modalities,[7] so do they.
Come collection time, the cards read "White Only"
In the Community Chest. Like a gambler's coin
Both sides heads or tails, the "Chance" cards read:
Go to jail. Go straight to jail. Do not pass "GO."
Do not collect a hundredth rand. Fishes feast,

---

[3] *sjambok*— a nightstick used by the police.

[4] **talons**—claws.

[5] Robben Island—the island where Mandela was kept imprisoned for twenty-eight years. Many other political prisoners were also kept on the island.

[6] **serf**—feudal slave, required to serve a lord.

[7] modalities—ceremonial patterns of behavior; rules.

I think, on those who sought to by-pass "GO"
On Robben Island.

Your logic frightens me, Mandela, your logic
Humbles me. Do you tame geckos?
Do grasshoppers break your silences?
Bats' radar pips pinpoint your statuesque
Gaze transcending distances at will?
Do moths break wing
Against a light bulb's fitful glow
That brings no searing illumination?
Your sight shifts from moth to bulb,
Rests on its pulse-glow fluctuations—
Are kin feelings roused by a broken arc
Of tungsten[8] trapped in vacuum?

Your pulse, I know, has slowed with earth's
Phlegmatic[9] turns. I know your blood
Sagely warms and cools with seasons,
Responds to the lightest breeze
Yet scorns to race with winds (or hurricanes)
That threaten change on tortoise pads.

Is our world light-years away, Mandela?
Lost in visions of that dare supreme
Against a dire supremacy of race,
What brings you back to earth? The night guard's
Inhuman tramp?[10] A sodden eye transgressing through
The Judas hole?[11] Tell me Mandela,
That guard, is he *your* prisoner?

---

[8] tungsten—a rare metallic element.

[9] **Phlegmatic**—not easily excited to action or emotion.

[10] tramp—a firm, heavy step.

[11] Judas hole—peep hole.

Your bounty threatens me, Mandela, that **taut**[12]
Drumskin of your heart on which our millions
Dance. I fear we latch, fat leeches
On your veins. Our daily imprecisions
Dull keen edges of your will.
Compromises deplete your act's repletion—
Feeding will-voided stomachs of a continent,
What will be left of you, Mandela?

---

[12] **taut**—stretched tight.

QUESTIONS TO CONSIDER

1. What does Mandela represent for Soyinka?

2. What does Soyinka mean by the line "That guard, is he *your* prisoner" in stanza nine?

3. Describe what Soyinka means by Mandela's "logic." Why does it frighten Soyinka? Does it frighten you?

Three Poems

LÉOPOLD SENGHOR

Léopold Senghor (1906–   ) was born in the French colony of Senegal. Raised a Catholic, Senghor was sent to the Sorbonne in Paris to complete his education. Here he met Aimé Césaire (see page 273) and Leon Damas, two students from the Caribbean who felt, like Senghor, exiled from their homelands. While all three wrote in French, they felt a great commitment to their cultures and out of their discussions came the idea of Négritude. As a literary movement, Négritude was about celebrating the history, beliefs, and culture of the colonial peoples of Africa and the Caribbean. It also decried the devastation wrought by the colonial powers. For Senghor, Négritude was a way to create a distinctly African and distinctly modern culture. Senghor's poetry created a sense of African cultural identity, and his political work helped the African colonies of France achieve independence. In 1960 Senghor became the first president of independent Senegal, a post he held until 1981.

Prayer to the Masks

Masks! O Masks!
Black mask, red mask, You white-and-black masks
Masks of the four cardinal[1] points where the Spirit blows
I greet you in silence !
And, not the least of all, Ancestor with the lion head.
You keep this place safe from women's laughter
And any wry, **profane**[2] smiles.
You exude the immortal air where I inhale
The breath of my Fathers.

---

[1] cardinal—of great significance.

[2] **profane**—unholy or vulgar.

Masks with faces without masks, stripped of every dimple
And every wrinkle
You created this portrait, my face leaning
On an altar of blank paper
And in your image, listen to me!
The Africa of empires is dying—it is the agony
Of a sorrowful princess
And Europe, too, tied to us at the navel.
Fix your steady eyes on your oppressed children
Who give their lives like the poor man his last garment.
Let us answer "present" at the rebirth of the World
As white flour cannot rise without the leaven.[3]
Who else will teach rhythm to the world
Deadened by machines and cannons?
Who will sound the shout of joy at daybreak to wake orphans and the dead?
Tell me, who will bring back the memory of life
To the man of gutted hopes?
They call us men of cotton, coffee, and oil
They call us men of death.
But we are men of dance, whose feet get stronger
As we pound upon firm ground.

Letter to a Poet

to Aimé Césaire

To my Brother *aimé*, beloved friend, my bluntly fraternal greetings!
Black sea gulls like seafaring boatmen have brought me a taste
Of your tidings mixed with spices and the noisy fragrance of Southern Rivers
And Islands. They showed your influence, your distinguished brow,
The flower of your delicate lips. They are now your disciples,
A hive of silence, proud as peacocks. You keep their breathless zeal
From fading until moonrise. Is it your perfume of exotic fruits,
Or your wake of light in the fullness of day?
O, the many plum-skin women in the harem of your mind!

---

[3] leaven—in cooking, an ingredient like yeast or baking powder that causes fermentation or expansion of dough or batter.

Still charming beyond the years, embers aglow under the ash
Of your eyelids, is the Music we stretched our hands
And hearts to so long ago. Have you forgotten your nobility?
Your talent to praise the Ancestors, the Princes,
And the Gods, neither flower nor drops of dew?
You were to offer the Spirits the virgin fruits of your garden
—You ate only the newly harvested millet blossom
And stole not a petal to sweeten your mouth.
At the bottom of the well of my memory, I touch your face
And draw water to refresh my long regret.
You recline royally, elbow on a cushion of clear hillside,
Your bed presses the earth, easing the toil of wetland drums
Beating the rhythm of your song, and your verse
Is the breath of the night and the distant sea.
You praised the Ancestors and the legitimate princes.
For your rhyme and counterpoint you scooped a star from the heavens.
At your bare feet poor men threw down a mat of their year's wages,
And women their amber hearts and soul-wrenching dance.

My friend, my friend—Oh, you will come back, come back!
I shall await you under the mahogany tree, the message
Already sent to the woodcutter's boss. You will come back
For the feast of first fruits when the soft night
In the sloping sun rises steaming from the rooftops
And athletes, befitting your arrival,
Parade their youthfulness, adorned like the beloved.

Black Woman

Naked woman, black woman
Dressed in your color that is life, in your form that is beauty!
I grew up in your shadow. The softness of your hands
Shielded my eyes, and now at the height of Summer and Noon,
From the crest of a charred hilltop I discover you, Promised Land
And your beauty strikes my heart like an eagle's lightning flash.

Naked woman, dark woman
Ripe fruit with firm flesh, dark raptures of black wine,
Mouth that gives music to my mouth
Savanna of clear horizons, savanna quivering to the fervent caress
Of the East Wind, sculptured **tom-tom**,[4] stretched drumskin
Moaning under the hands of the conqueror
Your deep contralto[5] voice is the spiritual song of the Beloved.

Naked woman, dark woman
Oil no breeze can ripple, oil soothing the thighs
Of athletes and the thighs of the princes of Mali
Gazelle with **celestial**[6] limbs, pearls are stars
Upon the night of your skin. Delight of the mind's riddles,
The reflections of red gold from your shimmering skin
In the shade of your hair, my despair
Lightens in the close suns of your eyes.

Naked woman, black woman
I sing your passing beauty and fix it for all Eternity
before jealous Fate reduces you to ashes to nourish the roots of life.

---

[4] **tom-tom**—drum, commonly played with the hands.

[5] contralto—the lowest female voice or voice part, between soprano and tenor.

[6] **celestial**—related to the sky or heaven.

QUESTIONS TO CONSIDER

1. What idea is Senghor presenting in both "Prayer to the Masks" and "Black Woman"? What is Senghor saying about the relationship between European and African culture?

2. What is there about Césaire that Senghor is praising in "Letter to a Poet"?

3. Describe the many things about African and Caribbean culture that Senghor praises in these poems. What does he believe is their fundamental strength?

Three Poems

KOFI AWOONOR

Kofi Awoonor (1935–   ) is Ghana's leading literary figure and one of Africa's most acclaimed writers. In the 1950s, the prosperous Gold Coast was chosen by Great Britain to be the first of its African colonies to gain independence. When the former colony became the nation of Ghana on March 6, 1957, its first president, Kwame Nkrumah, quickly rose to be Africa's most prominent statesman. However, as the years passed he made himself president for life and his rule grew more oppressive; he jailed opposition leaders and spent vast sums on grandiose building projects. In 1966, he was replaced by a military government. In 1969, the military transferred power to a civilian government, but there were further coups in 1972, 1978, and 1979, when Jerry Rawlings, an air force officer, established himself as the power in the country. Rawlings has brought stability to Ghana, but he is essentially a dictator. Ghana's history is a metaphor for what occurred in the immediate aftermath of independence in Africa; high hopes were crushed by the greed, corruption, and lust for power of a small number. Awoonor went into exile when Nkrumah was overthrown. After a decade in Europe and the United States, Awoonor returned home, only to be jailed for a year on charges of subversion. Awoonor's powerful poems decrying the military regime and his experiences in prison only increased the poet's international reputation.

Song of War

I shall sleep in white calico;[1]
War has come upon the sons of men
I shall sleep in calico;
Let the boys go forward,
Kpli and his people should go forward;
Let the white man's guns boom,
We are marching forward;
all shall sleep in calico.

[1] calico—cotton cloth.

When we start, the ground shall shake;
The war is within our very huts;
Cowards should fall back
And live at home with the women;
They who go near our wives
While we are away in battle
Shall lose their calabashes² when we come.

Where has it been heard before
That a snake has bitten a child
In front of its own mother;
The war is upon us
It is within our very huts
And the sons of men shall fight it
Let the white man's guns boom
And its smoke cover us
We are fighting them to die.

We shall die on the battlefield
We shall like death at no other place,
Our guns shall die with us
And our sharp knives shall perish with us
We shall die on the battlefield.

---

² calabashes—gourdlike fruits whose dried shell is used to make bottles, bowls, and the like.

The Sea Eats the Land at Home

At home the sea is in the town,
Running in and out of the cooking places,
Collecting the firewood from the hearths
And sending it back at night;
The sea eats the land at home.
It came one day at the dead of night,
Destroying the cement walls,
And carried away the fowls,
The cooking-pots and the ladles,
The sea eats the land at home;
It is a sad thing to hear the wails,
And the mourning shouts of the women,
Calling on all the gods they worship,
To protect them from the angry sea.
Aku stood outside where her cooking-pot stood,
With her two children shivering from the cold,
Her hands on her breast,
Weeping mournfully.
Her ancestors have neglected her,
Her gods have deserted her,
It was a cold Sunday morning,
The storm was raging,
Goats and fowls were struggling in the water,
The angry water of the cruel sea;
The lap-lapping of the bark water at the shore,
And above the sobs and the deep and low moans,
Was the eternal hum of the living sea.
It has taken away their belongings
Adena has lost the trinkets which
Were her **dowry**[3] and her joy,
In the sea that eats the land at home,
Eats the whole land at home.

---

[3] **dowry**—property given to a husband by his bride.

At the Gates

I do not know which god sent me,
to fall in the river
and fall in the fire.
These have failed.
I move into the gates
demanding which war it is;
which war it is?
the dwellers in the gates
answer us; we will let that war come
they whom we followed to come
sons of our own mothers and fathers
bearing upon our heads nothing
save the thunder that does roar
who knows when evil matters will come.

Open the gates!
It is Akpabli Horsu[4] who sent me
Open the gates, my mother's children
and let me enter
our thunder initiates have **run amok**[5]
and we sleep in the desert land
not moving our feet
we will sleep in the desert
guns in our hands we cannot fire
knives in our hands we cannot throw
the death of a man is not far away.

I will drink it; it is my god who gave it to me
I will drink this calabash
for it is god's gift to me
bachelor, never go too far
for the drummer boys will cook and let you eat.

---

[4] Akpabli Horsu, a famous warrior who is commemorated in songs.

[5] **run amok**—gotten out of control.

Don't cry for me
my daughter, death called her
it is an offering of my heart
the ram has not come to stay
three days and it has gone
elders and chiefs whom will I trust
a snake has bitten my daughter
whom will I trust?
walk on gently; give me an offering
that I will give it to God
and he will be happy.

Uproot the yams you planted
for everything comes from God
it is an evil god who sent me
that all I have done
I bear the magic of the singer that has come
I have no paddle, my wish,
to push my boat into the river.

QUESTIONS TO CONSIDER

1. What sort of war is Awoonor describing in "Song of War"? What is the poem meant to express?

2. What do the last two lines of "The Sea Eats the Land at Home" suggest?

3. What does the title "At the Gates" refer to?

Taken

STEVE CHIMOMBO

Steve Chimombo (1945–   ) has been one of the leading writers and intellectuals in Malawi over the last three decades. Malawi became an independent country in 1964. For its first thirty years as a nation, it was ruled by Hastings Banda, one of the leaders of the anti-colonial movement in the 1950s. The longer he held power, the greater a dictator Banda became. In the 1970s, large numbers of intellectuals and politicians who opposed Banda's government were forced into exile or imprisoned. Chimombo's story "Taken" captures the injustices and insecurities of that era, and the tragedy that engulfed many African countries when their leaders became dictators.

I

It was a few minutes before noon, and I was packing my briefcase slowly, when Zinenani, an old friend now working in the capital city, burst in.

"Alekeni!" he shouted **unceremoniously**.[1]

"Hi!"

"When did you get back?"

"Get back?"

"I thought you'd gone abroad."

"It won't be for a month or so."

"But the whole capital is full of rumors of your having gone already, and decided to stay on."

"Stay on?"

"**Defected**[2] is the word."

"Defected? Why?"

"Because of what happened to Ndasauka."

"But I wasn't involved in that."

"Rumor has it that since your fellow writer was detained you decided to skip the country."

"But why should I do that? I haven't done anything that would make me go into exile."

"Believe me, when I saw you walk up to your office a few minutes ago, I thought I was seeing a ghost. The rumors were that strong. I came up just to make sure I was seeing right."

"But I was on the radio two days ago."

"That could have been prerecorded."

---

[1] **unceremoniously**—abruptly, lacking courtesy.

[2] **Defected**—deserted, changed loyalty to another country or party.

"That's true. Anyway, you can tell my well-wishers in the capital that I'm still around."

"But you'll still be going abroad?"

"I can't miss that opportunity."

"The rumors aren't anticipating your exile?"

"Believe me, if I had wanted to go into exile, I would have done so years ago when I was away studying in the U.K. and U.S.A. The thought seriously occurred to me then, but after toying with it, I realized I'm, deep down, an ancestor worshiper. I also discovered that I cannot write the genuine stuff when I'm on foreign soil. I decided to brave my own country."

"It's good the rumors were just that. We need fellows like you around."

"What are you doing here?"

"Consultations."

The phone rang. I let it ring.

"It's nice to see you, all the same."

"I've got to be going." Zinenani turned to the door.

I waved him off and lifted the receiver. "Hello?"

"This is Chodziwa-dziwa."

It was my kid brother. He had not been in touch for a long time. He, too, worked in the capital.

"How are you?"

"Fine. I'm actually speaking from your house."

"When did you come down?"

"I just arrived. I wanted to talk to you."

"I'll be right over. It's lunchtime, anyhow."

As I finished packing my briefcase, I puzzled over what Zinenani had said. The rumor was getting slightly stale. Just yesterday, I had been waylaid by a colleague's wife in the supermarket.

"Alekeni, come here!"

She took me by the hand and literally dragged me between two food counters. She was so enthusiastic I worried someone might suspect we were going to embrace or something, the way she furtively looked around and then drew near me as if she wanted to touch me.

"So"—she heaved a sigh of relief—"you're not gone!"

"Gone where?"

"Taken by the police."

"Why should the police take me?"

"Because of Ndasauka."

"But I don't even know what he's inside for."

"You don't need to know to be **implicated**.[3] You're a friend of his, and a writer, too.

"Even then."

It had ended like that, leaving me thoroughly **peeved**[4] at the source of the rumor. In Mtalika, rumor **diffused**[5] at the speed of sound: word of mouth, telephone, letter, even **telepathy**.[6] It was said that before you decided to seduce your friend's wife, people would already know about it and actively make sure it came about.

---

[3] **implicated**—included, involved.

[4] **peeved**—irritated, upset.

[5] **diffused**—spread out.

[6] **telepathy**—communication using only the mind.

Before long, I would end up believing in the rumor myself, even when right now I was still in Mtalika, getting into my own car to drive from my office home to have lunch with my family and kid brother. A free man.

"Daddy! Daddy!"

My five-year-old always ran up to the garage doors to meet me as soon as he heard the car in the driveway. Between our dog and him, I could not tell who gave me the warmer welcome. Sometimes they almost tripped over each other in the rush to meet me with cries and barks. It was overwhelming.

"Your brother is in the sitting room" were my wife's welcoming words.

I walked through the dining room to the lounge to find Chodziwa-dziwa flipping through a popular magazine. He looked up and grinned sheepishly. Something was bothering him.

"So it's not true" was his greeting.

"What?"

"That you are missing."

"Missing?" This was getting to be too enormous to be funny.

"A man came round to my place two days ago to say that something had happened involving a friend of yours, that your friend had been taken, and that you had disappeared without a trace."

"This is ridiculous. Who was the man?"

"I don't know, and he refused to identify himself. He said he just wanted your relatives to know that you could not be found."

It was **wearisome,**[7] if not monstrous. I reviewed my involvement with Ndasauka again.

2

I was going too fast but could do nothing about it. I was too agitated to be driving at that speed, yet I still maintained it, even when I kept going off the road at each minor bend. I had had one too many, but it was too late to start regretting that. I could not talk about Ndasauka rationally with his best friend by my side.

"Surely"—I detected the hoarseness in my voice—"you must know something he was involved in?"

"I'm telling you I don't."

"You don't know, or you don't want to discuss it?"

"I don't know anything that he was doing for the police to be interested in him."

"You're his closest friend."

"That doesn't mean he told me his entire life history."

"You were there when the police came to get him."

"It's very simple. I had invited him out to lunch at the club for a change. We had just finished the meal and were having a drink before going back to work when they found us at the bar."

"They knew you were there?"

"That's where they found us. I didn't know what was happening at first. One of them came over and called Ndasauka out. After a few minutes, another one came in, looking for nothing in particular. When Ndasauka didn't come back after fifteen minutes, I went out to investigate. I found him in handcuffs."

---

[7] **wearisome**—causing tiredness.

"You mean they handcuffed him right outside the club?"

"It created quite a sensation. There was a small crowd when I went out. I followed the police van to the office. There was another crowd as they took him up to his office."

"Still in handcuffs?"

"Yes. Another **contingent**[8] was already in the office going through his papers. I learned this from the secretary."

"How did she take it?"

"Scared. So gray she looked almost white. She couldn't type, read, crochet, or phone. I understand they threatened to arrest her, too, if she so much as moved from her chair."

"What were they looking for?"

"Search me."

"It comes back to what you know about all this. If you don't know, and his colleagues don't either, who is there to tell us what is happening?"

"The police."

I nearly exploded, the car swerved, and I hastily righted it again.

I felt cheated out of something in life and frustrated by the **tantalizing**[9] thought that perhaps beneath it all there was really nothing at all to discover. Perhaps the police did not even know what they were looking for. Maybe they only had Ndasauka on suspicion, pending further investigations. If that was the case, Ndasauka would be in for a long, long time. He might not ever come out.

The normal detention orders operated for twenty-eight days without formal charges. After that period, formal charges had to be filed, a statement issued, or the detainee released. The Republic of Mandania, however, operated neither with normal detention procedures nor with formal charges. A decade or so before, the country had gone through a spate of detentions of several highly placed persons in the civil service, the armed forces, and the university. All were supposedly suspected of planning a **coup**.[10] Although five years later most of the detainees had been released, some members of that group were still rotting in the numerous camps dotted around the country.

"Are we going back to the seventies?" was the question everyone asked as soon as Ndasauka was taken, and it was rumored—but never verified—that other members of the citizenry had also been or were about to be detained.

"When the police behave like that, it means they have reached the final act," someone who had lived through the terrors of the seventies said, meaning that the swoop was too dramatic and public to be followed by others of a similar nature.

In the seventies, enough terror had been generated for you to distrust even your closest relative and neighbor, for fear they might turn out to be one of the numerous informers in the pay of the police. People had disappeared into

---

[8] **contingent**—group.

[9] **tantalizing**—tempting; disappointing, after having had high hopes.

[10] **coup**—coup d'etat, a violent or illegal change of government.

detention, demise, or exile. The whole period was shrouded in such a terrifying cloak of mystery the media never covered it, no one talked about it in public, social places were emptied because it was safer to retire to your home after work. However, even within the safety of your home, you feared your servant, even your wife and children, and dreaded a knock at the door, lest it should be your turn to be taken.

> **"Who's spreading all these rumors?" I exploded. "I was at home and in bed the whole of last night."**

3

"Don't get involved in this."

It was the parish priest. He had gone to visit Ndasauka's family and then dropped in to see me.

"How can I get involved in something I don't know anything about?"

I was **exasperated**.[11] Why was everyone implicating me in the whole thing? The first hint that people thought I would be the next one to go was the surprised faces I met at work the day after Ndasauka was taken.

"When did they let you out?" the secretary had asked me.

"Who? What?"

"People said you were also taken yesterday. Someone saw the flashing lights of a police van in your drive at seven o'clock last night."

"It's a long drive and the driver might have been reversing."

"But what was it doing there, of all places, and at that hour?"

I could never figure out the answer to that one. Nor to the next, which I got from a colleague at coffee time the same day. "Someone told me you were taken for at least a few hours, if not the whole of last night."

"Who's spreading all these rumors?" I exploded. "I was at home and in bed the whole of last night. Why don't people ask me or my wife or my children before jumping to conclusions based on non-evidence? I know I went to Ndasauka's office after I'd heard what had happened to him. I saw the police there. I know I went to his house when I didn't find him at the office. I found the police and Ndasauka there. I was there to see him finally bundled into the police Land Rover to be heard of no more. But that was all I did."

It had not been all I did, though. I'd arrived at Ndasauka's home just as he was writing postdated checks to give to his children—his wife was away in the capital on a six-month course. I paced up and down outside, not knowing whether or not I could go in to speak to him, or, in fact, what I would say to him if I could.

The police crowded him out of the house.

---

[11] **exasperated**—frustrated, irritated.

"You must take me, too!" Ndasauka's seventy-year-old mother cried as she **tottered**[12] on crutches, following the group outside. It was the only clear sign of emotion that was expressed by any member of the family. I do not think the children fully understood what was happening, the oldest being only thirteen.

"Don't worry, Mother, he'll come back soon," one of the plainclothesmen said unconvincingly as they went over to the Land Rover parked just beyond the garage. Another police wagon was next to it. So many cars and officers for just one man.

"Excuse me," I introduced myself. "I'm a friend of Ndasauka's and I would like to know what's happening."

"Orders from the government: We are to take him to the capital."

"Where in the capital?" It was an automatic question.

"We can't say."

"But I have to tell his wife where he's being taken."

"You can't do that. You must not discuss with anyone what has happened today, until you hear from us."

"When will that be?"

"Tomorrow morning."

"But these kids will be alone all night with their old grandmother if his wife is not informed immediately. Who's going to look after them tonight?"

"I'm sorry, those are our instructions."

"Can I talk to Ndasauka?"

"Of course."

I went over to him.

"Look," I whispered, although the police could hear me, "do you know what this is all about?"

"All I know," he said loudly, "is that I'm being taken to the capital on government orders."

"What would you like me to do?"

He looked at his mute children. I thought someone would burst into tears.

He cleared his throat. "Look after the kids." He straightened up.

I watched him walk to the police car, flanked by the Special Branch men. They climbed in the back door of the Land Rover, putting him in the middle. The wagon followed. No sirens. No tears. That was the last we saw of him.

"Pirira is arriving by the trailer tonight." The parish priest brought me back to the present.

"She knows?"

"Of course. Could you pick her up? I have a meeting with the bishop, and it threatens to be a long one."

"That's all right. I'll meet her."

And so began the longest night in my life. The "trailer," as the late-night bus was called, was aptly nicknamed. It took the whole night to reach Mtalika from the capital, when other buses took no more than three hours. I had not known these details before and had gone to the bus station at nine o'clock to check on Ndasauka's wife. They told me the bus would arrive at eleven. At eleven, it still did not appear. Nor at one.

---

[12] **tottered**—walked unsteadily or weakly.

I parked by one of the shops with lighted fronts near the bus station and tried to sleep in the car. At three, another car came and parked behind mine. I raised a sleepy head.

The other man recognized me. "You're not waiting for the trailer, are you?"

"Yes."

"You're too early. It won't be here till four-thirty or later."

"But why didn't they tell me that before, so I could sleep at home?"

"They didn't know, either. It's quite erratic."

"Surely they could have phoned?"

"Once it has left the capital, it stops to drop or pick up any mail or passengers at every single trading center. It's useless to try to keep track of it. Those who know about its unpredictability wait until dawn before venturing to meet it."

I looked at my watch: three-fifteen. If I went home, I would probably sleep until midday. I decided to stay where I was.

The trailer groaned to a halt at four-thirty, dragging the mail van, from whence its nickname. I walked across the lot.

"Pirira," I greeted Ndasauka's wife. It was painful to try to smile.

"What happened?" She sobbed. She looked as if she had been crying all the way and was on the verge of collapse.

"The car is over there."

I got her bag and walked briskly. She had to trot after me.

"It's like this," I said as I drove off. "We really don't know what's happening."

It was no **consolation**.[13] I let her get what was left out of her system and drove in silence all the way to her house.

"Mommy!" was the delighted cry of the youngest boy as he rushed out to my car. The joy of seeing his mother and the reason for her being there were **irreconcilable**.[14]

"I'll be in touch." I hastily drove off.

"I'm sorry to get you involved like this," the parish priest had continued.

"You're a fellow writer and a friend of his. You should check your travel documents."

4

I turned into the side road leading up to the police camp and stopped at the barrier just inside the iron gates. There was a flurry of activity in the little hut on the side of the road. Two armed men emerged.

One marched purposefully toward the car. "Name and address?"

He leaned through the open window, surveyed me and the interior of the car. He paused by my left hand, which was still holding the gearshift. I ignored the bayonet waving half a foot away from my throat and supplied the information.

"Can we help you?"

I mentioned my desire to visit one of the top-ranking officers.

"Just a moment, sir." He marched back to the hut. I could see him phoning.

---

[13] **consolation**—relief of disappointment or sadness.

[14] **irreconcilable**—not compatible.

I wondered why there were roadblocks manned by heavily armed police at several points on either side of Mtalika town. It seemed as if Mandania was in a perpetual state of siege or under **curfew**.[15] As far as I knew, the nearest war was across the border, and it had nothing to do with us.

"Just obeying orders, sir." The man came back. "I have to ask his permission to let you through."

I shrugged and asked for directions. The barrier was lifted, I drove past slowly, and waved back at the mock salute I was given by the other man.

"Alekeni! Long time no see!"

The officer, in civilian clothes, pumped my hand with exaggerated enthusiasm, as I got out of the car. "Come in."

I didn't know if my mission could be discussed in the house with so many children milling around. "Thank you!" I said all the same.

The sitting room was filled with enough furniture for two houses. He waved me to a sumptuous chair, into which I sank up to my waist. I bobbed up again and sat forward on the edge of the seat.

"This is Alekeni, my old schoolmate." He introduced me to a parade of sons and daughters, who detached themselves from various corners and rooms and advanced an arm and a shy smile. They filed back to their occupations afterwards like a small **regiment**.[16]

Brief pause.

I decided to plunge straight into the purpose of my visit.

He jerked forward. "Yes." He spoke rapidly. "Ndasauka. I heard about it. Routine, of course. I'm kept informed of what is happening."

"The problem is," I continued, "that we don't know what is happening and we are really worried about it. It's a week now, and there's no news of his whereabouts or even the reasons for his being taken in."

"But why come to me?" He was very agitated. "It's not really my department."

"For the simple reason that we were at school together, we were friends. His wife also said you go to the same church. She, in fact, is the one who suggested I should come to see you."

"You realize this is a delicate matter?"

"But we don't know anything."

"I'm telling you it's a delicate matter. If anyone knew you came to see me about it, I would be in trouble."

"Surely you can mention at least to his wife the nature of the suspicions or the speculations as to why he was taken?"

"It's too sensitive."

"I take it it's not a criminal charge, then."

"In his case, it wouldn't be that."

"It's political, then?"

> *It seemed as if Mandania was in a perpetual state of siege or under curfew.*

---

[15] **curfew**—requirement that people stay indoors during certain hours, usually at night.

[16] **regiment**—organized group of soldiers.

"Look, I only got to know about it as a matter of routine. I didn't inquire further into the details, although I saw his name on the list."

"There are others involved, too?"

"Yes, and I trust you appreciate the fact that I can't just lift the phone and call the Special Branch?"

"I do, but surely on the list there was some explanation why the people had to be taken?"

"That's why I'm saying it's too delicate to discuss with you at the moment. Give me a few days and perhaps I can let you know what can be safely told."

"When can I get in touch with you again?"

"I'll get in touch with you."

When we parted, I had a strong suspicion he would not contact me again and that I had lost an old school friend forever. As I drove out past the armed guards, I wondered if the country hadn't been in a state of emergency all along and I hadn't known. It was too delicate to announce publicly, and so, too, would it be when the next one was taken.

QUESTIONS TO CONSIDER

1. Why does everyone think that something has happened to Alekeni?

2. Why is Alekeni's school friend so evasive?

3. What does the final sentence in the story suggest?

4. What is the tone of the story?

5. Why would a government want to detain or imprison writers? List all the reasons that you can think of.

On African Writing

JACK MAPANJE

Jack Mapanje (1945–   ) was born in Malawi in southeastern Africa. Malawi gained its independence from Great Britain in 1964 and has been ruled since then by Hastings Banda, who moved from being a leading nationalist to a repressive dictator. When Mapanje's first book of poems, Of Chameleons and Gods, *was published in 1981, he was denounced by the government for attacking the corruption he saw all around him. Mapanje was imprisoned from 1987 until 1991 with no formal charge ever leveled against him. Mapanje described his poems as an attempt "to find a voice or voices as a way of preserving some sanity."*

You've rocked at many passage rites, at drums
Mothers clapping their admiration of your
Initiation[1] voices—now praises of decay
That still **mesmerize**[2] some; at times you've
Yodeled like you'd never become men gallant
Hunting, marrying, hating, killing. But
In your masks you've sung on one praise
After another. You have sung mouth-songs!
Men struggling to justify what you touched
Only, heard merely! Empty men! Do you realize
You are still singing initiation tunes?
You have not **chimed**[3] hunting-marrying—

---

[1] **Initiation**—the ceremony of acceptance into a group.
[2] **mesmerize**—to hypnotize or fascinate.
[3] **chimed**—sung in unison.

Fighting-killing praises until you've
Stopped all this nonsense about drinking
Palm wine from plastic tumblers!
And these **doggerels**,[4] these sexual-tribal
Anthropological-political doggerels!
Don't you think even mothers will stop
Quaking some day? Don't you realize
Mothers also ache to see their grand
Children at home playing *bau*[5] on sofas?
Why do you always suppose mothers
Never want to see you at these conferences
They are for ever hearing about?
Why do you imagine they never understand
Things? They too can be alert to all this
Absurdity about what you think they think!
You've sung many songs, some superb
But these lip-songs are most despicable!

---

[4] **doggerels**—crudely written verse.
[5] *bau*—African game played with pieces.

QUESTIONS TO CONSIDER

1. What does Mapanje mean by "lip-songs"? Who is he criticizing?

2. What is Mapanje saying is more important than the songs?

3. What do the rituals represent to Mapanje in this poem? Is he praising them?

There Is No Exile

ASSIA DJEBAR

Assia Djebar (1936–   ) is the pen name of Fatima-Zohra Imalayene, an Algerian born into a middle-class family in Algiers. Djebar was one of the first Algerian women to receive schooling in France. While studying she began to write, and in 1957 her first novel La Soif ("The Thirst") was accepted for publication. Fearing that her family would disapprove of her writing and subject matter, the young writer chose the pseudonym, changed her birth date, and had her hair cut off for press photos. In 1958, Djebar was swept up in the conflict between an Algeria wanting independence and her colonial master, France. Djebar worked for the National Liberation Front (FLN) and was finally able to return to Algeria in 1962 when independence was granted. After independence, Djebar began to make films and adapt works for the theater. She has produced a body of work that has led to her being called "the most gifted woman writer to come out of the Moslem world in this century." "There is No Exile" is from Djebar's 1980 collection of stories Women of Algiers in Their Apartment *and focuses as so often in her fiction on the changing roles of women in Algerian society.*

That particular morning, I'd finished the housework a little earlier, by nine o'clock. Mother had put on her veil, taken her basket; in the opening of the door, she repeated as she had been repeating every day for three years: "Not until we had been chased out of our own country did I find myself forced to go out to market like a man."

"Our men have other things to do," I answered, as I'd been answering every day for three years.

"May God protect us!"

I saw Mother to the staircase, then watched her go down heavily because of her legs: "May God protect us," I said again to myself as I went back in.

The cries began around ten o'clock, more or less. They were coming from the apartment next door and soon changed into shrieks. All three of us, my two sisters —Aicha, Anissa, and I—recognized it by the way in which the women received it: it was death.

Aicha, the eldest, ran to the door, opened it in order to hear more clearly: "May misfortune stay away from us," she mumbled. "Death has paid the Smain family a visit."

At that moment, Mother came in. She put the basket on the floor, stopped where she stood, her face distraught, and began to beat her chest **spasmodically**[1] with her hands. She was uttering little stifled cries, as when she was about to get sick.

Anissa, although she was the youngest of us, never lost her calm. She ran to close the door, lifted Mother's veil, took her by the shoulders and made her sit down on a mattress.

"Now don't get yourself in that state on account of someone else's misfortune," she said. "Don't forget you have a bad heart. May God shelter and keep us always."

While she repeated the phrase several more times, she went to get some water and sprinkled it on Mother, who now, stretched out full length on the mattress, was moaning. Then Anissa washed her entire face, took a bottle of cologne from the wardrobe, opened it, and put it under her nostrils.

"No!" Mother said. "Bring me some lemon."

And she started to moan again.

Anissa continued to bustle about. I was just watching her. I've always been slow to react. I'd begun to listen to the sobs outside that hadn't ceased, would surely not cease before nightfall. There were five or six women in the Smain family, and they were all lamenting in chorus, each one settling, forever it seemed, into the muddled outbreak of their grief. Later, of course, they'd have to prepare the meal, busy themselves with the poor, wash the body. . . . There are so many things to do, the day of a burial.

For now, the voices of the hired mourners, all alike without any one of them distinguishable from the other if only by a more anguished tone, were making one long, gasping chant, and I knew that it would hang over the entire day like a fog in winter.

"Who actually died over there?" I asked Mother, who had almost quieted down.

"Their young son," she said, inhaling the lemon deeply. "A car drove over him in front of the door. I was coming home when my eyes saw him twisting one last time, like a worm. The ambulance took him to the hospital, but he was already dead."

Then she began to sigh again.

"Those poor people," she was saying, "they saw him go out jumping with life and now they're going to bring him back in a bloodstained sheet."

She raised herself halfway, repeated: "jumping with life." Then she fell back down on the mattress and said nothing other than the ritual formulas to keep misfortune away. But the low voice she always used to address God had a touch of hardness, vehemence.

"This day has an evil smell," I said, still standing in front of Mother, motionlessly. "I've sensed it since this morning, but I didn't know then that it was the smell of death."

"You have to add: May God protect us!" Mother said sharply. Then she raised her eyes to me. We were alone in the room,

---

[1] **spasmodically**—suddenly, briefly, and with great energy.

Anissa and Aicha had gone back to the kitchen.

"What's the matter with you?" she said. "You look pale. Are you feeling sick, too?"

"May God protect us!" I said and left the room.

At noon, Omar was the first one home. The weeping continued. I'd attended to the meal while listening to the **threnody**[2] and its **modulations**.[3] I was growing used to them. I thought Omar would start asking questions. But no. He must have heard about it in the street.

He pulled Aicha into a room. Then I heard them whispering. When some important event occurred, Omar spoke first to Aicha in this way, because she was the eldest and the most serious one. Previously, Father used to do the same thing, but outside, with Omar, for he was the only son.

So there was something new; and it had nothing to do with death visiting the Smain family. I wasn't curious at all. Today is the day of death, all the rest becomes immaterial.

"Isn't that so?" I said to Anissa, who jumped.

"What's the matter now?"

"Nothing," I said without belaboring the point, for I was familiar with her always disconcerted answers whenever I'd start thinking out loud. Even this morning . . .

But why this sudden, blatant desire to stare at myself in a mirror, to confront my own image at some length, and to say, while letting my hair fall down my back so that Anissa would gaze upon it: "Look. At twenty-five, after having been married, after having lost my two children one after

the other, having been divorced, after this exile and after this war, here I am busy admiring myself, smiling at myself like a young girl, like you . . ."

"Like me!" Anissa said, and she shrugged her shoulders.

Father came home a little late because it was Friday and he'd gone to say the prayer of *dhor*[4] at the mosque. He immediately asked why they were in mourning.

"Death has visited the Smains," I said, running toward him to kiss his hand. "It has taken their young son away."

"Those poor people," he said after a silence.

I helped him get settled in his usual place, on the same mattress. Then, as I put his meal in front of him and made sure he didn't have to wait for anything, I forgot about the neighbors for a while. I liked to serve Father; it was, I think, the only household task I enjoyed. Especially now. Since our departure, Father had aged a great deal. He gave too much thought to those who weren't with us, even though he never spoke of them, unless a letter arrived from Algeria and he asked Omar to read it.

In the middle of the meal I heard Mother murmur: "They can't possibly feel like eating today."

I wasn't curious at all. Today is the day of death, all the rest becomes immaterial.

---

[2] **threnody**—a poem, song, or speech of grief.
[3] **modulations**—musical sound variations.
[4] *dhor*—the noontime prayer in Islam.

"The body is still at the hospital," someone said.

Father said nothing. He rarely spoke during meals.

"I'm not really hungry," I said, getting up, to excuse myself.

The sobs outside seemed more muffled, but I could still distinguish their **singsong**.[5] Their gentle singsong. This is the moment, I said to myself, when grief becomes familiar, and pleasurable, and nostalgic. This is the moment when you weep almost voluptuously, for this gift of tears is a gift without end. This was the moment when the bodies of my children would turn cold fast, so fast, and when I knew it. . . .

At the end of the meal, Aicha came into the kitchen, where I was by myself. First she went to close the windows that looked out over the neighboring terraces, through which the weeping reached me. But I could still hear it. And, oddly, it was that which made me so tranquil today, a little gloomy.

"There are some women coming this afternoon to see you and to propose marriage," she began. "Father says the candidate is suitable in every way."

Without answering, I turned my back to her and went to the window.

"Now what's your problem?" she said a little sharply.

"I need some air," I said and opened the window all the way, so that the song could come in. It had already been a while since the breathing of death had become, for me, "the song."

Aicha remained a moment without answering. "When Father goes out, you'll attend to yourself a little," she said at last. "These women know very well that we're refugees like so many others, and that they're not going to find you dressed like a queen. But you should look your best, nevertheless."

"They've stopped weeping," I remarked, "or perhaps they're already tired," I said, thinking of that strange fatigue that grasps us at the depth of our sorrow.

"Why don't you keep your mind on the women who're coming?" Aicha replied in a slightly louder voice.

Father had left. Omar too, when Hafsa arrived. Like us, she was Algerian and we'd known her there, a young girl of twenty with an education. She was a teacher but had been working only since her mother and she had been exiled, as had so many others. "An honorable woman doesn't work outside her home," her mother used to say. She still said it, but with a sigh of helplessness. One had to live, and there was no man in their household now.

Hafsa found Mother and Anissa in the process of preparing pastries, as if these were a must for refugees like us. But her sense of **protocol**[6] was instinctive in Mother; an inheritance from her past life that she could not readily abandon.

"These women you're waiting for," I asked, "who are they?"

---

[5] **singsong**—a monotonous rising and falling in pitch of the voice when speaking.

[6] **protocol**—customs and regulations related to proper behavior.

"Refugees like us," Aicha exclaimed. "You don't really think we'd give you away in marriage to strangers?" Then with heart and soul: "Remember," she said, "the day we return to our own country, we shall all go back home, all of us, without exception."

"The day that we return," Hafsa, standing in the middle of the room, suddenly cried out, her eyes wide with dreams. "The day that we return to our country!" she repeated. "How I'd like to go back there on foot, the better to feel the Algerian soil under my feet, the better to see all our women, one after the other, all the widows, and all the orphans, and finally all the men, exhausted, sad perhaps, but free—free! And then I'll take a bit of soil in my hands, oh, just a tiny handful of soil, and I'll say to them: 'See, my brothers, see these drops of blood in these grains of soil in this hand, that's how much Algeria has bled throughout her body, all over her vast body, that's how much Algeria has paid for our freedom and for this, our return, with her own soil. But her martyrdom now speaks in terms of grace. So you see, my brothers . . .' "

"The day that we return," Mother repeated softly in the silence that followed . . . "if God wills it."

It was then that the cries began again through the open window. Like an orchestra that brusquely starts a piece of music. Then, in a different tone, Hafsa reminded us: "I'm here for the lesson."

Aicha pulled her into the next room.

During their meeting, I didn't know what to do. The windows of the kitchen and of the other two rooms looked out over the terraces. I went from one to the other, opening them, closing them, opening them again. All of this without hurrying, as if I weren't listening to the song.

Anissa caught me in my rounds.

"You can tell they're not Algerian," she said. "They're not even accustomed to being in mourning."

"At home, in the mountains," Mother answered, "the dead have nobody to weep over them before they grow cold."

"Weeping serves no purpose," Anissa was stoic, "whether you die in your bed or on the bare ground for your country."

"What do you know about it?" I suddenly said to her. "You're too young to know."

"Soon they're going to bury him," Mother whispered.

Then she raised her head and looked at me. I had once again closed the window behind me. I couldn't hear anything anymore.

"They're going to bury him this very day," Mother said again a little louder, "that's our custom."

"They shouldn't," I said. "It's a hateful custom to deliver a body to the earth when beauty still shines on it. Really quite hateful. . . . It seems to me they're burying him while he's still shivering, still. . ." (but I couldn't control my voice any longer).

"Stop thinking about your children!" Mother said. "The earth that was thrown on them is a blanket of gold. My poor daughter, stop thinking about your children!" Mother said again.

"I'm not thinking about anything," I said. "No, really. I don't want to think about anything. About anything at all."

It was already four o'clock in the afternoon when they came in. From the kitchen where I was hiding, I heard them exclaim, once the normal phrases of courtesy had been uttered: "What is that weeping?"

"May misfortune stay far away from us! May God protect us!"

"It gives me goose bumps," the third one was saying. "I've almost forgotten death and tears, these days. I've forgotten them, even though our hearts are always heavy."

"That is the will of God," the second one would respond.

In a placid voice, Mother explained the reason for the mourning next door as she invited them into the only room we had been able to furnish decently. Anissa, close by me, was already making the first comments on the way the women looked. She was questioning Aicha, who had been with Mother to welcome them. I had opened the window again and watched them exchange their first impressions.

"What are you thinking?" Anissa said, her eye still on me.

"Nothing," I said feebly; then, after a pause: "I was thinking of the different faces of fate. I was thinking of God's will. Behind that wall, there is a dead person and women going mad with grief. Here, in our house, other women are talking of marriage . . . I was thinking of that difference."

"Just stop 'thinking,'" Aicha cut in sharply. Then to Hafsa, who was coming in: "You ought to be teaching *her*, not me. She spends all her time thinking. You'd almost believe she's read as many books as you have."

"And why not?" Hafsa asked.

"I don't need to learn French," I answered. "What purpose would it serve? Father has taught us all our language. 'That's all you need,' he always says."

"It's useful to know languages other than your own," Hafsa said slowly. "It's like knowing other people, other countries."

I didn't answer. Perhaps she was right. Perhaps you ought to learn and not waste your time letting your mind wander, like mine, through the deserted corridors of the past. Perhaps I should take lessons and study French, or anything else. But I, I never felt the need to jostle my body or my mind. . . . Aicha was different. Like a man: hard and hard working. She was thirty. She hadn't seen her husband in three years, who was still **incarcerated**[7] in Barberousse prison, where he had been since the first days of the war. Yet, she was getting an education and didn't settle for household work. Now, after just a few months of Hafsa's lessons, Omar no longer read her husband's infrequent letters, the few that might reach her. She managed to decipher them

---

[7] **incarcerated**—imprisoned.

by herself. Sometimes I caught myself being envious of her.

"Hafsa," she said, "it's time for my sister to go in and greet these ladies. Please go with her."

But Hafsa didn't want to. Aicha insisted, and I was watching them play their little game of politeness.

"Does anyone know if they've come for the body yet?" I asked.

"What? Didn't you hear the chanters just now?" Anissa said.

"So that's why the weeping stopped for a moment," I said. "It's strange, as soon as some parts of the Koranic verses are chanted, the women immediately stop weeping. And yet, that's the most painful moment, I know it all too well myself. As long as the body is there in front of you, it seems the child isn't quite dead yet, can't be dead, you see? . . . Then comes the moment when the men get up, and that is to take him, wrapped in a sheet, on their shoulders. That's how he leaves, quickly, as on the day that he came. . . . For me, may God forgive me, they can chant Koranic verses all they want, the house is still empty after they've gone, completely empty. . . ."

Hafsa was listening, her head leaning toward the window. With a shiver, she turned toward me. She seemed younger even than Anissa, then.

"My God," she said, emotion in her voice, "I've just turned twenty and yet I've never encountered death. Never in my whole life!"

"Haven't you lost anyone in your family in this war?" Anissa asked.

"Oh yes," she said, "but the news always comes by mail. And death by mail, you see, I can't believe it. A first cousin of mine died under the guillotine[8] as one of the first in Barberousse. Well, I've never shed a tear over him because I cannot believe that he's dead. And yet he was like a brother to me, I swear. But I just can't believe he's dead, you understand?" she said in a voice already wrapped in tears.

"Those who've died for the Cause aren't really dead," Anissa answered with a touch of pride.

> *"Those who've died for the Cause aren't really dead," Anissa answered with a touch of pride.*

"So, let's think of the present. Let's think about today," Aicha said in a dry voice. "The rest is in God's hand."

There were three of them: an old woman who had to be the suitor's mother and who hastily put on her glasses as soon as I arrived; two other women, seated side by side, resembled each other. Hafsa, who'd come in behind me, sat down next to me. I lowered my eyes.

I knew my part, it was one I'd played before; stay mute like this, eyes lowered, and patiently let myself be examined until the very end: it was simple. Everything is simple, beforehand, for a girl who's being married off.

---

[8] guillotine—a device for beheading a person, consisting of a heavy blade that drops between two posts that guide its fall.

Mother was talking. I was barely listening. I knew the themes to be developed all too well: Mother was talking about our sad state as refugees; then they'd be exchanging opinions on when the end might be announced: ". . . another Ramadan[9] to be spent away from home . . . perhaps this was the last one . . . perhaps, if God wills it! Of course, we were saying the same thing last year, and the year before that. . . . Let's not complain too much. . . . In any event, victory is certain, all our men say the same thing. And we, we know the day of our return will come. . . . We should be thinking of those who stayed behind. . . . We should be thinking of those who are suffering. . . . The Algerian people are a people whom God loves. . . . And our fighters are made of steel. . . ." Then they'd come back to the tale of the flight, to the different means by which each one had left her soil where the fires were burning. . . . Then they'd evoke the sadness of exile, the heart yearning for its country . . . . And the fear of dying far from the land of one's birth . . . . Then. . . . "But may God be praised and may he grant our prayers!"

This time it lasted a bit longer; an hour perhaps, or more. Until the time came to serve coffee. By then, I was hardly listening at all. I too was thinking in my own way of this exile, of these somber days.

I was thinking how everything had changed, how on the day of my first engagement we had been in the long, bright living room of our house in the hills of Algiers; how we'd been prosperous then, we had prosperity and peace; how Father used to laugh, how he used to give thanks to God for the abundance of his home . . . And I, I wasn't as I was today, my soul grey, gloomy and with this idea of death beating faintly inside me since the morning. . . . Yes, I was thinking how everything had changed and that, still, in some way everything remained the same. They were still concerned with marrying me off. And why exactly? I suddenly wondered. And why exactly? I repeated to myself, feeling something like fury inside me, or its echo. Just so I could have worries that never change whether it's peace or wartime, so I could wake up in the middle of the night and question myself on what it is that sleeps in the depths of the heart of the man sharing my bed. . . . Just so I could give birth and weep, for life never comes unaccompanied to a woman, death is always right behind, furtive, quick, and smiling at the mothers. . . . Yes, why indeed? I said to myself.

Coffee had now been served. Mother was inviting them to drink.

"We won't take even one sip," the old woman began, "before you've given us your word about your daughter."

"Yes," the other one said, "my brother impressed upon us that we weren't to come back without your promising to give her to him as his wife."

I was listening to Mother avoid answering, have herself be begged hypocritically, and then again invite them to drink. Aicha joined in with her. The women were repeating their request. . . . It was all as it should be.

---

[9] Ramadan—Islamic season of fasting.

The game went on a few minutes longer. Mother invoked the father's authority: "I, of course, would give her to you. . . . I know you are people of means. . . . But there is her father."

"Her father has already said yes to my brother," one of the two women who resembled each other replied. "The question remains only to be discussed between us."

"Yes," said the second one, "it's up to us now. Let's settle the question."

I raised my head; it was then, I think, that I met Hafsa's gaze. There was, deep in her eyes, a strange light, surely of interest or of irony, I don't know, but you could feel Hafsa as an outsider, attentive and curious at the same time, but an outsider. I met that look.

"I don't want to marry," I said. "I don't want to marry," I repeated, barely shouting.

There was much commotion in the room: Mother got up with a deep sigh; Aicha was blushing, I saw. And the two women who turned to me, with the same slow movement of shock: "And why not?" one of them asked.

"My son," the old woman exclaimed with some arrogance, "my son is a man of science. In a few days he is leaving for the Orient."

"Of course," Mother said with touching haste. "We know he's a scholar. We know him to have a righteous heart. . . . Of course. . . ."

"It's not because of your son," I said. "But I don't want to get married. I see the future before my eyes, it's totally black. I don't know how to explain it, surely it must come from God. . . . But I see the future totally black before my eyes!" I said again, sobbing, as Aicha led me out of the room in silence.

Later, but why even tell the rest, except that I was consumed with shame and I didn't understand. Only Hafsa stayed close to me after the women had left.

"You're engaged," she said sadly. "Your mother said she'd give you away. Will you accept?" and she stared at me with imploring eyes.

"What difference does it make?" I said and really thought inside myself: What difference does it make? "I don't know what came over me before. But they were all talking about the present and its changes and its misfortunes. And I was saying to myself: of what possible use is it to be suffering like this, far away from home, if I have to continue here as before in Algiers, to stay home and sit and pretend. . . . Perhaps when life changes, everything should change with it, absolutely everything. I was thinking of all that," I said, "but I don't even know if that's bad or good. . . . You, you're smart, and you know these things, perhaps you'll understand. . . ."

"I do understand," she said, hesitating as if she were going to start talking and then preferred to remain silent.

"Open the window," I said. "It's almost dark."

She went to open it and then came back to my bed where I'd been lying down to cry, without reason, crying for shame and fatigue all at the same time. In the silence that followed, I was feeling distant, pondering the night that little by little engulfed the room. The sounds from the kitchen, where my sisters were, seemed to be coming from somewhere else.

Then Hafsa began to speak: "Your father," she said, "once spoke of exile, of our present exile, and he said—oh, I remember it well, for nobody speaks like your father—he said: 'There is no exile for any man loved by God. There is no exile for the one who is on God's path. There are only trials.'"

She went on a while, but I've forgotten the rest, except that she repeated *we* very often with a note of passion. She said that word with a peculiar **vehemence**,[10] so much so that I began to wonder toward the end whether that word really meant the two of us alone, or rather other women, all the women of our country.

To tell the truth, even if I'd known, what could I have answered? Hafsa was too knowledgeable for me. And that's what I would have liked to have told her when she stopped talking, perhaps in the expectation that I would speak.

But it was another voice that answered, a woman's voice that rose, through the open window, rose straight as an arrow toward the sky, that rounded itself out, spread out in its flight, a flight ample as a bird's after the storm, then came falling back down in sudden torrents. "The other women have grown silent," I said. "The only one left to weep now is the mother. . . . Such is life," I added a moment later. "There are those who forget or who simply sleep. And then there are those who keep bumping into the walls of the past. May God take pity on them!"

"Those are the true exiles," said Hafsa.

---

[10] **vehemence**—passion.

QUESTIONS TO CONSIDER

1. Compare and contrast Aicha and Anissa. What role does each play in the household?

2. Why does the narrator respond to the marriage proposal with such fear?

3. How would you describe the role of men and women in the society presented in Djebar's story? What can you infer about how it has changed in modern times?

from

The Dark Child

CAMARA LAYE

Camara Laye (1928–1980) was born in Guinea, but received much of his education in France. When he was twenty-six, Laye published his first book, The Dark Child, *a nostalgic memoir of his youth in a village. In it, Laye established one of the key themes of his writing: the contrast between his traditional upbringing and his modern education. The book is a lament for the passing of one way of life written while Laye was in school embarking on a new way. When Guinea became an independent nation in 1958, Laye became a cultural ambassador. His novels quickly established him as a major voice in African literature—certainly the finest African novelist writing in French. His criticism of the repressive rule of Guinea's leader Sékou Touré led to Laye's being forced into exile in 1966. He continued to write, but died in exile longing for his homeland.*

Of all the different kinds of work my father engaged in, none fascinated me so much as his skill with gold. No other occupation was so noble, no other needed such a delicate touch. And then, every time he worked in gold it was like a festival—indeed it was a festival—that broke the **monotony**[1] of ordinary working days.

So, if a woman, accompanied by a go-between, crossed the **threshold**[2] of the workshop, I followed her in at once. I knew what she wanted: she had brought some gold, and had come to ask my father to transform it into a trinket. She had collected it in the placers[3] of Siguiri where, crouching over the river for months on end, she had patiently extracted grains of gold from the mud.

These women never came alone. They knew my father had other things to do than make trinkets. And even when he had the time, they knew they were not the first to ask a favor of him, and that, consequently, they would not be served before others.

Generally they required the trinket for a certain date, for the festival of Ramadan[4] or the Tabaski[5] or some other family ceremony or dance.

---

[1] **monotony**—the state of being dull and unchanging.

[2] **threshold**—point of entry.

[3] placers—deposits of gravel or sand on a stream bed that contain valuable minerals.

[4] Ramadan—in Islam, it is the holy month during which the devout fast during each day.

[5] Tabaski—Islamic religious festival.

Therefore, to enhance their chances of being served quickly and to more easily persuade my father to interrupt the work before him, they used to request the services of an official praise-singer, a go-between, arranging in advance the fee they were to pay him for his good offices.

The go-between installed himself in the workshop, tuned up his *cora,* which is our harp, and began to sing my father's praises. This was always a great event for me. I heard recalled the lofty deeds of my father's ancestors and their names from the earliest times. As the couplets were reeled off it was like watching the growth of a great genealogical tree that spread its branches far and wide and flourished its boughs and twigs before my mind's eye. The harp played an accompaniment to this vast **utterance**[6] of names, expanding it with notes that were now soft, now shrill.

I could sense my father's vanity being inflamed, and I already knew that after having sipped this milk-and-honey he would lend a favorable ear to the woman's request. But I was not alone in my knowledge. The woman also had seen my father's eyes gleaming with contented pride. She held out her grains of gold as if the whole matter were settled. My father took up his scales and weighed the gold.

"What sort of trinket do you want?" he would ask.

"I want. . . ."

And then the woman would not know any longer exactly what she wanted because desire kept making her change her mind, and because she would have liked all the trinkets at once. But it would have taken a pile of gold much larger than she had brought to satisfy her whim, and from then on her chief purpose in life was to get hold of it as soon as she could.

"When do you want it?"

Always the answer was that the trinket was needed for an occasion in the near future.

"So! You are in that much of a hurry? Where do you think I shall find the time?"

"I am in a great hurry, I assure you."

"I have never seen a woman eager to deck[7] herself out who wasn't in a great hurry! Good! I shall arrange my time to suit you. Are you satisfied?"

He would take the clay pot that was kept specially for **smelting**[8] gold, and would pour the grains into it. He would then cover the gold with powdered charcoal, a charcoal he prepared by using plant juices of exceptional purity. Finally, he would place a large lump of the same kind of charcoal over the pot.

As soon as she saw that the work had been duly undertaken, the woman, now quite satisfied, would return to her household tasks, leaving her go-between to carry on with the praise-singing which had already proved so advantageous.

At a sign from my father the apprentices began working two sheepskin **bellows**.[9] The skins were on the floor, on opposite sides

---

[6] **utterance**—something spoken.

[7] **deck**—add beauty to or decorate.

[8] **smelting**—related to the melting of metal.

[9] **bellows**—device that forces air into a fire, to increase its heat.

of the forge, connected to it by earthen pipes. While the work was in progress the apprentices sat in front of the bellows with crossed legs. That is, the younger of the two sat, for the elder was sometimes allowed to assist. But the younger—this time it was Sidafa—was only permitted to work the bellows and watch while waiting his turn for promotion to less **rudimentary**[10] tasks. First one and then the other worked hard at the bellows: the flame in the forge rose higher and became a living thing, a **genie**[11] implacable and full of life.

Then my father lifted the clay pot with his long tongs and placed it on the flame.

Immediately all activity in the workshop almost came to a halt. During the whole time that the gold was being smelted, neither copper nor aluminum could be worked nearby, lest some particle of these base metals fall into the container which held the gold. Only steel could be worked on such occasions, but the men, whose task that was, hurried to finish what they were doing, or left it abruptly to join the apprentices gathered around the forge. There were so many, and they crowded so around my father, that I, the smallest person present, had to come near the forge in order not to lose track of what was going on.

If he felt he had inadequate working space, my father had the apprentices stand well away from him. He merely raised his hand in a simple gesture: at that particular moment he never uttered a word, and no one else would: no one was allowed to utter a word. Even the go-between's voice was no longer raised in song. The silence was broken only by the panting of the bellows and the faint hissing of the gold. But if my father never actually spoke, I know that he was forming words in his mind. I could tell from his lips, which kept moving, while, bending over the pot, he stirred the gold and charcoal with a bit of wood that kept bursting into flame and had constantly to be replaced by a fresh one.

> *The silence was broken only by the panting of the bellows and the faint hissing of the gold.*

What words did my father utter? I do not know. At least I am not certain what they were. No one ever told me. But could they have been anything but **incantations**?[12] On these occasions was he not invoking the genies of fire and gold, of fire and wind, of wind blown by the blast-pipes of the forge, of fire born of wind, of gold married to fire? Was it not their assistance, their friendship, their **espousal**[13] that he **besought**?[14] Yes. Almost certainly he was invoking these genies, all of whom are equally indispensable for smelting gold.

The operation going on before my eyes was certainly the smelting of gold, yet something more than that: a magical operation that the guiding spirits could regard with favor or disfavor. That is why, all

---

[10] **rudimentary**—basic, simple.

[11] **genie**—spirit.

[12] **incantations**—spells.

[13] **espousal**—marriage or partnership.

[14] **besought**—asked or begged for.

around my father, there was absolute silence and anxious expectancy. Though only a child, I knew there could be no craft greater than the goldsmith's. I expected a ceremony; I had come to be present at a ceremony; and it actually was one, though very protracted. I was still too young to understand why, but I had an inkling as I watched the almost religious concentration of those who followed the mixing process in the clay pot.

When finally the gold began to melt I could have shouted aloud—and perhaps we all would have if we had not been forbidden to make a sound. I trembled, and so did everyone else watching my father stir the mixture—it was still a heavy paste—in which the charcoal was gradually consumed. The next stage followed swiftly. The gold now had the fluidity of water. The genies had smiled on the operation!

"Bring me the brick!" my father would order, thus lifting the ban that until then had silenced us.

The brick, which an apprentice would place beside the fire, was hollowed out, generously greased with Galam butter. My father would take the pot off the fire and tilt it carefully, while I would watch the gold flow into the brick, flow like liquid fire. True, it was only a very sparse trickle of fire, but how vivid, how brilliant! As the gold flowed into the brick, the grease sputtered and flamed and emitted a thick smoke that caught in the throat and stung the eyes, leaving us all weeping and coughing.

But there were times when it seemed to me that my father ought to turn this task over to one of his assistants. They were experienced, had assisted him hundreds of times, and could certainly have performed the work well. But my father's lips moved and those inaudible, secret words, those incantations he addressed to one we could not see or hear, was the essential part. Calling on the genies of fire, of wind, of gold and **exorcising**[15] the evil spirits—this was a knowledge he alone possessed.

By now the gold had been cooled in the hollow of the brick, and my father began to hammer and stretch it. This was the moment when his work as a goldsmith really began. I noticed that before embarking on it he never failed to stroke the little snake stealthily as it lay coiled up under the sheepskin. I can only assume that this was his way of gathering strength for what remained to be done, the most trying part of his task.

But was it not extraordinary and miraculous that on these occasions the little black snake was always coiled under the sheepskin? He was not always there. He did not visit my father every day. But he was always present whenever there was gold to be worked. His presence was no surprise to *me*. After that evening when my father had spoken of the guiding spirit of his race I was no longer astonished. The snake was there intentionally. He knew what the future held. Did he tell my

---

[15] **exorcising**—driving away.

father? I think that he most certainly did. Did he tell him everything? I have another reason for believing firmly that he did. The craftsman who works in gold must first of all purify himself. That is, he must wash himself all over and, of course, abstain from all sexual commerce during the whole time. Great respecter of ceremony as he was, it would have been impossible for my father to ignore these rules. Now, I never saw him make these preparations. I saw him address himself to his work without any apparent preliminaries. From that moment it was obvious that, forewarned in a dream by his black guiding spirit of the task which awaited him in the morning, my father must have prepared for it as soon as he arose, entering his workshop in a state of purity, his body smeared with the secret potions hidden in his numerous pots of magical substances; or perhaps he always came into his workshop in a state of ritual purity. I am not trying to make him out a better man than he was—he was a man and had his share of human **frailties**[16]— but he was always uncompromising in his respect for ritual observance.

The woman for whom the trinket was being made, and who had come often to see how the work was progressing, would arrive for the final time, not wanting to miss a moment of this spectacle—as marvelous to her as to us—when the gold wire, which my father had succeeded in drawing out from the mass of molten gold and charcoal, was transformed into a trinket.

There she would be. Her eyes would devour the fragile gold wire, following it in its tranquil and regular spiral around the little slab of metal which supported it. My father would catch a glimpse of her and I would see him slowly beginning to smile. Her avid attention delighted him.

The craftsman who works in gold must first of all purify himself.

"Are you trembling?" he would ask. "Am I trembling?"

And we would all burst out laughing at her. For she would be trembling! She would be trembling with **covetousness**[17] for the spiral pyramid in which my father would be inserting, among the convolutions, tiny grains of gold. When he had finally finished by crowning the pyramid with a heavier grain, she would dance in delight.

No one—no one at all—would be more enchanted than she as my father slowly turned the trinket back and forth between his fingers to display its perfection. Not even the praise-singer whose business it was to register excitement would be more excited than she. Throughout this metamorphosis he did not stop speaking faster and ever faster, increasing his tempo, accelerating his praises and flatteries as the trinket took shape, shouting to the skies my father's skill.

For the praise-singer took a curious part—I should say rather that it was direct

---

[16] **frailties**—weaknesses.

[17] **covetousness**—desire or jealousy for another's possessions.

and effective—in the work. He was drunk with the joy of creation. He shouted aloud in joy. He plucked his *cora* like a man inspired. He sweated as if he were the trinket-maker, as if he were my father, as if the trinket were his creation. He was no longer a hired censer-bearer,[18] a man whose services anyone could rent. He was a man who created his song out of some deep inner necessity. And when my father, after having **soldered**[19] the large grain of gold that crowned the summit, held out his work to be admired, the praise-singer would no longer be able to contain himself. He would begin to intone the *douga*, the great chant which is sung only for celebrated men and which is danced for them alone.

> *He would begin to intone the* **douga,** *the great chant which is sung only for celebrated men and which is danced for them alone.*

But the *douga* is a formidable chant, a provocative chant, a chant which the praise-singer dared not sing, and which the man for whom it is sung dared not dance before certain precautions had been taken. My father had taken them as soon as he woke, since he had been warned in a dream. The praise-singer had taken them when he concluded his arrangements with the woman. Like my father he had smeared his body with magic substances and had made himself invulnerable to the evil genies whom the *douga* inevitably set free; these potions made him invulnerable also to rival praise-singers, perhaps jealous of him, who awaited only this song and the exaltation and loss of control which attended it, in order to begin casting their spells.

At the first notes of the *douga* my father would arise and emit a cry in which happiness and triumph were equally mingled; and **brandishing**[20] in his right hand the hammer that was the symbol of his profession and in his left a ram's horn filled with magic substances, he would dance the glorious dance.

No sooner had he finished, than work-men and apprentices, friends and customers in their turn, not forgetting the woman for whom the trinket had been created, would flock around him, congratulating him, showering praises on him and compli-menting the praise-singer at the same time. The latter found himself laden with gifts—almost his only means of support, for the praise-singer leads a wandering life after the fashion of the troubadours of old. Aglow with dancing and the praises he had received, my father would offer every-one cola nuts, that small change of Guinean courtesy.

Now all that remained to be done was to redden the trinket in a little water to which chlorine and sea salt had been added. I was at liberty to leave. The festi-val was over! But often as I came out of the

---

[18] censer-bearer—servant responsible for burning incense.

[19] **soldered**—joined one metal object to another.

[20] **brandishing**—waving.

workshop my mother would be in the court, pounding millet or rice, and she would call to me:

"Where have you been?" although she knew perfectly well where I had been.

"In the workshop."

"Of course. Your father was smelting gold. Gold! Always gold!"

And she would beat the millet or rice furiously with her pestle.

"Your father is ruining his health!"

"He danced the *douga*."

"The *douga*! The *douga* won't keep him from ruining his eyes. As for you, you would be better off playing in the court-yard instead of breathing dust and smoke in the workshop."

My mother did not like my father to work in gold. She knew how dangerous it was: a trinket-maker empties his lungs blowing on the blow-pipe and his eyes suffer from the fire. Perhaps they suffer even more from the microscopic precision which the work requires. And even if there had been no such objections involved, my mother would scarcely have relished this work. She was suspicious of it, for gold can not be smelted without the use of other metals, and my mother thought it was not entirely honest to put aside for one's own use the gold which the alloy had displaced. However, this was a custom generally known, and one which she herself had accepted when she took cotton to be woven and received back only a piece of cotton cloth half the weight of the original bundle.

QUESTIONS TO CONSIDER

1. What roles does the praise-singer play in the gold-working process?

2. Why does Laye so enjoy seeing his father work as a goldsmith? Why does his mother dislike it?

3. What are the two points of view in this memoir?

Chapter 2

The Middle East

Troubled Times

**Modern Faces in
Ancient Garb**

◀ *Return of Flock,* by the Iranian artist Mohammad Reza Irani
(1954–1994), glimpses timeless village life in contemporary Iran.

The Conjuror Made Off with the Dish

NAGUIB MAHFOUZ

Naguib Mahfouz (1911–   ) was the first Arab writer to win the Nobel Prize for literature. He has published nearly forty novels, almost all of them set in his beloved city of Cairo, the Egyptian capital. Egypt has passed through many periods during Mahfouz's life, all documented in his writing. When he was born, Egypt was run by the British, who installed a king during the 1920s. Various degrees of independence were granted over the next three decades, until 1952 when a military coup removed the British-backed king and created an independent country. Since the 1950s, Egypt has been dominated by a series of military leaders. At first the country was resolutely secular, but in the 1970s, the government began to encourage Islamic fundamentalists as a way to prop up its authoritarian regime. In 1981, Islamic radicals assassinated the president, and since then a war has been waged in Egypt between the military government and the fundamentalists. The real casualties of this conflict have been secular intellectuals like Mahfouz and the middle class. Mahfouz was stabbed in the neck in 1994 by Islamic fundamentalists who accused him of blasphemy, and he now experiences great physical pain when writing.

"The time has come for you to be useful," said my mother to me. And she slipped her hand into her pocket, saying, "Take this piaster[1] and go off and buy some beans. Don't play on the way and keep away from the carts."

I took the dish, put on my clogs, and went out, humming a tune. Finding a crowd in front of the bean seller, I waited until I discovered a way through to the marble counter.

"A piaster's worth of beans, mister," I called out in my shrill voice.

He asked me impatiently, "Beans alone? With oil? With cooking butter?"

I did not answer, and he said roughly, "Make way for someone else."

I withdrew, overcome by embarrassment, and returned home defeated.

"Returning with the dish empty?" my mother shouted at me. "What did you do—spill the beans or lose the piaster, you naughty boy?"

[1] piaster—smallest Egyptian coin.

"Beans alone? With oil? With cooking butter?—you didn't tell me," I protested.

"Stupid boy! What do you eat every morning?"

"I don't know."

"You good-for-nothing, ask him for beans with oil."

I went off to the man and said, "A piaster's worth of beans with oil, mister."

With a frown of impatience he asked, "Linseed oil? Vegetable oil? Olive oil?"

I was taken aback[2] and again made no answer.

"Make way for someone else," he shouted at me.

I returned in a rage to my mother, who called out in astonishment, "You've come back empty-handed—no beans and no oil."

"Linseed oil? Vegetable oil? Olive oil? Why didn't you tell me?" I said angrily.

"Beans with oil means beans with linseed oil."

"How should I know?"

"You're a good-for-nothing, and he's a **tiresome**[3] man—tell him beans with linseed oil."

I went off quickly and called out to the man while still some yards from his shop, "Beans with linseed oil, mister."

"Put the piaster on the counter," he said, plunging the ladle into the pot.

I put my hand into my pocket but did not find the piaster. I searched for it anxiously. I turned my pocket inside out but found no trace of it. The man withdrew the ladle empty, saying with disgust, "You've lost the piaster—you're not a boy to be depended on."

"I haven't lost it," I said, looking under my feet and round about me. "It was in my pocket all the time."

"Make way for someone else and stop bothering me."

I returned to my mother with an empty dish.

"Good grief, are you an idiot, boy?"

"The piaster. . ."

"What of it?"

"It's not in my pocket."

"Did you buy sweets with it?"

"I swear I didn't."

"How did you lose it?"

"I don't know."

"Do you swear by the Koran you didn't buy anything with it?"

"I swear."

"Is there a hole in your pocket?"

"No, there isn't."

"Maybe you gave it to the man the first time or the second."

"Maybe."

"Are you sure of nothing?"

"I'm hungry."

She clapped her hands together in a gesture of resignation. "Never mind," she said. "I'll give you another piaster but I'll take it out of your money-box, and if you come back with an empty dish, I'll break your head."

I went off at a run, dreaming of a delicious breakfast. At the turning leading to the alleyway where the bean seller was, I saw a crowd of children and heard merry,

---

[2] taken aback—surprised.

[3] **tiresome**—boring or annoying.

festive sounds. My feet dragged as my heart was pulled toward them. At least let me have a fleeting glance. I slipped in among them and found the conjurer looking straight at me. A **stupefying**[4] joy overwhelmed me; I was completely taken out of myself. With the whole of my being I became involved in the tricks of the rabbits and the eggs, and the snakes and the ropes. When the man came up to collect money, I drew back mumbling, "I haven't got any money."

He rushed at me savagely, and I escaped only with difficulty. I ran off, my back almost broken by his blow, and yet I was utterly happy as I made my way to the seller of beans.

"Beans with linseed oil for a piaster, mister," I said.

He went on looking at me without moving, so I repeated my request.

"Give me the dish," he demanded angrily.

The dish! Where was the dish? Had I dropped it while running? Had the conjurer made off with it?

"Boy, you're out of your mind!"

I retraced my steps, searching along the way for the lost dish. The place where the conjurer had been, I found empty, but the voices of children led me to him in a nearby lane. I moved around the circle. When the conjurer spotted me, he shouted out threateningly, "Pay up or you'd better scram."

"The dish!" I called out despairingly.

"What dish, you little devil?"

"Give me back the dish."

"Scram or I'll make you into food for snakes."

He had stolen the dish, yet fearfully I moved away out of sight and wept in grief. Whenever a passerby asked me why I was crying, I would reply, "The conjurer made off with the dish."

Through my misery I became aware of a voice saying, "Come along and watch!"

I looked behind me and saw a peep show had been set up. I saw dozens of children hurrying toward it and taking it in turns to stand in front of the peepholes, while the man began his tantalizing commentary to the pictures.

"There you've got the gallant knight and the most beautiful of all ladies, Zainat al-Banat."

My tears dried up, and I gazed in fascination at the box, completely forgetting the conjurer and the dish. Unable to overcome the temptation, I paid over the piaster and stood in front of the peephole next to a girl who was standing in front of the other one, and enchanting picture stories flowed across our vision. When I came back to my own world I realized I had lost both the piaster and the dish, and there was no sign of the conjurer. However, I gave no thought to the loss, so taken up was I with the pictures of chivalry, love, and deeds of daring. I forgot my hunger. I forgot even the fear of what threatened me at home. I took a few paces back so as to lean against the ancient wall of what had once been a treasury and the chief cadi's[5] seat of office, and gave

---

[4] **stupefying**—causing one to be unaware or stupid.

[5] cadi's—of an Islamic judge.

myself up wholly to my reveries. For a long while I dreamed of chivalry, of Zainat al-Banat and the ghoul.[6] In my dream I spoke aloud, giving meaning to my words with gestures. Thrusting home the imaginary lance, I said, "Take that, O ghoul, right in the heart!"

"And he raised Zainat al-Banat up behind him on the horse," came back a gentle voice.

I looked to my right and saw the young girl who had been beside me at the performance. She was wearing a dirty dress and colored clogs and was playing with her long **plait**[7] of hair. In her other hand were the red-and-white sweets called "lady's fleas," which she was leisurely sucking. We exchanged glances, and I lost my heart to her.

"Let's sit down and rest," I said to her.

She appeared to go along with my suggestion, so I took her by the arm and we went through the gateway of the ancient wall and sat down on a step of its stairway that went nowhere, a stairway that rose up until it ended in a platform behind which there could be seen the blue sky and minarets.[8] We sat in silence, side by side. I pressed her hand, and we sat on in silence, not knowing what to say. I experienced feelings that were new, strange, and obscure. Putting my face close to hers, I breathed in the natural smell of her hair mingled with an odor of dust, and the fragrance of breath mixed with the aroma of sweets. I kissed her lips. I swallowed my saliva, which had taken on a sweetness from the dissolved "lady's fleas." I put my

arm around her, without her uttering a word, kissing her cheek and lips. Her lips grew still as they received the kiss, then went back to sucking at the sweets. At last she decided to get up. I seized her arm anxiously. "Sit down," I said.

"I'm going," she replied simply.

"Where to?" I asked dejectedly.

"To the midwife[9] Umm Ali," and she pointed to a house on the ground floor of which was a small ironing shop.

"Why?"

"To tell her to come quickly."

"Why?"

"My mother's crying in pain at home. She told me to go to the midwife Umm Ali and tell her to come along quickly."

"And you'll come back after that?"

She nodded her head in assent and went off. Her mentioning her mother reminded me of my own, and my heart missed a beat. Getting up from the ancient stairway, I made my way back home. I wept out loud, a tried method by which I would defend myself. I expected she would come to me, but she did not. I wandered from the kitchen to the bedroom but found no trace of her. Where had my mother gone? When would she return? I was fed up with being in the empty house. A good idea occurred to me. I took a dish from the kitchen and a piaster from my savings and went off immediately to the

---

[6] ghoul—a spirit in Muslim folklore that feeds on corpses.

[7] **plait**—braid.

[8] minarets—slender towers attached to Muslim buildings of worship (mosques).

[9] midwife—a person trained to assist women in childbirth or illness.

seller of beans. I found him asleep on a bench outside the shop, his face covered by his arm. The pots of beans had vanished and the long-necked bottles of oil had been put back on the shelf and the marble counter had been washed down.

"Mister," I whispered, approaching.

Hearing nothing but his snoring, I touched his shoulder. He raised his arm in alarm and looked at me through reddened eyes.

"Mister."

"What do you want?" he asked roughly, becoming aware of my presence and recognizing me.

"A piaster's worth of beans with linseed oil."

"Eh?"

"I've got the piaster and I've got the dish."

"You're crazy, boy," he shouted at me. "Get out or I'll bash your brains in."

When I did not move, he pushed me so violently I went sprawling onto my back. I got up painfully, struggling to hold back the crying that was twisting my lips. My hands were clenched, one on the dish and the other on the piaster. I threw him an angry look. I thought about returning home with my hopes **dashed**,[10] but dreams of heroism and valor altered my plan of action. Resolutely I made a quick decision and with all my strength threw the dish at him. It flew through the air and struck him on the head, while I took to my heels, heedless of everything. I was convinced I had killed him, just as the knight had

killed the ghoul. I did not stop running till I was near the ancient wall. Panting, I looked behind me but saw no signs of any pursuit. I stopped to get my breath, then asked myself what I should do now that the second dish was lost? Something warned me not to return home directly, and soon I had given myself over to a wave of indifference that bore me off where it willed. It meant a beating, neither more nor less, on my return, so let me put it off for a time. Here was the piaster in my hand, and I could have some sort of enjoyment with it before being punished. I decided to pretend I had forgotten I had done anything wrong—but where was the conjurer, where was the peep show? I looked everywhere for them to no **avail**.[11]

Worn out by this fruitless searching, I went off to the ancient stairway to keep my appointment. I sat down to wait, imagining to myself the meeting. I yearned for another kiss **redolent**[12] with the fragrance of sweets. I admitted to myself that the little girl had given me lovelier sensations than I had ever experienced. As I waited and dreamed, a whispering sound came from behind me. I climbed the stairs cautiously, and at the final landing I lay down flat on my face in order to see what was beyond, without anyone being able to notice me. I saw some ruins surrounded by a high wall, the last of what remained of the treasury and the chief cadi's seat of office. Directly

---

[10] **dashed**—thrown with great force in order to break or shatter.

[11] **avail**—help or benefit.

[12] **redolent**—having a strong odor.

under the stairs sat a man and a woman, and it was from them that the whispering came. The man looked like a tramp; the woman like one of those Gypsies that tend sheep. A suspicious inner voice told me that their meeting was similar to the one I had had. Their lips and the looks they exchanged spoke of this, but they showed astonishing expertise in the unimaginable things they did. My gaze became rooted upon them with curiosity, surprise, pleasure, and a certain amount of **disquiet**.[13] At last they sat down side by side, neither of them taking any notice of the other. After quite a while the man said, "The money!"

"You're never satisfied," she said irritably.

Spitting on the ground, he said, "You're crazy."

"You're a thief."

He slapped her hard with the back of his hand, and she gathered up a handful of earth and threw it in his face. Then, his face soiled with dirt, he sprang at her, fastening his fingers on her windpipe, and a bitter fight ensued. In vain she gathered all her strength to escape from his grip. Her voice failed her, her eyes bulged out of their sockets, while her feet struck out at the air. In dumb terror, I stared at the scene till I saw a thread of blood trickling down from her nose. A scream escaped from my mouth. Before the man raised his head, I had crawled backward. Descending the stairs at a jump, I raced off like mad to wherever my legs might carry me. I did not stop running till I was breathless. Gasping for breath, I was quite unaware

of my surroundings, but when I came to myself I found I was under a raised **vault**[14] at the middle of a crossroads. I had never set foot there before and had no idea of where I was in relation to our quarter. On both sides sat sightless beggars, and crossing from all directions were people who paid attention to no one. In terror I realized I had lost my way and that countless difficulties lay in wait for me before I found my way home. Should I resort to asking one of the passersby to direct me? What, though, would happen if chance should lead me to a man like the seller of beans or the tramp of the waste plot? Would a miracle come about whereby I would see my mother approaching so that I could eagerly hurry toward her? Should I try to make my own way, wandering about till I came across some familiar landmark that would indicate the direction I should take?

I told myself that I should be resolute and make a quick decision. The day was passing, and soon mysterious darkness would descend.

---

[13] **disquiet**—worry or unease.
[14] **vault**—an arched roof.

QUESTIONS TO CONSIDER

1. Do you think the boy is to blame for what happens? Explain your answer.

2. What future does the end of the story seem to indicate for the boy?

3. Is this story set in Egypt today or a long time ago? Explain your answer.

Three Poems

YEHUDA AMICHAI

Yehuda Amichai (1924–   ) was born in Germany, but when he was twelve, his family moved to Jerusalem. They were part of the Zionist movement, which called for the creation of a Jewish national state in Palestine. After World War I, Jews had begun moving to the British-controlled area, where they reclaimed land, set up farms, harnessed the Jordan River for power, and established factories. In 1938, a civil war began between Arabs and Jews, and the outbreak of World War II only postponed the struggles to come. When the British pulled their troops out of Palestine in May 1948, the Jewish communal government proclaimed the state of Israel. A full-scale war erupted immediately. Armies from Egypt, Syria, Lebanon, Jordan, and Iraq poured across the frontiers to assist the Palestinians, but the better-organized Jewish forces more than held their own in the so-called Palestine War. While the fighting between the Arab states and Israel would continue for decades, the state of Israel was firmly established in Palestine. Amichai has been one of Israel's leading writers, with much of his writing centered on the conflicting claims to Palestine and the horrors of war.

Of Three or Four in a Room

Of three or four in a room
there is always one who stands beside the window,
He must see the evil among thorns
and the fires on the hill.
And how people who went out of their houses whole
are given back in the evening like small change.[1]
Of three or four in a room
there is always one who stands beside the window,
his dark hair above his thoughts.

---

[1] small change—something trivial or insignificant.

Behind him, words.
And in front of him, voices wandering without a knapsack,[2]
hearts without **provisions**,[3] **prophecies**[4] without water,
large stones that have been returned
and stay sealed, like letters that have no
address and no one to receive them.

Jerusalem

On a roof in the Old City
laundry hanging in the late afternoon sunlight:
the white sheet of a woman who is my enemy,
the towel of a man who is my enemy,
to wipe off the sweat of his brow.[5]

In the sky of the Old City
a kite.
At the other end of the string,
a child
I can't see
because of the wall.

We have put up many flags,
they have put up many flags.
To make us think that they're happy.
To make them think that we're happy.

---

[2] knapsack—backpack.
[3] **provisions**—food and drink.
[4] **prophecies**—predictions of future events.
[5] brow—forehead.

An Arab Shepherd Is Searching for His Goat on Mount Zion

An Arab shepherd is searching for his goat on Mount Zion[6]
and on the opposite mountain I am searching
for my little boy.
An Arab shepherd and a Jewish father
both in their temporary failure.
Our voices meet above the Sultan's Pool[7]
in the valley between us. Neither of us wants
the child or the goat to get caught in the wheels
of the terrible *Had Gadya*[8] machine.

Afterward we found them among the bushes
and our voices came back inside us, laughing and crying.
Searching for a goat or a son
has always been in the beginning
of a new religion in these mountains.

---

[6] Mount Zion—site of Jerusalem.

[7] Sultan's Pool—a pool in a valley just outside the walls of Jerusalem.

[8] *Had Gadya*—Hebrew for "one kid" and alludes to a Passover poem that describes a sequence of events in which a goat is bitten by a cat which in turn is bitten by a dog, and so on. The poem is meant to describe retribution for evil deeds and symbolize the journey of the soul from creation until Judgment Day.

QUESTIONS TO CONSIDER

1. What are the attitudes being depicted in "Of Three or Four in a Room"?

2. How would you describe the various kinds of "flags" that are depicted in "Jerusalem"? What do they stand for?

3. What is the new religion in "An Arab Shepherd Is Searching for His Goat on Mount Zion"? What were the old ones?

4. What is the overall tone of Amichai's poems? How do you think he feels about what has happened in Israel in the half-century since its creation?

Two Poems

MAHMOUD DARWISH

The Palestine War of 1948–1949 established Israel as an independent state and turned 750,000 Palestinians into refugees. With neighboring Arab states unwilling to accept them, the Palestinians became a people without a country. The refugees were forced to move to camps on the West Bank of the Jordan River and the narrow Gaza Strip. Mahmoud Darwish (1942–   ) was born in a Palestinian village that was destroyed in the war. Raised in Israel, Darwish became involved in the political opposition and was imprisoned by the government. In 1971, he went into exile and has become the most famous literary voice of the Palestinian movement. His poetry relates what it is like to be without a homeland, to be a permanent refugee.

Identity Card

Put it on record.
  I am an Arab
And the number of my card is fifty thousand
I have eight children
And the ninth is due after summer.
What's there to be angry about?

Put it on record.
  I am an Arab
Working with comrades of toil in a quarry.[1]
I have eight children
For them I wrest the loaf of bread,
The clothes and exercise books

---

[1] quarry—a mine or other place from which stone is gathered.

From the rocks
And beg for no alms at your door,
    Lower not myself at your doorstep.
    What's there to be angry about?

Put it on record.
    I am an Arab.
I am a name without a title,
Patient in a country where everything
Lives in a whirlpool of anger.
    My roots
    Took hold before the birth of time
    Before the **burgeoning**[2] of the ages,
    Before cypress and olive trees,
    Before the **proliferation**[3] of weeds.

My father is from the family of the plough
    Not from highborn nobles.
And my grandfather was a peasant
    Without line or **genealogy**.[4]
My house is a watchman's hut
    Made of sticks and reeds.
Does my status satisfy you?
    I am a name without a surname.[5]

Put it on record.
    I am an Arab.
Color of hair: jet black.
Color of eyes: brown.
My distinguishing features:
On my head the 'iqal cords over a keffiyeh[6]
    Scratching him who touches it.

---

[2] **burgeoning**—the act of beginning to grow rapidly, thriving.

[3] **proliferation**—the act of rapidly increasing in number, multiplying.

[4] **genealogy**—a line of descent traced from an ancestor.

[5] surname—family name, as opposed to a first name.

[6] '*iqal . . . keffiyeh*—In the traditional Palestinian headdress, a cloth (the *keffiyeh*) is held on the head by a hanging braid (the '*iqal*).

My address:
I'm from a village, remote, forgotten,
Its streets without name
And all its men in the fields and quarry.

What's there to be angry about?

Put it on record.
    I am an Arab.
You stole my forefathers' vineyards
    And land I used to till,[7]
    I and all my children,
And you left us and all my grandchildren
    Nothing but these rocks.
Will your government be taking them too
    As is being said?

So!
    Put it on record at the top of page one:
    I don't hate people,
    I trespass on no one's property.
And yet, if I were to become hungry
    I shall eat the flesh of my usurper.[8]
    Beware, beware of my hunger
    And of my anger!

---

[7] **till**—prepare soil to grow crops.
[8] **usurper**—one who seizes power wrongfully.

On Wishes

Don't say to me:
 Would I were a seller of bread in Algiers
 That I might sing with a rebel.
Don't say to me:
 Would I were a herdsman in the Yemen[9]
 That I might sing to the **shudderings**[10] of time.
Don't say to me:
 Would I were a café waiter in Havana[11]
 That I might sing to the victories of sorrowing women.
Don't say to me:
 Would I worked as a young laborer in Aswan[12]
 That I might sing to the rocks.

My friend,
The Nile will not flow into the Volga,
Nor the Congo or the Jordan into the Euphrates.[13]
Each river has its source, its course, its life.
My friend, our land is not barren.
Each land has its time for being born,
Each dawn a date with a rebel.

---

[9] Yemen—a country at the tip of the Arabian peninsula.

[10] **shudderings**—vibrations or tremors.

[11] Havana—the capital of Cuba, where there was a popular revolution against a corrupt government in 1959.

[12] Aswan—city in Egypt where a huge dam was built to make more land arable in Egypt.

[13] Nile . . . Volga . . . Congo . . . Jordan . . . Euphrates—large rivers in Egypt, Russia, central Africa, the Middle East, and Iraq, respectively.

QUESTIONS TO CONSIDER

1. What is the tone of "Identity Card"? From where does the poet draw his strength to resist?

2. What is the dominant idea of "On Wishes"?

3. From reading these poems, how would you describe the Palestinian struggle as Darwish sees and experiences it?

Four Poems

NIZAR QABBANI

Nizar Qabbani (1923–   ) is one of the Arab world's most famous writers. Born in Damascus, Syria, he studied law before entering the diplomatic corps. Qabbani's poems are written in everyday speech that is clear and concise, and they are on two main themes: love and the disaster of modern Arab politics. Qabbani has particularly attacked the corrupt leadership of the Arab states, and he is a virulent critic of Israel. Qabbani's first collection was published in 1943, and his numerous publications since have kept him always at the forefront of Arabic poetry. His themes and his clarity make his poems immensely appealing to the majority of Arabic-speakers.

I Conquer the World with Words

I conquer the world with words,
conquer the mother tongue,
verbs, nouns, **syntax,**[1]
I sweep away the beginnings of things
and with a new language
that has the music of water the message of fire
I light the coming age
and stop time in your eyes
and wipe away the line
that separates
time from this single moment.

---

[1] **syntax**—the arrangement of words and their meanings in relation to one another.

Equation

I love you
therefore I am
in the present.
I write, beloved,
and retrieve the past.

Language

When a man is in love
how can he use old words?
Should a woman
desiring her lover
lie down with
grammarians[2] and linguists?

I said nothing
to the woman I loved
but gathered
love's adjectives into a suitcase
and fled from all languages.

Fragments from *Notes on the Book of Defeat*

If an audience[3] could be arranged
and also my safe return
this is what I'd tell the Sultan
This is what he'd learn:
O Sultan, my master, if my clothes

---

[2] grammarians—experts in grammar.
[3] audience—a formal appointment to meet with a person of authority.

are ripped and torn
it is because your dogs with claws
are allowed to tear me.
And your informers every day are those
who dog[4] my heels, each step
unavoidable as fate.
They interrogate my wife, at length,
and list each friend's name.
Your soldiers kick and beat me,
force me to eat from my shoes,
because I dare approach these walls
for an audience with you.
You have lost two wars
and no one tells you why.
Half your people have no tongues.
What good their unheard sigh?
The other half, within these walls,
run like rabbits and ants,
silently inside.
If I were given safety
from the Sultan's armed guards
I would say, O Sultan,
the reason you've lost wars twice
was because you've been walled in from
mankind's cause and voice.

---

[4] dog—to follow closely and persistently.

QUESTIONS TO CONSIDER

1. What act is Qabbani describing in "I Conquer the World with Words"? What does the last sentence of the poem suggest?

2. What is the comparison Qabbani is making in both "Equation" and "Language"? Why do you think he is making it?

3. What is the political message of "Fragments from *Notes on the Book of Defeat*"? What and whom does the speaker need protection from?

4. From reading these poems, do you think Qabbani feels that the poet must speak out in difficult times? Point to lines in the poems that support your answer.

The Butcher

ARI SILETZ

Ari Siletz (1953–   ) grew up in Iran when it was still ruled by the Shah Muhammad Reza Pahlavi. The shah was an autocrat who spent the country's huge oil profits on building a large army and on grandiose industrial projects. Iran had the look of a modern country, but the government had never introduced public education. Businesses were run by foreign workers, and most Iranians were mired in poverty. What middle class did exist was frustrated by Iran's repressive society. The shah's most serious opposition came from the Muslim clergy who bitterly opposed his promotion of Western values. The clergy, led by Ayatollah Ruhollah Khomeini, evoked powerful religious and nationalist sentiments to encourage resistance. During the 1970s, strikes crippled the Iranian economy, and by the end of 1978 a popular revolution was under way in the streets. The shah fled. On February 1, Iran was declared an Islamic republic. Siletz's story "The Butcher" is set in the 1970s when the seeds of revolution were already sown.

The call to noon prayer was beating down from the sun. A laborer **mutters**[1] his devotion in the scant shade of a **sapling**.[2]

> *Guide us along the straight path*
> *The path of those You have favored*
> *Not of those with whom You are angry*
> *Not of those who are lost.*

Enough playing and sightseeing at the marketplace. Time to go home for lunch. I had spent the day watching the grape flies at the fruitseller's shade. They float silently in the fragrant air, their wings blurred around them like halos. They read your mind. Try to grab one and it has already drifted serenely out of the way.

No hurry, no panic. They know the future.

On the short walk home memories of the fruitseller's paradise are already being **bleached**[3] by the sun.

> *Guide us along the straight path . . .*

Why do we need guiding along the straight path? I wonder.

I reach the house, but the gate is locked. I don't feel like knocking; there is an easier way. The neighbors are building their house and there are piles of bricks every

---

[1] **mutters**—speaks softly.

[2] **sapling**—a young tree.

[3] **bleached**—whitened.

where. After many trips back and forth I have enough bricks to make a step stool with which to climb the wall into the house. My arms are scraped pink by the effort. I sneak to the kitchen and try to startle my mother.

"You better go put those bricks back before the neighbor sees them," she says.

The next day I pass by the fruitseller's and go straight to the **cobbler's**[4] tiny shop. A pair of my mother's shoes need mending. The cobbler flashes a "two" with his finger, and goes back to the shoe at hand. His hair and beard look just like the bristles he uses on the shoes.

"I will wait for them here," I say as I pull up a stool. He does not hear me. The walls are covered with unfinished shoes waiting to be soled. They look like faces with their mouths wide open.

"They are shouting at each other," I say, pointing to the walls. The cobbler cannot hear them; he is deaf-mute. He emphatically flashes two fingers again. Come back in two hours. So I walk next door to the butcher's shop to look at the ghastly picture on his window and try to figure out what it means. I hesitate to ask him. Some things are better left alone.

The butcher is a decent man. He has to be, for he is entrusted with doing all our killing. Even though we pass on the act, we are still responsible for the deaths we cause. The killing must be done mercifully and according to the rules of God. The killer must be pure of heart and without **malice**[5] for the world.

Our butcher was a man of great physical and moral strength. My mother said he reminded her of the legendary champion, Rustam. Rustam was so strong that he asked God to take away some of his strength so that he would not make potholes wherever he walked. The butcher was very big. Every time he brought down the cleaver,[6] I feared he might split the butcher's block. His **burly**[7] hands carried the power of life and death. The carcasses hanging on the hooks and the smell of raw meat testified to this. Above the scales was a larger-than-life picture of the first Shiite[8] imam,[9] Ali, who supervised this Judgment-Day atmosphere with a stern but benevolent presence. Across Ali's lap lay his undefeated sword, Zulfaghar.

But the true object of my terror was the picture in the shop window.

A man was chopping off his own arm with a cleaver.

The artwork was eerie, as the man's face had no expression—he stared blankly at the viewer while the blood ran out. This was the butcher's logo. Underneath it the most common name for a butcher shop was beautifully calligraphed: Javanmard (man of integrity).

---

[4] **cobbler**—a person who repairs shoes.

[5] **malice**—hostility.

[6] cleaver—a heavy chopping tool used by butchers.

[7] **burly**—big and strong.

[8] Shiite—a member of one of the main branches of Islam, which rejects the first three successors of Muhammmed, believing that Muslim leadership passed directly from Muhammed to his son-in-law Ali.

[9] imam—a Muslim leader. To Shiites the imams were the twelve legitimate successors of Muhammed beginning with Ali.

I had asked my mother what the **mutilation**[10] signified. She had said it was a traditional symbol attesting the butcher's honesty, but she could not explain further.

"Is the butcher honest?" I had asked.

"Yes, he is very honest. We never have to worry about spoiled meat or bad prices."

"He would rather chop off his arm than be dishonest? Is that what his sign means?"

"Yes."

"What about other shopkeepers? What have they vowed to do in case they are dishonest?"

"I don't know."

"What about the cobbler? Did he do something dishonest? Is that what happened to him?"

"I don't know."

"Is that why people kill themselves? Because they have been very dishonest?"

"Look, it is just a picture. It's not worth having nightmares over. Next time you are there, you can ask him what it means."

I did not ask him about it until I was forced to by my conscience.

One day my mother sent me out to buy half a kilo of ground meat. She told me to tell the butcher that she wanted it without any fat. She knew it would be more expensive and gave me extra money to cover it. I got to the butcher shop at the busiest time of the day. One good thing about the butcher was that he, unlike other shopkeepers, helped the customers on a first-come, first-served basis. Status had no meaning for him and he could not be

bribed.[11] People knew this about him and respected it. When he asked whose turn it was, instead of the usual elbowing and jostling, he got a unanimous answer from the crowd. People do not lie to an honest man.

This gave great meaning to the picture of Ali above the scales. Ali, the Prophet's son-in-law and one-man army, is known for his uncompromising idealism. His guileless methods were interpreted as lack of political wisdom, and he was passed over three times for succession to Mohammad. When he did finally become **caliph,**[12] he became an easy target for the assassin as he, like the Prophet, refused bodyguards for himself. Shiites regard him as the true successor to Mohammad and disregard the three caliphs that came before him.

When my turn came up, I asked for a half a kilo of ground meat with no fat. The butcher sliced off some meat from a **carcass**[13] and ground it. Then he wrapped it in wax paper and wrapped that in someone's homework. Sometimes he used newspapers, but because of the Iranian habit of forcing students to copy volumes of text for homework, old notebook paper was as common as newsprint. He gave me the meat and I gave him the money and started to walk out, but he called me back and gave me some change. This was free money; my mother had not expected change. I took the money and immediately spent it on sweets.

---

[10] **mutilation**—act of cutting or tearing off.

[11] **bribed**—persuaded by gifts or money.

[12] **caliph**—the leader of the Islamic religion.

[13] **carcass**—the dead body of an animal.

When I went home, I did not tell her that she had given me too much money. I worried that she would know I had spent the change on candy and that she would yell at me for it.

Around noontime my mother called me into the kitchen. She asked me if I had told the butcher to put no fat in the meat. I said I had told him.

"I thought he was an honest man. He gave you meat with fat and charged you the higher price," she said sadly.

Now I knew where the extra money came from. In the heat of business he had forgotten about the "no fat" and had given me regular ground meat. But he had *not* charged me the higher price.

"We will go there now and straighten this out with him," she said sternly.

I thought about confessing, but I **deluded**[14] myself into thinking the change had nothing to do with it. After all, *he* made the mistake. How much change had he given me anyway? Or maybe my mother was wrong about the quality of the meat. I was just a victim of the butcher's and my mother's stupidity.

It was still noontime as we set off to straighten out the butcher. The call to prayer was being sung. Across the neighborhood devout supplicants beseeched their maker.

Guide us along the straight path
The path of those You have favored
Not of those with whom You are angry
Not of those who are lost.

I was certainly lost. I was fighting the delusion like a drug, now dispelling it, now overwhelmed by it. When things were clear, I could see that I had done nothing wrong except fail to get permission to buy candy. The butcher made a mistake. I did not know about it, and I bought unauthorized candy. All I had to do was tell my mother and no crime would have been committed. The real crime was still a few minutes in the future, when I would endanger the reputation and livelihood of an honest man. I still had time to avert that.

Guide us along the straight path . . .

When delusion reigned, I felt I had committed a grave, irreversible sin that, paradoxically, others should be blamed for. The straight path was so simple, so forgiving; the other was harsh and muddled. How much more guidance did I need? The prayer did not say "chain us to the straight path." When we reached the shop, the butcher was cleaning the surfaces in preparation for lunch. He usually gathered with the cobbler and the fruitseller in front of the cobbler's shop. They spread their lunch cloth and ate a meal of bread and meat

> **"I thought he was an honest man. He gave you meat with fat and charged you the higher price,"** she said sadly.

[14] **deluded**—misled or deceived.

soup. In **accordance**[15] with tradition, passersby were invited to join them, and in accordance with tradition, the invitation was declined with much apology and gratitude.

My mother told him that when she finished frying the meat, there was too much fat left over and she thought the wrong kind of meat had been sold. She asked if he remembered selling me the meat. The butcher was unclear. He remembered having to call me back to give me some change, but he was too busy at the time to remember more. My mother said that no change would have been involved as she had given me exact change. This confused the butcher and he decided that he did not remember the incident at all. His changing of his recollection added to my mother's suspicions. Meanwhile, Ali was **glowering**[16] at me from the top of the scales, his Zulfaghar ready to strike. My face was hot and my fingers felt numb.

Finally, the butcher, who was not one to argue in the absence of evidence, ground the right amount of the right kind of meat, wrapped it in wax paper, wrapped that in someone's homework, and gave it to my mother. She offered to pay for it, but the butcher refused to accept the money and apologized for making the mistake. When we left, he was taking apart the meat grinder in order to clean it again.

On the way back I felt sleepy. My mother asked if I was all right.

"I'm fine," I said weakly.

"Your father will be home in a few more days," she reassured.

"Mother, do you think the butcher was dishonest?" I asked.

"No, I think he really made a mistake."

"How do you know that?"

"Because he gave us the new meat so willingly. If he was a greedy man, he would not have done that. He probably feels very bad."

A terrible thought occurred to me. "Bad enough to chop off his own arm?" I asked urgently.

"I don't think so," she said.

But I was not convinced. She did not know what awful things could happen off the straight path. "I have to go back," I said as I started to run.

"Where are you going, you crazy boy?"

"I have to ask him about the picture," I yelled.

"Ask him later, now is not the time. . . ." She gave up—I was already a whorl of dust.

I was panting and swallowing when I saw the butcher. He was having lunch with the cobbler and the fruitseller. What did I want now?

"Please, help yourself," said the butcher, inviting me to the spread. I just stood for a while.

"Why do you have a picture of the man chopping off his arm?" I finally asked. The cobbler was tapping the fruitseller on the back, asking what was going on. The fruitseller indicated a chopping motion

---

[15] **accordance**—agreement.
[16] **glowering**—staring in an angry or a threatening way.

over his own arm and pointed toward the butcher shop. The cobbler smiled and repeated the fruitseller's motions.

"That is the Javanmard," the butcher said. "He cheated Ali."

"Why?" I asked.

"Even when he was caliph, Ali did not believe in servants. One day a man came to the butcher's shop and bought some meat. The butcher put his thumb on the scale and so gave him less meat. Later he found out that the customer was Ali himself. The butcher was so distraught and ashamed that he got rid of the guilty thumb along with the arm," he said.

I was greatly relieved. One did not mutilate oneself for committing a wrong against just anybody. It had to be someone of Ali's stature. Our butcher was safe even if he was to blame himself for the mistake. But I had to be absolutely sure.

"So if one were to cheat someone not as holy as Ali, one would not have to feel so bad?" I asked. Looking back, I see that he interpreted this as a criticism of the moral of the **parable.**[17] He was transfixed in thought for a long time. The cobbler was tapping the fruitseller again, but the fruitseller could not find the correct gestures; he kept shrugging irritably.

The butcher finally came to life again. "Ali was good at reminding us of the difference between good and bad," he explained.

I was glad I was not so gifted.

"Would he have killed the butcher with Zulfaghar?" I asked.

"No, in fact I think once he found out what the butcher had done, he went to him and healed the arm completely," he said, displaying his arms. I looked carefully at his arms, but there was not even a trace of an injury. "A miracle," he explained.

The fruitseller was able to translate this and the cobbler agreed vigorously. He had something to add to the story, but we could not understand him.

During lunch I told my mother the butcher's story.

"Now why couldn't this wait until tomorrow?" she asked, collecting the dishes.

"Mother?"

"Yes?"

"If I were to get some change and not bring it back, what would you do?"

"Did you get change and not bring it back?" She smelled a guilty conscience.

"No, I was just wondering."

"It depends on what I had sent you to buy," she said deviously.

"Like meat for instance."

She pondered this while she did the dishes. When she was done, she donned her chador[18] and asked me to put on my shoes.

"Where are we going?" I wondered.

"To the butcher's," she said curtly. "You are going to apologize and give him the money we owe him."

"It was *his* mistake," I protested guiltily.

---

[17] **parable**—a story of imagined events used to teach a lesson.

[18] chador—a large sheet of cloth, worn as a combination veil, shawl, and head covering.

"And you stood there all that time, under Ali's eyes, and watched him grind us the new meat without saying anything."

I followed her dolorously out the gate. I could tell she was upset because she was walking fast and did not care if her chador blew around. But halfway there she changed her mind and with a swish[19] of her chador ordered me to follow her back home.

"Why are we going back, Mother?"

"If this gets out, they will never trust you at the marketplace again," she said angrily.

"So we are not going to apologize?"

"Of course you will apologize. You are going to give him your summer homework so he can wrap his meat in it."

The summer homework filled two whole notebooks. The school had made us copy the entire second grade text. Completing it had been a torturous task and a major accomplishment. My mother had patiently encouraged me to get it out of the way early in the vacation so that it would not loom over me all summer.

"What will I tell the teacher?" I begged.

"You will either do the homework again or face whatever you get for not having it. Or maybe instead of the homework you can show her the composition you are going to write."

"We did not have to write any compositions," I whined.

"You are going to write one explaining why you don't have your homework."

So, for the fourth time that day I went to the butcher shop. It was still quiet at the marketplace; the butcher was taking a nap. He woke up to my shuffling and chuckled groggily when he saw me.

"I was looking for you in the skies but I find you on earth (long time no see)," he said.

I gave him my notebooks and told him that my mother said he could wrap meat in them. He thanked my mother and apologized again for the mistake. My mother had told me not to discuss that with him, so I left quickly.

Within a few days, scraps of my homework, wrapped around chunks of lamb, found their way into kitchens across the neighborhood.

I opted for writing the composition explaining the publication of my homework. My mother signed it. The teacher accepted it enthusiastically, and while other students were writing "How I spent my summer vacation," I was permitted to memorize the opening verses of the Koran.[20] I had heard it many times before and knew the meaning, but I did not have it memorized. It goes:

Guide us along the straight path
The path of those You have favored . . .

A few summers later, the butcher became involved in the religious uprising

---

[19] swish—the act of swinging something audibly through the air.

[20] Koran—the sacred book of Islam.

against the Shah. He tacked a small picture of Khomeini[21] next to Ali and Zulfaghar and would not take it down. His customers, including my mother, urged him not to be so foolish.

"Was Ali foolish to refuse body guards?" he asked.

"You are not Ali, you are just a butcher. Khomeini is gone, exiled. At least hide his picture behind Ali's picture."

When he disappeared, we all worried that he would never come back. But a few days later, he opened his shop again and, as far as I know, never hid anything anywhere.

---

[21] Khomeini—Ruhollah Khomeini (1900–1989) was the ayatollah, or spiritual leader, of Shiite Muslims. He helped inspire the popular revolution in Iran in 1979 and guided the country until his death.

QUESTIONS TO CONSIDER

1. Why does the boy not tell his mother the truth as they return to the butcher shop?

2. What do you think is the meaning of what happens to the boy at the end? Why is he being rewarded at school?

3. What is the lesson that the butcher teaches? What in the story suggests that he understood what the homework the boy gave him meant?

The Slave Fort

GHASSAN KANAFANI

Ghassan Kanafani (1936–1972) was born in Acre, Palestine. In the wake of the war that established Israel in 1948, Kanafani's family fled their home. He grew up in exile, and all his writing is devoted to documenting the plight of the Palestinians: a people without a homeland. Kanafani was killed by a car bomb in Beirut in 1972, but by that time his fiction and his journalism had established him as one of the most important Palestinian writers. "The Slave Fort" is an allegory about how we live our lives.

Had he not been so sadly shabby one would have said of him that he was a poet. The site he had chosen for his humble hut of wood and beaten-out jerry cans was truly magnificent; right by the threshold[1] the might of the sea flowed under the feet of sharp rocks with a deep-throated, unvarying sound. His face was **gaunt**,[2] his beard white though streaked with a few black hairs, his eyes hollow under bushy brows; his cheek-bones protruded like two rocks that had come to rest either side of the large projection that was his nose.

Why had we gone to that place? I don't remember now. In our small car we had followed a rough, miry and featureless road. We had been going for more than three hours when Thabit pointed through the window and gave a piercing shout:

"There's the Slave Fort."

This Slave Fort was a large rock the base of which had been eaten away by the waves so that it resembled the wing of a giant bird, its head curled in the sand, its wing outstretched above the clamor of the sea.

"Why did they call it 'The Slave Fort?'"

"I don't know. Perhaps there was some historical incident which gave it the name. Do you see that hut?"

And once again Thabit pointed, this time towards the small hut lying in the shadow of the the gigantic rock. He turned off the engine and we got out of the car.

"They say that a half-mad old man lives in it."

"What does he do with himself in this waste[3] on his own?"

---

[1] threshold—doorway or entrance.

[2] **gaunt**—thin or grim in appearance.

[3] waste—empty or barren land.

"What any half-mad old man would do."

From afar we saw the old man squatting on his heels at the entrance to his hut, his head clasped in his hands, staring out to sea.

"Don't you think there must be some special story about this old man? Why do you insist he's half-mad?"

"I don't know, that's what I heard."

Thabit, having arrived at the spot of his choice, leveled the sand, threw down the bottles of water, took out the food from the bag, and seated himself.

"They say he was the father of four boys who struck it lucky and are now among the richest people in the district."

"And then?"

"The sons quarreled about who should provide a home for the father. Each wife wanted her own way in the matter and the whole thing ended with the old man making his escape and settling down here."

"It's a common enough story and shouldn't have turned the old man half-mad."

"There he is, only a few yards away—why not go over and ask him?"

Thabit looked at me uncomprehendingly, then lit the small heap of wood he had arranged and poured water into the metal water-jug and set it on the fire.

"The important thing in the story is to agree about whether his flight was a product of his mad half, or his sane half."

Thabit blew at the fire, then began rubbing his eyes as he sat up straight resting his body on his knees.

"I can't bear the idea which the sight of him awakens in me."

"What idea?"

"That the man should spend seventy years of his life so austerely, that he should work, exert himself, existing day after day and hour after hour, that for seventy long years he should gain his daily bread from the sweat of his brow, that he should live through his day in the hope of a better tomorrow, that for seventy whole years he should go to sleep each night—and for what? So that he should, at the last, spend the rest of his life cast out like a dog, alone, sitting like this. Look at him—he's like some polar animal that has lost its fur. Can you believe that a man can live seventy years to **attain**[4] to this? I can't stomach it."

Once again he stared at us; then, spreading out the palms of his hands, he continued his **tirade:**[5]

"Just imagine! Seventy useless, meaningless years. Imagine walking for seventy years along the same road; the same directions, the same boundaries, the same horizons, the same everything. It's unbearable!"

"No doubt the old man would differ with you in your point of view. Maybe he believes that he has reached an end which is distinct from his life. Maybe he wanted just such an end. Why not ask him?"

We got up to go to him. When we came to where he was he raised his eyes, coldly returned our greeting and invited us to sit

---

[4] **attain**—accomplish, arrive at.

[5] **tirade**—a long and passionate speech.

down. Through the half-open door we could see the inside of the hut; the threadbare mattress in one corner, while in the opposite one was a square rock on which lay a heap of unopened oyster shells. For a while silence **reigned**;[6] it was then broken by the old man's feeble voice asking:

"Do you want oyster shells? I sell oyster shells."

As we had no reply to make to him, Thabit inquired:

"Do you find them yourself?"

"I wait for low tide so as to look for them far out. I gather them up and sell them to those who hope to find pearls in them."

We stared at each other. Presently Thabit put the question that had been exercising all our minds.

"Why don't you yourself try to find pearls inside these shells?"

"I?"

He uttered the word as though becoming aware for the first time that he actually existed, or as though the idea had never previously occurred to him. He then shook his head and kept his silence.

"How much do you sell a heap for?"

"Cheaply—for a loaf or two."

"They're small shells and certainly won't contain pearls."

The old man looked at us with lustreless eyes under bushy brows.

"What do you know about shells?" he demanded sharply. "Who's to tell whether or not you'll find a pearl?" And as though afraid that if he were to be carried away still further he might lose the duel, he relapsed into silence.

"And can you tell?"

"No, no one can tell," and he began toying with a shell which lay in front of him, pretending to be unaware of our presence.

"All right, we'll buy a heap."

The old man turned round and pointed to the heap **arrayed**[7] on the square rock.

"Bring two loaves," he said, a concealed ring[8] of joy in his voice, "and you can take that heap."

On returning to our place bearing the heap of shells, our argument broke out afresh.

"I consider those eyes can only be those of a madman. If not, why doesn't he open the shells himself in the hope of finding some pearls?"

"Perhaps he's fed up with trying and prefers to turn spectator and make money."

It took us half the day before we had opened all the shells. We piled the gelatinous[9] insides of the empty shells around us, then burst into laughter at our madness.

In the afternoon Thabit suggested to me that I should take a cup of strong tea to the old man in the hope that it might bring a little joy to his heart.

As I was on my way over to him a slight feeling of fear stirred within me. However, he invited me to sit down and began sipping at his tea with **relish**.[10]

---

[6] **reigned**—ruled, held power.

[7] **arrayed**—displayed or arranged.

[8] ring—bell-like sound.

[9] gelatinous—jellylike.

[10] **relish**—great liking or enjoyment.

"Did you find anything in the shells?"

"No, we found nothing—you fooled us."

He shook his head sadly and took another sip.

"To the extent of two loaves!" he said, as though talking to himself, and once again shook his head. Then, suddenly, he glanced at me and explained sharply:

"Were these shells your life—I mean, were each shell to represent a year of your life and you opened them one by one and found them empty, would you have been as sad as you are about losing a couple of loaves?"

He began to shake all over and at that moment I was convinced that I was in the presence of someone who certainly was mad. His eyes, under their bushy brows, gave out a sharp and unnatural brightness, while the dust from his ragged clothes played in the afternoon sun. I could find not a word to say. When I attempted to rise to my feet he took hold of my wrist and his **frail**[11] hand was strong and convulsive. Then I heard him say:

"Don't be afraid—I am not mad, as you believe. Sit down. I want to tell you something; the happiest moments of my day are when I can watch disappointment of this kind."

I reseated myself, feeling somewhat calmer.

In the meantime, he began to gaze out at the horizon, seemingly unaware of my presence, as though he had not, a moment ago, invited me to sit down. Then he turned to me.

"I knew you wouldn't find anything. These oysters are still young and therefore can't contain the seed of a pearl. I wanted to know, though."

Again he was silent and stared out to sea. Then, as though speaking to himself, he said:

"The ebb tide will start early tonight and I must be off to gather shells. Tomorrow other men will be coming."

Overcome by bewilderment, I rose to my feet. The Slave Fort stood out darkly against the light of the setting sun. My friends were drinking tea around the heaps of empty shells as the old man began running after the **receding**[12] water, bending down from time to time to pick up the shells left behind.

---

[11] **frail**—fragile, delicate.

[12] **receding**—shrinking back or further away.

QUESTIONS TO CONSIDER

1. How would you describe the landscape of the Slave Fort and the old man who lives there? How is this symbolic?

2. How would you contrast Thabit's tirade and the old man's statement about the oysters? Explain the two different perspectives on how we live our lives.

3. What sort of commentary on life is Kanafani making in "The Slave Fort"? Can you draw any parallels between it and the Palestinians' difficulties after 1948? Explain.

From Behind the Veil

DHU'L NUN AYYOUB

Dhu'l Nun Ayyoub (1908–   ) is one of Iraq's most prominent writers, who often depicts the clash between Islamic tradition and modernity. The emphasis on modesty and honor in traditional Islamic society led over time to the practice of women wearing veils when they were in public. It became customary that the only men to look on a woman's face were her father and brothers and, eventually, her husband. This tradition began to die out in the 1920s, but has been revived in some Muslim countries in the last two decades. What seems to many in the West to be a symbol of oppression can often be to the wearer a symbol of faith and freedom. Ayyoub presents this view of the veil in the story "From Behind the Veil."

The street, although wide, was inconveniently full of strollers passing to and fro. The situation was not helped by the sleek swift cars, which sped by from time to time. They carried wealthy occupants, young women and ladies, who, protected from the curiosity of the outside world, displayed radiant faces. Their shining gaze **roved**[1] across the street, smiling or frowning as they took in sights which pleased or displeased them.

Among the surging crowd was an amazing mixture of different clothes and contrasting shapes, which, if nothing else, serve to emphasize the varying tastes of these passersby.

A European who had never been to the East before might be excused for thinking that its people were in the middle of a great festival. As time goes by, however, he is moved to say in amazement, "What long carnival celebrations you have in this country!" Our Western friend would think that people wear these amazing clothes for a festival, just as they would do in his own country.

You can also see women in the crowd, both veiled and unveiled. A man can be surprised to find himself turning involuntarily towards those figures, wearing long silk gowns, which give them such an **enticing**[2] and alluring shape, and make the observer yearn to uncover the magic and the secrets which lie beneath them.

---

[1] **roved**—wandered.

[2] **enticing**—tempting, inviting.

His desire is only increased when his gaze falls on the filmy[3] veil. Behind it he can catch a fleeting glimpse of fine features and penciled eyebrows, which serve to inflame the fires of his heart. It makes him want to devote the rest of his life to the exploration of this world full of shame-faced beauty.

Ihsan was one of those who would stroll along with the crowd displaying his smart and tasteful suit over his slim figure, patting his dark gleaming hair whenever he felt that the evening breezes had ruffled it, or spread a curl over his clear forehead.

This Ihsan was a young man of eighteen, good-looking with fine features which made him attractive to a number of women. Naturally he was aware of his appeal and attraction, and he had the youthful capacity to exploit it. That's why you can see him now, with his eyes wandering in search of a quarry.[4]

Ihsan was not interested in chasing unveiled girls. They exuded poise, which he found unattractive, and they were always looking anxiously to avoid criticism so they never looked the passersby directly in the face. They would walk by without turning their heads, paying no attention to the expressions of flattery which came their way from the gallants, who, after getting as much out of them as a dog gets out of barking at clouds, would give them no further attention.

This is the reason that makes Ihsan always sidle up to the girls with the long cloaks and the secret little movements which attract him: the burning sighs and the gentle laughter and the concealed glances.

Siham had gone out on the evening of that day as usual to take the air and stroll through the streets. This evening stroll had become a part of her life to such an extent that it was now indispensable. She couldn't remember exactly the date when she first set out to **saunter**[5] through the street, and did not really know the reason why she kept up her evening appointments. If she did, she did not admit it. Whatever the case, no sooner had Siham seen the bustle in the middle of the street than she headed for the pavement. She looked cautiously left and right until she saw Ihsan in the distance, and suddenly she felt the blood coursing through her veins.

She found herself unconsciously moving towards him until she was almost parallel with him, saw him staring at her from top to bottom, and felt a tremor throughout her body. When she saw his burning stare almost penetrating the cloak which covered her slender body her heart beat violently. She was used to seeing him every day at this time, and she used to stare at him freely each time until she had memorized his face. Of late, she had begun to feel her heart pounding whenever she saw him, and her face flushed with confusion. There

---

[3] filmy—thin and semitransparent.

[4] quarry—someone or something to pursue, an intended victim.

[5] **saunter**—walk slowly and without effort.

was nothing to stop her from feasting her eyes on him, however, because she knew that the veil covered her face and concealed the overwhelming attraction she felt for him.

We cannot be certain what it was that made this youth know that the girl was interested in him, and whether his first overture to her came in the course of one of his habitual overtures, which he made to any girl. Whatever it was, he went up to the girl boldly on that first day, and **sidled**[6] up to her, greeted her, and saw her turning round to look at him cautiously before hurrying on her way.

He knew immediately that she was not angry with him, and emboldened, he carried on behind her and saw her going into one of the public parks. She knew that he was following her, and hastened on her way, trembling with conflicting emotions of joy, fear, and caution.

He followed her into the park for a short distance, until he saw her sitting on her own, behind a big tree. He went up to her and spoke to her smilingly.

"Good evening."

"Good evening," she replied shyly.

Then she raised her veil from her brown face and her dark eyes, and Ihsan

She was having an adventure, nothing more, and she was drawn into it by her youth and by the warm blood which coursed in her veins.

was captivated by the long dark eyelashes which cast a shadow over her features.

The features of her face were fine, and inspired the beholder with the strongest feelings of awe and worship. She was fearful and breathless, turning from side to side like a timid gazelle. She knew that what she was doing amounted to an unpardonable crime, but drew comfort from one thing—the knowledge that this boy had not seen her before and did not know her. She was having an adventure, nothing more, and she was drawn into it by her youth and by the warm blood which coursed in her veins.

The boy's mind worked on some expressions of flattery and endearment. For his opening shot, he ventured: "I've seen you often, as you've passed by this street and then gone to walk among the trees. I wasn't able to talk to you because I respect you, and your whole appearance tells me that you are from a good family."

She replied, a little resentfully: "But I suppose you always try to talk with ordinary girls as well? Why don't you just chase the common girls, and satisfy your passions on them?"

"I'm sorry, really, I don't mean you any harm. But I'm alone, as you see, and I can't find a companion to share my walks with me. I saw that you were the only girl who found pleasure in these strolls, and so I felt that there was a link between us. Anyway, if you find my presence unpleasant in any way, I'll move off right now."

---

[6] **sidled**—walked in a timid or sneaky manner.

He made a move to get up, but she checked him and asked: "Do you know who I am?"

"I haven't the least idea, but this doesn't stop me from believing that I share your spirit," he replied softly.

"If you want to accompany me on these innocent walks, I don't see any objection," she mused. "There's no harm in strolling around with you for an hour or so, at intervals which we can agree on, on condition that you promise me that you won't try to follow me and try to find out who I am. I don't want you trying to contact me at any other times."

"I respect your wish and I shall honor it," he replied formally.

The two of them sat side by side on one of the stone benches, and a deep silence reigned over them, in which each felt the beating of their own hearts. This silence continued for a long time. Both of them had been overcome by the novelty of their strange and singular situation.

Ihsan, however, was a youth accustomed to flirtations, although he realized that this time he was faced with a girl who was pure and virtuous. There was something about her, a certain strength of purpose and character, which confused him, and stopped him from going too far. His mind worked to collect his thoughts and to rescue him from the situation into which he had unwittingly walked.

At length, he spoke, somewhat confused.

"What is your name, please?"

"Have you forgotten my condition that you should not try to identify me?"

"Of course. I'm sorry. But surely . . . in view of our future friendship . . ."

"Have you forgotten? We live in a society in which this situation is unforgivable. If my people knew anything of this they'd kill me. While society is like this, we must learn to deceive. We must use the follies of our society in order to break its **shackles**!"[7]

"What a penetrating mind you have!" said Ihsan admiringly.

"Thank you. Time's getting on and I must be getting back to the house. I will see you again in two days."

As she said goodbye he tried to put his arm around her waist, but she **rebuffed**[8] him sharply. Then she relented slightly, saying: "I don't know who you are. You might be one of those mean boys who take delight in trapping girls for their own pleasure and sport."

She went back to the house invigorated, but somewhat disturbed, for she had broken with the most binding and serious of traditions in one fell swoop. She didn't understand how it had begun and how it had ended, until it seemed to her that everything that had happened that day was a disturbing dream.

She threw her cloak on one side, and went to help her mother with the housework. She flattered her mother, made herself agreeable, and took delight in carrying out her orders and her arrangements. When her father returned home from work

---

[7] **shackles**—restraints, like handcuffs.
[8] **rebuffed**—rejected.

she welcomed him with smiling face, then she went to her room to get on with her studies.

She set about her work mechanically, with nervous high spirits, and had disturbing dreams at night.

The meetings went on longer, and the subjects of their conversations diversified. The relationship between them developed, and things became deeply involved. She no longer felt that there was anything strange or unusual about the meetings, but she kept her head, using her lively mind to conceal her relationship with this boy, and to prevent him from trying to find out who she was and getting in touch with her.

One day Siham was sitting with her father, talking to him after supper, while he was scanning the evening paper. His eye fell on a long article about women who had abandoned the veil, and, deciding to have his daughter's view, he read the article out aloud. No sooner had he finished than Siham roundly abused the author for trying to break with convention and introduce modern **heresies**.[9] Her father felt a greatly increased regard for his intelligent, well-brought-up daughter, who obviously knew the value of traditions and respected them. Such a difference between her and the rest of her irresponsible scandalous friends, who, no sooner had they learned to read and write, went around throwing overboard society's conventions without shame or respect!

Impulsively, he moved towards his daughter and kissed her forehead.

"God preserve you as a treasure for your father."

When she reached her room Siham could barely stop herself from laughing out loud. She picked up her veil and danced with glee, then stopped in the middle of the room and began to whisper to the veil: "You black shroud, you know how I despise you and make use of you to keep him apart from me! I don't care about you, and I feel nothing for you. I defy you. But I love you too. These poor girls take refuge behind you in order to preserve their virginity, and their honor, and good morals. If they were more truthful they would say they love you because you hide faults and scandals. I love you because you help me to enjoy my life in a way that only those who wear the veil can appreciate. I pity those wretched unveiled women. I scorn them."

---

[9] **heresies**—beliefs that are opposed to what is normally or traditionally accepted.

QUESTIONS TO CONSIDER

1. Why does Ihsan prefer veiled girls?

2. What are the differences between Siham's and her father's attitudes to the veil?

3. Why is "From Behind the Veil" an ironic story for most Western readers? What did you think of Ayyoub's attitude to the veil? Explain your answer.

At the Time of the Jasmine

ALIFA RIFAAT

Alifa Rifaat (1930–   ) is modern Egypt's great chronicler of domestic drama. A writer who has focused on short stories, Rifaat has taken little part in the literary world of Egypt, preferring to devote herself to her family and to maintaining her privacy. Rifaat has spent time living in the West, but her stories are exclusively set in Egypt. They depict the daily lives of Egyptians, often focusing on the clash between the modern world and the traditional Islamic world.

He leaned his head against the backrest of the seat as the all-station train to Upper Egypt took him joltingly along, producing a **doleful**[1] rhythm on the rails.

With his handkerchief he wiped his face, removing the specks of sand. Even so the view before his eyes remained blurred, the telegraph poles intermingling with the **spectral**[2] forms of date palms that broke up into misty phantoms that were soon erased, leaving the yellow surface of sky to others which no sooner made their appearance than they vanished with the same speed.

He caught sight of some young boys plunging naked into the long winding cleft of the lbrahimiyya Canal, cooling themselves in its shallow waters, while the sun's heat grew stronger, carrying with it what little breeze there was and turning it into a scorching **inferno**.[3]

Time was at a standstill, stifling his breathing. He began toying wearily with his black tie as he glanced distractedly at the platforms of the small stations the train was passing by, amused at seeing the hefty men proudly clasping their guns slung on their shoulders, and the women spread out on the platform, their children carried close to them, while alongside them lay the cages of chickens they would be trading in the markets.

The cable he had received that morning lay in his jacket pocket.

"Your father Hagg Aballah Shalabi has died. Respect for the dead demands speedy burial." The words fell heavy as gravel in his throat, despite the fact that for

---

[1] **doleful**—sad, mournful.

[2] **spectral**—ghostlike.

[3] **inferno**—raging fire or extreme heat.

a long time his father had, for him, been like someone already dead—ever since the day he had sent him away to the English school in Maadi some time after his mother's death.

Every morning his mother would place the silver ewer[4] before him and he would rush off to where his father would be sitting at the edge of the prayer mat, his sleeves rolled up and his hands stretched out above the little silver basin and he would pour the water over them slowly and carefully, in his eyes an expression of admiration for his father as he made his **ablutions**;[5] then he would pour the water over his feet from which he had removed his socks. He couldn't remember ever having opposed his father in anything, not even when he had carried him out to where the men were and had put him on Antar's back, laughing and boasting jubilantly:

"My son Hassan's a real man, a bold horseman—riding's in his blood."

He hadn't been scared that day and hadn't looked up towards the window from which his mother **surreptitiously**[6] gazed down on him, the kohl[7] mixing in her eyes with tears of pity. He had merely let his short legs hang down the warm flanks and, taking the end of his *galabia*[8] between his teeth, had clung with both hands to the long hair of the mane. Antar had rushed off with him, crossing the intersecting banked up tracks round the village, and had brought him back, prancing about amidst the admiring cries of the men.

Even when Muntaha, the sweet, shy girl with the thick black pigtails, had come to the house with her red box in her *howdah*[9] on top of the camel from the neighboring **hamlet**,[10] and his father had carried her and put her into his bed where his mother used previously to sleep, even Muntaha he had loved. He would cling to her bright-colored, scented dress as she went about the house, finding companionship in her from the loneliness he suffered after his mother had left him.

During the time away from home spent with foreign tutors his childhood quickly died, his love for his father froze and he himself became a sophisticated man not greatly concerned with emotions, subordinating everything to rational standards and to convention. The nostalgia within himself for his village Behbesheen was lost with the passing of the days, and the nights erased from his mind the memory of its rich pastures.

When he grew up he did his duty by visiting the place whenever his father was blessed with another child lest it be said of him that he was annoyed about brothers and sisters sharing with him his father's lands. Once he had opened his own accountancy office his visits grew less owing to his being taken up with business and then came to an end when he

---

[4] ewer—a large pitcher or jug of water.

[5] **ablutions**—ceremonial washings of the body or an object.

[6] **surreptitiously**—secretly, stealthily.

[7] kohl—a black powder used as eye makeup.

[8] *galabia*—a wide outer garment, worn like a wrap in Egypt.

[9] *howdah*—a seat fastened on the back of a camel or an elephant.

[10] **hamlet**—a small village.

married his Turkish colleague Louga Hanem Toubchi. That day he had sent his father a cable reading: "Am getting married tonight."

His father received the news with silence, and when he was blessed with a daughter he again informed his father of the good news. The father contented himself by replying with a cable which said: "Call her Jasmine."

As the days passed his wife turned into a person who was always grumbling, afflicted by the arrogance of her countrymen. He bore her patiently until the day when she shouted at him:

"I am Louga Hanem Toubchi—is my name to become Madame Shalabi?"

"Go back to them," he told her with frightening calm.

Taking her daughter, she had gone to the Toubchi household in Zamalek[11] and he had stayed on in his flat in the center of Cairo, not worried about being on his own. He let her be, thinking to break her **obstinacy**,[12] but she only grew more stubborn and did not return. After this he did not think of visiting the village owing to his having become wrapped up in his work. Today, after the death of his father, his link with the rest of his relations would no doubt be cut and he would remain without roots.

The train stopped at Boush, his village's main township, so he took up his suitcase in which he had, together with his pajamas, thrust the shroud he had bought before leaving Cairo. Duty demanded that he should bring with him a shroud that was in keeping with his father's position in the village. People would think badly of him if he didn't bring some white and green silk and a cashmere shawl and lay on a fine funeral night. In his pocket was a large sum he had drawn out from his savings at the bank to be spent on doing what was expected of him.

That day he had sent his father a cable reading: "Am getting married tonight."

As he got down from the train he was seized by the hands of men come to convey their condolences. Faraghalli, who used as a child to steal with a fish hook the chickens of Madame Carmel, wife of the Health clerk, and who had now become a spokesman for the peasants, wrapped him round in an embrace inside his rich *aba*[13] as he muttered:

"May God give you strength to bear this loss, Mr. Hassan."

He muttered some vague words in answer, then his hand was seized by the strong grasp of Sheikh Hammad, his father's overseer, as he passed him Antar's reins with the words:

"It's very hot, men, and it would be wrong of us to leave the dead man till midday."

Hassan jumped onto Antar's back, proudly sitting upright in order to assure

---

[11] Zamalek—upper-class residential district of Cairo, the capital of Egypt.

[12] **obstinacy**—stubbornness.

[13] *aba*—a sleeveless outergarment worn by Arabs.

Sheikh Hammad that a soft hand had nothing to do with being a real man. The sun was sending down its scorching vertical shafts on to his bare head. The men were pressing their mounts forward, having let down the ends of their turbans to protect them from the blazing heat. He himself lifted up the morning newspaper over his head as he used to do in Cairo, then lowered it again to his side when he saw the line of girls from the jasmine[14] factory standing and staring at him as he passed between them.

The blast of hot air brought with it the aroma of jasmine, whose pervasive smell clung to the flying specks of sand, penetrating deeply into men's chests so that, in time, all the people of the district suffered from a **chronic**[15] cough—and no sooner had things quieted down than the next season had made its appearance.

By staying in Cairo he had escaped the malady but now, breathing in the aroma, he began to cough badly. With the coughing his eyes watered, until they became reddened and puffy, while Antar took him along the banked up tracks between the fields and then came to a stop in front of the stone wall surrounding the house.

"The burial permit is ready," said Sheikh Hammad, "and the sheiks are here."

As soon as he entered voices were raised in wailing from the women seated on the ground, who were covering their heads with earth.

His young brother came forward carrying the silver basin and ewer for him

to make his ablutions, his face bearing the same dull dismay he himself had been afflicted with the day his mother had died.

He patted his shoulder consolingly, then made his ablutions and entered the dead man's room. His legs began shaking suddenly as he advanced towards the brass bed where his father's body lay. He drew back the end of the sheet covering the face and the flies buzzed, then settled again. Staring at his father's face, he muttered through dry lips:

"Peace be upon you and the mercy of Allah."

Then he pressed them to the cold forehead. Though incapable of returning the salutation, the dead man had certainly heard him. Crystal tears glinted in his eyes, putting the walls out of focus and setting dancing before his eyes the framed Qur'anic verse[16] in large Kufic[17] calligraphy that stood over the bed:

"Make ready for them such force and tethered horses as you are able—Allah the Great has spoken aright."

The voices of the sheiks grew louder as they recited the most beautiful names of Allah. Sheikh Abdul Maqsoud the corpse-washer came forward and drew off the white *galabia* and undid, from round the waist, the black snake-skin belt that the

---

[14] jasmine—a fragrant ornamental shrub, usually having yellow or white flowers.

[15] **chronic**—lasting for a long time.

[16] Qur'anic verse—a portion of the Qur'an or Koran, the sacred book of Islam.

[17] Kufic—a stylized Arabic alphabet, employed in making copies of the Qur'an.

Hagg used to wear, a snake he had shot after it had for long struck terror in Behbesheen.

Sheikh Abdul Maqsoud turned the belt over in his hands, his deep-set eyes gleaming with joy; he then took hold of the dead man's hand and pulled the large gold ring off it: all this had now become his, a contribution of alms made to him by the family in memory of the dead man. He then raised the rigid body with his assistant and laid it down on the wooden plank set over the large brass bowl.

He handed the brass cup to Hassan and advanced the container of pure water towards him, saying:

"Take hold of yourself, my son, otherwise your tears will make the water impure."

With steady hand Hassan poured the water over the head and body which Sheikh Abdul Maqsoud was rubbing down with soap.

When the voices began reciting the Qur'an they performed the rites of ablution on the dead man, then dried the body. They tore the winding sheets with a shrill screech that jolted Hassan's nerves. He took control of himself as they stitched up the pieces of cloth and wrapped them round the body, tying them securely at the legs and on top of the head. They spread the bed covering in the wooden bier[18] and laid the body on it, then covered it over with the cashmere shawl.

Sheikh Hammad entered and took the brass bedstead to pieces, while the women's voices rose loud with wailing. The brass bedstead had been set up ever since Hagg Aballah's first marriage; Hassan's mother had breathed her last in it, and to it he had brought Muntaha in marriage and in it she had had his other children. But with the death of the master of the house the bedstead must be done away with and not set up again till after the period of mourning.

Hassan gave a sharp cough as the aroma of incense inflamed the sensitivity of his nose and the tears flowed copiously[19] from his eyes. Stolidly, he passed the handkerchief over his face and went forward to take up one of the front shafts of the bier with Sheikh Hammad, who took the other, the rear ones being taken by two faithful retainers. Resting it on their shoulders, they went out into the courtyard.

Owais, the man in charge of the livestock, threw a young water buffalo to the ground in front of the bier and ran Hamid the butcher's knife over its throat and the blood spilt out on the hot, burning sands in a sacrifice to the dead man.

The men trod across the pool of blood as they bore the bier to the other side of the stone wall and the funeral cortège[20] arranged itself in ranks behind them.

They hurried along with the bier as they fervently uttered, in hoarse voices, the formula of the unity of Allah: there is no god but Allah. The women hastened behind

---

[18] bier—a movable frame on which a coffin or a corpse is placed or taken to a grave.

[19] **copiously**—abundantly.

[20] cortège—funeral procession.

them, clad in the *shagga*[21] that hung down over their bodies like a tent, allowing nothing to show but the gleam of their eyes.

The sun had passed the center point in the sky but still sent down its searing rays into the sands so that its heat penetrated stingingly through their sandals.

They passed along the winding village lanes till they came down to where the only **mosque**[22] stood, in the middle of the road that led to the other hill where the ruins of graves lay in ranks at the foot of the mountain.

Casting off their sandals, they took the dead man in and placed him in the *mihrab*.[23] Seven times they uttered the words "Allah is greatest," then said the funeral prayers, after which they again took up the bier and hurried along with it to the cemetery. The gravedigger had prepared the grave, opening the mouth and removing the earth from the entrance and collecting up the bones of the former inhabitants and tying them up in their decaying shrouds and placing them against the inner wall painted with lime; then he scattered the soft sand mixed with henna,[24] in preparation for laying down the new corpse.

The coffin grew heavier on its bearers as they hurried along, panting hard, their shoulders almost twisted from their bodies; it was as though the dead man was resisting the grave in terror, so that, as they advanced, the front of the bier turned them in the direction of the houses and they progressed with sideways steps. The stalks of maize[25] in the basins of cultivated land gave out, behind red sparks discharged

from the sharp blade of the sun, a white vapor that made their eyes smart. Having reached the opening, they put down the bier in front of it.

Sheikh Hammad placed a small pair of scissors in Hassan's hand, saying between his teeth:

"Come along, man, do your duty. Snip the **shroud**[26] or it will be stolen by those dirty thieves of gravediggers. I swear by the Almighty if one of them falls into my hands I'll hang him on the tree alongside the mosque."

Then he spat on the ground to show his disgust.

Hassan took the scissors and went down behind the corpse into the darkness of the grave.

The sound of the Qur'an reciters grew louder, speeding up their recitation, as though they had another appointment.

A lizard passed between his feet, then disappeared into the darkness. He squatted down on his knees alongside his father and stretched out his hand with the scissors and began cutting the shroud, careful not to touch the dead flesh. The gravedigger patted him on the shoulder as he muttered:

---

[21] *shagga*—a large sheet of cloth, worn as a combination veil, shawl, and head covering.

[22] **mosque**—Islamic place of worship and teaching.

[23] *mihrab*—niche in the wall of a mosque. It indicates the direction of Mecca, toward which Muslims face as they pray.

[24] *henna*—a tropical shrub or the reddish dye made from it.

[25] *maize*—corn.

[26] **shroud**—a sheetlike garment, often used to wrap a corpse for burial.

"Come along, man—may the Lord give him protection."

He got to his feet and walked backwards behind him, as he gave his salutations to the dead man and then came out into the sunlight. He stood amongst the men till the gravedigger had completed his task and had piled the earth against the entrance and poured water over it, then watered the nearby cactus with what was left.

The sun was now suspended over the peak of the mountain, and it cast forth red shafts of light that made long shadows, depicting vague specters. The tombs looked similar to the scattered houses in the dusky light of sunset.

Someone called out:

"Say that Allah is One!"

In a deep voice they all muttered fervently:

"There is no god but Allah."

"Everyone thereon passes away," quoted the gravedigger, "and there remains your Lord's face possessed of majesty and splendor."

"That which Allah has said is the truth," they all called out.

Stealthily Hassan passed some money to the gravedigger and set about returning, with the crowd following him, to the courtyard of the house.

The men seated themselves on the cane chairs that had been set out in rows with the kerosene lamps above their heads; each time the Qur'an reciter finished a chapter, cups of coffee were handed round. They would listen fervently, rocking to the rhythm, until the reciter concluded by reciting the Fatiha.[27] By this time it was midnight, and the men spread out the palms of their hands, then passed them over their faces in supplication.

Giving Hassan a sideways look, Sheikh Hammad said, "May Allah have mercy upon him, he was a loving father to everybody, and the greatest horseman in the whole district."

Faraghalli answered him:

"There are plenty of horsemen about, man. What was special about him was that he could put his ear to the ground and say 'So-and-so's going along such-and-such a track and he'll be arriving after such-and-such a time' and his words would ring true as a gold guinea."[28]

Hassan lowered his head in silence. Perhaps these men knew his father better than he did. Was it in fact he himself who was responsible for the estrangement[29] between himself and his father? He took out a wad of notes from his pocket and thrust them into Sheikh Hammad's hand.

"Spend them on what's required— tonight's at my expense."

Confused by Hassan's generosity, Sheikh Hammad exclaimed:

"What nobility—May the Lord bless you."

Trays with bowls of broth ranged round with pieces of boiled meat were set up on the low tables, and Hassan rose to

---

[27] Fatiha—the opening verse of the Qur'an or Koran, the sacred book of Islam. The verse is Islam's most commonly used prayer.

[28] gold guinea—an old English coin.

[29] estrangement—alienation, separation.

invite the men, while he himself ate a little with difficulty, waiting till everyone had dispersed and the pressure lamps had been put out.

Entering the house, he walked in loneliness through its rooms, passing among the women squatting on the mats, clad in black. From the ground there rose a black tent that moved towards him; from two tiny slits there looked out at him two eyes which he recognized as those of Muntaha, his father's wife. She held out her hand with a key, muttering in a voice choked by weeping:

"The Hagg Aballah handed over to me the key of the cupboard in trust for me to give to you."

"Be strong," he muttered, taking the key from her.

"Strength is with Allah."

He went to the cupboard he had known since childhood. As he did so his eyes fell for an instant on the glistening water on the floor, left over after the dead man had been washed.

His hand came across a large bundle of notes, also a piece of paper on which was recorded the names of those who were to benefit from the sum of money. His gaze came to rest on the name of his daughter Jasmine mentioned among those to inherit. The words became blurred and he sat down on the edge of the mattress that had been laid out on the ground for him to sleep on instead of the bed that had been dismantled and some of whose pieces were leaning in the corner against the wall. He placed his head between his hands and the papers between his outstretched legs. The smell of the jasmine whose flowers were opening in the night like white stars was wafted in to him by the breeze. He had said, "Call her Jasmine." He had loved her and had mentioned her among his own children in his will. He had no doubt thought about her and had perhaps sometimes longed to see her. Why had he not asked to meet her? More than once he'd said to Louga Hanem, before the final break: "We must take a train to the country so my father can see my child." She would put her elegant nose in the air and he would keep silent. Too often he kept silent. Once, during one of the rare times they met, his father had said:

"Next year, my son, we'll make the pilgrimage together," and he had burst into childish laughter.

The years had passed and a life had come to an end and the wish had not been fulfilled. He smiled sadly at the memory, beset by a feeling of **bafflement**.[30] The days had robbed the two of them and they had not gone. They hadn't even seen enough of each other, and a sensation of yearning for his father exploded suddenly in his breast. Which of them was to blame?

He woke up from his thoughts to the echoing howling of the mountain wolves. Had the grave robber done it? Had he left the opening of the grave unclosed after him?

---

[30] **bafflement**—confusion and frustration.

The blood rose up into his neck, as he choked with grief and anger and he let his body fall back as though struck by a blow from the Hagg's famous staff. He had never in fact suffered it. When he was young it was enough for Hagg Aballah to wave it in his face and shout "The rod's for the insubordinate," for his weak body to tremble under the imaginary blows.

"Father, you gave me a real beating tonight."

The winds whistled **forlornly**[31] through the branches of the date palms, then silence reigned while the jasmine buds carefully folded themselves against the rapidly spreading rays of the sun. The cooing of pigeons rose from the dove-cotes[32] on top of the houses.

Sheikh Hammad's voice called from outside:

"Mr. Hassan, the commissioner has sent the jeep to take you to the station—there's half an hour till the train goes."

Awwad entered carrying the basin and ewer, and in his wake Muntaha, her hair disheveled and in her nightgown, carrying a tray of breakfast.

He went out to the car. As he got into it he waved at the men who had gathered, then it moved off, leaving behind it a whirlpool of dust that enveloped the children who had risen from sleep and collected at the sound of the car and were now trying to catch up as, with the ends of their *galabias* in their teeth, they ran along on their thin brown legs.

---

[31] forlornly—sadly.

[32] dove-cotes—shelters with nesting holes for domesticated pigeons.

QUESTIONS TO CONSIDER

1. How did Hassan and his father grow estranged? How did Hassan and his wife grow estranged?

2. What is the "real beating" that Hassan mentions at the end of the story? Does he feel that he deserved it? Explain.

3. Compare and contrast the character of Hassan and that of his father. Who is more respected? Who was happier? Explain why.

from

A Portrait of Egypt

MARY ANNE WEAVER

Mary Anne Weaver is a staff writer for The New Yorker *magazine who has devoted much of her life to studying Egypt and Arabic culture. The following is a section of her book* A Portrait of Egypt *(1999), which depicts how Egypt has been changing in recent decades.*

The streets of Cairo are like no other streets in the world. Every corner, every crevice, every alleyway seems to be inhabited. Crowds of pedestrians and traffic jostle for space, and noise is everywhere—a pervasive din of car horns tooting, street vendors hawking their wares, and muezzins,[1] their voices shrilly amplified, calling the faithful to prayers. I imagine that there was a time when the streets of every great city resounded with hawkers' cries, but now they are to be found only in cities such as this. Here in Cairo, in the centuries-old Khan el-Khalili Bazaar, there are still itinerant sellers of roasted nuts, of discarded metal, of baskets and paraffin,[2] of shawls, of trinkets, and of ornaments. The calls that have vanished from other great cities still echo here. This is one of my most vivid impressions of that first day, a bright June morning in 1977, when I first ventured into Cairo's alleyways. In dark basements, old men were ironing old clothes. In dark alleys, young men dressed in Islamic robes were selling cassettes of sermons delivered at "popular"—as opposed to official government—mosques.[3] . . .

Modern Cairo was built in the early twentieth century to house three million people; by 1977 it was bursting with more than five million exuberant Cairenes. Brightly painted carts of garbage collectors, herds of goats and sheep competed with the city's 250,000 private cars. Even then Cairo—the Islamic world's largest city—was one of the most congested in the

---

[1] muezzins—criers who call Muslims to prayer five times a day.

[2] paraffin—waxy material used for candles and waterproofing.

[3] mosques—Muslim buildings of worship.

Middle East, perhaps in the world. I was told that it was a difficult, if not impossible, place in which to live. There were recurrent power failures; food shortages were sometimes acute. I could often find imported cheese and caviar in the market, but not flour or local soap. It was often impossible to telephone an apartment downstairs. Cairo specializes in a state of total **pandemonium.**[4]

Yet on the tony[5] island of Zamalek, where we lived, there was a sense of the world that came before—old Edwardian mansions, now mostly in disrepair, and large, untended lawns shaded by cypresses and eucalyptus; broad avenues spoke of being traversed by carriage and horse. Life remained gracious on this side of the Nile. There were hostesses and soirees, afternoon teas, poetry readings. The conversation was often of politics, of Voltaire and Kant.[6] There was the feeling that Egypt was drifting —no one knew where.

I remember those early evenings, when we sat on well-appointed terraces overhanging the Nile, and looked across the water at the slum of Imbaba; we speculated on *its* lifestyle. Its population density was 105,000 people per 2.2 square miles; an average of 3.7 people lived in every room. On our side of the Nile, the level of literacy was among the highest in the world; in Imbaba, the average income was thirty dollars a month. Here, four languages were normally spoken at dinner parties, served by candlelight; rooms were filled with books. There, hidden away in the alleys,

far from our understanding or view, sheep, goats, and children drank from open sewers, and, after dark, some neighborhoods yielded to packs of wild dogs. I remember one evening in particular as I watched with friends the flickering lights of a funeral procession passing through Imbaba. The next morning, we read in the newspaper that two children had been eaten alive by rats.

What I had only begun to glimpse during those early years was that the real Egypt was two Egypts—at least two. There was our world in Zamalek and theirs in Imbaba, separated by the **serpentine**[7] Nile. There was Upper Egypt and the Nile Delta hugging the Mediterranean Sea. There was the present and there was the past, but the future was indefinite and ill defined.

In much of the Middle East, the future has been buried by the past. Today's Egypt is a monument and also a hostage to its ancient past. It gave the world the Pharaonic dynasties, the Gezira Sporting Club, and the Pyramids, those most magnificent of all monuments. But it has a darker side as well, in which not only does its present battle its past but **secularists**[8] battle Islamists,[9] and Islamists battle Christian

---

[4] **pandemonium**—confusion, chaos.

[5] tony—stylish, fashionable.

[6] Voltaire and Kant—eighteenth-century European philosophers.

[7] **serpentine**—winding or coiling like a snake.

[8] **secularists**—people who are concerned with earthly things instead of spirituality or religion.

[9] Islamists—Muslims with a very traditional view of the Islamic religion.

Copts;[10] astonishing poverty **coalesces**[11] uneasily with astonishing wealth. Egyptians—unlike Westerners, who sometimes romanticize their ancient land—are their own fiercest critics, railing against their repression and corruption, their **apartheids**,[12] their lack of democracy, their prisons filled with forgotten men, and their barriers between their own people as unrelenting as India's system of **caste**.[13] . . .

> **Both history and the river have set Egypt apart.**

Looked at on a map, Egypt is large: 386,900 square miles, about the size of Spain and France combined. But if you look again, it's a very different image when you distinguish between the desert and the arable land. Viewed from a plane, flying south to north, the real Egypt—the land on which man can live—is small and lotus-shaped. A thin, two-to-eighteen-mile-wide strip of green, the flower's stem, follows the Nile north from Egypt's border with Sudan; then, near Cairo and on to the Mediterranean Sea, comes the Nile Delta, the blossom, as the river flows unhurriedly down to the sea. In that narrow strip of 13,800 square miles, about the size of Taiwan,[14] over sixty million people now live. Ninety-five percent of Egypt's population lives on less than 5 percent of its land. The rest of the country is desert, brutal and unchanged, scarcely touched since Pharaonic times.

It is easy to understand why the Nile has molded Egypt's character as well as its geography. Men needed to organize to cope with its **fickle**[15] **ebbs**[16] and floods; thus civilization emerged. They required means of surveying their tiny plots of **irrigated**[17] land; thus geometry emerged. Protected in their green river valley by the barriers the desert imposed, the ancient Egyptians constructed **perdurable**[18] institutions, like the Pyramids and the **effigies**[19] of Upper Egypt—cocoons to their immortality. With scarcely an interruption, Pharaoh succeeded Pharaoh and dynasty followed dynasty for nearly three thousand years before Christ, a continuity of government unmatched by any in the world.

Both history and the river have set Egypt apart.

The Persians broke the Pharaonic line and, for nearly twenty-three hundred years, Egypt was little more than a province of foreign conquerors: Greeks, Romans, Arabs, Mamluks, Turks, and French, and finally the British, until Egypt, forty-six years ago, reclaimed its past. Yet, through the centuries, the Nile flowed on, and the Egyptian determined his life by the

---

[10] Copts—natives of Egypt descended from the ancient Egyptians. They are Christians.

[11] **coalesces**—combines with something else.

[12] **apartheids**—forced systems of segregation or discrimination based on race.

[13] **caste**—social class or status.

[14] Taiwan— island country off the coast of mainland China.

[15] **fickle**—inconsistent.

[16] **ebbs**—falling levels of water.

[17] **irrigated**—supplied with water.

[18] **perdurable**—permanent.

[19] **effigies**—sculptures or models, usually of a person.

rise and fall of its waters, rather than by a foreign master's whims.

The Arabs arrived with Koran[20] and sword in the seventh century, and their conquest of Egypt made the Egyptians Muslim; whether it made them Arab, however, is far more debatable. The early Arab dynasties did impose their language, which replaced the widely spoken Greek and the old Pharaonic tongue; but after three hundred years of Arab rule Egypt fell, first to the Fatimids (who founded Cairo and al-Azhar, the oldest university in the world), then to the Ayyubids, the Mamluks, and the Ottomans—all of them Islamic but none of them Arab. History, like the river, again set Egypt apart.

A Hamitic strain prevails in the blood of its river people; by contrast, the desert Arabs are Semites. An Egyptian's physiognomy is different; his Arabic is different, peppered with odd words, some Pharaonic, others borrowed from European conquerors. His customs are different from those of the desert Arabs: his tombs; his veneration of saints; and his elaborate burials. His poetry is different, as is his literature. And although Arab by definition now, Egyptians—by emotion and inclination—still consider themselves Egyptians first.

I once met a man at a dinner party, a small, sparrowlike man, who told me that he had spent two days inside the Mugamma—the headquarters of Egypt's nightmarish bureaucracy—in order to get a much-needed stamp affixed to a document. He was slightly claustrophobic and hated crowds, he said. Inside the Mugamma, he

had been terrified. One of the cardinal rules of Egyptian life is that you do not queue.[21] Rather, you are somehow swept along by the sheer gravity of a crowd. And that is precisely what happened to this tiny, bespectacled man. "No left turns were permitted," he recalled of those two days, during which he was engulfed by "miles of people," he said, shuffling, pushing, and shoving as they moved, in disorderly **cadence**,[22] from room to room. At each stop, they each secured yet another form. Finally, the sparrowlike man reached the coveted door of the only bureaucrat who possessed the stamp for which he had come in search. He was totally devastated when he was told that the bureaucrat had died two weeks before. No successor had yet been named. And the stamp? It was probably secreted away in a locked drawer, along with the personal papers of the dead man.

I was duly impressed with his **apocryphal**[23] tale, and not at all prepared for the little man's bemusement or pride when he made his final point: Egypt's bureaucracy was the oldest in the world and had spun red tape for at least three thousand years before the Arabs arrived.

This was Egypt, with all of its curious juxtapositions and charms. The unexpected was always there, just around a corner or down an alleyway, and, even during those early years, it had begun to announce itself

---

[20] Koran—the sacred book of Islam.

[21] queue—get in line.

[22] **cadence**—rhythm.

[23] **apocryphal**—invented.

in our upper-class neighborhood of Zamalek, where, tucked away from public view, there were a growing number of unofficial, or storefront, mosques. . . .

The first one I visited, with a classmate named Nadine, a not at all conventional upper-class Cairene, was in an unpaved alley just off one of Zamalek's fashionable shopping streets, on the ground floor of a dun-colored[24] apartment building, with latticed windows and chocolate doors. Tattered streamers of yellow, red, and green flew above the doors, somehow defiant, yet faded and torn. As we waited for permission to enter the mosque, I watched a group of men transform a small adjacent empty square, spreading out straw mats for Friday evening prayers. The few women in evidence were shrouded in black abayas, covered from head to toe; anonymous forms, they glided in and out of storefront shops. The sounds, from amplified systems or from radios, were those of the Koran. The smells were of open sewers, wet wool, and mud.

A friend of Nadine's appeared and led us into the women's section of the mosque. I covered my head, as I had been instructed to do, and removed my shoes, before entering a damp, bare, and drafty room. In a far corner—which was difficult to see, since in the women's section we were hidden from the main prayer area by an improvised white sheet that fell from the ceiling beams—I was able to glimpse a high-backed wooden chair, which had been elevated slightly on a cluster of cement blocks. A single bare lightbulb was the only source of light except for tiny shafts that filtered through the room's dirty windows and its open doors. It seemed an unlikely setting for a powerful spiritual voice.

There was a stir as the "popular" Sheikh of Zamalek entered the room, wearing traditional Islamic dress—a long white robe and a tiny white crocheted prayer cap. He was a fiery speaker, whose views carried great weight, Nadine said. There was utter silence while he climbed into the high-backed wooden chair. I peeked out from behind the sheeting and was astonished by what I saw. For the "popular" Sheikh of Zamalek was a man whom I recognized at once: a polite and rather boring—or so I had thought— lecturer at the university. An agronomist! Yet when he began to speak, he was transformed. In amazement, I watched his flailing arms and heard his voice begin to rise as he admonished the crowd: "Islam is the solution!" He had begun to shout.

I glanced around our area, hidden behind the sheet, where all the women wore head scarves, or hijabs; a few wore veils. Some of them held their children by the hand. No one in our area appeared to be poor. The women stood and listened to the sheikh in silence, in crisply aligned rows.

A muezzin began chanting, his melancholy voice piped by a loudspeaker to the overflow crowd outside. The men in the prayer room began to chant, *Allahu akbar!*—"God is most great!" Behind the sheeting, the women did the same.

---

[24] dun-colored—dull, grayish brown in appearance.

Seemingly on cue, the "popular" Sheikh of Zamalek became vehement, and his voice rose to an even higher pitch.

"Dictators will go to hell!" he shouted. "Power goes to their heads!" He then spoke elliptically of chaos and betrayal. He never mentioned President Sadat by name, but everyone knew whom he meant.

I was struck by the realization, as I listened to the powerful voice of the sheikh—whom I had known before, albeit somewhat vaguely, as a timid professor dressed in button-down shirts and outrageously outdated ties—that so much of Egypt wore a mask, including Zamalek itself. And the deeper into its alleys I went, the more they became an expression of Islam.

Nadine was the one who taught me that. We met at the American University of Cairo (or AUC) in 1978. She was a graduate student in sociology, I in Arab affairs, and it was Nadine who introduced me to the tumultuous world of campus politics. We were mostly removed from it at AUC, which was a rarefied kind of place, whose students were largely drawn from Egypt's upper class. Yet even there I was becoming increasingly conspicuous in my jeans and Western dress.

"How *can* you not see what's happening?" Nadine used to rail, and her eyes would flash. She was one of the most spirited women that I have ever met. Tall and elegant, with large, luminous, kohl-rimmed[25] dark eyes and a swanlike neck, she had once worn blue jeans, studied American literature, and painted her nails. But on a late October morning in 1978, she had stood, along with three other young women, before the faculty of Cairo University's medical school, hooded and shrouded, in a faceless, Iranian-style black chador.[26] She had joined the others, all medical students, including a sister of hers, as a member of a national university council, which had been elected that spring, in elections in which the Islamists had captured more than 60 percent of the seats. She invited me to come along that morning, and I did. Standing outside the classroom, I watched a group of professors pass. As they glimpsed the young women through the open door, they were clearly aghast. Melodic in their chants praising Allah, graceful in their flowing robes, the women were nevertheless didactic in their demands: they refused to dissect male corpses; to be integrated academically with men; and they demanded that a dual curriculum be established, as well as university centers for prayer.

Nadine was then in her early twenties, a daughter of Zamalek's immensely wealthy upper class. And if it was a **paradox**[27] for the daughter of a patrician family to be preaching Islamist politics, then she failed to grasp it. It was just one of the anomalies of her life. She was an Eastern **fatalist**[28] by birth, a Western liberal

---

[25] kohl-rimmed—outlined with a black powder used in makeup.

[26] chador—a large sheet of cloth, worn as a combination veil, shawl, and head covering.

[27] **paradox**—a contradictory statement or event.

[28] **fatalist**—one who believes that all things are predetermined and unchangeable.

by education, a feminist who donned Islamic robes and maintained an abiding fascination with designer clothes.

I asked her later that afternoon, while we lolled on the grass of AUC—where, in deference to university regulations, she had abandoned her austere chador and was dressed instead in a long white robe—whether her recently acquired Islamic attire was a sign of protest, as it was increasingly becoming for young coeds in Iran. "It's more a matter of identity than of protest," she replied. "If you dress and behave Western, then you are compelled to *be* Western. Islam gives you yourself."

> *"If you dress and behave Western, then you are compelled to be Western. Islam gives you yourself."*

I glanced around the campus, and even here, it seemed to me, a growing number of women had begun to cover their heads in the Islamic fashion, and a growing number of men now sported full Islamic beards.

Students came and went as we continued to chat, and, in retrospect, our conversations seem to have always been the same: eyewitness accounts of clashes in Upper Egypt between Islamists and Christian Copts; vicious underground fights, often with knives flashing, both in Upper Egypt and at northern universities. Figures were not being officially released, but scores had been wounded. People had died. Egypt's 360-member rubber-stamp parliament had begun to debate a return to Shariah, or Islamic law; a rampant consumerism, bred in large part by the peace policies of President Sadat, had drawn **poignant**[29] distinction between Cairo's haves and have-nots. Certainly Egypt was becoming increasingly tied to Washington as a result of the Camp David Accords. It stood dangerously isolated in the Arab world.

That summer, much to the distress of her mother, and to the astonishment of some of her friends, Nadine left Cairo for military training, in a remote Islamist desert camp. She gave me a hug when we said our goodbyes. Then, hidden behind her enveloping black chador, she boarded the train for Upper Egypt, and was gone.

As I left the train station and walked through Cairo's fashionable streets with their handsomely stocked shops, I first sensed that growing tension between Western values and the currents of Islam.

The Islamic revival movement at Egypt's thirteen universities had clearly baffled university authorities. Hundreds of young women less committed than Nadine were "taking the veil," as it is called; others were demanding classes separate from men. Still others were covering themselves in robes from head to foot—to the dismay of most of their mothers, who had fought for the freedom to unveil their faces and to wear short skirts. What was perhaps even more unsettling, however, was the fact that the Islamists had begun to infiltrate

---

[29] **poignant**—sharp, piercing.

university faculties and had set up clandestine campus cells.[30] They were demanding the abrogation[31] of all Western influence in the schools and had begun publishing a large number of newspapers and tracts. Their funding came largely from the conservative, oil-rich kingdoms and sheikdoms of the Persian Gulf—most significantly from Saudi Arabia, with the encouragement of Anwar Sadat.

With strongholds at Alexandria University, the University of Asyut, Cairo University's medical and scientific schools, and the Technical Military Academy, the Islamists had backgrounds as **eclectic**[32] as their accents were diverse. Some were of peasant stock, from the villages of Upper Egypt; others were the sons and daughters of the merchant or the civil-servant class; still others, like Nadine, were the children of Egypt's most privileged class. Their common denominator was discontent. They bonded on their strict **adherence**[33] to Islam and on their intellect. They were generally high achievers scholastically, and they were largely drawn from Egypt's most demanding university faculties. They defied stereotyping, I quickly learned, and could not be called reactionary, as some were very progressive in thought; others wanted a return to a seventh-century caliphate,[34] and to Shariah law; still others **propagated**[35] violence, as a means of "**expurgating**[36] sin." They were a fusion of all Egyptian trends.

Nadine had told me (and I later confirmed) that the activists among them probably numbered no more than twenty thousand, but that they could draw on the support of a million or so sympathizers, or perhaps more. Western diplomats worried that, after the military, they were Egypt's best-organized social force.

One morning shortly after Nadine had left, I went in search of Dr. Sa'ad el-Din Ibrahim, a professor of sociology at AUC who had studied the Islamist movement more than many at the time, and found him at his desk, which was covered with piles of paper and with half-finished cups of tea. He told me that the reappearance of the movement was predictable in the context of the history of the Arab world—a history in which revival movements have appeared in the aftermath of what was perceived to be a great failure of existing regimes. The present cycle began in 1974 and 1975, he said, when disillusionment replaced the early **euphoria**[37] of Arab victories in the 1973 October War. "Students looked with alarm at the apparent **rapprochement**[38] with Israel, and generally with the West. They disdained the emphasis on a consumer society, and the corruption that it was seen to breed. There was also the socioeconomic dislocation of society," he went on, "the frustrations of the lower and

---

[30] cells—small groups of people who are involved in rebellious religious or political activity.

[31] abrogation—abolishing.

[32] **eclectic**—varied and well-rounded.

[33] **adherence**—faithful devotion.

[34] caliphate—when all Muslims were under the rule of a single religious leader.

[35] **propagated**—encouraged.

[36] **expurgating**—removing something objectionable.

[37] **euphoria**—feeling of happiness or well-being.

[38] rapprochement—reestablishment of relations.

middle class. In the January 1977 riots, we saw a massive symbol of floating discontent."

I remember what it had been like then.

For forty-eight hours, hundreds of thousands of outraged workers and students, slum dwellers, and government bureaucrats poured into Cairo's streets, rioted, burned, and looted when food subsidies—which benefit all Egyptians— were cut. Thousands more cheered them on from rooftops. The shadow of revolution seemed to loom over Egypt during those two days. And what the mobs attacked was as revealing as what they did not. They tried to burn government buildings (and sometimes succeeded); they gutted buses and trams and ripped up railroad tracks, a protest against the appalling system of public transport. But they directed most of their anger toward symbols of luxury and wealth. (They did not attack foreigners or embassies, nor did they paint anti-American slogans, although that was considered quite fashionable at the time.)

On the second morning of the riots, I watched a group of mullahs surging through the streets—bearded men, in large turbans, brandishing Korans. They were visible only sporadically, engulfed in the swelling crowd. Yet later that afternoon, as I looked down at the demonstrators from a balcony on Pyramid Road—a strip of sometimes stylish, often seedy, nightclubs and bars—they seemed a sea of flowing white prayer robes and caps as

they flailed bamboo clubs, iron pipes, and machetes in the air. The Venus Club, where visiting Saudi Arabian businessmen drank twenty-five-dollar bottles of whiskey, was sacked and burned. Mercedeses and other imported cars were gleefully smashed. Chants of "Sadat, O Sadat, you dress in the latest fashion, while we sleep twelve to a room" reverberated through the crowd and were picked up by its supporters on the rooftops.

Stunned by the depth of the rioters' passion—and by the 120 buses and hundreds of buildings that had been burned in Cairo alone—the government reversed its earlier decree that would have increased the cost of such basic necessities as bread, rice, and bottled gas by between 12 and 45 percent. The increases had shown a barely credible governmental insensitivity to a population where a worker's monthly pay was three times less than a bottle of imported French wine.

By the evening of the second day a reluctant Army was patrolling Cairo's streets. Camouflaged army trucks, their occupants in battle dress, guarded its bridges. Along the Nile, steel-helmeted troops manned barricades, which had been assembled hastily, mile after mile. Flames licked at overturned buses and cars, and in central Tahrir Square the loudest sound was the pop-pop-pop of exploding tear gas. The weight of the military had driven the mobs back to their dark streets. At least 160 people had died. Over a thousand were wounded; another two thousand were arrested, as a consequence of what the government announced, with an astonishing lack of reticence, was a "major Communist plot." Few Cairenes—including some within the government—took the allegations seriously. Yet even though the riots were generally considered to be a spontaneous outburst of rage, there certainly was some organization in some parts of town, where men could be seen directing the crowds and telling them which way to march.

I thought of all the flowing white prayer robes and caps I had seen on Pyramid Road. And I remembered what someone had told me earlier. Islam is the world's only major faith that can truly be defined as political.

QUESTIONS TO CONSIDER

1. How does the Nile River shape the geography of Egypt?

2. How do the Egyptians differ from other Arabs?

3. What disparities does Weaver see in Cairo? How does her friend Nadine embody some of these contradictions?

4. Why is it ironic that the Islamist movement represents a threat to the Egyptian government?

5. Does Weaver seem pessimistic or optimistic about the troubles in Egypt? Explain your answer with details from the essay.

World Events

▲

Rise of Nazism
In the mid-1930s, the National Socialist (or Nazi) Party, under the
leadership of Adolf Hitler (shown here in 1934) seized total control
of the German government.

◀ The Holocaust

When the Nazis took power in Germany, they began a campaign for "racial purity." With the coming of World War II, this campaign became the Holocaust, the systematic murder of millions of people throughout Europe, particularly Jews. The extermination program was carried out in concentration camps established in the areas controlled by the Nazis. This photo shows survivors of the Auschwitz concentration camp.

The Atomic Bomb

On August 6, 1945, at the end of World War II, the United States made the first use in history of nuclear weapons, dropping an atomic bomb that destroyed the Japanese city of Hiroshima. Three days later, a second bomb was dropped on another Japanese city, Nagasaki, producing the mushroom cloud shown here. ▶

◀ Partition of India

At midnight on August 15, 1947, the former British colony of India became two independent countries—the predominately Hindu nation of India and the Muslim nation of Pakistan. During the religious violence resulting from this partition, an estimated one million people died. In this photo, Muslims living in London are shown raising the Pakistani flag on that day to mark their independence.

◀ Korean War

When World War II ended, Korea became a divided nation. In 1950, North Korea, supported first by the Soviet Union and later by China, invaded South Korea, which asked the United Nations to intervene. Before the Korean War ended in 1953, approximately 5 million soldiers and civilians were killed. This photo shows UN troops bringing in North Korean POWs.

▲

Founding of Israel

On May 14, 1948, the independent state of Israel was founded as a Jewish homeland. In this photo, Jews are shown celebrating in Washington, DC, on the following day.

◀ Cuban Revolution

This photograph shows Cuban revolutionary Fidel Castro during his 1959 "March on Havana," which resulted in the overthrow of the government of Fulgencio Batista. While Castro did introduce reforms, he also imposed a harsh, left-wing dictatorship.

Vietnam War

Beginning in the late 1950s, the United States supported South Vietnam in its long war with communist North Vietnam. When American forces were withdrawn in 1973, the South Vietnamese were soon defeated. This photo shows U.S. helicopters landing American troops during an operation in February 1966.

▼

▲

China's Cultural Revolution

In 1966, Chinese communist leader Mao Zedong began the "Great Proletarian Cultural Revolution," a campaign against intellectuals and other elite groups within Chinese society. Under the leadership of fanatical youthful militias known as Red Guards, the Cultural Revolution rapidly got out of hand and resulted in widespread purges in which thousands of people died. With chaos threatening Chinese society, the Red Guard militias were disbanded in 1976 with Mao's approval. This photo shows a parade observing the 30th anniversary of the Cultural Revolution.

Military Coup in Chile

In September 1973, the Socialist government of Chilean president Salvador Allende (shown here) was overthrown by a military coup and replaced with a repressive right-wing government. ▶

Poland's Solidarity Movement

Political change in Eastern Europe was signaled in 1980 when shipyard workers in Poland, under the leadership of Lech Walesa, were successful in forcing the Communist government to recognize their union, Solidarity. In elections during 1989 and 1990, Poles voted overwhelmingly for Solidarity candidates, electing Walesa (shown here voting in the 1990 elections) president.

Death of Indira Gandhi

Religious fanaticism continued to plague India. In 1984, extremists among one religious sect, the Sikhs, were agitating for their own independent state. When Indian prime minister Indira Gandhi ordered troops to attack a group of Sikh terrorists, she was murdered in retaliation by two Sikh members of her own bodyguard. Gandhi's funeral is shown here.

▲

South African Elections

In 1994, South Africa held its first multiracial elections (shown here), ending decades of rule by the white minority. Although violence had been feared, the voting proceeded smoothly and resulted in the election of Nelson Mandela, who had been imprisoned 27 years for opposing South Africa's policy of racial segregation, as the country's first black president.

Arab-Israeli Peace Accords

In September 1993, Israeli Prime Minister Yitzhak Rabin and Yasir Arafat, head of the Palestine Liberation Organization, signed an agreement at the White House that granted the Palestinians self-rule in the Gaza Strip and the West Bank. ▶

Persian Gulf War

In August 1990, the Mideast nation of Iraq invaded neighboring Kuwait, seizing its oil fields and threatening those of Saudi Arabia. The following January, the United States, and its allies launched a massive counter-offensive to liberate Kuwait from Iraqi control. By the end of February, the Persian Gulf War was over. ▶

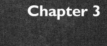

Chapter 3

East Asia

Finding a Space

Traditional Guideposts

◀ *Zuisho* ("Good Omen"), a watercolor by the 20th-century
Japanese artist Yoshinobu Yokoyama, shows a serene mountain
landscape shrouded in snow.

The Pearl

YUKIO MISHIMA

Yukio Mishima (1925–1970) came of age in postwar Japan, at a time when modernity was confronting traditional Japanese ideas and beliefs head-on. In the rebuilding after World War II, great efforts were put into fostering democracy and secular values. It was felt that Japan's traditional values and hierarchical society led to the destructive war. Much of Mishima's writing deals with what he saw as the spiritual void left in Japan by the abandonment of traditional values. This void was his obsession, and Mishima launched a personal crusade to restore bushido—the warrior code of ancient Japan that put great value on reciprocal loyalty and duty. Mishima founded a paramilitary society, and in 1970 they occupied a military base where the writer committed ritual suicide in an attempt to awaken Japan to its spiritual plight. In his writing, Mishima was a subtle chronicler of people's behavior. "The Pearl" offers a satirical look into upper-class society in Japan.

December 10 was Mrs. Sasaki's birthday, but since it was Mrs. Sasaki's wish to celebrate the occasion with the minimum of fuss, she had invited to her house for afternoon tea only her closest friends. Assembled were Mesdames Yamamoto, Matsumura, Azuma, and Kasuga—all four being forty-three years of age, exact contemporaries of their hostess.

These ladies were thus members, as it were, of a Keep-Our-Ages-Secret Society, and could be trusted implicitly not to divulge to outsiders the number of candles on today's cake. In inviting to her birthday party only guests of this nature Mrs. Sasaki was showing her customary prudence.

On this occasion Mrs. Sasaki wore a pearl ring. Diamonds at an all-female gathering had not seemed in the best of taste. Furthermore, pearls better matched the color of the dress she was wearing on this particular day.

Shortly after the party had begun, Mrs. Sasaki was moving across for one last inspection of the cake when the pearl in her ring, already a little loose, finally fell from its socket. It seemed a most inauspicious event for this happy occasion, but it would have been no less embarrassing to have everyone aware of the misfortune, so Mrs. Sasaki simply left the pearl close by the rim of the large cake dish and resolved to do something about it later. Around the cake were set out the plates, forks, and paper napkins for herself and the four guests. It now occurred to Mrs. Sasaki that she had no wish to be seen wearing a ring with no stone while cutting this cake, and accordingly she removed the ring from her finger and very deftly, without turning around, slipped it into a recess in the wall behind her back.

Amid the general excitement of the exchange of gossip, and Mrs. Sasaki's surprise and pleasure at the thoughtful presents brought by her guests, the matter of the pearl was very quickly forgotten. Before long it was time for the customary ceremony of lighting and extinguishing the candles on the cake. Everyone crowded excitedly about the table, lending a hand in the not untroublesome task of lighting forty-three candles.

Mrs. Sasaki, with her limited lung capacity, could hardly be expected to blow out all that number at one puff, and her appearance of utter helplessness gave rise to a great deal of hilarious comment.

The procedure followed in serving the cake was that, after the first bold cut, Mrs. Sasaki carved for each guest individually a slice of whatever thickness was requested and transferred this to a small plate, which the guest then carried back with her to her own seat. With everyone stretching out hands at the same time, the **crush**[1] and confusion around the table was considerable.

On top of the cake was a floral design executed in pink icing and liberally interspersed with small silver balls. These were silver-painted crystals of sugar—a common enough decoration on birthday cakes. In the struggle to secure helpings, moreover, flakes of icing, crumbs of cake, and a number of these silver balls came to be scattered all over the white tablecloth. Some of the guests gathered these stray particles between their fingers and put them on their plates. Others popped them straight into their mouths.

> *At the spot where she was sure she had left it, the pearl was no longer to be seen.*

In time all returned to their seats and ate their portions of cake at their leisure, laughing. It was not a homemade cake, having been ordered by Mrs. Sasaki from a certain high-class confectioner's, but the guests were unanimous in praising its excellence.

Mrs. Sasaki was bathed in happiness. But suddenly, with a tinge of anxiety, she recalled the pearl she had abandoned on the table, and, rising from her chair as casually as she could, she moved across to look for it. At the spot where she was sure she had left it, the pearl was no longer to be seen.

Mrs. Sasaki abhorred losing things. At once and without thinking, right in the middle of the party, she became wholly engrossed in her search, and the tension in

---

[1] **crush**—a crowded mass of people.

her manner was so obvious that it attracted everyone's attention.

"Is there something the matter?" someone asked.

"No, not at all, just a moment. . . ."

Mrs. Sasaki's reply was ambiguous, but before she had time to decide to return to her chair, first one, then another, and finally every one of her guests had risen and was turning back the tablecloth or **groping**[2] about on the floor.

Mrs. Azuma, seeing this commotion, felt that the whole thing was just too deplorable for words. She was incensed at a hostess who could create such an impossible situation over the loss of a solitary pearl.

Mrs. Azuma resolved to offer herself as a sacrifice and to save the day. With a heroic smile she declared: "That's it then! It must have been a pearl I ate just now! A silver ball dropped on the tablecloth when I was given my cake, and I just picked it up and swallowed it without thinking. It *did* seem to stick in my throat a little. Had it been a diamond, now, I would naturally return it—by an operation, if necessary—but as it's a pearl I must simply beg your forgiveness."

This announcement at once resolved the company's anxieties, and it was felt, above all, that it had saved the hostess from an embarrassing **predicament**.[3] No one made any attempt to investigate the truth or falsity of Mrs. Azuma's confession. Mrs. Sasaki took one of the remaining silver balls and put it in her mouth.

"Mm," she said. "Certainly tastes like a pearl, this one!"

Thus this small incident, too, was cast into the **crucible**[4] of good-humored teasing, and there—amid general laughter—it melted away.

When the party was over Mrs. Azuma drove off in her two-seater sportscar, taking with her in the other seat, her close friend and neighbor Mrs. Kasuga. Before two minutes had passed Mrs. Azuma said, "Own up! It was you who swallowed the pearl, wasn't it? I covered up for you, and took the blame on myself."

This unceremonious manner of speaking concealed deep affection, but, however friendly the intention may have been, to Mrs. Kasuga a wrongful accusation was a wrongful accusation. She had no recollection whatsoever of having swallowed a pearl in mistake for a sugar ball. She was—as Mrs. Azuma too must surely know—**fastidious**[5] in her eating habits, and, if she so much as detected a single hair in her food, whatever she happened to be eating at the time immediately stuck in her **gullet**.[6]

"Oh, really now!" protested the timid Mrs. Kasuga in a small voice, her eyes

---

[2] **groping**—feeling about or searching blindly with the hands.

[3] **predicament**—a difficult, unpleasant, or embarrassing situation.

[4] **crucible**—a severe test or trial.

[5] **fastidious**—fussy, very careful in matters of taste and choice.

[6] **gullet**—throat.

studying Mrs. Azuma's face in some puzzlement. "I just couldn't do a thing like that!"

"It's no good pretending. The moment I saw that green look on your face, I knew."

The little disturbance at the party had seemed closed by Mrs. Azuma's frank confession, but even now it had left behind it this strange awkwardness. Mrs. Kasuga, wondering how best to demonstrate her innocence, was at the same time seized by the fantasy that a solitary pearl was lodged somewhere in her intestines. It was unlikely, of course, that she should mistakenly swallow a pearl for a sugar ball, but in all that confusion of talk and laughter one had to admit that it was at least a possibility. Though she thought back over the events of the party again and again, no moment in which she might have inserted a pearl into her mouth came to mind—but, after all, if it was an unconscious act one would not expect to remember it.

Mrs. Kasuga blushed deeply as her imagination chanced upon one further aspect of the matter. It had occurred to her that when one accepted a pearl into one's system it almost certainly—its luster a **trifle**[7] dimmed, perhaps, by gastric juices—reemerged intact within a day or two.

And with this thought the design of Mrs. Azuma, too, seemed to have become transparently clear. Undoubtedly Mrs. Azuma had viewed this same prospect with embarrassment and shame, and had therefore cast her responsibility onto another, making it appear that she had considerately taken the blame to protect a friend.

Meanwhile Mrs. Yamamoto and Mrs. Matsumara whose homes lay in a similar direction, were returning together in a taxi. Soon after the taxi had started Mrs. Matsumura opened her handbag to make a few adjustments to her make-up. She remembered that she had done nothing to her face since all that commotion at the party.

Groping about with the tips of her fingers, Mrs. Matsumura retrieved the object, and saw to her amazement that it was a pearl.

As she was removing the powder compact her attention was caught by a sudden dull gleam as something tumbled to the bottom of the bag. Groping about with the tips of her fingers, Mrs. Matsumura retrieved the object, and saw to her amazement that it was a pearl.

Mrs. Matsumura stifled an exclamation of surprise. Recently her relationship with Mrs. Yamamoto had been far from cordial, and she had no wish to share with that lady a discovery with such awkward implications for herself.

Fortunately Mrs. Yamamoto was gazing out of the window and did not appear to have noticed her companion's momentary start of surprise.

Caught off balance by this sudden turn of events, Mrs. Matsumura did not pause to consider how the pearl had found its

---

[7] **trifle**—a small amount.

way into her bag, but immediately became a prisoner of her own private brand of school-captain morality.[8] It was unlikely—she thought—that she would do a thing like this, even in a moment of abstraction. But since, by some chance, the object had found its way into her handbag, the proper course was to return it at once. If she failed to do so, it would weigh heavily upon her conscience. The fact that it was a pearl, too—an article you could neither call all that expensive nor yet all that cheap—only made her position more ambiguous.

At any rate, she was determined that her companion, Mrs. Yamamoto, should know nothing of this incomprehensible development—especially when the affair had been so nicely rounded off, thanks to the selflessness of Mrs. Azuma. Mrs. Matsumura felt she could remain in the taxi not a moment longer, and, on the pretext of remembering a promise to visit a sick relative on her way back, she made the driver set her down at once, in the middle of a quiet residential district.

Mrs. Yamamoto, left alone in the taxi, was a little surprised that her practical joke should have moved Mrs. Matsumura to such abrupt action. Having watched Mrs. Matsumura's reflection in the window just now, she had clearly seen her draw the pearl from her bag.

At the party Mrs. Yamamoto had been the very first to receive a slice of cake. Adding to her plate a silver ball which had spilled onto the table, she had returned to her seat—again before any of the others—and there had noticed that the silver ball was a pearl. At this discovery she had at once conceived a malicious plan. While all the others were preoccupied with the cake, she had quickly slipped the pearl into the handbag left on the next chair by that insufferable **hypocrite**[9] Mrs. Matsumura.

Stranded in the middle of a residential district where there was little prospect of a taxi, Mrs. Matsumura fretfully gave her mind to a number of reflections on her position.

First, no matter how necessary it might be for the relief of her own conscience, it would be a shame indeed, when people had gone to such lengths to settle the affair satisfactorily, to go and stir up things all over again; and it would be even worse if in the process—because of the inexplicable nature of the circumstances—she were to direct unjust suspicions upon herself.

Secondly—notwithstanding these considerations—if she did not make haste to return the pearl now, she would forfeit her opportunity forever. Left till tomorrow (at the thought Mrs. Matsumura blushed) the returned pearl would be an object of rather disgusting speculation and doubt. Concerning this possibility Mrs. Azuma herself had dropped a hint.

It was at this point that there occurred to Mrs. Matsumura, greatly to her joy, a master scheme which would both salve her

---

[8] school-captain morality—reference to the rigorousness of the honor code at private schools.

[9] **hypocrite**—a person who claims to have beliefs or opinions that their actions do not support.

conscience and at the same time involve no risk of exposing her character to any unjust suspicion. Quickening her step, she emerged at length onto a comparatively busy thoroughfare, where she hailed a taxi and told the driver to take her quickly to a certain celebrated pearl shop on the Ginza. There she took the pearl from her bag and showed it to the attendant, asking to see a pearl of slightly larger size and clearly superior quality. Having made her purchase, she proceeded once more, by taxi, to Mrs. Sasaki's house.

Mrs. Matsumura's plan was to present this newly purchased pearl to Mrs. Sasaki, saying that she had found it in her jacket pocket. Mrs. Sasaki would accept it and later attempt to fit it into the ring. However, being a pearl of a different size, it would not fit into the ring, and Mrs. Sasaki—puzzled—would try to return it to Mrs. Matsumura, but Mrs. Matsumura would refuse to have it returned. Thereupon Mrs. Sasaki would have no choice but to reflect as follows: The woman has behaved in this way in order to protect someone else. Such being the case, it is perhaps safest simply to accept the pearl and forget the matter. Mrs. Matsumura has doubtless observed one of the three ladies in the act of stealing the pearl. But at least, of my four guests, I can now be sure that Mrs. Matsumura, if no one else, is completely without guilt. Whoever heard of a thief stealing something and then replacing it with a similar article of greater value?

By this device Mrs. Matsumura proposed to escape forever the infamy of suspicion, and equally—by a small outlay of cash—the pricks of an uneasy conscience.

To return to the other ladies. After reaching home, Mrs. Kasuga continued to feel painfully upset by Mrs. Azuma's cruel teasing. To clear herself of even a ridiculous charge like this—she knew—she must act before tomorrow or it would be too late. That is to say, in order to offer positive proof that she had not eaten the pearl it was above all necessary for the pearl itself to be somehow produced. And, briefly, if she could show the pearl to Mrs. Azuma immediately, her innocence on the gastronomic count (if not on any other) would be firmly established. But if she waited until tomorrow, even though she managed to produce the pearl, the shameful and hardly mentionable suspicion would inevitably have intervened.

The normally timid Mrs. Kasuga, inspired with the courage of impetuous action, burst from the house to which she had so recently returned, sped to a pearl shop in the Ginza, and selected and bought a pearl which, to her eye, seemed of roughly the same size as those silver balls on the cake. She then telephoned Mrs. Azuma. On returning home, she explained, she had discovered in the folds of the bow of her sash the pearl which Mrs. Sasaki had lost, but, since she felt too ashamed to return it by herself, she wondered if Mrs. Azuma would be so kind as to go with her, as soon as possible. Inwardly Mrs. Azuma considered the story a little unlikely, but since it was the request of a good friend she agreed to go.

Mrs. Sasaki accepted the pearl brought to her by Mrs. Matsumura and, puzzled at its failure to fit the ring, fell obligingly into that very train of thought for which Mrs. Matsumura had prayed; but it was a surprise to her when Mrs. Kasuga arrived about an hour later, accompanied by Mrs. Azuma, and returned another pearl.

Mrs. Sasaki hovered perilously on the brink of discussing Mrs. Matsumura's prior visit, but checked herself at the last moment and accepted the second pearl as unconcernedly as she could. She felt sure that this one at any rate would fit, and as soon as the two visitors had taken their leave she hurried to try it in the ring. But it was too small, and wobbled loosely in the socket. At this discovery Mrs. Sasaki was not so much surprised as dumbfounded.

On the way back in the car both ladies found it impossible to guess what the other might be thinking, and, though normally relaxed and **loquacious**[10] in each other's company, they now lapsed into a long silence.

Mrs. Azuma, who believed she could do nothing without her own full knowledge, knew for certain that she had not swallowed the pearl herself. It was simply to save everyone from embarrassment that she had cast shame aside and made that declaration at the party—more particularly it was to save the situation for her friend, who had been fidgeting about and looking conspicuously guilty. But what was she to think now? Beneath the peculiarity of Mrs.

Kasuga's whole attitude, and beneath this elaborate procedure of having herself accompany her as she returned the pearl, she sensed that there lay something much deeper. Could it be that Mrs. Azuma's intuition had touched upon a weakness in her friend's make-up which it was forbidden to touch upon, and that by thus driving her friend into a corner she had transformed an unconscious, impulsive kleptomania[11] into a deep mental derangement beyond all cure?

Mrs. Kasuga, for her part, still retained the suspicion that Mrs. Azuma had genuinely swallowed the pearl and that her confession at the party had been the truth. If that was so, it had been unforgivable of Mrs. Azuma, when everything was smoothly settled, to tease her so cruelly on the way back from the party, shifting the guilt onto herself. As a result, timid creature that she was, she had been panic-stricken, and besides spending good money had felt obliged to act out that little play—and was it not exceedingly ill-natured of Mrs. Azuma that, even after all this, she still refused to confess it was she who had eaten the pearl? And if Mrs. Azuma's innocence was all pretense, she herself—acting her part so painstakingly—must appear in Mrs. Azuma's eyes as the most ridiculous of third-rate comedians.

To return to Mrs. Matsumura. That lady, on her way back from obliging Mrs.

---

[10] **loquacious**—talkative.

[11] kleptomania—the recurring urge to steal, usually not because of need or profit.

Sasaki to accept the pearl, was feeling now more at ease in her mind and had the notion to make a leisurely reinvestigation, detail by detail, of the events of the recent incident. When going to collect her portion of cake, she had most certainly left her handbag on the chair. Then, while eating the cake, she had made liberal use of the paper napkin—so there could have been no necessity to take a handkerchief from her bag. The more she thought about it the less she could remember having opened her bag until she touched up her face in the taxi on the way home. How was it, then, that a pearl had rolled into a handbag which was always shut?

She realized now how stupid she had been not to have remarked this simple fact before, instead of flying into a panic at the mere sight of the pearl. Having progressed this far, Mrs. Matsumura was struck by an amazing thought. Someone must purposely have placed the pearl in her bag in order to incriminate her. And of the four guests at the party the only one who would do such a thing was, without doubt, the detestable Mrs. Yamamoto. Her eyes glinting with rage, Mrs. Matsumura hurried toward the house of Mrs. Yamamoto.

From her first glimpse of Mrs. Matsumura standing in the doorway, Mrs. Yamamoto knew at once what had brought her. She had already prepared her line of defense.

However, Mrs. Matsumura's cross-examination was unexpectedly severe, and from the start it was clear that she would accept no evasions.

"It was you, I know. No one but you could do such a thing," began Mrs. Matsumura, deductively.

"Why choose me? What proof have you? If you can say a thing like that to my face, I suppose you've come with pretty conclusive proof, have you?" Mrs. Yamamoto was at first icily composed.

To this Mrs. Matsumura replied that Mrs. Azuma, having so nobly taken the blame on herself, clearly stood in an incompatible relationship with mean and despicable behavior of this nature; and as for Mrs. Kasuga, she was much too weak-kneed for such dangerous work; and that left only one person—yourself.

Mrs. Yamamoto kept silent, her mouth shut tight like a clamshell. On the table before her gleamed the pearl which Mrs. Matsumura had set there. In the excitement she had not even had time to raise a teaspoon, and the Ceylon tea she had so thoughtfully provided was beginning to get cold.

"I had no idea that you hated me so." As she said this, Mrs. Yamamoto dabbed at the corners of her eyes, but it was plain that Mrs. Matsumura's resolve not to be deceived by tears was as firm as ever.

"Well, then," Mrs. Yamamoto continued, "I shall say what I had thought I must never say. I shall mention no names, but one of the guests . . ."

Someone must purposely have placed the pearl in her bag in order to incriminate her.

"By that, I suppose, you can only mean Mrs. Azuma or Mrs. Kasuga?"

"Please, I beg at least that you allow me to omit the name. As I say, one of the guests had just opened your bag and was dropping something inside when I happened to glance in her direction. You can imagine my amazement! Even if I had felt *able* to warn you, there would have been no chance. My heart just throbbed and throbbed, and on the way back in the taxi—oh, how awful not to be able to speak even then! If we had been good friends, of course, I could have told you quite frankly, but since I knew of your apparent dislike for me . . ."

"I see. You have been very considerate, I'm sure. Which means, doesn't it, that you have now cleverly shifted the blame onto Mrs. Azuma and Mrs. Kasuga?"

"Shifted the blame! Oh, how can I get you to understand my feelings? I only wanted to avoid hurting anyone."

"Quite. But you didn't mind hurting me, did you? You might at least have mentioned this in the taxi."

"And if you had been frank with me when you found the pearl in your bag, I would probably have told you, at that moment, everything I had seen—but no, you chose to leave the taxi at once, without saying a word!"

For the first time, as she listened to this, Mrs. Matsumura was at a loss for a reply.

"Well, then. Can I get you to understand? I wanted no one to be hurt."

Mrs. Matsumura was filled with an even more intense rage.

"If you are going to tell a string of lies like that," she said, "I must ask you to repeat them, tonight if you wish, in my presence, before Mrs. Azuma and Mrs. Kasuga."

At this Mrs. Yamamoto started to weep.

"And thanks to you," she sobbed reprovingly, "all my efforts to avoid hurting anyone will have come to nothing."

It was a new experience for Mrs. Matsumura to see Mrs. Yamamoto crying, and, though she kept reminding herself not to be taken in by tears, she could not altogether dismiss the feeling that perhaps somewhere, since nothing in this affair could be proved, there might be a modicum of truth even in the assertions of Mrs. Yamamoto.

In the first place—to be a little more objective—if one accepted Mrs. Yamamoto's story as true, then her reluctance to disclose the name of the guilty party, whom she had observed in the very act, argued some refinement of character. And just as one could not say for sure that the gentle and seemingly timid Mrs. Kasuga would never be moved to an act of malice, so even the undoubtedly bad feeling between Mrs. Yamamoto and herself could, by one way of looking at things, be taken as actually lessening the likelihood of Mrs. Yamamoto's guilt. For if she were to do a thing like this, with their relationship as it was, Mrs. Yamamoto would be the first to come under suspicion.

We have differences in our natures," Mrs. Yamamoto continued tearfully, "and I cannot deny that there are things about yourself which I dislike. But, for all that, it is really too bad that you should suspect me of such a petty[12] trick to get the better of you. . . . Still, on thinking it over, to submit quietly to your accusations might well be the course most consistent with what I have felt in this matter all along. In this way I alone shall bear the guilt, and no other will be hurt."

After this pathetic pronouncement Mrs. Yamamoto lowered her face to the table and abandoned herself to uncontrolled weeping.

Watching her, Mrs. Matsumura came by degrees to reflect upon the impulsiveness of her own behavior. Detesting Mrs. Yamamoto as she had, there had been times in her **castigation**[13] of that lady when she had allowed herself to be blinded by emotion.

When Mrs. Yamamoto raised her head again after this prolonged bout of weeping, the look of resolution on her face, somehow remote and pure, was apparent even to her visitor. Mrs. Matsumura, a little frightened, drew herself upright in her chair.

"This thing should never have been. When it is gone, everything will be as before." Speaking in riddles, Mrs. Yamamoto pushed back her disheveled hair and fixed a terrible, yet hauntingly beautiful gaze upon the top of the table. In an instant she had snatched up the pearl from before her, and, with a gesture of no ordinary resolve, tossed it into her mouth. Raising her cup by the handle, her little finger elegantly extended, she washed the pearl down her throat with one gulp of cold Ceylon tea.

Mrs. Matsumura watched in horrified fascination. The affair was over before she had time to protest. This was the first time in her life she had seen a person swallow a pearl, and there was in Mrs. Yamamoto's manner something of that desperate finality one might expect to see in a person who had just drunk poison.

However, heroic though the action was, it was above all a touching incident, and not only did Mrs. Matsumura find her anger vanished into thin air, but so impressed was she by Mrs. Yamamoto's simplicity and purity that she could only think of that lady as a saint. And now Mrs. Matsumura's eyes too began to fill with tears, and she took Mrs. Yamamoto by the hand.

"Please forgive me, please forgive me," she said. "It was wrong of me."

For a while they wept together, holding each other's hands and vowing to each

In an instant she had snatched up the pearl from before her, and, with a gesture of no ordinary resolve, tossed it into her mouth.

---

[12] petty—mean.

[13] **castigation**—severe scolding or punishment.

other that henceforth they would be the firmest of friends.

When Mrs. Sasaki heard rumors that the relationship between Mrs. Yamamoto and Mrs. Matsumura, which had been so strained, had suddenly improved, and that Mrs. Azuma and Mrs. Kasuga, who had been such good friends, had suddenly fallen out, she was at a loss to understand the reasons and contented herself with the reflection that nothing was impossible in this world.

However, being a woman of no strong **scruples**,[14] Mrs. Sasaki requested a jeweler to refashion her ring and to produce a design into which two new pearls could be set, one large and one small, and this she wore quite openly, without further mishap.

Soon she had completely forgotten the small commotion on her birthday, and when anyone asked her age she would give the same untruthful answers as ever.

---

[14] **scruples**—regard for the morality or appropriateness of an action.

QUESTIONS TO CONSIDER

1. How would you describe the character of each of the ladies in the story? What seems to motivate the ladies?

2. What is the dominant tone of this story? Do you think Mishima wants the reader to like or dislike certain characters more than others?

3. From your reading of this story, how would you describe Japanese society? What seems to dominate its social interactions?

Three Poems

BEI DAO

Bei Dao (1949–   ) is the pen name of China's most prominent poet. Born Zhao Zhenkai in the year of China's Communist revolution, Bei grew up under Communism and witnessed the worst excesses of the Cultural Revolution (1966–1976), a movement that tried to remake Chinese society by destroying all vestiges of intellectual and cultural life. It was a period of great violence and repression. Bei's poetry is part of the reaction against the Cultural Revolution that began in the late 1970s. He founded a literary magazine and became a prominent leader of the democracy movement. In 1989, when the Chinese government massacred democratic protesters in Tiananmen Square, Bei was in Berlin at a conference. He chose to remain in exile rather than return to certain imprisonment. Since then he has lived in Scandinavia and the United States.

One Step

the pagoda's[1] shadow moves across the grass, pointing at you
or at me, at different moments
we are only one step away
parting or meeting again
is an ever-repeating
theme: hate only one step away
the sky **sways**[2] on its foundation of fear
the buildings open windows in every direction
we live inside them
or outside: death only one step away

---

[1] pagoda—a Hindu or Buddhist temple, especially a many-tiered tower.

[2] **sways**—swings back and forth.

the child has learned to talk to walls
the history of the city is sealed by old men
in their hearts: **dotage**[3] only one step away

Language

many languages
fly around the world
producing sparks when they collide
sometimes of hate
sometimes of love

reason's mansion
collapses without a sound
baskets woven of thoughts
as flimsy as bamboo splints[4]
are filled with blind toadstools

the beasts on the cliff
run past, trampling the flowers
a dandelion grows secretly
in a certain corner
the wind has carried away its seeds

many languages
fly around the world
the production of languages
can neither increase nor decrease
mankind's silent suffering

---

[3] **dotage**—feeble-mindedness or stupidity caused by age.
[4] splints—thin strips of wood.

A Perpetual Stranger

a perpetual[5] stranger
am I to the world
I don't understand its language
my silence it can't comprehend
all we have to exchange
is a touch of contempt
as if we meet in a mirror

a perpetual stranger
am I to myself
I fear the dark
but block with my body
the only lamp
my shadow is my beloved
heart the enemy

---

[5] **perpetual**—never-ending, permanent.

QUESTIONS TO CONSIDER

1. In the first poem, what does Bei mean by the "step"? Why is it so close?

2. What is "mankind's silent suffering" in "Language"? In the final poem, who is the "perpetual stranger"? What do these images and ideas have in common?

3. How would you describe Bei's pessimism? Do you agree with his point of view? Why or why not?

The Mao Button

FENG JICAI

Feng Jicai (1942–   ) grew up during the Chinese Revolution. He worked for many years as a painter, but was forced to stop during the Cultural Revolution (1966–1976), and turned to writing. The Cultural Revolution was a time when people informed on each other for the slightest deviation from the Communist party line, and average citizens went to great lengths to prove their zeal and loyalty. Many of Feng's stories are satirical, and he was unable to publish any of his writings until 1977. The Cultural Revolution had ended the year before with the death of Mao Zedong, the leader of Communist China. Mao was worshipped in China, his image and his sayings revered. "The Mao Button" satirizes this worship and people's constant striving to better their neighbors.

He vowed to get himself a **stupendous**[1] Mao button tonight after work.

Actually, the one he had worn to the office today was big and novel enough to arouse a good deal of envy.

His brother-in-law had gotten it specially for him from a certain unit in the navy and had brought it to his place just last night. Everyone in his family had wanted it. After squabbling over it for about half an hour, they had agreed to take turns: each would have it for a day until it had circulated once, then each would keep it for a week at a time. He had gotten it first, not because he was head of the house, but because he had wanted so desperately

to show it off at work. He had insisted, and he had won.

He was delighted with himself all morning at the office. He created a real sensation. "You've outdone us all today, Mr. Kong!" said everyone who saw him, as they bent down to pore over the button as if it were some kind of jewel.

Their envious looks went straight to his head. He was certain that his Mao button was the best at the office today. At lunch he paraded around the cafeteria to make sure everyone noticed him. But then

---

[1] **stupendous**—amazing, especially in terms of size.

Mr. Chen, from the production department, approached him sporting an even bigger, newer, more eye-catching button on his neatly pressed jacket. An **embossed**[2] portrait of the Leader was centered in a great red enamel sun, below which a giant golden steamship forged through the waves. The Leader was depicted from the front instead of the usual profile. He was wearing an army cap, and his cap and collar bore insignia. The gilding was superb: the flash of gold against red dazzled the eye. The button was a collector's item. Kong felt his own button darken like a light that had gone out. And it was so small by comparison—his whole button was no bigger than the portrait on Mr. Chen's, whose entire button must have been more than three inches across: about as big as a sesame cake.

Mr. Chen was extremely coolheaded and always kept a straight face. As they walked by each other, Mr. Chen just eyed Kong's chest and passed him like some champion athlete meeting a young amateur. Hurt, jealous, and angry, Kong made up his mind to go right out and get an enormous Mao button, even if it cost him his life's savings. He just had to bring Mr. Chen down a peg or two.

When he got home in the evening he told his family about his failure. After a quick dinner he found all the Mao buttons in the house, wrapped them in a handkerchief, and stuffed them into his pocket. He even snatched up the buttons his wife and son were wearing. Then he

dashed out to The East Is Red Avenue, the busiest shopping street in town. He had heard that the open space beyond the parking lot of the big department store was the place to go to trade Mao buttons. People said you could get all the latest styles there. He had never been before.

By the time he got there the sky was dark and all the lights were on, but shoppers still crowded the street. Practically everyone was wearing Mao buttons; they seemed to have become another part of the human body. Some people wore four or five across their chests, the way European generals used to wear their medals a hundred years ago. It seemed to Kong that people with unusual Mao buttons held their heads higher than the rest, while those with ordinary little **outmoded**[3] buttons moved drearily through the crowd. No matter how much status, income, or power you had, the quality of your Mao button was all-determining at this particular moment. Had the Mao button become the acid test of the wearer's political stance and loyalty to the Leader? A touchstone? A monitor of the heart?

As he walked he paid no attention to the people coming toward him; he had eyes only for their Mao buttons. Colorful, glittering buttons of all sizes were rushing at him like stars shooting by a rocket ship in outer space. Then he spotted a button exactly like Mr. Chen's. He reached out and grabbed its wearer by the arm.

---

[2] **embossed**—carved or molded onto a surface.
[3] **outmoded**—out of date or fashion.

"Just what do you think you're doing?" the man demanded, obviously startled.

Kong took a closer look at him: a short, fat, paunchy old soldier. Perhaps he was an officer.

"Excuse me, uh—" Kong asked with an ingratiating laugh, "could you spare your Mao button? I have all kinds—you could have your pick. Do you think we could make a deal?"

The soldier sneered as if to say that his button was a priceless family heirloom. He looked annoyed at Kong's **effrontery**.[4] Kong was still clutching his sleeve. "No way," he snapped, shoving Kong aside, and waddled away.

Kong was angry, but he comforted himself with the thought that even if he had gotten the button, it would merely have put him on an equal footing with Mr. Chen. What he wanted was to outdo him. Then he caught sight of the swarm of button traders beyond the parking lot. His heart began to pound like that of a fisherman who spots a shimmering school of fish, and he broke into a run.

Once in the crowd, Kong felt hot and flushed, but the sight was mind-boggling: an endless variety of Mao buttons and an assortment of hawkers to match.

Some wore the buttons they hoped to trade and called out what kinds they were looking for:

"Who has a Wuhan Steelworks 'two-and-a-half'?"—a button two-and-a-half inches in diameter—"I'll swap you for it!"

Some displayed their buttons on hand towels; others, who mistook flashy colors for beauty, had their wares in flat glass cases lined with colored paper on the sides and green satin on the bottom. Still others pinned their buttons to their caps so that people had to crane their necks to see them. The crowd thronged the south and east edges of the parking lot. Some people had even spilled over into the lot and squeezed their way in between the cars. With their haggling, shouts, and laughter, the place was noisier than an open-air market at the busiest hour of the morning.

Someone tapped him on the shoulder. "What kind are you looking for?"

The speaker was a big, tall middle-aged man with the unctuous[5] manner of a practiced salesman. But he was wearing a baggy blue jacket with only a single bottlecap-sized Mao button on the chest. He did not look as though he had any special goods.

"I want a big one. At least a 'three-and-a-half.' Do you have any?"

"Oh-ho—no little trinkets for you, eh! Do you mind if the workmanship is a bit rough?" the man asked. He seemed to have what Kong wanted.

"Let me see it."

"First tell me what you have," the man replied without batting an eyelid. He was as **haughty**[6] as a Mao-button millionaire.

---

[4] **effrontery**—shameful disrespect.

[5] unctuous—oily.

[6] **haughty**—arrogant and proud.

"I've got dozens of different kinds," said Kong, reaching for his pocket.

The man touched Kong's wrist. "Don't take them out in this mob. Somebody'll swipe them. Come with me!"

They elbowed their way out of the crowd, crossed the street, and entered the dark alley beside the Revolution Hat and Shoe Store. The man led him to the second lamppost.

"Let me see your goods," he ordered.

Kong handed the man his handkerchief of Mao buttons. The man inspected them, shaking his head and clucking in disapproval, and gave them back.

"You got any better ones?" he asked after a moment's thought.

"No, these are all I have."

The man paused again. "You're going to have a hard time trading that bunch of buttons for a 'three-and-a-half,'" he said, pointing at Kong's handkerchief of buttons. "Don't forget—the big ones are hot items now."

"Well, I should have a look at yours, whether you're going to trade or not. Then we'll see what's what," Kong retorted scornfully. After all, he had not even seen the man's wares.

Instead of answering, the man unfastened his outer jacket and whisked it open. Kong's eyes nearly popped out of his head: at least a hundred different Mao buttons were pinned to the man's inner jacket. He was a walking Mao button treasure house. Kong had never seen any of the styles before.

"You haven't seen anything yet," the man said before Kong could look his fill. "Take a peek inside—that's where the big ones are." And he opened the button-covered jacket to reveal yet another garment laden with row upon row of shiny buttons. They were huge: all were at least as big as a fist, and one, the size of the lid of a mug, caught the eye like a crane among chickens.

Kong's eyes nearly popped out of his head: at least a hundred different Mao buttons were pinned to the man's inner jacket.

"That's the one I want!" cried Kong in delight, his heart thumping.

"What? This one?" the man asked with a chuckle. "Do you know how big it is? It's a 'four.' You see where it says 'Loyalty' three times in gold along here? This is a 'Triple Loyalty' button from Xinjiang. Nobody around here has seen these yet. I guess you don't know the market: even four times the buttons you've got here wouldn't buy you one of these. All your buttons put together are worth at most a 'three-and-a-half.' And that's only if you trade with me—nobody else would give you such a good deal. Your buttons are too little and too ordinary."

"Why don't you just let me have this 'four'? I've got forty or fifty buttons here, and—" Kong pleaded. He was madly in love with the button. If only he could just wear it tomorrow, Mr. Chen and everyone else at the office would be green with envy.

Just then a swarthy little man appeared on the left and approached to look at the Mao buttons on the tall man's chest.

The tall man glanced at the newcomer and yanked his outer jacket shut. "No deal!" he announced rudely, and stalked away, jingling like a horse in bell harness.

Kong thought, "I can't let him get away—at least I've got to trade him for a 'three-and-a-half.'" He was about to run after the tall man when the swarthy little man put out an arm to stop him. With his chin of bristly black stubble and his dark clothes, he looked as if he were carved in jet. His round gleaming eyes seemed to cast a black luster over his entire person.

"Don't trade with him—gypping beginners is his racket," he said in a rasping voice. "Those 'Triple Loyalty' buttons from Xinjiang are a dime a dozen; they're considered passé. Now tell me what you've got — I'll make you a deal. I've got a Mao button like nothing you've ever seen before."

"Is it big?"

"Big! Well, it's bigger than that 'Triple Loyalty' button of his. But it's not just big—it's a real novelty. But let me see yours first."

Kong produced his package of buttons again and let the man examine them like a customs inspector. Then the man led him deeper into the alley. The streetlights were burned out, and it was pitch-dark. Kong was afraid that the stranger was going to mug him. The farther they went, the darker it got, until the man's murky silhouette almost blended into the gloomy black shadows.

"Couldn't I take a look at it here?" he asked, making a supreme effort to be brave.

"All right," agreed the swarthy little man, and like the tall man before him he unfastened his jacket, but his chest was a dark blur without a single Mao button. Before Kong could ask any questions he heard a click, and a round, glowing, moon-like object magically appeared on the man's left breast. It seemed to Kong that a luminous hole had opened up in the man's chest or that his heart had lit up. And inside was a picture: a color portrait of Chairman Mao waving from the Tiananmen Rostrum![7]

When he recovered from his momentary stupefaction, Kong understood: the man was wearing a round glass case lit by a flashlight bulb. In the case a color photo of the Leader waving a giant hand was mounted behind a red cardboard railing. The light bulb was probably between the photo and the cardboard. The battery was concealed on the man's person; the wiring hung down from the back of the case; and the switch was in his hand. A flip of the switch and presto! The Mao button would light up like a color television. A truly great invention!

The man clicked the light off. "Well, how do you like it?" came his smug, wheedling voice in the dark. "Isn't it incredible? What'll you give me for it? But

---

[7] Tiananmen Rostrum—speaker's platform in Tiananmen Square, a vast public space in Beijing, the capital of China.

don't forget that the batteries and switch alone are worth a lot of money!"

Kong had to agree that the button was a real novelty. But his interest quickly faded. This was some homemade contraption, not a proper button. And you had to carry around a complete set of electrical equipment—wiring, batteries, a switch— as if you were an electric fan. Besides, it might be eye-catching at night, but it would be totally lackluster by day.

"It's very nice," he said politely after a moment's thought, "but I think I won't take it, since it's not a proper button. What I'd like is a regular button, at least a 'three-and-a-half' if you have any."

The man launched into a sales pitch, but Kong would not change his mind. Then the man grabbed him eagerly by the wrist. Kong, who had been afraid to start with, thought the man was going to rob him of his Mao buttons. Jerking his arm free, he ran for the brightly lit entrance to the alley.

"Stop him!" he heard the man shout behind him.

It occurred to Kong that some of the man's cronies might be lurking nearby. He shot out of the alley and into the street, where he almost collided with an approaching bicycle. Skittish as a hare, he jumped over the front wheel and darted back into the crowd of button traders by the parking lot. For fear that the swarthy little man might spot him, he stooped over, hiding his face, and stole through the crowd. Luckily he escaped without further mishap and ran all the way home.

When his wife saw how pale and breathless he was, she thought he was ill. She scolded him, once she found out what had happened, and poured him a hot cup of tea to calm him down.

"You've got Mao buttons on the brain!" she said. "You never do what you're supposed to when you get home from work—and tonight, of all things, you run out onto the streets to swap buttons. Don't you know what kind of riffraff you could have run into out there? And you took the kid's and my buttons too! If they'd been stolen, what would we have worn tomorrow? People would say I'd gone without my button because I didn't love Chairman Mao. They'd arrest me as a counterrevolutionary, and there wouldn't be anybody here to cook for you when you got home from work every day. It takes finesse to get good Mao buttons. Look at Mr. Wang—now there's a real operator. He may be unassuming, but he's got more buttons than anybody."

"Which Mr. Wang?"

"The one who lives on the third floor of the front building. You still don't know who I mean? Of course you do—Mrs. Wang's husband. What's the matter with you? Did they scare you silly out there?"

"Oh—yes—I see. So where does he get so many buttons?"

"He's on the staff of a badge factory where they make nothing but Mao buttons.

> *People would say I'd gone without my button because I didn't love Chairman Mao.*

His boss gives him hundreds of them to take along on every business trip. You have to grease palms with them nowadays to get a hotel room, buy train tickets, or ask anyone a favor. They're worth more than cash. A little while ago Mrs. Wang told me that her husband paid for a new truck for his factory with nothing but Mao buttons."

"How many buttons did that cost?"

"The man's clever—he may not have parted with all that many. My guess is that a shrewd fellow like him lines his own pocket on the sly whenever he has the chance. Why else would Mrs. Wang have a new Mao button every time I see her? When I ask her about them she just laughs it off instead of answering, but I'm sure she gets them all from her husband. Just now I went over there to collect their water bill and found them gloating over their buttons. I burst in without knocking and really got an eyeful."

"Did you get a good look at them? What kinds did they have?"

"I couldn't begin to tell you. There were at least a thousand—the bed and table were both covered with them."

"Were there any big ones?"

"Big ones? I swear one of them was as big as a saucepan lid."

So the object of his far-flung search had been right next door all along. Leaving his tea untouched on the table, he ran to the front building as fast as his legs could carry him. "Mr. Wang!" he began to shout, even before he got to the third floor. Like some invisible hand, joy clutched at his vocal cords and made his voice tremble.

Once inside Mr. Wang's apartment, he begged him to show his treasures. Mr. Wang **grudgingly**[8] obliged, since Kong was an old neighbor. Now here was a great Mao-button collection! Mr. Wang was a Mao-button millionaire if there ever was one. Kong was developing an inferiority complex.

Then he spotted the enormous button that his wife had mentioned. Mr. Wang said that it was a "five-and-a-half." Kong weighed it in his palm. It was surprisingly heavy: at least half a pound. But the picture was commonplace: a big red sun with a profile of the Leader in the middle and a chain of nine sunflowers across the bottom. The flowers looked more like coarse sieves. The buffing, painting, and gilding were shoddy. However, it was definitely the biggest in the world—Mr. Chen's would look tiny by comparison. Kong wanted a big one: they were the best—they stood out and really made a statement. He begged Mr. Wang for it and showed his buttons one more time. Luckily he had one with a picture of the globe and the caption: "The People of the World Yearn for the Red Sun." Mr. Wang happened to need this one to complete a set of four, so Kong gave it to him, along with two others, in exchange for the biggest button in history. He arrived home cradling his treasure in trembling hands.

"Wow!" his wife and son exclaimed when they saw it.

---

[8] **grudgingly**—with reluctance or hesitation.

The next morning he rose early, shaved, washed his face and neck, and put on clean clothes, as carefully as if he were going to be awarded a medal. Next, ignoring his wife's protests, he used one of her soft new handkerchiefs to polish the huge button with petroleum jelly He had some trouble pinning it on. It covered half of his narrow chest when he wore it on the side, but placed in the middle it looked **frivolous**,[9] like the breastplate of an ancient general. And his jacket sagged under its tremendous weight. Worst of all, since the pin was right in the center of the back, the button tilted outward like a picture frame instead of lying flat. Kong was at a loss until his wife suggested that he change into his denim jacket; although the weather was still too warm for denim, the stiff material allowed the button to lie flat the way it was supposed to.

With the button on, he struck a few poses and admired himself in the mirror.

"Hooray!" his son cheered, clapping his hands. "My dad is tops! My dad is number one!"

The child was adorable—his compliments were the icing on the cake.

Yes, he really was the sensation of the day! People ogled him as he rode his bicycle down the street. Some pointed him out to their companions, but he sped past them before they could get a good look at him. He was on cloud nine. To prolong the gratification, he took the long way to work. People on a passing bus pressed their noses flat against the windows to stare. As he approached the gate of his office building he tensed up like an actor about to take his first plunge through a brightly lit stage door. He was headed for the **limelight**.[10]

He entered the gate and locked his bicycle in the yard.

"Hey, everybody," someone shouted, "come see Mr. Kong's Mao button!" In no time flat he was surrounded by a crowd. People were jostling each other and craning their necks to see. They were looking at his button with amazement and envy, and at him with a new respect. Everyone was yelling, which attracted more people.

"Now that's a big button. Where did you get it?"

"Mr. Kong, you're a real go-getter!"

"Of course! I'm loyal to Chairman Mao," he said with a **smug**[11] laugh, keeping one hand on the button in case anyone tried to snatch it.

Some people tried to move his fingers out of the way so that they could get a better look at the button; others tried to peek at the back to find out where it was made.

"It doesn't say anything on the back," he cried, clutching the button. "It was produced by a classified military factory. Please quit yanking on it, the pin is too small—" He seemed anxious, but in fact he was jubilant. The excitement he was causing was a sign that his button was without compare not only at the office,

---

[9] **frivolous**—silly.

[10] **limelight**—focus of attention.

[11] **smug**—overconfident and satisfied.

but probably in the whole city. Unless someone made a button as big as a crock lid, which only a giant could wear. Then he remembered Mr. Chen: where was yesterday's victor now?

The crowd had swelled to thirty or forty people. Everyone was babbling at once. He could not hear anything. His heavy denim jacket had brought the sweat out on his forehead. Unable to stand it any longer, he began to wriggle his way out of the unbearable crush, away from the hands that were pulling on him.

"Let me out, you're squashing me!"

He was tickled pink.

Finally he squeezed his way out like a noodle out of a noodle machine. He was exhilarated. But just then he heard a clank, as though a heavy metal platter had fallen to the ground. Then he heard it rolling around. He did not realize what the sound was until he reached up and found that his Mao button was gone.

"Oh, oh! My button fell off!" he cried. Everyone froze and he began a frantic search. It was not on the ground in front of him, so he stepped back to turn around and look behind him. He felt something hard and slippery underfoot.

"Oh, no! You're standing on a button with a portrait of Chairman Mao!" he heard a woman say, before he could grasp what had happened.

In terror he looked down and saw the Mao button under his heel. He should have been able to lift his foot quickly, but it was as unresponsive as a piece of wood. His body went limp and his weight sank

into the offending leg. With all eyes riveted upon him, he stood rooted to the spot.

This blunder was a heinous[12] crime that brought him to the brink of destruction. There is no need to recount the details here. Suffice it to say that he recovered from his Mao-button mania and came to look upon these former objects of his affection with fear and trembling. These events are all behind him now. But there is one question that puzzles him to this day. Perhaps the only clue to its answer lies in the following "natural phenomenon": you can travel the entire three million seven hundred and seven thousand square miles of our country today and see hardly a single Mao button. . . .

---

[12] heinous—shockingly evil.

QUESTIONS TO CONSIDER

1. At the beginning of the story, why does Mr. Kong vow to get a "stupendous" Mao button?

2. Do you sympathize with Mr. Kong or do you feel he gets what he deserves? Explain your answer.

3. What is the lesson that Feng is trying to teach in his satire?

The Explosion in the Parlor

BAI XIAO-YI

Bai Xiao-Yi is a prizewinning short story writer in China. He particularly favors the miniature, or short short story, as a form conducive to what he wants to say. Bai has published widely in China, and his stories depict the variety of social interaction in China. They are particularly good at expressing the ironies of the way people interact.

The host poured tea into the cup and placed it on the small table in front of his guests, who were a father and daughter, and put the lid on the cup with a clink. Apparently thinking of something, he hurried into the inner room, leaving the thermos on the table. His two guests heard a chest of drawers opening and a **rustling**.[1]

They remained sitting in the parlor, the ten-year-old daughter looking at the flowers outside the window, the father just about to take his cup, when the crash came, right there in the parlor. Something was hopelessly broken.

It was the thermos, which had fallen to the floor. The girl looked over her shoulder abruptly, startled, staring. It was mysterious. Neither of them had touched it, not even a little bit. True, it hadn't stood steadily when their host placed it on the table, but it hadn't fallen then.

The crash of the thermos caused the host, with a box of sugar cubes in his hand, to rush back from the inner room. He **gawked**[2] at the steaming floor and **blurted**[3] out, "It doesn't matter! It doesn't matter!"

The father started to say something. Then he muttered, "Sorry, I touched it and it fell."

"It doesn't matter," the host said.

Later, when they left the house, the daughter said, "Daddy, *did* you touch it?"

"No. But it stood so close to me."

"But you *didn't* touch it. I saw your reflection in the windowpane. You were sitting perfectly still."

---

[1] **rustling**—making a gentle sound like leaves blowing in the wind.

[2] **gawked**—stared stupidly.

[3] **blurted**—spoke abruptly or without thinking.

The father laughed. "What then would you give as the cause of its fall?"

"The thermos fell by itself. The floor is uneven. It wasn't steady when Mr. Li put it there. Daddy, *why* did you say that you . . ."

"That won't do, girl. It sounds more acceptable when I say I knocked it down. There are things which people accept less the more you defend them. The truer the story you tell, the less true it sounds."

The daughter was lost in silence for a while. Then she said, "Can you explain it only this way?"

"Only this way," her father said.

QUESTIONS TO CONSIDER

1. Why does the father accept blame for something he did not do?

2. Who do you think is right: the father or the daughter? Why?

3. Though the father says he can explain "only this way," how would you put his lesson into your own words?

The Grasshopper and the Bell Cricket

YASUNARI KAWABATA

Yasunari Kawabata (1899–1972) was Japan's first winner of the Nobel Prize in literature, in 1968. One of Japan's finest novelists, he is also celebrated for his very short stories, which he called "palm-of-the-hand stories." Kawabata intended these stories to be miniature works of art, rather like a poem or a painting in the way they depict delicate and beautiful images and events. Kawabata was an imagistic writer whose writing is dominated by two themes: love and loneliness, and the conflict between tradition and modernity in twentieth-century Japan. "The Grasshopper and the Bell Cricket" reflects many traditional aspects of Japanese culture, including a reverence for the natural world and for crafts.

Walking along the tile-roofed wall of the university, I turned aside and approached the upper school. Behind the white board fence of the school playground, from a dusky clump of bushes under the black cherry trees, an insect's voice could be heard. Walking more slowly and listening to that voice, and furthermore reluctant to part with it, I turned right so as not to leave the playground behind. When I turned to the left, the fence gave way to an embankment planted with orange trees. At the corner, I exclaimed with surprise. My eyes gleaming at what they saw up ahead, I hurried forward with short steps.

At the base of the embankment was a **bobbing**[1] cluster of beautiful varicolored lanterns, such as one might see at a festival in a remote country village. Without going any farther, I knew that it was a group of children on an insect chase among the bushes of the embankment. There were about twenty lanterns. Not only were there crimson, pink, indigo, green, purple, and yellow lanterns, but one lantern glowed with five colors at once. There were even some little red store-bought lanterns. But most of the lanterns were beautiful square ones which the children had made themselves with love and care. The bobbing

---
[1] **bobbing**—moving quickly up and down.

lanterns, the coming together of children on this lonely slope—surely it was a scene from a fairy tale?

Each day, with cardboard, paper, brush, scissors, penknife, and glue, the children made new lanterns out of their hearts and minds.

One of the neighborhood children had heard an insect sing on this slope one night. Buying a red lantern, he had come back the next night to find the insect. The night after that, there was another child. This new child could not buy a lantern. Cutting out the back and front of a small carton and papering it, he placed a candle on the bottom and fastened a string to the top. The number of children grew to five, and then to seven. They learned how to color the paper that they stretched over the windows of the cutout cartons, and to draw pictures on it. Then these wise child-artists, cutting out round, three-cornered, and lozenge leaf shapes in the cartons, coloring each little window a different color, with circles and diamonds, red and green, made a single and whole decorative pattern. The child with the red lantern discarded it as a tasteless object that could be bought at a store. The child who had made his own lantern threw it away because the design was too simple. The pattern of light that one had had in hand the night before was unsatisfying the morning after. Each day, with cardboard, paper, brush, scissors, penknife, and glue,

the children made new lanterns out of their hearts and minds. Look at my lantern! Be the most unusually beautiful! And each night, they had gone out on their insect hunts. These were the twenty children and their beautiful lanterns that I now saw before me.

Wide-eyed, I **loitered**[2] near them. Not only did the square lanterns have old-fashioned patterns and flower shapes, but the names of the children who had made them were cut out in squared letters of the syllabary.[3] Different from the painted-over red lanterns, others (made of thick cutout cardboard) had their designs drawn onto the paper windows, so that the candle's light seemed to **emanate**[4] from the form and color of the design itself. The lanterns brought out the shadows of the bushes like dark light. The children crouched eagerly on the slope wherever they heard an insect's voice.

"Does anyone want a grasshopper?" A boy, who had been peering into a bush about thirty feet away from the other children, suddenly straightened up and shouted.

"Yes! Give it to me!" Six or seven children came running up. Crowding behind the boy who had found the grasshopper, they peered into the bush. Brushing away their outstretched hands and spreading out his arms, the boy stood as if guarding the bush where the insect

---

[2] **loitered**—hung around.

[3] **syllabary**—characters or symbols representing syllables.

[4] **emanate**—issue, originate.

was. Waving the lantern in his right hand, he called again to the other children.

"Does anyone want a grasshopper? A grasshopper!"

"I do! I do!" Four or five more children came running up. It seemed you could not catch a more precious insect than a grasshopper. The boy called out a third time.

"Doesn't anyone want a grasshopper?"

Two or three more children came over.

"Yes. I want it."

It was a girl, who just now had come up behind the boy who'd discovered the insect. Lightly turning his body, the boy gracefully bent forward. Shifting the lantern to his left hand, he reached his right hand into the bush.

"It's a grasshopper."

"Yes. I'd like to have it."

The boy quickly stood up. As if to say "Here!" he thrust out his fist that held the insect at the girl. She, slipping her left wrist under the string of her lantern, enclosed the boy's fist with both hands. The boy quietly opened his fist. The insect was transferred to between the girl's thumb and index finger.

"Oh! It's not a grasshopper. It's a bell cricket." The girl's eyes shone as she looked at the small brown insect.

"It's a bell cricket! It's a bell cricket!" The children echoed in an envious chorus.

"It's a bell cricket. It's a bell cricket."

Glancing with her bright intelligent eyes at the boy who had given her the cricket, the girl opened the little insect cage hanging at her side and released the cricket in it.

"It's a bell cricket."

"Oh, it's a bell cricket," the boy who'd captured it **muttered**.[5] Holding up the insect cage close to his eyes, he looked inside it. By the light of his beautiful many-colored lantern, also held up at eye level, he glanced at the girl's face.

Oh, I thought. I felt slightly jealous of the boy, and sheepish. How silly of me not to have understood his actions until now! Then I caught my breath in surprise. Look! It was something on the girl's breast which neither the boy who had given her the cricket, nor she who had accepted it, nor the children who were looking at them noticed.

In the faint greenish light that fell on the girl's breast, wasn't the name "Fujio" clearly discernible? The boy's lantern, which he held up alongside the girl's insect cage, inscribed his name, cut out in the green papered **aperture**,[6] onto her white cotton kimono. The girl's lantern, which dangled loosely from her wrist, did not project its pattern so clearly, but still one could make out, in a trembling patch of red on the boy's waist, the name "Kiyoko." This chance interplay of red and green—if it was chance or play—neither Fujio nor Kiyoko knew about.

Even if they remembered forever that Fujio had given her the cricket and that Kiyoko had accepted it, not even in dreams would Fujio ever know that his name had been written in green on Kiyoko's breast or

---

[5] **muttered**—spoke quietly.

[6] **aperture**—a space or hole through which light passes.

that Kiyoko's name had been inscribed in red on his waist, nor would Kiyoko ever know that Fujio's name had been inscribed in green on her breast or that her own name had been written in red on Fujio's waist.

Fujio! Even when you have become a young man, laugh with pleasure at a girl's delight when, told that it's a grasshopper, she is given a bell cricket; laugh with affection at a girl's **chagrin**[7] when, told that it's a bell cricket, she is given a grasshopper.

Even if you have the wit to look by yourself in a bush away from the other children, there are not many bell crickets in the world. Probably you will find a girl like a grasshopper whom you think is a bell cricket.

And finally, to your clouded, wounded heart, even a true bell cricket will seem like a grasshopper. Should that day come, when it seems to you that the world is only full of grasshoppers, I will think it a pity that you have no way to remember tonight's play of light, when your name was written in green by your beautiful lantern on a girl's breast.

---

[7] **chagrin**—embarrassment or shame.

QUESTIONS TO CONSIDER

1. What does the narrator think of the lanterns? What does the children's attitude toward this utilitarian object suggest about Japanese culture?

2. What does Kawabata mean by the phrase "a grasshopper whom you think is a bell cricket"?

3. What does the interaction between Fujio and Kiyoko mean to the narrator?

Two Poems

ISHIGAKI RIN
IBARAGI NORIKO

Ishigaki Rin (1920–   ) and Ibaragi Noriko (1926–   ) are two of Japan's most highly regarded poets. Writing poetry is an ancient and common tradition in Japan. Perhaps because of this, Japan has probably produced more women poets than any other country in the world. Ishigaki and Ibaragi both began writing at an early age and coupled their writing with a traditional Japanese family life. They are representative of what is best in the Japanese writing tradition and how it has adapted to the changes in the modern world.

The Pan, the Pot, the Burning Fire I Have in Front of Me

ISHIGAKI RIN

For a long time
these things have always been placed
in front of us women:

a pan of a reasonable size
suited to one's strength,
a pot in which it's convenient for rice
to begin to swell and shine, grain by grain,
the heat of the fire inherited since time **immemorial**[1]—
in front of these there have always been
    mothers, grandmothers, and their mothers

---

[1] **immemorial**—old and forgotten or unrecorded.

What measures of love and sincerity
they must have poured
into these utensils—
sometimes red carrots,
sometimes black kelp,[2]
sometimes smashed fish

in the kitchen, always accurately
for morning, noon, and evening, preparations have been made
and in front of the preparations, some pairs of
warm knees and hands have always been lined up.

Ah without those people lining up
how could women have repeated
cooking happily?
their **unflagging**[3] care,
so daily a service they become unconscious of it.

Cooking has oddly been
the woman's assigned role,
but I don't think that's unfortunate;
because of that, her knowledge and social position
may have **lagged**[4] behind the times
but it isn't too late:
the things we have in front of us,
the pan and the pot, and the burning fire,

in front of these familiar utensils,
let us also study government, economy, literature
as sincerely
as we cook potatoes and meat,

not for vanity and promotion
but so all
may be served for mankind
so all may work for love.

---

[2] kelp—seaweed.

[3] **unflagging**—tireless, persistent.

[4] **lagged**—fallen.

When My Beauty Was at Its Best

IBARAGI NORIKO

When my beauty was at its best
town after town came tumbling down, giving us
glimpses of blue sky stuck up in
the least expected places.

When my beauty was at its best
many people around me died
in factories, at sea, on unknown islands, and
I had no chance to make the best of myself.

When my beauty was at its best
I had no young man bringing me lovely presents.
All they did was raise their hands in **salute**,[5] and soon
left for the front, leaving me with nothing more than pure looks.

When my beauty was at its best
I was empty-headed,
I was stubborn-hearted,
my limbs were a glossy brown.

When my beauty was at its best
my country was defeated.
"How can that be?"
I strode around the **humbled**[6] town, my sleeves rolled up.

When my beauty was at its best
I heard jazz streaming from the radio,
and I plunged myself as **rapturously**[7] into its sweet melodies
of when I first knew the forbidden pleasure of smoking.

---

[5] **salute**—a gesture of respect or recognition.
[6] **humbled**—of low status or importance.
[7] **rapturously**—with great joy or delight.

When my beauty was at its best
I was very unhappy
I was very awkward,
I was very, very lonely.
That's why I've decided to live a long time if I can,
like Monsieur Rouault,[8] the dear old man who
painted those marvelously beautiful pictures in his old age.
—Yes, in his old age!

---

[8] Monsieur Rouault—Georges Rouault (1871–1958), French expressionist painter.

QUESTIONS TO CONSIDER

1. Does Ishigaki resent the "pan," "pot," and "fire"? What do they represent to her?

2. What is the message of "When My Beauty Was at Its Best"? How does Ibaragi present it?

3. Do these poems seem like the work of women who are very modern or very traditional in their outlook? Explain your answer using examples from the poems.

Four Poems

SHU TING

Shu Ting (1952–   ) is one of China's most highly regarded lyric poets, but it was not always so. When she was in high school, her father was accused of political crimes by the Communist government, and she was sent to work in a cement factory in the countryside. In her loneliness, Shu began writing poems, and with the thaw in the cultural climate of China after Mao Zedong's death in 1976 she began publishing. In the 1980s, Shu became famous as an innovative poet, combining ancient Chinese poetic techniques with modern ones to create a direct, powerful style. Shu's poems are almost always about people's emotional lives.

Missing You

A multi-colored chart without a boundary;
An equation chalked on the board, with no solution;
A one-stringed lyre[1] that tells the **beads**[2] of rain;
A pair of useless oars that never cross the water.

Waiting buds in suspended animation;
The setting sun is watching from a distance.
Though in my mind there may be an enormous ocean,
What emerges is the sum: a pair of tears.

Yes, from these **vistas**,[3] from these depths,
Only this.

---

[1] lyre—an ancient stringed instrument.
[2] **beads**—drops.
[3] **vistas**—views.

Bits of Reminiscence

A toppled wine-cup,
A stone path floating beneath the moon
Where the grass was trampled:
One azalea branch left lying there . . .

Eucalyptus trees begin to spin
In a **collage**[4] of stars
As I sit on the rusted anchor,
The dizzy sky reflected in my eyes.

A book held up to shut out candlelight;
Fingers lightly at your mouth;
In the fragile cup of silence
A dream, half-illumined,[5] half-obscure.

Gifts

My dream is the dream of a pond
Not just to mirror the sky
But to let the willows and ferns
Suck me dry.
I'll climb from the roots to the veins,
And when leaves **wither**[6] and fade
I will refuse to mourn
Because I was dying to live.

My joy is the joy of sunlight.
In a moment of creation
I will leave shining words
In the pupils of children's eyes

---

[4] **collage**—a collection of things arranged artfully.

[5] half-illumined—partially lit up.

[6] **wither**—to become dry and shriveled.

Igniting golden flames.
Whenever seedlings sprout
I shall sing a song of green.
I'm so simple I'm profound!

My grief is the grief of birds.
The Spring will understand:
Flying from hardship and failure
To a future of warmth and light.
There my blood-stained pinions[7]
Will scratch hieroglyphics[8]
On every human heart
For every year to come.

Because all that I am
Has been a gift from earth.

Fairy Tales

for Gu Cheng

You believed in your own story
Then climbed inside it—
A turquoise flower.
You gazed past ailing trees,
Past crumbling walls and rusty railings.
Your least gesture beckoned a constellation
Of wild vetch,[9] grasshoppers, and stars
To sweep you into immaculate distances.

The heart may be tiny
But the world is enormous.

---

[7] pinions—wings or the feathers on a bird's wing.

[8] hieroglyphics—pictures of objects that represent words, syllables, or sounds.

[9] vetch—a climbing herb.

And the people in turn believe—
In pine trees after rain,
Ten thousand tiny suns, a mulberry branch
Bent over water like a fishing-rod,
A cloud tangled in the tail of a kite.
Shaking off dust, in silver voices
Ten thousand memories sing from your dream.

The world may be tiny
But the heart's enormous.

QUESTIONS TO CONSIDER

1. What is the common thread that connects the images in "Missing You"?

2. How does the poet capture the sense of memory and imagination in "Bits of Reminiscence"?

3. What is the meaning of the title "Gifts"?

4. What seems traditional and what seems modern in Shu Ting's lyric poems? Put as many things as you can into each category.

Three Poems

SO CHONG-JU

So Chong-Ju (1915–   ) is Korea's most famous modern poet. Having witnessed the many tragedies of Korea in the twentieth century, So has concentrated on writing poetry as a salve for the country's wounds. As a writer, he combines modern and traditional techniques, but his outlook is deeply traditional. The modern world has been tragic for many Koreans, and there is a sense of longing for the past in So's work. He once described writing poetry as broadcasting "his earnest longing for things to a world afflicted with disinterest."

Flower-Patterned Snake

A back path, steeped in musk[1] and mint.
A beautiful snake.
Into what monstrous sorrow must you have been born
to bear a form so repulsive.

Like flower-patterned anklets.
Your grandfather's eloquent, Eve-beguiling[2] tongue,
voiceless, flickers round your red mouth.

The blue skies—bite them,
in your **resentment**[3] bite them

and flee, take your face away!

---

[1] musk—a strong-smelling substance produced by a gland in male deer and used as an ingredient in perfumes.

[2] Eve-beguiling—To *beguile* means "to deceive." The speaker refers to the story in the Bible where the serpent tempts Eve to disobey God.

[3] **resentment**—bitter or angry feelings.

I follow,
hurling stone upon stone after you
down the scented, grass-choked path,
gasping as if I had swallowed oil,
but not because Eve was an ancestor's wife.

How I would like to wear your colors
more lovely than flower-patterned anklets.

The lovely mouth, gleaming red
as if wet with Cleopatra's blood.[4]
Sink down my snake!

Twenty-year-old Sunie's mouth, beautiful
as a cat's . . . Sink down, my snake!

Beside a Chrysanthemum

To bring one chrysanthemum[5]
to flower, the cuckoo has cried
since spring.

To bring one chrysanthemum to bloom,
thunder has rolled
through the black clouds.

Flower, like my sister returning
from distant, youthful **byways**[6]
of throat-tight longing
to stand by the mirror:

---

[4] Cleopatra's blood—The Egyptian queen Cleopatra committed suicide by allowing a poisonous snake to bite her.

[5] chrysanthemum—a type of plant with brightly colored flowers.

[6] **byways**—rarely traveled roads, or unimportant activities.

for your yellow petals to open
last night such a frost fell,
and I could not sleep.

Untitled

"Pine flower's blooming," says
a friend on the phone
a hundred miles away.
"Just think of the scent!"

"I am
            thinking of it," I say
to myself, facing
a thousand years away.
"Can you imagine
                        this scent?"

QUESTIONS TO CONSIDER

1. In "Flower-Patterned Snake," what different feelings does the snake inspire in the speaker?

2. What relationship does the speaker in "Beside a Chrysanthemum" see between beauty and pain?

3. What point about the imagination do you think is being made in "Untitled"?

from

Japan, the Ambiguous, and Myself

KENZABURO OE

Kenzaburo Oe (1935–   ) was the second Japanese writer to win the Nobel Prize. Much of his writing has explored the difficulty of life in post-World War II Japan—to him a country dominated by alienation and relentless pursuit of modernity and economic success. To many in Japan, Oe is not only the finest writer of his generation but also the intellectual conscience of the nation. He has written widely about the atomic bombings and struggled to see that this catastrophe is never forgotten. Oe has been controversial because his writing style is innovative and wholly modern, flouting almost all of the traditional conventions of Japanese literature. The following is an excerpt from a speech Oe delivered in Scandinavia in which he described his view of modern Japan and what he has tried to do in his writing.

I want to talk today about Japanese culture as seen through the filter of literature, and to do so I will focus on three main subjects, the first of which is *The Tale of Genji*. This tenth-century "novel," considered the pride and joy of Japanese culture, appeared three hundred years before Dante's *Divine Comedy*.[1] Some fifty-four chapters in length, it was written by Murasaki Shikibu, a lady-in-waiting at the imperial court. The theme of particular interest to me in this work is introduced in the chapter entitled "The Maiden," in which Genji, the hero, now in his mid-thirties, has risen to the post of first minister, the highest position in court

politics, second only to the emperor himself. The chapter deals with the youthful love affairs and education of Genji's son, Yugiri, and I would like to comment specifically on the latter: his son's education.

Yugiri is to attend university, or, to be more exact, enter the university dormitory at court where young boys his age are **matriculated**.[2] But when Genji sends him to the dormitory, Yugiri's grandmother, an

---

[1] *Divine Comedy*—fourteenth-century epic poem, which is one of the landmarks of European literature.

[2] **matriculated**—enrolled in a college or university.

imperial princess, objects strenuously to the idea of a child of noble birth being forced into the kind of studies usually left to striving commoners. "This," she laments, "is the very height of absurdity. How pitiful!" And the narrator seconds the grandmother's objection, agreeing that Genji's proposal is inappropriate. Yet Murasaki Shikibu has Genji reason with the old princess, arguing in favor of the importance of learning and saying that he himself had benefited from even the inadequate knowledge he was able to acquire in the service of his father, the emperor. "Only after we have had enough book learning," Genji explains, "can we bring our Yamato spirit into full play"— Yamato being an old name for Japan. By "book learning" Genji means knowledge of Chinese literature; so he is arguing that it is only after establishing a solid foundation in the Chinese classics that **intrinsically**[3] Japanese talents will be treated with due respect.

"Yamato spirit." Those of you who have studied modern history may hear an **ominous**[4] echo in this expression, for it came to take on a dangerous overtone in the earlier half of this century as the battle cry of Japanese soldiers pressing forward on their march of aggression into China. But I would like to note here that the words first appeared in *The Tale of Genji*, coined by a woman writer with the specific and limited meaning I have just described. I believe she had in mind something not unlike what Aristotle[5] calls *sensus communis*, that is, a shared sensibility. And if we

further define this *sensus communis* as an **innate**[6] quality that exists in human beings at a higher level comprising our intellect, emotions, and imagination, we could say that when Murasaki Shikibu speaks of "Yamato spirit," she is referring to nothing more than a particular sensibility inherent in her fellow countrymen. "Having Yamato spirit is important," she has Genji say, and he goes on to argue that this "shared sensibility" should influence one's behavior as a human being. But without a solid foundation in Chinese learning, its benefits are limited, and so, he concludes, his son should study at the university.

Such formal education has, in fact, been the means by which the Japanese have, from ancient times, sought to learn about foreign cultures. Traditionally, that meant Chinese culture, which the Japanese in the past studied with a certain confidence in their own "shared sensibility." Nor, I think, was this confidence a sign of hubris[7] or intolerance; rather, it was marked by the kind of gentle sensitivity characteristic of human beings who know what it means to doubt. Such was Genji's confidence, born of a clear-eyed practicality and realism— and contrasted here with the class-bound notions of the old princess.

---

[3] **intrinsically**—naturally or characteristically.

[4] **ominous**—threatening, indicating disaster or difficulty.

[5] Aristotle—(384–322 B.C.) Greek philosopher whose work is one of the cornerstones of European thought.

[6] **innate**—natural.

[7] hubris—arrogant pride.

After the Meiji Restoration of 1868,[8] "foreign culture" came to mean not Chinese but European learning, with all the implications that had for the modernization of Japan; but fundamentally there was no real change in the attitude toward learning from those outside. Once again, however, the notion of "Yamato spirit" was brought into play, as Meiji politicians used it to unify the people's cultural consciousness in the interests of creating a modern state. This was done, in large part, by stressing the absolute nature of Japanese culture, with the emperor as its central feature. From there, however, it was only a short step for the concept of "Yamato spirit" to assume its role as a slogan for imperialist Japan.

In the same period, the similar expression *wakon-kansai*, or "Yamato spirit with Chinese learning," was replaced by *wakon-yosai*, "Yamato spirit with Western learning"; and this, too, gradually took on a **belligerent**,[9] militaristic **connotation**.[10] No one would have denied that we learned extensively from Western science, art, and technology, yet Japan's ideology, which held the emperor to be absolute, was always placed above all that. This sort of absolutism, which showed none of the tolerance and sensitivity that characterized the spirit to which Genji was referring, led eventually to the fanatic belief that Japan could win a war despite trailing far behind in modern weapons technology and other similar areas. I know firsthand about such fanaticism, since it was **instilled**[11] in me as a child.

Like everyone else at that time, I was made to believe this mad conviction so alien to the "Yamato spirit" of Murasaki Shikibu. She put it very well when she said that "without *learning* it serves no purpose."

Japan's greatest writer after the Meiji Restoration is Soseki Natsume, who lived during a period of rapid modernization, and it is his work I would like to take up next.

Among his best-known works is a novel entitled *Sorekara* or, in English, *And Then*. Written in 1909, in the relatively peaceful years following the Russo-Japanese War,[12] it portrays the life of Daisuke, a young, well-to-do intellectual who falls in love with the wife of a friend and finds himself entangled in all the torments this **entails**.[13] The novel is of particular interest to me because the hero is in the habit of bluntly expressing his criticism of the society he lived in. At one point, for example, when a friend asks him why he refuses to work and remains dependent on his wealthy father, he unleashes the following **tirade**.[14] (I quote here from Norma Field's translation.)

---

[8] Meiji Restoration of 1868—the date at which the feudal system collapsed in Japan and was replaced by a modern form of government under the Emperor Meiji. It was the beginning of a period of intensive modernization.

[9] **belligerent**—constantly fighting or aggressive.

[10] **connotation**—an implied or unstated meaning.

[11] **instilled**—gradually introduced into a person's mind.

[12] Russo-Japanese War—war between Russia and Japan in 1905 which established Japan as a major world power.

[13] **entails**—requires.

[14] **tirade**—a long and passionate speech.

Why not?—well, it's not my fault. That's to say, it's the world's fault. Or, to exaggerate a little, it's because the relationship between Japan and the West is no good that I won't work. . . .

The point is, Japan can't get along without borrowing from the West. . . . But it poses as a first-class power. And it's straining to join the ranks of the first-class powers. That's why, in every direction it puts up the façade of a first-class power and cheats on what's behind. . . . And see, the consequences are reflected in each of us as individuals. A people so oppressed by the West have no mental leisure, they can't do anything worthwhile. They get an education that's stripped to the bare bones, and they're driven with their noses to the grindstone until they're dizzy—that's why they all end up with nervous breakdowns. . . . Unfortunately, exhaustion of the spirit and deterioration of the body come hand-in-hand. And that's not all. The decline of morality has set in too. Look where you will in this country, you won't find one square inch of brightness. It's all pitch black. So what difference would it make, what I said or what I did, me standing all alone in the middle of it?"

This is, of course, Soseki himself speaking his mind, as is the following. (Again I quote from Field's translation.)

Contemporary society, in which no human being could have contact with another without feeling **contemptuous**,[15] constituted what Daisuke called the decadence of the twentieth century. The life appetites, which had suddenly swollen of late, exerted extreme pressure on the instinct for morality and threatened its collapse. Daisuke regarded this phenomenon as a clash between the old and new appetites. And finally, he understood that the striking growth of the life appetites was, in effect, a tidal wave that had swept from European shores.

The two forces would have to come to an equilibrium at some point. But Daisuke believed that until the day came when feeble Japan could stand shoulder to shoulder financially with the greatest powers of Europe, that balance would not be achieved. And he was resigned to the likelihood that the sun would never shine upon such a day.

Elsewhere in the novel Soseki refers to the Japanese as "an unfortunate people **beset**[16] by the fierce appetites of life," and he laments that European morality is unknown to them. I would only add that this description applies equally well to the Japanese today. The "fierce appetites" of the Japanese in the 1990s, manifested in

---

[15] **contemptuous**—hateful.

[16] **beset**—attacked or harassed.

every aspect of our greedy consumerism, all but dwarf those of Soseki's time and continue to be driven by what he calls "tidal waves that sweep from European shores." Status-conferring brand-name products from Europe fill the shelves of Japanese stores from Tokyo to the smallest provincial town, and the anonymous mass of Japanese consumers line up to buy them, eager to satisfy this strange craving of theirs. The young are especially ravenous in this regard, but corporate moguls are not far behind, as they have shown recently with such conspicuous purchases as Rockefeller Center and van Gogh's *Sunflowers*. One might imagine that these world-class shopping sprees would come under attack from the Japanese public, but they haven't, in large part because people realize that the corporate giants are only doing on a grander scale what each of them is doing privately. People who live in glass houses, as we all know, do not throw stones.

Soseki's gloomy judgments were prophetic in every way but one: he could never have known that the day would come when Japan would be able to "stand shoulder to shoulder financially with the greatest powers of Europe." That day *has* come, but without the beneficial effect that Soseki imagined it would have: the balance between "appetites" and morality has not been restored, and the spiritual deficit has become more **acute**.[17] True, Japan has been modernized, but at the cost of an ugly war which it started in China and which left neighboring Asian countries devastated.

Japan itself was reduced to a **smoldering**[18] ruin; Tokyo was razed to the ground, and a worse fate befell Hiroshima and Nagasaki.[19] Still, modernization continued with the postwar reconstruction and the subsequent period of rapid economic growth; but these have, in effect, led to a deeper kind of decline, a state of outright spiritual poverty. In this sense, Soseki was correct, frighteningly correct.

Soseki's astute predictions present us, however, not only with a bleak vision but with a task to fulfill, one that has to do with what he called an "appetite for morality." From *Sorekara*, it is clear that Japanese intellectuals of Soseki's time possessed a European sense of morality, which they were able to connect with that held by the Japanese before the beginning of their march toward modernization. If Japan is to find a way out of its current predicament—by which I mean its lack of any moral direction—then it must do so by establishing a sense of morality that can be shared with Western nations but that, for its own purposes, is founded firmly on the traditions of Japan's pre-modern period. Only then will Japan be able to shed its "black sheep" image and play an appropriate role in the world community.

The world is changing, and not just in Eastern Europe. Values are becoming ever more diverse, and with this diversification

---

[17] **acute**—intense, sharp, or clearly defined.

[18] **smoldering**—burning slowly with smoke but not flame.

[19] Hiroshima and Nagasaki—the Japanese cities destroyed by atomic bombs in August 1945.

come new goals and aspirations. In this changed world, Japan will inevitably have a new part to play, perhaps not the least important aspect of which will be in its relationship with a changing China.

The third writer I would like to talk about is myself, though I should hasten to add that I am not suggesting that I belong in the same league as Murasaki or Soseki. Still, if you will indulge me, I would like to spend a few minutes on two of my works that have been translated into several European languages.

A Personal Matter is the story of a young man whose first child is born with a **cranial**[20] deformity. The work describes what might be called a rite of passage, as the young father struggles to accept the infant as a member of his family. When he first sees the baby lying in the hospital crib, he hopes it will die, thinking that in life it would be just a vegetable and fearing the burden that he and his wife would face for the rest of their lives. In the course of the story, the young man in fact does more than merely wish for the baby's death; he desperately searches the city for a doctor who will agree to let the child die.

The young man I describe is, in a sense, a romantic. Before marrying, he had dreamed of going to Africa, and it is this dream that comes back to him with a vengeance when faced with the reality of having become the father of a deformed child. Having the child killed, divorcing his wife, and fleeing Japan—these are the nightmare fantasies that occur to him, prompted in part by a former girlfriend who does everything she can to make them come true. In the end, however, the young man experiences a kind of **epiphany**,[21] realizing that abandoning the child to die is **tantamount**[22] to destroying himself. He sheds his romanticism, parts with the girl-friend who is bound for Africa, and accepts the child, deciding in favor of a life-saving operation. His decision is for reality: to build a family on reality, to live reality.

The novel *Man'en gannen no futtoboru*, translated into English as *The Silent Cry*, is structurally more complex than *A Personal Matter*. It has to do with two very symbolic years in Japanese history: 1860 and 1960. In 1860, just before embarking on its pro-gram of modernization, the feudal govern-ment sent delegates to America for the first time; and in 1960, exactly one hundred years later, the security treaty with America, negotiated at the end of the Pacific War,[23] was extended. In that year, a popular movement demanding the treaty's nullifi-cation swept the nation, but the will of the people who took part in anti-treaty demonstrations was ignored. One of the heroes of *The Silent Cry* is a college student named Takashi who takes part in these demonstrations. After the defeat of the movement, he has a change of heart, con-verting to the pro-treaty side and going to America as a member of a theatrical troupe to give performances expressing his remorse to the American public. Returning

---

[20] **cranial**—of or relating to the skull.

[21] **epiphany**—moment of clarity, revelation.

[22] **tantamount**—the same as, equivalent to.

[23] Pacific War—the Japanese name for World War II.

to Japan, he decides to leave Tokyo, the scene of his political activities, and go back to the land of his ancestors, a village in a valley in Shikoku surrounded by forests. And he invites his elder brother, Mitsusaburo, to make the journey with him, though neither has visited the village in a long time. Mitsusaburo, who was no more than a disinterested observer of the anti-treaty movement, reluctantly agrees to join him.

Soon after their arrival in the village, the brothers, while searching an old storehouse attached to their family residence, discover records telling of events that had taken place a hundred years earlier. Their great-grandfather had been a village official who had crushed a peasant rebellion led by his own younger brother. They learn, too, from village legend, that their great-grandfather had lured his brother to the very same storehouse and had murdered him there. As the story unfolds, Takashi, on the pretext of organizing a football team, gathers a group of young men together and trains them to attack a new supermarket that has been built with Korean money. The attack throws the village into a state of **anarchy**,[24] and the two brothers, almost despite themselves, begin to take on the roles played by their counterparts a hundred years earlier. Before the drama can fully play itself out, however, Takashi's rebellion, which he calls "a riot of the imagination," runs aground on his involvement in a sex crime perpetrated in the **guise**[25] of an accident. Cornered, he

commits suicide, but his death awakens Mitsusaburo to a life of action.

One of the motives I had for writing this novel was my growing awareness at the time of a culture in Japan that was very different from the dominant Tokyo one. The work is set in my native village in Shikoku, but even that village is a part of Japan that was undergoing a major transition then. After the defeat in the Pacific War, reconstruction according to a mandate[26] issued by Tokyo was carried out in every corner of the country, my village being no exception. This was, in fact, part of the reason I had to leave to study at a university in Tokyo, though this has been the pattern for nearly every intellectual in Japan in recent times, and I was merely following a well-trodden path. In my case, I majored in French literature and began my career as a writer. I remained in Tokyo after graduating, and, like Takashi in the novel, I was involved in the 1960 movement against the U.S.-Japan Security Treaty. But for me, at the time, this experience led not so much back to my village but to a growing awareness of and interest in Okinawa, a prefecture[27] that was then still under U.S. occupation. In particular, it was the cultural independence of this island prefecture that planted in me a seed that has grown into a new

---

[24] **anarchy**—political or social disorder.

[25] **guise**—make-believe or deceptive appearance.

[26] mandate—an official command or instruction.

[27] prefecture—a district or region under military command.

perspective on Japanese culture as a whole. For no matter how Japanized (or "Yamatoized") it may outwardly appear now, Okinawa still retains its non-Yamato cultural identity; and, unlike the insular, unaccommodating, and emperor-focused culture of the rest of Japan, it is blessed with a richness and diversity peculiar to **peripheral**[28] cultures. Its people possess an openness to the world that comes from knowing the meaning of relative values.

What I did in *The Silent Cry*, with the understanding I gained from Okinawan culture, was to identify elements in the legends of my own village that reach out to similar legends from Korea and other Asian nations. In a sense, the novel becomes what Mikhail Bakhtin[29] calls, in the phraseology of European culture, "an image system of grotesque realism"; and it was, in fact, Bakhtin's theory that enabled me to make these cultural connections. In the process of doing so, moreover, I was able to rediscover and represent aspects of Okinawa that are embedded deep within other peripheral Japanese cultures.

The surname or, more accurately perhaps, the clan name of the brothers in the novel is Nedokoro, which means "the place of one's roots." I took the name from the Okinawan word *nendukuruu*, meaning "a house that shelters the roots of one's clan members' souls." The word appealed to me because, as someone who left his native village for Tokyo and whose eyes had been opened by the study of European culture there, I had rediscovered—through my encounter with Okinawa—my own forest home, the fertile ground in which my writing has developed.

And now, as I approach sixty and look back on my career, I realize that everything I have written has been, in one way or another, an **extrapolation**[30] of the two novels I have just discussed. The baby with the deformity was in reality my son, the fact of whose birth has overshadowed my life and writing. Over the years, I have often written on the theme of living with his mental handicap, and this same theme also informs my writing on Hiroshima and Nagasaki. I have tried to define the meaning that the experience of these two cities has for people in Japan and elsewhere, and I have been involved in activities associated with what I have written on this subject; but my fundamental perspective has always been that of the parent of a handicapped child. This is the experience that influences everything I write and everything I do. Thus, for example, my realization that life with a mentally handicapped child has the power to heal the wounds that family members inflict on one another led me to the more recent insight that the victims and survivors of the atomic bombs have the same sort of power to heal all of us who live in this nuclear age. This, though, seems almost

---

[28] **peripheral**—on the fringe or of minor importance.

[29] Mikhail Bakhtin—(1895–1975) Russian philosopher and literary critic.

[30] **extrapolation**—a continuation of (or estimation based upon) a limited set of things that are already known.

self-evident when one sees the survivors of Hiroshima and Nagasaki, by now **frail**[31] and elderly, speaking up and taking an active part in the movement to abolish all nuclear weapons. They are, to me, the embodiment of a prayer for the healing of our society, indeed the planet as a whole.

As for the theme of Japan's peripheral cultures which I dealt with in *The Silent Cry*, this too has featured in many of my other novels, where I have often portrayed groups independent of, or even in opposition to, the main Tokyo-centered culture. In the world of the novel, I have repeatedly tried to picture a village culture rooted in a cosmology that revolves around the cycle of life, death, and rebirth. This has been my way of resisting, on a mythological level, the **homogenizing**,[32] centristic culture that has exerted its influence even over my own home in Shikoku. If you read my *M/T to mori no fushigi no monogatari*, which has been translated into Swedish and French, you will see that this novel, with others like it, is a record of my attempts to develop a model for this cultural alternative.

Japan's emperor system, which had apparently lost its social and political influence after the defeat in the Pacific War, is beginning to flex its muscles again, and in some respects it has already recouped much of its lost power—with two differences: first, the Japanese today will not accept the prewar ideology-cum theology that held the emperor to be both absolute ruler and living **deity**.[33] Nevertheless, imperial rites performed quite recently were done in such a manner as to impress upon us that the emperor's lineage can be traced to a deity; I am referring here to the rituals associated with the present emperor's enthronement and the so-called Great Thanksgiving Service that followed it. These ceremonies provoked little objection from either the government or the people, indeed most Japanese seemed to take it all very much for granted.

The second difference from the prewar situation is that the emperor is no longer the supreme commander of Japan's military forces. Under the present constitution, the so-called Self-Defense Forces should not even exist, yet Japan's military buildup has been enormous. The conservative party, perpetually in power, controls these forces and conducts itself as if the holy nimbus[34] of the emperor were shining from behind it. This has been the state of affairs through-out the postwar years, and it can be thought of as the cause of one of the most sensational events of that period: the suicide of Yukio Mishima.[35]

Mishima committed hara kiri after calling for a coup d'état[36] by the unconsti-tutional Self-Defense Forces, which he could not bear to see **relegated**[37] to a status that virtually denied their very existence.

---

[31] **frail**—delicate, fragile.

[32] **homogenizing**—making all parts the same, standardizing.

[33] **deity**—a god or goddess.

[34] nimbus—a halo or bright cloud.

[35] Yukio Mishima—major Japanese writer (see page 134).

[36] coup d'état—the violent or illegal seizure of power.

[37] **relegated**—assigned to an unimportant or inferior position.

He wanted to restore them to their role as the emperor's army, just as he wanted to restore the emperor himself to his place at the center of Japanese culture. The emperor at the heart of things—that was the core of Mishima's philosophy, but it was a philosophy founded on his own very peculiar ideas of traditional culture, and it served him and his kind alone. There is a wide range of opinion regarding the emperor system in Japan today, but it is alarming to see it regaining any popular support, for it has the kind of power that tends to override differing views.

In such an environment, I suspect that my novels may fall further out of the mainstream, insofar as they are based on folktales and mythology that pose a direct challenge to the emperor system. I do not mind this, however, since **alienation**[38] from such a system can only help outline my literary **microcosm**[39] even more sharply. I suppose my only regret is that my writing, in the sense that it is an act of resistance against reactionary tendencies in postwar Japan, has not had sufficient power to push back a rising tide of conformity.

As I said a moment ago, the world today is undergoing a major transition, and Japan, too, is in the midst of change. So, with some urgency, I find myself trying to answer a question that I believe all writers are asking: what is the role of a writer in times like these? What can our words accomplish? For my own part, I trust that the discussions I will have with the writers and students of Scandinavia will help me find an answer. That is why I have come here.

---

[38] **alienation**—the condition of being or feeling isolated from friends or society.

[39] **microcosm**—a tiny representation of a community, region, or world.

QUESTIONS TO CONSIDER

1. What is "Yamato spirit"? Does Oe approve or disapprove of it? Explain his reasons.

2. Why does Oe think that Japan lacks moral direction? What does he propose to counter this?

3. What have been the two main themes of Oe's writing? What has been his goal in writing about these themes?

Chapter 4

Southeast Asia and Australia

Finding a Home

Redefining Borders

◀ This painting shows a dance performed by Aborigines, the native people of Australia.

Scent of Apples

BIENVENIDO SANTOS

Bienvenido Santos (1911–   ) is a writer who seems to have always lived his life between two countries: the Philippines and the United States. The Philippines was a U.S. colony from 1899 until 1946, and thereafter remained closely tied economically and politically. Santos deeply loves his homeland but has always been drawn to the United States: for education, for job opportunities, and for sanctuary from war and the corrupt government of Ferdinand Marcos (1965–1986). Because of this divide, the main subject of Santos's writing has been exile and the longing for home. Santos fled the Philippines during World War II and spent much of the war touring the United States for the U.S. government's Office of Education. During this time, he met many other Filipinos. "Scent of Apples" describes one of these experiences.

When I arrived in Kalamazoo it was October and the war was still on. Gold and silver stars[1] hung on pennants above silent windows of white and brick-red cottages. In a backyard, an old man burned leaves and twigs while a gray-haired woman sat on the porch, her red hands quiet on her lap, watching the smoke rising above the elms, both of them thinking of the same thought perhaps about a tall, grinning boy with blue eyes and flying hair, who went to war, where could he be now this month when leaves were turning into gold and the fragrance of gathered apples was in the wind.

It was a cold night when I left my room at the hotel for a usual speaking engagement. I walked but a little way.

A heavy wind coming up from Lake Michigan was icy on the face. It felt like winter straying early in the northern woodlands. Under the lamp posts the leaves shone like bronze. And they rolled on the pavements like the ghost feel of a thousand autumns long dead, long before the boys left for faraway lands without great icy winds and promise of winter early in the air, lands without apple trees, *the singing and the gold*!

It was the same night I met Celestino Fabia, "just a Filipino farmer" as he called himself, who had a farm about thirty miles east of Kalamazoo.

---

[1] Gold and silver stars—indicating the families of soldiers fighting in World War II.

"You came all that way on a night like this just to hear me talk?" I asked.

"I've seen no Filipino for so many years now," he answered quickly. "So when I saw your name in the papers where it says you come from the Islands and that you're going to talk, I come right away."

Earlier that night I had addressed a college crowd, mostly women. It appeared that they wanted me to talk about my country; they wanted me to tell them things about it because my country had become a lost country. Everywhere in the land the enemy **stalked**.[2] Over it a great silence hung; and their boys were there, unheard from, or they were on their way to some little known island on the Pacific, young boys all, hardly men, thinking of harvest moons and smell of forest fire.

It was not hard talking about our own people. I knew them well and I loved them. And they seemed so far away during those terrible years that I must have spoken of them with a little **fervor**,[3] a little nostalgia.

In the open forum that followed, the audience wanted to know whether there was much difference between our women and the American women. I tried to answer the question as best as I could, saying, among other things, that I did not know much about American women, except that they looked friendly, but differences or similarities in inner qualities such as naturally belonged to the heart or to the mind, I could only speak about with vagueness.

While I was trying to explain away the fact that it was not easy to make comparisons, a man rose from the rear of the hall, wanting to say something. In the distance, he looked slight and old and very brown. Even before he spoke, I knew that he was, like me, a Filipino.

"I'm a Filipino," he began, loud and clear, in a voice that seemed used to wide open spaces, "I'm just a Filipino farmer out in the country." He waved his hand towards the door. "I left the Philippines more than twenty years ago and have never been back. Never will perhaps. I want to find out, sir, are our Filipino women the same like they were twenty years ago?"

As he sat down, the hall filled with voices, hushed and intrigued. I weighed my answer carefully. I did not want to tell a lie, yet I did not want to say anything that would seem **platitudinous**,[4] insincere. But more important than these considerations, it seemed to me that moment as I looked towards my countryman, I must give him an answer that would not make him so unhappy. Surely, all these years, he must have held on to certain ideals, certain beliefs, even illusions peculiar to the exile.

"First," I said as the voices gradually died down and every eye seemed upon me. "First, tell me what our women were like twenty years ago."

The man stood to answer. "Yes," he said, "you're too young. . . . Twenty years ago our women were nice, they were modest, they wore their hair long, they

---

[2] **stalked**—hunted or pursued stealthily.

[3] **fervor**—passion.

[4] **platitudinous**—dull or commonplace, but presented with great seriousness.

dressed proper and went for no monkey business. They were natural, they went to church regular, and they were faithful." He had spoken slowly, and now in what seemed like an afterthought, added, "It's the men who ain't."

Now I knew what I was going to say.

"Well," I began, "it will interest you to know that our women have changed—but definitely! The change, however, has been on the outside only. Inside, here," pointing to the heart, "they are the same as they were twenty years ago, God fearing, faithful, modest, and *nice*."

The man was visibly moved. "I'm very happy, sir," he said, in the manner of one who, having stakes on the land, had found no cause to regret one's sentimental investment.

After this, everything that was said and done in that hall that night seemed like an **anti-climax**;[5] and later, as we walked outside, he gave me his name and told me of his farm thirty miles east of the city.

We had stopped at the main entrance to the hotel lobby. We had not talked very much on the way. As a matter of fact, we were never alone. Kindly American friends talked to us, asked us questions, said goodnight. So now I asked him whether he cared to step into the lobby with me and talk shop.

"No, thank you, " he said, "you are tired. And I don't want to stay out too late."

"Yes, you live very far."

"I got a car," he said, "besides . . ."

Now he smiled, he truly smiled. All night I had been watching his face and I wondered when he was going to smile.

"Will you do me a favor, please," he continued smiling almost sweetly. "I want you to have dinner with my family out in the country, I'd call for you tomorrow afternoon, then drive you back. Will that be all right?"

"Of course," I said. "I'd love to meet your family." I was leaving Kalamazoo for Muncie, Indiana, in two days. There was plenty of time.

"You will make my wife very happy," he said.

"You flatter me."

"Honest. She'll be very happy. Ruth is a country girl and hasn't met many Filipinos. I mean Filipinos younger than I, cleaner looking. We're just poor farmer folk, you know, and we don't get to town very often. Roger, that's my boy, he goes to school in town. A bus takes him early in the morning and he's back in the afternoon. He's a nice boy."

"I bet he is," I agreed. "I've seen the children of some of the boys and their American wives and the boys are tall, taller than the father, and very good looking."

"Roger, he'd be tall. You'll like him."

Then he said goodbye and I waved to him as he disappeared in the darkness.

The next day he came, at about three in the afternoon. There was a mild, ineffectual sun shining; and it was not too cold. He was wearing an old brown tweed jacket and worsted[6] trousers to match. His shoes

---

[5] **anti-climax**—a disappointing end to something significant or impressive.

[6] worsted—firm-textured wool.

were polished, and although the green of his tie seemed faded, a colored shirt hardly accentuated it. He looked younger than he did the night before now that he was clean shaven and seemed ready to go to a party. He was grinning as we met.

"Oh, Ruth can't believe it. She can't believe it," he kept repeating as he led me to his car—a nondescript thing in faded black that had known better days and many hands. "I says to her, I'm bringing you a first class Filipino, and she says, aw, go away, quit kidding, there's no such thing as first class Filipino. But Roger, that's my boy, he believed me immediately. What's he like, daddy, he asks. Oh, you will see, I says, he's first class. Like you, daddy? No, no, I laugh at him, your daddy ain't first class. Aw, but you are, daddy, he says. So you can see what a nice boy he is, so innocent. Then Ruth starts **griping**[7] about the house, but the house is a mess, she says. True it's a mess, it's always a mess, but you don't mind, do you? We're poor folks, you know."

The trip seemed interminable. We passed through narrow lanes and disappeared into thickets, and came out on barren land overgrown with weeds in places. All around were dead leaves and dry earth. In the distance were apple trees.

"Aren't those apple trees?" I asked wanting to be sure.

"Yes, those are apple trees," he replied. "Do you like apples? I got lots of 'em. I got an apple orchard, I'll show you."

All the beauty of the afternoon seemed in the distance, on the hills, in the dull soft sky.

"Those trees are beautiful on the hills," I said.

"Autumn's a lovely season. The trees are getting ready to die, and they show their colors, proud-like."

"No such thing in our own country," I said.

That remark seemed unkind, I realized later. It touched him off on a long deserted tangent, but one ever there perhaps. How many times did the lonely mind take unpleasant detours away from the familiar winding lanes toward home for fear of this, the remembered hurt, the long lost youth, the grim shadows of the years; how many times indeed, only the exile knows.

It was a rugged road we were traveling and the car made so much noise that I could not hear everything he said, but I understood him. He was telling his story for the first time in many years. He was remembering his own youth. He was thinking of home. In these odd moments there seemed no cause for fear, no cause at all, no pain. That would come later. In the night perhaps. Or lonely on the farm under the apple trees.

In this old Visayan[8] town, the streets are narrow and dirty and strewn with coral shells. You have been there? You could not have missed our house, it was the biggest in town, one of the oldest, ours was a big family. The house stood right on the edge of the street. A door opened heavily and you enter a dark hall leading to the stairs. There is the smell of

---

[7] **griping**—complaining.

[8] *Visayan*—a large island group in the central Phillippines.

chickens roosting on the low-topped walls, there is the familiar sound they make and you grope your way up a massive staircase, the bannisters smooth upon the trembling hand. Such nights, they are no better than the days, windows are closed against the sun; they close heavily.

Mother sits in her corner looking very white and sick. This was her world, her domain. In all these years I cannot remember the sound of her voice. Father was different. He moved about. He shouted. He ranted.[9] He lived in the past and talked of honor as though it were the only thing.

I was born in that house. I grew up there into a pampered[10] brat. I was mean. One day I broke their hearts. I saw mother cry wordlessly as father heaped his curses upon me and drove me out of the house, the gate closing heavily after me. And my brothers and sisters took up my father's hate for me and multiplied it numberless times in their own broken hearts. I was no good.

But sometimes, you know, I miss that house, the roosting chickens on the low-topped walls. I miss my brothers and sisters. Mother sitting in her chair, looking like a pale ghost in a corner of the room. I would remember the great live posts, massive tree trunks from the forests. Leafy plants grew on the sides, buds pointing downwards, wilted and died before they could become flowers. As they fell on the floor, father bent to pick them and throw them out into the coral streets. His hands were strong. I have kissed those hands . . . many times, many times.

Finally we rounded a deep curve and suddenly came upon a **shanty**,[11] all but ready to crumble in a heap on the ground, its plastered walls were rotting away, the floor was hardly a foot from the ground. I thought of the cottages of the poor colored folk in the south, the **hovels**[12] of the poor everywhere in the land. This one stood all by itself as though by common consent all the folk that used to live here had decided to stay away, despising it, ashamed of it. Even the lovely season could not color it with beauty.

A dog barked loudly as we approached. A fat blonde woman stood at the door with a little boy by her side. Roger seemed newly scrubbed. He hardly took his eyes off me. Ruth had a clean apron around her shapeless waist. Now as she shook my hands in sincere delight I noticed shamefacedly (that I should notice) how rough her hands, how coarse and red with labor, how ugly! She was no longer young and her smile was **pathetic**.[13]

As we stepped inside and the door closed behind us, immediately I was aware of the familiar scent of apples. The room was bare except for a few ancient pieces of second-hand furniture. In the middle of the room stood a stove to keep the family warm in winter. The walls were bare. Over the dining table hung a lamp yet unlighted.

---

[9] **ranted**—lectured or preached theatrically.

[10] **pampered**—spoiled by luxury or overindulgence.

[11] **shanty**—a crudely built hut or cabin.

[12] **hovels**—small, miserable homes.

[13] **pathetic**—causing pity, sadness, or contempt.

Ruth got busy with the drinks. She kept coming in and out of a rear room that must have been the kitchen and soon the table was heavy with food, fried chicken legs and rice, and green peas and corn on the ear. Even as we ate, Ruth kept standing, and going to the kitchen for more food. Roger ate like a little gentleman.

"Isn't he nice looking?" his father asked.

"You are a handsome boy, Roger," I said.

The boy smiled at me. "You look like Daddy," he said.

Afterwards I noticed an old picture leaning on the top of a dresser and stood to pick it up. It was yellow and soiled with many fingerings. The faded figure of a woman in Philippine dress could yet be distinguished although the face had become a blur.

"Your . . . " I began.

"I don't know who she is, " Fabia hastened to say. "I picked that picture many years ago in a room on La Salle Street in Chicago. I have often wondered who she is."

"The face wasn't a blur in the beginning?"

"Oh, no. It was a young face and good."

Ruth came with a plate full of apples.

"Ah," I cried, picking out a ripe one, "I've been thinking where all the scent of apples came from. The room is full of it."

"I'll show you, " said Fabia.

He showed me a backroom, not very big. It was half-full of apples.

"Every day," he explained, "I take some of them to town to sell to the groceries. Prices have been low. I've been losing on the trips."

"These apples will spoil," I said.

"We'll feed them to the pigs."

Then he showed me around the farm. It was twilight now and the apple trees stood bare against a glowing western sky. In apple blossom time it must be lovely here, I thought. But what about wintertime?

In apple blossom time it must be lovely here, I thought. But what about wintertime?

One day, according to Fabia, a few years ago, before Roger was born, he had an attack of acute appendicitis. It was deep winter. The snow lay heavy everywhere. Ruth was pregnant and none too well herself. At first she did not know what to do. She bundled him in warm clothing and put him on a cot near the stove. She shoveled the snow on their front door and practically carried the suffering man on her shoulders, dragging him through the newly made path towards the road where they waited for the U.S. mail car to pass. Meanwhile snowflakes poured all over them and she kept rubbing the man's arms and legs as she herself nearly froze to death.

"Go back to the house, Ruth!" her husband cried; "you'll freeze to death."

But she clung to him wordlessly. Even as she scrubbed her arms and legs, her tears rolled down her cheeks. "I won't leave you, I won't leave you," she repeated.

Finally the U.S. mail car arrived. The mailman, who knew them well, helped them board the car, and, without stopping on his usual route, took the sick man and his wife direct to the nearest hospital.

Ruth stayed in the hospital with Fabia. She slept in a corridor outside the patients' ward and in the day time helped in scrubbing the floor and washing the dishes and cleaning the men's things. They didn't have enough money and Ruth was willing to work like a slave.

"Ruth's a nice girl," said Fabia; "like our own Filipino women."

Before nightfall, he took me back to the hotel. Ruth and Roger stood at the door holding hands and smiling at me. From inside the room of the shanty, a low light flickered. I had a last glimpse of the apple trees in the orchard under the darkened sky as Fabia backed up the car. And soon we were on our way back to town. The dog had started barking. We could hear it for some time, until finally, we could not hear it any more, and all was darkness around us, except where the head lamps revealed a stretch of road leading somewhere.

Fabia did not talk this time. I didn't seem to have anything to say myself. But when finally we came to the hotel and I got down, Fabia said, "Well, I guess I won't be seeing you again."

It was dimly lighted in front of the hotel and I could hardly see Fabia's face. He had not come down from the car, but he had moved to my side, and I saw his hand, extended. I gripped it.

"Tell Ruth and Roger," I said, "I love them."

He dropped my hand quickly. "They'll be waiting for me now," he said.

"Look," I said, not knowing why I said it, "one of these days, very soon, I hope, I'll be going home. I could go to your town."

"No," he said softly, sounding very much defeated but brave. "Thanks a lot. But, you see, nobody would remember me now."

Then he started the car, and as it moved away, he waved his hand.

"'Goodbye," I said, waving back into the darkness. And suddenly the night was cold like winter **straying**[14] early in these northern woodlands.

I hurried inside. There was a train the next morning that left for Muncie, Indiana, at a quarter after eight.

---

[14] **straying**—wandering away from the right place.

QUESTIONS TO CONSIDER

1. Why does Celestino Fabia have the photograph of an unknown Filipino woman in his home?

2. How does Celestino Fabia feel about his youth in the Philippines?

3. What is the narrator feeling at the end of the story? What does it imply about his identity as a Filipino?

A Gentleman's Agreement

ELIZABETH JOLLEY

Elizabeth Jolley (1923–   ) is one of Australia's most prominent novelists. She was born and raised in England, but moved to Australia in 1959 and has often said that she considers herself an Australian, particularly in her writing. She did not begin to write until the 1960s and to publish until the 1970s. Jolley is fascinated by eccentric and quirky characters who make of life what they want. Her story "A Gentleman's Agreement" is about such characters, but it also describes the classic divide of Australian society between those who live and work on the land and those who live in cities. Australia is a vast country that is heavily populated only in its coastal cities. Land is readily available, if you can make a living from farming it.

In the home science lesson I had to unpick my darts[1] as Mrs. Kay said they were all wrong and then I scorched the collar of my dress because I had the iron too hot. And then the sewing machine needle broke and there wasn't a spare and Mrs. Kay got really wild and Peril Page cut all the notches off her pattern by mistake and that finished everything.

"I'm not ever going back to that school," I said to Mother in the evening. "I'm finished with that place!" So that was my brother and me both leaving school before we should have and my brother kept leaving jobs too, one job after another. Sometimes not even staying long enough in one place to wait for his pay.

But Mother was worrying about what to get for my brother's tea.

"What about a bit of lamb's fry and bacon," I said. She brightened up then and, as she was leaving to go up the terrace for her shopping, she said, "You can come with me tomorrow then and we'll get through the work quicker." She didn't seem to mind at all that I had left school.

Mother cleaned in a large block of luxury apartments. She had keys to the flats and she came and went as she pleased and as her work demanded. It was while she was working there that she had the idea of letting the people from down our street taste the pleasures rich people took for granted in their way of living. While these people were away to their offices

---

[1] darts—tucks stitched into a piece of clothing.

or on business trips she let our poor neighbors in. We had wedding receptions and parties in the penthouse and the old folk came in to soak their feet and wash their clothes while Mother was doing the cleaning. As she said, she gave a lot of pleasure to people without doing anybody any harm, though it was often a terrible rush for her. She could never refuse anybody anything and, because of this, always had more work than she could manage and more people to be kind to than her time really allowed.

Sometimes at the weekends I went with Mother to look at Grandpa's valley. It was quite a long bus ride. We had to get off at the twenty-nine-mile peg,[2] cross the Medulla brook, and walk up a country road with scrub on either side till we came to some cleared acres of pasture which was the beginning of her father's land. She struggled through the wire fence hating the mud. She wept out loud because the old man hung on to his land and all his money was buried, as she put it, in the **sodden**[3] meadows of cape weed and stuck fast in the outcrops of granite higher up where all the topsoil had washed away. She couldn't sell the land because Grandpa was still alive in a Home for the Aged, and he wanted to keep the farm though he couldn't do anything with it. Even sheep died there. They either starved or got drowned depending on the time of the year. It was either drought there or flood. The weatherboard house was so neglected it was falling apart, the tenants were **feckless**,[4] and if a calf was born there

it couldn't get up, that was the kind of place it was. When we went to see Grandpa he wanted to know about the farm and Mother tried to think of things to please him. She didn't say the fence posts were crumbling away and that the castor oil plants had taken over the yard so you couldn't get through to the barn.

There was an old apricot tree in the middle of the meadow, it was as big as a house and a terrible burden to us to get the fruit at just the right time. Mother liked to take some to the hospital so that Grandpa could keep up his pride and self-respect a bit.

In the full heat of the day I had to pick with an apron tied round me; it had deep pockets for the fruit. I grabbed at the green fruit when I thought Mother wasn't looking and pulled off whole branches so it wouldn't be there to be picked later.

"Don't take that branch!" Mother screamed from the ground. "Them's not ready yet. We'll have to come back tomorrow for them."

I lost my temper and pulled off the apron full of fruit and hurled it down but it stuck on a branch and hung there quite out of reach either from up the tree where I was or from the ground.

"Wait! Just you wait till I get a holt of you!" Mother pranced round the tree and I didn't come down till we had missed our

---

[2] peg—marker, milestone.

[3] **sodden**—soaked through with liquid, saturated.

[4] **feckless**—lacking purpose or vitality.

bus and it was getting dark and all the dogs in the little township barked as if they were insane, the way dogs do in the country, as we walked through trying to get a lift home.

One Sunday in the winter it was very cold but Mother thought we should go all the same. We passed some sheep huddled in a natural fold of furze[5] and withered grass all frost sparkling in the morning.

"Quick!" Mother said. "We'll grab a sheep and take a bit of wool back to Grandpa."

"But they're not our sheep," I said.

"Never mind!" And she was in among the sheep before I could stop her. The noise was terrible but she managed to grab a bit of wool.

"It's terrible dirty and shabby," she complained, pulling at the shreds with her cold fingers. "I don't think I've ever seen such miserable wool."

All that evening she was busy with the wool, she did make me laugh.

"How will modom have her hair done?" She put the wool on the kitchen table and kept walking all round it talking to it. She tried to wash it and comb it but it still looked awful so she put it round one of my curlers for the night.

"I'm really ashamed of the wool," Mother said next morning.

"But it isn't ours," I said.

"I know but I'm ashamed all the same," she said. So when we were in the penthouse at South Heights she cut a tiny

piece off the bathroom mat. It was so soft and silky. And later we went to visit Grandpa. He was sitting with his poor paralyzed legs under his tartan rug.

"Here's a bit of the wool clip Dad," Mother said, bending over to kiss him. His whole face lit up.

"That's nice of you to bring it, really nice." His old fingers stroked the little piece of nylon carpet.

"It's very good, deep and soft," he smiled at Mother.

"They do wonderful things with sheep these days Dad," she said.

"They do indeed," he said, and all the time he was feeling the bit of carpet.

"Are you pleased Dad?" Mother asked him anxiously. "You are pleased aren't you?"

"Oh yes I am," he assured her.

I thought I saw a moment of disappointment in his eyes, but the eyes of old people often look full of tears.

On the way home I tripped on the steps. "Ugh! I felt your bones!" Really Mother was so thin it hurt to fall against her.

"Well what d'you expect me to be, a boneless wonder?"

> *I thought I saw a moment of disappointment in his eyes, but the eyes of old people often look full of tears.*

---

[5] furze—spiny, yellow-colored shrubs that grow in European wastelands.

Really Mother had such a hard life and we lived in such a cramped and **squalid**[6] place. She longed for better things and she needed a good rest. I wished more than anything the old man would agree to selling his land. Because he wouldn't sell I found myself wishing he would die and whoever really wants to wish someone to die! It was only that it would sort things out a bit for us.

In the supermarket Mother thought and thought what she could get for my brother for his tea. In the end all she could come up with was fish fingers and a packet of jelly beans.

"You know I never eat fish! And I haven't eaten sweets in years." My brother looked so tall in the kitchen. He lit a cigarette and slammed out and Mother was too tired and too upset to eat her own tea.

Grandpa was an old man and though his death was expected it was unexpected really and it was a shock to Mother to find she suddenly had eighty-seven acres to sell. And there was the house too. She had a terrible lot to do as she decided to sell the property herself and at the same time, she did not want to let down the people at South Heights. There was a man interested to buy the land, Mother had kept him up her sleeve for years, ever since he had stopped once by the bottom paddock[7] to ask if it was for sale. At the time Mother would have given her right arm to be able to sell it and she promised he should have first refusal if it ever came on the market.

We all three, Mother and myself and my brother, went out at the weekend to tidy things up. We lost my brother and then we suddenly saw him running and running and shouting, his voice lifting up in the wind as he raced up the slope of the valley.

"I do believe he's laughing! He's happy!" Mother just stared at him and she looked so happy too.

I don't think I ever saw the country look so lovely before.

The **tenant**[8] was standing by the shed. The big tractor had crawled to the doorway like a sick animal and had stopped there, but in no time my brother had it going.

It seemed there was nothing my brother couldn't do. Suddenly after doing nothing in his life he was driving the tractor and making fire breaks, he started to paint the sheds and he told Mother what fencing posts and wire to order. All these things had to be done before the sale could go through. We all had a wonderful time in the country. I kept wishing we could live in the house, all at once it seemed lovely there at the top of the sunlit meadow. But I knew that however many acres you have they aren't any use unless you have money too. I think we were all thinking this but no one said anything though Mother kept looking at my brother and the change in him.

---

[6] **squalid**—disgustingly dirty.

[7] **paddock**—small field or enclosure for keeping horses in.

[8] **tenant**—a person who rents land or property.

There was no problem about the price of the land, this man, he was a doctor, really wanted it and Mother really needed the money.

"You might as well come with me," Mother said to me on the day of the sale. "You can learn how business is done." So we sat in this lawyer's comfortable room and he read out from various papers and the doctor signed things and Mother signed. Suddenly she said to them, "You know my father really loved his farm but he only managed to have it late in life and then he was never able to live there because of his illness." The two men looked at her.

"I'm sure you will understand," she said to the doctor, "with your own great love of the land. My father's love for his valley, I feel if I could live there just to plant one crop and stay while it matures, my father would rest easier in his grave."

"Well I don't see why not." The doctor was really a kind man. The lawyer began to protest, he seemed quite angry.

"It's not in the agreement," he began to say. But the doctor silenced him, he got up and came round to Mother's side of the table.

"I think you should live there and plant your one crop and stay while it matures," he said to her. "It's a gentleman's agreement," he said.

"That's the best sort," Mother smiled up at him and they shook hands.

"I wish your crop well," the doctor said, still shaking her hand.

The doctor made the lawyer write out a special clause which they all signed. And then we left, everyone satisfied. Mother had never had so much money and the doctor had the valley at last but it was the gentleman's agreement which was the best part.

My brother was impatient to get on with improvements.

"There's no rush," Mother said.

"Well one crop isn't very long," he said.

"It's long enough," she said.

So we moved out to the valley and the little weatherboard cottage seemed to come to life very quickly with the pretty things we chose for the rooms.

"It's nice whichever way you look out from these little windows," Mother was saying and just then her crop arrived. The carter set down the boxes along the edge of the verandah[9] and, when he had gone, my brother began to unfasten the hessian coverings. Inside were hundreds of **seedlings**[10] in little plastic containers.

"What are they?" he asked.

"Our crop," Mother said.

"Yes I know, but what is the crop? What are these?"

"Them," said Mother, she seemed unconcerned, "oh they're a jarrah[11] forest," she said.

---

[9] verandah—porch.

[10] **seedlings**—young plants.

[11] jarrah—a type of Eucalyptus tree in Australia.

"But that will take years and years to mature," he said.

"I know," Mother said. "We'll start planting tomorrow. We'll pick the best places and clear and plant as we go along."

"But what about the doctor?" I said, somehow I could picture him pale and patient by his car out on the lonely road which went through his valley. I seemed to see him looking with longing at his paddocks and his meadows and at his slopes of scrub and bush.

"Well he can come on his land whenever he wants to and have a look at us," Mother said. "There's nothing in the gentleman's agreement to say he can't."

QUESTIONS TO CONSIDER

1. Why does the mother want to plant a jarrah forest?

2. How do you feel about the doctor in the story? Explain your answer.

3. What does the farm represent to the family?

Reflections of Spring

DUONG THU HUONG

Duong Thu Huong (1947–   ) is one of Vietnam's most prominent writers. During the Vietnam War she served for seven years in a Communist Youth Brigade and then took up journalism. However, in the 1980s she grew disillusioned with the Communist government in Vietnam. In 1989, she was expelled from the Communist Party, and two years later was imprisoned for seven months for making speeches advocating democracy. Her books were runaway bestsellers in Vietnam, as they spoke to the plight of ordinary Vietnamese under Communism. Duong's books are currently banned in Vietnam.

It's not because of that evening. But since then, thoughts of her hadn't left his mind. They would **linger**[1] for a while, then rush at him like a **gust**[2] of wind, throwing his thoughts into chaos and disrupting his equanimity, leaving behind vague and anguished longings. That evening, he was returning to Hanoi from a midland province. An economic planner, he was used to these long, **tedious**[3] trips. Dozing in his seat on the bus, he was awoken by loud clanking sounds coming from the engine. The driver lifted the hood and moaned:

"Can't make it to Hanoi this evening. The radiator is broken . . ."

The passengers got off the bus to walk around and to breathe in the pleasant air of the midland area. Yellow fields ran to the horizon. In the distance, one could see the uneven peaks of dark green hills, like a **clique**[4] of moss-covered snails resting on a carpet of rice paddies. The yellow of ripe rice was pale in the fading sun, but it flared up in spots, as if still soaked in light. At the edge of the road, the harvested field had a soft pink glow, as gentle as adolescent love. The autumn breeze made him feel light-headed: He was free from projects, reports, criticisms, approvals—all **hindrances**[5] and distractions. It was an unusual feeling, this clarity. He walked briskly along.

---

[1] **linger**—hang around or about.
[2] **gust**—a stong sudden rush or burst.
[3] **tedious**—uninteresting, tiringly boring, or overly long.
[4] **clique**—a small, exclusive social group.
[5] **hindrances**—obstacles.

By the side of the road was a row of houses. Their uneven roofs and white walls gave a strong warmth to the landscape. Butted up against each other, the houses were fronted by a mishmash of verandahs in different styles. In the small yards were tree stumps and piles of bricks. Nearby, pigeon coops perched on tree branches. At the base of a mound of shiny yellow straw, smelling of harvest, an old hen led her chicks, cluck-clucking, searching for food. A crude red and green sign announced a bicycle repair shop. In front, a **dangling**[6] flat tire wobbled with each gust of wind. Bunches of bananas, suspended from hooks, hovered over the heads of diners in the cheap restaurants.

The serenity and **melancholic**[7] air of the small town enchanted him. He didn't know what he was thinking, but he walked up and down the streets admiring the familiar views, especially the shrubs and poinciana plants behind the houses. The yellow flowers bloomed in the quiet evening.

"Uncle, come in for a drink. We have country rice pies and sticky-rice cakes."

An old woman behind a small glass display case leaned forward to greet her customer. He was a little surprised; it had been a long time since he heard such a natural, friendly greeting from a shopkeeper. He walked in and sat down on a long bench. He didn't know why he had walked in; he wasn't hungry, thirsty or in need of a smoke from the water pipe. But he had a strong **intuition**[8] he was waiting for something. It was vague yet urgent. His heart beat anxiously. The shopkeeper leisurely poured out a bowl of green tea for her customer. Then she sat back, chewed her betel nut[9] and said nothing. He raised the bowl of tea, took a sip and looked around. A gust of wind whirled some yellow leaves. From a distance, they looked like tiny gold grains that nature had generously scattered.

He had known all of this at one time. They were images from his past, although he wasn't aware of it. He felt increasingly **uneasy**.[10]

"Grandma, should I make more rice wafers?"

A girl's voice echoed from inside the house. The sound of her voice startled him. He almost got up to rudely peer into the other room. But he restrained himself. The shop owner's granddaughter came out from the back:

"I baked ten more rice wafers, Grandma. There's none left in the basket!"

Seeing him, the girl stepped back cautiously. The old woman opened the bag and took out a bunch of small rice pancakes. "Bake twenty small ones for Grandma. They're easier to sell." The girl answered "yes" in a low voice and leaned

---

[6] **dangling**—hanging and swaying back and forth.

[7] **melancholic**—depressing, gloomy.

[8] **intuition**—understanding without using thought or the senses.

[9] betel nut—leaf chewed by many people in Asian countries.

[10] **uneasy**—disturbed or uncomfortable.

over the earthenware basin to blow into the fire. The white ashes flew up, danced in the air and gently landed on her shiny black hair. Her teenage face was smooth and ruddy as a ripe fruit. Her nose was straight and graceful. She had a simple haircut, parted down the middle. He couldn't take his eyes off her; his heart beat excitedly.

"This is it!"

This unspoken sentiment had echoed within him as the girl came out . . . Twenty-three years ago, when he was in the tenth grade and a boarder in a small town, there was a similarly pretty and well-behaved girl. The same earthenware basin with red coals throwing off cinders, the same ruddy cheeks and round wrists . . . but the girl from his memory had a long hollow trace on her forehead. There were the same poinciana flowers and tiny yellow leaves, scattered by gusts of wind, dotting the ground in autumn, when sounds from the radio mixed with rustling from the unharvested rice paddies and the **incessant**[11] noises of insects—the lazy, for-lorn music of a small town.

It was odd how deeply buried these memories were. He was very poor then. Each month, his mother would send him only three *dong*[12] for pocket money and 10 kilograms of rice. But he studied harder than all the other boys in his class, who called him a bookworm. The pretty girl lived next door to the house where he rented his room. She used to lean her arms against the fence and listen to him memorize poems out loud. Her mother

was a food vendor; she would squat in front of the earthenware basin to bake rice wafers for her mother. At night, when he studied, she also lit an oil lamp and sat under the carambola tree to do her homework. At 10 o'clock, as his face was still buried in a book, she would hoist a carrying pole onto her shoulder to go get water for her family. She was a good student and never needed his help. Still, she would look at him admiringly as he diagrammed a geometric problem, or as he closed his eyes and recited, smooth as soup, a long poem. By the time she came back with the water, he would be ready for bed. He was so hungry he had to literally tighten his belt. It was then she would bring him a piping hot rice wafer. The two of them didn't say much. Usually, he just smiled:

"What luck, my stomach was growling."

He never bothered to thank her. But they both felt that they needed to see each other, look at each other's faces and talk about nothing. Neither of them dared to ask too deeply about the other. Truth is, there was nothing more to ask . . . Her piping hot wafers; the hollow trace on her forehead; the bright face; the understanding looks when he was homesick, sitting all bunched up during cold, rainy evenings.

He suddenly remembered all these things. All of them. He now understood what he had been waiting for that evening.

---

[11] **incessant**—continual, never-ending.

[12] *dong*—basic unit of Vietnamese currency.

It had arrived. That beautiful, sweet, distant memory. A memory, buried for more than twenty years, awakened suddenly by a gust of wind.

The young girl, who was fanning the fire, looked up: "Grandma, I've finished ten . . . Give me a hand . . ."

She gave the stack of yellow cakes to the old woman and glanced curiously at the strange customer. He rotated the tea bowl in his hands while staring at her. She became flustered and clumsily swatted a lump of coal to the ground with her fan. She picked it up immediately, threw it back into the basin, then blew on her two fingers to cool them off, her brows knit in a frown.

"Now she looks like a twelve-year-old. The other girl was older, and more pretty," he thought.

Once, he didn't have enough money to buy textbooks. It wasn't clear how she found out. That night, along with the wafers, she also gave him a small envelope. He opened it: inside was a small stack of bills. The notes were so new you could smell the aroma of paper and ink. It was her New Year's money. He sat motionless. It looked like she had been hoarding it for ten months and hadn't touched it. "But what did I do that day?" After graduating, he was preoccupied with taking the university admissions exam. After his acceptance, knowing he was going away, he excitedly took care of the paperwork, merrily said goodbye to everyone, then took a train straight for Hanoi.

"Why didn't I say goodbye to the girl? No, I was about to, but it was getting too close to my departure date. I was rushed by my relatives. And **intimidated**[13] by such an opportunity . . ."

And after that? A fresh environment; a strange city; life's frantic rhythm made him dizzy; bright lights; streetcars; the first parties where he felt awkward, provincial, out of place; teahouses; the blackboard in the classroom; new girlfriends . . .

"Eat the hot rice wafers, Uncle. It's **aromatic**[14] in your mouth. In Hanoi, you don't get country treats like this." The old shopkeeper gave him a small rice wafer. Its fluffy surface was **speckled**[15] with golden sesame seeds—very appetizing. He broke off a small piece and put it in his mouth. It was a taste he had long forgotten about.

"I used to think rice wafers were the most delicious food on earth," he thought. He remembered studying at night, particularly nights when he had to memorize history and biology lessons—two damnable subjects, when he was so hungry waiting for her footsteps near the fence that his mouth could taste the deliciously baked rice flour and the fatty sesame seeds . . . that taste and smell . . . and her wet eyes looking at him, as she rested her arms on the windowsill and smiled:

"I knew you were hungry, Brother. I get pretty hungry at night also. Mother told me to go into town tomorrow to buy

---

[13] **intimidated**—frightened, awed.
[14] **aromatic**—pleasantly sharp or strong.
[15] **speckled**—covered with spots.

cassava so we can have something extra to eat at night." The next day she brought him pieces of boiled cassava. At eighteen, eating them, he also thought her boiled cassava was the most delicious food on earth. Once, she gave him cassava wrapped in banana leaves. It was steaming hot. As he yanked his arms back, she grabbed both his hands and the hot cassava. She let go immediately, her eyes wide in astonishment. As for him, he was as dizzy as he had been that one holiday morning, when he had drunk too much sweet wine . . .

"I really did love her back then. . . I really did love. . ." Then why hadn't he gone back to that town to find her? Finished with his studies, he was assigned a job by the government. Then he had to apply for housing. Then he was involved with a female colleague. Life worries. There was a secret agreement, then the marriage license. That was his wife, unattractive yet **dogged**[16] in her pursuit of his love, who used every trick imaginable to make him yield to the harsh demands of necessity. . . And then what? Children. Problems at work. A promotion. Steps forward and backward. Years spent overseas to get a doctorate degree. . . Everything has to be **tabulated**.[17]

"Is the wafer good, Uncle?" the old woman asked.

"Very good, Grandmother," he answered. Crumbs fell onto his knees and he brushed them off. The old hen came over, cluck clucking for her chicks to come pick the crumbs.

"Why didn't I look for her? Why did I . . . Well, I had to achieve, at all costs, the planning targets for operative 038. . . And, to raise my kids, I had to teach to supplement my income. My daughters don't resemble me; they are like their mother, ugly, stuck-up. . . But do I love my wife? Probably not. . . Most likely not. I've never **tingled**[18] because of that woman like I did years ago waiting for the sounds of the little girl's footsteps. Especially in the afternoon, with everyone gone, when she washed her hair—with her cheeks dripping wet and strands of hair nappy on her temples. As she dried her hair, one hand on the fence, she would smile because she knew I was secretly admiring her. . . As for my wife, there's never any suspense; I never look forward to seeing her, nor feel empty when we're apart. Back then, going home to get rice, how I anticipated seeing the little girl again, even after only a day. . . My wife needed a husband and she found me. As for me. . ."

This thought nearly drove him mad. He stood up abruptly. The girl fanning the fire stared at him, her eyes black as coal, a deep dimple on one cheek.

He paid the old woman and started walking toward the bus. He wanted to return to Hanoi immediately. He wanted to forget these thoughts . . .

---

[16] **dogged**—grimly persistent.

[17] **tabulated**—listed and ordered.

[18] **tingled**—felt a slight prickling, stinging, or throbbing.

But the bus wasn't fixed until 2 in the morning. They returned to Hanoi by dawn. He returned to his daily life, to his daily business and worries . . . The thoughts of the little girl never left him. They would circle back like the hands on a watch.

"Why didn't I go find her back then? I surely would have had a different wife. And who knows . . ." The little girl is thirty-eight now, but to him she's still fifteen. She is his true love, but why do people only find out these things twenty years later? He flicked the cigarette ashes into the fancy pink ashtray and watched the tiny **embers**[19] slowly die. On the bed, his wife sleepily raised her head:

"Why are you up so late, dear? Are you admiring me?"

"Yes, yes, I'm admiring you," he answered, squashing the cigarette butt in the ashtray. His wife had just bought an embroidered dress from Thailand and had asked what he thought of it three times already.

"Go to bed, dear."

"I still have work to do."

"I wonder where the little girl is living now? What is she doing? Maybe I can take a bus there tomorrow. No, no, that's not possible." He saw clearly that to walk away silently twenty-three years ago was wrong. How could he possibly go back, when he had dismissed love so easily?

He retrieved the cigarette butt and lit it again. The ember returned to his lips.

A garden full of shades. Carambolas on the ground like fallen stars. And the smell of ripe carambolas. And her wet eyes. Her head tilted as she stood near the fence . . .

"But I was very shy then. I didn't dare to make any vow . . . Stop denying it—it is useless when it comes to love." He knew he had loved her and she had loved him, but he was impatient to get out of there because he was **dazzled**[20] by his own prospects. During the last hectic days, he did brood over a petty calculation. He did plan to . . . but never realized it.

"It wasn't like that, because . . .

"Sure it was.

"It wasn't like that . . .

"Yes, and you can't be forgiven . . ."

He threw the cigarette butt into the ashtray and flopped into an armchair. The polyester-covered cushions weren't as comfortable as usual. He stood up again, went to the window and pushed the glass panes open.

"It's cold, honey," his wife shrieked.

He didn't turn around, but answered gruffly:

"Then use the blanket."

Many stars lit up the night sky. He suddenly smelled the scent of fresh straw, of harvest. This familiar smell shrouded the neighborhood, a fragrance to stir one's soul. The poinciana flowers bloomed in the evening . . . Everything revived—vague, **spurious**,[21] yet stark enough to make him bitter. His head was spinning.

---

[19] **embers**—small pieces of wood or coal glowing in a dying fire.

[20] **dazzled**—confused, stunned, or blinded.

[21] **spurious**—not genuine, false.

He lit a second cigarette and slapped himself on the forehead.

"What is going on?"

There was no answer. Only a rising **tremolo**[22] of rice stalks and leaves rustling. Again, the swirling sky over the crown of the carambola tree; her smooth, firm arms on the windowsill as she smiled at him. White teeth like two rows of corn. His love had returned, right now, within him. He walked unconsciously to the mirror. His hair had begun to gray. Lines were etched all over his cheeks. Behind the glasses, his eyes had started to become lifeless. He drew deeply on the cigarette then exhaled. The pale blue smoke billowed shapelessly, like the confusions in his life.

His report contained many interesting proposals and was very well received, a complete success. Both his bosses and rivals were equally impressed. He himself didn't know how he had managed to do it. All the endless nights, walking back and forth, watching smoke rise then evaporate, when he had thought of her. She, the object of his true love—a love not shared, not articulated, what does it all add up to? But these soothing, melancholic memories had kept him awake at night, and he had written his report during these late hours, as he tried to recover what had disappeared from his life.

At the conference, people were admiring the exhibits illustrating his proposals. He had succeeded almost completely. Even his enemies were congratulating him. He smiled, shook hands and thanked everybody before slipping out into the hallway. Alone.

His closest colleague ran out to find him. The man looked him in the eye and said:

"The newspaper photographers are waiting for you. What's wrong, Brother? Are you in love?"

"Me, in love?," he chuckled, then snapped, "Me, love?! Are you mad? Me still in love . . . a steel-and-cement man, a . . . and with my hair turning . . ."

He didn't finish his sentence, but rushed out the gate. He walked down a little lane. For some reason, his eyes were stinging, as if smoke had blown into them. Where's that hamlet, that town? With pigeon coops and piles of straw in the yards. And poinciana flowers blooming in the evening sun. And the windswept rice paddies, with their ripe stalks rustling. And the harvested fields glowing, a soft pink, distant . . .

---

[22] **tremolo**—wavering or trembling sound.

QUESTIONS TO CONSIDER

1. What happens to the narrator at the tea shop? Why does this cause such an upheaval in his life?

2. What made the narrator abandon the girl he claims to have loved? What does the ending reflect about the narrator?

3. How do you interpret the title of this story?

4. What is Duong saying in this story about the choices each of us makes in life? How do you think she would define home? Would the narrator of the story define it the same way?

The Making of a New Zealander

FRANK SARGESON

Frank Sargeson (1903–1982) was the first important New Zealand writer not to leave the country for more literarily developed countries such as England and America. Sargeson worked every conceivable job through the 1920s and 1930s, from farmhand to lawyer, and experienced various ways of life in his homeland. New Zealand is a small country and one in which the immigrant experience is a defining factor. Sargeson was fascinated with the variety of cultures represented in his land and he was an absolute master of dialogue. "The Making of a New Zealander" takes up the issue of identity and immigration. Though the story is humorous, it also has a serious message.

When I called at that farm they promised me a job for two months so I took it on, but it turned out to be tough going. The boss was all right, I didn't mind him at all, and most days he'd just settle down by the fire and get busy with his crochet.[1] It was real nice to see him looking happy and contented as he sat there with his ball of wool.

But this story is not about a cocky[2] who used to sit in front of the fire and do crochet. I'm not saying I haven't got a story about him, but I'll have to be getting round to it another time.

Yes, the boss was all right, it was his missus that was the trouble. Some people say, never work for a woman, women'll never listen to reason. But that's not my experience. Use your block and in no time you'll be unlucky if you don't have them eating out of your hand.

But this time I was unlucky. This Mrs. Crump was a real tough one. She and the boss ran a market garden besides the cows. She'd tie a flour-bag over her head, get into gumboots, and not counting the time she put in in the house, she'd do about twelve hours a day, and she had me doing the same. Not that I minded all that much. The best of working on the land is that you're not always wishing it was time to knock off. Nor thinking of pay-day, either,

---

[1] crochet—craft in which a hooked needle is used to turn yarn into fabric.

[2] cocky—New Zealand slang for a small landholder with a reputation for being tight with money and hard on his farm labor.

particularly if there isn't a pub handy. I'm not going to explain. If you don't believe me, try it yourself and see.

But twelve hours a day, every day. I'll admit I used to get tired. Mrs. Crump would see I was done in and tell me to stop working, and that was just what I was waiting for her to do. But there'd be a look in her eye. She'd say that I wasn't built for hard work, but she wasn't surprised because she'd never met a man she couldn't work to a **standstill**.[3] Well, after she'd said that I'd just go on working, and if I was feeling cheeky[4] I'd tell her I didn't mind giving her a run for her money. And before those two months were up I was feeling cheeky pretty often. Once she got going about my wages and everything else she had to pay out. She couldn't keep the wolf from the door, she said. Well then, I said, if you can't you'll just have to keep the door shut.

Now I'm running on ahead so I'd better break off again, because this isn't just a no-account story about how I began to get cheeky and put wisecracks across Mrs. Crump. It's not about Mrs. Crump, she only comes into it. I'm not saying I haven't got a story about her too, but it's another one I'll be getting round to another time.

What I want to tell is about how I sat on a hillside one evening and talked with a man. That's all, just a summer evening and a talk with a man on a hillside. Maybe there's nothing in it and maybe there is.

The man was one of two young Dallies who ran an orchard up at the back of Mrs.

Crump's place. These two had come out from Dalmatia[5] and put some money down on the land, not much, just enough to give them the chance to start working the land. They were still paying off and would be for a good many, many years. There was a shed where they could live, and to begin with they took it in turns to go out and work for the money they needed to live and buy trees.

All that was some years before I turned up. The Dallies had worked hard, but it wasn't all plain sailing. They had about twenty-five acres, but it **sloped**[6] away from the sun. They'd planted pines for shelter, but your shelter has to make a lot of growth before it's any use on land with a good slope to the south. And it was poor land, just an inch or two of dark soil on top of clay. You could tell it was poor from the tea-tree, which made no growth after it was a few feet high. Apples do best on land like that, so it was apple-trees the Dallies had mainly gone in for.

Of course Mrs. Crump gossiped to me about all this. When I was there the Dallies weren't keeping a cow, so she was letting them have milk at half the town price. She didn't mind doing that much for them, she said, they worked so hard. And my last job each day was to take a billy[7] up to the back fence. I'd collect an empty billy that would be hanging on a hook, and I'd

---

[3] **standstill**—complete stop.

[4] cheeky—rude, without respect.

[5] Dalmatia—a region of Croatia, along the Adriatic Sea.

[6] **sloped**—angled.

[7] billy—New Zealand slang for a bucket.

always consider going on and having a yarn with the Dallies. It wasn't far across to their shed but it would be getting dark, I'd be feeling like my tea so I'd tell myself I'd go over another time.

Then one evening the billy wasn't on the hook and I went on over, but the door was shut and there was no one about. The dog went for me but he never had a show. He'd had distemper,[8] he couldn't move his hind[9] legs and just had to pull himself along. I had a look round but there wasn't much to see, just two flannels and a towel hanging on the line, and a few empty barrels splashed with bluestone. Close to the shed there were grape vines growing on wires, then the trees began. They were carrying a lot of fruit and looked fine and healthy, but just a bit too healthy I thought. You could tell from the growth that the Dallies had put on a lot of fertilizer. For a while I waited about, kidding to the dog until he wagged his tail, then I went back.

The next day one of the Dallies brought the billy over but I didn't see him. When we were milking Mrs. Crump told me. He was the one called Nick, and the evening before he'd had to take his mate into hospital. He'd had a spill off his bike and broken some ribs and his collar-bone. Mrs. Crump thought perhaps there'd been some drinking, she said they made wine. Anyhow Nick was upset. If his mate died, he said, he would die too. He'd have nothing left, nothing. And how could he work and live there by himself when his mate was lying all broken up in the hospital? Every afternoon he would leave off working and ride into town to see his mate.

There's a pal for you, Mrs. Crump said.

Well, up at the fence the billy would always be on the hook, but if Nick was in town seeing his cobber[10] I'd think it would be no use going over. Then one evening he was just coming across with the billy so I went over to meet him. We greeted each other, and I think we both felt a bit shy. He was small and dark, almost black, and his flannel and denims were pretty far gone the same as mine were. I gave him my tin and told him to roll a cigarette, and when he lit up he went cross-eyed. I noticed that, and I saw too that there was a sort of sadness on his face.

I asked him how his cobber was, and he said he was good.

In two days he will be here, he said. You could see he was excited about it and his face didn't look so sad. In two weeks, he said, it will be just as if it never happened.

That's great, I said, and we sat down and smoked.

How's the dog? I said.

He is getting better too, Nick said.

He whistled, and the dog pulled himself over to us by his front paws and put his chin on Nick's leg, and somehow with the dog there it was easier to talk.

I asked Nick about his trees and he said they were all right, but there were too many diseases.

---

[8] distemper—disease of some animals that causes fever and coughing, among other symptoms.

[9] hind—back, rear.

[10] cobber—New Zealand slang for a friend.

Too much quick manure, I said.

He said yes, but what could they do? It would take a long time to make the soil deep and sweet like it was in the part of Dalmatia he came from. Out here everybody wanted money quick, so they put on the manure. It was money, money, all the time. But he and his mate never had any. Everything they got they had to pay out, and if the black-spot got among the apples they had to pay out more than they got. Then one of them had to go out and try for a job.

It's the manure that gives you the black-spot, I said.

Sometimes I think it is God, Nick said.

Well, maybe you're right, I said, but what about the grapes?

On no, Nick said, they grow, yes. But they are not sweet. To make wine we must put in sugar. In Dalmatia it is not done. Never.

Yes, I said, but you don't go back to Dalmatia.

Oh, he said, now I am a New Zealander.

No, I said, but your children will be.

I have no children and I will never marry, Nick said.

No? I said, then your cobber will.

He will never marry either, Nick said.

Why? I said, there are plenty of Dalmatian girls out here. I bet you could get New Zealand girls too.

But Nick only said no no no no no.

If you were in Dalmatia I bet you'd be married, I said.

But I am not in Dalmatia, Nick said, now I am a New Zealander. In New Zealand everybody says they cannot afford to get married.

Yes, I said, that's what they say. But it's all wrong.

Yes, Nick said, it is all wrong. Because it is all wrong I am a Communist.[11]

Good, I said. Well, I thought, spoil a good **peasant**[12] and you might as well go the whole hog.

I bet you don't tell Mrs. Crump you're a Communist, I said.

Oh no, Nick said, she would never be a Communist.

No fear, I said.

I will tell you about Mrs. Crump, Nick said. She should go to Dalmatia. In Dalmatia our women wear bags on their heads just like her, and she would be happy there.

Yes, I said, I believe you're right. But Nick, I said, I thought you'd be a Catholic.

No, Nick said. It is all lies. In Dalmatia they say that Christ was born when there was snow on the ground in Palestine.[13] But now I have read in a book there is no snow in Palestine. So now I know that they tell lies.

---

[11] Communist—a person who favors the economic and social system based on ownership of land and the means of economic production by the people of a state.

[12] **peasant**—a rural person.

[13] Palestine—region of the Middle East that was once known as the Holy Land as it contained Bethlehem where Jesus was born. It is today mostly divided between Israel and Jordan.

So you're a Communist instead, I said.

Yes, I am a Communist, Nick said. But what is the good of that? I am born too soon, eh? What do you think?

Maybe, I said.

You too, Nick said. You think that you and me are born too soon? What do you think?

He said it over and over, and I couldn't look him in the face. It had too much of that sadness. . . . I mightn't have put it the way Nick had, I mightn't have said I was born too soon, but Nick knew what he was talking about. Nick and I were sitting on the hillside and Nick was saying he was a New Zealander, but he knew he wasn't a New Zealander. And he knew he wasn't a Dalmatian any more.

He knew he wasn't anything any more.

Listen, Nick said, do you drink wine?

Yes, I said.

Then tomorrow night you come up here and we will drink wine, Nick said.

Yes, I said, that's O.K. with me.

There is only tomorrow night, Nick said, then my mate will be here. We will drink a lot of wine, I have plenty and we will get very, very drunk. Oh, heaps drunk.

Yes, I said. Sure thing.

Tomorrow night, he said.

He got up and I got up, he just waved his hand at me and walked off. He picked the dog up under his arm and walked off, and I just stood there and watched him go.

But it turned out I never went up to Nick's place. When I was having my tea that evening Mrs. Crump told me about how a woman she knew had worked too hard and dropped dead with heart failure. But there's nothing wrong with my heart, she said.

No, I said, except that maybe it's not in the right place.

Of course it must have sounded like one of my wisecracks, but I was thinking of Dalmatia.

Anyhow Mrs. Crump said she'd stood enough from me, so when I'd finished my tea I could go.

I wasn't sorry. I stood on the road and wondered if I'd go up to Nick's place, but instead I walked into town, and for a few days I never left off drinking.

I wanted to get Nick out of my mind. He knew what he was talking about, but maybe it's best for a man to hang on.

QUESTIONS TO CONSIDER

1. What does Nick mean by saying he was born too soon? Do you agree or disagree? Explain your answer.

2. Why does the narrator want to get Nick out of his mind at the end of the story?

3. What do you think it means to be a member of a nation? How is this different for a native citizen than it is for an immigrant?

At the River

PATRICIA GRACE

Patricia Grace (1937–   ) is of Maori descent, and most of her writing concerns the experiences of Maori in New Zealand. The Maori are the aboriginal settlers of New Zealand, and they violently opposed the European settlers in the 1800s. This conflict led to a great drop in the Maori population. But in the twentieth century, the Maori have emerged as an economically self-sufficient and culturally independent part of New Zealand. Grace's stories celebrate this independence.

Sad I wait, and see them come slow back from the river. The torches move slow.

To the tent to rest after they had gone to the river, and while asleep the dream came. A dream of death. He came to me in the dream, not sadly but smiling, with hand on heart and said I go but do not weep. No weeping, it is my time.

Woke then and out into the night to watch for them with sadness on me, sadness from the dream. And waiting, there came a morepork[1] with soft wingbeat and rested above my head. "Go," I said to the bird. "He comes not with you tonight. He is well and strong. His time is not here."

But it cried, the morepork. Its call went out. Out and out until the tears were on my face. And now I wait and I see the torches come, they move slow back from the river. Slow and sad they move and I

think of him. Many times have we come to this place for eels. Every year we come at this time. Our children come and now our grandchildren, his and mine. This is the river for eels and this the time of year.

A long way we have traveled with our tents and food stores our lamps and bedding and our big eel drums. Much work for us today preparing our camp. But now our camp is ready and they have gone with the torches downriver to the best eel place. And this old lady stays behind with her old kerosene lamp and the campfire dying, and the little ones sleeping in their beds. Too tired for the river tonight, too old for the work of catching eels. But not he.

---

[1] morepork—an owl native to New Zealand.

He is well and strong. No aching back or tired arms he. No bending, no sadness on him or thoughts of death like this old one.

His wish but not mine to come here this year. "Too old," I said to him. "Let the young ones go. Stay back we two and **tend**[2] our sweet potatoes and corn."

"This old body," he said. "It hungers for the taste of eel."

"The drums will be full when they return," I said. "Let them bring the eels to us, as they would wish to do."

"Ah no," he said. "Always these hands have fetched the food for the stomach. The eels taste sweeter when the body has worked in fetching."

"Go then," I said, and we prepared.

I think of him now as I await their return. "My time is here," he said in the dream, and now the bird calls out. And I think too of the young ones who spoke to him today in a new way, a way I did not like.

Before the night came they worked, all of them, to make their torches for the river. Long sticks from the tea-tree, long and straight. **Tins**[3] tied at the tops of the sticks, and in the tins rags soaked in oil. A good light they made as they left tonight for the river. Happy and singing they went with their torches. But I see the lights return now, **dim**.[4] Dim and slow they come and sadly I await them.

And the young ones, they made their eel hooks. Straight sticks with strong hooks tied for catching eels. He smiled to see the hooks, the straight sticks with the strong hooks tied.

"Your hooks," he said. "They work for the hands?" But the young ones did not speak, instead bent heads to the work of tying hooks.

Then off, the young ones, to the hills for **hare**[5] bait as the sun went down. Happy they went with the gun. Two shots went out and we awaited their return. The young ones, they came back laughing. Happy they came with the hare. "Good bait this," they said. "Good bait and good hooks. Lots of eels for us tonight."

But their nanny said to them, "A hook is good for the eel but bad for the leg. Many will be there at the river tonight, your uncles, aunties, big cousins, your nanny too. Your hooks may take a leg in place of an eel. The old way, with the stick, and the bait tied is a safe way and a good way. You waste your time with hooks."

But the young ones rolled on the ground. "Ho, Grandpa," they called, "You better watch your leg tonight. The hook might get your leg, Grandpa."

"And watch your hand, Grandpa, the eel might get your hand."

"Bite your hand off, Grandpa. You better watch out."

Did not like their way of talking to their nanny but he has patience with the young.

---

[2] **tend**—take care of.

[3] **Tins**—metal boxes made of tin.

[4] **dim**—not bright, barely visible.

[5] **hare**—animal that resembles a large rabbit.

"You'll see," he said. "You want to know how to get eels then you watch your grandpa."

They did not keep quiet, the young ones after that. Called out to him in a way I did not like, but he is patient.

"Ah, Grandpa, that old way of yours is no good. That way is old like you, Grandpa."

"You might end up in the river with your old way of catching eels."

Spoke sharply to them then in our own language.

"Not for you to speak in this manner. Not our way to speak like this. It is a new thing you are doing. It is a bad thing you have learned."

No more talk from these two then, but laughing still, and he spoke up for them.

"They make their torches, the boys, and they make the hooks, and then they go to the hills for hare. They think of the river and the eels in the river, and then they punch each other and roll on the ground. Shout and laugh waiting for the night to come. The funny talk it means nothing."

"Enough to shout and fight," I said. "Enough to roll on the ground and punch each other, but the talk needs to stay in the mouth."

Put my head down then not pleased, and worked at my task of kneading[6] the bread for morning.

Now I wait and stir the ashes round the oven while the morning bread cooks, and on the ashes I see my tears fall. The babies sleep behind me in the tent, and above me the bird cries.

Much to do after a night of eeling when the drum is full. From the fire we scrape away the dead ashes to put into the drum of eels. All night our eels stay there in the drum of ashes to make easier the task of scraping. Scrape off the ashes and with it comes the sticky eel slime. Cut the eels, and open them out then ready for smoking. The men collect green wood from the tea-tree for our smoke drum. Best wood this, to make a good smoke. Good and clear. All day our smoke house goes. Then wrap our smoked eel carefully and pack away before night comes and time for the river again.

But no eels for us this night. No scraping and smoking and packing this time. Tonight our camp comes down and we return. The dim lights come and they bring him back from the river. Slow they bring him.

Now I see two lights come near. The two have come to bring me sad news of him. But before them the bird came, and before the bird the dream—he in the dream with hand on heart.

And now they stand before me, the boys, heads down. By the dim torchlight I see the tears on their faces, they do not speak.

"They bring your nanny back," I say. "Back from the river." But they do not speak.

---

[6] kneading—pressing and folding.

"Hear the morepork," I say to them. "It calls from the trees. Out and out it cries. They bring him back from the river, I see your tears."

"We saw him standing by the river," they say. "Saw him bend, looking into the water, and then we saw him fall."

They stand, the young ones in the dim torchlight with tears on their faces, the tears fall. And now they come to me, kneeling by me, weeping.

"We spoke bad to him," they say. "They were bad things we said. Now he has fallen and we have said bad things to him."

So I speak to them to comfort them. "He came to me tonight with hand on heart. 'Do not weep,' he said. 'It is my time.' Not your words that made him fall. His hand was on his heart. Hear the morepork cry. His time is here."

And now we weep together, this old lady and these two young ones by her. No weeping he said. But we will weep a little while for him and for ourselves. He was our strength.

We weep and they return. His children and mine return from the river hearing him. Sad they come in the dim light of torches. The young ones help me to my feet, weeping still, and I go toward them as they come.

And in my throat I feel a cry well up. Lonely it sounds across the night. Lonely it sounds, the cry that comes from in me.

QUESTIONS TO CONSIDER

1. Why does the old man want to go to fish for eels? What does this desire indicate?

2. Why do the young speak so boldly to the old man? Why do they regret it later?

3. What inferences can you draw about the values of Maori culture from this story? Make as many as you can.

Three Poems

OODGEROO NOONUCCAL

HYLLUS MARIS

JUDITH WRIGHT

The Australian aborigines are the native inhabitants of Australia; it is thought that they may have lived there for 40,000 years. When English settlers arrived in Australia in the late eighteenth century, the aborigines quickly came to be marginalized. Pacification policies by the settlers led to a massive drop in the aboriginal population and the incorporation of many aborigines as permanent menial laborers. In the twentieth century, the aboriginal population made a comeback and their culture thrived. The following poems all express something of aboriginal culture. Oodgeroo Noonuccal (1920–1993) and Hyllus Maris (1930–1986) both helped lead the aboriginal culture movement. Judith Wright (1915–   ) is an Australian poet descended from the British settlers; nonetheless she shares Noonuccal's and Maris's faith in and love of aboriginal culture.

Municipal Gum

OODGEROO NOONUCCAL

Gumtree in the city street,
Hard bitumen[1] around your feet,
Rather you should be
In the cool world of leafy forest halls
And wild bird calls.

---

[1] bitumen—tarlike substance used for road surfacing and roofing.

Here you seem to me
Like that poor cart-horse
Castrated, broken, a thing wronged,
Strapped and buckled, its hell prolonged,
Whose hung head and **listless**[2] mien[3] express
Its hopelessness.
Municipal gum, it is **dolorous**[4]
To see you thus
Set in your black grass of bitumen—
O fellow citizen,
What have they done to us?

Spiritual Song of the Aborigine

HYLLUS MARIS

I am a child of the Dreamtime People
Part of this Land, like the **gnarled**[5] gumtree
I am the river, softly singing
Chanting our songs on my way to the sea
My spirit is the dust-devils
Mirages, that dance on the plain
I'm the snow, the wind and the falling rain
I'm part of the rocks and the red desert earth
Red as the blood that flows in my veins
I am eagle, crow and snake that glides
Through the rain-forest that clings to the mountainside
I awakened here when the earth was new
There was emu, wombat, kangaroo[6]
No other man of a different hue
I am this land
And this land is me
I am Australia.

---

[2] **listless**—without energy or enthusiasm.

[3] mien—a person's look or way of carrying him- or herself.

[4] **dolorous**—painful, distressing.

[5] **gnarled**—twisted, bent, bumpy.

[6] emu, wombat, kangaroo—animals native to Australia.

Bora Ring[7]

JUDITH WRIGHT

The song is gone; the dance
is secret with the dancers in the earth,
the ritual useless, and the tribal story
lost in an alien tale.

Only the grass stands up
to mark the dancing-ring: the apple-gums[8]
posture and mime a past corroboree,[9]
murmur a broken chant.

The hunter is gone: the spear
is splintered underground; the painted bodies
a dream the world breathed sleeping and forgot.
The nomad feet are still.

Only the rider's heart
halts at a sightless shadow, an unsaid word
that fastens in the blood the ancient curse,
the fear as old as Cain.[10]

---

[7] Bora Ring—the sacred place where the *bora* ritual is performed indicating a boy's passage into manhood.

[8] apple-gums—eucalyptus trees in Australia.

[9] corroboree—an aborigine festival.

[10] Cain—In the Bible, Cain is the eldest son of Adam and Eve. He kills his brother Abel and is cursed by God.

QUESTIONS TO CONSIDER

1. How would you contrast the two gumtrees presented in "Municipal Gum?" What is Noonuccal's message in the poem?

2. What elements of the aborigine religion does Maris depict in "Spiritual Song of the Aborigine"?

3. What is the event that Wright is describing in "Bora Ring"? What does the ring symbolize for the character in the poem?

4. How would you describe the aborigine's philosophy of life from reading these three poems? Explain how you made your inferences.

The Birth

PRAMOEDYA ANANTA TOER

Pramoedya Ananta Toer (1926–   ) is Indonesia's most prominent writer. Born when the country was still under Dutch colonial rule, his father ran a school that promoted Indonesian culture and nationalism. The Dutch lost control of Indonesia when the Japanese invaded in 1942. In 1945, colonial control passed to the British, who were violently opposed by the general population. Two years of civil war ended with Indonesian independence in 1949. Toer had been active in the struggle against all three outside powers, and with independence he devoted himself to writing. He quickly became one of the country's leading novelists and journalists. In 1965, a military coup overthrew the democratically elected government, and many intellectuals were jailed. Toer was in prison, uncharged and untried, for fourteen years. His four-part novel describing his prison experiences is one of the landmarks of Indonesian literature. "The Birth" is a story that describes a part of the protest movement against the Dutch.

I

One of the adopted children in our house was a student called Hurip. He had finished government high school in the provincial[1] capital, Semarang. A number of young men, still students, stayed with us too. The older boys often gathered to talk. I could not understand many of the things they talked about, and I certainly couldn't understand Hurip when he said, "We need dynamism. Our society is too **static**.[2] We should have the courage to do something other than being civil servants."

I was curious to find out as much as I could, and often left father's books and desk in a mess. I asked mother about things I couldn't understand. I asked her what Hurip meant. She told me politely that when I was grown up I would understand readily enough.

I worried about it. I asked my friends what he meant and they didn't know. I asked the servant who was seven times as old as I was and she didn't understand either.

Hurip's opinions were respected in our house because he had passed through the Dutch school system. Even mother

---

[1] provincial—pertaining to an administrative district of a country.

[2] **static**—passive or unchanging.

respected him. It was scarcely surprising that he became the center of attention and that everyone paid close attention to whatever he said. He dominated every conversation. Mother said he had joined a political party.

I was amazed to hear of this. To me politics meant the police and our whole house hated anything to do with the police.

"Isn't father angry he's joined the police?" I asked.

She smiled at my question. Then explained simply what politics was and told me: "Those who join the parties are the enemies of the police."

I understood a little. I tried to explain it to my friends but they laughed in disbelief. Our servant refused to believe it. I felt surrounded by thick **impenetrable**[3] walls.

Then came that afternoon. We had washed; the older boys had not yet begun to play chess, study or paint. They sat on a mat around a low table—a desk—and engaged in earnest conversation. I sat behind Hurip, who spoke with great fire: "It must be boring being a civil servant. They go to work at a set time, stay in the office for a set period, go home at a set time, play with their wives and have children at regular intervals. They live like that year after year. Really boring. They dream like donkeys of a bundle of hay, a drink of water and quiet rest. Beautiful thoughts about their next pay rise. Then they jump about like dogs, a pat on the head from their boss and they dream of promotion. They get scared like rabbits: a frown from the boss and they'll lose their jobs."

The other boys listened carefully. I tried to, but couldn't follow it all. One thing stayed with me: you would get babies if you played with your wife.

Hurip continued about how boring it would be to be a civil servant. "Never any variety," he said. "You need change to be creative. And when the month was safely over, they carried their salaries home looking pleased with themselves, light in the head—and a little flushed. From the middle to the end of the month they sweated because they didn't have enough money. Bills, chits,[4] invoices and pawnshop tickets danced in their heads. And those who never got bored with themselves became solid gold civil servants in the top **echelons**.[5] Their lives never changed. They just kept having more kids . . . "

This was before the second world war, when the Dutch and their civil service seemed likely to stay forever.

And I still didn't understand what he meant, so I just listened quietly.

After lunch I asked mother if you really got babies by playing with your wife. She

> *I was amazed to hear of this. To me politics meant the police and our whole house hated anything to do with the police.*

---

[3] **impenetrable**—unable to be penetrated or crossed.

[4] chits—vouchers written on small slips of paper.

[5] **echelons**—levels or ranks.

didn't answer me. Without changing her expression she ordered me to go and study and to call Hurip on my way. When she saw I still wanted an answer, she said firmly: "Go and study! Don't put it off. There'll always be study until you're grown up. Go on."

And I repeated my question. She was angry. I never saw her uncertain about anything, even the smallest thing—she was always **resolute**.[6] It was of great value to her in running the house.

I went. And shortly after I heard her calling Hurip. From then on, my adopted brother was more careful when I was around. He would joke noisily with the others and then, when I came, turn the conversation to serious matters.

2

The ordinariness of our smalltown existence suddenly changed. I could not have described it **explicitly**[7] but I felt it strongly. From the conversations I heard, I found out that there was turmoil among the nobles. And among the merchants. And among the farmers and artisans. Hurip spoke of India and *swadesi*,[8] of the Japanese and of the rise of Asia. He spoke fiercely, as father did when he made his speeches: "From the time of the first kings in the fatherland, the nobles have been the most powerful class in society—power they have wrongly **usurped**.[9] They claim the right—although no-one admits or practices the right other than themselves— to be called 'lord' by the lower-classes. They try to be **contemplative**[10] rather than

active. They are at peace only because they cannot see what is going on around them. The only thing they are interested in is promotion, prestige and their salary. Sometimes their fine dreams turn into groundless fears: retrenchment, the anger of their superiors, a drop in their salary. But we are organizing. If they don't want to join us, we will sweep them aside."

As usual I couldn't follow all he had to say.

3

Life in our small town was passing through a **ferment**.[11] A football club was established and soon each part of town had three football clubs of its own. Football clubs grew like mushrooms among the young. Among the nobles there were artistic circles: theater, shadow-play, classical dance, singing and the traditional *gamelan*.[12] Among the young people there were modern theater groups and pop orchestras. Father was a **patron**[13] of several artistic, sporting and social clubs. And mother was patron of a women's club.

---

[6] **resolute**—certain or determined.

[7] **explicitly**—clearly, leaving nothing implied.

[8] *swadesi*—Indonesian word for the Indian leader Mohandas Gandhi's concept of self-sufficiency as a means of opposing colonial rule. Gandhi suggested that Indians make everything they need and so not support the textile industry in Britain.

[9] **usurped**—seized or assumed wrongfully.

[10] **contemplative**—thoughtful, meditative.

[11] **ferment**—period of activity or excitement.

[12] *gamelan*—a Javanese orchestra of percussion instruments.

[13] **patron**—a person who gives financial or other support to a person, cause, or work of art.

Many of the people in our neighborhood joined the police. They reported that the government was strengthening its police forces. But the people still came in droves when Engineer Sukarno[14] came to speak in our town. And they weren't stopped from gathering in their thousands when Doctor Sosrokartono came to visit, and from asking him to turn water into holy water. The head of almost every family came home in great delight with half a bottle of salt water, as if his family's salvation were assured forever.

In the early morning squads of men would be out running. And almost every Sunday there was a football game. Often the children would line up and sing the popular nationalist song:

As the sun in the east begins to rise
Let us stand and go forth in our
    strength. . .

Father ordered us to join the scouts. And at a grand campfire a line of old men were sworn in as honorary members of the Boy Scouts of Indonesia. Among them, in scout's uniform, was father. The number of scouts quadrupled.[15] Two new troops were formed, one Muslim and one using the medium of Dutch.

Slowly but surely we began to hate the Dutch. And the hate finally spread.

"Don't think Europeans will always be more important than we," father once told mother, happily. I noticed her stomach was slightly full.

Mother enjoyed the taste of the words. I still remember him saying that, although I was only seven. She was holding a book. It was, as I found out ten or eleven years later, a book on the political consequences of the cotton trade. Cotton was an important **commodity**[16] and a disguised political issue.

She fondly looked at me and then said, while looking at father, "There are other ways of earning a living than working in an office. What do you want to be when you grow up, my son?"

"A farmer!" I exclaimed with delight.

"A farmer?" asked father. I said "yes." Mother continued: "If you really want to be a farmer you can't be lazy like you are now." And she told me about the ranches in the United States, Australia, and in the Hawaiian islands.

Her simple words made me eager to hoe the small plot of ground prepared for me. Often she helped me. And once as we planted sweet potato she said hopefully, "The fruit of one's own labor is sweetest, my son. Look! you're starting to sweat. That's good for your blood and your health."

She even told me that one day the highest officials ruling over Indonesia would no longer be Dutch, but our own people. Then, "You're still young. Later, when you've done with your schooling

---

[14] Engineer Sukarno—Achmad Sakarno (1902–1970) was the first president of independent Indonesia.

[15] quadrupled—increased by four times.

[16] **commodity**—a useful thing that can be bought and sold.

and like to read big books like your father does, you'll know a lot—and the seed I've planted will bear fruit. As will the labors of those who want to see our own people in control. But you can't understand yet. Do you know what father's doing?"

"He's not home very often," I said interrupting.

"No, he's not, he's still planting for the future—for future decades—and the crop will never be exhausted."

"Never? Sweet potato?"

"Sweet potato. Not the kind you eat. But something you can enjoy when you've grown up. Something better than this. Better for you then than now. And for your friends."

I stopped hoeing and looked at her for a while. Seeing my hoe still, she too stopped and looked at me. "You don't understand," she said regretfully. "One day you'll understand without all the riddles."

I never forgot her words. Or the vitality which gripped our small town.

4

Hurip no longer talked as much as he had. He was obliged by father to teach in his school, a private school established nine years before I was born. After Hurip came home from school, he slept. In the early evening he corrected his students' work, later he studied. He had no time to sit around talking or to play chess or practice the violin.

Once—I remember—on the afternoon prior to the weekly holiday, a group sat around the study table. I was there, as usual sitting behind Hurip. And in a controlled but firm voice he said: "The government taxes are crippling us. They tax anything and everything, And we all suffer because of it. We have to pay tax for every meter of cloth we buy and every time we walk on the road."

I could understand what he was saying and could imagine how happy people would be if there were no taxes. He finished up: "The Dutch haven't come here to make you all senior civil servants. They've come to take our money away from us in taxes. And if we don't pay and have nothing they can pillage, we have to do forced labor in prison. The *Samin* rebels to the south of us were smart. They refused ever to pay any taxes."

His voice always carried conviction. And that made the other children believe every word he uttered.

The change in attitude became clear when people began to wear *lurik*, a coarse, quickly-fading, village-woven striped cloth. Even the nobles wore it. I was not rich, but I had never felt drawn to *lurik* either. Wash it two or three times and the color was a mess. But father wore pyjamas and shirts made of *lurik*. And one day we all received a set of *lurik* shirts each. My confusion was increased. When Hurip, in the company of the other boys said, "The people in India are wearing *lurik* too, and burning overseas cloth," I said, automatically, "What a pity. If they gave it to me, I'd have it."

Everyone laughed and I fell silent. I realized then how unimportant I was and that I was expected to listen and not to try to make myself heard. Hurip put me on his lap and said: "When you make your own cloth and burn overseas clothing, that's called *swadesi*. It makes work for your own countrymen, and when they work they get the benefits. If you wear foreign clothing, foreigners do the work and they get all the benefits."

I nodded uncomprehendingly. The conversation which I could neither follow nor understand went on until midnight. I slept on the mat and was allowed to stay there until morning when the cold air began to bite my skin.

At that time wearing *lurik* made you a more respected person. I wasn't surprised when mother told an old village woman: "Make me twelve lengths of *lurik*— nicely colored and well-patterned, for the children."

The cloth had to be for us. Mother ordered none for herself because she disliked wearing it.

The weaver said happily, "Lots of people are wearing *lurik* nowadays."

"It's *swadesi*, dear," mother explained.

"The villagers are starting to use that word," the weaver said. "It's *swadesi*. My neighbors are weaving day and night, just like when I was a kid. And they're starting to plant cotton in their yards. Even the sandalman—he makes sandals out of old tires—is getting more trade. Every week people come from the cooperatives to buy this many or that many dozen. He's got a lot of people working for him. He used to have just himself. And now he's got fifteen men."

Mother listened delightedly. I still cannot understand why she was so pleased. When the weaver left she said to herself, as she looked at me, "*Swadesi* is bringing industry to the villages. If this can keep going for twenty or thirty years, the little man—" she pointed to the south where a bamboo craftsman lived, "will be well off, not miserable like he is now. He has so many children. Eight. And each basket is only worth a farthing.[17] And it takes a person over half a day to make one."

I heard much about *swadesi* but still do not know how important it was. I was never very interested.

Mother's stomach began to expand. She seldom worked. The weaving equipment she bought stayed in the shed. She had been shown how to use it, and had studied seven more days on her own. But she couldn't bear to weave for more than three hours at a time. Her stomach and whole body ached, she said. So she usually sat in the rotunda,[18] where she

> *I heard much about* swadesi *but still do not know how important it was. I was never very interested.*

---

[17] farthing—the smallest British coin in the old-style currency.

[18] rotunda—building with a circular ground plan, especially one with a dome.

could see the scenery, and read a foreign book. Father was seldom at home. Planting for the future, she said. And when he did come, he always had three or four people with him. Then they talked about things I couldn't understand, stopping occasionally to laugh or to whisper in great earnestness. They spiced their talk with the now common words: *swadesi*, co-operatives, the people's bank, education, mass literacy and **indigenous**[19] enterprise.

I was pleased to know as much as I did. I never felt guilty listening in the corner. Children in our district were not supposed to do that, but father never forbade me. Once a guest even singled me out and said, half to me, half to father: "He must carry on the work we have begun." I listened harder, hoping for more of such sweet praise.

Father said nothing. He smiled and his thick moustache was stretched a little.

His guests wore *lurik* and sandals made out of old tires, or were barefooted. Their faces shone with the passion and spirit the *lurik* reflected.

5

Gradually more and more guests came to our house. Neighbors who were illiterate came to talk with father. And others whom I did not recognize at all, village owls from far away, came to meet him. Then other old men—who were far from illiterate—came and asked to be allowed to follow courses in politics, economics and general studies. And many students who had only finished primary school and then worked for the government or themselves came to undertake teaching or trade courses. My older "brothers" organized it all. Father administered, with a look of victory on his face.

Several weeks later we gained some new furniture: two duplicators, a large box of paper and five typewriters. Our house was suddenly an office. The machines typed all the time and the duplicator spun off lessons for the students.

In the admission register I read: Three hundred new students for the literacy course. Forty to be teachers. Three to learn a trade. Fifty for general studies. Fifteen in the kindergarten and twenty for the English course. Eleven for the Dutch course, all government schoolteachers.

"We're starting," father said to Hurip.

From then on father was the center of attention in our small town. He was always busy, often away for long periods. The pile of books he had to mark continually increased. Sometimes my older brothers helped him. Mother enjoyed the new situation. Many women came to the house and asked about this and that. And she always accepted the patronage of newly-formed women's groups. She went to the meetings even though her stomach hurt.

Whenever father was home the police came by frequently, looking in from astride their bikes. But they did no more than look. I didn't understand why they did that. When I asked mother why, she explained:

---

[19] **indigenous**—originating naturally in a region.

"They like to make sure your father's up to no mischief."

"He's only teaching people how to work, isn't he?"

"They don't want too many of us to understand and be able to read and write as well."

She refused to explain more, even though I kept on asking. I had to be content to wait for a few years until I could understand for myself.

Great changes took place in the family. Industry filled the time which had once been empty and relaxed. When I walked in the streets, people would sometimes say to each other, "That's his son." They even asked me to stop and talk about my father and sometimes gave me money. I liked that. I grew to feel that father was an important man in town.

Father came home after teaching and ate with mother. Once he looked sullen and pale. I was helping get the meal ready. Mother asked him "Don't you feel well? You're working too hard."

Father said he didn't feel well.

"You'd better take a week off."

"It's not the work. It's this—we have to be the boss here before we can do what we want. Certainly before we can do anything that will benefit society."

"Explain yourself," she said.

"I've got a letter."

"Go on."

"From the government."

"What about?"

"It's a threat. Or more politely, a reminder. I have to stop everything I'm doing."

Mother looked at him sharply. I left.

I always liked to spread anything I knew. So I told Hurip. He wasn't surprised. His face suddenly tired, like father's. He didn't accept the news as I had expected him to. Disappointedly I sat in the doorway of the kitchen waiting until mother and father had finished eating. And I thought of father's pale, **sullen**[20] face.

"Aren't you eating with your father?" the servant asked.

I shook my head.

"Why not?"

"Father can't work." I complained and informed at the same time.

"Who's stopped him? No-one would dare. Even the mayor's afraid of him."

I considered that, repeated it to myself to tell others. But his pale, sullen face quickly wiped that thought away. I went quickly to a fifteen-year-old who was in fifth grade. I told him what I had heard from father and mother. He interrupted me: "The inspector and five of his men came when father was teaching us civics."

"Why didn't I see them?"

"Your class had gone home."

I understood now. He continued, "All the books he had printed in Semarang— for the first and second literacy courses— have been **confiscated**.[21] Over seven thousand of them. It's a shame. He worked

---

[20] **sullen**—brooding, gloomy.

[21] **confiscated**—taken or seized by an authority.

hard on them. And the printing was expensive. We had no classes for over three hours. All the teachers were rounded up. We had to wait in our rooms. We watched the police taking the books away. They cut the school's power lines too. No-one can study at night now."

The rest of the story was irrelevant. Only father's cold, sullen face and the disaster it portended mattered.

When I returned to the dining table they had finished. Mother was asking "And how about the people's bank you put fifty thousand Rupiah[22] into?" He shook his head. The expression contained a greater threat: "Any loss will be ours."

Slowly and deliberately he said, "Our only responsibility was that we should make the effort. And we did. If the out-come is other than we hoped, that is none of our business."

Mother agreed, repressing a moan. Then, trying to hide the disappointment she felt, she said, "I believe that what you have done will endure. I have prayed for the safe progress and rapid completion of your work. But if evil comes—it is indeed none of our business."

6

From that time on, few people came to our house. Even the school children who usually came to play stayed away. Our house became an island. Mother was more solitary than usual. Hurip regularly sat with a book in his hand, thinking, but never reading. When he realized what he was doing, his eyes returned to the rows of print but focused on nothing. He would sigh and get up and go out of the house. When I went to bed he would still be out.

The number of pupils in the school gradually fell away. A friend whose father was a civil servant told me, "Civil servants with children in non-state schools have no hope of promotion."

In the primary school I attended the numbers dropped from nearly four hundred to eighty-four. The school buildings no longer shone as brightly and nobly as before. They were dark and gloomy.

And once I overheard mother complain to herself as she lay on her bed, "How could they relieve them of their duties and position just for being members of a club?" I saw her cry. The tears turned me dumb and I ran away.

One night I woke to hear a hard, cruel voice coming from the room next to mine, Hurip's room: "They're strangling us. I can't bear living in a small town with so many problems."

It was Hurip's voice. The tone was one of extreme anger. I didn't know why he was angry. But the next day he saw father and asked his permission to leave.

He never wrote to us to tell us how he was, where he was staying, whether he was working or studying.

Mother advised me to read as much as Hurip used to: he even took a book to the toilet. After he left his name was often

---

[22] Rupiah—basic Indonesian unit of money.

recalled with genuine affection. But he never sent us any news of himself.

As before when he was busy, father was away more and more. Sometimes no-one saw him for three days and nights at a time. He wasn't at school. At home he never read or marked the students' books; he never walked in the garden and he never took us walking in the early morning. He seldom smiled—or even talked, except when it was strictly necessary. It was a swift and extraordinary change. I realized in my own way that something had happened over which neither father nor mother had any control.

When the schoolyard was overgrown with weeds, the gloom and the sullen chill began to lift from his face. He began to teach regularly, although still he often did not come home at night. And one night when he was absent, mother said to me "We made life too easy for the foreigners. They've given us back nothing but trouble and deceit, force and threats, lies and oppression." Her voice was harsh, threatening.

I tried to understand her in my childish way. But couldn't. I didn't understand. It was hopeless. And I didn't dare ask any questions. The memory of the bite in her voice terrified me. I was silent. And it made no difference to her.

"I hope," she continued, this time without the threat, the harshness or the despair; her voice was soft and **coaxing**,[23] "that you'll study properly, my son. Hurip was clever but the situation was too much for him. He had to run away to forget his

disappointment. Your father's clever but he can't do anything. So you have to be cleverer than them both. If you are cleverer—far cleverer than they—you won't fail."

I did not fully understand her. The softness of her voice stirred me but I did not know what I should say. Mother embraced me and kissed my neck. I felt the warmth of her tears. I still did not understand. When she had calmed a little, I asked, "Daddy can't work any more but he still keeps going out. Why?"

> *You're still a child and can't feel the disappointment grown-ups can feel. Your father is sad and needs amusement.*

"He can't forget his students' studies, my dear."

"But there's no electricity and he doesn't come home at night. How can he work then?"

"Your father's a very disappointed man. You cannot possibly understand how disappointed he is. You're still a child and can't feel the disappointment grown-ups can feel. Your father is sad and needs amusement."

The answer stopped any desire in me to ask further. Not just because I didn't understand, but also because the rhythm of her voice terrified me.

When I was a child I often used to wander all over the district. The first place

---

[23] **coaxing**—persuasive.

I visited was the market after selling was over, and before the sweepers began their work. I gathered the labels from balls of thread and put them in a box. Many of my friends had hundreds, some even had thousands. Whoever had the most felt the richest—like adults with their coins. The one with the most had pride of place in any conversation. People were reluctant to contradict him because they secretly hoped for some of his labels.

I often saw father gambling at other people's places, sometimes at a Chinese man's place. And I would pass by pretending not to notice. So I found out what mother meant by amusement. But I could never bring my understanding into line with my discovery.

Too I often heard people mocking father for shifting his interests to gambling, away from the various areas of nationalist endeavor. I never said anything. But because of the strong influence of mother's **ethical**[24] teachings I knew, childishly, how offensive they thought gambling was. I never told her until one day she asked "Have you seen your father anywhere?"

It was late afternoon. I knew father had not come home.

"I saw him . . ."

"Find him. Tell him I asked him to come home."

I found him over his cards. When he saw me coming his expression muddied. But, despite that, I told him mother wanted him to come home. He said, "I'll come in a little while."

Shortly after I arrived home he came. Mother did not say much. Nor did he. At night he read a Dutch book. I don't know what it was about. And as I went to sleep I heard mother say to him, "You've comforted your grief long enough now."

I didn't hear his answer. Two days and nights passed peacefully. Father went nowhere. He came home from school each day. But he was restless. And then, quite suddenly, he went out. Mother saw him go and said nothing. And when he came home from school and again went out, she let him go. Until one day: "He's been gone four days," mother said from her bed.

I saw an expression of despair pass across her face. And I answered "yes."

"Find a pen and some paper," she ordered.

She wrote, finding it difficult to use the words she wanted. Wrote briefly. Then handed the short letter to me silently and returned to her bed.

"For father?" I asked nervously.

For a long time she said nothing. I watched her anxiously. Finally she nodded. I went. I searched for hours but couldn't find him. The places he usually played in were empty. And each time I went to one of the houses where he played, I was smartly told, "Your father's not here."

"Do you know where he is, please?"

"Perhaps at So-and-so's house."

I went to So-and-so's house. He wasn't there either. I walked around the town for four or five hours. Without success. And,

---

[24] **ethical**—relating to morals.

remembering how mother had looked, I didn't dare return home. Despondently I sat under a tamarind tree at the edge of the street. I thought of sad things. Very sad things! I don't know why. The confiscation of his books, the failure of the bank, the dwindling number of students, the duplicator sitting useless, the typewriters silent, the schoolyard overgrown with weeds. And the co-operative store at the edge of the city, which I had often visited with him, now closed down. I thought of these. Then the trial plantation in front of our house, which had to be sold to meet the bank's debts and now belonged to the government.

I thought of that. Suddenly I thought of how he looked and the moustache and beard he shaved so seldom recently. They made him look much older. An uncomprehending but deep feeling of despair swept over me. I rested against the tree, and took out the letter. I was afraid to read it, but my curiosity to know anything and everything overcame my fear. So I read it:

> Have you no thought for the child in my womb? Honor him by devoting yourself to Almighty God, so that the child may grow to be wise and virtuous.
>
> Come home.
>
> If you don't want to come home when you get this letter, pray that I die and take your unborn child with me to the grave.

The letter had no date and no signature. The force of the words was sufficient to drive me to tears. I put the letter back in my trouser pocket, quickly. My dreams returned, more beautiful than ever. The faces suddenly grew dark. Hope vanished, from the land, sea and sky, from other people, from myself.

The letter forced me to get up again and find father. Eventually I found him on the back verandah[25] of a Chinese house. As usual when he was asked to come he looked annoyed. But he took the letter, and read it. Then he said "I'll be home soon," a formula which always made me feel better.

Actually he was always home soon after me. He did not go at once to mother but talked with the children instead. He spoke louder than usual, it seemed to me, so that she would hear him. I don't know what happened between them but he stayed home after that. He helped us with our homework. A week passed.

Three men came. They chatted for ten to fifteen minutes. I prepared light refreshments for them. And as I carried them in, father and mother were talking in her room. I heard her slowly say, "This is the house where all my children except the first were born. I don't care—I don't want it turned into a gambling den. You must think of your children."

I still remember: it was two o'clock. And afterwards he and his guests went to another of our houses, four hundred meters to the north of our residence. It was

---

[25] verandah—porch.

the first time she had never received his guests. What really surprised me was the way that as soon as father and his guests had left, she got quickly out of bed and ordered the oldest adopted child to buy six loaves of bread.

She went skittishly to the kitchen and made a bread-pudding. She forbade the servant to help. She put in a lot of cinnamon so that it would be sweet. Towards twilight, about six o'clock, four of my brothers and I took it to the men. Father was at first surprised to see so much food but then shouted with pleasure: "Well! Pudding, how nice."

And the guests all laughed, although the white cards were more important than food. They shifted their eyes from their cards to the food and then to the host and shouted with more attention to politeness than was necessary: "How nice."

We went home, not saying a word the whole way.

7

Once, unexpectedly, the weaver came to see mother. I met her too.

"No-one's buying *lurik* anymore," she said. "Everyone wanted it before. Now no-one does. In fact the only ones who want it are the people in villages and they don't have any money. Wouldn't you like to buy some?"

Mother had gently to say "no": she still had a lot in her cupboards. The woman sighed. She continued: "My neighbor's sandal factory has folded up completely. He's left town to go and be a coolie in the city. And laborers aren't very well off—they're worse than my family."

"I'm afraid *swadesi* is over," mother explained sadly and hollowly. As she spoke her eyes glazed. She used to like talking to villagers. Now she didn't.

The weaver tiredly returned across the river to her village.

No-one spoke very much of *swadesi* anymore. Times had changed. The villagers were sorry that they had put their money into co-operatives and lost the lot. The *swadesi* fever had retreated and vanished. The town returned to its usual quiet ways. Civil servants no longer played out great dramas of nationalism in their heads. They forced themselves back into their routine: going to work, staying in the office for a set period, going home, playing with their wives, sleeping; getting up in the morning again—for a while.

Gambling took over from *swadesi*. Gambling! Gambling! Even small children with two or five cent pieces a day gambled. Cock fighting gained new life and spread rapidly. It was announced in the villages that the government had fifty **vacancies**[26] for policemen and young men fought for the positions. Other news told of large numbers of men being arrested for gambling, cock fighting, robbery and murder.

Both the duplicators and all the typewriters were put in boxes. Mother explained: "They have to go back to the shop because father can't keep up the payments."

---

[26] **vacancies**—empty positions or spaces.

And a few days later men came and took away our furniture. I asked mother where they were taking it but she only shook her head. I fell silent, but later learned that they had been taken by a man to whom father was in debt. At night she called us and ordered one of us to go and find him. I had to do the cooking with the servant. Two hours later the search for father was declared unsuccessful.

That night the fourth child was safely born: a boy! It screamed lustily.

The next morning, as the sun bathed the earth in its glow, I went to mother's room to see my new brother and to kiss him—the child who was my blood-brother forever. Mother greeted me with a smile. My brother slept on. All signs of suffering were gone from mother's face. At that moment father came, and walked straight into her room. He shouted happily: "It's a boy! He'll be bigger than either of us."

And mother greeted him hollowly, tiredly, forcing herself to speak, full of pride: "He'll get nothing from you. Or from here. Or from this particular cycle of time. He'll do it all by himself."

I left.

8

And with the birth of my brother, *swadesi* breathed its last and left, never to be spoken of again by those it had destroyed. So did the co-operatives and the literacy campaign. And cock fighting and thieving, robbery and murder retreated to the outskirts of the region, to return to the center occasionally. Ten new policemen were taken on.

Finally everything returned to the way it had been before. Blora was quiet and peaceful. And then the age of the rising sun, slowly advancing, sometimes startling, began to penetrate the darkness of the night.

And life went on as usual.

QUESTIONS TO CONSIDER

1. From whose point of view is this story told? How does this point of view color the story?

2. Why do the villagers take up *swadesi?* Why does the movement end?

3. Why does the father take to gambling? What do you think he is going to do at the end of the story?

Ah Bah's Money

CATHERINE LIM

Catherine Lim (1942–   ) was born on the Malay peninsula in what is now Malaysia when it was still a British colony. The colony became an independent country in 1957, but terrorism and violence plagued the multiethnic population. In 1965, the island city of Singapore peacefully seceded. Malaysia is dominated by its Malay majority, while Singapore has almost equal Chinese and Malay populations. When Singapore became independent, Catherine Lim, like many Malaysians of Chinese heritage, chose to live there. In the 1970s, Lim established herself as one of Singapore's most important writers, focusing on the events and ironies of daily life in the economically powerful city. "Ah Bah's Money" is a story about a child growing up, but it is also a commentary on life in Singapore, a city dominated by business and monetary success.

Ah Bah's money, in 2 one-dollar notes and an assortment of coins, lay in a pile on the old handkerchief, but Ah Bah was reluctant to pull up the corners into a bundle to put inside the cigarette tin. Ah Bah was reluctant because the sight of his money gave him so much pleasure. He had already done the following things with his money: spread out the notes and ranged[1] the coins in a row beside them, stacked up the coins according to their denominations,[2] stacked up the coins to make each stack come to a dollar. But still he wanted to go on touching his money. He could tell exactly which coin came from whom or where. The twenty-cent coin with the greenish stain on the edge was given to him by Ah Lam Soh, who was opening her purse when the coin dropped out and he picked it up for her.

"You may keep it," she said, and thereafter Ah Bah watched closely every time Ah Lam Soh opened her purse or put her hand into her blouse pocket. The ten-cent coin, which had a better shine than all the rest, he had actually found near a rubbish dump, almost hidden from sight by an old slipper. And the largest coin of all, the fifty-cent coin, he had earned. He was still rather puzzled about why Kim Heok Soh had given him so much money; he had been required merely to stand in the front portion of the house and to say to any visitor, "Kim Heok Soh has gone to the dry goods shop and will not be back till an hour later. She has asked

---

[1] ranged—lined up.
[2] denominations—values, sizes, or units.

me to take care of her house for her." But all the time Kim Heok Soh was in the house; he knew because he could hear her in the room and there was somebody with her.

He counted his money—five dollars and eighty-five cents, and his heart glowed. Very carefully, he pulled up the corners of the hankerchief at last into a tight bundle which he then put inside the cigarette tin. Then he put the cover on firmly, and his money, now safe and secure, was ready to go back into its hiding place in a corner of the cupboard behind the stacks of old clothes, newspapers and calendars.

And now Ah Bah became uneasy, and he watched to see if his father's eyes would rest on the old broken-down cupboard that held his treasure, for once his father had found his money—two dollars in twenty- and ten-cent coins—tied up in a piece of rag and hidden under his pillow, and had taken it away for another bottle of beer. His father drank beer almost every night. Sometimes he was in a good mood after his beer and he would talk endlessly about this or that, smiling to himself. But generally he became **sullen**[3] and bad-tempered, and he would begin shouting at anyone who came near. Once he threw an empty beer bottle at Ah Bah's mother; it missed her head and went crashing against the wall. Ah Bah was terrified of his father, but his mother appeared **indifferent**.[4] "The lunatic," she would say, but never in his hearing. Whenever he was not at home, she would slip out and play cards in Ah Lam Soh's house. One evening she returned, flushed with excitement and gave him fifty

cents; she said it had been her lucky day. At other times she came back with a **dispirited**[5] look, and Ah Bah knew she had lost all her money in Ah Lam Soh's house.

The New Year was coming and Ah Bah looked forward to it with an intensity that he could barely conceal. New Year meant *ang pows*;[6] Ah Bah's thin little fingers closed round the red packets of money given him by the New Year visitors with such energy that his mother would scold him and shake her head in **doleful**[7] apology, as she remarked loudly to the visitors, "My Ah Bah, he feels no shame whatever!"

His forefinger and thumb feeling expertly through the red paper, Ah Bah could tell immediately how much was in the red packet; his heart would sink a little if the fingers felt the hard edges of coins, for that would be forty cents or eighty cents at most. But if nothing was felt, then joy of joys! Here was at least a dollar inside.

This year Ah Bah had *eight* dollar notes. He could hardly believe it when he took stock of his wealth on the last day of the festive season. Eight new notes, crisp, still smelling new, and showing no creases except where they had been folded to go into the red packets. Eight dollars! And a small pile of coins besides. Ah Bah experienced a thrill such as he had never felt before.

---

[3] **sullen**—brooding, moody.

[4] **indifferent**—having no interest in or sympathy for.

[5] **dispirited**—discouraged.

[6] *ang pows*—little red envelopes of money given to children to celebrate the new year.

[7] **doleful**—sad, joyless.

And then it was all anxiety and fear, for he realized that his father knew about his *ang pow* money; indeed his father had referred to it once or twice, and would, Ah Bah was certain, be searching the bedding, cupboard and other places in the house for it.

Ah Bah's heart beat with the violence of angry **defiance**[8] at the thought. The total amount in his cigarette tin was now seventeen dollars and twenty-five cents, and Ah Bah was determined to protect his money at all costs. Nobody was going to take his money from him. Frantically, Ah Bah went to the cupboard, took out the bundle of money from the cigarette tin and stuffed it into his trouser pocket. It made a **conspicuous**[9] bulge. Ah Bah didn't know what to do, and his little mind worked feverishly to find a way out of this very **direful**[10] situation.

He was wandering about in the village the next day as usual, and when he returned home, he was crying bitterly. His pocket was empty. When his mother came to him and asked him what the matter was, he bawled. He told her, between sobs, that a rough-looking Indian had pushed him to the ground and taken away his money. His father who was in the bedroom rushed out, and made Ah Bah tell again what had happened. When Ah Bah had finished, sniffling miserably, his father hit him on the head, snarling, "You idiot! Why were you so anxious to show off your *ang pow* money? Now you've lost it all!" And when he was told that the sum was seventeen dollars and twenty-five cents, his **vexation**[11] was extreme, so that he would not be contented till he had hit the boy again.

Ah Bah's mother cleaned the bruise on the side of his face where he had been pushed to the ground, and led him away from his father.

"You are a silly boy," she **scolded**.[12] "Why did you carry so much money around with you? Someone was sure to rob you!" And feeling sorry for him, she felt about in her blouse pocket and found she could spare fifty cents, so she gave it to him, saying, "Next time, don't be so silly, son."

He took the coin from her, and he was deeply moved. And then, upon impulse, he took her by the hand, and led her outside their house to the old hen-house, near the well, under the trees, and he whispered to her, his heart almost bursting with the excitement of a **portentous**[13] secret successfully kept, "It's there! In the cigarette tin, behind that piece of wood!" To prove it, he squeezed into the hen house and soon emerged, reeking of hen-house odors, triumphantly clutching the tin. He took off the lid and showed her the money inside.

She was all amazement. Then she began to laugh and to shake her head over the ingenuity of it all, while he stood looking up at her, his eyes bright and bold with victory.

"You're a clever boy," she said, "but take care that you don't go near the hen house often. Your father's pocket is empty

---

[8] **defiance**—open disobedience or resistance.

[9] **conspicuous**—clearly visible, obvious.

[10] **direful**—terrible, awful.

[11] **vexation**—irritation, distress, or anger.

[12] **scolded**—lectured.

[13] portentous—important, as a good omen.

again, and he's looking around to see whose money he can get hold of, that devil."

Ah Bah earned twenty cents helping Ah Lau Sim to scrape coconut, and his mother allowed him to have the ten cents which he found on a shelf, under a comb. Clutching his money, he stole out of the house; he was just in time to back out of the hen house, straighten himself and pretend to be looking for dried twigs for firewood for his father stood at the doorway, looking at him. His father was in a restless mood again, pacing the floor with a dark look on his face, and this was the sign that he wanted his beer very badly but had no money to pay for it. Ah Bah bent low, **assiduously**[14] looking for firewood, and then through the corner of his eye, he saw his father go back into house.

That night Ah Bah dreamt that his father had found out the hiding place in the hen house, and early next morning, his heart beating wildly, he stole out and went straight to the hen house. He felt about in the darkness for his cigarette tin; his hand touched the damp of the hen droppings and caught on a nail, and still he searched— but the cigarette tin was not there.

He ran sniffling to his mother, and she began to scold him, "I told you not to go there too often, but you wouldn't listen to me. Didn't you know your father has been asking for money? The devil's found you out again."

The boy continued to sniff, his little heart aching with the terrible pain of the loss.

"Never mind," his mother said, "you be a good boy and don't say anything about it; otherwise your father's sure to rage like a mad man." She led him inside the house and gave him a slice of bread with some sugar.

She was glad when he quieted down at last, for she didn't want to keep Ah Lam Soh and the others waiting. The seventeen dollars and twenty-five cents (she had hurriedly hidden the handkerchief and the cigarette tin) was secure in her blouse pocket, and she slipped away with eager steps for, as the fortune teller had told her, this was the beginning of a period of good luck for her.

---

[14] **assiduously**—carefully and persistently.

QUESTIONS TO CONSIDER

1. How would you compare and contrast Ah Bah's parents? Which is the more sympathetic character? Explain why.

2. Why does Ah Bah confide in his mother?

3. What defines his life to Ah Bah? Do you think this is a good, a bad, or an indifferent thing?

4. If "Ah Bah's Money" is a metaphor for life in Singapore, what do you think is the message Lim wants to get across?

Cambodia: Back to Sierra Leone?

ROBERT D. KAPLAN

Robert D. Kaplan is a journalist who has made a career out of covering the war- and poverty-torn parts of the world. The following essay is from his book The Ends of the Earth, *which chronicled a journey through the developing parts of the world as the twenty-first century arrived. This essay describes the tragedies that have plagued Cambodia and seem likely to haunt it in the new millennium.*

In the picture gallery of twentieth-century horrors, Cambodia is a consummate icon:[1] its towering sugar palms, green paddy fields, and dark monsoon[2] clouds racked by the violent forces of communist ideology and class warfare, colonialism and anticolonialism, and the utopian ideals of the French intellectual left, stretched out of all proportion by a peculiarly Asian tendency for literalness and chilling abstraction. Between 1975 and 1979, the result of these forces was one of history's great holocausts. Under the communist regime of "Democratic Kampuchea," between 1 and 1.5 million Cambodians out of a population of 8 million were shot, **bludgeoned**,[3] starved, or worked to death, or died of disease, in the most intense and awful attempt at social transformation history has ever recorded.

It was also the mass murder that will prove hardest to explain to future generations. In 1959, a Cambodian exchange student at the Sorbonne[4] in Paris, Khieu Samphan, argued in a doctoral thesis that cities and towns were inhabited by "parasites" and should, therefore, be emptied out by "mass transfer" in order to stimulate agricultural growth, since the "parasites" could be used for farm labor. Crackpot doctoral dissertations are nothing unusual, especially those by third world peasants who go directly from their villages to the Left Bank of the Seine and, without any

---

[1] consummate icon—a perfect symbol.
[2] monsoon—rainy season.
[3] **bludgeoned**—beaten with clubs.
[4] Sorbonne—France's greatest university.

intellectual underpinnings, begin imbibing[5] Marxist economic theory. But who would expect that such a thesis would actually be carried out?

Samphan was part of a **coterie**[6] of Cambodians, born in the 1920s and 1930s, who studied at the Sorbonne. Their leader was one Saloth Sar, born in 1928, the son of a well-off landowner. He would later call himself Pol Pot. These students converted to Marxism-Leninism, went back to the rural countryside of Cambodia in the early 1960s and began a movement to be known as the Khmer Rouge, or Red Khmers. According to one version, it was King Norodom Sihanouk, the dilettantish[7] Cambodian leader, who first used the term Khmer Rouge, almost as a term of endearment.

The Cambodian countryside to which these French-educated radicals returned was different from the rest of Indochina. Ever since 1431, when the Thais captured the medieval Khmer capital of Angkor in northwestern Cambodia, Khmer fortunes have been in gradual decline. Angkor's great sandstone temples, or "wats," had been reclaimed by the jungle: rediscovered by French colonialists only in the nineteenth century. For hundreds of years, Cambodia was a weak and enticing chunk of real estate wedged between the stronger states of Thailand and Vietnam: sparsely populated yet easily accessible, and *rich*, with alluvial[8] soil and the Tonle Sap, or "Great Lake," the richest freshwater fishing zone in the world. In the nineteenth century,

Thailand and Vietnam fought for influence in Cambodia, and had the French not established their protectorate in 1863, Cambodia east of the Mekong River may well have become part of Vietnam, just as Cambodia west of the Mekong may have become part of Thailand. Rather than fortify Cambodian nationhood, however, the French added to Khmer feelings of inferiority by favoring the Vietnamese. The French strengthened Vietnamese bureaucratic institutions rather than build Cambodian ones, and shipped Cambodian raw materials to Vietnam. When the French departed in 1954, Thailand and South Vietnam, now aligned with the United States, renewed their historic ambitions against Cambodia for which their anticommunist ideology was mere **pretext**.[9] Prince Sihanouk's response was neutralism, which would earn only the disdain of the West and its allies, and of the Khmer Rouge as well.

Once in the forest, the Khmer Rouge were prone to several extremely powerful psychological undercurrents that rather than soften their ideological certainties only intensified them. For one thing, there was the Khmer warrior tradition, evinced by the hideous violence of the battle scenes carved in relief upon the hundreds of temples at Angkor. The Khmer Rouge

---

[5] imbibing—absorbing.

[6] **coterie**—an exclusive social group sharing similar interests.

[7] dilettantish—unserious, playful, amateurish.

[8] alluvial—relating to a flood plain.

[9] **pretext**—a reason or an excuse.

mentality did not emerge from a vacuum. Barbarity had been a constant in Cambodia. During the 1970–75 civil war that had preceded the Khmer Rouge takeover, two members of the legislature were killed and their livers publicly eaten by an angry crowd. During the five years of fighting before the Khmer Rouge victory, a half million Cambodians, mainly civilians, were killed. Abetting this violent streak was a deliberate Khmer Rouge policy of recruiting young teenagers and children as young as ten or twelve as fighters and cadres. Khmer Rouge leaders thus created an army whose troops had yet to be fully "socialized."

It was an army of children without a trace of compassion. These heavily armed youngsters rarely left the forest. They knew nothing of an outside world except what their leaders told them: a world that had exploited the countryside and was synonymous with foreign imperialists. Truly, nowhere else in Indochina has there been such a divide between town and country as in Cambodia, where forests are dense and towns, especially the capital city of Phnom Penh, are laid out in a grid pattern of streets marked by colonial-style European architecture.

In Khmer Rouge minds, these towns and cities were populated not by fellow Cambodians but by "parasites" and "enemies," like the Vietnamese immigrant community, members of a group that throughout history had exploited Cambodia. Helping the southern Vietnamese were the French colonialists and the urban parasites, and in recent years the American imperialists.

While the kids with the AK-47 assault rifles were learning how to hate and kill such enemies, the top **echelon**[10] of Khmer Rouge leadership was also ensconced in the jungle, developing models of abstract purity for the revolution to come. These models derived from several sources, including the terror regime of the French Revolution,[11] the collectivization[12] of agriculture as practiced under Stalin,[13] the "total mobilization" of the population as it was carried out in 1950s China during the Great Leap Forward,[14] the unrestrained class warfare of Mao's Great Cultural Revolution,[15] and the self-reliance of communist North Korea. Former U.S. diplomat and Cambodian specialist David P. Chandler writes in *The Tragedy of Cambodian History: Politics, War and Revolution since 1945* that "the literalness and speed with which these models were" later to be "followed made them especially destructive." Just as the encroaching forest had engulfed the great monuments of civilization at Angkor,

---

[10] **echelon**—level or rank.

[11] French Revolution—the events in 1789 that toppled the French monarchy. In the 1790s, France collapsed into a period of terror, which ended when Napoleon gained power.

[12] collectivization—organization of ownership and responsibilities for the benefit of all.

[13] Stalin, Josef—(1879–1953) leader who presided over the Soviet Union during its most repressive period.

[14] Great Leap Forward—an economic policy in China from 1957–1960. It attempted to industrialize and collectivize all parts of the Chinese economy but instead led to mass starvation.

[15] Great Cultural Revolution—the period from 1966–1976 in China when teachers and intellectuals were targeted as enemies of the state. It was a period of great repression and violence.

the armed teenagers from the forest—foot soldiers of Sorbonne ideologues—were to trample down the civilization of Cambodian cities.

The top leadership of the Khmer Rouge didn't even use noms de guerre.[16] They sometimes referred to themselves as "Brother Number One" or "Brother Ninety-nine." Actual names were considered bourgeois extravagances. But such realizations about the Khmer Rouge are mainly after-the-fact wisdom. As the Khmer Rouge capture of Phnom Penh approached in 1975, these details either weren't known in the West or were ignored. Author William Shawcross contends that in Washington, the Khmer Rouge were assumed to be merely another band of communists, like those in Vietnam, and that such **idiosyncracies**[17] as the ethnic hatred with which the Khmer Rouge looked toward the North Vietnamese communists were discounted. The clumsiness of Nixon's policy[18] was evinced by its secret bombing of Cambodia in 1969, followed by more bombing in 1973. As the B-52s wasted the Cambodian countryside, they only drove more and more furious peasants into the arms of the Khmer Rouge, while the Khmer Rouge itself intensified its hatred of the West and urban Cambodians. Nixon and Kissinger's apparent ignorance of Cambodia and the Khmer Rouge was a foreign policy disaster with few parallels in modern history.

The weeks preceding the collapse of the pro-American regime of Marshal Lon Nol in Phnom Penh in 1975 were to be burned not only into historical memory,

but into literary memory as well: a result of the enormity of what happened immediately after the Khmer Rouge arrived in the capital, and of the Westerners who happened to witness it, including the British poet James Fenton and Sidney Schanberg of *The New York Times*, whose reports of the horror have become classics.

Not Stalingrad, not Hiroshima, never before had a city been so completely emptied of its inhabitants.

APRIL 17, 1975, Day One of the Year Zero by Khmer Rouge reckoning, was the day that the Khmer Rouge occupied Phnom Penh and a Khmer Rouge government spokesman proudly annnounced that "more than two thousand years" of Cambodian history had come to an end. In a matter of hours, prodded by heavily armed Khmer Rouge soldiers, often in black pajamas and red-checkered kerchiefs, many of them hardly more than children, the inhabitants of Cambodia's capital were marched out of the city in a broad river of humanity. Not Stalingrad,[19] not Hiroshima,[20] never before had a city been

---

[16] noms de guerre—French for "war names," specifically the names taken by guerrillas to hide their real identities.

[17] **idiosyncracies**—individual or unique traits.

[18] Nixon's policy—Richard M. Nixon was U.S. president from 1969 to 1974. Henry Kissinger served as his secretary of state from 1973 on.

[19] Stalingrad—the site of a massive battle in 1942–1943 between the German and Russian armies. The city was mostly destroyed in street fighting.

[20] Hiroshima, Japan—the first city struck by an atomic bomb.

so completely emptied of its inhabitants. Within two weeks, Phnom Penh and several other major cities were empty: several million Cambodians had been forcibly evicted to the countryside. Concerning a second evacuation later that year, from the rural southwest of Cambodia to the northwest, diplomat Chandler says:

"The image of tens of thousands of people jammed upright into trucks and slow-moving freight cars, making their way through an empty landscape toward an uncertain but **ominous**[21] future, hauntingly echoes the Jewish experience in World War II. There was an important difference, however: in Cambodia the oppressors had the same nationality and (until shortly before the evacuations) the same religion as the oppressed."

This, after all, is the point where all explanations become inadequate, where the madness of twentieth-century ideology takes over. By Cambodian standards, even Rwanda, where one ethnic group, the Hutus, killed hundreds of thousands of members of another ethnic group, the Tutsis, seemed almost comprehensible, for in many instances the opposing sides had at least some distinct physical characteristics. But in Cambodia, "base people" killed "April 17 people": base people being those Cambodians who were rural, and April 17 people being those Cambodians who moved from the cities to the countryside only on April 17, 1975, when the mass transfers began. The base people showed no mercy, for in the minds of the Khmer Rouge leadership, the April 17 people—

women, children, and babies, too—were simply the slag[22] of history.

History, according to the plan of the Khmer Rouge, now had to be propelled forward. Besides the evacuation of cities and towns, money was abolished. So were mail delivery and all forms of formal education, such as public schools and universities. All newspapers were shut down. The Buddhist religion was prohibited. Everyone was made to wear a peasant costume, and all meals, henceforth, had to be eaten in "collective" groups. "As in Thomas More's *Utopia*,[23] strict rules for behavior (clothing, haircuts, vocabulary . . .) were laid down," writes Chandler. Anyone with post-secondary school education was marked for execution. Because the Khmer Rouge forest children thought that all people who wore glasses were intellectuals, glasses were as deadly as the yellow star[24] in Nazi Germany. Ninety percent of the country's medical doctors were murdered between 1975 and 1979. Babies were bashed to death against trees.

Chandler writes that under the Khmer Rouge, "Cambodia soon became a gigantic prison farm." Many thousands, perhaps more, of the 1 to 1.5 million casualties of the Khmer Rouge regime were executed by having their heads smashed in with hoes

---

[21] **ominous**—threatening, disastrous, or difficult.

[22] slag—waste material after a metal has been extracted.

[23] Thomas More's *Utopia*—the 1516 book that describes an ideal state.

[24] yellow star—all Jews in Nazi Germany had to wear a yellow star to indicate their "inferior" status.

and shovels, since ammunition had to be hoarded for fighting fellow communists across the border, whose crime was that they were Vietnamese. (The murder of an estimated two hundred thousand Vietnamese civilians, who had lived peacefully in Cambodia for generations— but who represented in Khmer Rouge minds a potential fifth column[25]—was at least one Khmer Rouge **atrocity**[26] that made some "sense," since it had racial **connotations**[27] and thus is no more inexplicable than what would later occur in Rwanda.)

Regarding the Cambodian deaths, though, the most extraordinary thing was that the top echelon of the Khmer Rouge— isolated within their Marxist abstractions— never intended them to happen. Pol Pot, Khieu Samphan, and the others actually thought that their plan of rapid social transformation would provide a better material life for most Cambodians without the need for killing anyone. "When their program failed," writes Chandler, "the leaders were confused. . . ." The brutality had gotten out of hand. Perhaps the problem was a flaw in Khieu Samphan's doctoral thesis?

Fighting between Cambodian and Vietnamese communists in the late 1970s flared into open war that ended in January 1979, when the Vietnamese marched into Phnom Penh and the Khmer Rouge fled into the forests. Next came famine in Cambodia, which led to an international relief effort. However, because the Vietnamese communists were allied with the Soviet Union, throughout the 1980s the United States and its ally, Thailand backed—of all groups—the Khmer Rouge, who were armed by China and were now fighting the Vietnamese occupation authorities.

With the end of the Cold War, the United Nations organized a national reconciliation process, which involved twenty-two thousand UN troops and cost $2 billion, the biggest UN operation in history. The reconciliation process was capped by elections held in May 1993, which the UN, with much fanfare, declared a success. What happens in Cambodia hereafter will say much about the long-term value of such UN operations. Cambodia's future will be crucial to any historical reckoning of the UN.

Less than an hour after leaving Bangkok's modern airport, I saw through the plane window a succession of red laterite[28] roads, corrugated-iron roofs glinting in the sunlight, and intense tropical greenery. From the air Thailand had looked like a manicured lawn. Cambodia was a weedy garden. The ragged landscape indicated a poor country, as did the absence of both paving and traffic on the country roads. The fact that I had to fly into Cambodia was another bad sign. Phnom Penh is no further from Bangkok than Nong Khai, which is easily reached by train

---

[25] fifth column—people of a country who aid an invader.

[26] **atrocity**—evil or cruel act.

[27] **connotations**—implied meanings.

[28] laterite—red or yellow clay that is used for making roads in tropical climates.

or bus. Phnom Penh isn't, since the Khmer Rouge still controlled the border areas on the Cambodian side.

From the vantage point of Thailand, everything that I had recently heard about Cambodia seemed unreal. Thailand was booming economically, Laos was full of promise, and Vietnam was about to emerge as a dynamic oil-producing power of the early twenty-first century. Yet Cambodia was said to be back-breakingly poor, politically unstable, and dangerous, not unlike the West African countries I had visited. But wasn't I in prosperity-bound Southeast Asia?

On July 26, 1994, a few months before my trip, three Western backpackers—a Briton, a Frenchman, and an Australian— were kidnapped by Khmer Rouge guerrillas only about seventy miles south of the capital of Phnom Penh, where the Khmer Rouge ambushed the train the three were traveling in. In November 1994, while I was in Cambodia, I would read a Reuters dispatch describing the eventual murder of the backpackers by the Khmer Rouge, the recovery of the victims' bodies, and the autopsies that followed. The dispatch said:

> They were bound. The three died
> from massive head injuries. . . .
> The method of execution bore
> all the hallmarks of a classic
> "Killing Fields"-style murder—
> a blow from a hoe to the back
> of the head.

In addition, *The Cambodia Daily* of November 4–6, 1994, reported that the Khmer Rouge had murdered forty villagers in western Cambodia. Some were "bludgeoned and axed to death with hoes." Others were bound together in pairs and shot.

In 1994, the very existence of the Khmer Rouge seemed, like much else about Cambodia, absurd. The Cold War had ended. Vietnam was on the road to becoming a new vacation destination for Americans. Yet in Cambodia, the Khmer Rouge were still in the forest: It was as if the SS[29] were still roaming through Germany.

The landscape outside my plane window helped explain why. I had seen such landscapes before, when I flew into Guinea and Sierra Leone.[30] Show me a poor country with bad, potholed roads and, often enough, I'll show you a country with bandit soldiers or a guerrilla insurgency. Thailand was fifty minutes and a million miles away.

Graham Miller, the Cambodia office director of CARE, greeted me with a bear hug at plane-side. Graham and I were friends from the days of the 1984–85 Ethiopian famine and hadn't seen each other for years. A tall and bluff South Africa-born Australian, Graham had lived in eleven troubled third world countries and had worked in forty-three. A veteran geologist, his specialty was digging water wells in rural areas. He could just look at a

---

[29] SS—elite military unit of the Nazi Party that served as a security force during World War II.

[30] Guinea and Sierra Leone—countries in West Africa.

landscape and tell you how far down the water table was. Graham is what foreign affairs **sophisticates**[31] call an "expat" working for an "NGO (non-governmental organization)." In other words, he is an expatriate[32] employed by a private Western relief agency—in this case, C A R E. As human disasters multiply on account of ethnic wars, famines, the collapse of states, and refugee migrations, NGOs have filled the gap left vacant by Western governments and their militaries. Diplomats and journalists often rely on NGOs for their information as to what is going on in-country—that is, away from the capital city. Indeed, while the American public appears increasingly unwilling to put its soldiers at risk, it apparently thinks little of putting its relief volunteers—American "expats"—in extremely dangerous situations. Cambodia in 1994 had as many as ninety NGOs operating around the country, staffed by as many as one thousand expats, including Americans. With a population of under 10 million Cambodia may have had more resident expats and NGOs per capita than any other third world country. Cambodia is, thus, at the cutting edge of this little-mentioned but pivotal foreign policy evolution.

"Cambodia, mate, well, it's a bloody mess. But you never know. Here at the airport, for instance, they seem to be getting their act together." Without Graham's help, I stood quietly on line, purchased a visa for twenty dollars, and got my immigration stamp. There was a system, in other words. We jumped into Graham's four-wheel-drive vehicle for the twenty-minute drive to his house. Along the way, I stuck my head out the window while listening to Graham's briefing. This is what I saw and heard:

The air had that dense and dirty fish-tank quality of the poor and crowded tropics: garbage, stray dogs, and crying babies. I saw relatively few cars but encountered many motorbikes and rickety, rusted bicycle-rickshaws driven by men wearing wraparound sunglasses and baseball hats. Other men were rebuilding auto parts in stalls along the dusty streets. Yet it was "charming," in the heartbreaking sense in which that word is often applied to the underdeveloped world—with the usual banana groves, flame trees, and those old and scabby lemon-colored colonial buildings with rotting balconies. There were the water lilies floating in urban swamps, and little boys selling jasmine blossoms stuck into the ends of sugarcane sticks. Phnom Penh had something else besides, something particularly Cambodian, which I would learn to appreciate at Angkor: those mottled, weather-stained Buddhist temple buildings of autumnal stone, with fungus growing on the red tiles, which only seemed to

The air had that dense and dirty fish-tank quality of the poor and crowded tropics.

---

[31] **sophisticates**—knowledgeable people, experts.
[32] expatriate—someone who leaves his or her homeland and lives in a foreign country.

increase their preciousness. The somber facades[33] more evocative of medieval cloisters[34] in Europe than of the sun-splashed tropics, help give Cambodia a visual texture that other third world countries lack. It was my first intimation of Cambodia's specialness. I thought of what a relief worker had told author William Shawcross about Cambodia: "It had everything—temples, starving brown babies and an Asian Hitler figure [Pol Pot]—it was like sex on a tiger skin."

Phnom Penh is named after a hill, or *phnom* in Cambodian, topped by a Buddhist temple built by a woman named Penh. It had been a ghost town between 1975 and 1979. Then it came under Vietnamese occupation, and now was still coming back to life. The city's mood and character had yet to be buried beneath the high-rises that dominated Bangkok. The population had risen to 1–3 million because of recent migration from the countryside, but Phnom Penh is small compared to other Asia capitals, and has relatively little industry, a more crowded and sprawling version of Vientiane.[35]

It was the people that gripped my throat: those buttery, cocoa-brown faces blending Melanesian,[36] Indian, and Oriental features, and bearing an archetypal[37] forest-spirit quality, enhanced by eyes of such smiling brightness that each face was like a charity poster.

I also noticed many beggars and amputees in the streets.

"Ten million land mines, my friend," Graham informed me, "one for every person in the country. Cambodia has one of the highest per capita ratio of amputees in the world, maybe the highest. There are two hundred to three hundred injuries per month from mines. Legacy of the civil war and the Khmer Rouge war with the Vietnamese. The Western community here is operating some interesting de-mining programs you may want to look at. But the Khmer Rouge now re-mine in days what it takes us two to three months to de-mine. It costs the Khmer Rouge an average of one to four dollars to lay a mine. De-mining costs thousands . . .

"The city looks beautiful now, doesn't it?" Graham went on cheerily. "Last summer many of the streets were flooded. No drainage. By the way, I hope you brought lots of U.S. dollars in small denominations. The dollar's more or less the currency here. Credit cards are pretty useless. Not much of a financial or tax system in Cambodia. There's probably a lot of dirty drug money around, too. Army's a mess: 2,004 generals for an army of only 80,000. I've observed the soldiers quite a bit—they're drunk, bored, and underpaid. The government roadblocks outside Phnom Penh can be lethal. Peasants are as fearful of the soldiers as they are of the Khmer Rouge. That's the heart of the problem: the Khmer Rouge are weak and corrupt, but so is the government."

---

[33] facades—the faces or fronts of buildings.

[34] cloisters—monasteries or convents.

[35] Vientiane—the capital of Laos in southeast Asia.

[36] Melanesian—of or having to do with Melanesia, the Pacific islands just north of Australia.

[37] archetypal—primitive.

"What about disease?" I asked Graham.

"Cerebral malaria. But it's not like Africa, it only exists in isolated pockets deep in the bush. Though in Phnom Penh there's quite a bit of dengue fever, which is also carried by mosquitoes."

"What about river blindness—onchocerciasis, like in West Africa?"

"None here. But there's quite a bit of schistosomiasis—bilharzia—in the irrigation canals."

Graham pulled to a stop. My heart sank as he reached his hand down and retrieved a Club to lock onto his steering wheel. The Club is an anticar theft device familiar to those in American cities and crime-plagued suburbs. Seeing my questioning eyes, Graham explained, "No choice, mate. We've already had some vehicles stolen." He continued:

"Crime's high here. Lots of robberies, carjackings even. Our French neighbors were robbed at gunpoint; the six-year-old was shot. The thing about this place is, with a bandit, drunken army, too many people around here have guns." Two slightly menacing street urchins with baseball hats appeared out of nowhere. "I'll pay these boys to watch the car," Graham explained.

My melancholy intensified, and I could feel it in my belly. I was light-headed. It was not the fear of crime that I felt or the fear of disease, but the deeper writer's fear of having oversimplified something—in this case, the idea of culture, which now seemed like a greater mystery to me than it had at the beginning of my journey in West Africa. I had assumed that the random crime and other social chaos of West Africa were the result of an already-fragile cultural base, the lack in most places of a written language until this century, and geographical isolation from other major civilizations: It was now coming further undone as a consequence of high birthrates and urbanization. But here I was, in the heart of Buddhist-Confucian Southeast Asia, in a land where the written script was one thousand two hundred years old and every surrounding country was in some stage of impressive economic growth. Yet Cambodia was eerily similar to Sierra Leone: with random crime, mosquito-borne disease, a government army that was more like a mob, and a countryside that was ungovernable because of guerrilla insurgents. True, Cambodia's literacy rate was higher than Sierra Leone's: 35 percent compared to 21 percent. But so was the population growth rate; a shocking 4.4 percent, higher than anywhere in West Africa.

I know, I know. Nixon, Kissinger, and especially the Khmer Rouge had inflicted destruction upon Cambodia. It was in the crosshairs of twentieth-century ideological and superpower politics, while West Africa was an ideological and strategic backwater. Cambodia's plight could be blamed on outside forces to a degree that Sierra Leone's plight could not. Moreover, Cambodia might simply be the exception that proves the rule about Asian cultural vitality. But I doubted this.

After all, it was Cambodians who had killed 1.5 million other Cambodians, and they were still killing them: The murderers weren't Americans or Martians. To absolve Cambodian culture of responsibility is as illogical as to heap all the blame for what had happened on Henry Kissinger. Culture, I suspected, was still crucial to the question of why some states like Cambodia and Sierra Leone failed. Perhaps, to paraphrase Leo Tolstoy's remark about families—while all successful cultures share similar traits, unsuccessful ones fail in their own highly complex ways.[38]

Perhaps indigenous people like the Khmers are simply less dynamic than groups whose history has been marked by large-scale migration, like the Thais and Vietnamese. Perhaps the special problems of Cambodia had something to do with its dense forests, which, like Liberia's, **engendered**[39] isolation and suspicion. I didn't know. All I could do was poke around and use my **intuition**.[40] But to avoid the subject of culture as a determinant would be to avoid a principal cause for the difference in development patterns.

The issue of development is even more complex than I can describe, since the most extraneous event of the briefest duration in a country's history might have the most fundamental and long-term repercussions. For example:

Between 1948 and 1968, Cambodia's population more than doubled, from 3 million to 6.6 million; and by 1968 the Cambodian economy was a shambles. Agricultural production was **stagnant**[41] and the annual deficit amounted to an eighth of the entire budget. Sihanouk's

solution was to open government casinos in Phnom Penh and the port city of Sihanoukville, so that money spent on illegal gambling would be diverted to the national treasury. The casinos opened in early 1969 and operated twenty-four hours a day. Students, peasants, cyclo-drivers, soldiers, and officials lost their savings at the casinos as gambling fever gripped Phnom Penh and Sihanoukville. Still worse, Sihanouk's relatives were stealing most of the casino profits. The casinos closed in January 1970, shortly before Marshal Lon Nol toppled Sihanouk. Many Cambodians to this day believe that had Sihanouk not decided to open the casinos, he would not have been overthrown and the trajectory of Cambodian history, including the Khmer Rouge holocaust, would have been different. Who can say for sure?

Moreover, in early 1971 Lon Nol suffered a stroke. It was mild and he recovered quickly. But coming as it did after a Vietnamese communist commando attack on the airport that destroyed the Cambodian air force, news of the illness seriously convinced Cambodians that his rule was doomed. What if Lon Nol had not taken ill and what if the casinos never opened—would the Khmer Rouge still

---

[38] complex ways—In *Anna Karenina*, Tolstoy wrote that while happy families are all alike, unhappy ones are each unhappy in their own way.

[39] **engendered**—caused, brought about.

[40] **intuition**—knowledge without using reason or the senses.

[41] **stagnant**—inactive, motionless.

have come to power and wrought the havoc[42] that so damaged the local culture? No one knows.

I'm not suggesting, for instance, that the distress of a whole continent, like Africa, can be the result of a series of unlucky accidents like those mentioned above. On the other hand, the idea that the source of national success or failure can be discovered by scientific study, as many political scientists hope, struck me as absurd by the time I reached Cambodia.

For example, "controlled case comparisons" are the basis for much political science analysis. A researcher might select several cases of conflict around the world that are identical except for the one variable under study—scarcity of farmland, let's say. The political scientist could then, perhaps, draw conclusions about whether land scarcity causes upheaval. But this is nonsense! How can there be such a thing as "controlled case comparisons" when every single conflict around the world is different from every other one for a plethora[43] of complex cultural and accidental reasons, such as Sihanouk's flirtation with casinos? Human cultures aren't bacteriological ones—so many microbes[44] of this kind and so many microbes of that kind. A political scientist can do little more than what a journalist does: go to places where there appear to be interesting linkages between, say, land scarcity and violence, and see if causal[45]

relationships exist. From this, some useful ideas or theories might emerge. To call it science, though, is an overstatement.

"Manny, I want you to meet Robert, an old friend of mine from Africa," Graham announced.

"I'll stand you a beer, Robert," Manny replied. Manny was an ethnic Greek former Australian diplomat who had *stayed on* in Phnom Penh and opened a bar-restaurant. Manny's bar was the unofficial information clearinghouse for the expat and NGO community in Cambodia, the place where expats returning from the countryside fortified themselves with steaks and beer while trading war stories. Given that foreign diplomats in Phnom Penh got much of their information from relief workers, who had told their stories first to Manny, I figured Manny, who wore shorts and a loud Hawaiian-print shirt, was worth talking to.

"There's a lot of banditry and too many firearms," Manny said. "Many Cambodian generals have their own private militias in the countryside—like warlords, actually. In the government, everyone is trying to steal what they can, in case this whole UN-engineered democracy collapses. Gold's the thing, mate. Everybody who can is hoarding gold. The Vietnamese, Thais, Singaporeans

---

[42] **havoc**—widespread destruction, confusion, or disorder.

[43] **plethora**—an oversupply or excess.

[44] microbes—tiny organisms such as bacteria, viruses, or fungi.

[45] **causal**—relating to cause and effect.

are all in Phnom Penh buying up pieces of Cambodia. The place is ripe for plunder. Of course, much of what everybody will tell you—including what I'm telling you— has to be regarded as hearsay, conjecture. Outside of Phnom Penh, for instance, it's difficult to know what is happening."

One unassailable truth emerged from Manny's monologue: the fact that, like little Sierra Leone, Cambodia was "big." The smallest country in Southeast Asia in square mileage, Cambodia was the largest country in Southeast Asia in the danger and difficulty of land travel, and it was hard to know in advance what lurked in the countryside. Kampot was only eighty-eight miles south of Phnom Penh, on the Gulf of Siam, but trains to Kampot were periodically held up by both bandits and Khmer Rouge. The last Westerners to ride the train—the three backpackers—had been kidnapped and murdered. Kratie, upriver on the Mekong, was only one hundred miles to the northeast, but the "slow boat" there took more than a day and was sometimes shot at by Khmer Rouge hiding in the forested banks or was boarded and robbed by government soldiers. A "fast boat," however, took five and a half hours and was considered safe. The fast boat, privately operated by Singaporeans, was the only reliable link to the town from Phnom Penh. Nong Khai, by contrast, was three hundred miles north of Bangkok—or three times the distance between Phnom Penh and Kratie—but could be comfortably reached by train or bus, or by airplane and air-conditioned coach in a journey that took under two hours. Information about Nong Khai, complete with fax numbers of hotels and businesses there, was readily available in Bangkok, whereas news of Kampot and Kratie in Phnom Penh was sparse and laced with rumor.

Officially, Cambodian and Western observers in Phnom Penh said that the elected government controlled 80 percent of Cambodian territory, while the Khmer Rouge held the rest—mainly in the mountainous and heavily forested areas in the south near the Gulf of Siam, and in the west near the Thai border. But in 1994, the situation on the ground was less clear-cut. Of the area that the government controlled, only about half, or 40 percent of Cambodia's total land area, was assumed to be safe. The other half was safe during the day but overrun by Khmer Rouge patrols at night. Or it was safe during the dry season but was deserted by government troops when the rains started. John Holloway, Australia's former ambassador to Cambodia, reported that "during the . . . wet season, while the government forces are **marooned**[46] in their barracks playing cards, the Khmer Rouge will send out cadres on foot through the mud into remote villages to sit and talk with villagers and ascertain their needs. Sometimes these needs are for protection from government troops, in which case the Khmer Rouge cadre will return with weapons and mines . . ." Later, when I visited the northeast of the country, a German

---

[46] **marooned**—stranded or abandoned.

expat showed me a map of Cambodia and said, "Basically, wherever you see large tracts of thick forests, that's Khmer Rouge territory."

Three to four percent of Cambodia's old growth forests were being lost yearly to illegal hardwood logging. With the Cold War ended, the Khmer Rouge had begun to lose allies in the disintegrating Asian communist bloc. But they were gaining them among Thai, Malaysian, and Singaporean businessmen willing to pay in U.S. dollars for hardwood timber, which Khmer Rouge patrols escorted on heavy trucks out of the forest. The alliance between the Khmer Rouge and Thai generals and businessmen involved the transfer of lumber, gems, and even children for Bangkok sex markets: worth tens of millions of dollars per year. Hardwood logging in the Thai-Cambodian border region had led to massive soil erosion in the upper reaches of Cambodia's Tonle Sap, or Great Lake, and silted up parts of the lake where fish spawn. Not only was this critical freshwater fish reserve dying out, but as the Great Lake silted up, it closed off an exit valve for the lower reaches of the Mekong River. This increased the frequency of flooding in eastern Cambodia and in Vietnam's Mekong Delta. Cambodia's Great Lake region, which dominated the center of the country, was becoming a smaller version of the Amazon: a lawless netherworld of illegal logging and similar environmental devastation. Meanwhile, the Khmer Rouge were gradually transforming themselves from ideological warriors of the twentieth century to nihilistic road warriors of the twenty-first. "Just as it makes no sense to ask why people eat or what they sleep for," writes Martin van Creveld, an Israel-based military historian, "so fighting in many ways is not a means but an end." However elusive, that was one of the best explanations I could find for why the Khmer Rouge kept fighting.

In the middle of the last decade of the twentieth century, Cambodia was, like some other third world countries including Angola and Afghanistan, a land of internal exiles, land mines, disorder, and disease. According to Dr. Tea Phalla, a Cambodian government health expert, "2 million" of the country's 10 million inhabitants could die "directly or indirectly" from HIV infections in the future. The World Health Organization reports that "trends among blood donors suggest that Phnom Penh may experience an even larger HIV epidemic than has occurred in northern Thailand."

Perhaps the most telling and frightening aspect of recent Cambodian history, one that might be a **harbinger**[47] for other places in the twenty-first century, is its very lack of theme. Chandler refers to the successive collapse of "one-reign dynasties." There was the monarchial rule of King Sihanouk, then the military regime of Lon Nol, then the Marxist-Leninist "central committee" structure of the Khmer Rouge,

---

[47] **harbinger**—a person or thing that announces or signals the approach of another.

then Vietnamese occupation, and since 1993 a democratically elected coalition of royalists linked to Sihanouk and communists linked formerly to both the Vietnamese and the Khmer Rouge. The king, Lon Nol's military, and the Khmer Rouge all advertised a new and stable phase of Cambodian history. Would democracy fare any better than they had?

Graham had to stop at the market to run errands. As I looked around, I saw things that did not track with the negative image of Cambodia I had been developing. In the rickety shops made of scrap wood, corrugated iron, and cement were electric lights, air-conditioning units, photocopy machines, some computers and fax machines, and photographic development equipment. Electronic appliances everywhere looked clean and well maintained. Furthermore, as I learned, public electricity and water systems were fairly reliable. Many of these appliances were not being run off private generators as in West Africa and even Pakistan. Graham, who had run office operations in Sudan, Kenya, and Angola, told me that "people here maintain equipment better than in Africa." I checked this with other expats who had lived in both Southeast Asia and sub-Saharan Africa, and they agreed. In fact, the clean and well-lit shops in Phnom Penh were familiar to me: They looked like the shops run by the Lebanese and Syrian merchants in Freetown, Sierra Leone, and those of Indian merchants I had seen in East African cities during my visits in the 1980s. Then I recalled how much more

orderly the immigration procedure had been at Phnom Penh airport compared to airports in West Africa. Was Cambodia an unusual combination of efficiency and chaos? Was the ability to organize death camps and to repair a photocopy machine the result of a common cultural trait? Or was I now too protective of Africa? Were these well-functioning shops proof that even violent, chaotic Cambodia was about to pull steeply ahead of most places in sub-Saharan Africa?

Probably the biggest difference, though, between Cambodia and Sierra Leone was that whereas Sierra Leone was engulfed by the failed and semi-failed states of Liberia and Guinea, Cambodia **adjoined**[48] the two powerboat economies of Thailand and Vietnam, with tigers such as Malaysia and Singapore close by. As a result, Cambodian cities were being modernized even as Cambodia's natural resources were being plundered.

Inflation[49] had fallen from 100 to 30 percent between 1992 and 1994. And every day that the unwieldy coalition between royalists and communists (who weren't really communists) survived was a victory for the UN process and a defeat for the Khmer Rouge. A provincial governor in the northeast would tell me: "In people's minds, there are only two parties, that of the government and that of Pol Pot. The differences between royalists and

---

[48] **adjoined**—bordered.

[49] inflation—increase in prices and decrease in the value of money.

communists may seem big to us, but to the peasants they are increasingly seen as the same party."

There were two views about the UN in Cambodia. The first held that the much-trumpeted elections were "an expensive stunt" that got rave reviews while it happened but, like many attempts to "force history" in the third world, was gradually looking less worthwhile. It seemed **futile**[50] to impose an American-style election system on a country that had never known individual freedom and where a communications infrastructure barely existed. Democracy for Cambodia seemed an effort that should begin with economic development and the establishment of schools.

Instead, Cambodians, many of them illiterate, were exposed cold turkey to a Western election campaign.

I listened to stories about how the UN had moved in with an army of expensive vehicles and high-tech communications gear, and sent the Cambodian economy, especially the real estate market, into overdrive to meet the need for Western-style villas and restaurants. After the elections were over, the UN deserted and monthly rental rates for villas dropped from $3,700 back to $1,200. "It was an event, not a process," said one expat. "Had the UN spent $2 billion for roads, schools, and rural development rather than on an election, the Khmer Rouge would be weaker in rural Cambodia than they are now," said a second expat. A third said, "Elections should have come last, not first, in the process of regeneration." A number of Cambodians told me, "The UN, it came, now it's gone."

The other view held that as long as the democratic government survived, the UN elections would constitute a pivotal turn in Cambodian history, in which for the first time Cambodians experienced the dignity of voting in secrecy in a closed booth. And in the course of my journey beyond Phnom Penh, I would meet Cambodians who volunteered praise for the UN reconciliation process.

Graham packed up his wife, Elizabeth, and the three of us went for a meal at the Phnom Penh Foreign Correspondents' Club. It was the most alluring foreign journalists' club I had ever seen: a Somerset Maugham cliché-in-waiting[51] for a glossy magazine feature, composed of dark, varnished wood and bamboo, with wicker chairs, mustard-yellow walls, and Corinthian pilasters[52]—and, of course, the obligatory slow-moving fans. The club had an open-air bar, from which I could look out over the confluence[53] of the Mekong River and an egress[54] of the Great Lake. With no glass to separate us from the street below, I could enjoy Campari and soda with steak and

---

[50] **futile**—unproductive, worthless.

[51] Somerset Maugham cliché-in-waiting—Kaplan means the club resembles the settings of the fiction of Somerset Maugham (1876–1965), an English writer known for his stories about Englishmen in the tropics.

[52] pilasters—rectangular columns.

[53] confluence—joining of waterways.

[54] egress—outlet.

eggs while watching Cambodian children sift through the garbage a few feet away.

It occurred to me that rather than dissolve into poverty and chaos or be lifted into prosperity, Cambodia was moving in both directions simultaneously—with its powerful neighbors taking economic advantage of the chaos while helping to generate the prosperity. Either way, the region was looking more and more like a late-seventeenth-century French map of Indochina that I had purchased in Thailand, with the Mekong River valley as both an informal dividing line between Thai-dominated Cambodian lands and Vietnamese-dominated areas, as well as a major zone of settlement in its own right. In *The Warrior Heritage*, Seanglim Bit writes that until the arrival of the French in 1863, "the concept of nationhood was embodied in a cultural version of political geography. Cambodia was where Cambodian was spoken in the village. . . ." In an age of open borders, whether the UN process succeeded or failed, nationhood would probably return to something like that.

Graham took me to Tuol Sleng, a school in the heart of Phnom Penh that the Khmer Rouge had converted into a prison and torture facility after they emptied out the city. Experts estimate that between sixteen and twenty thousand persons passed through Tuol Sleng between 1976 and early 1979. Except for six known cases, none came out alive. After the Vietnamese liberated Phnom Penh and opened the prison to the public, comparisons between

Tuol Sleng and Auschwitz and Dachau were inescapable. Actually, as both Shawcross and Chandler are careful to note, the better comparison is between Tuol Sleng and Stalin's Lubyanka prison during the purges of the 1930s. Almost all the victims of Tuol Sleng were themselves Khmer Rouge, or relatives of Khmer Rouge, who fell afoul of party doctrine at a time when that doctrine, in addition to changing almost daily, was actually known only to a select and increasingly paranoiac inner circle that included Pol Pot and Khieu Samphan.

But Tuol Sleng was different from Auschwitz and Dachau in a more important way. Auschwitz and Dachau had been converted into museums. They had been sanitized by Western curators with heating and air-conditioning, polished-glass display cases, stage lighting, museum shops, and modern toilets for the visiting public. Tuol Sleng had gone through no such sterilization process. The display cases were crude. It was miserably hot. Rats scavenged in the hallways and wretched toilets. I saw dust balls, spiderwebs, and dried blood splattered on the peeling walls. For all I knew, the Khmer Rouge might have left yesterday. The building, with a wire net stretched over the balconies so that torture victims could not commit suicide, had literally been left as it was. The smells of human feces, human sweat, and dead flesh had been erased—that was the only difference. In such a setting, the sight of chains, fingernail and nipple pliers, and photographs of young women with swollen and blackened eyes achieve an effect that you do not find in Europe's particular hells.

In the courtyard, the gallows were next to a child's swing. I noticed a pile of split coconuts that reminded me of the pile of smashed skulls I had seen as I entered the building. I recalled reading about how a Bosnian Serb militia leader had taken a poor and illiterate farm boy and converted him into a genocidal monster by having the youth slaughter pigs over and over again. The difference between killing hogs and people had become, with practice, trivial.

Nine miles south of Phnom Penh was Choeng Ek, a Khmer Rouge extermination site where 129 mass graves holding 8,985 corpses of men, women, children, and infants had been unearthed. Choeng Ek was the original killing field from which the film got its name. The drive from Phnom Penh through flat paddy fields graced by swaying sugar palms was reminiscent of the film footage. Water buffaloes meandered over the grave pits. White water-lilies dotted nearby wetlands.

Two tomato-colored tour buses pulled up. One unloaded a group of Thais and the another a group of Greek tourists. The groups looked alike: prosperously middle-class, with expensive cameras, sunglasses, and "casual" clothes. Each group contained the usual one or two shouters, fifty-year-old men who acted like teenage boys. The shouters insisted on being photographed while holding one of the bleached human limbs lying about. Some of the Thais and Greeks appeared uncomfortable about this, and remained quiet. But by the time both tour buses departed, everyone was back in good cheer. This year Cambodia, next year Hawaii.

QUESTIONS TO CONSIDER

1. From reading Kaplan's essay, how would you describe a Cambodian? List as many traits as you can.

2. Why did the United States support the Khmer Rouge?

3. What was the controversy over the UN-sponsored elections in Cambodia? Do you think the UN was right?

4. What is the contrast between West Africa and Cambodia that Kaplan keeps exploring in his essay? What are his final thoughts on the subject?

Writers and Politics

▲

Isabel Allende

Shortly after the 1973 military coup in Chile that toppled the socialist government of her uncle Salvador Allende, Chilean writer Isabel Allende is shown listening to speeches at the International Conference for Solidarity with the People of Chile, held in Helsinki, Finland.

Pramoedya Ananta Toer

Indonesian writer Pramoedya Ananta Toer, shown here in his Jakarta home in 1986, first told his tales to his fellow-inmates during the 14 years he spent as a political prisoner. ▶

Mahmoud Darwish

Born in a village that was destroyed in 1947 at the beginning of the Arab-Israeli conflict, Palestinian poet Mahmoud Darwish was raised in Israel, joined the political opposition, and was imprisoned by the government. ▶

◄ Assia Djebar
Algerian writer Assia Djebar worked for the National Liberation Front, which staged a long, violent struggle to gain Algeria's independence from France.

Ghassan Kanafani
Growing up in exile in Lebanon, Palestinian writer Ghassan Kanafani devoted himself to documenting the plight of his people until he was killed by a car bomb in Beirut in July 1972. **▶**

▲

Feng Jicai

This 1986 photo shows Chinese writer Feng Jicai looking at letters he had received from many people in China reporting their experiences of the repression that took place during the period of the Cultural Revolution.

▲

Bei Dao

A leader of the pro-democracy movement in China, poet Bei Dao was out of the country when government troops massacred hundreds of protestors in Beijing's Tiananmen Square and has since lived in self-imposed exile in Scandanavia and the United States.

▲

Salman Rushdie

Indian-born writer Salman Rushdie was forced to go into hiding in 1989 when the Islamic fundamentalist government of Iran sentenced him to death for writings which they considered disrespectful of Muhammad.

Jamaica Kincaid

Jamaica Kincaid was born on the West Indian island of Antigua when it was still a British colony and has used her writing to expose the cultural damage of colonialism on subject peoples.

▼

Chapter 5

Canada and the Caribbean

Coming to Terms

Observing One's Life

 This painting of farmers trying to keep birds from eating their crops is by the Haitian artist Micius Stephane (1912–   ).

His Chosen Calling

V. S. NAIPAUL

V. S. Naipaul (1932–) was born on the island of Trinidad into an Indian family. Naipaul won one of the four scholarships awarded annually to students in the Caribbean islands and went to Oxford in 1950. He remained in England after graduation and began writing. A prolific writer of fiction and travel books, Naipaul's work is dominated by questions of identity and place. An Indian born in the West Indies, a West Indian educated in England, and a writer steeped in the European tradition, Naipaul has used his writing to examine societies and how we belong to them. "His Chosen Calling" is from his first book, Miguel Street, *a series of sketches of a poor community in Trinidad.*

After midnight there were two regular noises in the street. At about two o'clock you heard the sweepers; and then, just before dawn, the **scavenging**[1] carts came and you heard the men scraping off the rubbish the sweepers had gathered into heaps.

No boy in the street particularly wished to be a sweeper. But if you asked any boy what he would like to be, he would say, "I going be a cart-driver."

There was certainly a glamor to driving the blue carts. The men were aristocrats. They worked early in the morning, and had the rest of the day free. And then they were always going on strike. They didn't strike for much. They struck for things like a cent more a day; they struck if someone was laid off. They struck when the war began; they struck when the war ended. They struck when India got independence. They struck when Gandhi[2] died.

Eddoes, who was a driver, was admired by most of the boys. He said his father was the best cart-driver of his day, and he told us great stories of the old man's skill. Eddoes came from a low Hindu caste, and there was a lot of truth in what he said. His skill was a sort of family skill, passing from father to son.

One day I was sweeping the pavement in front of the house where I lived, and

---

[1] **scavenging**—collecting something useful from garbage or other discarded material.

[2] Gandhi—Mohandas Gandhi (1869–1948) was an Indian nationalist who led India to independence from Britain in 1947.

Eddoes came and wanted to take away the broom from me. I liked sweeping and didn't want to give him the broom.

"Boy, what you know about sweeping?" Eddoes asked, laughing.

I said, "What it have so much to know?"

Eddoes said, "This is my job, boy. I have experience. Wait until you big like me."

I gave him the broom.

I was sad for a long time afterwards. It seemed that I would never grow as big as Eddoes, never have that thing he called experience. I began to admire Eddoes more than ever; and more than ever I wanted to be a cart-driver.

But Elias was not that sort of boy.

When we who formed the Junior Miguel Street Club squatted on the pavement, talking, like Hat and Bogart and the others, about things like life and cricket and football, I said to Elias, "So you don't want to be a cart-driver? What you want to be then? A sweeper?"

Elias spat neatly into the gutter and looked down. He said very earnestly, "I think I going be a doctor, you hear."

If Boyee or Errol had said something like that, we would all have laughed. But we recognized that Elias was different, that Elias had brains.

We all felt sorry for Elias. His father George brutalized the boy with blows, but Elias never cried, never spoke a word against his father.

One day I was going to Chin's shop to buy three cents' worth of butter, and I asked Elias to come with me. I didn't see George about, and I thought it was safe.

We were just about two houses away when we saw George. Elias grew scared. George came up and said sharply, "Where you going?" And at the same time he landed a powerful **cuff**[3] on Elias's jaw.

George liked beating Elias. He used to tie him with rope, and then beat him with rope he had soaked in the gutters of his cow-pen. Elias didn't cry even then. And shortly after, I would see George laughing with Elias, and George used to say to me, "I know what you thinking. You wondering how me and he get so friendly so quick."

The more I disliked George, the more I liked Elias.

I was prepared to believe that he would become a doctor some day.

Errol said, "I bet you when he come doctor and thing he go forget the rest of we. Eh, Elias?"

A small smile appeared on Elias's lips.

"Nah," he said. "I wouldn't be like that. I go give a lot of money and thing to you and Boyee and the rest of you fellows." And Elias waved his small hands, and we thought we could see the Cadillac and the black bag and the tube-thing that Elias was going to have when he became a doctor.

Elias began going to the school at the other end of Miguel Street. It didn't really

---

[3] **cuff**—a blow with the fist or open hand.

look like a school at all. It looked just like any house to me, but there was a sign outside that said:

Titus Hoyt, I.A., (London, External)
Passes in the Cambridge
School Certificate Guaranteed

The odd thing was that although George beat Elias at the slightest opportunity, he was very proud that his son was getting an education. "The boy learning a hell of a lot, you know. He reading Spanish, French and Latin, and he writing Spanish, French and Latin."

The year before his mother died, Elias sat for the Cambridge Senior School Certificate.

Titus Hoyt came down to our end of the street.

"That boy going pass with honors," Titus Hoyt said. "With honors."

We saw Elias dressed in neat khaki trousers and white shirt, going to the examination room, and we looked at him with awe.

Errol said, "Everything Elias write not remaining here, you know. Every word that boy write going to England."

It didn't sound true.

"What you think it is at all?" Errol said. "Elias have brains, you know."

Elias's mother died in January, and the results came out in March.

Elias hadn't passed.

Hat looked through the list in the *Guardian* over and over again, looking for Elias's name, saying, "You never know. People always making mistake, especially when it have so much names."

Elias's name wasn't in the paper.

Boyee said, "What else you expect? Who correct the papers? English man, not so? You expect them to give Elias a pass?"

Elias was with us, looking sad and not saying a word.

Hat said, "Is a damn shame. If they know what hell the boy have to put up with, they woulda pass him quick quick."

Titus Hoyt said, "Don't worry. Rome wasn't built in a day. This year! This year, things going be much much better. We go show those Englishmen and them."

Elias left us and he began living with Titus Hoyt. We saw next to nothing of him. He was working night and day.

One day in the following March, Titus Hoyt rode up to us and said, "You hear what happen?"

"What happen?" Hat asked.

"The boy is a genius," Titus Hoyt said.

"Which boy?" Errol asked.

"Elias."

"What Elias do?"

"The boy gone and pass the Cambridge Senior School Certificate."

Hat whistled. "The Cambridge Senior School Certificate?"

Titus Hoyt smiled. "That self. He get a third grade. His name going to be in the papers tomorrow. I always say it, and I saying it again now, this boy Elias have too much brains."

Hat said later, "Is too bad that Elias father dead. He was a good-for-nothing, but he wanted to see his son a educated man."

Elias came that evening, and everybody, boys and men, gathered around him. They talked about everything but books, and Elias, too, was talking about things like pictures and girls and cricket. He was looking very solemn, too.

There was a pause once, and Hat said, "What you going to do now, Elias? Look for work?"

Elias spat. "Nah, I think I will write the exam again."

I said, "But why?"

"I want a second grade."

We understood. He wanted to be a doctor.

Elias sat down on the pavement, and said, "Yes, boy. I think I going to take that exam again, and this year I going to be so good that this Mr. Cambridge go **bawl**[4] when he read what I write for him."

We were silent, in wonder.

"Is the English and litricher that does beat me."

In Elias's mouth litricher was the most beautiful word I heard. It sounded like something to eat, something rich like chocolate.

Hat said, "You mean you have to read a lot of poultry and thing?"

Elias nodded. We felt it wasn't fair, making a boy like Elias do litricher and poultry.

Elias moved back into the pink house which had been empty since his father died. He was studying and working. He went back to Titus Hoyt's school, not as pupil, but as a teacher, and Titus Hoyt said he was giving him forty dollars a month.

We felt it wasn't fair, making a boy like Elias do litricher and poultry.

Titus Hoyt added, "He worth it, too. He is one of the brightest boys in Port of Spain."

Now that Elias was back with us, we noticed him better. He was the cleanest boy in the street. He bathed twice a day and scrubbed his teeth twice a day. He did all this standing up at the tap in front of the house. He swept the house every morning before going to school. He was the opposite of his father. His father was short and fat and dirty. He was tall and thin and clean. His father drank and swore. He never drank and no one ever heard him use a bad word.

My mother used to say to me, "Why you don't take after Elias? I really don't know what sort of son God give me, you hear."

And whenever Hat or Edward beat Boyee and Errol, they always said, "Why you beating we for? Not everybody could be like Elias, you know."

---

[4] **bawl**—to cry or wail.

Hat used to say, "And it ain't only that he got brains. The boy Elias have nice *ways* too."

So I think I was a little glad when Elias sat the examination for the third time, and failed.

Hat said, "You see how we catch these Englishmen and them. Nobody here can tell me that the boy didn't pass the exam, but you think they go want to give him a better grade? Ha!"

And everybody said, "Is a real shame."

And when Hat asked Elias, "What you going to do now, boy?" Elias said, "You know, I think I go take up a job. I think I go be a **sanitary**⁵ inspector."

We saw him in Khaki uniform and khaki topee,⁶ going from house to house with a little note-book.

"Yes," Elias said. "Sanitary inspector, that's what I going to be."

Hat said, "It have a lot of money in that, I think. I hear your father George uses to pay the sanitary inspector five dollars a month to keep his mouth shut. Let we say you get about ten or even eight people like that. That's—let me see . . . ten fives is fifty, eight fives is forty. There, fifty, forty dollars straight. And mark you, that ain't counting your salary."

Elias said, "Is not the money I thinking about. I really like the work."

It was easy to understand that.

Elias said, "But it have a exam, you know."

Hat said, "But they don't send the papers to England for that?"

Elias said, "Nah, but still, I fraid exams and things, you know. I ain't have any luck with them."

Boyee said, "But I thought you was thinking of taking up doctoring."

Hat said, "Boyee, I going to cut your little tail if you don't shut up."

But Boyee didn't mean anything bad.

Elias said, "I change my mind. I think I want to be a sanitary inspector. I really like the work."

For three years Elias sat the sanitary inspectors' examination, and he failed every time.

Elias began saying, "But what the hell you expect in Trinidad? You got to bribe everybody if you want to get your toenail cut."

Hat said, "I meet a man from a boat the other day, and he tell me that the sanitary inspector exams in British Guiana much easier. You could go to B.G. and take the exams there and come back and work here."

Elias flew to B.G., wrote the exam, failed it, and flew back.

Hat said, "I meet a man from Barbados. He tell me that the exams easier in Barbados. It easy, easy, he say."

Elias flew to Barbados, wrote the exam, failed it, and flew back.

Hat said, "I meet a man from Grenada the other day—"

---

⁵ **sanitary**—relating to health or conditions affecting health, especially cleanliness and precautions against disease.

⁶ topee—a hat made to ward off the sun, also called a pith helmet.

Elias said, "Shut your arse up, before it have trouble between we in this street."

A few years later I sat the Cambridge Senior School Certificate Examination myself, and Mr. Cambridge gave me a second grade. I applied for a job in the Customs,[7] and it didn't cost me much to get it. I got a khaki uniform with brass buttons, and a cap. Very much like the sanitary inspector's uniform.

Elias wanted to beat me up the first day I wore the uniform.

"What your mother do to get you that?" he shouted, and I was going for him, when Eddoes put a stop to it.

Eddoes said, "He just sad and jealous. He don't mean anything."

For Elias had become one of the street aristocrats. He was driving the scavenging carts.

"No theory here," Elias used to say. "This is the **practical**.[8] I really like the work."

---

[7] Customs—government department that monitors and taxes imports and exports.

[8] **practical**—of or concerned with ordinary activities or work.

QUESTIONS TO CONSIDER

1. How would you describe Elias's character? Compare him to his father and Mr. Titus Hoyt.

2. How does the narrator and Elias's relationship change in the story? Is this reflected in the narrator's attitude toward Elias?

3. What is Naipaul saying about assumptions and idealism in "His Chosen Calling"? What is the lesson Naipaul's story teaches about self-knowledge?

Two Poems

DEREK WALCOTT

Derek Walcott (1930–   ) was born in St. Lucia. His father was a painter, and his mother a drama teacher. Walcott inherited both his parents' talents as well as an immense gift for poetry. Before he was twenty, Walcott had already published a book of poems and had a play produced. He helped to found the Trinidad Theatre Workshop, which he directed from 1959 to 1971, writing numerous plays for the company. Though highly regarded as a dramatist, it is for his poetry that Walcott has achieved international fame and for which he won the Nobel Prize in 1992. The two poems below both have a verve that captures life in Walcott's West Indies. "A Sea-Chantey," in particular, is dominated by the names of islands in the West Indies. As you read, look carefully at the rhythm and rhyme of Walcott's poems.

A Sea-Chantey

Là, tout n'est qu'ordre et beauté,
Luxe, calme, et volupté.[1]
　　　　　　　　—Baudelaire

Anguilla, Adina,
Antigua, Cannelles,
Andreuille, all the *l*'s,
Voyelles, of the liquid Antilles,
The names tremble like needles

---

[1] *Là ... volupté*—lines from the poem "Invitation to the Voyage" by Charles Baudelaire. The French translates as "There, all is ordered and elegant/ Pleasure, peace, and opulence."

Of anchored frigates,[2]
Yachts tranquil as lilies,
In ports of calm coral,
The **lithe**,[3] ebony hulls
Of strait-stitching schooners,[4]
The needles of their masts
That thread **archipelagoes**[5]
Refracted embroidery
In feverish waters
Of the seafarer's islands,
Their shorn, leaning palms,
Shaft of Odysseus,[6]
Cyclopic[7] volcanoes,
Creak their own histories,
In the peace of green anchorage;
Flight, and Phyllis,
Returned from the Grenadines,
Names entered this Sabbath,
In the port clerk's register;
Their baptismal names,
The sea's liquid letters,
Repos donnez à cils[8]. . .
And their blazing cargoes
Of charcoal and oranges;
Quiet, the fury of their ropes.
Daybreak is breaking
On the green chrome water,
The white **herons**[9] of yachts
Are at **Sabbath**[10] **communion**,[11]

---

[2] frigates—sailing vessels.

[3] **lithe**—graceful.

[4] schooners—sailing vessels having a foremast and a mainmast, and with their sails rigged fore-and-aft.

[5] **archipelagoes**—groups of islands.

[6] Odysseus—the hero of the Homeric epic poem *The Odyssey*, which describes Odysseus's ten-year journey home from the Trojan War. In one episode, Odysseus blinds a Cyclops.

[7] **Cyclopic**—having a single round opening in the center.

[8] *Repos donnez à cils*—French for "Rest, close your eyes."

[9] **herons**—long-necked wading birds.

[10] **Sabbath**—the first day of the week, Sunday, observed by most Christians in commemoration of the Resurrection of Christ.

[11] **communion**—sacrament of bread and wine.

The histories of schooners
Are murmured in coral,
Their cargoes of sponges
On sandspits of islets,
Barques[12] white as white salt
Of **acrid**[13] St. Maarten,
Hulls crusted with barnacles,
Holds foul with great turtles,
Whose ship-boys have seen
The blue heave of Leviathan,[14]
A seafaring, Christian,[15]
And intrepid people.

Now an apprentice washes his cheeks
With salt water and sunlight.

In the middle of the harbor
A fish breaks the Sabbath
With a silvery leap.
The scales fall from him
In a tinkle of church bells;
The town streets are orange
With the week-ripened sunlight,
Balanced on the bowsprit[16]
A young sailor is playing
His grandfather's **chantey**[17]
On a trembling mouth organ;
The music curls, dwindling
Like smoke from blue **galleys**,[18]

---

[12] Barques—sailing vessels having three or more masts, square-rigged on all but the aft-most.

[13] **acrid**—harsh or bitter in taste or smell, irritating to the eyes and nose.

[14] Leviathan—a great sea monster and symbol of evil.

[15] Christian—the hero of John Bunyan's religious novel *The Pilgrim's Progress* (1678). The book recounts Christian's journey from the city of destruction to the celestial paradise.

[16] bowsprit—a pole projecting from the upper end of the bow of a sailing vessel.

[17] **chantey**—a sailor's song, especially sung in rhythm to work.

[18] **galleys**—kitchens.

To dissolve near the mountains.
The music uncurls with
The soft vowels of inlets,
The christening of vessels,
The titles of portages,
The colors of sea grapes,
The tartness of sea-almonds,
The alphabet of church bells,
The peace of white horses,
The pastures of ports,
The litany of islands,
The rosary of archipelagoes,
Anguilla, Antigua,
Virgin of Guadeloupe,
And stone-white Grenada
Of sunlight and pigeons,
The amen of calm waters,
The amen of calm waters,
The amen of calm waters.

A City's Death by Fire

After that hot gospeller[19] had leveled all but the churched sky,
I wrote the tale by tallow[20] of a city's death by fire;
Under a candle's eye, that smoked in tears, I
Wanted to tell, in more than **wax**,[21] of faiths that were snapped like wire.
All day I walked abroad among the rubbled tales,
Shocked at each wall that stood on the street like a liar;
Loud was the bird-rocked sky, and all the clouds were **bales**[22]
Torn open by looting, and white, in spite of the fire.

---

[19] gospeller—a person who reads or sings the Gospel.
[20] tallow—fat that has been melted down and used to make candles and soap.
[21] **wax**—a fit of anger.
[22] **bales**—large bundles.

By the smoking sea, where Christ walked, I asked, why
Should a man wax tears, when his wooden world fails?
In town, leaves were paper, but the hills were a flock of faiths;
To a boy who walked all day, each leaf was a green breath
Rebuilding a love I thought was dead as nails,
Blessing the death and the baptism by fire.[23]

---

[23] baptism by fire—initiation by severe circumstances, generally used to mean the first experience of combat.

QUESTIONS TO CONSIDER

1. Describe the sound of "A Sea-Chantey." What is Walcott trying to capture and how has he accomplished it?

2. What is the love that Walcott thought was "as dead as nails" in "A City's Death by Fire"?

3. Point to things in Walcott's poems that show how Walcott represents both West Indian and English culture. Do you think he has found a way to come to terms with his identity in his poems?

Three Poems

AIMÉ CÉSAIRE

Aimé Césaire (1913–   ) was born in Martinique, a French possession in the Caribbean. He went to Paris in 1931 to continue his education at France's most prestigious university. In Paris he met two African poets, Leon Damas and Leopold Senghor (see page 31). They founded a journal called L'Etudiant Noir ("The Black Student") that gave birth to the Négritude movement. In fact, Césaire coined the term in his famous 1939 poem "Cahier d'un retour au pays natal" ("Notebook of a Return to My Native Land"). As a literary movement, Négritude was about celebrating the history, beliefs, and culture of the colonial peoples of Africa and the Caribbean. It also attacked the devastation wrought by colonial powers. With the outbreak of World War II, Césaire returned to Martinique. His poetry is often difficult, with surrealistic imagery and complex rhythms and rhymes. The subjects are almost always Martinican culture and the tragedy of French influence on it.

To Know Ourselves

Reflect then

to know ourselves
   in the rain in the ashes in the **ford**[1]
   in the flooding

ourselves who dreamt

---

[1] **ford**—a place where a river or an other body of water is shallow enough to be waded across.

too litle there
without numbers or **rune**[2]
flung through hills and **vales**[3]
in ourselves to know this heavy heart

huge rock tumbled hollowed from within
by some **ineffable**[4] music the prisoner
of a melody nevertheless to be saved from Disaster

Merciless Great Blood

from the depths of a land of silence
of charred bones of burned vine shoots of storms of screams
held back and muzzled
of a land of desires inflamed by a restlessness of branches
of a shipwreck right against (the very black sand having been
force fed with a peculiar silence
in the quest for prints of bare feet and sea birds)
from the depths of a land of thirst
where to cling to the absurd profile of a totem pole and
drums is **futile**[5]
of a deaf land savagely sealed at all ends
of a land of a red mare galloping the desperate length
of the towpaths of the sea and of the lasso of the most
perfidious[6] currents

Defeat Defeat vast desert
where fiercer than the Egyptian Khamsin[7]
the Assouan[8] wind whistles

---

[2] **rune**—a character from any of several ancient alphabets.

[3] **vales**—valleys.

[4] **ineffable**—impossible to express or describe in words.

[5] **futile**—useless, ineffective.

[6] **perfidious**—deliberately treacherous, deceitful.

[7] Khamsin—a hot southerly wind in Egypt, often bringing dust storms.

[8] Assouan—city in Egypt also known as Aswan. It is one of the driest places on earth.

for which **silential**[9] grief shall we choose to be the drum
   and by whom mounted
   by what triumphant heel
   toward the strange **bayous**[10]
shall we moan shall we twist
shall we scream until a night **haggard**[11] enough to fell
the armed vigilance
installed in the dead of the night of ourselves
by the **insidious**[12] impurity of the wind

It Is Myself, Terror, It Is Myself

Stranded dried up dreams flush with the **muzzles**[13] of rivers create
formidable piles of mute bones
the too swift hopes crawl scrupulously
like tamed snakes
one does not leave one never leaves
as for me I have halted, faithful, on the island
standing like Prester John[14] slightly sideways to the sea
and sculptured at snout level by waves and bird droppings
things things it is to you that I give
my crazed violent face ripped open in the whirlpool's depths
my face tender with fragile coves where **lymphs**[15] are warming
it is myself terror it is myself
the brother of this volcano which certain without saying a word
ruminates[16] an indefinable something that is sure

---

[9] **silential**—unspoken.

[10] **bayou**—marshy arm, inlet, or outlet of a river or lake.

[11] **haggard**—exhausted in appearance, as from prolonged suffering or strain.

[12] **insidious**—operating without being noticed, but with serious effect.

[13] muzzles—the projecting parts of the head of an animal, including jaws, mouth, and nose.

[14] Prester John—legendary ruler of a vast Christian empire in Africa.

[15] lymphs—a stream or spring of clear, pure water.

[16] **ruminates**—ponders.

and passage as well for birds of the wind
which often stop to sleep for a season
it is thyself sweetness it is thyself
run through by the eternal sword
and the entire day advancing
branded with the red-hot iron of **foundered**[17] things
and of recollected sun

---

[17] **foundered**—sunken, wrecked.

QUESTIONS TO CONSIDER

1. What is Césaire saying about the importance of knowing ourselves?

2. How would you describe the landscape of "Merciless Great Blood" and the landscape of "It Is Myself, Terror, It Is Myself"? What do these landscapes metaphorically represent?

3. How would you describe Césaire's poetry to someone else? What is the poet trying to get across? What do you feel you have learned about the poet from the three poems?

Mother, the Great Stones Got to Move

LORNA GOODISON

Lorna Goodison (1947–   ) was born in Jamaica and is a part of an important generation of Caribbean women writers who began to come to prominence in the 1980s. Like the Antiguan Jamaica Kincaid (see page 310), Goodison has focused on the lives of women, finally giving their thoughts, feelings, and ideas a voice in literature. Goodison has published six volumes of poetry, a collection of short stories, and is well known as a painter. "Mother, the Great Stones Got to Move" takes up one of Caribbean women writers' most prominent themes: the mother and her role.

Mother, one stone is wedged across the hole in our history
and scaled with blood wax.
In this hole is our side of the story, exact figures,
headcounts,[1] burial artifacts, documents, lists, maps
showing our way up through the stars; lockets of brass
containing all textures of hair clippings.
It is the half that has never been told,
and some of us must tell it.

Mother, there is the stone on the hearts of some women and
    men
something like an onyx,[2] cabochon[3]-cut,

---

[1] **headcounts**—counts of individuals in a group.

[2] onyx—a semiprecious type of quartz or stone that is often used for decoration and ceremony.

[3] cabochon—a gemstone, usually round or oval, cut and polished, but not faceted.

which hung on the wearer seeds[4] bad dreams. Speaking for
     the small
dreamers of this earth, plagued with nightmares, yearning
for healing dreams
we want the stone to move.

Upon an evening like this, mother, when one year is making
     way
for another, in a ceremony attended by a show of silver stars,
mothers see the moon, milk-fed, herself a nursing mother
and we think of our children and the stones upon their future
and we want these stones to move.

For the year going out came in fat at first
but toward the harvest it grew lean,
and many mouth corners gathered white
and another kind of poison, powdered white
was brought in to replace what was green.
And death sells it with one hand
and with the other death palms a gun
then death gets death's picture
in the papers asking

"where does all this death come from?"
Mother, stones are pillows
for the homeless sleep on concrete sheets.
Stone flavors soup, stone is now meat,
the hard-hearted giving our children
stones to eat.

Mother, the great stones over mankind got to move.
It's been ten thousand years we've been watching them now
from various points in the universe.
From the time of our birth as points of light
in the eternal coiled workings of the cosmos.

---

[4] seeds—implants, establishes.

Roll away stone of poisoned powders come
to blot out[5] the hope of our young.
Move stone of sacrificial lives we breed
to feed to suicide god of **tribalism**.[6]
From across the pathway to mount morning
site of the rose quartz fountain
brimming anise[7] and star water
bright fragrant for our children's future
Mother these great stones got to move.

---

[5] blot out—destroy or hide.

[6] **tribalism**—strong loyalty to one's own group.

[7] anise—a Mediterranean plant of the parsley family.

QUESTIONS TO CONSIDER

1. Who does Goodison mean by "our side" in line three of the poem?

2. What does the stone in the poem symbolize? How many different things can you identify?

3. What is the message Goodison is trying to convey in this poem? What is she saying about how we lead our lives?

A Class of New Canadians

CLARK BLAISE

Clark Blaise (1940–) was born in the United States to a French-Canadian father and a British-Canadian mother. After his education he returned to Canada and his multiple identities—being part of both French-speaking and English-speaking Canada, being American, being an immigrant to Canada—have informed almost all of his fiction. Canada has always been divided along linguistic lines, with the province of Quebec, and its capital Montreal, maintaining its French language against the predominance of English throughout the rest of the country. Canada has a long history of welcoming immigrants and in the twentieth century has been a haven for many persecuted people. Blaise's story "A Class of New Canadians" describes the realities of Canada's accepting and incorporating of many peoples and cultures.

Norman Dyer hurried down Sherbrooke Street, collar turned against the snow. "Suberb!" he muttered, passing a basement gallery next to a French bookstore. Bleached and fanned women in furs dashed from hotel lobbies into waiting cabs. Even the neon clutter of the side streets and the honks of slithering taxis seemed remote tonight through the peaceful snow. *Superb,* he thought again, waiting for a light and backing from a slushy curb: a word reserved for wines, cigars, and delicate sauces; he was feeling superb this evening. After eighteen months in Montreal, he still found himself freshly impressed by everything he saw. He was proud of himself for having steered his life north, even for jobs that were **menial**[1] by standards

he could have demanded. Great just being here no matter what they paid, looking at these buildings, these faces and hearing all the languages. He was learning to be insulted by simple bad taste, wherever he encountered it.

Since leaving graduate school and coming to Montreal, he had sampled every **ethnic**[2] restaurant downtown and in the old city, plus a few Levantine[3] places out in Outremont. He had worked on conversational French and mastered much of the

---

[1] **menial**—degrading, suitable for servants.

[2] **ethnic**—related to the culture and traditions of a people or country.

[3] Levantine—of the Middle Eastern countries that border the Mediterranean Sea.

local **dialect**,[4] done reviews for local papers, translated French-Canadian poets for Toronto quarterlies, and tweaked his colleagues for not sympathizing enough with Quebec separatism. He attended French performances of plays he had ignored in English, and kept a small but elegant apartment near a colony of *émigré*[5] Russians just off Park Avenue. Since coming to Montreal he'd witnessed a hold-up, watched a murder, and seen several riots. When stopped on the street for directions, he would answer in French or accented English. To live this well and travel each long academic summer, he held two jobs. He had no intention of returning to the States. In fact, he had begun to think of himself as a semi-permanent, semi-political exile.

Now, stopped again a few blocks farther, he studied the window of Holt-Renfrew's exclusive men's shop. Incredible, he thought, the authority of simple good taste. Double-breasted chalk-striped suits he would never dare to buy. Knitted sweaters, and fifty-dollar shoes. One tanned mannequin was decked out in a brash checkered sportscoat with a burgundy vest and dashing ascot. Not a price tag under three hundred dollars. Unlike food, drink, cinema, and literature, clothing had never really involved him. Some day, he now realized, it would. Dyer's clothes, thus far, had all been bought in a chain department store. He was a walking violation of American law, clad shoes to scarf in Egyptian cottons, Polish leathers, and woolens from the People's Republic of China.

He had no time for dinner tonight; this was Wednesday, a day of lectures at one university, and then an evening course in English as a Foreign Language at McGill, beginning at six. He would eat afterwards.

Besides the money, he had kept this second job because it flattered him. There was to Dyer something fiercely **elemental**,[6] almost existential, about teaching both his language and his literature in a foreign country—like Joyce in Trieste, Isherwood and Nabokov in Berlin, Beckett in Paris.[7] Also it was necessary for his students. It was the first time in his life that he had done something socially useful. What difference did it make that the job was beneath him, a recent Ph.D., while most of his colleagues in the evening school at McGill were idle housewives and bachelor civil servants? It didn't matter, even, that this job was a **perversion**[8] of all the sentiments he held as a **progressive**[9] young teacher. He was a god two evenings a week, sometimes suffering and fatigued, but nevertheless an **omniscient**,[10]

---

[4] **dialect**—a regional variation of a language.

[5] *émigré*—French for "immigrant."

[6] **elemental**—essential, basic.

[7] Joyce in Trieste, Isherwood and Nabokov in Berlin, Beckett in Paris—important twentieth-century writers who lived in exile from their homelands and hence were immersed in foreign languages.

[8] **perversion**—something that is misguided, distorted, or misinterpreted.

[9] **progressive**—in favor of progress and reform.

[10] **omniscient**—all-knowing.

benevolent[11] god. His students were silent, ignorant, and dedicated to learning English. No discussions, no demonstrations, no dialogue.

I love them, he thought. They need me.

He entered the room, pocketed his cap and ear muffs, and dropped his briefcase on the podium. Two girls smiled good evening.

They love me, he thought, taking off his boots and hanging up his coat; I'm not like their English-speaking bosses.

I love myself, he thought with amazement even while conducting a drill on word order. I love myself for tramping down Sherbrooke Street in zero weather just to help them with noun clauses. I love myself standing behind this podium and showing Gilles Carrier and Claude Veilleux the difference between the past continuous and the simple past; or the sultry Armenian girl with the bewitching half-glasses that "put on" is not the same as "take on"; or telling that clashing Mr. Miguel Mayor, late of Madrid, that simple futurity can be expressed in four different ways, at least.

This is what mastery is like, he thought. Being superb in one's chosen field, not merely in one's mother tongue. A respected performer in the lecture halls of the major universities, equipped by twenty

> *This is what mastery is like, he thought. Being superb in one's chosen field, not merely in one's mother tongue.*

years' research in the remotest libraries, and slowly giving it back to those who must have it. Dishing it out **suavely**,[12] even wittily. Being a legend. Being loved and a little feared.

"Yes, Mrs. David?"

A *sabra*,[13] freckled, reddish hair, looking like a British model, speaks with a nifty British accent, and loves me.

"No," he smiled, "I *were* is not correct except in the present subjunctive, which you haven't studied yet."

The first hour's bell rang. The students closed their books for the intermission. Dyer put his away, then noticed a page of his Faulkner[14] lecture from the afternoon class. *Absalom, Absalom!*, his favorite.

"Can anyone here tell me what *the impregnable citadel of his passive rectitude* means?"

"What, sir?" asked Mr. Vassilopoulos, ready to copy.

"What about the *presbyterian and lugubrious effluvium of his passive vindictiveness?*" A few girls giggled. "O.K.," said Dyer, "take your break."

In the halls of McGill they broke into the usual groups. French Canadians and South Americans into two large circles, then the Greeks, Germans, Spanish, and French into smaller groups. The patterns interested Dyer. Madrid Spaniards and

---

[11] **benevolent**—good, helpful.

[12] **suavely**—agreeably, politely.

[13] *sabra*—an Israeli Jew born in Israel.

[14] Faulkner—William Faulkner (1897–1962), American novelist who documented life in the South. *Absalom, Absalom!* is a novel about racism and identity.

Parisian French always spoke English with their New World co-linguals. The Middle Europeans spoke German together, not Russian, preferring one occupier to the other. Two Israeli men went off alone. Dyer decided to join them for the break.

Not *sabras,* Dyer concluded, not like Mrs. David. The shorter one, dark and wavy-haired, held his cigarette like a violin bow. The other, Mr. Wienrot, was tall and pot-bellied, with a ruddy face and thick stubby fingers. Something about him suggested truck-driving, perhaps of beer, maybe in Germany. Neither one, he decided, could supply the name of a good Israeli restaurant.

"This is really hard, you know?" said Weinrot.

"Why?"

"I think it's because I'm not speaking much of English at my job."

"French?" asked Dyer.

"French? Pah! All the time Hebrew, sometimes German, sometimes little Polish. Crazy thing, eh? How long you think they let me speak Hebrew if I'm working in America?"

"Depends on where you're working," he said.

"Hell, I'm working for the Canadian government, what you think? Plant I work in—I'm engineer, see—makes boilers for the turbines going up North. Look. When I'm leaving Israel I go first to Italy. Right away—bamm I'm working in Italy I'm speaking Italian like a native. Passing for a native."

"A native Jew," said his dark-haired friend.

"Listen to him. So in Rome they think I'm from Tyrol—that's still native, eh? So I speak Russian and German and Italian like a Jew. My Hebrew is bad, I admit it, but it's a lousy language anyway. Nobody likes it. French I understand but English I'm talking like a bum. Arabic I know five dialects. Danish fluent. So what's the matter I can't learn English?"

"It'll come, don't worry," Dyer smiled. *Don't worry, my son;* he wanted to pat him on the arm. "Anyway, that's what makes Canada so appealing. Here they don't force you."

"What's this *appealing*? Means nice? Look, my friend, keep it, eh? Two years in a country I don't learn the language means it isn't a country."

"Come on," said Dyer. "Neither does forcing you."

"Let me tell you a story why I come to Canada. Then you tell me if I was wrong, O.K.?"

"Certainly," said Dyer, flattered.

In Italy, Weinrot told him, he had lost his job to a Communist union. He left Italy for Denmark and opened up an Israeli restaurant with five other friends. Then the six Israelis decided to rent a bigger apartment downtown near the restaurant. They found a perfect nine-room place for two thousand kroner a month, not bad shared six ways. Next day the landlord told them the deal was off. "You tell me why," Weinrot demanded.

No Jews? Dyer wondered. "He wanted more rent," he finally said.

"More—you kidding? More we expected. *Less* we didn't expect. A couple with eight kids is showing up after we're gone and the law in Denmark says a man has a right to a room for each kid plus hundred kroner knocked off the rent for each kid. What you think of that? So a guy who comes in *after us* gets a nine-room place for a thousand kroner *less*. Law says no way a bachelor can get a place ahead of a family, and bachelors pay twice as much."

Dyer waited, then asked, "So?"

"So, I make up my mind the world is full of communism, just like Israel. So I take out applications next day for Australia, South Africa, U.S.A., and Canada. Canada says come right away, so I go. Should have waited for South Africa."

"How could you?" Dyer cried. "What's wrong with you anyway? South Africa is fascist. Australia is racist."

The bell rang, and the Israelis, with Dyer, began walking to the room.

"What I was wondering, then," said Mr. Weinrot, ignoring Dyer's outburst, "was if my English is good enough to be working in the United States. You're American, aren't you?"

It was a question Dyer had often avoided in Europe, but had rarely been asked in Montreal. "Yes," he admitted, "your English is probably good enough for the States or South Africa, whichever one wants you first."

He hurried ahead to the room, feeling that he had let Montreal down. He wanted to turn and shout to Weinrot and to all the others that Montreal was the greatest city on the continent, if only they knew it as well as he did. If they'd just break out of their little ghettos.

At the door, the Armenian girl with the half-glasses caught his arm. She was standing with Mrs. David and Miss Parizeau, a jolly French-Canadian girl that Dyer had been thinking of asking out.

"Please, sir," she said, looking at him over the tops of her tiny glasses, "what I was asking earlier—*put on*—I heard on the television. A man said *You are putting me on* and everybody laughed. I think it was supposed to be funny but *put on* we learned means get dressed, no?"

"Ah—*don't put me on*," Dyer laughed.

"I yaven't erd it neither," said Miss Parizeau.

"To put somebody on means to make a fool of him. To put some*thing* on is to wear it. O.K.?" He gave examples.

"Ah, now I know," said Miss Parizeau. "Like bullshitting somebody. Is it the same?"

"Ah, yes," he said, smiling. French Canadians were like children learning the language. "Your example isn't considered polite. 'Put on' is very common now in the States."

"Then maybe," said Miss Parizeau, "we'll ave it ere in twenty years."

The Armenian giggled.

"No—I've heard it here just as often," Dyer protested, but the girls had already entered the room.

He began the second hour with a smile which slowly soured as he thought of the Israelis. America's anti-communism was bad enough, but it was worse hearing it echoed by immigrants, by Jews, here in Montreal. Wasn't there a psychological type who chose Canada over South Africa? Or was it just a matter of visa and slow adjustment? Did Johannesburg[15] lose its Greeks, and Melbourne[16] its Italians, the way Dyer's students were always leaving Montreal?

And after class when Dyer was again feeling content and thinking of approaching one of the Israelis for a restaurant tip, there came the flood of small requests: should Mrs. Papadopoulos go into a more advanced course; could Mr. Perez miss a week for an interview in Toronto; could Mr. Giguère, who spoke English perfectly, have a harder book; Mr. Coté an easier one?

Then as he packed his briefcase in the empty room, Miguel Mayor, the vain and **impeccable**[17] Spaniard, came forward from the hallway.

"Sir," he began, walking stiffly, ready to bow or salute. He wore a loud gray checkered sportscoat this evening, blue shirt, and matching ascot-handkerchief, slightly mauve. He must have shaved just before class, Dyer noticed, for two fresh **daubs**[18] of antiseptic cream stood out on his jaw, just under his earlobe.

"I have been wanting to ask *you* something, as a matter of fact," said Dyer. "Do you know any good Spanish restaurants I might try tonight?"

"There are not any good Spanish restaurants in Montreal," he said. He stepped closer. "Sir?"

"What's on your mind, then?"

"Please—have you the time to look on a letter for me?"

He laid the letter on the podium.

"Look *over* a letter," said Dyer. "What is it for?"

"I have applied," he began, stopping to emphasize the present perfect construction, "for a job in Cleveland, Ohio, and I want to know if my letter will be good. Will an American, I mean—"

"Why are you going there?"

"It is a good job."

"But Cleveland—"

"They have a black man mayor, I have read. But the job is not in Cleveland."

"Let me see it."

Most honourable Sir: I humbly beg consideration for a position in your grand company . . .

"Who are you writing this to?"

"The president," said Miguel Mayor.

I am once a student of Dr. Ramiro Gutierrez of the Hydraulic Institute of Sevilla, Spain . . .

"Does the president know this Ramiro Gutierrez?"

"Oh, everybody is knowing him," Miguel Mayor assured, "he is the most famous expert in all Spain."

---

[15] Johannesburg—the capital of South Africa.
[16] Melbourne—the capital of Australia.
[17] **impeccable**—without fault or flaw.
[18] **daubs**—lumps, globs.

"Did he recommend this company to you?"

"No—I have said in my letter, if you look—"

An ancient student of *Dr. Gutierrez, Salvador del Este, is actually a boiler expert who is being employed like supervisor is formerly a friend of mine . . .*

"Is he still your friend?"

Whenever you say come to my city Miguel Mayor for talking I will be coming. I am working in Montreal since two years and am now wanting more money than I am getting here now . . .

"Well . . ." Dyer sighed.

"Sir—what I want from you is knowing in good English how to interview me by this man. The letters in Spanish are not the same to English ones, you know?"

I remain humbly at your orders . . .

"Why do you want to leave Montreal?"

"It's time for a change."

"Have you ever been to Cleveland?"

"I am one summer in California. Very beautiful there and hot like my country. Montreal is big port just like Barcelona.[19] Everybody mixed together and having no money. It is just a place to land, no?"

"Montreal? Don't be silly."

"I thought I come here and learn good English but where I work I get by in Spanish and French. It's hard, you know?"

He smiled. Then he took a few steps back and gave his cuffs a gentle tug, exposing a set of jade cufflinks.

Dyer looked at the letter again and calculated how long he would be correcting it, then up at his student. How old is he? My age? Thirty? Is he married? Where do the Spanish live in Montreal? He looks so **prosperous,**[20] so confident, like a male model off a page of *Playboy*. For an instant Dyer felt that his student was mocking him, somehow pitting his astounding confidence and wardrobe, sharp chin and matador's bearing against Dyer's command of English and mastery of the side streets, bistros,[21] and ethnic restaurants. Mayor's letter was painful, yet he remained somehow competent. He would pass his interview, if he got one. What would he care about America, and the odiousness he'd soon be supporting? It was as though a superstucture of exploitation had been revealed, and Dyer felt himself abused by the very people he wanted so much to help. It had to end someplace.

He scratched out the second "humbly" from the letter, then folded the sheet of foolscap.[22] "Have it typed right away," he said. "Good luck."

"Thank you, sir," said his student, with a bow. Dyer watched the letter disappear in the inner pocket of the checkered sports-coat. Then the folding of the cashmere

---

[19] Barcelona—a port city on the southern coast of Spain.

[20] **prosperous**—having good fortune, success, or wealth.

[21] bistros—small, modest European-style restaurants or cafés.

[22] foolscap—a type of expensive writing paper.

> **Montreal is big port just like Barcelona. Everybody mixed together and having no money.**

scarf, the draping of the camel's hair coat about the shoulders, the easing of the fur hat down to the rims of his ears. The meticulous filling of the pigskin gloves. Mayor's patent leather galoshes glistened.

"Good evening, sir," he said.

"*Buenas noches*," Dyer replied.

He hurried now, back down Sherbrooke Street to his daytime office where he could deposit his books. Montreal on a winter night was still mysterious, still magical. Snow blurred the arc lights. The wind was dying. Every second car was now a taxi, crowned with all orange crescent. Slushy curbs had hardened. The window of Holt-Renfrew's was still attractive. The legless dummies invited a final stare. He stood longer than he had earlier, in front of the sporty mannequin with a burgundy waistcoat, the mauve and blue ensemble, the jade cufflinks.

Good evening, sir, he could almost hear. The ascot, the shirt, the complete outfit, had leaped off the back of Miguel Mayor. He pictured how he must have entered the store with three hundred dollars and a prepared speech, and walked out again with everything off the torso's back.

I want that.

What, Sir?

That.

The coat, sir?

Yes.

Very well, sir.

And *that.*

Which, sir?

All that.

"Absurd man!" Dyer whispered. There had been a moment of fear, as though the naked body would leap from the window, and legless, chase him down Sherbrooke Street. But the moment was passing. Dyer realized now that it was comic, even touching. Miguel Mayor had simply tried too hard, too fast, and it would be good for him to stay in Montreal until he deserved those clothes, that touching vanity and confidence. With one last look at the window, he turned sharply, before the clothes could speak again.

QUESTIONS TO CONSIDER

1. How would you describe Norman Dyer? Do you think he is a good or bad person? Explain your answer.

2. What is Dyer's reaction to Mayor's letter? Why does he do what he does with it?

3. What does Clark think about the way people should view themselves and their lives in "A Class of New Canadians"? Do you feel his view is idealistic or realistic?

Three Poems

MARGARET ATWOOD

Margaret Atwood (1939–   ) is probably Canada's best-known writer. Her novels, particularly The Handmaid's Tale, *which was made into a feature film in 1990, have a wide international readership, and through them she has created a platform for her political ideas. Atwood first became known as a poet in Canada in the 1960s. She caused an uproar in the Canadian literary community in 1972 with the publication of* Survival, *a study of themes in Canadian literature that argued that Canadian writers had remained rooted in a colonial mentality, subservient to England.*

True Stories

Don't ask for the true story;
why do you need it?

It's not what I set out with
or what I carry.

What I'm sailing with,
a knife, blue fire,

luck, a few good words
that still work, and the **tide**.[1]

---

[1] **tide**—the rise and fall of ocean waters.

Notes Towards a Poem That Can Never Be Written

for Carolyn Forché

i

This is the place
you would rather not know about,
this is the place that will inhabit you,
this is the place you cannot imagine,
this is the place that will finally defeat you

where the word *why* **shrivels**[2] and empties
itself. This is **famine**.[3]

ii

There is no poem you can write
about it, the sandpits
where so many were buried
& unearthed, the unendurable
pain still traced on their skins.

This did not happen last year
or forty years ago but last week.
This has been happening,
this happens.

---

[2] **shrivels**—shrinks and wrinkles.
[3] **famine**—extreme and widespread shortage of food or other resources.

We make wreaths of adjectives for them,
we count them like beads,
we turn them into statistics & litanies
and into poems like this one.

Nothing works.
They remain what they are.

iii

The woman lies on the wet cement floor
under the unending light,
needle marks on her arms put there
to kill the brain
and wonders why she is dying.

She is dying because she said.
She is dying for the sake of the word.
It is her body, silent
and fingerless, writing this poem.

iv

It resembles an operation
but it is not one

nor despite the spread legs, grunts
and blood, is it a birth.

Partly, it's a job,
partly it's a display of skill
like a concerto.

It can be done badly
or well, they tell themselves.

Partly, it's an art.

The facts of this world seen clearly
are seen through tears;
why tell me then
there is something wrong with my eyes?

to see clearly and without flinching,
without turning away,
this is agony, the eyes taped open
two inches from the sun.

What is it you see then?
Is it a bad dream, a hallucination?
Is it a vision?
What is it you hear?

The razor across the eyeball
is a detail from an old film.
It is also a truth.
Witness is what you must bear.

vi

In this country you can say what you like
because no one will listen to you anyway,
it's safe enough, in this country you can try
      to write
the poem that can never be written,
the poem that invents
nothing and excuses nothing,
because you invent and excuse yourself
      each day.

Elsewhere, this poem is not invention.
Elsewhere, this poem takes courage.
Elsewhere, this poem must be written
because the poets are already dead.

Elsewhere, this poem must be written
as if you are already dead,
as if nothing more can be done
or said to save you.

Elsewhere you must write this poem
because there is nothing more to do.

Dreams of the Animals

Mostly the animals dream
of other animals   each
according to its kind

    (though certain mice and small rodents
    have nightmares of a huge pink
    shape with five claws descending)

moles dream of darkness and delicate
mole smells

frogs dream of green and golden frogs
sparkling like wet suns
among the lilies[4]

red and black
striped fish, their eyes open
have red and black striped
dreams   defense, attack, meaningful
patterns

---

[4] lilies—water lilies, aquatic plants that have large floating leaves and showy flowers.

birds dream of territories
enclosed by singing.

Sometimes the animals dream of evil
in the form of soap and metal
but mostly the animals dream
of other animals.

There are exceptions:

    the silver fox in the roadside zoo
    dreams of digging out
    and of baby foxes, their necks bitten

    the caged armadillo
    near the train
    station, which runs
    all day in figure eights
    its piglet feet **pattering**,[5]
    no longer dreams
    but is insane when waking;

    the iguana
    in the petshop window on St. Catherine
        Street
    crested, royal-eyed, ruling
    its kingdom of water-dish and sawdust

    dreams of sawdust

---

[5] **pattering**—making a rapid series of light taps.

QUESTIONS TO CONSIDER

1. What does Atwood see as the difference between true stories and her stories?

2. How does observing one's life affect the living of it?

3. How would you describe the differences between the animals in the wild and in captivity in "Dreams of Animals"?

Mammie's Form at the Post Office

E.A. MARKHAM

E. A. Markham (1939–   ) was born on the small West Indian island of Montserrat. In 1956 he went to England to finish his education and spent many years there teaching and writing. His poems and stories generally use humor to explain life in Montserrat and particularly the experience of Caribbean immigrants. Markham was part of the first wave of postwar immigrants to England, who went in search of education, jobs, and opportunity. His experiences allowed him to document a way of life typical since the 1950s: the colonial immigrant living in the former ruling country. "Mammie's Form at the Post Office" is a story that focuses on the difficulties for immigrants to England.

She remembered it just in time and panicked; but there must be a way of getting the money there today. Her children were heartless, telling her it wasn't necessary: they had no respect for the dead.

At the Post Office, she went to the wrong end of the counter, and felt a fool when they directed her to the right queue,[1] as if she couldn't read; so she tried to explain. There were a lot of openings but most of them said CLOSED, so she had to join a queue. It embarrassed her that all these Post Offices now had bullet-proof glass shutting out the customer: really, it was offensive to treat people like this—she was almost beginning to feel like a criminal. She thought of Teacher Tudy's Post Office at home where people from the village would come and stand in the yard with their back to the Stables[2] (which Tudy had converted to a garage) while their names were read out from the dining-room door. Of course, Mammie never had to stand in the yard; she would either send over Sarah or Franco, or if she didn't think of it, Tudy would put the letters aside, and probably bring them over herself the next night.

---

[1] queue—line of people waiting their turn.
[2] Stables—buildings used for keeping horses.

Queuing behind the bullet-proof glass, Mammie couldn't help feeling that she'd been reduced to standing with her back to Teacher Tudy's Stables, waiting for her name to be called out.

When it was at last her turn, she told the boy behind the counter that she wanted to send some money to the West Indies, she wanted to send $100 home. But the boy pretended he didn't understand what she was saying, and then asked if she wanted to send money ABROAD. She had to correct him and tell him she was sending her money HOME: that's where she was from. She was **indignant**[3] that first they treated you like a foreigner, and then they denied you your home. He was just a child, and she wondered why they didn't have anyone bigger who could deal with the customers and understand what they wanted. She wanted to send $100 home.

"D'you want to send dollars?"

"Yes. Yes. A Hundred."

"$100. To the West Indies."

"To Murial."

"Yes. Not sure if you can do that, actually. Look, I'll just . . ."

"And I'm in a hurry."

He was just moving off, apparently to look for something, and stopped.

"Look, I've just got to check on this, all right?"

"Yes. Go ahead. As long as it gets there in a hurry."

"I have to send it by Telegraph in that case. Can you . . . just hang on . . ." He reached under the counter and took out a Form. "I'll just go and check on the rates. If you'll just fill out this meanwhile." He slipped the Form under the bullet-proof glass, and told her to fill out both sides.

Mammie took the Form and started searching for her glasses. And after that, the Form didn't make sense. It was all to do with people sending money to Bangladesh and Pakistan, and not one word about the West Indies; so the young fellow must have given her the wrong Form.

When he came back—with a big book— Mammie returned the Form and asked for one for the West Indies; and he said it didn't matter: West Indies was the same as Bangladesh. It was the first time in her life she'd ever heard anyone say that the West Indies, where she was born and grew up and where all her family came from and where her mother and the rest of her relations died and were buried, was the same as Bangladesh which was somewhere in India, where the people were Indian, and she'd never set foot in her life. But she kept all this to herself, and filled out the Form nevertheless.

She put down Murial's name. Murial didn't live in a "Road or Street"; she lived in the village (she had a lovely house in the village), so Mammie had to leave out that line and go right on to "Village or Town" and "Country of Destination" having again left out "District, State, or Province." While she was doing this, someone pushed her to

---

[3] **indignant**—feeling displeasure at something thought to be unjust, offensive, or insulting.

one side as if she was a beggar, and took her place; but she wasn't going to argue with any of them.

On the other side of the Form, she had to make a decision. Murial wasn't a DEPENDENT,[4] so that took care of that. She was tempted to sign her name under PURPOSE OF PAYMENT, but the money had nothing to do with:

a) for goods imported into the UK up to £50 in value . . . subject for the possession of an import license if necessary;

b) of subscriptions and entrance fees to clubs/societies other than for travel services up to £50 per year per club/society;

c) of maintenance payments under Orders of Court;

d) in settlement of commercial and professional debts up to £50 (See paragraph below).

She was sending the money to repair her uncle's headstone and to weed the family plot. As Murial was kind enough to look after her affairs at home, Mammie thought it might upset her if she sent the money as PAYMENT, for Murial wasn't someone she employed, Murial was a friend. So in the end, she entered it under CASH GIFT.

The boy took the Form and said she'd have to send it in Pounds, and they could change it at the other end. That was all right. Then he started filling out another Form, checking with his book, and showing it to the man working next to him, so that the whole world would soon know her business. Then he looked up and smiled at her, and asked if it was urgent.

The boy was a fool, she had already told him it was urgent.

"Then, that'll be . . . £45.50 plus THREE and SEVEN TWENTY. That would be . . . £55.20. O.K.?"

He was crazy. She had £30 which was plenty. He was joking.

"You joking?"

"Sorry . . . ?"

"Last time it cost only £24. Or Twenty Three."

Then he said something that she didn't really follow. So she asked him to repeat it, because then he'd surely find out his mistake.

He was treating her like a child now. "That'll be £45.50 for the $100. And there's THREE POUNDS charge for sending it urgently. You want it urgent, don't you . . .

"Yes. Yes."

". . . and then there's the message, and that's going to cost you another . . ."

"Cut it out. Cut out the message." The message wasn't important.

The message itself was all right, the message was free. But . . .

Mammie wanted the message out.

He read as he crossed it out "THIS IS TO WEED THE HEADSTONES."

---

[4] **dependent**—a person who relies on someone else for aid or support.

"Not weed. To weed the *graves*."

"Yes, well it don't matter now, I've crossed . . ."

"It does matter. I'm not **illiterate**.[5] You can't weed the headstones, you repair them."

"It doesn't cost any more, it's the address that's expensive. Look, do you have to send it . . . It'd be cheaper by *Telegraph Letter*."

"Will it get there today?"

His friend, working next to him made a comment and laughed, young lad himself didn't laugh. He came very close to the glass and she didn't like his look.

"It'll get there in a few days. I mean, it's not exactly *urgent*, is it?"

"All right, all right."

"You'll send it the cheaper way?"

"It's all right, I'll go to another Post Office."

This time he was very rude.

"It didn't cost so much last time," Mammie wasn't going to be defeated. But by then he was dealing with another customer, complaining.

She was too busy to go to the other Post Office now; she had to look after the living as well as the dead *the quick and the dead*:[6] she smiled to herself. The joke pleased her. It occurred to her then that at the Post Office she had just said "Dollars" to the young lad; she didn't specify West Indian Dollars which were only about Four Shillings and Twopence, which would be less than 25p in the new money (at least, that's what it was in the old days). Last year, it had only cost her £24 to send the money to Murial. At the other Post Office. This year, she was prepared to allow for another £4 for **inflation**[7] and for Telegraphing it . . . Unless the boy was talking about some other dollar; but he must know she was West Indian, even though he wasn't qualified to work behind the bullet-proof glass. But what could she do; she was tired: her mother would have to wait another day, choking in grass.

---

[5] **illiterate**—unable to read or write.

[6] "the quick and the dead"—phrase from the Bible referring to the "living and the dead" who will be judged at the Second Coming.

[7] **inflation**—a steady rise in the level of prices over time.

QUESTIONS TO CONSIDER

1. What does sending the money to the West Indies represent for Mammie?

2. What is the real confusion between Mammie and the clerk? What causes this misunderstanding?

3. Do you think the clerk behind the counter is prejudiced against Mammie? Point to details in the story that support your response. What do you think Markham would say?

Two Poems

MICHAEL ONDAATJE

Michael Ondaatje (1943–   ) was born in Sri Lanka, but at nineteen emigrated to Canada. He began his writing career as a poet with the collection The Dainty Monsters *(1967). Ondaatje has published more than ten collections of poetry, and he began writing novels in the 1970s. His novel* The English Patient *won England's most important fiction award, the Booker Prize, in 1992, and was made into a popular feature film. In all his writing, Ondaatje examines cultural and national identity. The exotic lyricism of much of his poetry can be attributed to growing up in Sri Lanka, but he has also been influenced by the knowledge that he is a product of the British Empire, moving from one colony to another.*

The Story

i

For his first forty days a child
is given dreams of previous lives,
journeys, winding paths,
a hundred small lessons
and then the past is erased.

Some are born screaming,
some full of **introspective**[1] wandering
into the past—that bus ride in winter,
the sudden arrival within

---

[1] **introspective**—related to the examination of one's own mental or emotional state.

a new city in the dark.
And those departures from family bonds
leaving what was lost and needed.
So the child's face is a lake
of fast moving clouds and emotions.

A last chance for the clear history of the self.[2]
All our mothers and grandparents here,
our dismantled childhoods
in the buildings of the past.

Some great forty-day daydream
before we bury the maps.

ii

There will be a war, the king told his pregnant wife.
In the last phase seven of us will cross
the river to the east and disguise ourselves
through the farmlands.
We will approach the markets
and befriend the rope-makers. Remember this.

She nods and strokes the baby in her belly.

After a month we will enter
the halls of that king.
There is dim light from small high windows.
We have entered with no weapons,
just rope in the baskets.
We have trained for years
to move in silence, invisible,
not one creak of bone,
not one breath,
even in lit rooms,
in order to disappear into this building
where the guards live in half-light.

---

[2] self—a person's sense of individuality.

When a certain night falls
the seven must enter the **horizontal**[3] door
remember this, face down,
as in birth.
Then (he tells his wife)
there is the corridor of dripping water,
a noisy rain, a sense
of creatures at your feet.
And we enter halls of further darkness,
cold and wet among the enemy warriors.
To overcome them we **douse**[4] the last light.

After battle we must leave another way
avoiding all doors to the north . . .

(The king looks down
and sees his wife is asleep
in the middle of the adventure.

He bends down and kisses through the skin
the child in the body of his wife.
Both of them in dreams. He lies there,
watches her face as it catches a breath.
He pulls back a wisp across her eye
and bites it off. Braids[5] it
into his own hair, then sleeps beside them.)

---

[3] **horizontal**—flat or level in relation to the ground.

[4] **douse**—extinguish.

[5] Braids—weaves.

With all the **swerves**[6] of history
I cannot imagine your future.
Would wish to dream it, see you
in your teens, as I saw my son,
your already philosophical air
rubbing against the speed of the city.
I no longer guess a future.
And do not know how we end
nor where.

Though I know a story about maps, for you.

iv

After the death of his father,
the prince leads his warriors
into another country.
Four men and three women.
They disguise themselves and travel
through farms, fields of turnip.
They are private and shy
in an unknown, uncaught way.

In the hemp[7] markets
they court friends.
They are dancers who tumble
with lightness as they move,
their long hair wild in the air.
Their shyness slips away.

They are charming with desire in them.
It is the dancing they are known for.

---

[6] **swerves**—sudden changes in direction.
[7] hemp—a plant with strong fibers that can be used to make rope and fabrics.

One night they leave their beds.
Four men, three women.
They cross open fields where nothing grows
and swim across the cold rivers
into the city.

Silent, invisible among the guards,
they enter the horizontal door
face down so the blades of poison
do not touch them. Then
into the rain of the tunnels.

It is an old story—that one of them
remembers the path in.
They enter the last room of faint light
and douse the lamp. They move
within the darkness like dancers
at the center of a maze
seeing the enemy before them
with the unlit habit of their journey.

There is no way to behave after victory.

*

And what should occur now is unremembered.

The seven stand there.
One among them, who was that baby,
cannot recall the rest of the story
—the story his father knew, unfinished
that night, his mother sleeping.

We remember it as a tender story,
though perhaps they perish.
The father's lean arm across
the child's shape, the taste
of the wisp of hair in his mouth . . .

The seven embrace in the destroyed room
where they will die without
the dream of exit.
We do not know what has happened.
From the high windows the ropes
are not long enough to reach the ground.
They take up the knives of the enemy
and cut their long hair and braid it
onto one rope and they descend
hoping it will be long enough
into the darkness of night.

Sweet Like a Crow

for Helli Corea, 8 years old

"The Sinhalese[8] are beyond a doubt one of the least musical
people in the world. It would be quite impossible to have
less sense of pitch, line or rhythm." —Paul Bowles

Your voice sounds like a scorpion being pushed
through a glass tube
like someone has just trod on a peacock
like wind howling in a coconut
like a rusty bible, like someone pulling barbed wire
across a stone courtyard, like a pig drowning,
a vattacka[9] being fried
a bone shaking hands
a frog singing at Carnegie Hall.

Like a crow swimming in milk,
like a nose being hit by a mango
like the crowd at the Royal-Thomian match,

---

[8] Sinhalese—the principal race of Sri Lanka.
[9] vattacka—pumpkin.

a womb full of twins, a **pariah**[10] dog
with a magpie[11] in its mouth
like the midnight jet from Casablanca[12]
like Air Pakistan curry,
a typewriter on fire, like a hundred
pappadams[13] being crunched, like someone
trying to light matches in a dark room,
the clicking sound of a reef when you put your head into
    the sea,
a dolphin reciting epic poetry to a sleepy audience,
the sound of a fan when someone throws brinjals[14] at it,
like pineapples being sliced in the Pettah[15] market
like betel[16] juice hitting a butterfly in mid-air
like a whole village running naked onto the street
and tearing their sarongs,[17] like an angry family
pushing a jeep out of the mud, like dirt on the needle,
like 8 sharks being carried on the back of a bicycle
like 3 old ladies locked in the lavatory
like the sound I heard when having an afternoon sleep
and someone walked through my room in ankle bracelets.

---

[10] **pariah**—outcast.

[11] magpie—a noisy bird in the jay family that has a long tail and black and white feathers.

[12] Casablanca—a port city in Morocco in North Africa.

[13] pappadams—thin rounds of peppered lentil dough fried in deep fat.

[14] brinjals—eggplants.

[15] Pettah—Anglo-Indian slang for a market outside a fortified town or city.

[16] betel—the leaf of a pepper plant that is wrapped around a betel nut and chewed. The chewer spits the bright red juice out as he chews.

[17] sarongs—loose-fitting, skirtlike garments.

QUESTIONS TO CONSIDER

1. Why do the seven not know the way out in "The Story"? Do you think they got away in the end? Why or why not?

2. What do you think Ondaatje is trying to do in "Sweet Like a Crow"? Is he successful? Why or why not?

3. How might "Sweet Like a Crow" be a reflection of Ondaatje's own life? Do you like the poem more or less because of this? Explain your answer.

Three Poems

HERBERTO PADILLA

Cuba became an independent country in 1898, but it was heavily influenced by the United States government and the vast U.S. business interests in the island. Corrupt dictators dominated the country until 1959 when Fidel Castro led a popular revolution. He set up a Communist government and nationalized all the U.S. holdings on the island. Cuba has been almost entirely closed to the world at large since then. The early years of the revolution were idealistic, but the country is now one of the poorest and most repressive in the Caribbean. Herberto Padilla (1932–) is a poet who has seen both sides of Cuba's revolution. After 1959, he worked for the official news service and was awarded literary prizes for his poetry. However, in the 1960s his opposition to the regime's policies led to his arrest and imprisonment. He was exiled in 1980 and now lives in the United States.

Landscapes

You can see them everywhere in Cuba.
Green or red or yellow, flaking off from the water
and the sun, true landscapes of these times
of war.
The wind tugs at the Coca-Cola signs.
The clocks courtesy of Canada Dry are stopped
at the old time.
The neon signs, broken, crackle and splutter[1] in the rain.
Esso's is something like this
    S   O   S
and above there are sonic crude letters
reading P A T R I A O M U E R T E.[2]

---

[1] splutter—to make explosive popping or sizzling sounds.

[2] Patria o Muerte—Spanish for "Country or Death."

Man on the Edge

He is not the man who goes over the wall,
feeling himself enclosed by his times,
nor is he the fugitive breathing hard
hidden in the back of a truck
fleeing from the terrorists,
nor is he the poor guy with the canceled passport
who is always trying to cross a new border.
He lives on this side of heroics
—in that dark part—
but never gets rattled or surprised.
He does not want to be a hero,
not even a romantic
around whom we might
weave a legend.
He is sentenced to this life, and, what terrifies him more,
condemned **irretrievably**[3] to his own time.
He is headless at two in the morning,
going from one room to another
like an enormous wind
which barely survives in the wind outside,
Every morning he begins again
as if he were an Italian actor.[4]
He stops dead
as if someone had just stolen his being.
No looking glass[5] would dare reflect
this fallen mouth, this wisdom gone bankrupt.

---

[3] **irretrievably**—unable to be returned or restored.

[4] Italian actor—a reference to the *commedia dell'arte*, improvisational perfomances by actors playing stock characters.

[5] looking glass—mirror.

A Fountain, a House of Stone

(Zurbarán[6])

A fountain, a house of stone,
a bridge, a chapel with a weather vane[7]
and a squeaking hinge in the door,
a road bordered by flowers
and, farther on, a river.

Can we describe the world this way,
eyes wide open, shoes up on the table
with a dusky halo like a lantern,
and the still face, distant and ever-demanding,
nailing us down with its eyes,
hunting down in our **innards**[8]
the cowardly **swagger**[9] of **allegory**?[10]
It is possible. The world can be described
   in any way you like. You might
come out with one last twist of the facts, as they say,
our last coin
to take us back again to that river
   that attends our childhood as it does old age.
One might cross the bridge
among the bamboo which creaks once again
like a bridge across a river,
in such a way that the hinge[11] we have hung on to
   since we were children
    becomes stronger as time passes.
The house, the road bordered by flowers, and the chapel
   thereby belong to us,
or we belong to them. It's all the same.

---

[6] *Zurbarán*—Francisco de Zurbarán (1598–1664) was a Spanish Baroque painter famed for his austere religious paintings.

[7] vane—a spinning pointer used to show the direction of the wind.

[8] **innards**—internal parts.

[9] **swagger**—strutting about arrogantly.

[10] **allegory**—the symbolic presentation of meaning through the actions of fictional characters.

[11] hinge—the object, person, or event on which something else depends.

QUESTIONS TO CONSIDER

1. What are the "times of war" in "Landscapes"?

2. What sort of images does Padilla use in "Man on the Edge"? How do these images help you figure out what the poem means?

3. What does Padilla mean by the last sentence, "It's all the same," in "A Fountain, a House of Stone"?

4. How would you describe the tone of these three poems? How do you think Padilla's experiences in jail and exile affected his outlook in these poems and in his own life?

On Seeing England for the First Time

JAMAICA KINCAID

Jamaica Kincaid (1949–   ) was born Elaine Potter Richardson in Antigua, which at that time was still a British colony. In 1966 she emigrated to the United States, and in 1976 joined The New Yorker *magazine as a staff writer. Almost all of her writing has been published first in that magazine. Kincaid has emerged as one of the major West Indian literary voices through her stories and such novels as* Annie John *(1985) and* Lucy *(1990). Much of Kincaid's writing decries the woeful influence of Britain on Antigua; she deeply hates all colonial culture. The following essay, which was published in 1991, describes growing up in a British colony.*

When I saw England for the first time, I was a child in school sitting at a desk. The England I was looking at was laid out on a map gently, beautifully, delicately, a very special jewel; it lay on a bed of sky blue—the background of the map—its yellow form mysterious, because though it looked like a leg of mutton,[1] it could not really look like anything so familiar as a leg of mutton because it was England—with shadings of pink and green, unlike any shadings of pink and green I had seen before, squiggly veins of red running in every direction. England was a special jewel all right, and only special people got to wear it. The people who got to wear England were English people. They wore it wet and they wore it everywhere: in jungles, in deserts, on plains, on top of the highest mountains, on all the oceans, on all the seas. When my teacher had pinned this map up on the blackboard, she said, "This is England"—and she said it with authority, seriousness, and adoration, and we all sat up. It was as if she had said, "This is Jerusalem,[2] the place you will go to when you die but only if you have been good." We understood then—we were meant to understand then—that England was to be our source of myth and the source from which we got our sense of reality, our

---

[1] mutton—flesh of a sheep that is used as food.

[2] Jerusalem—an ancient holy city for Jews, Christians, and Muslims.

sense of what was meaningful, our sense of what was meaningless—and much about our own lives and much about the very idea of us headed that last list.

At the time I was a child sitting at my desk seeing England for the first time, I was already very familiar with the greatness of it. Each morning before I left for school, I ate a breakfast of half a grapefruit, an egg, bread and butter and a slice of cheese, and a cup of cocoa; or half a grapefruit, a bowl of oat porridge, bread and butter and a slice of cheese, and a cup of cocoa. The can of cocoa was often left on the table in front of me. It had written on it the name of the company, the year the company was established, and the words "Made in England." Those words, "Made in England," were written on the box the oats came in too. They would also have been written on the box the shoes I was wearing came in; the bolt of gray linen cloth lying on the shelf of a store from which my mother had bought three yards to make the uniform that I was wearing had written along its edge those three words. The shoes I wore were made in England; so were my socks and cotton undergarments and the satin ribbons I wore tied at the end of two plaits of my hair. My father, who might have sat next to me at breakfast, was a carpenter and cabinetmaker. The shoes he wore to work would have been made in England, as were his khaki shirt and trousers, his underpants and undershirt, his socks and brown felt hat. Felt was not the proper material from which a hat that was expected to provide shade from the hot sun should

have been made, but my father must have seen and admired a picture of an Englishman wearing such a hat in England, and this picture that he saw must have been so compelling that it caused him to wear the wrong hat for a hot climate most of his long life. And this hat—a brown felt hat—became so central to his character that it was the first thing he put on in the morning as he stepped out of bed and the last thing he took off before he stepped back into bed at night. As we sat at breakfast, a car might go by. The car, a Hillman or a Zephyr, was made in England. The very idea of the meal itself, breakfast, and its substantial quality and quantity, was an idea from England; we somehow knew that in England they began the day with this meal called breakfast, and a proper breakfast was a big breakfast. No one I knew liked eating so much food so early in the day; it made us feel sleepy, tired. But this breakfast business was "Made in England" like almost everything else that surrounded us, the exceptions being the sea, the sky, and the air we breathed.

At the time I saw this map—seeing England for the first time—I did not say to myself, "Ah, so that's what it looks like," because there was no longing in me to put a shape to those three words that ran through every part of my life no matter how small; for me to have had such a longing would have meant that I lived in a certain atmosphere, an atmosphere in which those three words were felt as a burden. But I did not live in such an atmosphere. When my teacher showed us the map, she asked us to study it carefully, because no test we would ever take would be complete without this statement: "Draw a map of England." I did not know then that the statement "Draw a map of England" was something far worse than a declaration of war, for a flat-out[3] declaration of war would have put me on alert. In fact, there was no need for war—I had long ago been conquered. I did not know then that this statement was part of a process that would result in my erasure—not my physical erasure, but my erasure all the same. I did not know then that this statement was meant to make me feel awe[4] and small whenever I heard the word "England": awe at the power of its existence, small because I was not from it.

> *I did not know then that this statement was meant to make me feel awe and small whenever I heard the word "England": awe at the power of its existence, small because I was not from it.*

After that there were many times of seeing England for the first time. I saw England in history. I knew the names of all the kings of England. I knew the names of their children, their wives, their disappointments, their triumphs, the names of people who betrayed them. I knew the dates on which they were born and the dates they died. I knew their conquests and was made to feel good if I figured in them; I knew their defeats.

This view—the naming of the kings, their deeds, their disappointments—was the vivid[5] view, the forceful view. There were other views, subtler[6] ones, softer, almost not there—but these softer views were the ones that made the most lasting impression on me, the ones that made me really feel like nothing. "When morning touched the sky" was one phrase, for no morning touched the sky where I lived. The morning where I lived came on abruptly, with a shock of heat and loud noises. "Evening approaches" was another. But the evenings where I lived did not approach; in fact, I had no evening—I had night and I had day, and they came and went in a mechanical way: on, off, on, off. And then there were gentle mountains and low blue skies and moors over which people took walks for nothing but pleasure, when where I lived a walk was an act of labor, a burden, something only death or the automobile could relieve. And the weather there was so remarkable because the rain fell gently always, and the wind blew in gusts that were sometimes deep, and the air was various shades of gray, each an appealing shade for a dress to be worn when a portrait was being painted; and when it rained at twilight, wonderful

---

[3] flat-out—direct and immediate.

[4] awe—overwhelming feeling of admiration, fear, or wonder.

[5] vivid—clear, distinct, and striking.

[6] subtler—more difficult to perceive or understand.

things happened: People bumped into each other unexpectedly and that would lead to all sorts of turns of events—a plot, the mere weather caused plots.

The reality of my life, the life I led at the time I was being shown these views of England for the first time, for the second time, for the one hundred millionth time, was this: The sun shone with what sometimes seemed to be a deliberate cruelty; we must have done something to deserve that. My dresses did not rustle in the evening air as I strolled to the theater (I had no evening, I had no theater; my dresses were made of a cheap cotton, the weave of which would give way after not too many washings). I got up in the morning, I did my chores (fetched water from the public pipe for my mother, swept the yard), I washed myself, I went to a woman to have my hair combed freshly every day (because before we were allowed into our classroom our teachers would inspect us, and children who had not bathed that day, or had dirt under their fingernails, or whose hair had not been combed anew that day might not be allowed to attend class. I ate that breakfast. I walked to school. At school we gathered in an auditorium and sang a hymn, "All Things Bright and Beautiful," and looking down on us as we sang were portraits of the queen of England and her husband; they wore jewels and medals and they smiled. I was a Brownie.[7] At each meeting we would form a little group around a flagpole, and after raising the Union Jack,[8] we would say, "I promise to do my best, to do my duty to God and the queen, to help other people every day and obey the scouts' law."

But who were these people and why had I never seen them? I mean, really seen them, in the place where they lived? I had never been to England. England! I had seen England's representatives. I had seen the governor-general at the public grounds at a ceremony celebrating the queen's birthday. I had seen an old princess and I had seen a young princess. They had both been extremely not beautiful, but who among us would have told them that? I had never seen England, really seen it. I had only met a representative, seen a picture, read books, memorized its history. I had never set foot, my own foot, in it.

The space between the idea of something and its reality is always wide and deep and dark. The longer they are kept apart—idea of thing, reality of thing—the wider the width, the deeper the depth, the thicker and darker the darkness. This space starts out empty, there is nothing in it, but it rapidly becomes filled up with obsession or desire or hatred or love—sometimes all of these things, sometimes some of these things. That the idea of something and its reality are often two completely different things is something no one ever remembers; and so when they meet and find that they are not compatible, the weaker of the two, idea or reality, dies.

---

[7] Brownie—a Girl Scout who is 6 to 8 years old.

[8] Union Jack—the British national flag.

And so finally, when I was a grown-up woman, the mother of two children, the wife of someone, a person who resides in a powerful country that takes up more than its fair share of a continent, the owner of a house with many rooms in it and of two automobiles, with the desire and will (which I very much act upon) to take from the world more than I give back to it, more than I deserve, more than I need, finally then, I saw England, the real England, not a picture, not a painting, not through a story in a book, but England, for the first time. In me, the space between the idea of it and its reality had become filled with hatred, and so when at last I saw it I wanted to take it into my hands and tear it into little pieces and then crumble it up as if it were clay, child's clay. That was impossible, and so I could only **indulge**[9] in not-favorable opinions.

If I had told an English person what I thought, that I find England ugly, that I hate England; the weather is like a jail sentence; the English are a very ugly people; the food in England is like a jail sentence; the hair of English people is so straight, so dead-looking; the English have an unbearable smell so different from the smell of people I know, real people of course, I would have been told that I was a person full of **prejudice**.[10] Apart from the fact that it is I—that is, the people who look like me—who would make that English person aware of the unpleasantness of such a thing, the idea of such a thing, prejudice, that person would have been only partly right, sort of right: I may be

capable of prejudice, but my prejudices have no weight to them, my prejudices have no force behind them, my prejudices remain opinions, my prejudices remain my personal opinion. And a great feeling of rage and disappointment came over me as I looked at England, my head full of personal opinions that could not have public, my public, approval. The people I come from are powerless to do evil on a grand scale.

The moment I wished every sentence, everything I knew, that began with England would end with "and then it all died, we don't know how, it just all died" was when I saw the white cliffs of Dover.[11] I had sung hymns and recited poems that were about a longing to see the white cliffs of Dover again. At the time I sang the hymns and recited the poems, I could really long to see them again because I had never seen them at all, nor had anyone around me at the time. But there we were, groups of people longing for something we had never seen. And so there they were, the white cliffs, but they were not that pearly, majestic thing I used to sing about, that thing that created such a feeling in these people that when they died in the place where I lived they had themselves buried facing a direction that would allow them to see the white cliffs of Dover when they were resurrected, as surely they

---

[9] **indulge**—to follow an inclination or desire.

[10] **prejudice**—bias or preconceived opinion.

[11] white cliffs of Dover—picturesque chalk cliffs on the Southeast coast of England from which one can view France on a clear day.

would be. The white cliffs of Dover, when finally I saw them, were cliffs, but they were not white; you could only call them that if the word "white" meant something special to you; they were steep;[12] they were so steep, the correct height from which all my views of England, starting with the map before me in my classroom and ending with the trip I had just taken, should jump and die and disappear forever.

---

[12] steep—high, towering.

QUESTIONS TO CONSIDER

1. Is Kincaid describing her childhood from her point of view as a child or as an adult? Explain your answer.

2. What does Kincaid mean when she writes that the "space between the idea of something and its reality is always wide and deep and dark"? Do you agree with this statement? Why or why not?

3. Do you think Jamaica Kincaid has come to terms with having been born in a British colony? Why or why not? How would you describe her attitude toward England?

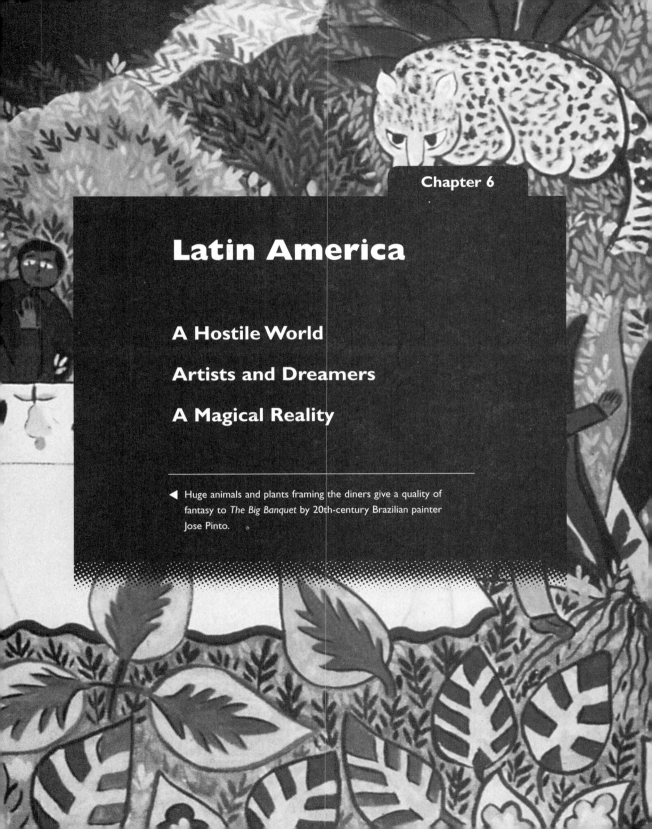

Chapter 6

Latin America

A Hostile World

Artists and Dreamers

A Magical Reality

◀ Huge animals and plants framing the diners give a quality of
fantasy to *The Big Banquet* by 20th-century Brazilian painter
Jose Pinto.

Three Poems

CLARIBEL ALEGRÍA

Claribel Alegría (1924–) was born in Nicaragua, but has spent most of her life in exile in El Salvador and the United States. Her parents were involved in the opposition to Nicaragua's American-backed dictator Somoza, and Alegría was not able to live in Nicaragua until Somoza was overthrown by a leftist revolution in 1979. For Alegría, a writer must be a political activist who exposes injustice. Her poetry bears witness to the poverty and violence of life in Central American countries ruled by dictators and multinational corporations. Alegría's poems remember the silent victims of civil war and third-world economies where poverty-stricken populations are oppressed by corrupt governments.

Savoir Faire[1]

My black cat doesn't know
he will die one day
he doesn't cling to life
as I do
he leaps from the rooftop
light as air
climbs the tamarind[2] tree
barely scratching it
doesn't dread crossing bridges
or dark alleyways

---

[1] **Savoir Faire**—French phrase for "know-how."

[2] tamarind—a tropical evergreen tree.

nor the **perfidious**[3] scorpion
my black cat falls in love
with every cat he meets
he refuses to be **snared**[4]
by a single love
the way I did.

Nocturnal Visits

I think of our anonymous boys
of our burnt-out heroes
the amputated
the cripples
those who lost both legs
both eyes
the **stammering**[5] teen-agers.
At night I listen to their phantoms
shouting in my ear
shaking me out of **lethargy**[6]
issuing me commands
I think of their tattered lives
of their feverish hands
reaching out to seize ours.
It's not that they're begging
they're demanding
they've earned the right to order us
to break up our sleep
to come awake
to shake off once and for all
this **lassitude**.[7]

---

[3] **perfidious**—dangerous and deceptive.

[4] **snared**—trapped.

[5] **stammering**—stuttering, speaking with pauses or repetitions of the same syllable.

[6] **lethargy**—lack of energy, sleepiness.

[7] **lassitude**—weariness, lack of interest in exerting oneself.

Documentary

Come, be my camera.
Let's photograph the ant heap
the queen ant
extruding[8] sacks of coffee,
my country.
It's the harvest.
Focus on the sleeping family
cluttering the ditch.
Now, among trees:
rapid,
dark-skinned fingers
stained with honey.
Shift to a long shot:
the file of ant men
trudging down the ravine
with sacks of coffee.
A contrast:
girls in colored skirts
laugh and chatter,
filling their baskets
with berries.
Focus down.
A close-up of the pregnant mother
dozing in the hammock.
Hard focus on the flies
spattering her face.
Cut.
The terrace of polished **mosaics**[9]
protected from the sun.
Maids in white aprons
nourish the ladies
who play canasta,[10]

---

[8] **extruding**—thrusting or pushing out.

[9] **mosaics**—pictures or patterns created by arranging small and many-colored pieces of such materials as stone and glass.

[10] canasta—a card game.

celebrate invasions
and feel sorry for Cuba.
Izalco[11] sleeps
beneath the volcano's eye.
A subterranean growl
makes the village tremble.
Trucks and ox-carts
laden with sacks
screech down the slopes.
Besides coffee
they plant angels
in my country.
A chorus of children
and women
with the small white coffin
move politely aside
as the harvest passes by.
The riverside women,
naked to the waist,
wash clothing.
The truck drivers
exchange **jocular**[12] obscenities
for insults.
In Panchimalco,[13]
waiting for the ox-cart to pass by,
a peasant
with hands bound behind him
by the thumbs
and his escort of soldiers
blinks at the airplane:
a huge bee
bulging with coffee growers
and tourists.

---

[11] Izalco—town at the base of the most active volcano in Central America.

[12] **jocular**—merry, humorous.

[13] Panchimalco—town on the Pacific Coast of El Salvador.

The truck stops in the market place.
A **panorama**[14] of iguanas,
chickens,
strips of meat,
wicker baskets,
piles of *nances,*
nísperos,
oranges,
zunzas,
zapotes,
cheeses,
bananas,
dogs, *pupusas, jocotes,*[15]
acrid[16] odors,
taffy candies,
urine puddles, tamarinds.
The virginal coffee
dances in the millhouse.
They strip her,
rape her,
lay her out on the patio
to doze in the sun.
The dark storage sheds
glimmer.
The golden coffee
sparkles with malaria,[17]
blood,
illiteracy,
tuberculosis,[18]
misery.

---

[14] **panorama**—an unbroken view of a surrounding area.

[15] *nances, nísperos… zunzas, zapotes… pupusas, jocotes*—Spanish names for a number of different fruits.

[16] **acrid**—sharp or bitter.

[17] malaria—fever caused by the bite of a mosquito.

[18] tuberculosis—an infectious disease characterized by small, round areas of swelling, especially in the lungs.

A truck roars
out of the warehouse.
It bellows uphill
drowning out the lesson:
A for alcoholism,
B for battalions,
C for corruption,
D for dictatorship,
E for exploitation,
F for the feudal power
of fourteen families
and etcetera, etcetera, etcetera.
My etcetera country,
my wounded country,
my child,
my tears,
my obsession.

QUESTIONS TO CONSIDER

1. How would you describe Alegría's attitude toward her cat in "Savoir Faire"?

2. Who is Alegría describing in "Nocturnal Visits"? Why do they have the right described in the last sentence?

3. What is the tragedy Alegría depicts in "Documentary"? Who does she blame for it?

4. What makes the world of Alegría's poems so hostile? Do you think things will get better or worse? Explain your answer.

A Story and Two Essays

CLARICE LISPECTOR

In her lifetime, Clarice Lispector (1925–1977) was Brazil's most important woman writer. Her style of writing—honest, intellectual, and providing psychological portraits of single characters—was innovative and influential. Lispector reflected on the world around her, avoiding social or political commentary, which she felt often absorbed the literary talents of writers. Lispector was one of the first Brazilian writers to gain an international following. The following three prose pieces are typical of Lispector's imaginative and descriptive writing, which uses the techniques of both fiction and nonfiction.

The Sharing of Bread

It was Saturday and we had been invited to lunch out of a sense of obligation. But we were all much too fond of Saturday to go wasting it in the company of people whom we did not care for. Each of us had experienced happiness at some time or other and had been left with the mark of desire. As for me, I desired everything. And there we were, trapped, as if our train had been **derailed**[1] and we had been forced to settle down among perfect strangers. No one there cared for me and I did not care for them. As for my Saturday—it swayed outside my windows in acacias[2] and shadows. Rather than spend it badly, I preferred to hold it in my clenched fist, where it could be crumpled like a handkerchief. Waiting for lunch to be served, we half-heartedly drank a toast to the health of resentment: tomorrow it would be Sunday. I have no desire to be with you, our gaze was saying without any warmth, as we slowly blew smoke from our dry cigarettes. The **avarice**[3] of refusing to share our Saturday eroded little by little and advanced like rust, until any happiness would have been an insult to a greater happiness.

---

[1] **derailed**—caused to leave the rails.

[2] acacias—trees with small yellow or white flowers.

[3] **avarice**—extreme greed for money or other gain.

Only the mistress of the household did not appear to save her Saturday in order to exploit it on a Thursday evening. But how could this woman, whose heart had experienced other Saturdays, have forgotten that people crave more and more? She did not even betray impatience with this **heterogeneous**[4] gathering in her home, daydreaming and resigned, as if waiting for the next train to leave, any train—rather than remain in that deserted railway station, rather than have to restrain the horse from **bolting**[5] furiously to join more and more horses.

We finally moved into the dining room for a lunch without the blessing of hunger. When taken by surprise, we came face to face with the table. This could not be for us . . .

It was a table prepared for men of good will. Who could the expected guest be who had simply failed to turn up? But it was we ourselves. So that woman served the best no matter the guest? And she was content to wash the feet of the first stranger. We watched, feeling uneasy.

The table had been covered with solemn abundance. Sheaves[6] of wheat were piled up on the white table-cloth. And rosy apples, enormous yellow carrots, round tomatoes with their skins ready to burst, green marrows[7] with translucent skins, pineapples of a malign savageness, oranges golden and tranquil, gherkins[8] bristling like porcupines, cucumbers stretched tight over watery flesh, red, hollow peppers that caused our eyes to smart—were all entangled in moist whiskers of maize,[9] as auburn as if bordering human lips. And the berries of the grape. The purplest of the grapes that could barely wait to be pressed. Nor did they mind who pressed them. The tomatoes were circular for no one: for the atmosphere, for the circular atmosphere. Saturday belonged to anyone who cared to turn up. The oranges would sweeten the tongue of the first person to arrive. Beside the plate of each unwanted guest, the woman who washed the feet of strangers had placed—even without choosing or loving us—a sheaf of wheat, a bunch of fiery radishes, or a crimson slice of water-melon with its merry seeds. All dissected by the Spanish acidity visible in the green lemons. In the earthenware jugs there was milk, as if it had crossed a rocky desert with the goats. Wine that was almost black after being thoroughly trampled shuddered in the clay vessels. Everything was set before us. Everything cleansed of perverse human desire. Everything as it really is, and not as we would wish it to be. Simply existing and intact. Just as a field exists. Just as the mountains exist. Just as man and woman exist, but not those of us who are consumed by greed. Just as Saturday exists. Simply existing. It exists.

---

[4] **heterogeneous**—diverse, varied.

[5] **bolting**—suddenly running away.

[6] Sheaves—bundles.

[7] marrows—squashes.

[8] gherkins—small cucumbers used for pickling.

[9] whiskers of maize—cornsilk.

On behalf of nothing, it was time to eat. On behalf of no one, it was good. Without any dream. And on a par with day, we gradually became anonymous, growing, rising, to the height of possible existence. Then, like the landed[10] aristocracy, we accepted the table.

There was no holocaust: everything there was anxious to be eaten just as we were anxious to eat it. Saving nothing for the following day, there and then I offered my feelings to that which aroused those feelings. It was a feast for which I had not paid in advance with the suffering of waiting, the hunger that comes as we bring the food to our lips. For now we felt hungry, an all-consuming hunger which embraced the entire spread[11] down to the crumbs. Those who drank wine kept a watchful eye on the milk. Those who slowly sipped milk could taste the wine that the others were drinking. Just outside, God among the acacias. Acacias which existed. We ate. Like someone giving water to a horse. The carved meat was shared out. The friendly exchanges were homely and rustic. No one spoke ill of anyone because no one spoke well of anyone. It was a harvest reunion and a truce was declared. We ate. Like a horde of living creatures, we slowly covered the earth. As busy as someone who cultivates existence, and plants, and reaps, and kills, and lives, and dies, and eats. I ate with the honesty of the man who does not belie what he is eating; I ate the food and not its name. God was never so possessed by what He is. The food was saying, **brusque**,[12] happy, austere: eat, eat and

share. Everything there was mine, it was my father's table. I ate without affection, I ate without the passion of mercy. Without offering myself to hope. I ate without any longing whatsoever. And I was wholly deserving of that food. For I cannot always be my brother's keeper, just as I can no longer be my own keeper, for I have ceased to love myself. Nor do I wish to form life because existence already exists. It exists like some territory where we all advance. Without a single word of love. Without a word. But your pleasure comprehends mine. We are strong and we eat. For bread is love among strangers.

An Angel's Disquiet

Upon leaving the building, I was taken by surprise. What had been simply rain on the window-panes and been shut out by the curtains and cozy warmth indoors, was tempest and darkness outside on the street. Had this change taken place while I was going down in the lift? A Rio[13] downpour without any shelter in sight. Copacabana[14] with water seeping under the doorways of shops at street-level, thick muddy currents reaching half-way up my legs, as I probed

---

[10] landed—landowning.

[11] spread—an elaborate meal.

[12] **brusque**—abrupt or informal way of acting or speaking.

[13] Rio—Rio de Janeiro, the largest city in Brazil, formerly the capital.

[14] Copacabana—a section of Rio famed for its hotels, skyscrapers, and nightlife.

with one foot to try and make contact with the invisible pavement. It was like an incoming tide which brought enough water in its wake to activate the moon's secret influence: there was already a tidal ebb and flow. Worst of all was that age-long fear engraved on the flesh: I am without shelter and the world has banished me to my own world. I, who can only be accommodated in a house, will never again possess a house. I am these soaking clothes. My drenched hair will never dry again, and I know that I shall not be among those destined to enter the Ark,[15] for the best couple of my species has already been chosen.

On street-corners, cars have been abandoned, their engines paralyzed, and there is not a taxi in sight. The ferocious happiness of several men who find it impossible to return to their homes is unmistakable. The **diabolical**[16] happiness of men on the loose presented an even greater threat to a woman whose only desire was to return home as quickly as possible. I walked at random along street after street, dragging myself rather than walking: to stop, even for a second, would have meant danger. I barely managed to hide my overwhelming sense of desolation. Some fortunate soul under an improvised tent, called out: By Jove, you're a courageous lady! It was not courage, it was definitely fear. Because everything was paralyzed, I who am terrified of that moment in which everything comes to a standstill, felt I had to go on.

When suddenly, through the downpour, a taxi appeared. It advanced cautiously, moving centimeter by centimeter, as if testing the ground with its wheels. How was I to secure that taxi? I approached it. I could not afford the luxury of asking; I remembered all the times when, however sweetly I pleaded, my plea was refused. Suppressing my panic, which gave a false impression of strength, I said to the taxi-driver: "I must get home! It's late! I have small children who must be wondering where I am, it's already dark, do you hear me?" To my great surprise, the man simply answered: yes. Still puzzled, I got in. The taxi could scarcely move through the muddy currents, but it was moving—and it would eventually arrive. I was only thinking: this is more than I deserve. Soon I was thinking: it never occurred to me that I should be so deserving. And very soon, I was the mistress of my very own taxi. I had taken possession as if by right of something which had been given to me **gratuitously**,[17] and I briskly set about tidying myself up: I wrung the water from my hair and clothes, pulled off my squelching shoes, and dried my face which looked tear-stained. I confess without shame that I had been weeping. Not much and for different reasons, but I had been weeping. After settling into my new domain, I leaned back comfortably in what was mine, and from my Ark, I watched the world come to an end.

---

[15] Ark—the boat Noah built to survive the flood.

[16] **diabolical**—disgracefully bad, evil.

[17] **gratuitously**—without having been requested or charged for.

Just then, a woman approached the car. As the taxi slowly advanced, she succeeded in accompanying it, holding on to the door-handle in a state of distress. And she literally implored me to allow her to share my taxi. I was already very late, and her route would have meant making a lengthy detour. I remembered, however, my own desperation five minutes earlier, and decided that she should not suffer a similar crisis. When I said yes, her note of pleading immediately ceased, and was replaced with an extremely practical tone of voice: "Good, but wait a minute while I go across the road to collect a parcel which I left with the dressmaker so that it wouldn't get soaked." "Is she taking advantage of me?" I asked myself in my customary doubt as to whether I should or should not let people take advantage of me. I ended up by giving in. The woman took her time. And she came back carrying an enormous parcel which she held on outstretched arms, as if contact with her own body might stain the dress. She made herself comfortable on the back seat beside me, making me feel inhibited in my own home.

And my Calvary[18] for being an angel began at once—for the woman, with that authoritarian voice of hers, had already started to call me an angel. Her situation could scarcely have been less endearing: there was to be a première that night and, were it not for my generosity, her dress would have been soaked in the rain or she would have been late and missed the première. I had already experienced my own premières, and had not been enthusiastic about any of them. "You have no idea what a miracle this has been," she told me firmly. "I started to pray in the street, to pray that God would send an angel to my rescue; I made a vow that I would fast all day tomorrow. —And God sent you." Feeling ill at ease, I fidgeted in my seat. Was I an angel destined to salvage premières? The divine irony left me disconcerted. But the woman, with all the force of her practical faith, and she was a forceful woman, vehemently insisted upon acknowledging me as an angel, something which very few people have ever acknowledged in the past, and even then with the greatest discretion. I tried to shrug it off with some mild sarcasm. "Don't over-estimate me, I am merely a means of transport." While she made no attempt to grasp my meaning, I unwillingly conceded that the argument did not really excuse me: angels are also a means of transport. Intimidated, I remained silent. I am always greatly impressed by anyone who shouts at me: the woman was not shouting, but she was clearly towering over me. Incapable of facing up to her, I took refuge in sweet **cynicism**[19]: that woman who handled her own ecstasy with such vigor, must be a woman who was accustomed to paying with money, and almost certainly she would end up by rewarding her angel with a cheque, also bearing in mind that the rain

---

[18] Calvary—the hill near Jerusalem where Jesus was crucified.
[19] **cynicism**—disbelief in human sincerity or goodness.

must have washed away all my distinction. With a little more consoling cynicism, I silently informed her that money would be as legitimate a way as any other of thanking me, since her money was really money. Or—I thought in amusement—she could easily give her dress for the première as a token of her gratitude, because what she really ought to be grateful for was not that she had protected her dress from the rain, but that she had attained a state of grace through me as it were. With ever mounting cynicism, I thought to myself, "Everyone gets the angel they deserve, and just look at the angel she got: here I am, out of pure curiosity, coveting a dress which I have never seen. Now let's see how her soul is going to conform to the idea of an angel who is interested in dresses." It struck me in my arrogance, that I had no desire to be assigned as an angel to the fervid[20] stupidity of that woman.

To be frank, being an angel was beginning to weigh upon me. I am all too familiar with the ways of the world: they call me good-hearted, and at least for some time I am disturbed by my own malice. I also began to understand why angels get upset: they are at everybody's beck and call. This had never occurred to me before. Unless I happened to be an angel rather low down in the hierarchy of angels. Who knows, perhaps I was just a novice angel. The complacent happiness of that woman began to depress me: she had exploited me to the full. She had converted my indecisive nature into a definite profession, she had transformed my spontaneity into an obligation, she had enslaved me, I who was an angel. Who knows, however, if I had not been sent into the world just for that moment of usefulness. This then, was my true worth. In the taxi I was not a fallen angel: I was an angel who came to her senses. I came to my senses and showed my displeasure. Any more nonsense and I would tell that woman in open revolt whose guardian angel I was: do me the favor of getting out of this taxi at once! But I **curbed**[21] my tongue and supported the weight of my wings which felt ever more contrite because of the woman's enormous parcel. As my protégée,[22] she continued to say nice things about me, or rather, about my function. I fumed inwardly. The woman sensed this and fell silent as if confused. By the time we reached Viveiros de Castro there was mute hostility between us.

—Listen, I said to her abruptly, because my spontaneity is a double-edged knife even for others, the taxi will drop me first then take you on.

—But, she said in surprise, a note of indignation creeping into her voice, then I shall have to make an enormous detour and end up by being late! You, on the other hand, would only have the slightest detour if you were to drop me off first.

> **In the taxi I was not a fallen angel: I was an angel who came to her senses.**

---

[20] fervid—passionate.

[21] curbed—restrained or suppressed.

[22] protégée—woman or girl under the care or protection of another person.

—Of course, I replied dryly. But I will not allow any detours.

—I'll pay the whole fare! she insulted me with the same money with which she would have remembered to reward me.

—I shall pay the whole fare, I insulted her in return.

Upon alighting from the taxi, like someone who asks for nothing, I took great care to leave my wings folded on the taxi seat. I alighted with that profound lack of finesse which has saved me from angelical **abysses**.[23] Free of wings, with a great swish of my invisible tail and with the **hauteur**[24] which I reserve for taxi-drivers, I swept through the imposing entrance of the Visconde de Pelotas apartment block as **regal**[25] as a queen.

Five Days in Brasilia

Brasilia[26] is built on the line of the horizon. —Brasilia is artificial. As artificial as the world must have been when it was created. When the world was created, it was necessary to create a human being especially for that world. We are all deformed through adapting to God's freedom. We cannot say how we might have turned out if we had been created first, and the world had been deformed afterwards to meet our needs. Brasilia has no inhabitants as yet who are typical of Brasilia. If I were to say that Brasilia is pleasant, you would realize immediately that I like the city. But if I were to say that Brasilia is the image of my insomnia,

you would see this as a criticism: but my insomnia is neither pleasant nor awful: my insomnia is I, it is lived, it is my terror.

The two architects who planned Brasilia were not interested in creating something beautiful. That would be too simple; they created their own terror, and left that terror unexplained. Creation is not an understanding, it is a new mystery. — When I died, I opened my eyes one day and there was Brasilia. I found myself alone in the world. There was a stationary taxi. Without any driver—Lucio Costa and Oscar Niemeyer[27] are two solitary men. —I look at Brasilia the way I look at Rome: Brasilia began with a final simplification of ruins. The ivy had not yet grown. — Besides the wind there is another thing which blows. —It can only be recognized in the supernatural rippling of the lake. — Wherever you stand, you have the impression of being on the margin of a dangerous precipice. Brasilia stands on the margin. — Were I to live here, I should let my hair grow down to my feet. —Brasilia belongs to a glorious past which no longer exists. That type of civilization disappeared thousands of years ago. In the 4th century B.C., Brasilia was inhabited by men and women who were fair and very tall, who were neither American nor Scandinavian,

---

[23] **abysses**—deep or seemingly bottomless openings.

[24] **hauteur**—pride, haughtiness.

[25] **regal**—grand or magnificent in appearance, manner, or size.

[26] Brasilia—capital of Brazil since 1960. It was designed and built in the 1950s.

[27] Lúcio Costa and Oscar Niemeyer—the architects who designed the original plan for Brasilia.

and who shone brightly in the sun. They were all blind. That explains why there is nothing to collide with in Brasilia. The inhabitants of Brasilia dressed in white gold. The race became extinct because few children were born. The more beautiful the natives of Brasilia, the more blind, pure, and radiant they became, and the fewer children they produced. The natives of Brasilia lived for nearly three hundred years. There was no one in whose name they could die. Thousands of years later the location was discovered by a band of fugitives who would not be accepted in any other place; they had nothing to lose. There they lit a bonfire, set up their tents, and gradually began excavating the sands which buried the city. Those men and women were short and dark-skinned, with shifty, restless eyes, and because they were fugitives and desperate, there was someone in whose name they could both live and die. They occupied the houses which were in ruins and multiplied themselves, thus forming a human race which was much given to contemplation. —I awaited the night, like someone awaiting the shadows in order to steal away unobserved. When the night came, I perceived with horror that it was hopeless: wherever I might go, I should be seen. The thought terrified me: seen by whom?—The city was built without any escape route for rats. A whole part of myself, the worst part, and precisely that part of me which has a horror of rats, has not been provided for in Brasilia. Its founders tried to ignore the importance of human beings. The dimensions of the city's buildings were calculated for the heavens. Hell has a better understanding of me. But the rats, all of them enormous, are invading the city. That is an invisible headline in the newspapers. — Here I am afraid. —The construction of Brasilia: that of a totalitarian state. —This great visual silence which I love.

In Brasilia there is no place where one may enter, no place where one may leave.

Even my insomnia might have created this piece of never-never-land. Like those two monks, I would also meditate in the desert where there are no opportunities for temptation. But I see black vultures flying high overhead. What is perishing, dear God? —I did not shed a single tear in Brasilia. There was no place for tears. —It is a shore without any sea. —In Brasilia there is no place where one may enter, no place where one may leave.

Mummy, it's nice to see you standing there with your white cape waving in the breeze. (The truth is that I have perished, my son.) —A prison in the open air. Besides, there is nowhere to escape to. For anyone escaping would probably find himself heading for Brasilia. They ensnared me in freedom. But freedom is simply what is conquered. When they strike me, they are ordering me to be free. —The human indifference which lurks in my nature is something I discover here in Brasilia, and it flowers cold and patient, the cold strength of Nature. Here is the place where my crimes (not the worst of them, but those which I should fail to recognize in myself)—where my cold crimes find sufficient scope. I am leaving. Here my crimes would not be crimes of love. I am leaving for my other crimes, those which God and I understand. But I know that I shall return. I am drawn here by all that is terrifying in my nature. —I have never seen anything like it in the world. But I recognize this city at the very core of my dream. The core of my dream is lucidity. —For as I was saying, Flash Gordon . . . —If they were to photograph me standing in Brasilia, upon developing the film only the landscape would emerge. —Where are the giraffes of Brasilia? —A certain twitching on my part, certain moments of silence, provoke my son into commenting: Gosh, grown-ups are the limit. —It is urgent. Were Brasilia not populated, or rather, not overpopulated, it would be inhabited in some other way. And should that happen, it would be much too late: there would be no place for people. They would feel themselves tacitly expelled. —Here the soul casts no shadow on the ground. During the first two days I had no appetite. Everything had the appearance of the food they serve on board aeroplanes. —At night, I turned my face towards silence. I know that there is a secret hour when manna[28] falls and moistens the lands of Brasilia. —However close one is, everything here is seen from afar. I have found no means of touching it. But at least there is one thing in my favor:

before arriving here, I already knew how to touch things from afar. I never became too desperate: from afar, I was able to touch things. I possessed a great deal, and not even that which I have touched, suspects this. A rich woman is like that. It is pure Brasilia. —The city of Brasilia lies outside the city. —"Boys, boys come here, will you. Look who's coming on the street, all dressed up in modernistic style. It ain't nobody but . . ." (*Aunt Hagar's Blues*, played by Ted Lewis and his Band, with Jimmy Dorsey on the clarinet.) —That astonishing beauty, this city traced out in the air. —Meantime, no samba[29] is likely to emerge in Brasilia. —Brasilia does not permit me to feel weary. It persecutes me to some extent. I feel fine. I feel fine. I feel fine. I felt just fine. Besides, I have always cultivated my weariness, as my most precious manifestation of **inertia**.[30] —Everything just for today. God alone knows what will happen to Brasilia. Here the fortuitous[31] takes one by surprise—Brasilia is haunted. It is the motionless profile of something. —Unable to sleep. I look out of my hotel window at three o'clock in the morning. Brasilia is a landscape of insomnia. It never sleeps. —Here the organic being does not disintegrate. It becomes petrified. —I should like to see five hundred eagles of the blackest onyx scattered throughout Brasilia. —Brasilia is asexual. —The first time you set eyes on the city you feel inebriated:[32] your

---

[28] manna—In the Bible, manna is a miraculous food provided by God to the Israelites in the desert.

[29] samba—Brazilian dance.

[30] **inertia**—unwillingness to act or move.

[31] fortuitous—chance event.

[32] inebriated—intoxicated, drunk.

feet do not touch the ground. —How deeply the people breathe in Brasilia. Anyone who breathes here starts to experience desire. And that is to be avoided. Desire does not exist here. Will it ever exist? I cannot see how. —It would not surprise me to encounter Arabs on the street. Arabs of another age and long since dead. —Here my passion dies. And I gain **lucidity**[33] which makes me feel **grandiose**[34] for no good reason. I am immense and futile, I am of the purest gold. And almost endowed with a medium's powers. —If there is still some crime which humanity has not committed, that new crime will be initiated here. It is so very open, so well adjusted to the plateau, that no one will ever know. This is the place where space most closely resembles time. —I am certain that this is the right place for me. But I have become much too corrupted on earth. I have acquired all of life's bad habits. —**Erosion**[35] will strip Brasilia to the bone. —The religious atmosphere which I sensed from the outset, and denied. This city was achieved through prayer. Two men beatified[36] by solitude created me here, on foot, restless, exposed to the wind. —One greatly longs to see white horses unleashed in Brasilia. At night, they would change to green under the light of the moon —I know what those two men wanted: that peace and silence which also conform to my idea of eternity. Those two men created the image of an eternal city. —There is something here which frightens me. When I shall discover what it is, I shall also discover what I like about this place. Fear has always guided me to the things I love; and because I love, I am afraid. It was often fear which took me by the hand and led me. Fear leads me to danger. And everything I love has an element of risk.

In Brasilia you find the craters of the Moon. —The beauty of Brasilia is to be found in those invisible statues.

---

[33] **lucidity**—clarity of thought, understanding.

[34] **grandiose**—impressive, imposing.

[35] **Erosion**—the wearing away of a surface by water, wind, or friction.

[36] beatified—sanctified.

QUESTIONS TO CONSIDER

1. Why does the hostess in "The Sharing of Bread" serve such a good meal? How does the narrator feel when eating it?

2. Why is the narrator of "An Angel's Disquiet" hostile to the woman who shares the taxi? Do you think she is being unfair? Why or why not?

3. From reading "Five Days in Brasilia," do you think that Lispector likes or dislikes Brasilia? Explain how you arrived at your answer.

4. How would you describe the world of Lispector's stories? Is it a happy or hostile place? Explain your answer.

A Story and a Poem

JORGE LUIS BORGES

Jorge Luis Borges (1899–1986) was born in Buenos Aires, Argentina, but received his education in Europe. Thanks to this education and his English grandmother, Borges had a command of European languages and their literatures. He began writing stories and poems in his youth. Most of Borges's writing is elliptical and metaphysical. The descriptions are precise, but not of the world we know. He reveled in mystery and paradoxes. Borges also suffered from a degenerative eye condition that eventually caused him to go completely blind. Dreams and visions, and imagery of light and darkness, play a large role in both his prose and poetry. The short stories Borges wrote in the 1940s made him internationally famous—one of the very first Latin American writers to gain such a reputation. He is rightly regarded as one of the century's most innovative and important writers.

The Circular Ruins

And if he left off dreaming about you . . .
—*Through the Looking Glass*, VI.

No one saw him disembark in the unanimous night, no one saw the bamboo canoe sink into the sacred mud, but in a few days there was no one who did not know that the **taciturn**[1] man came from the South and that his home had been one of those numberless villages upstream in the deeply **cleft**[2] side of the mountain, where the Zend language has not been contaminated by Greek and where leprosy[3] is infrequent. What is certain is that the gray man kissed the mud, climbed up the bank without pushing aside (probably, without feeling) the blades which were **lacerating**[4] his flesh, and crawled, nauseated and bloodstained, up to the circular enclosure crowned with a stone tiger or horse, which sometimes was the color of flame and now was that of ashes. This circle was a temple which had been devoured by ancient fires, profaned by the miasmal[5] jungle, and whose god no longer received the homage of men. The stranger stretched

---

[1] **taciturn**—saying little, uncommunicative.

[2] **cleft**—split, partly divided.

[3] leprosy—moral corruption or contagion.

[4] **lacerating**—tearing or mangling.

[5] miasmal—having a strong or unpleasant smelling vapor.

himself out beneath the pedestal. He was awakened by the sun high overhead. He was not astonished to find that his wounds had healed; he closed his **pallid**[6] eyes and slept, not through weakness of flesh but through determination of will. He knew that this temple was the place required for his invincible intent; he knew that the incessant trees had not succeeded in strangling the ruins of another **propitious**[7] temple downstream which had once belonged to gods now burned and dead; he knew that his immediate obligation was to dream. Toward midnight he was awakened by the **inconsolable**[8] shriek of a bird. Tracks of bare feet, some figs and a jug warned him that the men of the region had been spying respectfully on his sleep, soliciting his protection or afraid of his magic. He felt a chill of fear, and sought out a **sepulchral**[9] niche[10] in the **dilapidated**[11] wall where he concealed himself among unfamiliar leaves.

The purpose which guided him was not impossible, though supernatural. He wanted to dream a man; he wanted to dream him in minute entirety and impose him on reality. This magic project had exhausted the entire expanse of his mind; if someone had asked him his name or to relate some event of his former life, he would not have been able to give an answer. This uninhabited, ruined temple suited him, for it contained a minimum of visible world; the proximity of the workmen also suited him, for they took it upon themselves to provide for his **frugal**[12] needs. The rice and fruit they brought him were nourishment enough for his body,

which was consecrated to the sole task of sleeping and dreaming.

At first, his dreams were chaotic; then in a short while they became dialectic[13] in nature. The stranger dreamed that he was in the center of a circular amphitheater which was more or less the burnt temple; clouds of taciturn students filled the tiers of seats; the faces of the farthest ones hung at a distance of many centuries and as high as the stars, but their features were completely precise. The man lectured his pupils on anatomy, cosmography,[14] and magic: the faces listened anxiously and tried to answer understandingly, as if they guessed the importance of that examination which would redeem one of them from his condition of empty illusion and interpolate[15] him into the real world. Asleep or awake, the man thought over the answers of his phantoms, did not allow himself to be deceived by impostors, and in certain perplexities he sensed a growing intelligence. He was seeking a soul worthy of participating in the universe.

---

[6] **pallid**—pale, especially from illness.

[7] **propitious**—favorable.

[8] **inconsolable**—despairing, broken-hearted.

[9] **sepulchral**—tomblike.

[10] niche—a shallow recess.

[11] **dilapidated**—rundown, in a state of disrepair or ruin.

[12] **frugal**—sparing or economical with regard to food or money.

[13] dialectic—forming a synthesis or structure.

[14] cosmography—a description or mapping of the general features of the universe.

[15] interpolate—insert.

After nine or ten nights he understood with a certain bitterness that he could expect nothing from those pupils who accepted his doctrine passively, but that he could expect something from those who occasionally dared to oppose him. The former group, although worthy of love and affection, could not ascend to the level of individuals; the latter pre-existed to a slightly greater degree. One afternoon (now afternoons were also given over to sleep, now he was only awake for a couple of hours at daybreak) he dismissed the vast illusory[16] student body for good and kept only one pupil. He was a taciturn, sallow[17] boy, at times intractable,[18] and whose sharp features resembled those of his dreamer. The brusque elimination of his fellow students did not disconcert him for long; after a few private lessons, his progress was enough to astound[19] the teacher. Nevertheless, a catastrophe took place. One day, the man emerged from his sleep as if from a viscous desert, looked at the useless afternoon light which he immediately confused with the dawn, and understood that he had not dreamed. All that night and all day long, the intolerable lucidity[20] of insomnia fell upon him. He tried exploring the forest, to lose his strength; among the hemlock he barely succeeded in experiencing several short snatches of sleep, veined with fleeting,

> **All that night and all day long, the intolerable lucidity of insomnia fell upon him.**

rudimentary[21] visions that were useless. He tried to assemble the student body but scarcely had he articulated a few brief words of exhortation when it became deformed and was then erased. In his almost perpetual vigil,[22] tears of anger burned his old eyes.

He understood that modeling the incoherent and vertiginous[23] matter of which dreams are composed was the most difficult task that a man could undertake, even though he should penetrate all the enigmas[24] of a superior and inferior order; much more difficult than weaving a rope out of sand or coining the faceless wind. He swore he would forget the enormous hallucination which had thrown him off at first, and he sought another method of work. Before putting it into execution, he spent a month recovering his strength, which had been squandered by his delirium. He abandoned all premeditation of dreaming and almost immediately succeeded in sleeping a reasonable part of each day. The few times that he had dreams during this period, he paid no attention to them. Before resuming his task, he waited until the moon's disk was

---

[16] **illusory**—imagined or deceptive.

[17] **sallow**—colored a sickly yellow or pale brown.

[18] **intractable**—hard to control or deal with.

[19] **astound**—amaze.

[20] lucidity—clarity.

[21] rudimentary—undeveloped, incomplete.

[22] **vigil**—keeping awake during a time usually spent sleeping in order to carefully watch something or pray.

[23] **vertiginous**—causing a sensation of spinning and dizziness.

[24] enigmas—puzzles

perfect. Then, in the afternoon, he purified himself in the waters of the river, worshipped the planetary gods, pronounced the prescribed syllables of a mighty name, and went to sleep. He dreamed almost immediately, with his heart throbbing.

He dreamed that it was warm, secret, about the size of a clenched fist, and of a garnet color within the penumbra[25] of a human body as yet without face or sex; during fourteen lucid nights he dreamt of it with **meticulous**[26] love. Every night he perceived it more clearly. He did not touch it; he only permitted himself to witness it, to observe it, and occasionally to rectify it with a glance. He perceived it and lived it from all angles and distances. On the fourteenth night he lightly touched the pulmonary[27] artery with his index finger, then the whole heart, outside and inside. He was satisfied with the examination. He deliberately did not dream for a night; he then took up the heart again, invoked the name of a planet, and undertook the vision of another of the principal organs. Within a year he had come to the skeleton and the eyelids. The innumerable hair was perhaps the most difficult task. He dreamed an entire man—a young man, but who did not sit up or talk, who was unable to open his eyes. Night after night, the man dreamt him asleep.

In the Gnostic[28] cosmogonies, demiurges[29] fashion a red Adam who cannot stand; as clumsy, crude and elemental as this Adam of dust was the Adam—of dreams forged by the wizard's nights. One afternoon, the man almost destroyed his entire work, but then changed his mind. (It would have been better had he destroyed it.) When he had exhausted all supplications to the deities of the earth, he threw himself at the feet of the effigy[30] which was perhaps a tiger or perhaps a colt and implored its unknown help. That evening, at twilight, he dreamt of the statue. He dreamt it was alive, tremulous:[31] it was not an **atrocious**[32] bastard of a tiger and a colt, but at the same time these two fiery creatures and also a bull, a rose, and a storm. This multiple god revealed to him that his earthly name was Fire, and that in this circular temple (and in others like it) people had once made sacrifices to him and worshipped him, and that he would magically animate the dreamed phantom, in such a way that all creatures, except Fire itself and the dreamer, would believe it to be a man of flesh and blood. He commanded that once this man had been instructed in all the rites, he should be sent to the other ruined temple whose pyramids were still standing downstream, so that some voice would glorify him in that deserted edifice. In the dream of the man that dreamed, the dreamed one awoke.

---

[25] penumbra—shadow.

[26] **meticulous**—giving great attention to details.

[27] pulmonary—of or relating to the lungs.

[28] Gnostic—concerning the occult or the mystical.

[29] demiurges—heavenly creatures who serve a Supreme Being.

[30] effigy—image.

[31] tremulous—trembling.

[32] **atrocious**—very bad or unpleasant.

The wizard carried out the orders he had been given. He devoted a certain length of time (which finally proved to be two years) to instructing him in the mysteries of the universe and the cult of fire. Secretly, he was pained at the idea of being separated from him. On the pretext of **pedagogical**[33] necessity, each day he increased the number of hours dedicated to dreaming. He also remade the right shoulder, which was somewhat defective.

> **Not to be a man, to be a projection of another man's dreams—what an incomparable humiliation, what madness!**

At times, he was disturbed by the impression that all this had already happened. . . . In general, his days were happy; when he closed his eyes, he thought: *Now I will be with my son.* Or, more rarely: *The son I have* **engendered**[34] *is waiting for me and will not exist if I do not go to him.*

Gradually, he began accustoming him to reality. Once he ordered him to place a flag on a faraway peak. The next day the flag was fluttering on the peak. He tried other **analogous**[35] experiments, each time more **audacious**.[36] With a certain bitterness, he understood that his son was ready to be born—and perhaps impatient. That night he kissed him for the first time and sent him off to the other temple whose remains were turning white downstream, across many miles of **inextricable**[37] jungle and marshes. Before doing this (and so that

his son should never know that he was a phantom, so that he should think himself a man like any other) he destroyed in him all memory of his years of apprenticeship.

His victory and peace became blurred with boredom. In the twilight times of dusk and dawn, he would prostrate himself before the stone figure, perhaps imagining his unreal son carrying out identical rites in other circular ruins downstream; at night he no longer dreamed, or dreamed as any man does. His perceptions of the sounds and forms of the universe became somewhat pallid: his absent son was being nourished by these diminutions of his soul. The purpose of his life had been fulfilled; the man remained in a kind of ecstasy. After a certain time, which some chroniclers prefer to compute in years and others in decades, two oarsmen awoke him at midnight; he could not see their faces, but they spoke to him of a charmed man in a temple of the North, capable of walking on fire without burning himself. The wizard suddenly remembered the words of the god. He remembered that of all the creatures that people the earth, Fire was the only one who knew his son to be a phantom. This memory, which at first calmed him, ended by tormenting him. He feared lest his son should meditate on this

---

[33] **pedagogical**—related to teaching or instruction.

[34] **engendered**—created, brought about.

[35] **analogous**—similar or parallel.

[36] **audacious**—daring, bold.

[37] **inextricable**—inescapable.

abnormal privilege and by some means find out he was a mere simulacrum.[38] Not to be a man, to be a projection of another man's dreams—what an incomparable humiliation, what madness! Any father is interested in the sons he has **procreated**[39] (or permitted) out of the mere confusion of happiness; it was natural that the wizard should fear for the future of that son whom he had thought out entrail by entrail, feature by feature, in a thousand and one secret nights.

His misgivings ended abruptly, but not without certain forewarnings. First (after a long drought) a remote cloud, as light as a bird, appeared on a hill; then, toward the South, the sky took on the rose color of leopard's gums; then came clouds of smoke which rusted the metal of the nights; afterwards came the panic-stricken flight of wild animals. For what had happened many centuries before was repeating itself.

The ruins of the sanctuary of the god of Fire was destroyed by fire. In a dawn without birds, the wizard saw the **concentric**[40] fire licking the walls. For a moment, he thought of taking refuge in the water, but then he understood that death was coming to crown his old age and absolve him from his labors. He walked toward the sheets of flame. They did not bite his flesh, they caressed him and flooded him without heat or combustion. With relief, with humiliation, with terror, he understood that he also was an illusion, that someone else was dreaming him.

---

[38] simulacrum—an image of something.

[39] **procreated**—brought into existence by the natural process of reproduction.

[40] **concentric**—having a common center.

In Praise of Darkness

Old age (this is the name that others give it)
may prove a time of happiness.
The animal is dead or nearly dead;
man and soul go on.
I live among vague whitish shapes
that are not darkness yet. Buenos Aires,
which once broke up in a tatter of slums and open lots
out toward the endless plain,
is now again the graveyard of the Recoleta, the Retiro square,
the shabby streets of the old Westside,
and the few vanishing decrepit houses
that we still call the South.
All through my life things were too many.
To think, Democritus[41] tore out his eyes;
time has been my Democritus.
This growing dark is slow and brings no pain;
it flows along an easy slope
and is akin to eternity.
My friends are faceless,
women are as they were years back,
one street corner is taken for another,
on the pages of books there are no letters.
All this should make me uneasy,
but there's a restfulness about it, a going back.
Of the many generations of books on earth
I have read only a few,
the few that in my mind I go on reading still
reading and changing.
From south and east and west and north,
roads coming together have led me
to my secret center.

---

[41] Democritus—Greek philosopher (460?–370? B.C.)

These roads were footsteps and echoes,
women, men, agonies, rebirths,
days and nights,
falling asleep and dreams,
each single moment of my yesterdays
and of the world's yesterdays,
the firm sword of the Dane and the moon of the Persians,
the deeds of the dead,
shared love, words,
Emerson,[42] and snow, and so many things.
Now I can forget them. I reach my center,
my algebra and my key,
my mirror.
Soon I shall know who I am.

---

[42] Emerson—Ralph Waldo Emerson (1803–1882), American writer and philosopher.

QUESTIONS TO CONSIDER

1. Who is the "wizard" in "The Circular Ruins"? What is he trying to do?

2. What do you think Borges intended "The Circular Ruins" to describe? What lessons can you draw from it?

3. What is Borges describing in "In Praise of Darkness"? What does he mean by the last line of the poem?

4. How would you describe the role of the artist, or creator and thinker, as Borges depicted him? How autobiographical do you think he intended these works to be?

Three Poems

OCTAVIO PAZ

Octavio Paz (1914–1998) began writing poetry in his teens and published his first book at age nineteen. In his writing, Paz has tried to come to terms with the glory of Mexico's past contrasted with her poverty and underdevelopment. He has been horrified by Mexico's continually repressive and corrupt governments. Paz's poetry is suffused with Mexico's cultural and historical legacy. He believes that poetry is an "operation capable of changing the world, poetic activity is revolutionary by nature." Paz has made many people believe that the intellectual has an important role to play in the development of Latin America. He was awarded the Nobel Prize in 1990.

Poet's Epitaph[1]

He tried to sing, singing
not to remember
his true life of lies
and to remember
his lying life of truths.

The Street

A long and silent street.
I walk in blackness and I stumble and fall
and rise, and I walk blind, my feet
stepping on silent stones and dry leaves.

---

[1] **epitaph**—words written in memory of a person who has died.

Someone behind me also stepping on stones, leaves:
if I slow down, he slows;
if I run, he runs. I turn: nobody.

Everything dark and doorless.
Turning and turning among these corners
which lead forever to the street
where nobody waits for, nobody follows me,
where I pursue a man who **stumbles**[2]
and rises and says when he sees me: nobody

Small Variation[3]

Like music come back to life—
who brings it from over there, from the other side,
who conducts it through the **spirals**[4]
of the mind's ear?—
like the vanished
moment that returns
and is again the same
presence erasing itself,
the syllables unearthed
make sound without sound:
and at the hour of our death, amen.

In the school chapel
I spoke them many times
without conviction. Now I hear them
spoken by a voice without lips,
a sound of sand sifting away,
while in my skull the hours toll
and time takes another turn around my night.

---

[2] **stumbles**—trips and almost falls.

[3] **variation**—departure from a standard or type.

[4] **spirals**—curves or coils that wind around themselves in an enlarging or a decreasing circular motion.

I am not the first man on earth—
I tell myself in the **manner**[5] of Epictetus[6]—
who is going to die.
And as I say this
the world breaks down in my blood.

The sorrow
of Gilgamesh[7] when he returned
from the land without **twilight**[8]
is my sorrow. On our shadowy earth
each man is Adam:[9]
with him the world begins,
with him it ends.

Between after and before—
brackets[10] of stone—
for an instant that will never return I shall be
the first man and I shall be the last.
And as I say it, the instant—
bodiless, weightless—
opens under my feet
and closes over me and is pure time.

---

[5] **manner**—way or style.

[6] Epictetus—(fl. A.D. 100) Greek philosopher who advocated a serene life where death was faced with equanimity.

[7] Gilgamesh—hero of a Sumerian epic poem, who goes to the underworld in search of immortality, but returns knowing that no man can escape death.

[8] **twilight**—decline or destruction.

[9] Adam—In the Bible, Adam is the first man.

[10] **brackets**—fixtures or printed marks that enclose something.

QUESTIONS TO CONSIDER

1. What does Paz mean by the "true life of lies" and the "lying life of truths" in "Poet's Epitaph"?

2. What is Paz describing in "The Street"?

3. What is "Small Variation" about? What is Paz's message on this subject?

4. From reading these three poems, how would you describe Paz's idea of the writer and his goals?

Four Poems

PABLO NERUDA

Commonly regarded as the most important Latin American poet of the century, Pablo Neruda (1904–1973) began writing poetry at an early age. Pablo Neruda was a pseudonym chosen by Neftalí Ricardo Eliecer Reyes Basoalto at sixteen to hide from his father the fact that he was publishing poetry. The young writer entered the diplomatic corps, and it was through his various postings that Neruda discovered the modern poetry being published in Europe. It was also in Europe in the 1930s that he discovered radical politics. In the following years, Neruda declared himself a Communist and spent many years in exile from Chile. In 1971, Neruda was awarded the Nobel Prize. When he died he was living in Chile during a period of liberalization, which had collapsed in a military coup just a few days before the poet's death.

We Are Many

Of the many men whom I am, whom we are,
I cannot settle on a single one.
They are lost to me under the cover of clothing,
They have departed for another city.

When everything seems to be set
to show me off as a man of intelligence,
the fool I keep concealed in my person
takes over my talk and occupies my mouth.

On other occasions, I am dozing in the midst
of people of some distinction,
and when I summon my courageous self,

a coward completely unknown to me
swaddles[1] my poor skeleton
in a thousand tiny reservations.

When a stately home bursts into flames,
instead of the fireman I summon,
an **arsonist**[2] bursts on the scene,
and he is I. There is nothing I can do.
What must I do to single out myself?
How can I put myself together?

All the books I read
lionize[3] dazzling hero figures,
always brimming with self-assurance.
I die with envy of them;
and, in films where bullets fly on the wind,
I am left in envy of the cowboys,
left admiring even the horses.

But when I call upon my **dashing**[4] being,
out comes the same old lazy self,
and so I never know just who I am,
nor how many I am, nor who we will be being.
I would like to be able to touch a bell
and call up my real self, the truly me,
because if I really need my proper self,
I must not allow myself to disappear.

While I am writing, I am far away;
and when I come back, I have already left.
I should like to see if the same thing happens
to other people as it does to me,
to see if as many people are as I am,

---

[1] **swaddles**—wraps, as in garments or bandages.

[2] **arsonist**—a person who intentionally sets property on fire.

[3] **lionize**—glorify, treat as a celebrity.

[4] **dashing**—spirited or lively.

and if they seem the same way to themselves.
When this problem has been thoroughly explored,
I am going to school myself so well in things
that, when I try to explain my problems,
I shall speak, not of self, but of geography.

Too Many Names

Mondays are **meshed**[5] with Tuesdays
and the week with the whole year.
Time cannot be cut
with your weary scissors,
and all the names of the day
are washed out by the waters of night.

No one can claim the name of Pedro,
nobody is Rosa or Maria,
all of us are dust or sand,
all of us are rain under rain.
They have spoken to me of Venezuelas,
of Chiles and of Paraguays;[6]
I have no idea what they are saying.
I know only the skin of the earth
and I know it is without a name.

When I lived amongst the roots
they pleased me more than flowers did,
and when I spoke to a stone
it rang like a bell.

---

[5] **meshed**—interwoven.

[6] Venezuelas . . . Chiles . . . Paraguays—Venezuela, Chile, and Paraguay are countries in South America.

It is so long, the spring
which goes on all winter.
Time lost its shoes.
A year is four centuries.

When I sleep every night,
what am I called or not called?
And when I wake, who am I
if I was not I while I slept?

This means to say that scarcely
have we landed into life
than we come as if new-born;
let us not fill our mouths
with so many **faltering**[7] names,
with so many sad formalities,
with so many **pompous**[8] letters,
with so much of yours and mine,
with so much signing of papers.

I have a mind to confuse things,
unite them, bring them to birth,
mix them up, undress them,
until the light of the world
has the oneness of the ocean,
a generous, vast wholeness,
a **crepitant**[9] fragrance.

---

[7] **faltering**—wavering or hesitating.

[8] **pompous**—self-important.

[9] **crepitant**—making a cracking sound.

Poet's Obligation

To whoever is not listening to the sea
this Friday morning, to whoever is **cooped**[10] up
in house or office, factory or woman
or street or mine or harsh prison cell:
to him I come, and, without speaking or looking,
I arrive and open the door of his prison,
and a vibration starts up, vague and insistent,
a great fragment of thunder sets in motion
the rumble of the planet and the foam,
the raucous rivers of the ocean flood,
the star vibrates swiftly in its corona,
and the sea is beating, dying and continuing.

So, drawn on by my destiny,
I ceaselessly must listen to and keep
the sea's lamenting in my awareness,
I must feel the crash of the hard water
and gather it up in a **perpetual**[11] cup
so that, wherever those in prison may be,
wherever they suffer the autumn's **castigation**,[12]

I may be there with an errant wave,
I may move, passing through windows,
and hearing me, eyes will glance upward
saying "How can I reach the sea?"
And I shall broadcast, saying nothing,
the starry echoes of the wave,
a breaking up of foam and of quicksand,
a rustling of salt withdrawing,
the grey cry of sea-birds on the coast.

So, through me, freedom and the sea
will make their answer to the shuttered heart.

---

[10] **cooped**—confined or imprisoned.
[11] **perpetual**—never-ending.
[12] **castigation**—severe scolding or punishment.

Poetry

And it was at that age . . . Poetry arrived
in search of me. I don't know, I don't know where
it came from, from winter or a river.
I don't know how or when,
no, they were not voices, they were not
words, nor silence,
but from a street I was summoned,
from the branches of night,
abruptly from the others,
among violent fires
or returning alone,
there I was without a face
and it touched me.

I did not know what to say, my mouth
had no way
with names,
my eyes were blind,
and something started in my soul,
fever or forgotten wings,
and I made my own way,
deciphering
that fire,
and I wrote the first faint line,
faint, without substance, pure
nonsense,
pure wisdom of someone who knows nothing,
and suddenly I saw
the heavens
unfastened
and open,
planets,

palpitating[13] plantations,
shadow perforated,
riddled
with arrows, fire and flowers,
the winding night, the universe.

And I, infinitesimal[14] being,
drunk with the great starry
void,
likeness, image of
mystery,
felt myself a pure part
of the abyss,
I wheeled with the stars,
my heart broke loose on the wind.

---

[13] **palpitating**—throbbing, pulsating.

[14] **infinitesimal**—very or infinitely small.

QUESTIONS TO CONSIDER

1. Who is the "we" in "We Are Many"? Do you agree with Neruda's idea? Why or why not?

2. Why does Neruda "have a mind to confuse things" in "Too Many Names"? What is his point?

3. What is the "poet's obligation"? Contrast it with Neruda's definition in "Poetry." Which do you find more interesting as an idea? Explain your answer.

4. After reading these four poems, how would you describe Neruda as a poet? What does he think the poet does and should do?

The Spirits Were Willing

ISABEL ALLENDE

Isabel Allende (1942–   ) was born into an important Chilean family. Her father was one of the country's ambassadors, and she was the niece of Salvador Allende, who was president from 1970–1973. Allende began her career as a journalist, but when Salvador Allende's government was overthrown by a military coup in 1973, she went into exile. This experience and the brooding of exile led Allende to begin writing fiction, in particular, a vast novel about many generations of a single family much like her own. This novel, The House of the Spirits *(1982), made her reputation. In the following essay she describes the genesis of that novel and her writing career.*

Someone has said that books have a guardian angel. The angel doesn't always do its job, but sometimes it does it so well that the book avoids every obstacle in its travels through the world. Born under a lucky star, *The House of the Spirits* has had this good fortune. It was published a few months ago in Spain, and one day I saw it for the first time on a bookstore counter. It was hiding in a corner, **timid**[1] and frightened. I was afraid for my novel; I knew that it no longer belonged to me, that now there would be nothing I could do to help it. There it was, exposed to the gaze of persons who might judge it without mercy. But as time passed I began to relax, and I now believe that there really is a spirit that watches over it.

They say that every first novel is autobiographical, especially those written by women. That's not exactly true in my case, because I'm not in the book. I am not any of the characters, but I don't deny that I have known many of them and that their passions and suffering have touched me very deeply. Some of the anecdotes in its pages are things I heard from the lips of my mother or grandfather or read in my grandmother's notebooks of daily life. I could say that all together these stories **comprise**[2] a kind of family tradition.

---

[1] **timid**—easily frightened, shy.

[2] **comprise**—make up, compose.

People often ask me why I chose to write something as vast and complex as a family saga. The answer is that you don't choose a theme, the theme chooses you. Somehow this story began to grow inside me. I carried it in my heart for many years and fed it tirelessly. For this reason, in order to talk about the history of this book I'm going to have to talk about the history of my family and of my country.

My father disappeared from my life when I was very young, leaving so few traces that even if I **ransack**[3] my memory I cannot even remember his face. My mother went back to her parents' home to live, along with her children, an event that had a critical impact on my childhood. I think that this explains why the book gives such importance to the big house full of spirits where the Truebas live out their lives. Our house was neither so large nor so luxurious as theirs; it didn't have a garden with singing fountains and Olympian statues nor an army of servants like the house built by the protagonist of my novel. But to me it seemed enormous, shadowy and drafty, and I was sure it was haunted by ghosts who rattled the wardrobes and slipped in and out of mirrors. There I grew up, absorbed in solitary games and excursions to the basement, a mysterious treasure trove of useless junk. That place was my Pandora's box. It contained the past, captured in old love letters, travel diaries, and portraits of bishops, maidens, and explorers with one foot on a Bengal tiger. My fantasy was fed by all that and also by my books. My legacy from my father was a great stack of books: novels by Jack London, Jules Verne, Emilio Salgari;[4] the Tesoro de Juventud collection; classic works of all times. Two eccentric bachelor uncles lived with us, one of whom had more books than you could even count. No one guided or censored my reading, so at ten I wept over the tragedies of Shakespeare, tried to decipher Freud,[5] and became thoroughly confused reading the Marquis de Sade.[6] I envied people who could write and I filled countless notebooks with my impossible tales. Thirty years later, when I could not **postpone**[7] any longer the decision to write a novel, I took some dreams, experiences, and fears from that era of my life and concocted a group of characters who go up in a balloon, invent fabulous machines, travel to India in search of the 999 names of God, get lost in the jungle looking for treasure, or die in a tenement[8] disguised as the Queen of Austria.

My grandfather was a patriarch, a strong, intolerant man shaken by uncontrollable passions who died when he was

---

[3] **ransack**—thoroughly search, go through or over.

[4] London . . . Verne . . . Salgari—nineteenth-century writers of adventure stories.

[5] Freud—Sigmund Freud (1856–1939) was an Austrian physician who developed psychoanalysis.

[6] Marquis de Sade—(1740–1814) French author whose writings about perversion and cruelty gave rise to the term "sadism."

[7] **postpone**—delay.

[8] tenement—urban housing with low standards of sanitation, safety, and comfort.

nearly a hundred in full possession of his faculties, **frail**[9] and **lame**,[10] but without a wrinkle, with a lion's mane of hair and the piercing blue eyes of a boy of twenty. He was a marvelous character for a book.

I had a magnificent grandmother who died too young but whose spirit still accompanies me. She was a luminous, transparent being whom I named Clara in my book. There was little to invent; I took her from reality, although I did exaggerate a bit. Perhaps it was true that my grand-mother could move a three-legged table with the power of her thought, that she helped the poor, sheltered poets, and float-ed above human frailties with an eternal smile and the most limpid eyes in the world.

I grew up in my grandparents' house and lived there until my mother married a diplomat, and we set out on a trip that took us to several countries. Later I was separated from her for long periods. I am bound to my mother by a profound, happy, and absolute affection. We developed the habit of writing letters to each other every day, which trained me to be an alert observer of the world, to be aware of people's emotions, to decipher symbols and discover keys, perceiving the hidden side of reality. It also gave me the discipline of writing, something I am grateful for every time I sit down before a blank sheet of paper.

I have no vocation for the nomadic life. All the years I spent wandering about the world I kept **yearning**[11] to recover the stability of my childhood. That's why when I finally returned to Chile, I took a very deep breath of the air of my country, looked up at its snow-covered peaks and set about putting down roots. "This is where I'm staying; I will live here and be buried here one day under a **bough**[12] of jasmine," I said.

How can I put into words what I felt then or what I feel even now every time I pronounce the name of Chile? Pablo Neruda described the country as a long petal. . . . He wrote poems to its forests, lakes, and volcanoes and to the *cordillera*[13] that accom-panies it from north to south, crumbling into a dust of islands before it disappears in the ice of the Antarctic.

It is a region of balmy valleys where grapes grow, of lunar deserts, copper mountains, and steep cliffs battered by the waves of the Pacific Ocean. A mad geogra-phy inhabited by a hospitable people steeped in poverty and suffering. The Chileans are accustomed to **calamity**;[14] they live on the crest of catastrophe, waiting for the next earthquake, flood, drought, or political upheaval. It is a land to love with passion and serve with joy, a land to tell about in books.

---

[9] **frail**—fragile, delicate.

[10] **lame**—disabled or weak, usually referring to the inability to walk.

[11] **yearning**—strongly desiring.

[12] **bough**—branch of a tree.

[13] *cordillera*—a range of mountains, usually parallel and connected by plateaus.

[14] **calamity**—a disaster or great misfortune.

When I wrote *The House of the Spirits*, my ambition was to paint in broad strokes a **fresco**[15] of all Latin America. I am aware of the many differences that exist among our countries, but I think that the similarities and **affinities**[16] are even more striking. I am convinced that a single inexorable and prodigious destiny unites us all and that one day there will be a single country stretching from the Rio Grande to the frozen reaches of the South Pole. In honor of that Utopia I did not place the Trueba family in a particular country. The Truebas could exist anywhere on the continent, and their turbulent passions, their collective, shared suffering, their victories, and their defeats would be identical. This is so much the case that I receive letters from all over South America from readers who tell me that they have identified with the characters and their story, which is similar to their own.

I returned to Chile when I was fifteen years old, beginning to sense my womanhood and to dream about love. I wrote some dreadful poetry, **belligerent**[17] prose, and the inevitable letters to my mother. I think I already knew then that I wanted to be a writer. Agatha Christie was my ideal because she produced many novels and still had free time for afternoon tea and rose gardening in the English countryside. I had no idea how arduous writing was.

One night at a party a boy asked me to dance. It was the chance I had been waiting for, and after arguing with him for four years, I succeeded in convincing him that we should get married. We have been together ever since. I knew love, had children, and a very full era of my life began. It was the age of the twist, the miniskirt, hippies and marijuana, women's liberation, and the political and social struggles of my country. I worked as a journalist, which is a kind of **oblique**[18] way of approaching literature. An older colleague gave me my first lessons. He gave me a bit of advice I still heed because it never fails: "Tell the truth. Only the truth can touch your reader's heart."

When I wrote **The House of the Spirits,** *my ambition was to paint in broad strokes a fresco of all Latin America.*

My life was passionate and active. I was always at the forefront of whatever was going on; nevertheless, a part of me was always looking toward the past.

And so, loving and working and storing up history, I went on living my life. Until one fateful Tuesday—September 11, 1973—when I woke up to a new reality. That day a military coup overthrew the constitutional government of Chile, putting an end to a history of democratic rule that distinguished my country on a continent plagued by dictatorships. What happened

---

[15] **fresco**—a painting done in watercolor on a wall or ceiling while the plaster is still wet.

[16] **affinities**—common characteristics that suggest a relationship.

[17] **belligerent**—hostile, argumentative, or combative.

[18] **oblique**—indirect.

in Chile has special characteristics, but it is not very different from what happens in other tyrannies. Outside the country one merely has to read the international press to get information. Inside the dictatorship, on the other hand, information is censored, because control of public opinion is critical to the regime. Thanks to my job as a journalist I knew exactly what was happening in my country; I experienced it firsthand, and those **cadavers**,[19] torture victims, widows, and orphans left an **indelible**[20] impression in my memory. The last chapters of *The House of the Spirits* recount those events. I based that account on what I saw with my own eyes and on the direct testimony of people who lived through the brutal experience of the repression.

For those who know and love liberty, it is impossible to adapt to a dictatorship. Many people around us were imprisoned, killed, or forced underground. The time came for me to leave, despite the promise I had made myself to live and die in that country. My husband spread out a map of the world, and we looked for a place to go. That's how we arrived in Venezuela, a hot, green country that took us in together with many other refugees and emigrants. We arrived with our children, with very little luggage, and with sorrow in our hearts.

The enchanted trunks of my uncles were left behind along with the books in the basement, the family portraits, the letters and travel diaries, my grandmother's three-legged table, and her crown of orange blossoms. My grandfather stayed behind also, sitting in a rocking chair, infinitely desolate and lonely, with a hundred years of memories and no one to share them with.

Far away from my country, I felt like a tree whose roots have been cut off and which is doomed to **shrivel**[21] and die. Nostalgia, rage, and sadness kept me paralyzed for a long time. Nevertheless, little by little, my emotions were purified, I acquired a larger perspective of reality, and the new country won my heart. Then I felt the necessity of recovering the benevolent spirits of the past, the landscape of my country, the people I knew, the streets of my city, the winter rains, and the peaches of summer. In January of 1981 I woke up one morning with an extravagant idea. I had the thought that if I set down in writing what I wanted to rescue from oblivion, I could reconstruct that lost world, revive the dead, unite the dispersed, capture the memories forever, and make them mine. Then no one could ever take them away from me. I bought paper and sat down to write a story.

When I put the first piece of paper in the typewriter, I didn't know how to accomplish any of this, but I knew I should write. I remembered the words of my old reporter friend: tell the truth. I wanted to talk about the suffering of my people and of other people of that tormented continent so that the truth would touch the hearts of my readers.

---

[19] **cadavers**—dead bodies.

[20] **indelible**—unable to be erased or removed.

[21] **shrivel**—to shrink into a wrinkled, folded, rolled-up, or dried-up state.

It's true that I wrote for the pleasure of writing and because I had waited almost forty years for that moment. But I also did it because of an unavoidable obligation.

Latin America is living a tragic moment of its history. In our lands fifty percent of the population is **illiterate**[22] and yet writers are listened to and respected. They are the voice of those who suffer in silence. All of us who write and who are fortunate enough to be published should assume the commitment of serving the cause of freedom and justice. We have a mission to accomplish at the front lines. We must combat the **obscurantism**[23] that oppresses several countries of our continent through the force of our words, with reason, and with hope. We must put letters at the service of mankind. The worst enemy of barbarism is ideas.

I wanted what I wrote to be part of the effort to make our reality known. I wrote the story of a family like mine and like many others, of a country like mine and like any other in Latin America. The story spans almost a century; I started at the beginning, with the things most remote in time, things that had been told to me—transformed, of course, by magic, emotion and the vagaries of memory. Once I had begun, I kept recounting things in order and without pause straight to the end.

I did not know that this book would change my life. I lacked experience in literature, and I did not imagine the impact that the written word could have.

While the ink was still fresh I had the opportunity to prove that there were spirits that protected my book: its acceptance in Spain was immediate and very warm. That surprised me, since I had thought that Europe was very far from Latin America. Later I learned that this is not so and that human beings are alike all over the world. All that is needed is a little effort for us to understand and accept one another.

Because of the strict censorship in Chile in 1982, I thought that *The House of the Spirits* would not be read in my country. I resigned myself to the idea that my compatriots would never read that story, one that speaks of injustice, fear, and suffering, but also of **solidarity**,[24] courage, and love as they exist in a country like ours.

I never could have imagined what happened.

The book entered Chile like a pirate, hidden in the suitcases of brave travelers or sent by mail without covers and cut into two or three pieces so that it could not be identified. The few copies that entered the country this way multiplied by magic art.

> *I wrote the story of a family like mine and like many others, of a country like mine and like any other in Latin America.*

---

[22] **illiterate**—unable to read or write.

[23] **obscurantism**—resistance to knowledge and enlightenment.

[24] **solidarity**—unity in feeling or action among a group of individuals.

People who had a copy made photocopies, that passed from hand to hand. There were lists of people who wanted to read it, and I am told that there were even a few people who rented out copies of it.

Months later the government decided that it was necessary to lift the censorship of books in order to improve its image, although there is still a suffocating muzzle over the mouths of those using the mass media. Along with other books that had been banned for the previous ten years, *The House of the Spirits* entered Chile legally and has headed sales lists since last August. It moves me to think that the book is being translated into so many languages and that the spirits that live in its pages will be in contact with readers in remote places, offering them a breath of this fabulous continent where I was born. It's hard for me to imagine the Truebas speaking English, German or Norwegian, but I trust they will get along just fine.

I wrote out of urgent need, as I said in the first line of the book: "to reclaim the past and overcome my terrors." I did not suspect that the **benevolent**[25] spirit of my grandmother would protect those pages, watching over them in their travels through the world. I like to think about this, to imagine, for example, that Clara, clear, **clairvoyant**[26] Clara, is here at my side at this moment, wearing her white gown and her woolen gloves, with her false teeth hanging on a chain around her neck.

Yes . . . It's a beautiful idea that books have their own guardian spirit.

---

[25] **benevolent**—actively friendly and helpful.
[26] **clairvoyant**—having extraordinary insight or perception.

QUESTIONS TO CONSIDER

1. Why does Allende begin writing *The House of the Spirits?*

2. Where is *The House of the Spirits* set? Why did Allende choose this setting?

3. What does Allende feel is the role of the writer in Latin America? What does she find ironic about this?

Light Is Like Water

GABRIEL GARCÍA MÁRQUEZ

Gabriel García Márquez (1928–   ) is one of the world's most highly regarded writers. Born in Colombia, García Márquez is the most prominent exponent of magic realism. This distinctly Latin American genre incorporates realistic description with magical and mythological events. It began as a way to depict the vast culture and history of Latin America, particularly the ancient and modern religions. García Márquez brought magic realism international attention through his stories, particularly his classic novels, One Hundred Years of Solitude *(1967) and* Love in the Time of Cholera *(1985). García Márquez won the Nobel Prize in 1982.*

At Christmas the boys asked again for a rowboat.

"Okay," said their papa, "we'll buy it when we get back to Cartagena."[1]

Totó, who was nine years old, and Joel, who was seven, were more determined than their parents believed.

"No," they said in chorus. "We need it here and now."

"To begin with," said their mother, "the only navigable water here is what comes out of the shower."

She and her husband were both right. Their house in Cartagena de Indias had a yard with a dock on the bay, and a shed that could hold two large yachts. Here in Madrid,[2] on the other hand, they were crowded into a fifth-floor apartment at 47 Paseo de la Castellana. But in the end neither of them could refuse, because they had promised the children a rowboat complete with sextant[3] and compass if they won their class prizes in elementary school, and they had. And so their papa bought everything and said nothing to his wife, who was more reluctant than he to pay gambling debts. It was a beautiful aluminum boat with a gold stripe at the waterline.

"The boat's in the garage," their papa announced at lunch. "The problem is,

---

[1] Cartagena—port city in Colombia in South America.

[2] Madrid—the capital of Spain, located in the central plains.

[3] sextant—an instrument with an arc of 60° used in navigation and surveying.

there's no way to bring it up in the elevator or by the stairs, and there's no more space available in the garage."

On the following Saturday afternoon, however, the boys invited their classmates to help bring the boat up the stairs, and they managed to carry it as far as the maid's room.

"Light is like water," I answered. *"You turn the tap and out it comes."*

"Congratulations," said their papa. "Now what?"

"Now nothing," said the boys. "All we wanted was to have the boat in the room, and now it's there."

On Wednesday night, as they did every Wednesday, the parents went to the movies. The boys, lords and masters of the house, closed the doors and windows and broke the glowing bulb in one of the living room lamps. A jet of golden light as cool as water began to pour out of the broken bulb, and they let it run to a depth of almost three feet. Then they turned off the electricity, took out the rowboat, and navigated at will among the islands in the house.

This fabulous adventure was the result of a **frivolous**[4] remark I made while taking part in a seminar on the poetry of household objects. Totó asked me why the light went on with just the touch of a switch, and I did not have the courage to think about it twice.

"Light is like water," I answered. "You turn the tap and out it comes."

And so they continued sailing every Wednesday night, learning how to use the sextant and the compass, until their parents came home from the movies and found them sleeping like angels on dry land. Months later, longing to go farther, they asked for complete skin-diving outfits: masks, fins, tanks, and compressed-air rifles.

"It's bad enough you've put a rowboat you can't use in the maid's room," said their father. "To make it even worse, now you want diving equipment too."

"What if we win the Gold Gardenia Prize for the first semester?" said Joel.

"No," said their mother in alarm. "That's enough."

Their father reproached her for being intransigent.

"These kids don't win so much as a nail when it comes to doing what they're supposed to," she said, "but to get what they want they're capable of taking it all, even the teacher's chair."

In the end the parents did not say yes or no. But in July, Totó and Joel each won a Gold Gardenia and the public recognition of the headmaster. That same afternoon, without having to ask again, they found the diving outfits in their original packing in their bedroom. And so the following Wednesday, while their parents were at the movies seeing *Last Tango in Paris*, they filled the apartment to a depth of two fathoms,[5]

---

[4] **frivolous**—silly or irresponsible.

[5] fathoms—units of measure, each equal to six feet.

dove like tame sharks under the furniture, including the beds, and **salvaged**[6] from the bottom of the light things that had been lost in darkness for years.

At the end-of-the-year awards ceremony, the brothers were acclaimed as examples for the entire school and received certificates of excellence. This time they did not have to ask for anything, because their parents asked them what they wanted. They were so reasonable that all they wanted was a party at home as a treat for their classmates.

Their papa, when he was alone with his wife, was radiant.

"It's a proof of their maturity," he said.

"From your lips to God's ear," said their mother.

The following Wednesday, while their parents were watching *The Battle of Algiers*, people walking along the Paseo de la Castellana saw a cascade of light falling from an old building hidden among the trees. It spilled over the balconies, poured in torrents down the **façade**,[7] and rushed along the great avenue in a golden flood that lit the city all the way to the Guadarrama.

In response to the emergency, firemen forced the door on the fifth floor and found the apartment **brimming**[8] with light all the way to the ceiling. The sofa and easy chairs covered in leopard skin were floating at different levels in the living room, among the bottles from the bar and the grand piano with its Manila shawl that fluttered half submerged like a golden manta ray.

Household objects, in the fullness of their poetry, flew with their own wings through the kitchen sky. The marching-band instruments that the children used for dancing drifted among the bright-colored fish freed from their mother's aquarium, which were the only creatures alive and happy in the vast illuminated marsh. Everyone's toothbrush floated in the bathroom, along with Papa's condoms and Mama's jars of creams and her spare bridge,[9] and the television set from the master bedroom floated on its side, still tuned to the final episode of the midnight movie for adults only.

At the end of the hall, moving with the current and clutching the oars, with his mask on and only enough air to reach port, Totó sat in the stern of the boat, searching for the lighthouse, and Joel, floating in the **prow**,[10] still looked for the north star with the sextant, and floating through the entire house were their thirty-seven classmates, eternalized in the moment of peeing into the pot of geraniums, singing the school song with the words changed to make fun of the headmaster, sneaking a glass of brandy from Papa's bottle. For they had turned on so many lights at the same time that the apartment had flooded, and two entire

---

[6] **salvaged**—rescued from loss, damage, or destruction.

[7] **façade**—the face of a building, especially the front.

[8] **brimming**—full.

[9] **bridge**—a removable partial denture.

[10] **prow**—the front part of a ship.

classes at the elementary school of Saint Julian the Hospitaler drowned on the fifth floor of 47 Paseo de la Castellana. In Madrid, Spain, a remote city of burning summers and icy winds, with no ocean or river, whose landbound **indigenous**[11] population had never mastered the science of navigating on light.

---

[11] **indigenous**—native.

QUESTIONS TO CONSIDER

1. How would you describe the tone of "Light Is Like Water"? Do you think the tone is appropriate to the events in the story?

2. What does the last sentence of the story seem to mean? What is García Márquez commenting on?

3. Based on your reading of this story, how would you describe the hallmarks of magic realism? What do you think of it as a style of writing?

Continuity of Parks

JULIO CORTÁZAR

Julio Cortázar (1914–1984) began his literary career as a poet and translator. In the 1940s he started writing fiction and his first stories were published by another Argentinean writer, Jorge Luis Borges (see page 334). The two writers are often compared because of their deep knowledge of European literature and the metaphysical questing of their stories. However, unlike Borges, Cortázar was extremely political. In 1951 he was forced into exile because of his opposition to the dictator Juan Perón. Even when Perón lost power, Cortázar was unable to return to Argentina as the country was controlled by repressive military regimes. It was only in 1983, the year before Cortázar's death, that a democratically elected government took office in Argentina.

He had begun to read the novel a few days before. He had put it down because of some urgent business conferences, opened it again on his way back to the estate by train; he permitted himself a slowly growing interest in the plot, in the **characterizations**.[1] That afternoon, after writing a letter giving his power of attorney and discussing a matter of joint ownership with the manager of his estate, he returned to the book in the **tranquility**[2] of his study which looked out upon the park with its oaks. Sprawled in his favorite armchair, its back toward the door—even the possibility of an intrusion would have irritated him, had he thought of it—he let his left hand caress repeatedly the green velvet upholstery and set to reading the final chapters. He remembered effortlessly the names and his mental image of the characters; the novel spread its glamour over him almost at once. He tasted the almost **perverse**[3] pleasure of disengaging himself line by line from the things around him, and at the same time feeling his head rest comfortably on the green velvet of the chair with its high back, sensing that the cigarettes rested within reach of his hand, that beyond the great windows the air of afternoon danced under the oak trees in the park. Word by word, licked up by the **sordid**[4] dilemma of the hero and heroine, letting himself be

---

[1] **characterizations**—descriptions of characters.

[2] **tranquility**—peace, calmness.

[3] **perverse**—improper.

[4] **sordid**—unclean or corrupt.

absorbed to the point where the images settled down and took on color and movement, he was witness to the final encounter in the mountain cabin. The woman arrived first, apprehensive; now the lover came in, his face cut by the backlash of a branch. Admirably, she **stanched**[5] the blood with her kisses, but he **rebuffed**[6] her caresses, he had not come to perform again the ceremonies of a secret passion, protected by a world of dry leaves and furtive paths through the forest. The dagger warmed itself against his chest, and underneath liberty pounded, hidden close. A lustful, panting dialogue raced down the pages like a **rivulet**[7] of snakes, and one felt it had all been decided from eternity. Even to those caresses which **writhed**[8] about the lover's body, as though wishing to keep him there, to dissuade him from it; they sketched abominably the frame of that other body it was necessary to destroy. Nothing had been forgotten: alibis, unforeseen hazards, possible mistakes. From this hour on, each instant had its use minutely assigned. The cold-blooded, twice-gone-over re-examination of the details was barely broken off so that a hand could caress a cheek. It was beginning to get dark.

Not looking at one another now, rigidly fixed upon the task which awaited them, they separated at the cabin door. She was to follow the trail that led north. On the path leading in the opposite direction, he turned for a moment to watch her running, her hair loosened and flying. He ran in turn, crouching among the trees and hedges until, in the yellowish fog of dusk, he could distinguish the avenue of trees which led up to the house. The dogs were not supposed to bark, they did not bark. The estate manager would not be there at this hour, and he was not there. He went up the three porch steps and entered. The woman's words reached him over the thudding of blood in his ears: first a blue chamber, then a hall, then a carpeted stairway. At the top, two doors. No one in the first room, no one in the second. The door of the salon, and then, the knife in hand, the light from the great windows, the high back of an armchair covered in green velvet, the head of the man in the chair reading a novel.

---

[5] **stanched**—stopped or slowed the flow of.

[6] **rebuffed**—rejected.

[7] **rivulet**—a small stream.

[8] **writhed**—wiggled, squirmed.

QUESTIONS TO CONSIDER

1. What happens at the end of the story? How do you know?

2. Why do the hero and heroine meet at the cabin?

3. What elements of magic and fantasy are in "Continuity of Parks"? What purpose do they serve?

Two Words

ISABEL ALLENDE

Isabel Allende (see page 352) is one of Latin America's most prominent writers. She is one of the most popular exponents of magic realism in the generation after that of García Márquez (see page 359).

She went by the name of Belisa Crepusculario, not because she had been baptized with that name or given it by her mother, but because she herself had searched until she found the poetry of "beauty" and "twilight" and cloaked herself in it. She made her living selling words. She journeyed through the country from the high cold mountains to the burning coasts, stopping at fairs and in markets where she set up four poles covered by a canvas awning under which she took refuge from the sun and rain to minister[1] to her customers. She did not have to peddle her merchandise because from having wandered far and near, everyone knew who she was. Some people waited for her from one year to the next, and when she appeared in the village with her bundle beneath her arm, they would form a line in front of her stall. Her prices were fair. For five centavos she delivered verses from memory; for seven she improved the quality of dreams; for nine she wrote love letters; for twelve she invented insults for **irreconcilable**[2] enemies. She also sold stories, not fantasies but long, true stories she recited at one telling, never skipping a word. This is how she carried news from one town to another. People paid her to add a line or two: our son was born; so-and-so died; our children got married; the crops burned in the field. Wherever she went a small crowd gathered around to listen as she began to speak, and that was how they learned about each others' doings, about distant relatives, about what was going on in the civil war.

[1] minister—supply, take care of.

[2] **irreconcilable**—unable to make peace.

To anyone who paid her fifty centavos in trade, she gave the gift of a secret word to drive away melancholy. It was not the same word for everyone, naturally, because that would have been collective deceit. Each person received his or her own word, with the assurance that no one else would use it that way in this universe or the Beyond.

> **To anyone who paid her fifty centavos in trade, she gave the gift of a secret word to drive away melancholy.**

Belisa Crepusculario had been born into a family so poor they did not even have names to give their children. She came into the world and grew up in an inhospitable land where some years the rains became avalanches of water that bore everything away before them and others when not a drop fell from the sky and the sun swelled to fill the horizon and the world became a desert. Until she was twelve, Belisa had no occupation or virtue other than having withstood hunger and the exhaustion of centuries. During one **interminable**[3] drought, it fell to her to bury four younger brothers and sisters; when she realized that her turn was next, she decided to set out across the plains in the direction of the sea, in hopes that she might trick death along the way. The land was **eroded**,[4] split with deep cracks, strewn with rocks, fossils of trees and thorny bushes, and skeletons of animals bleached by the sun. From time to time she ran into families who, like her, were heading south, following the **mirage**[5] of water. Some had begun the march carrying their belongings on their back or in small carts, but they could barely move their own bones, and after a while they had to abandon their possessions. They dragged themselves along painfully, their skin turned to lizard hide and their eyes burned by the **reverberating**[6] glare. Belisa greeted them with a wave as she passed, but she did not stop, because she had no strength to waste in acts of compassion. Many people fell by the wayside, but she was so stubborn that she survived to cross through that hell and at long last reach the first trickles of water, fine, almost invisible threads that fed spindly vegetation and farther down widened into small streams and marshes.

Belisa Crepusculario saved her life and in the process accidentally discovered writing. In a village near the coast, the wind blew a page of newspaper at her feet. She picked up the **brittle**[7] yellow paper and stood a long while looking at it, unable to determine its purpose, until curiosity overcame her shyness. She walked over to a man who was washing his horse in the muddy pool where she had **quenched**[8] her thirst.

---

[3] **interminable**—endless or seemingly endless.

[4] **eroded**—gradually worn away.

[5] **mirage**—optical illusion.

[6] **reverberating**—reflecting or echoing.

[7] **brittle**—hard, fragile, and likely to break.

[8] **quenched**—satisfied or extinguished.

"What is this?" she asked.

"The sports page of the newspaper," the man replied, concealing his surprise at her ignorance.

The answer astounded the girl, but she did not want to seem rude, so she merely inquired about the significance of the fly tracks scattered across the page.

"Those are words, child. Here it says that Fulgencio Barba knocked out El Negro Tiznao in the third round."

That was the day Belisa Crepusculario found out that words make their way in the world without a master, and that anyone with a little cleverness can appropriate them and do business with them. She made a quick assessment of her situation and concluded that aside from becoming a prostitute or working as a servant in the kitchens of the rich there were few occupations she was qualified for. It seemed to her that selling words would be an honorable alternative. From that moment on, she worked at that profession, and was never tempted by any other. At the beginning, she offered her merchandise unaware that words could be written outside of newspapers. When she learned otherwise, she calculated the infinite possibilities of her trade and with her savings paid a priest twenty pesos to teach her to read and write; with her three remaining coins she bought a dictionary. She poured over it from A to Z and then threw it into the sea, because it was not her intention to **defraud**[9] her customers with packaged words.

One August morning several years later, Belisa Crepusculario was sitting in her tent in the middle of a plaza, surrounded by the uproar of market day, selling legal arguments to an old man who had been trying for sixteen years to get his pension. Suddenly she heard yelling and thudding hoofbeats. She looked up from her writing and saw, first, a cloud of dust, and then a band of horsemen come galloping into the plaza. They were the Colonel's men, sent under orders of El Mulato, a giant known throughout the land for the speed of his knife and his loyalty to his chief. Both the Colonel and El Mulato had spent their lives fighting in the civil war, and their names were **ineradicably**[10] linked to devastation and **calamity**.[11] The rebels swept into town like a stampeding herd, wrapped in noise, bathed in sweat, and leaving a hurricane of fear in their trail. Chickens took wing, dogs ran for their lives, women and children **scurried**[12] out of sight, until the only living soul left in the market was Belisa Crepusculario. She had never seen El Mulato and was surprised to see him walking toward her.

"I'm looking for you," he shouted, pointing his coiled whip at her; even before the words were out, two men rushed her—knocking over her canopy and shattering her inkwell—bound her hand and foot,

---

[9] **defraud**—to cheat by criminal deception.

[10] **ineradicably**—irremovably.

[11] **calamity**—a disaster or great misfortune.

[12] **scurried**—moved hurriedly.

and threw her like a sea bag across the rump of El Mulato's mount. Then they thundered off toward the hills.

Hours later, just as Belisa Crepusculario was near death, her heart ground to sand by the pounding of the horse, they stopped, and four strong hands set her down. She tried to stand on her feet and hold her head high, but her strength failed her and she slumped to the ground, sinking into a confused dream. She awakened several hours later to the **murmur**[13] of night in the camp, but before she had time to sort out the sounds, she opened her eyes and found herself staring into the impatient glare of El Mulato, kneeling beside her.

"Well, woman, at last you've come to," he said. To speed her to her senses, he tipped his canteen and offered her a sip of liquor laced with gunpowder.

She demanded to know the reason for such rough treatment, and El Mulato explained that the Colonel needed her services. He allowed her to splash water on her face, and then led her to the far end of the camp where the most feared man in all the land was lazing in a hammock strung between two trees. She could not see his face, because he lay in the deceptive shadow of the leaves and the indelible shadow of all his years as a bandit, but she imagined from the way his gigantic aide addressed him with such humility that he must have a very menacing expression. She was surprised by the Colonel's voice, as soft and well-modulated as a professor's.

"Are you the woman who sells words?" he asked.

"At your service," she **stammered**,[14] peering into the dark and trying to see him better.

The Colonel stood up, and turned straight toward her. She saw dark skin and the eyes of a ferocious **puma**,[15] and she knew immediately that she was standing before the loneliest man in the world.

"I want to be President," he announced.

The Colonel was weary of riding across that godforsaken land, waging useless wars and suffering defeats that no **subterfuge**[16] could transform into victories. For years he had been sleeping in the open air, bitten by mosquitoes, eating iguanas and snake soup, but those minor inconveniences were not why he wanted to change his destiny. What truly troubled him was the terror he saw in people's eyes. He longed to ride into a town beneath a triumphal arch with bright flags and flowers everywhere; he wanted to be cheered, and be given newly laid eggs and freshly baked bread. Men fled at the sight of him, children trembled, and women miscarried from fright; he had had enough, and so he had decided to become President. El Mulato had suggested that they ride to the capital, gallop up to the Palace, and take

---

[13] **murmur**—quiet continuous sound.

[14] **stammered**—spoke with pauses or repetitions of the same syllable, often because of embarrassment or fear.

[15] puma—a type of large, wild cat.

[16] **subterfuge**—an attempt to avoid blame or defeat.

over the government, the way they had taken so many other things without anyone's permission. The Colonel, however, did not want to be just another tyrant; there had been enough of those before him and, besides, if he did that, he would never win people's hearts. It was his aspiration to win the popular vote in the December elections.

"To do that, I have to talk like a candidate. Can you sell me the words for a speech?" the Colonel asked Belisa Crepusculario.

She had accepted many assignments, but none like this. She did not dare refuse, fearing that El Mulato would shoot her between the eyes, or worse still, that the Colonel would burst into tears. There was more to it than that, however; she felt the urge to help him because she felt a throbbing warmth beneath her skin, a powerful desire to touch that man, to fondle him, to clasp him in her arms.

All night and a good part of the following day, Belisa Crepusculario searched her **repertory**[17] for words adequate for a presidential speech, closely watched by El Mulato, who could not take his eyes from her firm wanderer's legs and virginal breasts. She discarded harsh, cold words, words that were too flowery, words worn from abuse, words that offered improbable promises, untruthful and confusing words, until all she had left were words sure to touch the minds of men and women's intuition. Calling upon the knowledge she had purchased from the priest for twenty pesos, she wrote the speech on a sheet of paper and then signaled El Mulato to untie the rope that bound her ankles to a tree. He led her once more to the Colonel, and again she felt the throbbing anxiety that had seized her when she first saw him. She handed him the paper and waited while he looked at it, holding it gingerly between thumbs and fingertips.

"What does this say," he asked finally.

"Don't you know how to read?"

"War's what I know," he replied.

She read the speech aloud. She read it three times, so her client could engrave it on his memory. When she finished, she saw the emotion in the faces of the soldiers who had gathered round to listen, and saw that the Colonel's eyes glittered with enthusiasm, convinced that with those words the presidential chair would be his.

"If after they've heard it three times, the boys are still standing there with their mouths hanging open, it must mean the thing's damn good, Colonel" was El Mulato's approval.

"All right, woman. How much do I owe you?" the leader asked.

"One peso, Colonel."

"That's not much," he said, opening the pouch he wore at his belt, heavy with proceeds from the last foray.

"The peso entitles you to a bonus. I'm going to give you two secret words," said Belisa Crepusculario.

"What for?"

---

[17] **repertory**—collection, especially of information and experiences.

She explained that for every fifty centavos a client paid, she gave him the gift of a word for his exclusive use. The Colonel shrugged. He had no interest at all in her offer, but he did not want to be impolite to someone who had served him so well. She walked slowly to the leather stool where he was sitting, and bent down to give him her gift. The man smelled the scent of a mountain cat issuing from the woman, a fiery heat radiating from her hips, he heard the terrible whisper of her hair, and a breath of sweetmint murmured into his ear the two secret words that were his alone.

"They are yours, Colonel," she said as she stepped back. "You may use them as much as you please."

El Mulato accompanied Belisa to the roadside, his eyes as entreating as a stray does, but when he reached out to touch her, he was stopped by an avalanche of words he had never heard before; believing them to be an **irrevocable**[18] curse, the flame of his desire was extinguished.

During the months of September, October, and November the Colonel delivered his speech so many times that had it not been crafted from glowing and durable words it would have turned to ash as he spoke. He traveled up and down and across the country, riding into cities with a triumphal air, stopping in even the most forgotten villages where only the dump heap betrayed a human presence, to convince his fellow citizens to vote for him. While he spoke from a platform erected in the middle of the plaza, El Mulato and his men handed out sweets and painted his name on all the walls in gold frost. No one paid the least attention to those advertising **ploys**;[19] they were dazzled by the clarity of the Colonel's proposals and the poetic lucidity of his arguments, infected by his powerful wish to right the wrongs of history, happy for the first time in their lives. When the Candidate had finished his speech, his soldiers would fire their pistols into the air and set off firecrackers, and when finally they rode off, they left behind a wake of hope that lingered for days on the air, like the splendid memory of a comet's tail. Soon the Colonel was the favorite. No one had ever witnessed such a phenomenon: a man who surfaced from the civil war, covered with scars and speaking like a professor, a man whose fame spread to every corner of the land and captured the nation's heart. The press focused their attention on him. Newspapermen came from far away to interview him and repeat his phrases, and the number of his followers and enemies continued to grow.

"We're doing great, Colonel," said El Mulato, after twelve successful weeks of campaigning.

But the Candidate did not hear. He was repeating his secret words, as he did more and more obsessively. He said them when he was mellow with nostalgia; he murmured them in his sleep; he carried them with him on horseback; he thought

---

[18] **irrevocable**—unable to be taken back, unalterable.
[19] **ploys**—schemes, cunning plans.

them before delivering his famous speech; and he caught himself savoring them in his leisure time. And every time he thought of those two words, he thought of Belisa Crepusculario, and his senses were inflamed with the memory of her feral scent, her fiery heat, the whisper of her hair, and her sweet-mint breath in his ear, until he began to go around like a sleepwalker, and his men realized that he might die before he ever sat in the presidential chair.

"What's got hold of you, Colonel," El Mulato asked so often that finally one day his chief broke down and told him the source of his befuddlement: those two words that were buried like two daggers in his gut.

"Tell me what they are and maybe they'll lose their magic," his faithful aide suggested.

I can't tell them, they're for me alone," the Colonel replied. Saddened by watching his chief decline like a man with a death sentence on his head, El Mulato slung his rifle over his shoulder and set out to find Belisa Crepusculario. He followed her trail through all that vast country, until he found her in a village in the far south, sitting under her tent reciting her rosary of news. He planted himself, spraddle-legged, before her, weapon in hand. "You! You're coming with me," he ordered.

She had been waiting. She picked up her inkwell, folded the canvas of her small stall, arranged her shawl around her shoulders, and without a word took her place behind El Mulato's saddle. They did not exchange so much as a word in all the trip; El Mulato's desire for her had turned into rage, and only his fear of her tongue prevented his cutting her to shreds with his whip. Nor was he inclined to tell her that the Colonel was in a fog, and that a spell whispered into his ear had done what years of battle had not been able to do. Three days later they arrived at the encampment, and immediately, in view of all the troops, El Mulato led his prisoner before the Candidate.

"I brought this witch here so you can give her back her words, Colonel," El Mulato said, pointing the barrel of his rifle at the woman's head. "And then she can give you back your manhood."

The Colonel and Belisa Crepusculario stared at each other, measuring one another from a distance. The men knew then that their leader would never undo the witchcraft of those accursed words, because the whole world could see the voracious-puma eyes soften as the woman walked to him and took his hand in hers.

QUESTIONS TO CONSIDER

1. How does Belisa Crepusculario make her living selling words? List all the things people pay her to do.

2. Why is the Colonel in a fog during his campaign?

3. What things seem magical in the story? What things seems absolutely realistic?

The Other America

ARTURO USLAR PIETRI

Arturo Uslar Pietri (1906–   ) is one of Venezuela's most important writers and intellectuals. He coined the term "magic realism" for Latin America's best-known style of fiction. As well as writing fiction, Uslar Pietri has written a great deal of journalism describing life in Venezuela and exploring the identity of Latin American writers. "The Other America" is from 1974, and in it Uslar Pietri attempts to understand the place Latin America occupies in the Western Hemisphere and the world.

What many people call "Latin America" is, in a very meaningful way, the world from which the name has been taken away. There has always been a metaphor, a **misnomer**,[1] or an understandable dissatisfaction about its name. The New World, the Indies, America, were all names dependent on chance and even ignorance. When in 1507 Martin Waldseemuller wrote the **auspicious**[2] name on his map, he wrote it on the border of the southern continental mass. The northern part of the hemisphere did not come to be called America until much later.

From the moment in 1776 when the old English colonies of the north declared their independence and for lack of a name opted for the simple political definition "United States of America," which **summarily**[3] described their form of government and their geographical situation, there arose the problem of what to call the South. When the new country's expansion and power became evident, the name "Americans" increasingly came to be ascribed to them. For the eighteenth-century French and English, Benjamin Franklin was "The American" while a man like Francisco de Miranda,[4] who had better title to embodying the reality of the New World, was a "*criollo*,"[5] an inhabitant of Terra Firma, or an exotic native.

That the name does not correspond to the thing exactly is not what matters. No

---

[1] **misnomer**—a name or term used wrongly.
[2] **auspicious**—favorable, prosperous.
[3] **summarily**—quickly, without delay.
[4] Francisco de Miranda—(1750–1816) revolutionary who fought for Venezuelan independence from Spain.
[5] *criollo*—a creole, a Spanish American of European descent.

name corresponds exactly to the thing it stands for. The origins of the names Asia, Africa, and Europe, not to mention Italy or Spain, were equally arbitrary. The problem has been the lack of a sufficient and secure identity.

It has gone on for four centuries; it has been long, **arduous**,[6] unending, this search for the identity of the sons of the other America, which is still called by such objectionable, almost provisional names as Spanish America, Latin America, Iberoamerica, and even Indoamerica. The presence of this changeable modifier reveals the necessity of a not clearly determined but specific difference from the **genus**[7] nearby.

Little importance would be given to the old or new, the ingenious or unaffected name, if behind its origin there were not hidden unsolved problems of definition and situation.

The peculiar attitude of the Latin American towards time and place has had much to do with all this. From the very beginning, his has been a situation that had to be changed. There, more than in any other place in history, one has thought in terms of future and distance. Tomorrow has always mattered more than today, the invisible more than the visible, the far more than the near. The search for El Dorado[8] is a perfect, if extreme, example of this mentality. What did their solitary, **meager**[9] cluster of huts matter in the face of the fact that they were on the road to El Dorado? They always found themselves facing a vastness to be conquered, compared with which what was known and possessed was disproportionately small. There was a Beyond in space and time where all would be good and plentiful.

From the arrival of the Conquistadores,[10] the future was more looked to than the present. They came to make "inroads," to explore new lands, to look for treasure, to build for tomorrow, with a project in their imagination.

The fact that America was man's first great encounter with a geographical area that was completely unknown and in great part uninhabited had much to do with this phenomenon. More important than what there was, was what could be done. The name itself, the New World, reveals this visionary conception. They did not come to conquer cities and countries, but rather to found what did not already exist, without much taking into account what already did exist. Kingdoms, territories, and provinces were created the way an architect outlines a building project on paper. More than the present, what could be done in the future was stressed. They were going to make a New Spain, a New Castile, or a New Toledo;[11] they were going to found the

---

[6] **arduous**—difficult, hard to achieve or overcome.

[7] **genus**—group of organisms that have traits in common.

[8] El Dorado—mythical city of gold sought by Spanish adventurers in Latin America.

[9] **meager**—lacking in amount or quality.

[10] Conquistadores—Spanish conquerors in South America in the sixteenth century.

[11] Castile . . . Toledo—Castile is a region of Spain; Toledo is a city.

Order of the Knights of the Golden Spur, or, purely, simply, the Utopia[12] of Sir Thomas More.

Latin America was conceived as a project. Everything the oldest official documents say refers to what can be done here. This runs from the letters of Columbus to the speeches of Bolívar,[13] from the futuristic, astonished vision of the Jesuit Acosta[14] in the sixteenth century to the description of the future's possibilities that fill Humboldt's[15] prophetic work at the end of the Colonial period.

Independence itself has more to do with a future project than with an actual present. This is its chief characteristic. For tomorrow, we must create the most perfect republic that humankind has ever seen. The limitations and obstacles of the present do not matter. When in 1811 the Venezuelan congress declared the first Spanish American Constitution, it did not appear to take into consideration the real situation of the country, or its actual institutions, or its social organization, or its economy; rather it rushed, **exempt**[16] and free from all ties to surrounding reality, to call for a political order which would require the complete transformation of existing reality to be able to function.

They turned to the remotest past, or they rushed toward the most **utopic**[17] future. Anything but the present. In any case, the remote past, updated or resuscitated, of a golden legend has been a traditional mode of revolutionary thought. Revolution is fundamentally a kind of **nostalgia**,[18] an attempt to return to the forgotten and lost Golden Age.

In the papers of the creators of the Spanish American revolution, this **disdain**[19] for the immediate stands out. Miranda's papers abound with the evidence of this attitude. Miranda observed and studied the basis of the most advanced political institutions of the Europe of his time, from the armies and hospitals to the gardens and parliaments, in order to transport them at some opportunity to the New World; but when it came to giving a title to the leader of this immense new State which was to extend from Mexico to Argentina, he could find none better than "Inca."[20] An "Inca" was to preside over the vast Mirandian republic, built upon the most modern political forms tested by England and Revolutionary France.

The first to take note of the hazards inherent in this position was Bolívar, whose Cartagena Manifesto and, above

---

[12] Utopia—a paradisal community envisioned by Thomas More in his 1516 work *Utopia*.

[13] Bolívar—Simon Bolívar (1783–1830) Venezuelan general who led a revolt against Spanish rule in South America.

[14] Acosta—José de Acosta (1539–1600) Jesuit missionary who wrote a history of the Spanish expansion into South America.

[15] Humboldt—Alexander von Humboldt (1769–1859) German naturalist who made a series of explorations of South America.

[16] **exempt**—free from responsibility, obligation, or liability.

[17] **utopic**—ideal, perfect.

[18] **nostalgia**—sentimental memory of or yearning for the past.

[19] **disdain**—rejection due to feelings of superiority.

[20] Inca—member of the ruling family of the Incas, the ancient culture of Peru.

all, whose Angostura Speech of 1819 point out the repeated error of not taking into consideration the social reality created by history. This call to order went unheard. The continual battling of the nineteenth century is expressed in utopian proclamations that had little to do with surrounding reality. An abstract political perfection was being sought after, and it was needed for the morrow.

All of this has never ceased being seen in caricature, has an undeniable tragic grandeur. So many years of struggle and destructive confrontation tragic among the Spanish American nations could be looked upon with prideful disdain by the United States of the time and by the great powers of Europe as a proof of inferiority or incapacity for civilized life. At the same time, the Positivists[21] arrived with their pessimistic diagnosis of the invincible factors of climate, race, and history that condemned us to barbarism or incapacity for civilized life. But a people who for so long and with so much passion have struggled in search of promises of justice, liberty, and equality reveal an extraordinary moral fiber. Certainly it would have been more useful and productive to resign themselves to the possible, to work within the given, and to give up looking for the superior forms of human dignity, but, stubbornly and almost unanimously, the hazardous and difficult path of the absolute was chosen.

In this connection, people have spoken of the Spanish American "nominalism"; to believe that the name is the thing itself, that to proclaim the republic is the republic, that to decree equality is equality. There is something of this, but this is not all. If this had been all, the countries would have remained quiet or hypnotized beside the renewed altars on which there had been set up the new idols of the great liberal principles. But this did not happen. Every time the promise or the hope did not become tangible reality, the struggle began anew. What caused the long wars that tore apart almost the entire Spanish American world in the past century and whose high points are such vast collective conflicts as the Mexican War of Reform, the Argentine crusade against Rosas, or the Venezuelan Federal war, was not only the proclamation of some political **dogma**,[22] but a thirst for justice which, in vastly differing and sometimes very **naive**[23] forms, reached all levels of society.

A world that has been able to struggle so much and for so long for the highest human ideals does not deserve such disdain and mocking commiseration.

Nonetheless, from the time of Queen Victoria and the French Third Republic, there has been an America worthy of admiration for its wealth, its virtues and its growing power, which was the one made up of the United States and perhaps also Canada; and another America, the hot countries, picturesque, primitive, at most

[21] Positivists—adherents of Positivism, a philosophical system that rejects abstract speculation in favor of realistic observation.

[22] **dogma**—a principle or belief system.

[23] **naive**—unsophisticated, simple.

good for colonization and exploitation. The land of parrots, vicuñas,[24] feathered Indians, cowboys, and ignorant chieftains. The land of exotic colonial products: cocoa, coffee, rum, molasses, tobacco, and hides; and strange and impure poets.

> *It was not easy— it never has been—to identify Latin America, which presents so many and such contradictory faces, inside and out.*

It was not easy— it never has been— to identify Latin America, which presents so many and such contradictory faces, inside and out. What appears to be contradictory is nothing but a form of its irreconcilable jumble. It is full of the conflict of relics and novelties. Half a century after an amazed Humboldt listened to a discussion about the world's most recent major political events on the rocky old path from La Guaira[25] to Caracas,[26] Sarmiento[27] was describing the stagnant life of seventeenth-century Mendoza.[28] And when Bolívar reached Cuzco[29] in 1825, he must have experienced the sensation of watching a deep, open cross-section through history. There, side by side, superimposed and barely fused, were the people, garments, and tones of the Incas and the Spanish churches, the **missionary**[30] and **doctrinaire**[31] priests, the doctors of Utraquism[32] and an army that brought, along with its coarse gun-powder,

Rousseau's and Montesquieu's[33] ideas. He could hold Pizarro's[34] standard in one hand and in the other, at the same time, a project for a democratic Constitution. They greeted him with the old ceremonial words proper for an Inca or Viceroy, while he spoke of "citizens" and "republic."

An Arrested Era

There was a Spanish era that remained arrested and backward on American soil. This is attested by the language, which evolved more slowly, by the archaism not only of idiomatic expressions but of customs that persisted in the life of *criollos* of the upper class. The Bourbons'[35] arrival on the Spanish throne was only felt slowly and superficially in America. In essentials, it was the world and values of the House of Hapsburg that survived.

That old Castilian Christian who was the heir of a long history of the encounter

---

[24] vicuñas—South American mammals related to the llama.

[25] La Guaira—the principal port of Venezuela.

[26] Caracas—capital of Venezuela.

[27] Sarmiento—Domingo Sarmiento (1811–1888) Argentine statesman and writer.

[28] Mendoza—city in western Argentina.

[29] Cuzco—city in southern Peru. It was the capital of the Inca empire.

[30] **missionary**—related to a religious task or goal, often conversion of nonbelievers or public service.

[31] **doctrinaire**—theoretical and impractical.

[32] Utraquism—moderate Protestant faith. Utraquists were followers of the reformer Jan Huss.

[33] Rousseau and Montesquieu—French philosophers of the Enlightenment who advocated equality and freedom.

[34] Pizarro—Francisco Pizarro (1471–1541) Spanish explorer who conquered Peru.

[35] Bourbons—the royal family of Spain.

of Christians, Moors,[36] and Jews on the Peninsula, and who arrived, as Américo Castro put it, full of indestructible Castilian breeding, found himself not only in a different geographical and social milieu, but in the presence of other races as well as other cultures. We still do not know much about the vast and profound process of cultural fusion which took place so dramatically, painfully, and richly in the new lands. From city planning to temple architecture, from language to working conditions, from worship to cuisine, from agricultural methods to family and societal relations, the presence of the Indian and the Black made itself felt through a great variety of contributions. What happened in Spanish America during those three centuries resembles nothing that occurred on other continents in the encounters between Europeans and natives. It did not happen in North America, or Africa or Asia in the spheres of English or French control.

There is no equivalent to the Inca Garcilaso[37] in Anglo-Saxon America. An Asian or an African baroque did not come into being as a legacy of the European encounter. No new social or artistic forms rose up; instead, the European was imposed upon the indigenous, the contact zone was narrow and lifeless, the Presbyterian church stood next to the Hindu temple, the European minority was isolated from the autochthonous[38] majority. It was impossible to produce an African Sarmiento or an American Caspicara or Aleijadinho.[39] Impossible because the basic fact out of

which arose those men and creations, a cultural and racial fusion, did not take place in any meaningful way in North America, or Africa, or Asia. Culturally there was *avant la lettre*,[40] **apartheid**.[41]

If the United States was able to appropriate to itself the name "America" in the eyes of the world, obliging the other three-quarters of the hemisphere to look for a surname or other name, it was not the result of a clever move or a successful advertising campaign. Fundamentally, it was the effect of the immense disparity of development and power between it and the rest of America. Immense consequences of all sorts the world around have come out of the spectacular fact that in less than two centuries, England's thirteen fringe colonies on the American North Atlantic coast became the greatest economic, technological, and military power on the planet.

With surprising speed and efficiency, they managed to take possession of the immense continental mass that stretched from ocean to ocean and to establish an economic system of the highest productivity that man has ever known and a system of simple and effective public freedoms.

---

[36] Moors—North African Muslims who conquered Spain in the eighth century.

[37] Garcilaso—Garcilaso de la Vega (1537?–1616?) historian of the Inca empire who was of both Spanish and Indian ancestry.

[38] autochthonous—native.

[39] Caspicara or Aleijadinho—Caspicara was an Ecuadoran painter; Aleijadinho was a Brazilian sculptor and architect.

[40] *avant la lettre*—French for "before the beginning."

[41] **apartheid**—a policy of segregation or discrimination based on race.

Many have been the causes and explanations given for such a great difference in growth, from climate and soil quality to the Protestant ethic and economic freedom.

In American territory, in cutting and dramatic form, the division of destiny and mentality occasioned by the Protestant Reformation in Europe has reappeared, between the North, which invented capitalism, rationalism, and parliamentarian[42] government, and the South, which remained faithful to the medieval heritage of absolutism, the master-and-slave economy, the dominance of religious dogma.

The other America did not decide its own path, but rather in great part it was the consequence of decisions that almost coincided with its birth.

The other America did not decide its own path, but rather in great part it was the consequence of decisions that almost coincided with its birth. As a result of the battle of Villahar it did not have representative government; owing to the Diet of Worms and seventeenth-century Hapsburg politics, it did not take part in the birth of capitalism, the development of scientific investigation, or the formulation of Rationalist thought.

In great part the difficulties in its history have derived from having to swim against the current, against the pull of those decisive factors that they inherited, in a desperate search for a possibility of incorporating themselves with another history and another era.

The antinomy[43] between the inherited soul and the vital need to keep up with the world of progress explains many of its contradictions.

While Carlos II was staging an anachronistic *auto-da-fé*[44] in Madrid's Plaza Mayor to celebrate his marriage to the past, in The Hague[45] the *Discours de la Méthode*[46] was being written, in London the Royal Society and the Bank of England were being founded, and Newton[47] was formulating his law of physics.

From that time on, the gap has not narrowed, and the leap which the countries of Hispanic heritage must attempt is of anxiety-provoking size. The times will change, or we ourselves must change.

The attempt to leap over the hereditary mentality has been the ferment of revolutionary disquiet in the Spanish American world, at least since the eighteenth century. The *criollos* soon discovered Rationalism, scientific progress, and the glitter of Enlightenment. Through the example of English America, through

---

[42] **parliamentarian**—government having a parliament as supreme legislative body.

[43] **antinomy**—a contradiction or conflict between two beliefs or conclusions that are both reasonable.

[44] *auto-da-fé*—the burning of a heretic in a public place.

[45] The Hague—the unofficial capital of the Netherlands.

[46] *Discours de la Méthode*—philosophical work (1637) by René Descartes in which he proposed "I think, therefore I am."

[47] Newton—Isaac Newton (1642–1727) English scientist who discovered the law of gravity.

journeys and the books that arrived along with other contraband from the heretic islands, a new urge arose to modernize and repudiate the past. New voices, new ideas, new Utopias to replace the already forgotten ones began to appear. It was precisely the sons and heirs of the Conquest's privileges who were most active in throwing themselves into the revolution. José Domingo Díaz, a Venezuelan monarchist contemporary with the War of Independence, was moved by astonishment to write in his book, *Recollections of the Caracas Rebellion:* "There for the first time was seen a revolution plotted and executed by the people who stood to lose the most by it."

Now, with its **equivocal**[48] name, its unsolved contradictions, its anxiety of the future and the absolute, its burden of defiant irrationality, the other America has entered the most unexpected and trying age the planet has known.

In the midst of the largest and swiftest transformation of all the relationships of value and change, in a confused panorama of new and growing possibilities of Utopia and risk, the old land of Utopia and risk must rethink its destiny and prepare itself for a future that can eventually be reconcilable with its visions.

New Forms of Power

New and large centers of power are forming of a size and consequence that the past never knew. It is no longer a question of the battleships and battalions of the old colonial powers. We are living in the nuclear bipolarity,[49] in the Cold War, in the new forms of power represented by technological monopoly and complex transitional enterprises. We now see the possibility of new concentrations of power rise up. Now it is not the United States and the Soviet Union alone with their respective spheres of influence, but we can clearly see the resurgence of the total power of a unified Europe. Japan appears as the major center of technological and industrial power in Asia. And the possibility should not be discarded that there will be an alliance of nations of Anglo-Saxon culture, which could comprise the United States, Canada, South Africa, Australia, and New Zealand, and to which Great Britain would have to belong in some way.

Someday, Black Africa will find a way to unite, and the destiny of China and India will take shape facing that of Japan. In the world that will come out of the growing concentration and disparate advance of technological and economic power, what role will Latin America play?

To contemplate this possibility, it should be considered in conjunction with an immense sum of geographical space, natural resources of all kinds, climates and forests and waters and human beings: one of the largest land masses of the planet, an extraordinarily homogeneous cultural unity, which could constitute one of the most unified of human concentrations in the world to come.

---

[48] **equivocal**—vague or ambiguous.

[49] **bipolarity**—having two extremes or sides.

Today, Spanish is the mother tongue of more than two hundred million persons. Numerically, it is the third largest language after Chinese and English. If we add up the countries speaking Spanish and Portuguese, whose linguistic border is very tenuous, they would represent more than three hundred million, the second largest linguistic community in the present world.

The possibility of a large total potential of power in the Hispanic world certainly exists. The organic complementing of its human and its natural resources, facilitated by its cultural and linguistic community, could create the bases for one of the important centers of world power in tomorrow's world.

The Hispanic world has experienced great moments of enlightenment in which it seems to have sensed some dark and powerful call of destiny.

The formation of the New World was one of those moments. We still have not justly evaluated everything meant by the **quantitative**[50] extension of the political, economic, and cultural space, nor even less the **qualitative**[51] changes introduced by this extension into its values and conceptions.

Another was the War of Independence; the Spanish Independence as well as the Latin American, two manifestations of a single phenomenon. The last vestige of the patrimonial myth of the Spanish Crown was broken, the lifeless flow of tradition was halted, and the countries had to face new circumstances. Throughout, there is a spiritual relationship and a coincidence of meaning in attitude and a contemporary correspondence of purpose which successively inspired Aranda, Miranda, Jovellanos, Bolívar, and Riego.[52] One moment in the history of the West demanded an appropriate, swift answer from the Hispanic world.

Another of these moments was the vast, multiple phenomenon which, at the end of the nineteenth century, provoked a wholly anguished and profound reevaluation of the past as well as a search for the future in the thought and literature of the Spanish language. This is represented by men separated in space, but not in intent or sentiment, such as Martí, Ganivet, Unamuno, Darío, and Rodó.[53] What in Spain is called the Generation of 1898 and in America is recognized as the Modernist movement, constitutes two **spontaneous**[54] and analogous reactions to a common situation.

We still do not know how much all of Spanish America participated morally and in spiritual anguish in the Spanish Civil War. It was felt as a new tragic episode in the old heritage and the old common calling.

---

[50] **quantitative**—measured or measurable by amount.

[51] **qualitative**—concerned with or depending on quality.

[52] Aranda… Riego—Spanish and Latin American political leaders of the late 1700s and early 1800s.

[53] Martí… Rodó—Spanish and Latin American writers involved in the modernismo literary movement beginning in the late 1800s.

[54] **spontaneous**—naturally occurring, without external cause.

Today, we are living in a similar period. Great concentrations of world power are forming. Scientific and technological power, which is at the same time the basis today of economic, military, and political dominance, with all its implications, continues to concentrate itself in the Anglo-Saxon countries, the Soviet Union and its family of satellites, and Japan.

What is the Hispanic world going to do? Revolve in a passive, sterile orbit around an alien power? Or gather its resources and its forces into an effective whole to enter a dialogue in the drama of the creation of man's future?

Should we say, as in Unamuno's tragic *boutade*,[55] "Let *them* invent," or should we ourselves begin to invent?

This is the time neither for optimisms nor for pessimisms, but rather for a cold, calculated realism that will take inventory of resources and define practical possibilities.

The other America, which is "other" not only because it is different from the Anglo-Saxon one, but because it needs to renew and redefine its present and find its future, and the other Spain, which must emerge, have no greater possibility than consciously to unite for the future what up till now has been nothing less than a tacit postponement, an unclaimed inheritance of the common past. The times are calling us.

---

[55] *boutade*—French for "joke."

QUESTIONS TO CONSIDER

1. What differences does Uslar Pietri see between North and South America? List as many as you can.

2. What does Uslar Pietri see as the potential of Latin America? What are the factors that contribute to this potential?

3. Does Uslar Pietri feel that Latin America is unjustly treated by the rest of the world? Explain your answer.

Nobel Laureates

Albert Camus
The fiction, drama, and essays of French writer Albert Camus, who was awarded the Nobel Prize in 1957, express a view of human beings struggling to find meaning in an absurd world. ▶

 Yasunari Kawabata

In 1968, novelist Yasunari Kawabata became the first Japanese writer to win the Nobel Prize for Literature.

Pablo Neruda

Chilean poet Pablo Neruda, who spent many years in exile from his country because of his left-wing political views, was awarded the Nobel Prize for Literature in 1971.

▼

▲

Czeslaw Milosz

Czeslaw Milosz, who fled the Communist regime of his native
Poland in 1951, won the Nobel Prize in 1980.

Gabriel García Márquez
Colombian novelist Gabriel García Márquez, best known for the "magic realism" of his fiction, won the Nobel Prize in 1982. ▶

◀ **Wole Soyinka**
In 1986, Nigerian poet and dramatist Wole Soyinka became the first African writer to win the Nobel Prize.

◀ Naguib Mahfouz
In 1988 the Nobel Committee gave the Prize for Literature to Egyptian novelist Naguib Mahfouz, the first writer from the Arab world to receive the award.

Octavio Paz
Mexican poet Octavio Paz won the Nobel Prize for Literature in 1990, becoming the first writer from Mexico to win the award.
▼

▲
Nadine Gordimer
When she received the Nobel Prize in 1991, novelist Nadine Gordimer became the first South African and the first woman from Africa to win the award.

▲
Derek Walcott
Born on the West Indian island of St. Lucia, poet and dramatist Derek Walcott received the Nobel Prize in 1992, becoming the first writer from the Caribbean to win the award.

▲
Seamus Heaney
Widely regarded as the finest poet writing in English today, Ireland's Seamus Heaney received the Nobel Prize in 1995.

◀ **Kenzaburo Oe**
The fiction of Japanese novelist Kenzaburo Oe, who won the Nobel Prize in 1996, has frequently written about the most catastrophic event in his country's recent history, the atomic bombing of Hiroshima and Nagasaki at the end of World War II.

Wislawa Szymborska

Immensely popular in her native Poland for the wit and humor of her writing, poet
Wislawa Szymborska was awarded the Nobel Prize for Literature in 1997.

▼

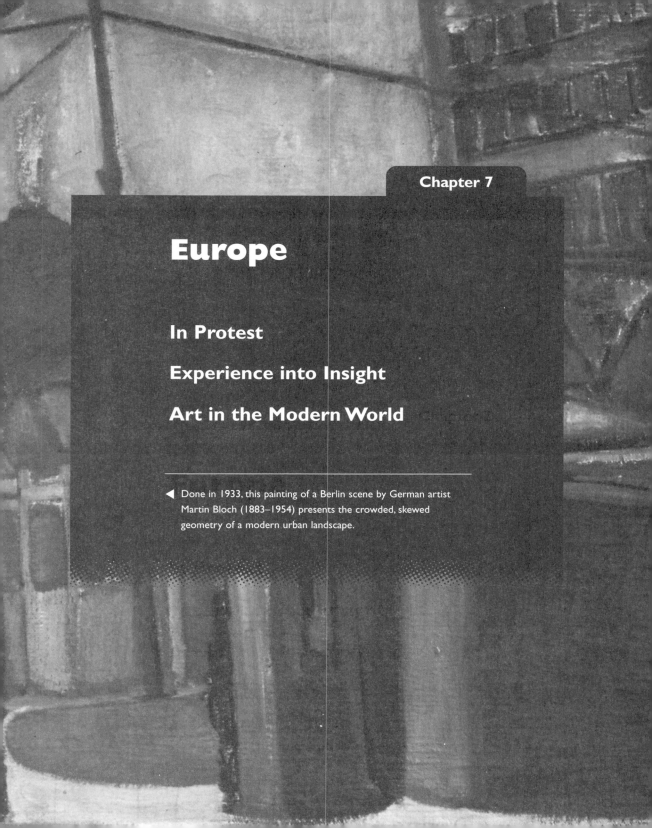

Chapter 7

Europe

In Protest

Experience into Insight

Art in the Modern World

◀ Done in 1933, this painting of a Berlin scene by German artist
Martin Bloch (1883–1954) presents the crowded, skewed
geometry of a modern urban landscape.

from

Survival in Auschwitz

PRIMO LEVI

Primo Levi (1919–1987) was an Italian chemist who during World War II was active in the anti-Fascist underground. In 1943, he was captured and, as a Jew, deported to the Auschwitz concentration camp. During the war, the Germans killed more than six million Jews in what has come to be known as the Holocaust. After the war, Levi began to write about his experience as a form of "interior liberation." His book, Survival in Auschwitz *(1947), is the first in a trilogy of memoirs that recount his time in Auschwitz and his liberation. Throughout the trilogy, which includes* The Reawakening *(1963) and* The Periodic Table *(1975), Levi employed a detached style of writing and reflection to portray what was a very personal horror.*

---

from *On the Bottom*

The journey did not last more than twenty minutes. Then the lorry[1] stopped, and we saw a large door, and above it a sign, brightly illuminated (its memory still strikes me in my dreams): ARBEIT MACHT FREI, work gives freedom.

We climb down, they make us enter an enormous empty room that is poorly heated. We have a terrible thirst. The weak gurgle of the water in the radiators makes us ferocious; we have had nothing to drink for four days. But there is also a tap— and above it a card which says that it is forbidden to drink as the water is dirty. Nonsense. It seems obvious that the card is a joke, "they" know that we are dying of thirst and they put us in a room, and there is a tap, and WASSERTRINKEN VERBOTEN.[2] I drink and I incite my companions to do likewise, but I have to spit it out, the water is **tepid**[3] and sweetish, with the smell of a swamp.

This is hell. Today, in our times, hell must be like this. A huge, empty room: We are tired, standing on our feet, with a tap which drips while we cannot drink the water, and we wait for something which will certainly be terrible, and nothing

---

[1] lorry—a truck or van.

[2] "Wassertrinken Verboten"—German for "Drinking the water is forbidden."

[3] **tepid**—slightly warm.

happens and nothing continues to happen. What can one think about? One cannot think anymore, it is like being already dead. Someone sits down on the ground. The time passes drop by drop.

We are not dead. The door is opened and an SS[4] man enters, smoking. He looks at us slowly and asks, *"Wer kann Deutsch?"*[5] One of us whom I have never seen, named Flesch, moves forward; he will be our interpreter. The SS man makes a long calm speech; the interpreter translates. We have to form rows of five, with intervals of two yards between man and man; then we have to undress and make a bundle of the clothes in a special manner, the woolen garments on one side, all the rest on the other; we must take off our shoes but pay great attention that they are not stolen.

Stolen by whom? Why should our shoes be stolen? And what about our documents, the few things we have in our pockets, our watches? We all look at the interpreter, and the interpreter asks the German, and the German smokes and looks him through and through as if he were transparent, as if no one had spoken.

I had never seen old men naked. Mr. Bergmann wore a truss[6] and asked the interpreter if he should take it off, and the interpreter hesitated. But the German understood and spoke seriously to the interpreter, pointing to someone. We saw the interpreter swallow and then he said: "The officer says, take off the truss, and you will be given that of Mr. Coen." One could see the words coming bitterly out of Flesch's mouth; this was the German manner of laughing.

Now another German comes and tells us to put the shoes in a certain corner, and we put them there, because now it is all over and we feel outside this world and the only thing is to obey. Someone comes with a broom and sweeps away all the shoes, outside the door in a heap. He is crazy, he is mixing them all together, ninety-six pairs, they will be all unmatched. The outside door opens, a freezing wind enters and we are naked and cover ourselves up with our arms. The wind blows and slams the door; the German reopens it and stands watching with interest how we **writhe**[7] to hide from the wind, one behind the other. Then he leaves and closes it.

Now the second act begins. Four men with razors, soap-brushes and clippers burst in; they have trousers and jackets with stripes, with a number sewn on the front; perhaps they are the same sort as those others of this evening (this evening or yesterday evening?); but these are **robust**[8] and flourishing. We ask many questions but they catch hold of us and in a moment we find ourselves shaved and sheared. What comic faces we have without hair! The four speak a language which does not seem of this world. It is certainly not German, for I understand a little German.

---

[4] SS—elite units of the German army during the Nazi era. They were in charge of the concentration camps.

[5] "Wer kann Deutsch?"—German for "Who knows German?"

[6] truss—medical device used to support a hernia.

[7] **writhe**—squirm, wiggle.

[8] **robust**—strong or sturdy.

Finally another door is opened: Here we are, locked in, naked, sheared[9] and standing, with our feet in water—it is a shower room. We are alone. Slowly the astonishment dissolves, and we speak, and everyone asks questions and no one answers. If we are naked in a shower room, it means that we will have a shower. If we have a shower it is because they are not going to kill us yet. But why then do they keep us standing, and give us nothing to drink, while nobody explains anything, and we have no shoes or clothes, but we are all naked with our feet in the water, and we have been traveling five days and cannot even sit down.

And our women?

Mr. Levi asks me if I think that our women are like us at this moment, and where they are, and if we will be able to see them again. I say yes, because he is married and has a daughter; certainly we will see them again. But by now my belief is that all this is a game to mock and **sneer**[10] at us. Clearly they will kill us, whoever thinks he is going to live is mad, it means that he has swallowed the bait, but I have not; I have understood that it will soon all be over, perhaps in this same room, when they get bored of seeing us naked, dancing from foot to foot and trying every now and again to sit down on the

Clearly they will kill us, whoever thinks he is going to live is mad, it means that he has swallowed the bait, but I have not.

floor. But there are two inches of cold water and we cannot sit down.

We walk up and down without sense, and we talk, everybody talks to everybody else, we make a great noise. The door opens, and a German enters; it is the officer of before. He speaks briefly, the interpreter translates. "The officer says you must be quiet, because this is not a rabbinical school." One sees the words which are not his, the bad words, twist his mouth as they come out, as if he was spitting out a foul taste. We beg him to ask what we are waiting for, how long we will stay here, about our women, everything; but he says no, that he does not want to ask. This Flesch, who is most unwilling to translate into Italian the hard cold German phrases and refuses to turn into German our questions because he knows that it is useless, is a German Jew of about fifty, who has a large scar on his face from a wound received fighting the Italians on the Piave.[11] He is a closed, **taciturn**[12] man, for whom I feel an instinctive respect as I feel that he has begun to suffer before us.

The German goes and we remain silent, although we are a little ashamed of our silence. It is still night and we wonder if the day will ever come. The door opens again, and someone else dressed in stripes

---

[9] sheared—with shaved heads.

[10] **sneer**—to smile or speak in a sarcastic or taunting manner.

[11] Piave—river in northeastern Italy, which saw fierce fighting between the Austrians and Italians during World War I.

[12] **taciturn**—quiet, uncommunicative.

comes in. He is different from the others, older, with glasses, a more civilized face, and much less robust. He speaks to us in Italian.

By now we are tired of being amazed. We seem to be watching some mad play, one of those plays in which the witches, the Holy Spirit, and the devil appear. He speaks Italian badly, with a strong foreign accent. He makes a long speech, is very polite, and tries to reply to all our questions.

We are at Monowitz, near Auschwitz, in Upper Silesia, a region inhabited by both Poles and Germans. This camp is a work camp (in German one says *Arbeitslager*); all the prisoners (there are about ten thousand) work in a factory which produces a type of rubber called Buna, so that the camp itself is called Buna.

We will be given shoes and clothes—no, not our own—other shoes, other clothes, like his. We are naked now because we are waiting for the shower and the disinfection, which will take place immediately after the reveille,[13] because one cannot enter the camp without being disinfected.

Certainly there will be work to do, everyone must work there. But there is work and work: He, for example, acts as doctor. He is a Hungarian doctor who studied in Italy and he is the dentist of the lager.[14] He has been in the lager for four and a half years (not in this one: Buna has only been open for a year and a half), but we can see that he is still quite well, not very thin. Why is he in the lager? Is he Jewish like us? "No," he says simply, "I am a criminal."

We ask him many questions. He laughs, replies to some and not to others, and it is clear that he avoids certain subjects. He does not speak of the women: He says they are well, that we will see them again soon, but he does not say how or where. Instead he tells us other things, strange and crazy things; perhaps he too is playing with us. Perhaps he is mad—one goes mad in the lager. He says that every Sunday there are concerts and football matches. He says that whoever boxes well can become cook. He says that whoever works well receives prize coupons with which to buy tobacco and soap. He says that the water is really not drinkable, and that instead a coffee substitute is distributed every day, but generally nobody drinks it as the soup itself is sufficiently watery to quench thirst. We beg him to find us something to drink, but he says he cannot, that he has come to see us secretly, against SS orders, as we still have to be disinfected, and that he must leave at once; he has come because he has a liking for Italians, and because, he says, he "has a little heart." We ask him if there are other Italians in the camp and he says there are some, a few, he does not know how many; and he at once changes the subject. Meanwhile a bell rang and he immediately hurried off and left us stunned and **disconcerted.**[15] Some feel refreshed

---

[13] reveille—a military wake-up signal played on a bugle or drums.

[14] lager—a concentration camp.

[15] **disconcerted**—upset.

but I do not. I still think that even this dentist, this incomprehensible person, wanted to amuse himself at our expense, and I do not want to believe a word of what he said.

> *We had reached the bottom. It is not possible to sink lower than this; no human condition is more miserable than this, nor could it conceivably be so.*

At the sound of the bell, we can hear the still dark camp waking up. Unexpectedly the water gushes out boiling from the showers—five minutes of bliss; but immediately after, four men (perhaps they are the barbers) burst in yelling and shoving and drive us out, wet and steaming, into the adjoining room, which is freezing; here other shouting people throw at us unrecognizable rags and thrust into our hands a pair of broken down boots with wooden soles; we have no time to understand and we already find ourselves in the open, in the blue and icy snow of dawn, barefoot and naked, with all our clothing in our hands, with a hundred yards to run to the next hut. There we are finally allowed to get dressed.

When we finish, everyone remains in his own corner and we do not dare lift our eyes to look at one another. There is nowhere to look in a mirror, but our appearance stands in front of us, reflected in a hundred **livid**[16] faces, in a hundred miserable and **sordid**[17] puppets. We are transformed into the phantoms glimpsed yesterday evening.

Then for the first time we became aware that our language lacks words to express this offense, the demolition of a man. In a moment, with almost prophetic **intuition**,[18] the reality was revealed to us: We had reached the bottom. It is not possible to sink lower than this; no human condition is more miserable than this, nor could it conceivably be so. Nothing belongs to us anymore; they have taken away our clothes, our shoes, even our hair; if we speak, they will not listen to us, and if they listen, they will not understand. They will even take away our name: and if we want to keep it, we will have to find ourselves the strength to do so, to manage somehow so that behind the name something of us, of us as we were, still remains.

We know that we will have difficulty in being understood, and this is as it should be. But consider what value, what meaning is enclosed even in the smallest of our daily habits, in the hundred possessions which even the poorest beggar owns: a handkerchief, an old letter, the photo of a cherished person. These things are part of us, almost like limbs of our body; nor is it conceivable that we can be deprived of them in our world, for we immediately find others to substitute [for] the old ones, other objects which are ours in their **personification**[19] and **evocation**[20] of our memories.

---

[16] **livid**—extremely angry, furious.

[17] **sordid**—dirty, sleazy.

[18] **intuition**—knowledge without using thought or the senses.

[19] **personification**—attribution of personal qualities to an object or thing.

[20] **evocation**—calling up or forth.

Imagine now a man who is deprived of everyone he loves, and at the same time of his house, his habits, his clothes, in short, of everything he possesses: He will be a hollow man, reduced to suffering and needs, forgetful of dignity and restraint, for he who loses all often easily loses himself. He will be a man whose life or death can be lightly decided with no sense of human **affinity**,[21] in the most fortunate of cases, on the basis of a pure judgment of utility. It is in this way that one can understand the double sense of the term "extermination camp" and it is now clear what we seek to express with the phrase "to lie on the bottom."

from *The Events of the Summer*

In this world shaken every day more deeply by the omens of its nearing end, amidst new terrors and hopes, with intervals of exasperated slavery, I happened to meet Lorenzo.

The story of my relationship with Lorenzo is both long and short, plain and **enigmatic**:[22] It is the story of a time and condition now **effaced**[23] from every present reality, and so I do not think it can be understood except in the manner in which we nowadays understand events of legends or the remotest history.

In concrete terms it amounts to little: An Italian civilian worker brought me a piece of bread and the remainder of his ration every day for six months; he gave me a vest of his, full of patches; he wrote a postcard on my behalf to Italy and brought me the reply. For all this he neither asked nor accepted any reward, because he was good and simple and did not think that one did good for a reward.

We are the untouchables to the civilians. They think, more or less explicitly —with all the **nuances**[24] lying between contempt and commiseration—that as we have been condemned to this life of ours, reduced to our condition, we must be tainted by some mysterious, grave sin. They hear us speak in many different languages, which they do not understand and which sound to them as grotesque as animal noises; they see us reduced to ignoble slavery, without hair, without honor and without names, beaten every day, more **abject**[25] every day, and they never see in our eyes a light of rebellion, or of peace, or of faith. They know us as thieves and untrustworthy, muddy, ragged and starving, and mistaking the effect for the cause, they judge us worthy of our abasement. Who could tell one of our faces from the other? For them we are *"Kazett,"*[26] a singular neuter word.

This naturally does not stop many of them throwing us a piece of bread or a potato now and again, or giving us their

---

[21] **affinity**—connection, closeness.

[22] **enigmatic**—puzzling, mysterious.

[23] **effaced**—wiped out.

[24] **nuances**—subtle shades or differences of meaning, feeling, or color.

[25] **abject**—miserable.

[26] *Kazett*—short for concentration camp (*konzentrationlager*); here used to refer to a prisoner.

bowls, after the distribution of *"Zivilsuppe"* in the workyards, to scrape and give back washed. They do it to get rid of some **importunate**[27] starved look, or through a momentary impulse of humanity, or through simple curiosity to see us running from all sides to fight each other or the scrap, bestially and without restraint, until the strongest one gobbles it up, whereupon all the others limp away, frustrated.

Now nothing of this sort occurred between me and Lorenzo. However little sense there may be in trying to specify why I, rather than thousands of others, managed to survive the test, I believe that it was really due to Lorenzo that I am alive today; and not so much for his material aid, as for his having constantly reminded me by his presence, by his natural and plain manner of being good, that there still existed a just world outside our own, something and someone still pure and whole, not corrupt, not savage, **extraneous**[28] to hatred and terror; something difficult to define, a remote possibility of good, but for which it was worth surviving.

The personages in these pages are not men. Their humanity is buried, or they themselves have buried it, under an offense received or inflicted on someone else. The evil and insane SS men, the kapos,[29] the politicals, the criminals, the prominents, great and small, down to the indifferent slave Häftlinge,[30] all the grades of the mad hierarchy created by the Germans paradoxically **fraternized**[31] in a uniform internal desolation.

But Lorenzo was a man; his humanity was pure and uncontaminated, he was outside this world of negation. Thanks to Lorenzo, I managed not to forget that I myself was a man.

---

[27] **importunate**—persistent.

[28] **extraneous**—coming from ouside of, external.

[29] kapos—the prisoners chosen to be in charge of the prison work groups.

[30] Häftlinge—German for "prisoner."

[31] **fraternized**—behaved as friends.

QUESTIONS TO CONSIDER

1. Why does Levi think so many people are amusing themselves at the prisoners' expense?

2. What is the reality revealed to Levi in the hut after the prisoners are given their clothes?

3. Why, according to Levi, can a man deprived of everything be more easily exterminated?

4. What is it that Lorenzo is able to remind Levi of? What is the implied contrast? What is the ultimate lesson?

Three Poems

HANS MAGNUS ENZENSBERGER

Hans Magnus Enzensberger (1929–) was born into a family of writers in Germany. He came to fame at an early age as a poet protesting against social injustice and industrialization. Enzensberger's writing criticizes many aspects of postwar German society. In 1968, he emigrated to Cuba, hoping to find his ideals and hopes realized by the revolution there. In the 1970s, however, he grew disillusioned with the power of radical and revolutionary politics to affect societal change. Enzensberger returned to Germany and has devoted himself more to lyric poetry that celebrates the individual.

For the Grave of a Peace-Loving Man

This one was no **philanthropist**,[1]
avoided meetings, stadiums, the large stores.
Did not eat the flesh of his own kind.

Violence walked the streets,
smiling, not naked.
But there were screams in the sky.

People's faces were not very clear.
They seemed to be battered
even before the blow had struck home.

---

[1] **philanthropist**—person of great charity or a lover of mankind.

One thing for which he fought all his life,
with words, tooth and claw, grimly,
cunningly,[2] off his own bat:

the thing which he called his peace,
now that he's got it, there is no longer a mouth
over his bones, to taste it with.

Middle-Class Blues

We can't complain.
We're not out of work.
We don't go hungry.
We eat.

The grass grows,
the social product,
the fingernail,
the past.

The streets are empty.
The deals are closed.
The sirens are silent.
All that will pass.

The dead have made their wills.
The rain's become a drizzle.
The war's not yet been declared.
There's no hurry for that.

---

[2] **cunningly**—cleverly.

We eat the grass.
We eat the social product.
We eat the fingernails.
We eat the past.

We have nothing to conceal.
We have nothing to miss.
We have nothing to say.
We have.

The watch has been wound up.
The bills have been paid.
The washing-up has been done.
The last bus is passing by.

It is empty.

We can't complain.

What are we waiting for?

Vanished Work

Rather remote, all of it.
As in a **saga**,[3] darkly,
the rag-and-bone-man
with his battered top hat,
the blue hand of the woad-miller,[4]
the corn-chandler[5] in his cool cellar.

The rush-man[6] has deserted his reed,
the beekeeper his hive,
the charcoal burner his flue.[7]
The woolcarder[8] threw her teasel[9] away,
the trough-maker his chisel.
Trades moldered away,
extinct skills.

What has happened to the bridoons,
the hames and the terrets?[10]

The cartwright[11] has passed away.
Only his name survives,
like an insect congealed in amber,[12]
in the telephone book.

---

[3] **saga**—legend, a long and involved story of heroic actions.

[4] woad-miller—person who processes woad, a plant used to make a blue dye.

[5] corn-chandler—dealer in grain.

[6] rush—marsh.

[7] flue—a passage for hot air or smoke.

[8] woolcarder—someone who prepares wool for spinning.

[9] teasel—a plant with bristles, once used to make a napped surface on wool.

[10] bridoons . . . hames . . . terrets—three parts of a horse's harness.

[11] cartwright—a maker of carts.

[12] amber—yellowish translucent fossilized resin derived from trees and used in jewelry.

But the shimmering block of light
I have lived to see
with my own eyes, heaved
easily, as if by magic
with an iron hook
onto the leathery shoulder-strap

of the iceman, on Wednesdays
at noon, **punctually,**[13] and the chips
melted like fire
in my chill mouth.

---

[13] **punctually**—exactly on time, promptly.

QUESTIONS TO CONSIDER

1. What are the different meanings of "peace" in "For the Grave of a Peace-Loving Man"? What is the tone of the poem?

2. What is the complaint of the middle class in "Middle-Class Blues"? Do you think it is justified? Explain why or why not.

3. What differentiates the iceman from the other professionals in "Vanished Work"? Why is he different?

4. What things is Enzensberger protesting against in these poems? Do you think he is justified in his protests? Explain why or why not.

An Insolvable Problem of Genetics

JOSEF SKVORECKY

Josef Skvorecky (1924–   ) became famous in Czechoslovakia when his first novel, The Cowards, *was banned by the Communist government in 1958. Despite this setback, Skvorecky was able to publish his stories in the 1960s and even a second novel in 1969. However, the liberalization and new freedoms that the Communist government allowed in Czechoslovakia in 1968—known as the Prague Spring—brought a Soviet invasion, and the Communist government grew extremely repressive. Skvorecky emigrated to Canada where he has lived, written, and taught ever since. Most of his stories and novels describe the ironies of life under Communism. Skvorecky described "An Insolvable Problem of Genetics" as "unfortunately, not a child of my imagination but something that actually happened to my friend Jan Bich."*

[From the secret diary of Vasil Krátký, a third-grade student at the Leonid Brezhnev High School in K.]

While offering a brotherly hand to many nations, our fatherland also harbors[1] a certain number of dark-skinned African students; some of these undergo preparatory courses in the Czech language in our town. Later they laud the good name of our nation far beyond the borders of our country, but my brother Adolf lost his lifelong happiness because of their overly friendly attitude toward the population.

This is how it happened: for two long years Adolf was secretly in love with the movie star Jana Brejchová and wrote her more than two hundred letters during this time. The interest shown by the film celebrity was not in the least comparable to my brother's effort, and so Adolf began to pursue Freddie Mourek, whose skinny figure and seemly features resembled somewhat those of the aforementioned actress.

The parents welcomed his decision because Freddie, as the illegitimate daughter of the Secretary of the Party cell at the Lentex linen factory in K., came from a

---

[1] harbors—holds or shelters.

family with an excellent class profile. Nothing but a single flaw disturbed the great impression made by Adolf's girl friend on our family, and that was her given name. One day while at our house, Freddie, to the accompaniment of Adolf's bass guitar, sang a certain loud song in a foreign language. To my father's uneasy inquiry concerning the origins of the song she answered that it was a black American song, whose lyrics protested against discrimination. Father applauded, then **extolled**[2] briefly the black struggle for equality; then he quite suddenly became very angry, and turning dark red, he began to curse the South African racists. Mother also became angry, and in the resulting friendly atmosphere Father asked Freddie why a girl as thoroughly progressive and an activist of the Young Communist League, would call herself by a name apparently of English origin.

At that Freddie blushed and said that she could now reveal to them the secret of her name because she had just agreed with Adolf to enter into wedlock in a civil ceremony prior to the final **matriculation**[3] examinations. Father was very heartened by the news as he happens to favor early **nuptials**[4] for youths finding themselves in their reproductive years, since these are called for by the appropriate authorities in an attempt to prevent population decrease. He then encouraged Freddie to reveal her secret without delay. "My name," she said, "I inherited from my father. He was a certain Frederick Positive Wasserman Brown, a migrant worker from South Carolina, who as a member of General Georgie Patton's Third U.S. Army seduced my mummy in Pilsen, and then had himself transferred to the Far East." "An American?" Father recoiled and turned gloomy. Then he partially recovered: "A migrant worker?" and Freddie, attempting to aid the complete recovery of my father who had earlier **lauded**[5] so eagerly the heroic struggle of the colored people, quickly added: "Yes. And besides my father was black." Against all expectations Father's gloom became permanent.

In the following days he began to bring home from the People's Municipal Library books of a certain Lysenko;[6] unable to find in them a satisfactory answer to what he was looking for, he borrowed a volume of the **friar**[7] Mendel[8] with pictures of various types of peas, white, gray, and black ones. He studied those very **diligently,**[9] and later when Freddie again sang at our house negro songs in a foreign language, he asked: "Listen, girl, that father of yours, was he a very black black or was he of a lighter hue?" "Very black," said Freddie,

---

[2] **extolled**—praised or celebrated.

[3] **matriculation**—enrollment at a college or university.

[4] **nuptials**—marriages, weddings.

[5] **lauded**—praised.

[6] Lysenko—Trofim Lysenko (1898–1976) geneticist who developed the false theory that heredity can be altered. His theories were propounded in the Soviet Union until 1965, and did uncountable damage to scientific and agricultural progress.

[7] **friar**—monk.

[8] Mendel—Gregor Mendel (1822–1884) Austrian botanist who discovered the laws of heredity and began the study of genetics.

[9] **diligently**—carefully and steadily.

who herself is very white, but has eyes which are very black, large and very beautiful. "So black that during the war they used him in reconnaissance, when, completely naked he would in the darkest night penetrate through the German lines, since he was completely invisible." And Father turned once again gloomy and said no more.

However, that evening he advised Adolf to break off without delay his relationship with the black man's daughter. Adolf resisted: "I'm not a racist!" "Neither am I," replied Father. "If Freddie were a dark-skinned girl I would welcome her as a daughter-in-law, because the union with an obvious member of an elsewhere persecuted race would doubtless even further **enhance**[10] the class profile of our family. But she is white. There arises the danger, that on the basis of the reactionary laws determined by the friar Mendel, she will bear you a black child, and there will be a scandal!" "What scandal? Black or white, it's all the same," Adolf rejoindered, and Father explained: "Nobody will believe that this black child is really yours. Everybody will think that it is the result of the efforts of our guests, the African students, and in that sense they will also **slander**[11] your wife." And he concluded: "Which is why you will break off the relationship before it is too late."

Adolf turned crimson and **ponderous**.[12] Then he said: "It is already too late. It is impossible to break off the relationship." A deadly silence prevailed, interrupted only by Mother's moaning and Father's fidgeting. From that day on, Adolf also started to carefully study the writings of the friar Mendel.

No doubt it was too late; it was, I imagine, because Adolf loved Freddie much more than he had ever loved Jana Brejchová, although he almost never sent her any letters. Freddie's mother, the textile worker and Party Secretary, was invited to our house, and I, hidden behind the large portrait of the Statesman, which conceals the hole where Grandfather's wall safe used to stand, overheard Mother emphasizing the terribly tender age of both the children and asking the esteemed Secretary's consent to apply to some sort of a committee in the matter of an absorption (or something that sounded like that). I really could not understand why the Comrade Mother (Mrs. Mourek) got upset to the point of refusing to co-operate with the committee, slammed the door and left, when on other occasions, as a class-conscious woman, she had always shown full confidence in committees, councils, and organs of all kinds.

It did not end there: the Comrade Secretary of the Party Cell at the Lentex linen factory in K. provided us with a

---

[10] **enhance**—heighten or intensify.

[11] **slander**—to make mean-spirited and false comments about a person.

[12] **ponderous**—heavy and clumsy.

further unexpected surprise. Soon after, when Father, Mother, my older sister Margaret, and even Adolf himself began spreading all around town that the father of Freddie was the migrant black Frederick Positive Wasserman Brown, and at the same time introducing the people to the laws of heredity according to which a completely white person can give birth to a black child thanks to the genes of its **progenitor**[13] (in order to preventively protect the reputation of Freddie in case of a child with other than Czech coloring), Comrade Mourek appeared again, and her squealing voice could be heard from the parlor, expressing herself to the effect that Father, Mother, Margaret, and Adolf were giving the girl (meaning Freddie) a bad name around town and causing trouble, of which she (Comrade Mourek) had had more than her fill throughout her life, the result of some youthful transgression. And although Father, having alertly declared himself the enemy of bourgeois morality, began to explain to her his intentions, he failed nonetheless.

As concerns Adolf, he deteriorated visibly, until finally he spoke about nothing else but the friar Mendel. This aroused the suspicion of the principal of the high school, Comrade Pavel Běhavka, who for several Sundays carefully observed, from his table at the Café Beránek, the entrance to the Catholic church in the town square (adding to his surveillance later on also the chapel of the Czech Protestants, and that of the Czech Evangelical Brethen), to find out whether Adolf, as a result of being converted to the **obscurantist**[14] faith of the friars, visited the services. He did not, but being psychologically uprooted, he would acquaint everyone at any occasion, even completely strange comrades, with the secret of the background of his fiancée Freddie, as well as with the laws of **genetics**.[15] Finally, after a large number of arguments, fights, and confrontations, Freddie one day broke up with him. To the accompaniment of his bass guitar they sang together for the last time the protest song "Get Me a New Dolly, Molly!" and then she declared (I overheard it secretly, hidden behind the portrait of the Statesman): "Your indiscretion is getting on my nerves, and I don't intend to put up with it any longer. Also, I would like you to know that I haven't told you everything: for your information, the mother of my father Frederick Positive Wasserman Brown was Japanese, his grandfather, who was brought over from Africa as a slave in chains, was a Pygmy, which, combined with the fact that my mother is one third a Jewish gypsy, leaves me with a very good chance of giving birth to a green dwarf, which your father will not be able to

> *Finally, after a large number of arguments, fights, and confrontations, Freddie one day broke up with him.*

---

[13] **progenitor**—ancestor, originator.

[14] **obscurantist**—opposed to knowledge and enlightenment.

[15] **genetics**—study of inherited traits and genes.

explain to the comrades with or without his Mendel. And it's good-bye forever, my little imbecile!"

Having said that, she left forever; and so my brother, deprived of his life-long happiness by the presence of the African students, did not become a father.

Somewhat later Freddie gave birth to twins: one is a boy and the other a girl, and both are completely pink. However, about that phenomenon, Mendel says nothing at all.

QUESTIONS TO CONSIDER

1. Why does Adolf's family like Freddie so much at first?

2. What is it that Freddie's mother objects to?

3. Would you describe Adolf's family's actions toward Freddie as racism? Why or why not?

4. What is Skvorecky protesting against in this story?

The Garden of Stubborn Cats

ITALO CALVINO

Italo Calvino (1923–1985) was Italy's most prominent fiction writer of the postwar era. He was a master of the fantastic and surreal, using absurdist techniques to draw comparisons with reality. His most famous work, If On a Winter's Night a Traveller (1979), is a series of stories that have no ending. Calvino's idea was to turn the reader into the protagonist of the novel. Calvino experimented in such ways in all of his writing, drawing readers into his surreal fiction with flair and humor. The following story displays Calvino's technique of using absurd events and ideas to comment on modern life.

The city of cats and the city of men exist one inside the other, but they are not the same city. Few cats recall the time when there was no distinction: the streets and squares of men were also streets and squares of cats, and the lawns, courtyards, balconies, and fountains: you lived in a broad and various space. But for several generations now domestic **felines**[1] have been prisoners of an uninhabitable city: the streets are uninterruptedly overrun by the mortal traffic of cat-crushing automobiles; in every square foot of terrain where once a garden extended or a vacant lot or the ruins of an old demolition, now condominiums loom up, welfare housing, brand-new skyscrapers; every entrance is crammed with parked cars; the courtyards, one by one, have been roofed by reinforced concrete and transformed into garages or movie houses or storerooms or workshops. And where a rolling plateau of low roofs once extended, copings, terraces, water tanks, balconies, skylights, corrugated-iron sheds, now one general superstructure rises wherever structures can rise; the intermediate differences in height, between the low ground of the street and the supernal[2] heaven of the penthouses, disappear; the cat of a recent litter seeks in vain the itinerary of its fathers, the point

---

[1] **felines**—cats.

[2] supernal—lofty.

from which to make the soft leap from balustrade[3] to cornice[4] to drainpipe, or for the quick climb on the roof-tiles.

But in this vertical city, in this compressed city, where all voids tend to fill up and every block of cement tends to mingle with other blocks of cement, a kind of counter-city opens, a negative city, that consists of empty slices between wall and wall, of the minimal distances ordained by the building regulations between two constructions, between the rear of one construction and the rear of the next; it is a city of cavities, wells, air conduits, driveways, inner yards, accesses to basements, like a network of dry canals on a planet of stucco and tar, and it is through this network, grazing the walls, that the ancient cat population still scurries.

On occasion, to pass the time, Marcovaldo would follow a cat. It was during the work-break, between noon and three, when all the personnel except Marcovaldo went home to eat, and he— who brought his lunch in his bag—laid his place among the packing-cases in the warehouse, chewed his snack, smoked a half-cigar and wandered around, alone and idle, waiting for work to resume. In those hours, a cat that peeped in at a window was always welcome company, and a guide for new explorations. He had made friends with a tabby, well fed, a blue ribbon around its neck, surely living with some well-to-do family. This tabby shared with Marcovaldo the habit of an afternoon stroll right after lunch; and naturally a friendship sprang up.

Following his tabby friend, Marcovaldo had started looking at places as if through the round eyes of a cat and even if these places were the usual environs of his firm he saw them in a different light, as settings for cattish stories, with connections practicable only by light, velvety paws. Though from the outside the neighborhood seemed poor in cats, every day on his rounds Marcovaldo made the acquaintance of some new face, and a miau, a hiss, a stiffening of fur on an arched back was enough for him to sense ties and intrigues and rivalries among them. At those moments he thought he had already penetrated the secrecy of the felines' society: and then he felt himself scrutinized by pupils that became slits, under the surveillance of the antennae of **taut**[5] whiskers, and all the cats around him sat impassive as sphinxes, the pink triangles of their noses convergent on the black triangles of their lips, and the only things that moved were the tips of the ears, with a vibrant jerk like radar. They reached the end of a narrow passage, between squalid blank walls; and, looking around, Marcovaldo saw that the cats that had led him this far had vanished, all of them together, no telling in which direction, even his tabby friend, and they had left

---

[3] balustrade—railing supported by short posts or pillars that forms a decorative wall to a balcony or bridge.

[4] cornice—decorative border around the wall of a room just below the ceiling.

[5] **taut**—tight, tense, or rigid.

him alone. Their realm had territories, ceremonies, customs that it was not yet granted to him to discover.

On the other hand, from the cat city there opened unsuspected peepholes onto the city of men: and one day the same tabby led him to discover the great Biarritz Restaurant.

Anyone wishing to see the Biarritz Restaurant had only to assume the posture of a cat, that is, proceed on all fours. Cat and man, in this fashion, walked around a kind of dome, at whose foot some low, rectangular little windows opened. Following the tabby's example, Marcovaldo looked down. They were transoms[6] through which the luxurious hall received air and light. To the sound of gypsy violins, partridges and quails swirled by on silver dishes balanced by the white-gloved fingers of waiters in tailcoats. Or, more precisely, above the partridges and quails the dishes whirled, and above the dishes the white gloves, and poised on the waiters' patent-leather shoes, the gleaming parquet floor, from which hung dwarf potted palms and tablecloths and crystal and buckets like bells with the champagne bottle for their clapper: everything was turned upside-down because Marcovaldo, for fear of being seen, wouldn't stick his head inside the window and confined himself to looking at the reversed reflection of the room in the tilted **pane**.[7]

But it was not so much the windows of the dining-room as those of the kitchens that interested the cat: looking through the former you saw, distant and somehow transfigured, what in the kitchens presented itself—quite concrete and within paw's reach—as a plucked bird or a fresh fish. And it was toward the kitchens, in fact, that the tabby wanted to lead Marcovaldo, either through a gesture of **altruistic**[8] friendship or else because it counted on the man's help for one of its raids. Marcovaldo, however, was reluctant to leave his belvedere[9] over the main room: first as he was fascinated by the luxury of the place, and then because something down there had riveted his attention. To such an extent that, overcoming his fear of being seen, he kept peeking in, with his head in the transom.

In the midst of the room, directly under that pane, there was a little glass fish tank, a kind of aquarium, where some fat trout were swimming. A special customer approached, a man with a shiny bald pate, black suit, black beard. An old waiter in tailcoat followed him, carrying a little net as if he were going to catch butterflies. The gentleman in black looked at the trout with a grave, intent air; then he raised one hand

Anyone wishing to see the Biarritz Restaurant had only to assume the posture of a cat, that is, proceed on all fours.

---

[6] transoms—windows divided by a horizontal bar or placed above a door or another window.

[7] **pane**—single sheet of glass in a window or door.

[8] **altruistic**—unselfish.

[9] belvedere—open-sided balcony or platform.

and with a slow, solemn gesture singled out a fish. The waiter dipped the net into the tank, pursued the appointed trout, captured it, headed for the kitchens, holding out in front of him, like a lance, the net in which the fish wriggled. The gentleman in black, solemn as a magistrate who has handed down a capital sentence, went to take his seat and wait for the return of the trout, sauteed "à la meuniére."

If I found a way to drop a line from up here and make one of those trout bite, Marcovaldo thought, I couldn't be accused of theft; at worst, of fishing in an unauthorized place. And ignoring the miaus that called him toward the kitchens, he went to collect his fishing tackle.

Nobody in the crowded dining room of the Biarritz saw the long, fine line, armed with hook and bait, as it slowly dropped into the tank. The fish saw the bait, and flung themselves on it. In the fray one trout managed to bite the worm: and immediately it began to rise, rise, emerge from the water, a silvery flash, it darted up high, over the laid tables and the trolleys of hors d'oeuvres, over the blue flames of the crêpes Suzette, until it vanished into the heavens of the transom.

Marcovaldo had yanked the rod with the brisk snap of the expert fisherman, so the fish landed behind his back. The trout had barely touched the ground when the cat sprang. What little life the trout still had was lost between the tabby's teeth. Marcovaldo, who had abandoned his line at that moment to run and grab the fish,

saw it snatched from under his nose, hook and all. He was quick to put one foot on the rod, but the snatch had been so strong that the rod was all the man had left, while the tabby ran off with the fish, pulling the line after it. Treacherous kitty! It had vanished.

But this time it wouldn't escape him: there was that long line trailing after him and showing the way he had taken. Though he had lost sight of the cat, Marcovaldo followed the end of the line: there it was, running along a wall; it climbed a parapet, wound through a doorway, was swallowed up by a basement... Marcovaldo, venturing into more and more cattish places, climbed roofs, straddled railings, always managed to catch a glimpse—perhaps only a second before it disappeared—of a moving trace that indicated a thief's path.

Now the line played out down a side-walk, in the midst of the traffic, and Marcovaldo, running after it, almost managed to grab it. He flung himself down on his belly: there, he grabbed it! He managed to seize one end of the line before it slipped between the bars of a gate.

Beyond a half-rusted gate and two bits of wall buried under climbing plants, there was a little **rank**[10] garden, with a small, abandoned-looking building at the far end of it. A carpet of dry leaves covered the path, and dry leaves lay everywhere under the boughs of the two plane trees, forming actually some little mounds in the yard. A layer of leaves was yellowing in the green water of a pool. Enormous buildings rose

---

[10] **rank**—overgrown, dense.

all around, skyscrapers with thousands of windows, like so many eyes trained disapprovingly on that little square patch with two trees, a few tiles, and all those yellow leaves, surviving right in the middle of an area of great traffic.

And in this garden, perched on the **capitals**[11] and balustrades, lying on the dry leaves of the flowerbeds, climbing on the trunks of the trees or on the drainpipes, motionless on their four paws, their tails making a question-mark, seated to wash their faces, there were tiger cats, black cats, white cats, calico cats, tabbies, angoras, Persians, house cats and stray cats, perfumed cats and mangy cats. Marcovaldo realized he had finally reached the heart of the cats' realm, their secret island. And, in his emotion, he almost forgot his fish.

It had remained, that fish, hanging by the line from the branch of a tree, out of reach of the cats' leaps; it must have dropped from its kidnapper's mouth at some clumsy movement, perhaps as it was defended from the others, or perhaps displayed as an extraordinary prize. The line had got tangled, and Marcovaldo, tug as he would, couldn't manage to yank it loose. A furious battle had meanwhile been joined among the cats, to reach that unreachable fish, or rather, to win the right to try and reach it. Each wanted to prevent the others from leaping: they hurled themselves on one another, they tangled in midair, they roiled around clutching each other, and finally a general war broke out in a whirl of dry, crackling leaves.

After many futile yanks, Marcovaldo now felt the line was free, but he took care not to pull it: the trout would have fallen right in the midst of that infuriated **scrimmage**[12] of felines.

It was at this moment that, from the top of the walls of the gardens, a strange rain began to fall: fish-bones, heads, tails, even bits of lung and lights. Immediately the cats' attention was distracted from the suspended trout and they flung themselves on the new delicacies. To Marcovaldo, this seemed the right moment to pull the line and regain his fish. But, before he had time to act, from a blind of the little villa, two yellow, skinny hands darted out: one was brandishing scissors; the other, a frying pan. The hand with the scissors was raised above the trout, the hand with the frying pan was thrust under it. The scissors cut the line, the trout fell into the pan; hands, scissors and pan withdrew, the blind closed: all in the space of a second. Marcovaldo was totally bewildered.

"Are you also a cat lover?" A voice at his back made him turn round. He was surrounded by little old women, some of them ancient, wearing old-fashioned hats on their heads; others, younger, but with the look of spinsters; and all were carrying in their hands or their bags packages of leftover meat or fish, and some even had little pans of milk. "Will you help me throw this package over the fence, for those poor creatures?"

---

[11] **capitals**—tops of columns.

[12] **scrimmage**—fight or struggle.

All the ladies, cat lovers, gathered at this hour around the garden of dry leaves to take the food to their protégés.

"Can you tell me why they are all here, these cats?" Marcovaldo inquired.

> *All the ladies, cat lovers, gathered at this hour around the garden of dry leaves to take the food to their protégés.*

"Where else could they go? This garden is all they have left! Cats come here from other neighborhoods, too, from miles and miles around . . ."

"And birds, as well," another lady added. "They're forced to live by the hundreds and hundreds on these few trees."

". . . And the frogs, they're all in that pool, and at night they never stop croaking . . . You can hear them even on the eighth floor of the buildings around here."

"Who does this villa belong to anyway?" Marcovaldo asked. Now, outside the gate, there weren't just the cat-loving ladies but also other people: the man from the gas pump opposite, the apprentices from a mechanic's shop, the postman, the grocer, some passers-by. And none of them, men and women, had to be asked twice: all wanted to have their say, as always when a mysterious and controversial subject comes up.

"It belongs to a Marchesa.[13] She lives there, but you never see her . . ."

"She's been offered millions and millions, by developers, for this little patch of land, but she won't sell . . ."

"What would she do with millions, an old woman all alone in the world? She wants to hold on to her house, even if it's falling to pieces, rather than be forced to move . . ."

"It's the only undeveloped bit of land in the downtown area . . . Its value goes up every year . . . They've made her offers—"

"Offers! That's not all. Threats, intimidation, persecution . . . You don't know the half of it! Those contractors!"

"But she holds out. She's held out for years . . ."

"She's a saint. Without her, where would those poor animals go?"

"A lot she cares about the animals, the old miser! Have you ever seen her give them anything to eat?"

"How can she feed the cats when she doesn't have food for herself? She's the last descendant of a ruined family!"

"She hates cats! I've seen her chasing them and hitting them with an umbrella!"

"Because they were tearing up her, flowerbeds!"

"What flowerbeds? I've never seen anything in this garden but a great crop of weeds!"

Marcovaldo realized that with regard to the old Marchesa opinions were sharply divided: some saw her as an angelic being, others as an egoist and a miser.

"It's the same with the birds; she never gives them a crumb!"

"She gives them hospitality. Isn't that plenty?"

---

[13] Marchesa—an Italian noblewoman.

"Like she gives the mosquitoes, you mean. They all come from here, from that pool. In the summertime the mosquitoes eat us alive, and it's all the fault of that Marchesa!"

"And the mice? This villa is a mine of mice. Under the dead leaves they have their **burrows,**[14] and at night they come out . . ."

"As far as the mice go, the cats take care of them . . ."

"Oh, you and your cats! If we had to rely on them . . ."

"Why? Have you got something to say against cats?"

Here the discussion degenerated into a general quarrel.

"The authorities should do something: confiscate the villa!" one man cried.

"What gives them the right?" another protested.

"In a modern neighborhood like ours, a mouse-nest like this . . . it should be forbidden . . ."

"Why, I picked my apartment precisely because it overlooked this little bit of green . . ."

"Green, hell! Think of the fine sky-scraper they could build here!"

Marcovaldo would have liked to add something of his own, but he couldn't get a word in. Finally, all in one breath, he exclaimed: "The Marchesa stole a trout from me!"

The unexpected news supplied fresh ammunition to the old woman's enemies, but her defenders exploited it as proof of the **indigence**[15] to which the unfortunate noblewoman was reduced. Both sides agreed that Marcovaldo should go and knock at her door to demand an explanation.

It wasn't clear whether the gate was locked or unlocked; in any case, it opened, after a push, with a mournful creak. Marcovaldo picked his way among the leaves and cats, climbed the steps to the porch, knocked hard at the entrance.

At a window (the very one where the frying pan had appeared), the blind was raised slightly and in one corner a round, pale blue eye was seen, and a clump of hair dyed an undefinable color, and a dry skinny hand. A voice was heard, asking: "Who is it? Who's at the door?" the words accompanied by a cloud smelling of fried oil.

"It's me, Marchesa. The trout man," Marcovaldo explained. "I don't mean to trouble you. I only wanted to tell you, in case you didn't know, that the trout was stolen from me, by that cat, and I'm the one who caught it. In fact the line . . ."

"Those cats! It's always those cats . . ." the Marchesa said, from behind the shutter, with a shrill, somewhat nasal voice. "All my troubles come from the cats! Nobody knows what I go through! Prisoner night and day of those horrid beasts! And with all the refuse people throw over the walls, to spite me!"

"But my trout . . ."

---

[14] **burrows**—holes or tunnels dug by animals and used as their homes.

[15] **indigence**—poverty, neediness.

"Your trout! What am I supposed to know about your trout!" The Marchesa's voice became almost a scream, as if she wanted to drown out the sizzle of oil in the pan, which came through the window along with the aroma of fried fish. "How can I make sense of anything, with all the stuff that rains into my house?"

"I understand, but did you take the trout or didn't you?"

"When I think of all the damage I suffer because of the cats! Ah, fine state of affairs! I'm not responsible for anything! I can't tell you what I've lost! Thanks to those cats, who've occupied house and garden for years! My life at the mercy of those animals! Go and find the owners! Make them pay damages! Damages? A whole life destroyed! A prisoner here, unable to move a step!"

"Excuse me for asking: but who's forcing you to stay?"

From the crack in the blind there appeared sometimes a round, pale blue eye, sometimes a mouth with two protruding teeth; for a moment the whole face was visible, and to Marcovaldo it seemed, bewilderingly, the face of a cat.

"They keep me prisoner, they do, those cats! Oh, I'd be glad to leave! What wouldn't I give for a little apartment all my own, in a nice clean modern building! But I can't go out . . . They follow me, they block my path, they trip me up!" The voice became a whisper, as if to confide a secret. "They're afraid I'll sell the lot . . . They won't leave me . . . won't allow me . . . When the builders come to offer me a contract, you

should see them, those cats! They get in the way, pull out their claws; they even chased a lawyer off! Once I had the contract right here, I was about to sign it, and they dived in through the window, knocked over the inkwell, tore up all the pages. . . ."

All of a sudden Marcovaldo remembered the time, the shipping department, the boss. He tiptoed off over the dried leaves, as the voice continued to come through the slats of the blind, enfolded in that cloud apparently from the oil of a frying pan. "They even scratched me . . . I still have the scar . . . All alone here at the mercy of these demons . . ."

Winter came. A blossoming of white flakes decked the branches and capitals and the cats' tails. Under the snow, the dry leaves dissolved into mush. The cats were rarely seen, the cat lovers even less; the packages of fish-bones were consigned to cats who came to the door. Nobody, for quite a while, had seen anything of the Marchesa. No smoke came now from the chimneypot of the villa.

One snowy day, the garden was again full of cats, who had returned as if it were spring, and they were miauing as if on a moonlit night. The neighbors realized that something had happened; they went and knocked at the Marchesa's door. She didn't answer: she was dead.

In the spring, instead of the garden, there was a huge building site that a contractor had set up. The steam shovels dug down to great depths to make room for the foundations, cement poured into the iron armatures, a very high crane passed beams to the workmen who were making the scaffoldings. But how could they get on with their work? Cats walked along all the planks, they made bricks fall and upset buckets of mortar, they fought in the midst of the piles of sand. When you started to raise an armature, you found a cat perched on top of it, hissing fiercely.

More treacherous pusses climbed onto the masons' backs as if to purr, and there was no getting rid of them. And the birds continued making their nests in all the trestles, the cab of the crane looked like an aviary . . . And you couldn't dip up a bucket of water that wasn't full of frogs, croaking and hopping . . .

QUESTIONS TO CONSIDER

1. Why does the Marchesa live in poverty on the most valuable piece of property in the city?

2. At the end of the story, does Calvino seem to indicate that the cats or the developers will prevail? Do you agree with him? Explain your answer.

3. If Calvino's story is a metaphor, what do the two opposing sets of neighbors represent? What does each side favor?

Three Poems

ANDREI VOZNESENSKY

Andrei Voznesensky (1933–   ) is one of the leading literary figures in Russia. Since his first books of poetry appeared in the 1960s, Voznesensky has commanded a massive audience in his native country. He believes that poetry is Russia's national art and that the poet's job is to ask the questions that will encourage people to act for themselves. Much of Voznesensky's poetry displays an immense outrage at the horrors of the century. As a boy during World War II, he lived as a refugee in the Ural Mountains. In 1942, his father brought him a copy of the Spanish painter Francisco Goya's book of etchings The Disasters of War. *These vibrant etchings depicted the horrors inflicted on Spain by Napoleon's invading army. To Voznesensky, they were equally appropriate for Russia during the war. His most famous poem, "I Am Goya," is about Goya's etchings and World War II.*

War Ballad

The piano has crawled into the quarry. Hauled
In last night for firewood, sprawled
With frozen barrels, crates and sticks,
The piano is waiting for the axe.

Legless, a black box, still polished;
It lies on its belly like a lizard,
Droning, heaving, hardly fashioned
For the quarry's **primordial**[1] art.

---

[1] **primordial**—existing at or from the beginning.

Blood red: his frozen fingers **cleft**,[2]
Two on the right hand, five on the left,
He goes down on his knees to reach the keyboard,
To strike the lizard's cord.

Seven fingers pick out rhymes and rhythm,
The frozen skin steaming, peeling off them,
As from a boiled potato. Their schemes,
Their beauty, ivory and **anthracite**,[3]
Flicker and flash like the great Northern lights.

Everything played before is a great lie;
The reflections of flaming chandeliers,
—Deceit, the white columns, the grand **tiers**[4]
In warm concert-halls—wild lies.

But the steel of the piano howls in me,
I lie in the quarry and I am deft
As the lizard. I accept the gift.

I'll be a song for Russia, I'll be
an étude,[5] warmth and bread for everybody.

---

[2] **cleft**—split.

[3] anthracite—a type of coal that burns with very little smoke.

[4] **tiers**—levels of a structure placed on each other.

[5] étude—a musical composition.

I Am Goya

I am Goya[6]
of the bare field, by the enemy's beak
    gouged[7]
till the craters of my eyes **gape**[8]
I am grief

I am the tongue
of war, the **embers**[9] of cities
on the snows of the year 1941[10]
I am hunger

I am the **gullet**[11]
of a woman hanged whose body like a bell
tolled over a blank square
I am Goya

O grapes of wrath!
I have hurled westward
       the ashes of the uninvited guest!
and hammered stars into the unforgetting
    sky—like nails
I am Goya

---

[6] Goya—Francisco Goya (1746–1828) Spanish painter and etcher.

[7] **gouged**—cut, gashed.

[8] **gape**—open wide.

[9] **embers**—small pieces of glowing wood or coal in a dying fire.

[10] 1941—the year the Germans invaded Russia during World War II.

[11] **gullet**—throat.

Two Poems

I

Over a dark and quiet empire
alone I fly—and envy you,
two-headed eagle[12] who at least
have always yourself to talk to.

II

To hang bare light bulbs from a ceiling
simple cord will always serve;
it's only the poet who must hang
by his **glaring**[13] white spinal nerve.

---

[12] two-headed eagle—the imperial symbol of both Russia and Germany. It originally symbolized eastern and western Europe united by the Holy Roman Emperor.

[13] **glaring**—brilliantly or blindingly shining.

QUESTIONS TO CONSIDER

1. What does the image of the piano and the player in "War Ballad" represent for Voznesensky? What does the music from the piano represent?

2. What does Goya represent in "I Am Goya"? Why has Voznesensky chosen such a figure for his image?

3. Who is the "I" in the first of the "Two Poems"? Contrast what is presented in the two poems. How do they reflect each other and what is Voznesensky's intention?

The Silent Men

ALBERT CAMUS

Albert Camus (1913–1960) was one of this century's most influential writers. Camus's novels, plays, and essays are the key works in the philosophy of the absurd known as existentialism. Although Camus himself rejected the term "existentialist," he propounded its basic doctrines that the world exists without reason or plan, and that people make their way through it on their own. The works that made Camus famous—his novel The Stranger, *his play* Caligula, *and his essay* The Myth of Sisyphus—*are all attempts to understand the world we live in and to tear down false philosophies of life. Camus began his career as a journalist, and during World War II when the Germans occupied France, he worked actively for the resistance.* The Stranger *(1946) made him one of France's premier intellectuals, and he was awarded the Nobel Prize in 1957. Camus was killed in a car accident at the height of his powers in 1960. His continuing influence can be seen by the fact that his unfinished novel,* The Last Man, *became an international bestseller when it was finally published in the 1990s.*

It was the dead of winter and yet a radiant sun was rising over the already active city. At the end of the jetty,[1] sea and sky fused in a single dazzling light. But Yvars did not see them. He was cycling slowly along the boulevards above the harbor. On the fixed pedal of his cycle his crippled leg rested stiffly while the other labored to **cope**[2] with the slippery road surface still wet with the night's moisture. Without raising his head, a slight figure astride the saddle, he avoided the rails of the former tram-line, suddenly turned the handlebars to let cars pass him, and occasionally elbowed back into place the bag in which Fernande had put his

lunch. At such moments he would think bitterly of the bag's contents. Between the two slices of coarse bread, instead of the Spanish omelet he liked or the beefsteak fried in oil, there was nothing but cheese.

The ride to the shop had never seemed to him so long. To be sure, he was aging. At forty, though he had remained as slim as a vine shoot, a man's muscles don't warm up so quickly. At times, reading sports commentaries in which a

---

[1] jetty—pier or breakwater built to protect or defend a harbor or coast.

[2] **cope**—handle, deal effectively with.

thirty-year-old athlete was referred to as a veteran, he would shrug his shoulders. "If he's a veteran," he would say to Fernande, "then I'm practically in a wheelchair." Yet he knew that the reporter wasn't altogether wrong. At thirty a man is already beginning to lose his wind without noticing it. At forty he's not yet in a wheelchair, but he's definitely heading in that direction. Wasn't that just why he now avoided looking towards the sea during the ride to the other end of town where the cooper's shop[3] was? When he was twenty he never got tired of watching it, for it used to hold in store a happy week-end on the beach. Despite or because of his lameness, he had always liked swimming. Then the years had passed, there had been Fernande, the birth of the boy, and, to make ends meet, the overtime, at the shop on Saturdays and on various odd jobs for others on Sundays. Little by little he had lost the habit of those violent days that used to **satiate**[4] him. The deep, clear water, the hot sun, the girls, the physical life—there was no other form of happiness in this country. And that happiness disappeared with youth. Yvars continued to love the sea, but only at the end of the day when the water in the bay became a little darker. The moment was pleasant on the terrace beside his house where he would sit down after work, grateful for his clean shirt that Fernande ironed so well and for the glass of anisette[5] all frosted over. Evening would fall, the sky would become all soft and mellow, the neighbors talking with Yvars would suddenly lower their voices. At those times

he didn't know whether he was happy or felt like crying. At least he felt in harmony at such moments, he had nothing to do but wait quietly, without quite knowing for what.

In the morning when he went back to work, on the other hand, he didn't like to look at the sea. Though it was always there to greet him, he refused to see it until evening. This morning he was pedaling along with head down, feeling even heavier than usual; his heart too was heavy. When he had come back from the meeting, the night before, and had announced that they were going back to work, Fernande had gaily said: "Then the boss is giving you all a rise?" The boss was not giving any rise; the strike had failed. They hadn't managed things right, it had to be admitted. An **impetuous**[6] walk-out, and the union had been right to back it up only half-heartedly. After all, some fifteen workers hardly counted; the union had to consider the other coopers' shops that hadn't joined in. You couldn't really blame the union. Cooperage, threatened by the building of tankers and tank trucks, was not thriving. Fewer and fewer barrels and large casks were being made; work consisted chiefly in repairing the huge tuns[7] already in

---

[3] cooper's shop—a shop where barrels are made and repaired.

[4] **satiate**—satisfy through overindulgence.

[5] anisette—a licorice-flavored liqueur particularly popular in the south of France.

[6] **impetuous**—rash, impulsive.

[7] tuns—large containers used for storing or making beer and wine.

existence. Employers saw their business compromised, to be sure, but even so they wanted to maintain a margin of profit and the easiest way still seemed to them to block wages despite the rise in living costs. What can coopers do when cooperage disappears? You don't change trades when you've gone to the trouble of learning one; this one was hard and called for a long apprenticeship. The good cooper, the one who fits his curved staves[8] and tightens them in the fire with an iron hoop, almost **hermetically,**[9] without caulking[10] with raffia or oakum,[11] was rare. Yvars knew this and was proud of it. Changing trades is nothing, but to give up what you know, your master craftsmanship, is not easy. A fine craft without employment and you're stuck, you have to resign yourself. But resignation isn't easy either. It was hard to have one's mouth shut, not to be able to discuss really, and to take the same road every morning with an accumulating fatigue, in order to receive at the end of every week merely what they are willing to give you, which is less and less adequate.

So they had got angry. Two or three of them had hesitated, but the anger had spread to them too after the first discussions with the boss. He had told them flatly, in fact, that they could take it or leave it. A man doesn't talk like that.

> *Changing trades is nothing, but to give up what you know, your master craftsmanship, is not easy.*

"What's he expect of us?" Esposito had said. "That we'll stoop over and wait to be kicked?" The boss wasn't a bad sort, however. He had inherited from his father, had grown up in the shop, and had known almost all the workers for years. Occasionally he invited them to have a snack in the shop; they would cook sardines or sausage meat over fires of shavings and, thanks partly to the wine, he was really very nice. At New Year he always gave five bottles of vintage wine to each of the men, and often, when one of them was ill or celebrated an event like marriage or first communion,[12] he would make a gift of money. At the birth of his daughter, there had been sugar-coated almonds for everyone. Two or three times he had invited Yvars to shoot on his coastal property. He liked his workmen, no doubt, and often recalled the fact that his father had begun as an apprentice. But he had never gone to their homes; he wasn't aware. He thought only of himself because he knew nothing but himself, and now you could take it or leave it. In other words, he had become obstinate likewise. But, in his position, he could allow himself to be.

---

[8] staves—curved pieces of wood that form the sides of a barrel or cask.

[9] **hermetically**—so as to be airtight or completely sealed.

[10] caulking—stopping up cracks or leaks.

[11] raffia or oakum—loose fibers that are used for sealing up cracks in wooden items.

[12] first communion—the first time a child receives the sacrament of bread and wine, an occasion for celebrating.

He had forced the union's hand, and the shop had closed its doors. "Don't go to the trouble of picketing," the boss had said; "when the shop's not working, I save money." That wasn't true, but it didn't help matters since he was telling them to their faces that he gave them work out of charity. Esposito was wild with fury and had told him he wasn't a man. The boss was hot-blooded and they had to be separated. But, at the same time, it had made an impression on the workers. Twenty days on strike, the wives sad at home, two or three of them discouraged, and, in the end, the union had advised them to give in on the promise of arbitration and recovery of the lost days through overtime. They had decided to go back to work. **Swaggering**,[13] of course, and Wag saying that it wasn't all settled, that it would have to be reconsidered. But this morning, with a fatigue that resembled defeat, cheese instead of meat, the illusion was no longer possible. No matter how the sun shone, the sea held forth no more promises. Yvars pressed on his single pedal and with each turn of the wheel it seemed to him he was aging a little. He couldn't think of the shop, of the fellow workers and the boss he would soon be seeing again without feeling his heart become a trifle heavier. Fernande had been worried: "What will you men say to him?" "Nothing," Yvars had straddled his bicycle, and had shaken his head. He had clenched his teeth; his small, dark, and wrinkled face with its delicate features had become hard. "We're going back to work. That's enough."

Now he was cycling along, his teeth still clenched, with a sad, dry anger that darkened even the sky itself.

He left the boulevard, and the sea, to attack the moist streets of the old Spanish quarter. They led to an area occupied solely by sheds, junkyards, and garages, where the shop was—a sort of low shed that was faced with stone up to half-way point and then glassed in up to the corrugated metal roof. This shop opened on to the former cooperage, a courtyard surrounded by a covered shed that had been abandoned when the business had enlarged and now served only as a storehouse for worn-out machines and old casks. Beyond the courtyard, separated from it by a sort of path covered with old tiles, the boss's garden began, at the end of which his house stood. Big and ugly, it was nevertheless prepossessing because of the Virginia creeper and the straggling honeysuckle surrounding the outside steps.

Yvars saw at once that the doors of the shop were closed. A group of workmen stood silently in front of them. This was the first time since he had been working here that he had found the doors closed when he arrived. The boss had wanted to emphasize that he had the upper hand. Yvars turned towards the left, parked his bicycle under the lean-to that prolonged the shed on that side, and walked towards the door. From a distance he recognized Esposito, a tall, dark, hairy fellow who

---

[13] **Swaggering**—walking in an arrogant or self-important manner.

worked beside him, Marcou, the union delegate, with his tenor's profile, Saïd, the only Arab in the shop, then all the others who silently watched him approach. But before he had joined them, they all suddenly looked in the direction of the shop doors, which had just begun to open. Ballester, the foreman, appeared in the opening. He opened one of the heavy doors and, turning his back to the workmen, pushed it slowly on its iron rail.

Ballester, who was the oldest of all, disapproved of the strike but had kept silent as soon as Esposito had told him that he was serving the boss's interests. Now he stood near the door, broad and short in his navy-blue jersey, already barefoot (he was the only one besides Saïd who worked barefoot), and he watched them go in one by one with his eyes that were so pale they seemed colorless in his old tanned face, his mouth downcast under his thick, drooping moustache. They were silent, humiliated by this return of the defeated, furious at their own silence, but the more it was prolonged the less capable they were of breaking it. They went in without looking at Ballester, for they knew he was carrying out an order in making them go in like that, and his bitter and downcast look told them what he was thinking. Yvars, for one, looked at him. Ballester, who liked him, nodded his head without saying a word.

Now they were all in the little locker-room on the right of the entrance: open stalls separated by unpainted boards to which had been attached, on either side, little locked cupboards; the farthest stall from the entrance, up against the walls of the shed, had been transformed into a shower above a gutter hollowed out of the earthen floor. In the center of the shop could be seen work in various stages, already finished large casks, loose-hooped, waiting for the forcing in the fire, thick benches with a long slot hollowed out in them (and in some of them had been slipped circular wooden bottoms waiting to be planed to a sharp edge), and finally cold fires. Along the wall, on the left of the entrance, the workbenches extended in a row. In front of them stood piles of staves to be planed. Against the right wall, not far from the dressing-room, two large power-saws, thoroughly oiled, strong and silent, gleamed.

Some time ago, the workshop had become too big for the handful of men who worked there. This was an advantage in the hot season, a disadvantage in winter. But today, in this vast space, the work dropped half finished, the casks abandoned in every corner with a single hoop holding the base of the staves spreading at the top like coarse wooden flowers, the sawdust covering the benches, the tool-boxes, and machines—everything gave the shop a look of neglect. They looked at it, dressed now in their old sweaters and their faded and patched trousers and they hesitated. Ballester was watching them. "So," he said, "we get started?" One by one, they went to their posts without saying a word. Ballester went from one to another, briefly reminding them of the work to be begun or finished. No one answered. Soon the first hammer resounded against the iron-tipped wedge sinking a hoop over the **convex**[14] part of a barrel, a plane[15] groaned as it hit a knot, and one of the saws, started up by Esposito, got under way with a great whirring of blade. Saïd would bring staves on request or light fires of shavings on which the casks were placed to make them swell in their corset of iron hoops. When no one called for him, he stood at a workbench riveting the big rusty hoops with heavy hammer blows. The scent of burning shavings began to fill the shop. Yvars, who was planing and fitting the staves cut out by Esposito, recognized the old scent and his heart relaxed somewhat. All were working in silence, but a warmth, a life was gradually beginning to reawaken in the shop. Through the broad windows a clean, fresh light began to fill the shed. The smoke rose bluish in the golden sunlight; Yvars even heard an insect buzz close to him.

At that moment the door into the former shop opened in the end wall and M. Lassalle, the boss, stopped on the threshold. Thin and dark, he was scarcely more than thirty. His white overall hanging open over a tan gabardine suit, he looked at ease in his body. Despite his very bony face cut like a hatchet, he generally aroused liking, as do most people who **exude**[16] vitality. Yet he seemed somewhat embarrassed as he came through the door. His greeting was less sonorous than usual; in any case, no one answered it. The sound of the hammers hesitated, lost the beat, and resumed even louder. M. Lassalle took a few hesitant steps, then he headed towards little Valery, who had been working with them for only a year.

Near the power-saw, a few feet away from Yvars, he was putting a bottom on a big hogshead[17] and the boss watched him. Valery went on working without saying anything. "Well, my boy," said M. Lassalle, "how are things?" The young man suddenly became more awkward in his movements. He glanced at Esposito, who was close to him, picking up a pile of staves in his huge arms to take them to Yvars. Esposito looked at him too while going on with his work, and Valery peered back into his hogshead without answering the boss. Lassalle, rather nonplussed, remained a moment planted in front of the young man, then he shrugged his shoulders and turned towards Marcou. The latter, astride his bench, was giving the finishing touches, with slow, careful strokes, to sharpening the edge of a bottom. "Hello, Marcou," Lassalle said in a flatter voice. Marcou did not answer, entirely occupied with taking very thin shavings off his wood. "What's got into you?" Lassalle asked in a loud voice as he turned towards the other workmen. "We didn't agree, to be sure. But that doesn't keep us from having to work together. So what's the use of this?" Marcou

> *"We didn't agree, to be sure. But that doesn't keep us from having to work together. So what's the use of this?"*

---

[14] **convex**—curving outward.

[15] plane—tool used to smooth a wooden surface by cutting shavings from it.

[16] **exude**—to give off or project.

[17] hogshead—a large barrel.

got up, raised his bottom piece, verified the circular sharp edge with the palm of his hand, squinted his languorous eyes with a look of satisfaction, and, still silent, went towards another workman who was putting together a hogshead. Throughout the whole shop could be heard nothing but the sound of hammers and of the power-saw. "O.K.," Lassalle said. "When you get over this, let me know through Ballester." Calmly, he walked out of the shop.

> **"Listen," said Lassalle, "you have all closed your minds. You'll get over it."**

Almost immediately afterwards, above the din of the shop, a bell rang out twice. Ballester, who had just sat down to roll a cigarette, got up slowly and went to the door at the end. After he had left, the hammers resounded with less noise; one of the workmen had even stopped when Ballester came back. From the door he said merely: "The boss wants you, Marcou and Yvars." Yvars's first impulse was to go and wash his hands, but Marcou grasped him by the arm as he went by and Yvars limped out behind him.

Outside in the courtyard, the light was so clear, so liquid, that Yvars felt it on his face and bare arms. They went up the outside stairs, under the honeysuckle on which a few blossoms were already visible. When they entered the corridor, whose walls were covered with diplomas, they heard a child crying and M. Lassalle's voice saying: "Put her to bed after lunch.

We'll call the doctor if she doesn't get over it." Then the boss appeared suddenly in the corridor and showed them into the little office they already knew, furnished with imitation **rustic**[18] furniture and its walls decorated with sports trophies. "Sit down," Lassalle said as he took his place behind the desk. They remained standing. "I called you in because you, Marcou, are the delegate and you, Yvars, my oldest employee after Ballester. I don't want to get back to the discussions, which are now over. I cannot, absolutely not, give you what you ask. The matter has been settled, and we reached the conclusion that work had to be resumed. I see that you are angry with me, and that hurts me, I'm telling you just as I feel it. I merely want to add this: what I can't do today I may perhaps be able to do when business picks up. And if I can do it, I'll do it even before you ask me. Meanwhile, let's try to work together." He stopped talking, seemed to reflect, then looked up at them. "Well?" he said. Marcou was looking out of the window. Yvars, his teeth clenched, wanted to speak but couldn't. "Listen," said Lassalle, "you have all closed your minds. You'll get over it. But when you become reasonable again, don't forget what I've just said to you." He rose, went towards Marcou, and held out his hand. "Ciao!" he said. Marcou suddenly turned pale, his popular tenor's face hardened and, for a second only, became mean-looking. Then he abruptly turned on

---

[18] **rustic**—of the country or plain, simple, unrefined.

his heel and went out. Lassalle, likewise pale, looked at Yvars without holding out his hand. "Go to hell!" he shouted.

When they went back into the shop, the men were lunching. Ballester had gone out. Marcou simply said: "Just wind," and returned to his bench. Esposito stopped biting into his bread to ask what they had answered; Yvars said they hadn't answered anything. Then he went to get his haversack and came back and sat down on his work-bench. He was beginning to eat when, not far from him, he noticed Saïd lying on his back in a pile of shavings, his eyes looking vaguely at the windows made blue by a sky that had become less luminous. He asked him if he had already finished. Saïd said he had eaten his figs. Yvars stopped eating. The uneasy feeling that hadn't left him since the interview with Lassalle suddenly disappeared to make room for a pleasant warmth. He broke his bread in two as he got up and, faced with Saïd's refusal, said that everything would be better next week. "Then it'll be your turn to treat me," he said. Saïd smiled. Now he bit into the piece of Yvars's sandwich, but in a gingerly way like a man who isn't hungry.

Esposito took an old pot and lighted a little fire of shavings and chips. He heated some coffee that he had brought in a bottle. He said it was a gift to the shop that his grocer had made when he learned of the strike's failure. A mustard jar passed from hand to hand. Each time Esposito poured out the already sugared coffee. Saïd swallowed it with more pleasure than he had taken in eating. Esposito drank the rest of the coffee right from the burning pot, smacking his lips and swearing. At that moment Ballester came in to give the back-to-work signal.

While they were rising and gathering papers and utensils into their haversacks, Ballester came and stood in their midst and said suddenly that it was hard for all, and for him too, but that this was no reason to act like children and that there was no use in sulking. Esposito, the pot in his hand, turned towards him; his long, coarse face had suddenly become flushed. Yvars knew what he was about to say—and what everyone was thinking at the same time— that they were not sulking, that their mouths had been closed, they had to take it or leave it, and that anger and helplessness sometimes hurt so much that you can't even cry out. They were men, after all, and they weren't going to begin smiling and **simpering**.[19] But Esposito said none of this, his face finally relaxed, and he slapped Ballester's shoulder gently while the others went back to their work. Again the hammers rang out, the big shed filled with the familiar din, with the smell of shavings and of old clothes damp with sweat. The big saw whined and bit into the fresh wood of the stave that Esposito was slowly pushing in front of him. Where the saw bit, damp sawdust spurted out and covered, with something like bread-crumbs, the big hairy hands firmly gripping the wood on each side of the moaning blade.

---

[19] **simpering**—giggling in a silly or an affected way.

Once the stave was ripped, you could hear only the sound of the motor.

At present Yvars felt only the strain in his back as he leaned over the plane. Generally the fatigue didn't come until later on. He had got out of training during these weeks of inactivity, it was clear. But he thought also of age, which makes manual labor harder when it's not mere precision work. That strain also fore-shadowed old age. Wherever the muscles are involved, work eventually becomes hateful, it precedes death, and on evenings following great physical effort sleep itself is like death. The boy wanted to become a schoolteacher, he was right; those who indulge in clichés about manual work don't know what they're talking about.

When Yvars straightened up to catch his breath, and also to drive away these evil thoughts, the bell rang out again. It was insistent, but in such a strange way, stops and imperious starts, that the men interrupted their work. Ballester listened, surprised, then made up his mind and went slowly to the door. He had disappeared for several seconds—when the ringing finally ceased. They resumed work. Again the door was flung open and Ballester ran towards the locker-room. He came out wearing canvas shoes and, slipping on his jacket, said to Yvars as he went by: "The child has had an attack. I'm off to get Germain," and he ran towards the main door. Dr. Germain took care of the shop's health; he lived in this outlying quarter. Yvars repeated the news without

commentary. They gathered around him and looked at one another, embarrassed. Nothing could be heard but the motor of the power-saw running freely. "It's perhaps nothing," one of them said. They went back to their places, the shop filled again with their noises, but they were working slowly, as if waiting for something.

A quarter of an hour later, Ballester came in again, hung up his jacket, and, without saying a word, went out through the little door. On the windows the light was getting dimmer. A little later, in the intervals when the saw was not ripping into the wood, the dull bell of an ambulance could be heard, at first in the distance, then nearer, finally just outside. Then silence. After a moment Ballester came back and everyone went up to him. Esposito had turned off the motor. Ballester said that while undressing in her room the child had suddenly **keeled**[20] over as if mowed down. "Did you ever hear anything like it!" Marcou said. Ballester shook his head and gestured vaguely towards the shop; but he looked as if he had had quite a turn. Again the ambulance bell was heard. They were all there, in the silent shop, under the yellow light coming through the glass panels, with their rough, useless hands hanging down along their old sawdust-covered trousers.

The rest of the afternoon dragged. Yvars now felt only his fatigue and his still heavy heart. He would have liked to talk. But he had nothing to say, nor had the

---

[20] **keeled**—fallen.

others. On their uncommunicative faces could be read merely sorrow and a sort of obstinacy. Sometimes the word "calamity" took shape in him, but just barely, for it disappeared immediately—as a bubble forms and bursts simultaneously. He wanted to get home, to be with Fernande again, and the boy, on the terrace. As it happened, Ballester announced closing-time. The machines stopped. Without hurrying, they began to put out the fires and to put everything in order on their benches, then they went one by one to the locker-room. Saïd remained behind; he was to clean up the shop and water down the dusty soil. When Yvars reached the locker-room, Esposito, huge and hairy, was already under the shower. His back was turned to them as he soaped himself noisily. Generally, they kidded him about his modesty; the big bear, indeed, obstinately hid. But no one seemed to notice on this occasion. Esposito backed out of the shower and wrapped a towel around him like a loincloth. The others took their turns, and Marcou was vigorously slapping his bare sides when they heard the big door roll slowly open on its cast-iron wheel. Lassalle came in.

He was dressed as at the time of his first visit, but his hair was rather **disheveled.**[21] He stopped on the threshold, looked at the vast deserted shop, took a few steps, stopped again, and looked towards the locker-room. Esposito, still covered with his loincloth, turned towards him. Naked, embarrassed he teetered from one foot to the other. Yvars thought that it was up to Marcou to say something. But Marcou remained invisible behind the sheet of water that surrounded him. Esposito grabbed a shirt and was nimbly slipping it on when Lassalle said: "Good night," in a rather too toneless voice and began to walk towards the little door. When it occurred to Yvars that someone ought to call him, the door had already closed.

Yvars dressed without washing, said good night likewise, but with his whole heart, and they answered with the same warmth. He went out rapidly, got his bicycle, and, when he straddled it, he felt the strain in his back again. He was cycling along now in the late afternoon through the trafficky city. He was going fast because he was eager to get back to the old house and the terrace. He would wash in the wash-house before sitting down to look at the sea, which was already accompanying him, darker than in the morning, above the parapet of the boulevard. But the little girl accompanied him too and he couldn't stop thinking of her.

At home, his boy was back from school and reading the picture papers. Fernande asked Yvars whether everything had gone

> *Sometimes the word "calamity" took shape in him, but just barely, for it disappeared immediately—as a bubble forms and bursts simultaneously.*

---

[21] **disheveled**—untidy, sloppy looking.

all right. He said nothing, cleaned up in he wash-house, then sat down on the bench against the low wall of the terrace. Mended washing hung above his head and the sky was becoming transparent; over the wall the soft evening sea was visible. Fernande brought the anisette, two glasses, and the jug of cool water. She sat down beside her husband. He told her everything, holding her hand as in the early days of their marriage. When he had finished, he didn't stir, looking towards the sea where already, from one end of the horizon to the other, the twilight was swiftly falling. "Ah! It's his own fault!" he said. If only he were young again, and Fernande too, they would have gone away, across the sea.

QUESTIONS TO CONSIDER

1. Why is Yvars so worried about growing old? What has changed in his outlook on life?

2. Why do you think Camus called this story "The Silent Men"?

3. Why does Yvars have a cheese sandwich and Säid have figs for lunch?

4. Describe the boss of the cooper's shop. Do you think he is a good or bad man? Explain your answer.

5. What is Yvars wishing for at the end of the story? What does Camus want us to realize about the way we live our lives?

Four Poems

TOMAS TRANSTRÖMER

Tomas Tranströmer (1931–   ) is considered to be Sweden's finest living poet. He has worked all his life as a psychologist, often with juvenile delinquents or the handicapped. Tranströmer's poems reflect his experiences as a psychologist; they are most often interior monologues that analyze who we are and how we should act. He has described his poems as "meeting places. Their intent is to make a sudden connection between aspects of reality that conventional languages and outlooks ordinarily keep apart. What looks at first like a confrontation turns out to be a connection." All of Tranströmer's poetry is about intense encounters or moments of revelation when the world seems a bit clearer.

Black Postcards

I

The calendar full, future unknown.
The cable hums the folksong from no country.
Falling snow on the lead-still sea. Shadows
                wrestle on the dock.

II

In the middle of life it happens that death comes
and takes your measurements. This visit
is forgotten and life goes on. But the suit is
                sewn in the silence.

Alone

One evening in February I came near to dying here.
The car skidded sideways on the ice, out
on the wrong side of the road. The approaching cars—
their lights—closed in.

My name, my girls, my job
broke free and were left silently behind
further and further away. I was anonymous
like a boy in a playground surrounded by enemies.

The approaching traffic had huge lights.
They shone on me while I pulled at the wheel
in a transparent terror that floated like egg white.
The seconds grew—there was space in them—
they grew big as hospital buildings.

You could almost pause
and breathe out for a while
before being crushed.

Then something caught: a helping grain of sand
or a wonderful gust of wind. The car broke free
and scuttled smartly right over the road.
A post shot up and cracked—a sharp clang—it
flew away in the darkness.

Then—stillness. I sat back in my seat-belt
and saw someone coming through the whirling snow
to see what had become of me.

II

I have been walking for a long time
on the frozen Östergötland fields.
I have not seen a single person.

In other parts of the world
there are people who are born, live and die
in a **perpetual**[1] crowd.

To be always visible—to live
in a swarm of eyes—
a special expression must develop.
Face coated with clay.

The **murmuring**[2] rises and falls
while they divide up among themselves
the sky, the shadows, the sand grains.

I must be alone
ten minutes in the morning
and ten minutes in the evening.
—Without a program.

Everyone is queuing at everyone's door.

Many.

One.

---

[1] **perpetual**—never ending.
[2] **murmuring**—making a quiet, continuous sound.

To Friends Behind a Frontier

I

I wrote so **meagerly**[3] to you. But what I couldn't write
swelled and swelled like an old-fashioned airship
and drifted away at last through the night sky.

II

The letter is now at the censor's. He lights his lamp.
In the glare my words fly up like monkeys on a grille,[4]
rattle it, stop, and bare their teeth.

III

Read between the lines. We'll meet in 200 years
when the microphones in the hotel walls are forgotten
and can at last sleep, become trilobites.[5]

Elegy

I open the first door.
It is a large sunlit room.
A heavy car passes outside
and makes the china **quiver.**[6]

I open door number two
Friends! You drank some darkness
and became visible.

---

[3] **meagerly**—inadequately, scantily, or poorly.

[4] grille—grating, cage, or screen.

[5] trilobites—prehistoric marine fossils.

[6] **quiver**—shake, tremble.

Door number three. A narrow hotel room.
View on an alley.
One lamppost shines on the asphalt.
Experience, its beautiful slag.[7]

---

[7] slag—waste material that rises in molten metal.

QUESTIONS TO CONSIDER

1. What is Tranströmer's message in "Black Postcards"?

2. What happens in the first part of "Alone"? How is this reflected in the second part? What is Tranströmer trying to say about how we must live?

3. What is the problem presented in "To Friends Behind a Frontier"? Is there an answer?

4. What is the contrast presented in each of the stanzas of "Elegy"? What is the contrast meant to remind us of?

The Majesty of the Law

FRANK O'CONNOR

Frank O'Connor (1903–1966) was one of Ireland's best-known short story writers. His stories combine realism and humor and offer a superb portrait of Ireland as it changed in the twentieth century. O'Connor had a gift for the flavor of Irish speech and the way people lived on the farms and in the cities. "The Majesty of the Law" shows how modernity clashed with the traditional way of life in many communities.

Old Dan Bride was breaking brosna[1] for the fire when he heard a step on the path. He paused, a bundle of saplings on his knee.

Dan had looked after his mother while the life was in her, and after her death no other woman had crossed his threshold. Signs on it, his house had that look. Almost everything in it he had made with his own hands in his own way. The seats of the chairs were only slices of log, rough and round and thick as the saw had left them, and with the rings still plainly visible through the grime and polish that coarse trouser-bottoms had in the course of long years imparted. Into these Dan had rammed stout[2] knotted ash-boughs that served alike for legs and back. The deal table, bought in a shop, was an inheritance from his mother and a great pride and joy to him though it rocked whenever he touched it. On the wall, unglazed and fly-spotted, hung in mysterious isolation a Marcus Stone print,[3] and beside the door was a calendar with a picture of a racehorse. Over the door hung a gun, old but good, and in excellent condition, and before the fire was stretched an old setter who raised his head expectantly whenever Dan rose or even stirred.

He raised it now as the steps came nearer and when Dan, laying down the bundle of saplings, cleaned his hands thoughtfully in the seat of his trousers, he gave a loud bark, but this expressed no more than a desire to show off his

---

[1] brosna—Irish word meaning "bundle of sticks."

[2] stout—strong, sturdy.

[3] Marcus Stone print—Marcus Stone (1840–1921) was a popular British painter of sentimental subjects.

own watchfulness. He was half human and knew people thought he was old and past his prime.

A man's shadow fell across the oblong of dusty light thrown over the half-door before Dan looked round.

"Are you alone, Dan?" asked an apologetic voice.

"Oh, come in, come in, sergeant, come in and welcome," exclaimed the old man, hurrying on rather uncertain feet to the door which the tall policeman opened and pushed in. He stood there, half in sunlight, half in shadow, and seeing him so, you would have realized how dark the interior of the house really was. One side of his red face was turned so as to catch the light, and behind it an ash tree raised its boughs of airy green against the sky. Green fields, broken here and there by clumps of red-brown rock, flowed downhill, and beyond them, stretched all across the horizon, was the sea, flooded and almost transparent with light. The sergeant's face was fat and fresh, the old man's face, emerging from the twilight of the kitchen, had the color of wind and sun, while the features had been so shaped by the struggle with time and the elements that they might as easily have been found impressed upon the surface of a rock.

"Begor, Dan," said the sergeant, "'tis younger you're getting."

"Middling I am, sergeant, middling," agreed the old man in a voice which seemed to accept the remark as a compliment of which politeness would not allow him to take too much advantage. "No complaints."

"Begor, 'tis as well because no one would believe them. And the old dog doesn't look a day older."

The dog gave a low growl as though to show the sergeant that he would remember this **unmannerly**[4] reference to his age, but indeed he growled every time he was mentioned, under the impression that people had nothing but ill to say of him.

"And how's yourself, sergeant?"

"Well, now, like the most of us, Dan, neither too good nor too bad. We have our own little worries, but, thanks be to God, we have our compensations."

"And the wife and family?"

"Good, praise be to God, good. They were away from me for a month, the lot of them, at the mother-in-law's place in Clare."

"In Clare, do you tell me?"

"In Clare. I had a fine quiet time."

The old man looked about him and then retired to the bedroom, from which he returned a moment later with an old shirt. With this he solemnly wiped the seat and back of the log-chair nearest the fire.

"Sit down now, sergeant. You must be tired after the journey. 'Tis a long old road. How did you come?"

"Teigue Leary gave me the lift. Wisha now, Dan, don't be putting yourself out. I won't be stopping. I promised them I'd be back inside an hour."

"What hurry is on you?" asked Dan. "Look, your foot was only on the path when I made up the fire."

---

[4] **unmannerly**—rude, discourteous.

"Arrah, Dan, you're not making tea for me?"

"I am not making it for you, indeed; I'm making it for myself, and I'll take it very bad of you if you won't have a cup."

"Dan, Dan, that I mightn't stir, but 'tisn't an hour since I had it at the barracks!"

"Ah, whisht, now, whisht! Whisht, will you! I have something here to give you an appetite."

The old man swung the heavy kettle onto the chain over the open fire, and the dog sat up, shaking his ears with an expression of the deepest interest. The policeman unbuttoned his tunic,[5] opened his belt, took a pipe and a plug of tobacco from his breast pocket, and crossing his legs in an easy posture, began to cut the tobacco slowly and carefully with his pocket knife. The old man went to the dresser and took down two handsomely decorated cups, the only cups he had, which, though chipped and handleless, were used at all only on very rare occasions; for himself he preferred his tea from a basin. Happening to glance into them, he noticed that they bore signs of disuse and had collected a lot of the fine white turf-dust that always circulated in the little smoky cottage. Again he thought of the shirt, and, rolling up his sleeves with a stately gesture, he wiped them inside and out till they shone. Then he bent and opened the cupboard. Inside was a quart bottle of pale liquid, obviously untouched. He removed the cork and smelt the contents, pausing for a moment in the act as though to recollect where exactly he had noticed that particular smoky smell before. Then, reassured, he stood up and poured out with a liberal hand.

"Try that now, sergeant," he said with quiet pride.

The sergeant, concealing whatever **qualms**[6] he might have felt at the idea of drinking illegal whisky, looked carefully into the cup, sniffed, and glanced up at old Dan.

"It looks good," he commented.

"It should be good," replied Dan with no mock modesty.

"It tastes good too," said the sergeant.

"Ah, sha," said Dan, not wishing to praise his own hospitality in his own house, " 'tis of no great excellence."

"You'd be a good judge, I'd say," said the sergeant without irony.

"Ever since things became what they are," said Dan, carefully guarding himself against a too-direct reference to the peculiarities of the law administered by his guest, "liquor isn't what it used to be."

"I've heard that remark made before now, Dan," said the sergeant thoughtfully. "I've heard it said by men of wide experience that it used to be better in the old days."

"Liquor," said the old man, "is a thing that takes time. There was never a good job done in a hurry."

"'Tis an art in itself."

"Just so."

"And an art takes time."

---

[5] tunic—a close-fitting short coat.

[6] **qualms**—doubts, second thoughts.

"And knowledge," added Dan with emphasis. "Every art has its secrets, and the secrets of **distilling**[7] are being lost the way the old songs were lost. When I was a boy there wasn't a man in the barony[8] but had a hundred songs in his head, but with people running here, there and everywhere, the songs were lost. . . . Ever since things became what they are," he repeated on the same guarded note, "there's so much running about the secrets are lost."

"There must have been a power of them."

"There was. Ask any man today that makes whisky do he know how to make it out of heather."[9]

"And was it made of heather?" asked the policeman.

"It was."

"You never drank it yourself?"

"I didn't, but I knew old men that did, and they told me that no whisky that's made nowadays could compare with it."

"Musha, Dan, I think sometimes 'twas a great mistake of the law to set its hand against it."

Dan shook his head. His eyes answered for him, but it was not in nature for a man to criticize the occupation of a guest in his own home.

"Maybe so, maybe not," he said noncommittally.

"But sure, what else have the poor people?"

"Them that makes the laws have their own good reasons."

"All the same, Dan, all the same, 'tis a hard law."

The sergeant would not be outdone in generosity. Politeness required him not to yield to the old man's defense of his superiors and their mysterious ways.

"It is the secrets I'd be sorry for," said Dan, summing up. "Men die and men are born, and where one man drained another will plough, but a secret lost is lost forever."

"True," said the sergeant mournfully. "Lost forever."

"Men die and men are born, and where one man drained another will plough, but a secret lost is lost forever."

Dan took his cup, rinsed it in a bucket of clear water by the door and cleaned it again with the shirt. Then he placed it carefully at the sergeant's elbow. From the dresser he took a jug of milk and a blue bag containing sugar; this he followed up with a slab of country butter and—a sure sign that he had been expecting a visitor— a round cake of homemade bread, fresh and uncut. The kettle sang and spat and the dog, shaking his ears, barked at it angrily.

"Go away, you brute!" growled Dan, kicking him out of his way.

He made the tea and filled the two cups. The sergeant cut himself a large slice of bread and buttered it thickly.

"It is just like medicines," said the old man, resuming his theme with the

---

[7] **distilling**—making liquor.

[8] barony—division of a county in Ireland.

[9] heather—an evergreen shrub.

imperturbability[10] of age. "Every secret there was is lost. And leave no one tell me that a doctor is as good a man as one that had the secrets of old times."

> **"Out there on the hillsides is the sure cure for every disease."**

"How could he be?" asked the sergeant with his mouth full.

"The proof of that was seen when there were doctors and wise people there together."

"It wasn't to the doctors the people went, I'll engage?"

"It was not. And why?" With a sweeping gesture the old man took in the whole world outside his cabin. "Out there on the hillsides is the sure cure for every disease. Because it is written"—he tapped the table with his thumb—"it is written by the poets 'wherever you find the disease you will find the cure.' But people walk up the hills and down the hills and all they see is flowers. Flowers! As if God Almighty—honor and praise to Him!—had nothing better to do with His time than be making old flowers!"

"Things no doctor could cure the wise people cured," agreed the sergeant.

"Ah, musha, 'tis I know it," said Dan bitterly. "I know it, not in my mind but in my own four bones."

"Have you the rheumatics[11] at you still?" the sergeant asked in a shocked tone.

"I have. Ali, if you were alive, Kitty O'Hara, or you, Nora Malley of the Glen,

'tisn't I'd be dreading the mountain wind or the sea wind; 'tisn't I'd be creeping down with my misfortunate red ticket for the blue and pink and yellow dribble-drabble of their ignorant dispensary."

"Why then indeed," said the sergeant, "I'll get you a bottle for that."

"Ah, there's no bottle ever made will cure it."

"That's where you're wrong, Dan. Don't talk now till you try it. It cured my own uncle when he was that bad he was shouting for the carpenter to cut the two legs off him with a handsaw."

"I'd give fifty pounds to get rid of it," said Dan **magniloquently**.[12] "I would and five hundred."

The sergeant finished his tea in a gulp, blessed himself and struck a match which he then allowed to go out as he answered some question of the old man. He did the same with a second and third, as though **titillating**[13] his appetite with delay. Finally he succeeded in getting his pipe alight and the two men pulled round their chairs, placed their toes side by side in the ashes, and in deep puffs, lively bursts of conversation, and long, long silences, enjoyed their smoke.

"I hope I'm not keeping you?" said the sergeant, as though struck by the length of his visit.

---

[10] **imperturbability**—calmness or inability to become excited.

[11] rheumatics—inflammation and pain of the joints or muscles.

[12] **magniloquently**—boastfully or grandiosely.

[13] **titillating**—pleasantly exciting.

"Ah, what would you keep me from?"

"Tell me if I am. The last thing I'd like to do is waste another man's time."

"Begor, you wouldn't waste my time if you stopped all night."

"I like a little chat myself," confessed the policeman.

And again they became lost in conversation. The light grew thick and colored and, wheeling about the kitchen before it disappeared, became tinged with gold; the kitchen itself sank into cool greyness with cold light on the cups and basins and plates of the dresser. From the ash tree a thrush began to sing. The open hearth gathered brightness till its light was a warm, even splash of crimson in the twilight.

Twilight was also descending outside when the sergeant rose to go. He fastened his belt and tunic and carefully brushed his clothes. Then he put on his cap, tilted a little to side and back.

"Well, that was a great talk," he said.

"'Tis a pleasure," said Dan, "a real pleasure."

"And I won't forget the bottle for you."

"Heavy handling from God to you!"

"Good-bye now, Dan."

"Good-bye, sergeant, and good luck."

Dan didn't offer to accompany the sergeant beyond the door. He sat in his old place by the fire, took out his pipe once more, blew through it thoughtfully, and just as he leaned forward for a twig to kindle it, heard the steps returning. It was the sergeant. He put his head a little way over the half-door.

"Oh, Dan!" he called softly.

"Ay, sergeant?" replied Dan, looking round, but with one hand still reaching for the twig. He couldn't see the sergeant's face, only hear his voice.

"I suppose you're not thinking of paying that little fine, Dan?"

There was a brief silence. Dan pulled out the lighted twig, rose slowly and shambled towards the door, stuffing it down in the almost empty bowl of the pipe. He leaned over the half door while the sergeant with hands in the pockets of his trousers gazed rather in the direction of the laneway, yet taking in a considerable portion of the sea line.

"The way it is with me, sergeant," replied Dan unemotionally, "I am not."

"I was thinking that, Dan; I was thinking you wouldn't."

There was a long silence during which the voice of the thrush grew shriller and merrier. The sunken sun lit up rafts of purple cloud moored high above the wind.

"In a way," said the sergeant, "that was what brought me."

"I was just thinking so, sergeant, it only struck me and you going out the door."

"If 'twas only the money, Dan, I'm sure there's many would be glad to oblige you."

"I know that, sergeant. No, 'tisn't the money so much as giving that fellow the satisfaction of paying. Because he angered me, sergeant."

The sergeant made no comment on this and another long silence ensued.

"They gave me the **warrant,**"[14] the sergeant said at last, in a tone which dissociated him from all connection with such an unneighborly document.

"Did they so?" exclaimed Dan, as if he was shocked by the thoughtlessness of the authorities.

"So whenever 'twould be convenient for you—"

"Well, now you mention it," said Dan, by way of throwing out a suggestion for debate, "I could go with you now."

"Ah, sha, what do you want going at this hour for?" protested the sergeant with a wave of his hand, dismissing the notion as the tone required.

"Or I could go tomorrow," added Dan, warming to the issue.

"Would it be suitable for you now?" asked the sergeant, scaling up his voice accordingly.

"But, as a matter of fact," said the old man emphatically, "the day that would be most convenient to me would be Friday after dinner, because I have some messages to do in town, and I wouldn't have the journey for nothing."

"Friday will do grand," said the sergeant with relief that this delicate matter was now practically disposed of. "If it doesn't they can damn well wait. You could walk in there yourself when it suits you and tell them I sent you."

"I'd rather have yourself there, sergeant, if it would be no inconvenience. As it is, I'd feel a bit shy."

"Why then, you needn't feel shy at all. There's a man from my own parish there, a warder; one Whelan. Ask for him; I'll tell him you're coming, and I'll guarantee when he knows you're a friend of mine he'll make you as comfortable as if you were at home."

"I'd like that fine," Dan said with profound satisfaction. "I'd like to be with friends, sergeant."

"You will be, never fear. Good-bye again now, Dan. I'll have to hurry."

"Wait now, wait till I see you to the road."

Together the two men strolled down the laneway while Dan explained how it was that he, a respectable old man, had had the grave misfortune to open the head of another old man in such a way as to require his removal to hospital, and why it was that he couldn't give the old man in question the satisfaction of paying in cash for an injury brought about through the victim's own unmannerly method of argument.

"You see, sergeant," Dan said, looking at another little cottage up the hill, "the way it is, he's there now, and he's looking at us as sure as there's a glimmer of sight in his weak, wandering, watery eyes, and nothing would give him more gratification than for me to pay. But I'll punish him. I'll lie on bare boards for him. I'll suffer for him, sergeant, so that neither he nor any of his children after him will be able to raise their heads for the shame of it."

---

[14] **warrant**—written order allowing police to search premises or arrest a suspect.

On the following Friday he made ready his donkey and butt and set out. On his way he collected a number of neighbors who wished to bid him farewell. At the top of the hill he stopped to send them back. An old man, sitting in the sunlight, hastily made his way indoors, and a moment later the door of his cottage was quietly closed.

Having shaken all his friends by the hand, Dan lashed the old donkey, shouted: "Hup there!" and set out alone along the road to prison.

QUESTIONS TO CONSIDER

1. Why does the sergeant come to see Dan? How does the sergeant feel about his task?

2. What has Dan done that he has to go to prison? Was he provoked into his actions?

3. What is the lesson Dan wants to teach by going to prison? Is he going to be successful?

4. Does O'Connor think the law is right or wrong in the story? Explain your answer.

Four Poems

EUGENIO MONTALE

Eugenio Montale (1896–1981) was one of the most perceptive and varied Italian poets of the century. He rose to prominence in the 1920s with descriptive lyric poetry that focused so tightly on objects that they took on far greater meaning. After World War II, Montale despaired of the survival of western civilization, and his poetry reflected on the intellectual ferment of the Cold War era. Montale's verse is a requiem for the united, traditional culture of Europe. Montale won the Nobel Prize in 1975. The first poem below is from Montale's earliest collection, Cuttlefish Bones *(1916), and the last three are from the 1950s when the destruction of World War II was still everywhere apparent in Italy and the Cold War tensions between the U.S. and the Soviet Union threatened to engulf the world in another vast war.*

The Eel

The eel, coldwater
siren, who leaves the Baltic[1] behind her
to reach these shores of ours,
our wetlands and marshes, our rivers,
who struggles upstream hugging the bottom, under a
    flood of the
downward torrent,
from branch to branch, thinning,
narrowing in, stem by stem,
snaking deeper and deeper into the rock core
of slab ledge, squirming through
stone interstices of slime until

---

[1] Baltic—sea in northern Europe. It divides Sweden from Germany and Poland.

one day, light,
exploding, blazes from the chestnut leaves,
ignites a wriggle in deadwater sumps
ravines spilling downhill toward the Romagna;[2] eel,
     torchlight, lash, arrow of Love on earth, whom
     only these dry gulches of ours or burned-out
     Pyrenean[3] gullies can draw back Edens of
     generation; the green soul seeking life where
     there's nothing but stinging drought, desolation;
     spark that says everything begins when every-
     thing seems dead ashes, buried stump; brief
     rainbow, twin of that other iris shining between
     your lashes, by which your virtue blazes out,
     unsullied among the sons of men floundering in
     your mud, can you deny a sister?

The Dead

The sea crashing against the opposing
shore lifts a cloud that spumes
till reabsorbed by the **shoals.**[4] Here one day,
against this iron coast, we hurled our hope
higher than the heaving sea,
and the barren abyss turns green again
as once in days that saw us
still here among the living.

Now that the north wind smoothes the raging knot
of brackish[5] currents, driving them back
where they began, someone has hung his nets
on the slashed boughs, draping
the path that sinks down

---

[2] Romagna—region in central Italy. It borders the Adriatic Sea.

[3] Pyrenean—of or pertaining to the Pyrenees, the great mountain range that separates France and Spain.

[4] **shoals**—areas of shallow water.

[5] brackish—slightly salty.

out of sight—
bleached nets drying in the late cold
touch of the light, while overhead
the blue crystal of the sky blinks
and plunges to an arc of storm-lashed
horizon.

More than seaweed dragged
by the boiling now revealed, our life stirs
against such **torpor**:[6] whatever in us
was resigned to limit, by one day stilled,
now seethes; between the strands weaving
branch to branch, the heart thrashes
like the gallinule[7]
trapped in the meshes
where an icy **stasis**[8] holds us fast,
motionless, migratory.

So too perhaps
even the dead in the ground may be denied
all repose: a force more pitiless
than life pulls them thence,[9] from all around
driving them toward this coast—ghosts
tortured by human memories, breaths
without voice or substance, betrayed
by darkness; and even now their thwarted
    flights,
so close to us still, brush by,
then drift down in the sea
that sifts them. . . .

---

[6] **torpor**—sluggishness, apathy.
[7] gallinule—long-toed wading bird.
[8] **stasis**—state of inactivity.
[9] thence—from that place.

Little Testament

This flickering at night
in the casing of my thoughts,
mother-of-pearl tracing of snail
or glass-grit trampled underfoot,
this is no light of factory or church
fed by **cleric**[10]
whether red or black.[11]
This rainbow is all
I can leave you in witness
of a faith that was fought for
a hope that burned more slowly
than a tough log on the grate.
Keep this powder in the mirror of your
    compact[12]
when every other light's gone out
and the wild sardana[13] turns hellish,
and a dark Lucifer swoops down on the
    shore
of Thames, Hudson, or Seine[14]
flapping pitchy wings half-
shorn away from his hard toil to tell you this:
    It's time.
It's no inheritance, no good luck charm
to stand against the hurricanes
battering the spiderweb of memory,
but a story only survives in ashes,

---

[10] **cleric**—official of the church.

[11] red or black—a reference to the two dominant strands of Italian political thought in the 1950s: Communism ("red") and Catholic ("black").

[12] compact—a small flat case usually used for makeup or a mirror.

[13] sardana—a Catalonian dance.

[14] Thames, Hudson, or Seine—rivers flowing through London, New York, and Paris, respectively.

persistence[15] is only **extinction.**[16]
The sign was right: he who recognized it
can't go wrong in finding you again.
Each man knows his own: pride
was not flight, humility was not
cowardice, that faint glow catching fire
beneath was not the striking of a match.

The Prisoner's Dream

Here, except for a few signs, you can't tell
    dawn from night.

The zigzag of starlings over the watchtowers
on days of fighting, my only wings,
a thread of arctic air,
the head-guard's eye at the peephole,
the crack of broken nuts, an oily
sputtering from the basements, roasting spits
imagined or real—but the straw is gold,
the winey[17] lantern is hearth enough for me,
if I can dream I'm sleeping at your feet.

The purge[18] never ends, no reasons given.
They say that those who **recant,**[19] who
    make signed statements
can save themselves from this massacre of
    silly geese;
that by breaking down and selling out the
    others,

---

[15] **persistence**—tireless determination.
[16] **extinction**—total destruction.
[17] winey—wine-colored; red or yellow.
[18] purge—cleaning, cleansing, or removal.
[19] **recant**—to take back or deny a statement or belief.

by confessing and informing, you get the
    spoon
instead of being dished up yourself in that
    stew
reserved for the gods of plague.

Slow-witted, and pricked
by this piercing mattress, I've fused
with the soaring moth whom the sole of
    my boot
pulverizes on the stony tiles;
with the shimmering kimonos[20] of light
strung out to dry from the towers at day-
    break;
I've sniffed on the wind the burnt fragrance
of sweet rolls from the ovens,
I've looked around, conjured up
rainbows on horizons of spiderwebs,
petals on the trellis of my bars,
I've risen only to fall back
into that gulf where a century's a second—
and the beatings go on and on, and the
    footsteps,
and I don't know whether I'll be at the feast
as stuffer or stuffing. It's a long wait,
and my dream of you isn't over.

---

[20] kimonos—long, loose Japanese robes.

QUESTIONS TO CONSIDER

1. How many sentences make up "The Eel"? How does the form contribute to the description of the eel? Who is the "you" in the second to last line? What has the eel come to represent?

2. Who are the dead referred to in the title of Montale's poem? What is he saying about how we live?

3. In "Little Testament," what is Montale referring to as the "rainbow," "powder," and "story"? What is the message of the last sentence of the poem?

4. In "The Prisoner's Dream," why is the prisoner in jail? How can he get out? What keeps him going? How many different references can you infer for the "you" in the last line?

5. How do "Little Testament" and "The Prisoner's Dream" seem to reflect the dark days of the Cold War, when the very survival of civilization seemed in doubt?

Two Poems

YEVGENY YEVTUSHENKO

Yevgeny Yevtushenko (1933–   ) was born in Russia. He started writing in the 1950s during a cultural thaw in the Soviet Union. Stalin was dead, and his repressive, murderous regime had given way to Communist leaders who allowed far more freedom of expression. Yevtushenko was one of the leaders of a new style of poetry, and, as he was allowed to publish and give readings in the West, he acquired an international following. However, Yevtushenko has always been dogged by a reputation for hypocrisy. He wrote in protest against the Communist regime, but he was well-treated by it and accepted its awards and honors while many of his contemporaries languished in prison. As the passions of the Cold War have faded, Yevtushenko has come to be seen in better perspective, as a powerful writer trapped by a system. Works like his poem "Babi Yar" and his memoirs helped expose the horrors of Soviet Communism; however, it is his lyrics about everyday life, love, and longing in Russia that live on.

Waiting

My love will come
will **fling**[1] open her arms and fold me in them,
will understand my fears, observe my changes.
In from the pouring dark, from the pitch night
without stopping to bang the taxi door
she'll run upstairs through the decaying porch
burning with love and love's happiness,
she'll run dripping upstairs, she won't knock,
will take my head in her hands,
and when she drops her overcoat on a chair,
it will slide to the floor in a blue **heap**.[2]

---

[1] **fling**—throw.
[2] **heap**—pile.

People

No people are uninteresting.
Their fate is like the chronicle of planets.

Nothing in them is not particular,
and planet is dissimilar from planet.

And if a man lived in **obscurity**[3]
making his friends in that obscurity
obscurity is not uninteresting.

To each his world is private,
and in that world one excellent minute.

And in that world one tragic minute.
These are private.

In any man who dies there dies with him
his first snow and kiss and fight.
It goes with him.

They are left books and bridges
and painted **canvas**[4] and machinery.

Whose fate is to survive.
But what has gone is also not nothing:

by the rule of the game something has gone.
Not people die but worlds die in them.

Whom we knew as faulty, the earth's creatures.
Of whom, essentially, what did we know?

---

[3] **obscurity**—the condition of being unseen or unnoticed.

[4] **canvas**—a strong, coarse cloth.

Brother of a brother? Friend of friends?
Lover of lover?

We who knew our fathers
in everything, in nothing.

They perish. They cannot be brought back.
The secret worlds are not **regenerated**.[5]

And every time again and again
I make my **lament**[6] against destruction.

---

[5] **regenerated**—regrown or reformed.
[6] **lament**—passionate expression of grief.

QUESTIONS TO CONSIDER

1. What does love seem to mean to Yevtushenko in "Waiting"?

2. What is Yevtushenko's "lament against destruction" in "People"? What does he mean when he says that "no people are uninteresting"?

3. How would you describe Yevtushenko's view of the human condition? Is he a pessimist or an optimist? What do you think shaped his view?

The Encyclopedia of the Dead

DANILO KIŠ

Danilo Kiš (1935–1989) was the finest Yugoslav writer of the twentieth century. He was born in Serbia of a Montenegrin mother and a Hungarian father. Kiš's life was dominated by two great oppressive ideologies: Fascism and Communism. He grew up in Nazi-occupied Yugoslavia, and his father, as a Jew, was sent to Auschwitz, where he died. After the war, Communists gained control of Yugoslavia and imposed their harsh rule. As a writer, Kiš resembles Argentina's great fantasist Jorge Luis Borges (see page 334). Both blend fact, fiction, and scholarship in their writing, arriving at a style that is highly entertaining and full of perceptions and insight about the modern world. Kiš's early death robbed Europe of one of its most innovative and thoughtful writers.

Last year, as you know, I went to Sweden at the invitation of the Institute for Theater Research. A Mrs. Johansson, Kristina Johansson, served as my guide and mentor. I saw five or six productions, among which a successful *Godot*[1]—for prisoners—was most worthy of note. When I returned home ten days later, I was still living in that far-off world as if in a dream.

Mrs. Johansson was a forceful woman, and she intended to use those ten days to show me everything there was to see in Sweden, everything that might interest me "as a woman." She even included the famous *Wasa*, the sailing ship that had been hauled out of the sludge after several hundred years, preserved like a pharaoh's mummy. One evening, after a performance of *Ghost Sonata*[2] at the Dramaten, my hostess took me to the Royal Library. I barely had time to wolf down a sandwich at a stand.

It was about eleven by then, and the building was closed. But Mrs. Johansson showed a pass to the man at the door, and he grudgingly let us in. He held a large ring of keys in his hand, like the guard who had let us into the Central Prison the day before to see *Godot*. My hostess, having delivered me into the hands of this

[1] *Godot—Waiting for Godot* (1952), a famous play by Samuel Beckett about the meaninglessness of life.
[2] *Ghost Sonata*—a piano trio by Beethoven.

Cerberus,[3] said she would call for me in the morning at the hotel; she told me to look through the library in peace, the gentleman would call me a cab, he was at my disposal . . . What could I do but accept her kind offer? The guard escorted me to an enormous door, which he unlocked, and then switched on a dim light and left me alone. I heard the key turn in the lock behind me; there I was, in a library like a dungeon.

A draft blew in from somewhere, rippling the cobwebs, which, like dirty scraps of gauze, hung from the bookshelves as over select bottles of old wine in a cellar. All the rooms were alike, connected by a narrow passageway, and the draft, whose source I could not identify, penetrated everywhere.

It was at that point, even before I had had a good look at the books (and just after noticing the letter *C* on one of the volumes in the third room), that I caught on: each room housed one letter of the alphabet. This was the third. And, indeed, in the next section all the books were marked with the letter *D*. Suddenly, driven by some vague **premonition,**[4] I broke into a run. I heard my steps reverberating, a multiple echo that faded away in the darkness. Agitated and out of breath, I arrived at the letter *M* and *with a perfectly clear goal in mind* opened one of the books. I had realized—perhaps I had read about it somewhere —that this was the celebrated *Encyclopedia of the Dead.* Everything had come clear in a flash, even before I opened the massive **tome.**[5]

The first thing I saw was his picture, the only illustration, set into the double-column text in roughly the middle of the page. It was the photograph you saw on my desk. It was taken in 1936, on November 12, in Maribor, just after his discharge. Under the picture were his name and, in parentheses, the years 1910–79.

You know that my father died recently and that I had been very close to him from my earliest years. But I don't want to talk about that here. What concerns me now is that he died less than two months before my trip to Sweden. One of the main reasons I decided to take the trip was to escape my grief. I thought, as people in adversity are wont to think, that a change of scene would help me escape the pain, as if we did not bear our grief *within* ourselves.

Cradling the book in my arms and leaning against the rickety wooden shelves, I read his biography completely **oblivious**[6] of time. As in medieval libraries, the books were fastened by thick chains to iron rings on the shelves. I did not realize this until I tried to move the heavy volume closer to the light.

I was suddenly overcome with anguish; I felt I had overstayed my welcome and Mr. Cerberus (as I called him) might come and ask me to halt my reading. I therefore started skimming through the paragraphs,

---

[3] Cerberus—three-headed dog that guards the underworld in Greek mythology.

[4] **premonition**—funny feeling, hunch, or suspicion, usually regarding future events.

[5] **tome**—a large, heavy book.

[6] **oblivious**—unaware.

turning the open book, insofar as the chain would allow, in the direction of the pale light shed by the lamp. The thick layer of dust that had gathered along their edges and the dangling scraps of cobwebs bore clear witness to the fact that no one had handled the volumes in a long time. They were fettered to one another like galley slaves, but their chains had no locks.

So this is the famous *Encyclopedia of the Dead*, I thought to myself. I had pictured it as an ancient book, a "venerable" book, something like the Tibetan Book of the Dead or the Cabala or the *Lives of the Saints*[7]—one of those **esoteric**[8] creations of the human spirit that only hermits, rabbis, and monks can enjoy. When I saw that I might go on reading until dawn and be left without any concrete trace of what I had read for either me or my mother, I decided to copy out several of the most important passages and make a kind of summary of my father's life.

The facts I have recorded here, in this notebook, are ordinary, encyclopedia facts, unimportant to anyone but my mother and me: names, places, dates. They were all I managed to jot down, in haste, at dawn. What makes the *Encyclopedia* unique (apart from its being the only existing copy) is the way it depicts human relationships, encounters, landscapes—the multitude of details that make up a human life. The reference (for example) to my father's place of birth is not only complete and accurate ("Kraljevčani, Glina township, Sisak district, Banija province") but is accompanied by both geographical and historical details.

Because *it* records everything. Everything. The countryside of his native region is rendered so vividly that as I read, or rather flew over the lines and paragraphs, I felt I was in the heart of it: the snow on distant mountain peaks, the bare trees, the frozen river with children skating past as in a Brueghel[9] landscape. And among those children I saw him clearly, my father, although he was not yet my father, only he who would become my father, who *had been* my father. Then the countryside suddenly turned green and buds blossomed on the trees, pink and white, hawthorn bushes flowered before my eyes, the sun arched over the village of Kraljevčani, the village church bells chimed, cows mooed in their barns, and the scarlet reflection of the morning sun glistened on the cottage windows and melted the icicles hanging from the gutters.

Then, as if it were all unfolding before my eyes, I saw a funeral procession headed in the direction of the village cemetery. Four men, hatless, were carrying a fir casket on their shoulders, and at the head of the procession walked a man, hat in hand, whom I knew to be—for that is what the book said—my paternal grandfather Marko, the husband of the deceased, whom they were laying to rest. The book

---

[7] Tibetan Book of the Dead . . . Cabala . . . *Lives of the Saints*—Buddhist, Jewish, and Christian religious texts.

[8] **esoteric**—understandable only by those with special knowledge.

[9] Brueghel—Pieter Brueghel (c. 1525–1569) was a Flemish painter famed for his landscapes and pictures of everyday life.

tells everything about her as well: date of birth, cause of illness and death, progression of disease. It also indicates what garments she was buried in, who bathed her, who placed the coins on her eyes, who bound her chin, who carved the casket, where the timber was felled. That may give you an idea—some idea, at least—of the copiousness of the information included in *The Encyclopedia of the Dead* by those who undertake the difficult and praiseworthy task of recording—in what is doubtless an **objective**[10] and **impartial**[11] manner— everything that can be recorded concerning those who have completed their earthly journey and set off on the eternal one. (For they believe in the miracle of biblical resurrection, and they compile their vast catalogue in preparation for that moment. So that everyone will be able to find not only his fellow men but also—and more important—his own forgotten past. When the time comes, this **compendium**[12] will serve as a great treasury of memories and a unique proof of resurrection.) Clearly, they make no distinction, where a life is concerned, between a provincial merchant and his wife, between a village priest (which is what my great-grandfather was) and a village bell ringer called Ćuk, whose name also figures in the book. The only condition—something I grasped at once, it seems to have come to me even before I could confirm it—for inclusion in *The Encyclopedia of the Dead* is that no one whose name is recorded here may appear in any other encyclopedia. I was struck from the first, as I leafed through the

book—one of the thousands of *M* volumes—by the absence of famous people. (I received immediate confirmation as I turned the pages with my frozen fingers, looking for my father's name.) The *Encyclopedia* did not include separate listings for Mažuranić or Meyerhold or Malmberg or Maretić, who wrote the grammar my father used in school, or Meštrović, whom my father had once seen in the street, or Dragoslav Maksimović, a lathe[13] operator and Socialist deputy whom my grandfather had known, or Tasa Milojević, Kautsky's translator, with whom my father had once conversed at the Russian Tsar Café. It is the work of a religious organization or sect whose democratic program stresses an egalitarian vision of the world of the dead, a vision that is doubtless inspired by some biblical precept and aims at redressing human injustices and granting all God's creatures an equal place in eternity. I was also quick to grasp that the *Encyclopedia* did not delve into the dark distance of history and time, that it came into being shortly after 1789. The odd caste of erudites must have members all over the world digging tirelessly and discreetly through obituaries and biographies, processing their data, and delivering them to headquarters in Stockholm. (Couldn't Mrs. Johansson be one of them? I wondered for

---

[10] **objective**—not influenced by outside opinions or prejudice.

[11] **impartial**—treating all sides equally.

[12] **compendium**—a summary or collection, usually collected in a single unit, box, or set.

[13] **lathe**—a machine for shaping wood or metal.

a moment. Couldn't she have brought me to the library, after I had confided my grief to her, so that I might discover *The Encyclopedia of the Dead* and find a **modicum**[14] of consolation in it?) That is all I can surmise, all I infer about their work. The reason for their secrecy resides, I believe, in the Church's long history of persecution, though work on an encyclopedia such as this understandably requires a certain discretion if the pressures of human vanity are to be avoided and attempts at corruption thwarted.

No less amazing than their secret activities, however, was their style, an unlikely **amalgam**[15] of encyclopedic conciseness and biblical eloquence. Take, for example, the meager bit of information I was able to get down in my notebook: *there* it is condensed into a few lines of such intensity that suddenly, as if by magic, the reader's spirit is overwhelmed by the radiant landscape and swift succession of images. We find a three-year-old boy being carried up a mountain path to see his maternal grandfather on a sweltering sunny day, while in the background—the second or third plane, if that is what it is called—there are soldiers, revenue officers, and police, distant cannon thunder and muffled barking. We find a pithy chronology of World War I: trains clanking past a market town, a brass band playing, water gurgling in the neck of a canteen, glass shattering, kerchiefs fluttering . . . Each item has its own paragraph, each period its own poetic essence and metaphor—not always in chronological order but in a strange

symbiosis[16] of past, present, and future. How else can we explain the **plaintive**[17] comment in the text—the "picture album" covering his first five years, which he spent with his grandfather in Komogovina—the comment that goes, if I remember correctly, "Those *would be* the finest years of his life"? Then come condensed images of childhood, reduced, so to speak, to **ideographs**:[18] names of teachers and friends, the boy's "finest years" against a backdrop of changing seasons, rain splashing off a happy face, swims in the river, a toboggan speeding down a snow-swept hill, trout fishing, and then—or, if possible, simultaneously—soldiers returning from the battlefields of Europe, a canteen in the boy's hands, a shattered gas mask abandoned on an embankment. And names, life stories. The widower Marko meeting his future wife, Sofija Rebrača, a native of Komogovina, the wedding celebration, the toasts, the village horse race, pennants and ribbons flapping, the exchange-of-rings ceremony, singing and kolo-dancing outside the church doors, the boy dressed up in a white shirt, a sprig of rosemary in his lapel.

Here, in my notebook, I have recorded only the word "Kraljevčani," but the *Encyclopedia* devotes several dense

---

[14] **modicum**—a little bit.

[15] **amalgam**—mixture or blend.

[16] **symbiosis**—a relationship formed to the benefit of all parties.

[17] **plaintive**—expressing great sadness or sorrow, mournful.

[18] **ideographs**—picture language.

paragraphs to this period, complete with names and dates. It describes how he awoke on that day, how the cuckoo in the clock on the wall roused him from his fitful sleep. It contains the names of the coachmen, the names of the neighbors who made up the escort, a portrait of the school-master, the guidance he offered to the boy's new mother, the priest's counsels, the words of those who stood at the outskirts of the village to wave them one last farewell.

Nothing, as I have said, is lacking, nothing omitted, neither the condition of the road nor the hues of the sky and the list of paterfamilias Marko's worldly possessions is complete to the last detail. Nothing has been forgotten, nor even the names of the authors of old textbooks and primers full of well-meaning advice, cautionary tales, and biblical **parables.**[19] Every period of life, every experience is recorded: every fish caught, every page read, the name of every plant the boy ever picked.

And here is my father as a young man, his first hat, his first carriage ride, at dawn. Here are the names of girls, the words of the songs sung at the time, the text of a love letter, the newspapers read—his entire youth compressed into a single paragraph.

Now we are in Ruma, where my father received his secondary-school education. Perhaps this example will give you an idea of how all-knowing, as they used to say, *The Encyclopedia of the Dead* actually is. The principle is clear, yet the **erudition,**[20] the need to record it all, everything a human

life is made of, is enough to take one's breath away. What we have here is a brief history of Ruma, a meteorological map, a description of the railway junction; the name of the printer and everything printed at the time—every newspaper, every book; the plays put on by **itinerant**[21] companies and the attractions of touring circuses; a description of a brickyard . . . where a young man, leaning against a locust tree, is whispering a mixture of romantic and rather **ribald**[22] words into a girl's ear (we have the complete text). And everything—the train, the printing press, the finale of *The Bumptious Bumpkin*, the circus elephant, the track forking off in the direction of Šabac—it all figures here only insofar as it pertains to the individual in question. There are also excerpts from school reports: grades, drawings, names of classmates, until the next-to-the-last year (section B), when the young man had words with Professor L.D., the history and geography teacher.

Suddenly we are in the heart of a new city. It is 1928; the young man is wearing a

> *Every period of life, every experience is recorded: every fish caught, every page read, the name of every plant the boy ever picked.*

---

[19] **parables**—an imagined story used to teach a lesson.

[20] **erudition**—learning.

[21] **itinerant**—traveling from place to place.

[22] **ribald**—harshly or disrepectfully humorous.

cap with a final-year insignia on it and has grown a mustache. (He will have it for the rest of his life. Once, fairly recently, his razor slipped and he shaved it off completely. When I saw him, I burst into tears: he was somebody else. In my tears there was a vague, fleeting realization of how much I would miss him when he died.) Now here he is in front of the Café Central, then at a cinema, where a piano plays while *Voyage to the Moon* unfolds on the screen. Later we find him looking over newly posted announcements on the notice board in Jecacic Square, one of which—and I mention it only as a curiosity—announces a lecture by Krleža. The name of Anna Eremija—a maternal aunt, in whose Jurišić Street flat in Zagreb he will later live—figures here side by side with the names of Križaj, the opera singer, whom he once passed in the Upper Town; Ivan Labus, the cobbler who repaired his shoes; and a certain Ante Dutina, in whose bakery he bought his rolls...

In that distant year of 1929, one approached Belgrade[23] via the Sava Bridge, probably with the same joy of arrival as one feels today. The train wheels clatter as they pass over the metal trestles, the Sava flows mud-green, a locomotive blows its whistle and loses speed, and my father appears at a second-class window, peering out at the distant view of an unfamiliar city. The morning is fresh, the fog slowly lifts off the horizon, black smoke puffs from the stack of the steamer Smederevo,

a muffled horn hoots the imminent departure of the boat for Novi Sad.

With brief interruptions, my father spent approximately fifty years in Belgrade, and the sum of his experiences—the total of some eighteen thousand days and nights (432,000 hours) is covered here, in this book of the dead, in a mere five or six pages! And yet, at least in broad outline, chronology is respected: the days flow like the river of time, toward the mouth, toward death.

In September of that year, 1929, my father enrolled in a school that taught surveying, and the *Encyclopedia* chronicles the creation of the Belgrade School of Surveying and gives the text of the inaugural lecture by its director, Professor Stojkovic (who enjoined the future surveyors to serve king and country loyally, for on their shoulders lay the heavy burden of mapping the new borders of their motherland). The names of the glorious-campaigns and no less glorious defeats of World War I—Kajmakčalan, Mojkovac, Cer, Kolubara, Drina—alternate with the names of professors and students who fell in battle, with my father's grades in trigonometry, draftsmanship, history, religion, and calligraphy. We find also the name Roksanda-Rosa, a flower girl with whom D.M. "trifled," as they said in those days, along with the names of Borivoj-Bora Ilić, who ran a café; Milenko Azanja, a tailor; Kosta Stavroski, at whose place he

---

[23] Belgrade—the capital of Yugoslavia.

stopped every morning for a hot *burek*;[24] and a man named Krtinić, who fleeced him once at cards. Next comes a list of films and soccer matches he saw, the dates of his excursions to Avala and Kosmaj, the weddings and funerals he attended, the names of the streets where he lived (Cetinjska, Empress Milica, Gavrilo Princip, King Peter I, Prince Miloš, Požeška, Kameniĉka, Kosmajska, Brankova), the names of the authors of his geography, geometry, and planimetry[25] texts, titles of the books he enjoyed (*King of the Mountain, Stanko the Bandit, The Peasant Revolt*), church services, circus performances, gymnastics demonstrations, school functions, art exhibits (where a watercolor done by my father was commended by the jury). We also find mention of the day he smoked his first cigarette, in the school lavatory, at the instigation of one Ivan Gerasimov, the son of a Russian **émigré**,[26] who took him one week later to a then celebrated Belgrade café, with a Gypsy orchestra and Russian counts and officers weeping to guitars and balalaikas[27]. . . Nothing is omitted: the ceremonial unveiling of the Kalemegdan monument, food poisoning from ice cream bought on the corner of Macedonia Street, the shiny pointed shoes purchased with the money his father gave him for passing his examinations.

The next paragraph tells of his departure for Užička Požega in 1933, in May. Traveling with him on the train, second class, is the unfortunate Gerasimov, the émigré's son. It is their first assignment: they are to survey the terrain of Serbia, make cadastral[28] and cartographic sketches. They take turns carrying the leveling rod and the theodolite;[29] protecting their heads with straw hats—it is summer by now, and the sun is beating down—they climb hills, call, shout back and forth to each other; the autumn rains begin; pigs start grubbing, the cattle start getting restless; the theodolite has to be kept sheltered: it attracts lightning. In the evenings they drink slivovitz[30] with Milenković, the village schoolmaster, the spit turns, Gerasimov curses first in Russian, then in Serbian, the brandy is strong. Poor Gerasimov will die of pneumonia in November of that year, with D.M. standing over his deathbed, listening to his ravings—just as he will stand over his grave, head bowed, hat in hand, meditating on the transitory nature of human existence.

That is what remains in my memory; that is what remains in the notes I hurriedly jotted down with my frozen fingers on that night or, rather, morning. And it represents two entire years, two seemingly monotonous years, when from May to November—bandit season—D.M. dragged the tripod

---

[24] *burek*—fried dumpling with filling of cheese or meat.

[25] planimetry—measurement of plane surfaces.

[26] **émigré**—a person who has left his or her country to settle in another, especially one who has been forced to do so for political reasons.

[27] balalaikas—three-stringed Russian musical instruments, rather like a triangular-shaped guitar.

[28] cadastral—showing a land's size, value, and ownership for tax purposes.

[29] theodolite—surveying instrument used to measure vertical and horizontal angles.

[30] slivovitz—strong plum brandy popular in eastern Europe.

and the theodolite up hill and down dale, the seasons changed, the rivers overflowed their banks and returned to them, the leaves turned first green, then yellow, and my father sat in the shade of blossoming plum trees, then took refuge under the eaves of a house as flashes of lightning illuminated the evening landscape and thunder reverberated through the ravines.

It is summer, the sun is blazing, and our surveyors (he has a new partner named Dragović) stop at a house (street and number noted) at noon, knock on the door, ask for water. A girl comes out and gives them a pitcher of ice-cold water, as in a folk tale. That girl—as you may have guessed—will become my mother.

I won't try to retell it all from memory, everything, the way it is recorded and depicted *there*—the date and manner of the **betrothal**,[31] the traditional wedding where money is no object, the range of picturesque folkways that were part of that life: it would all seem insufficient, fragmentary, compared with *the original*. Still, I can't help mentioning that the text gives a list of the witnesses and guests, the name of the priest who officiated, the toasts and songs, the gifts and givers, the food and drink. Next, chronologically, comes a period of five months, between November and May, when the newlyweds settled in Belgrade; the *Encyclopedia* includes the floor plan and furniture arrangement, the price of the stove, bed, and wardrobe, as well as certain intimate details that in such instances are always so alike and always so different. After

all—and this is what I consider the compilers' central message—nothing in the history of mankind is ever repeated, things that at first glance seem the same are scarcely even similar; each individual is a star unto himself, everything happens always and never, all things repeat themselves ad infinitum[32] yet are unique. (That is why the authors of the majestic monument to diversity that is *The Encyclopedia of the Dead* stress the particular; that is why every human being is sacred to them.)

Were it not for the compilers' obsession with the idea that every human being is unique, and every event singular, what would be the point of providing the names of the priest and the registrar, a description of the wedding dress, or the name of Gledić, a village outside Karljevo, along with all those details that connect man and place? For now we come to my father's arrival "in the field," his stay from May to November—bandit season again—in various villages. We find the name of Jovan Radojković (at whose inn, in the evenings, the surveyors drink chilled wine on credit) and of a child, Svetozar, who became my father's godson at the request of a certain Stevan Janjić, and of a Dr. Levstik, a Slovene[33] exile, who prescribed medication for my father's gastritis, and of a girl named Radmila-Rada Mavreva, with whom he had a roll in the hay off in a stable somewhere.

---

[31] **betrothal**—engagement to be married.

[32] ad infinitum—Latin for "to infinity" or "eternally."

[33] Slovene—referring to a Slavic people who live in the Slovenia region of Yugoslavia.

As for my father's military service, the book traces the marches he took with the Fifth Infantry stationed in Maribor, and specifies the names and ranks of the officers and N.C.O.s and the names of the men in his barracks, the quality of the food in the mess, a knee injury sustained on a night march, a **reprimand**[34] received for losing a glove, the name of the café at which he celebrated his transfer to Požarevac.

At first glance it may seem quite the same as any military service, any transfer, but from the standpoint of the *Encyclopedia* both Požarevac and my father's seven months in the barracks there were unique: never again, *never*, would a certain D.M., surveyor, in the autumn of 1935, draw maps near the stove of the Pozarevac barracks and think of how, two or three months before, on a night march, he had caught a glimpse of the sea.

The sea he glimpsed, for the first time, at twenty-five, from the slopes of the Velebit on April 28, 1935, would reside within him—a revelation, a dream sustained for some forty years with undiminished intensity, a secret, a vision never put into words. After all those years he was not quite sure himself whether what he had seen was the open sea or merely the horizon, and the only true sea for him remained the aquamarine of maps, where depths are designated by a darker shade of blue, shallows by a lighter shade.

That, I think, was why for years he refused to go away on holiday, even at a time when union organizations and tourist agencies sent people flocking to seaside resorts. His opposition betrayed an odd anxiety, a fear of being disillusioned, as if a close encounter with the sea might destroy the distant vision that had dazzled him on April 28, 1935, when for the first time in his life he glimpsed, from afar, at daybreak, the glorious blue of the Adriatic.[35]

All the excuses he invented to postpone that encounter with the sea were somehow unconvincing: he didn't want to spend his summers like a vulgar tourist, he couldn't spare money (which was not far from the truth), he had a low tolerance for the sun (though he had spent his life in the most blistering heat), and would we please leave him in peace, he was just fine in Belgrade behind closed blinds. This chapter in *The Encyclopedia of the Dead* goes into his romance with the sea in great detail, from that first lyric sighting, in 1935, to the actual encounter, face to face, some forty years later.

It took place—his first true encounter with the sea—in 1975, when at last, after an all-out family offensive, he agreed to go to Rovinj with my mother and stay at the house of some friends who were away for the summer.

He came back early, dissatisfied with the climate, dissatisfied with the restaurant service, dissatisfied with the television programs, put out by the crowds, the polluted water, the jellyfish, the prices and general "highway robbery." Of the sea

---

[34] **reprimand**—severe scolding.
[35] Adriatic—the sea between Italy and Yugoslavia.

itself, apart from complaints about pollution ("The tourists use it as a public toilet") and jellyfish ("They're attracted by human stench, like lice"), he said nothing, not a word. He dismissed it with a wave of the hand. Only now do we realize what he meant: his age-old dream of the Adriatic, that distant vision, was finer and keener, purer and stronger than the filthy water where fat men paddled about with oil-slathered "black as pitch" women.

That was the last time he went to the seaside for his summer holiday. Now I know that something died in him then, like a dear friend—a distant dream, a distant illusion (if it was an illusion) that he had borne within him for forty years.

As you can see, I've just made a forty-year leap forward in his life, but chronologically speaking we are still back in 1937, 1938, by which time D.M. had two daughters, myself and my sister (the son was yet to come), conceived in the depths of the Serbian hinterland, villages like Petrovac-on-the-Mlava or Despotovac, Stepojevac, Bukovac, Ćuprija, Jelašica, Matejevica, Ćečina, Vlasina, Knjaževac, or Podvis. Draw a map of the region in your mind, enlarging every one of the dots on the map or military chart (1:50,000) to their actual dimensions; mark the streets and houses he lived in; then walk into a courtyard, a house; sketch the layout of the rooms; inventory the furniture and the orchard; and don't forget the names of the flowers growing in the garden behind the house or the news in the papers he reads, news of

the, Ribbentrop-Molotov pact,[36] of the desertion of the Yugoslav royal government, of the prices of lard and of coal, of the feats of the flying ace Aleksić. . . That is how the master encyclopedists go about it.

As I've said before, each event connected with his personal destiny, every bombing of Belgrade, every advance of German troops to the east, and their every retreat, is considered from his point of view and in accordance with how it affects his life. There is mention of a Palmotićeva Street house, with all the essentials of the building and its inhabitants noted, because it was in the cellar of that house that he—and all of us—sat out the bombing of Belgrade; by the same token, there is a description of the country house in Stepojevac (name of owner, layout, etc., included) where Father sheltered us for the rest of the war, as well as the prices of bread, meat, lard, poultry, and brandy. You will find my father's talk with the Knjaževac chief of police and a document, dated 1942, relieving him of his duties, and if you read carefully you will see him gathering leaves in the Botanical Gardens or along Palmotićeva Street, pressing them and pasting them into his daughter's herbarium, writing out "Dandelion (*Taraxacum officinale*)" or "Linden (Tilia)" in the calligraphic hand he used when entering "Adriatic Sea" or "Vlasina" on maps.

---

[36] Ribbentrop-Molotov pact—a military alliance and nonaggression pact signed by Germany and Russia in 1939. It was a prelude to World War II.

The vast river of his life, that family novel, branches off into many tributaries, and parallel to the account of his **stint**[37] in the sugar refinery in 1943–44 runs a kind of digest or chronicle of the fate of my mother and of us, his children—whole volumes condensed into a few **cogent**[38] paragraphs. Thus, his early rising is linked to my mother's (she is off to one village or another to barter an old wall clock, part of her dowry, for a hen or a side of bacon) and to our, the children's, departure for school. This morning ritual (the strains of "Lilli Marlene" in the background come from a radio somewhere in the neighborhood) is meant to convey the family atmosphere in the sacked[39] surveyor's home during the years of occupation (meager breakfasts of chicory and zwieback[40]) and to give an idea of the "fashions" of the time, when people wore earmuffs, wooden-soled shoes, and army-blanket overcoats.

The fact that, while working at the Milišič Refinery as a day laborer my father brought home molasses under his coat, at great risk, has the same significance for *The Encyclopedia of the Dead* as the raid on the eye clinic in our immediate vicinity or the exploits of my Uncle Cveja Karakaševič, a native of Ruma, who would filch what he could from the German Officers' Club at 7 French Street, where he was employed as a "purveyor." The curious circumstance, also Cveja Karakaševič's doing, that several times during the German occupation we dined on fattened carp[41] (which would spend the night in the large enamel tub in our bathroom) and washed it down with French champagne from the same Officers' Club, the Drei Husaren, did not, of course, escape the attention of the *Encyclopedia's* compilers. By the same token, and in keeping with the logic of their program (that there is nothing insignificant in a human life, no hierarchy of events), they entered all our childhood illnesses—mumps, tonsillitis, whooping cough, rashes—as well as a bout of lice and my father's lung trouble (their diagnosis tallies with Dr. Djurović's: emphysema, due to heavy smoking). But you will also find a bulletin on the Bajlonova Marketplace notice board with a list of executed hostages that includes close friends and acquaintances of my father's; the names of patriots whose bodies swung from telegraph poles on Terazije, in the very center of Belgrade; the words of a German officer demanding to see his *Ausweis*[42] at the station restaurant in Niš; the description of a Četnik[43] wedding in Vlasotinci, with rifles going off all through the night.

The Belgrade street battles in October 1944 are described from his point of view and from the perspective of Palmotićeva Street: the artillery rolling by, a dead horse lying on the corner. The deafening roar of the caterpillar treads momentarily drowns

---

[37] **stint**—a fixed or alloted time of work.

[38] **cogent**—convincing or persuasive.

[39] sacked—raided, plundered, or destroyed.

[40] chickory and zwieback—an herb used as a substitute for coffee and sweetened bread, respectively.

[41] carp—a type of freshwater fish, often bred for use as food.

[42] *Ausweis*—identity card.

[43] Četnik—a Yugoslav soldier.

out the interrogation of a *Volksdeutscher*[44] named Franjo Hermann, whose supplications pass easily through the thin wall of a neighboring building where an OZNA[45] security officer **metes**[46] out the people's justice and revenge. The burst of machine-gun fire in the courtyard next door reverberating harshly in the abrupt silence that follows the passing of a Soviet tank, a splash of blood on the wall that my father would see from the bathroom window, and the corpse of the unfortunate Hermann, in fetal position— they are all recorded in *The Encyclopedia of the Dead*, accompanied by the commentary of a hidden observer.

> *For* **The Encyclopedia of the Dead,** *history is the sum of human destinies, the totality of ephemeral happenings.*

For *The Encyclopedia of the Dead*, history is the sum of human destinies, the totality of **ephemeral**[47] happenings. That is why it records every action, every thought, every creative breath, every spot height in the survey, every shovelful of mud, every motion that cleared a brick from the ruins.

The post my father held after the war in the Land Office, which undertook to remeasure and rerecord the land, as is usual after major historic upheavals, is accorded the detailed treatment it demands: quality of terrain, title deeds, new names for former German villages and new names for freshly colonized settlements.

Nothing, as I say, is missing: the clay caking the rubber boots bought from a drunken soldier; a bad case of diarrhea caused by some spoiled cabbage rolls eaten at a dive in Indjija; an affair with a Bosnian[48] woman, a waitress, in Sombor; a bicycle accident near Čantavir and the bruised elbow that came of it; a night ride in a cattle car on the Senta-Subotica line; the purchase of a plump goose to take home for a New Year's celebration; a spree with some Russian engineers in Banovići; a molar pulled, in the field, near a well; a rally at which he got soaked to the bone; the death of Steva Bogdanov, surveyor, who stepped on a trip-wire mine at the edge of some woods and with whom he had played billiards the previous day; the return of Aleksić, the stunt pilot, to the sky above Kalemegdan; serious alcohol poisoning in the village of Mrakodol; a ride in a crowded truck over the muddy road between Zrenjanin and Elemir; a quarrel with a new boss, a man named Šusput, somewhere in the region of Jaša Tomić; the purchase of a ton of Banovići coal after queuing from four in the morning at the Danube Railway Yard, in -15° weather; the purchase of a marble-top table at the flea market; a breakfast of "American" cheese and powdered milk in the Bosnia Workers' Canteen; his father's illness and death; the

---

[44] *Volksdeutscher*—a German soldier.

[45] OZNA—acronym for the Yugoslav security service during World War II.

[46] **metes**—hands or gives out.

[47] **ephemeral**—lasting for a short time.

[48] Bosnian—referring to a Slavic people who live in the central part of the former Yugoslavia.

prescribed visit to the cemetery forty days later; a bitter quarrel with one Petar Janković and one Sava Dragović, who advocated the Stalinist line;[49] their arguments and his counterarguments (which ended with my father's muffled "F——— Stalin!").

Thus, the *Encyclopedia* plunges us into the spirit of the time, into its political events.

The fear in which my father lived and the silence I myself remember—a heavy, oppressive silence—are construed by the book as infectious: one day he learned that that same Petar Janković, a colleague and distant relative, was reporting to the State Security Building every morning at six for a talk (as a result of having been denounced by the aforementioned Dragović), and would arrive at the office late, his face black and swollen from blows and lack of sleep; and on it went, every morning at sunup, for six months or so, until Petar recalled the names of some other people who shared his Russian delusions and listened to Radio Moscow.

Passing over the side streams—quarrels, reconciliations, spa visits (a whole family chronicle in miniature)—passing over the things that my father would bring home and that the *Encyclopedia* inventories with tender, loving care, I will mention only an Orion radio set, the *Collected Works* of Maxim Gorky,[50] an oleander in an enormous wooden bucket, and a barrel for pickling cabbage, as I find them more important than the other trifles the book goes into, such as the lined fabric I bought for him with my first wages and the bottle of Martell cognac he downed in a single evening.

But *The Encyclopedia of the Dead* is concerned with more than material goods: it is not a double-entry ledger or a catalogue, nor is it a list of names like the Book of Kings or Genesis,[51] though it is that as well; it deals with spiritual matters, people's views of the world, of God, their doubts about the existence of the beyond, their moral standards. Yet what is most amazing is its unique fusion of external and internal: it lays great stress on concrete facts, then creates a logical bond between the facts and man, or what we call man's soul. And whereas the compilers leave certain objective data without commentary —the conversion of tile stoves to electricity (1969), the appearance of a bald spot on my father's head or his abrupt slide into **gluttony,**[52] the refreshing elderberry drink he made from a *Politika* recipe—they do interpret his sudden passion for stamp collecting in old age as compensation for his prolonged immobility. They have no doubt that peering at stamps through a magnifying glass represents, in part, the repressed fantasies so often lurking in **staid,**[53] stable people with little proclivity for travel and adventure—the same frustrated **petit-bourgeois**[54] romanticism that

---

[49] Stalinist line—hard line Communism named for the dictatorial leader of Russia, Josef Stalin. It involved total subservience to rule from Moscow.

[50] Maxim Gorky—(1868–1936) Russian writer.

[51] Book of Kings or Genesis—books of the Old Testament in the Bible.

[52] **gluttony**—greed or excess when it comes to eating.

[53] **staid**—calm, restrained.

[54] **petit-bourgeois**—lower middle-class, conservative.

determined Father's attitude toward the sea. (He replaced journeys and distant horizons with more convenient, imaginary wanderings, using his first grandson's interest in the butterfly world of stamps to keep from appearing ridiculous in the eyes of others, and in his own.)

This, as you can see, is an area of the spiritual landscape quite near to the river's mouth, where friends' and relatives' funerals follow so closely on one another that every man—even a man less inclined than my father to silent meditation— turns philosopher, insofar as philosophy is the contemplation of the meaning of human existence.

Dissatisfied with his life, consumed by the melancholy of old age that nothing can assuage, neither devoted children nor affectionate grandchildren nor the relative calm of everyday life, he started grumbling and getting drunk more often. When he drank, he would burst into fits of anger quite unexpected in so mild a man with so gentle a smile. He would curse God, heaven, earth, the Russians, the Americans, the Germans, the government, and all those responsible for granting him such a miser- able pension after he had slaved a lifetime, but most of all he cursed television, which, insolent to the point of insult, filled the void of his evenings by bringing into the house the grand illusion of life.

The next day, himself again and mutely **contrite,**[55] he would feed the goldfinch on the balcony, talk to it, whistle to it, lifting the cage high above his head as if bran- dishing a lantern in the murk of human

tribulations.[56] Or, taking off his pajamas at last, he would dress with a groan, put on his hat, and walk to Takovska Street, to the main post office, and buy stamps. Then, in the afternoon, sipping coffee while perched on the edge of an armchair, his grandson at his side, he would arrange the stamps in albums with the help of delicate tweezers.

Occasionally, in moments of despair, he bemoaned his past, wailing as the elderly are wont to do: God hadn't granted him a real education, he would go ignorant to his grave, never having known well-being, never having known real seas or cities, never having known what a rich and cultivated man can know.

And his trip to Trieste ended as ingloriously as his trip to Rovinj.

It was, in his sixty-sixth year, his first border crossing, and it, too, took a good deal of pushing and pulling. Nor were his arguments any easier to counter: an intelligent person did not go to a country whose language he did not know; he had no intention of making a fortune on the black market; he had no craving for macaroni or Chianti and would much prefer an everyday Mostar *žilavka* or a Prokuplje white,[57] at home.

And yet we persuaded him to apply for a passport.

He came back ill-humored, ill-tempered, crushed: he had had a falling out with Mother (the shoes she had bought him

---

[55] **contrite**—filled with deep regret.

[56] **tribultations**—afflictions or oppressions.

[57] Mostar *žilavka* or a Prokuplje white—Yugoslav wines.

leaked and pinched), and the police had searched them and ransacked their luggage on the return trip to Belgrade.

Need I point out that the trip to Trieste—the downpour, with Father waiting umbrella-less under the awning of the Hotel Adriatico like a lost, drenched cur while Mother rummaged through shoes on the Ponte Rosso—receives in the *Encyclopedia* the place an episode of the sort deserves? His only consolation during the disastrous Trieste jaunt came from buying some flower seeds outside a shop there. (Fortunately, the packets had pictures of the flowers on them and clearly marked prices, so he didn't need to enter into negotiations with the saleswoman.) By then D.M. had become quite "involved in cultivating decorative flowers," as the *Encyclopedia* puts it. (It continues with an inventory of the flowers in pots and window boxes on the front and rear balconies.)

He had simultaneously begun to fill his time by painting floral patterns all over the house, a kind of floral **contagion.**[58] This sudden explosion of artistic talent came as a surprise. Dissatisfied—as he was dissatisfied with everything—with the way a retired officer, a neophyte housepainter, had plastered the bathroom (singing "The Partisans' March" all day long to pace his brushstrokes and leaving behind large, unevenly covered areas), my father rolled up his sleeves and set doggedly to work. Having failed to remove the dark spots on the wall, he decided to camouflage them with oil paint, following the outlines of the moisture stains. And thus the first flower—a gigantic bellflower or a lily, heaven only knows what it was—came into being.

We all praised him. The neighbors dropped in to view his handiwork. Even his favorite grandson expressed sincere admiration. That was how it all started. Next came the bathroom window, which he covered with tiny cornflower—blue posies, but he left them slanted and unfinished, so that the design, painted directly on the glass, gave the illusion of a windblown curtain.

From then on, he painted all day, unflaggingly, a cigarette dangling from his lips. (And in the silence we could hear the wheezing of his lungs, like bellows.) He painted flowers that bore little resemblance to real flowers, painted them all over old scratched trunks, china lampshades, cognac bottles, plain glass vases, Nescafé jars, and wooden cigar boxes. On the aquamarine background of a large soda-water siphon he painted the names of Belgrade cafés in the lettering he had once used for islands on maps: The Brioni, The Gulf of Kotor, The Seagull, The Sailor, The Daybreak, Café Serbia, The Vidin Gate, The Istanbul Gate, The Skadarlija, The Three Hats, The Two Deer, Under the Linden, Three Bunches of Grapes, The Šumatovac, The Seven Days, The March on the Drina, The Kalemegdan, The Kolarac, The Motherland, The Plowman, The Obrenovac, The Oplenac, The Town of Dušan, The River's Mouth, The Smederevo, The Hunter's Horn, The Question Mark, The Last Chance.

---

[58] **contagion**—infectious disease.

The curious fact that he died on his first grandson's twelfth birthday did not escape the compilers' attention. Nor did they fail to note his resistance to our naming his last grandson after him. We thought that we were indulging his vanity and that he would take it as a sign of special attention and favor, but all he did was grumble and I could see in his eyes a glimmer of the terror that would flash behind his glasses a year later when the certainty of the end suddenly dawned on him. The succession of the quick and the dead, the universal myth of the chain of generations, the vain solace man invents to make the thought of dying more acceptable—in that instant my father experienced them all as an insult; it was as though by the magical act of bestowing his name upon a newborn child, no matter how much his flesh and blood, we were "pushing him into the grave." I did not yet know that he had discovered a suspicious growth in the area of his groin and believed, or perhaps even knew, for sure, that, like a tuber, a strange, poisonous plant was sprouting in his intestines.

> **The curious fact that he died on his first grandson's twelfth birthday did not escape the compilers' attention.**

One of the last chapters of the *Encyclopedia* details the funeral ceremony: the name of the priest who administered the last rites, a description of the wreaths, a list of the people who accompanied him from the chapel, the number of candles lit for his soul, the text of the obituary in *Politika*.

The oration delivered over the bier[59] by Nikola Beševič, a Land Office colleague of many years' standing ("Comrade Djuro served his fatherland with equal honor before the war, during the occupation, and after the war in the period of the revitalization and reconstruction of our ravaged and sorely afflicted country"), is given in full, because, despite certain exaggerations and **platitudes,**[60] despite lapses in rhetoric, Beševič's oration over the body of his dead comrade and fellow countryman clearly exemplified something of the message and principles represented by the great *Encyclopedia of the Dead* ("His memory shall live forever and ever. Praise and glory be unto him!")

Well, that is more or less the end, where my notes stop. I shall not cite the sorry inventory of items he left behind: shirts, passport, documents, eyeglasses (the light of day glistening painfully in empty lenses just removed from their case)—in other words, the items passed on to my mother, at the hospital, the day after his death. It is all painstakingly set down in the *Encyclopedia*; not a single handkerchief is missing, not the Morava cigarettes or the issue of *Ilustrovana Politika* with a crossword puzzle partly completed in his hand.

Then come the names of the doctors, nurses, and visitors, the day and hour of the operation (when Dr. Petrović cut him open and sewed him shut, realizing it was useless to operate: the sarcoma[61] had

---

[59] bier—coffin and stand on which it is placed.

[60] **platitudes**—clichés, especially ones that are delivered with great seriousness.

[61] sarcoma—a cancer originating in the body's tissue.

spread to the vital organs). I haven't the strength to describe the look he gave me as he said goodbye on the hospital stairs a day or two before the operation; it contained all of life and all the terror that comes of knowing death. *Everything a living man can know of death.*

And so I managed in those few hours, frozen and in tears, to skim through all the pages dealing with him. I lost all track of time. Had I spent an hour in the icy library, or was day breaking outside? As I say, I lost all track of time and place. I hastened to put down as much information as possible; I wanted some evidence, for my hours of despair, that my father's life had not been in vain, that there were still people on earth who recorded and accorded value to every life, every affliction, every human existence. (Meager **consolation,**[62] but consolation nonetheless.)

Suddenly, somewhere in the final pages devoted to him, I noticed a flower, one unusual flower, that I first took for a vignette or the schematic drawing of a plant preserved in the world of the dead as an example of extinct flora. The caption, however, indicated that it was the *basic* floral pattern in my father's drawings. My hands trembling, I began to copy it. More than anything it resembled a gigantic peeled and cloven orange, crisscrossed with fine red lines like capillaries. For a moment I was disappointed. I was familiar with all the drawings my father had done in his leisure time on walls, boards, bottles, and boxes, and none was anything like this one. Yes, I

said to myself, even *they* can make a mistake. And then, after copying the gigantic peeled orange into my notebook, I read the concluding paragraph and let out a scream. I awoke drenched in sweat. I immediately wrote down all of the dream I remembered. And this is what remains of it . . .

Do you know what was in the last paragraph? That D.M. took up painting at the time the first symptoms of cancer appeared. And that therefore his obsession with floral patterns coincided with the progress of the disease.

When I showed the drawing to Dr. Petrović, he confirmed, with some surprise, that it looked exactly like the sarcoma in my father's intestine. And that the **efflorescence**[63] had doubtless gone on for years.

---

[62] **consolation**—comfort.
[63] **efflorescence**—blossoming, flowering of a plant.

QUESTIONS TO CONSIDER

1. To whom do you think "The Encyclopedia of the Dead" is being addressed? Explain your reasoning.

2. What does the sea represent to D.M.? What does it represent to the other members of his family?

3. What do the flower paintings and drawings by D.M. seem to mean? What do they represent to the daughter?

4. What is the *Encyclopedia of the Dead* in the story? Who wrote it? What is it a symbol of?

5. What are five contradictions in the story? What do you think Kiš was trying to accomplish with this technique?

Two Poems and a Lecture

SEAMUS HEANEY

Seamus Heaney (1939–   ) is widely regarded as the finest poet writing in English today. With his first book in 1966, Heaney placed himself at the forefront of Irish poetry, and he has moved from strength to strength over the years. His winning the Nobel Prize in 1995 was a widely expected acknowledgment of his achievement. Heaney writes with a lyric grace that is at once beautiful and unexpected. However, as an Irishman, Heaney has had to be more than simply a poet; he has also been a commentator on the war that has raged in Ireland during his whole life. Heaney is a Catholic born in Northern Ireland, the predominately Protestant counties which are not part of Ireland, but still ruled by Great Britain. Since Ireland became an independent state in 1921, a guerrilla war has raged over these counties between the British and the Irish Republican Army (IRA). Over the decades thousands have been killed in a conflict known as the "Troubles." Heaney is often called upon to comment on Ireland and the Troubles.

Whatever You Say, Say Nothing

I

I'm writing this just after an encounter
With an English journalist in search of "views
On the Irish thing." I'm back in winter
Quarters where bad news is no longer news,
Where media-men and stringers[1] sniff and point,
Where zoom lenses, recorders and coiled leads
Litter the hotels. The times are out of joint
But I incline as much to rosary beads

---

[1] stringers—part-time or freelance employees.

As to the **jottings**[2] and analyses
Of politicians and newspapermen
Who've scribbled down the long campaign from gas
And protest to gelignite and Sten,[3]

Who proved upon their pulses "**escalate**,"[4]
"Backlash" and "crack down," "the provisional wing,"[5]
"**Polarization**"[6] and "long-standing hate."
Yet I live here, I live here too, I sing,

Expertly civil-tongued with civil neighbors
On the high wires of first wireless reports,
Sucking the fake taste, the stony flavors
Of those **sanctioned**,[7] old, elaborate **retorts**:[8]

"Oh, it's disgraceful, surely, I agree."
"Where's it going to end?" "It's getting worse."
"They're murderers." "**Internment**,[9] understandably . . ."
The "voice of sanity" is getting **hoarse**.[10]

---

[2] **jottings**—notes.

[3] gelignite and Sten—bomb-making material and a type of machine gun, respectively.

[4] **escalate**—rapidly increase or raise.

[5] **provisional wing**—refers to the part of the IRA that is at war with the British.

[6] **Polarization**—division into two opposing groups.

[7] **sanctioned**—approved or encouraged.

[8] **retorts**—responses or retaliations.

[9] **Internment**—captivity, imprisonment.

[10] **hoarse**—rough, deep, and quiet.

III

"Religion's never mentioned here," of course.
"You know them by their eyes," and hold your tongue.
"One side's as bad as the other," never worse.
Christ, it's near time that some small leak was sprung

In the great dykes[11] the Dutchman made
To dam the dangerous tide that followed Seamus.
Yet for all this art and sedentary trade
I am incapable. The famous

Northern reticence, the tight gag of place
And times: yes, yes. Of the "wee six" I sing
Where to be saved you only must save face
And whatever you say, you say nothing.

Smoke-signals are loud-mouthed compared with us:
Maneuverings to find out name and school,
Subtle discrimination by addresses
With hardly an exception to the rule

That Norman, Ken and Sidney signaled Prod
And Seamus (call me Sean) was sure-fire Pape.[12]
O land of password, handgrip, wink and nod,
Of open minds as open as a trap,

Where tongues lie coiled, as under flames lie wicks,
Where half of us, as in a wooden horse,
Were cabin'd and confined like **wily**[13] Greeks,
Besieged within the siege, whispering morse.[14]

---

[11] dykes—walls built to prevent flooding from the sea.

[12] Prod . . . Pape—shorthand for Protestant and Catholic ("Papist"), the two groups fighting over Northern Ireland.

[13] **wily**—sneaky, clever, or calculating.

[14] morse—code used for transmitting messages.

IV

This morning from a dewy motorway
I saw the new camp for the internees:
A bomb had left a crater of fresh clay
In the roadside, and over in the trees

Machine-gun posts defined a real **stockade.**[15]
There was that white mist you get on a low ground
And it was déjà-vu, some film made
Of Stalag 17,[16] a bad dream with no sound.

Is there a life before death? That's chalked up
In Ballymurphy. Competence with pain,
Coherent miseries, a bite and sup:
We hug our little destiny again.

"Poet's Chair"

for Carolyn Mulholland

Leonardo[17] said: the sun has never
Seen a shadow. Now watch the sculptor move
Full circle round her next work, like a lover
In the sphere of shifting angles and fixed love.

---

[15] **stockade**—military prison.

[16] Stalag 17—a film about a prisoner of war camp in WW II.

[17] *Leonardo*—Leonardo da Vinci (1452–1519) Italian painter, sculptor, scientist, and architect.

I

Angling shadows of itself are what
Your "Poet's Chair" stands to and rises out of
In its sun-stalked inner-city courtyard.
On the *qui vive*[18] all the time, its four legs land
On their feet—cat's-foot, goat-foot, big soft splay-foot too;
Its straight back sprouts two bronze and leafy saplings.
Every flibbertigibbet in the town,
Old birds and boozers, late-night pissers, kissers,
All have a go at sitting on it some time.
It's the way the air behind them's winged and full,
The way a graft has seized their shoulderblades
That makes them happy. Once out of nature,
They're going to come back in leaf and bloom
And angel step. Or something like that. *Leaves*
On a bloody chair! Would you believe it?

II

Next thing I see the chair in a white prison
With Socrates[19] sitting on it, bald as a coot,[20]
Discoursing in bright sunlight with his friends.
His time is short. The day his trial began
A **verdant**[21] boat sailed for Apollo's shrine
In Delos, for the annual rite
Of commemoration. Until its **wreathed**[22]
And creepered rigging re-enters Athens
Harbor, the city's life is holy.

---

[18] *qui vive*—French phrase meaning "watchful" or "alert."

[19] Socrates—Greek philosopher (c. 470–399 B.C.) who was tried and executed by the Athenian government for "introducing new gods" and "corrupting the young."

[20] coot—stupid person.

[21] **verdant**—green, fresh-colored.

[22] **wreathed**—encircled or surrounded.

No executions. No hemlock bowl.[23] No tears
And none now as the poison does its work
And the expert jailer talks the company through
The stages of the numbness. Socrates
At the center of the city and the day
Has proved the soul immortal. The bronze leaves
Cannot believe their ears, it is so silent.
Soon Crito[24] will have to close his eyes and mouth,
But for the moment everything's an ache
Deferred, foreknown, imagined and most real.

III

My father's ploughing one, two, three, four sides
Of the lea ground where I sit all-seeing
At center field, my back to the thorn tree
They never cut. The horses are all hoof
And **burnished**[25] flank, I am all foreknowledge.
Of the poem as a ploughshare[26] that turns time
Up and over. Of the chair in leaf
The fairy thorn is entering for the future.
Of being here for good in every sense.

---

[23] hemlock bowl—Socrates died by drinking hemlock, a poison.

[24] Crito—a friend of Socrates who tried to convince him to escape before his execution. Crito was the last to talk with Socrates.

[25] **burnished**—polished by rubbing.

[26] ploughshare—or plowshare, the cutting blade of a plow.

from Nobel Lecture

When I first encountered the name of the city of Stockholm, I little thought that I would ever visit it, never mind end up being welcomed to it as a guest of the Swedish Academy and the Nobel Foundation. At that particular time, such an outcome was not just beyond expectation: it was simply beyond conception. In the nineteen-forties, when I was the eldest child of an ever-growing family in rural County Derry, we crowded together in the three rooms of a traditional thatched farmstead and lived a kind of den-life which was more or less emotionally and intellectually proofed against the outside world. It was an intimate, physical, creaturely existence in which the night sounds of the horse in the stable beyond one bedroom wall mingled with the sounds of adult conversation from the kitchen beyond the other. We took in everything that was going on, of course—rain in the trees, mice on the ceiling, a steam train rumbling along the railway line one field back from the house—but we took it in as if we were in the doze of hibernation. Ahistorical, pre-sexual, in suspension between the **archaic**[27] and the modern, we were as susceptible and impressionable as the drinking water that stood in a bucket in our scullery:[28] every time a passing train made the earth shake, the surface of that water used to ripple delicately, concentrically, and in utter silence.

But it was not only the earth that shook for us: the air around and above us was alive and signaling also. When a wind stirred in the beeches, it also stirred an aerial wire attached to the topmost branch of the chestnut tree. Down it swept, in through a hole bored in the corner of the kitchen window, right on into the innards of our wireless set where a little pandemonium of burbles and squeaks would suddenly give way to the voice of a BBC newsreader speaking out of the unexpected like a *deus ex machina*.[29] And that voice too we could hear in our bedroom, transmitting from beyond and behind the voices of the adults in the kitchen; just as we could often hear, behind and beyond every voice, the frantic, piercing signaling of Morse code.

We could pick up the names of neighbors being spoken in the local accents of our parents, and in the **resonant**[30] English tones of the newsreader the names of bombers and of cities bombed, of war fronts and army divisions, the numbers of planes lost and of prisoners taken, of casualties suffered and advances made; and always, of course, we would pick up too those other, solemn and oddly bracing words, "the enemy" and "the allies." But even so, none of the news of these world-spasms entered me as terror. If there was some

---

[27] **archaic**—ancient and no longer in widespread use.

[28] scullery—small kitchen or room at the back of the house used for cooking and washing dishes.

[29] *deus ex machina*—an unexpected power or event saving a seemingly hopeless situation.

[30] **resonant**—echoing, resounding.

thing ominous in the newscaster's tones, there was something **torpid**[31] about our understanding of what was at stake; and if there was something culpable about such political ignorance in that time and place, there was something positive about the security I inhabited as a result of it.

The wartime, in other words, was pre-reflective time for me. Pre-literate too. Pre-historical in its way. Then as the years went on and my listening became more deliberate, I would climb up on an arm of our big sofa to get my ear closer to the wireless speaker. But it was still not the news that interested me; what I was after was the thrill of story, such as a detective serial about a British special agent called Dick Barton or perhaps a radio adaptation of one of Capt. W.E. Johns's adventure tales about an RAF[32] flying ace called Biggles. Now that the other children were older and there was so much going on in the kitchen, I had to get close to the actual radio set in order to concentrate my hearing, and in that intent proximity to the dial I grew familiar with the names of foreign stations, with Leipzig and Oslo and Stuttgart and Warsaw and, of course, with Stockholm.[33]

I also got used to hearing short bursts of foreign languages as the dial hand swept round from the BBC to Radio Eireann, from the intonations of London to those of Dublin, and even though I did not understand what was being said in those first encounters with the gutturals[34] and sibilants[35] of European speech, I had already begun a journey into the wideness of the world. This in turn became a journey into the wideness of language, a journey where each point of arrival—whether in one's poetry or one's life—turned out to be a stepping stone rather than a destination, and it is that journey which has brought me now to this honored spot. And yet the platform here feels more like a space station than a stepping stone, so that is why, for once in my life, I am permitting myself the luxury of walking on air.

---

[31] **torpid**—sluggish, inactive, or dull.

[32] RAF—acronym for the Royal Air Force of England.

[33] Leipzig . . . Oslo . . . Stuttgart . . . Warsaw . . . Stockholm—major cities in Germany, Norway, Germany, Poland, and Sweden, respectively.

[34] gutturals—throaty, harsh sounds in a language.

[35] sibilants—hissing sounds in a language.

QUESTIONS TO CONSIDER

1. Where does Heaney seem to stand on the "Troubles" in "Whatever You Say, Say Nothing"?

2. How is a poem a "ploughshare" in "Poet's Chair"? What does Socrates represent in the poem?

3. How would you describe the journey that Heaney made to reach Stockholm and the Nobel Prize? What guided him through his journey?

Four Poems

ÁNGEL GONZÁLEZ

Ángel González (1925–   ) was marked during his youth by the Spanish Civil War when one of his brothers was killed and another sent into exile. The repressive dictatorship of Francisco Franco that followed the war dominated González's Spain until the 1970s, when democracy was established. He became a lawyer and from the 1950s onward, a lyric poet of great reputation. González's poems are a document of life in Spain under Franco, "not in what the words say but in what they imply, in the spaces of shadow, of silence, of anger, or of helplessness that they discover or cover. The existence of a censorship that was ruthless, and also frequently and fortunately inept, forced me at times to have recourse to an ironical and ambiguous language, and even to transfer to a distant objective correlative many of my more immediate and urgent concerns."

Before I Could Call Myself Ángel González

Before I could call myself Ángel González,
before the earth could support the weight of my body,
   a long time
and a great space were necessary:
men from all the seas and all the lands,
fertile[1] wombs of women, and bodies
and more bodies, **incessantly**[2] fusing
into another new body.

---

[1] **fertile**—productive, fruitful.

[2] **incessantly**—continually, repeatedly.

Solstices[3] and equinoxes[4] illuminated
with their changing lights, and **variegated**[5] skies,
the millenary trip of my flesh
as it climbed over centuries and bones.
Of its slow and painful journey,
of its escape to the end, surviving
shipwrecks, anchoring itself
to the last sigh of the dead,
I am only the result, the fruit,
what's left, rotting, among the remains;
what you see here,
is just that:
tenacious[6] trash resisting
its ruin, fighting against wind,
walking streets that go
nowhere. The success
of all failures. The insane
force of dismay . . .

Yesterday

Yesterday was Wednesday all morning.
By afternoon it changed:
it became almost Monday,
sadness invaded hearts
and there was a distinct
panic of movement toward
the trolleys
that take the swimmers down to the river.

---

[3] Solstices—two times during the year when the sun is furthest from the Earth's equator.

[4] equinoxes—times or dates when day and night are equal in length.

[5] **variegated**—marked with patches of different colors.

[6] **tenacious**—unwilling to give up.

At about seven a small plane slowly
crossed the sky, but not even the children
watched it.

       The cold
was unleashed,
someone went outdoors wearing a hat,
yesterday, and the whole day
was like that,
already you see,
how amusing,
yesterday and always yesterday and even now,
strangers
are constantly walking through the streets
or happily indoors snacking on
bread and coffee with cream: what
joy!

Night fell suddenly,
the warm yellow street lamps were lit,
and no one could
impede[7] the final dawn
of today's day,
so similar
and yet
so different in lights and aroma!

For that very same reason,
because everything is just as I told you,
let me tell you
about yesterday, once more
about yesterday: the incomparable
day that no one will ever
see again upon the earth.

---

[7] **impede**—block or prevent.

The Future

But the future is different
from that destiny seen from afar,
magical world, vast sphere
brushed by the long arm of desire,
brilliant ball the eyes dream,
shared dwelling
of hope and deception, dark
land
of illusion and tears
the stars predicted
and the heart awaits
and that is always, always, always distant.

But, I think, the future is also another thing:
a verb tense in motion, in action, in combat,
a searching movement toward life,
keel[8] of the ship that strikes the water
and struggles to open between the waves
the exact breach the rudder[9] commands.

I'm on this line, in this deep
trajectory[10] of agony and battle,
trapped in a tunnel or trench
that with my hands I open, close, or leave,
obeying the heart that orders,
pushes, determines, demands, and searches.

Future of mine . . . ! Distant heart
that dictated it yesterday:
don't be ashamed.
Today is the result of your blood,
pain that I recognize, light that I admit,

---

[8] keel—the timber or steel structure running lengthwise down the underside of a boat.

[9] rudder—a flat piece attached and hinged to a boat or plane that is used for steering.

[10] **trajectory**—flight path.

suffering that I assume,
love that I intend.

But still, nothing is definitive.
Tomorrow I have decided to go ahead
and advance,
tomorrow I am prepared to be content,
tomorrow I will love you, morning
and night,
tomorrow will not be exactly as God wishes.

Tomorrow, gray or luminous, or cold,
that hands shape in the wind,
that fists draw in the air.

Diatribe Against the Dead

The dead are selfish:
they make us cry and don't care,
they stay quiet in the most inconvenient places,
they refuse to walk, we have to carry them
on our backs to the tomb
as if they were children. What a burden!
Unusually rigid, their faces
accuse us of something, or warn us;
they are the bad conscience, the bad example,
they are the worst things in our lives always, always.

The bad thing about the dead
is that there is no way you can kill them.
Their constant destructive labor
is for that reason incalculable.
Insensitive, distant, **obstinate**,[11] cold,
with their **insolence**[12] and their silence
they don't realize what they undo.

---

[11] **obstinate**—stubborn, persistent, single-minded.

[12] **insolence**—disrespect or rudeness.

QUESTIONS TO CONSIDER

1. What is the trait that González says allowed him to survive in "Before I Could Call Myself Ángel González"? Does the poet admire this trait? Explain.

2. In the second poem, why is yesterday "incomparable"? Describe the poet's attitude to the past and present.

3. What does the future represent in "The Future"? Why is the speaker prepared to do all those things in the future?

4. What is the tone of "Diatribe Against the Dead"? What do you think was González's intention in writing it?

5. What do you think poetry represents to Ángel González?

Five Poems

WISLAWA SZYMBORSKA

CZESLAW MILOSZ

Czeslaw Milosz (1911–   ) and Wislawa Szymborska (1923–   ) are both Polish poets who won the Nobel Prize for literature—Milosz in 1980 and Szymborska in 1997. Milosz began writing poetry in the 1930s, and was active in the resistance to the Germans during World War II. In 1951, he fled Poland, horrified by the excesses of the Communist regime that took over after the war. In exile, Milosz's poetry came to be dominated by the themes of memory and the irony of life. Szymborska's poetry focuses on the individual and the singular. She began writing after the war and has explored the ironies of life in Poland under Communism, generally avoiding overt political statements. She is immensely popular in Poland for the wit and humor of her poems.

Some People Like Poetry

WISLAWA SZYMBORSKA

Some people—
that means not everyone.
Not even most of them, only a few.
Not counting school, where you have to,
and poets themselves,
you might end up with something like two per
     thousand.

Like—
but then, you can like chicken noodle soup,
or compliments, or the color blue,
your old scarf,
your own way,
petting the dog.

Poetry—
but what is poetry anyway?
More than one **rickety**[1] answer
has tumbled since that question first was raised.
But I just keep on not knowing, and I cling to that
like a redemptive[2] handrail.

A Contribution to Statistics

WISLAWA SZYMBORSKA

Out of a hundred people

those who always know better
—fifty-two,

doubting every step
—nearly all the rest,

glad to lend a hand
if it doesn't take too long
—as high as forty-nine,
always good
because they can't be otherwise
—four, well maybe five,

---

[1] **rickety**—built so as to be unsteady or flimsy.

[2] redemptive—helping, freeing.

able to admire without envy
—eighteen,

suffering illusions
induced by fleeting youth
—sixty, give or take a few,

not to be taken lightly
—forty and four,

living in constant fear
of someone or something
—seventy-seven,

capable of happiness
—twenty-something tops,

harmless singly,
savage in crowds
—half at least,

cruel
when forced by circumstances
—better not to know even **ballpark**[3] figures,

wise after the fact
—just a couple more
than wise before it,

taking only things from life
—thirty
(I wish I were wrong),

---

[3] **ballpark**—rough estimate.

hunched in pain,
no flashlight in the dark
—eighty-three
sooner or later,

righteous
—thirty-five, which is a lot,

righteous
and understanding
—three,

worthy of compassion
—ninety-nine,

mortal
—a hundred out of a hundred.
Thus far this figure still remains unchanged.

Ars Poetica?[4]

CZESLAW MILOSZ

I have always aspired to a more spacious form
that would be free from the claims of poetry or prose
and would let us understand each other without exposing
the author or reader to **sublime**[5] agonies.

In the very essence of poetry there is something indecent:
a thing is brought forth which we didn't know we had in us,
so we blink our eyes, as if a tiger had sprung out
and stood in the light, lashing his tail.

That's why poetry is rightly said to be dictated by a daimonion,[6]
though it's an exaggeration to maintain that he must be an angel.
It's hard to guess where that pride of poets comes from,
when so often they're put to shame by the disclosure of their **frailty.**[7]

What reasonable man would like to be a city of demons,
who behave as if they were at home, speak in many tongues,
and who, not satisfied with stealing his lips or hand,
work at changing his destiny for their convenience?

It's true that what is **morbid**[8] is highly valued today,
and so you may think that I am only joking
or that I've devised just one more means
of praising Art with the help of irony.

There was a time when only wise books were read,
helping us to bear our pain and misery.
This, after all, is not quite the same
as leafing through a thousand works fresh from psychiatric clinics.

---

[4] **Ars Poetica**—Latin for the "art of poetry."

[5] **sublime**—of the most lofty, grand, or noble kind.

[6] daimonion—demon.

[7] **frailty**—weakness, fragility.

[8] **morbid**—sickly, unwholesome, or grim.

And yet the world is different from what it seems to be
and we are other than how we see ourselves in our ravings.
People therefore preserve silent integrity,
thus earning the respect of their relatives and neighbors.

The purpose of poetry is to remind us
how difficult it is to remain just one person,
for our house is open, there are no keys in the doors,
and invisible guests come in and out at will.

What I'm saying here is not, I agree, poetry,
as poems should be written rarely and reluctantly,
under unbearable **duress**[9] and only with the hope
that good spirits, not evil ones, choose us for their instrument.

Return to Kraków in 1880

CZESLAW MILOSZ

So I returned here from the big capitals,
To a town in a narrow valley under the cathedral hill
With royal tombs. To a square under the tower
And the shrill trumpet sounding noon, breaking
Its note in half because the Tartar[10] arrow
Has once again struck the trumpeter.
And pigeons. And the garish kerchiefs of women selling flowers.
And groups chattering under the Gothic portico of the church.
My trunk of books arrived, this time for good.
What I know of my laborious life: it was lived.
Faces are paler in memory than on daguerreotypes.[11]
I don't need to write memos and letters every morning.
Others will take over, always with the same hope,
The one we know is senseless and devote our lives to.

---

[9] **duress**—threat or pressure.
[10] Tartar—another name for the Mongol warriors who conquered Asia and eastern Europe during the Middle Ages.
[11] daguerrotypes—early photographs.

My country will remain what it is, the backyard of empires,
Nursing its humiliation with provincial daydreams.
I leave for a morning walk tapping with my cane:
The places of old people are taken by new old people
And where the girls once strolled in their rustling skirts,
New ones are strolling, proud of their beauty.
And children trundle hoops for more than half a century.
In a basement a cobbler looks up from his bench,
A hunchback passes by with his inner **lament,**[12]
Then a fashionable lady, a fat image of the deadly sins.
So the Earth endures, in every petty matter
And in the lives of men, irreversible.
And it seems a relief. To win? To lose?
What for, if the world will forget us anyway.

Account

CZESLAW MILOSZ

The history of my stupidity would fill many volumes.

Some would be devoted to acting against consciousness,
Like the flight of a moth which, had it known,
Would have tended nevertheless toward the candle's flame.

Others would deal with ways to silence anxiety,
The little whisper which, though it is a warning, is ignored.

---

[12] **lament**—a passionate expression of grief or sadness.

I would deal separately with satisfaction and pride,
The time when I was among their adherents
Who strut victoriously, unsuspecting.

But all of them would have one subject, desire,
If only my own—but no, not at all; alas,
I was driven because I wanted to be like others.
I was afraid of what was wild and **indecent**[13] in me.

The history of my stupidity will not be written.
For one thing, it's late. And the truth is laborious.

---

[13] **indecent**—shockingly offensive.

QUESTIONS TO CONSIDER

1. In "Some People like Poetry," what things does Szymborska liken poetry to? Why does she care for it?

2. How would you describe the view of life presented in "A Contribution to Statistics"?

3. How would you describe Milosz's attitude toward poetry in "Ars Poetica?"?

4. What of the past and present is Milosz comparing in "Return to Kraków in 1880"? What is the message of the poem?

5. What does Milosz mean by his "stupidity" in "Account"?

6. How would you compare and contrast Szymborska's and Milosz's ideas about poetry?

L'viv / Lvov / Lwów

ANNE APPLEBAUM

L'viv is one of the major cities of Ukraine. Located in the western part of the country, it has traditionally been the center of the national movement, which since the mid-nineteenth century agitated for an independent Ukrainian nation. Ukrainians had been variously ruled by Poles, Russians, and Austrians for centuries. With the collapse of the Soviet Union in 1989, the Ukrainians got their wish, becoming a nation in 1991. Anne Applebaum is a journalist who has spent much of her career covering the changes that occurred in eastern Europe after the collapse of Communism in 1989. Applebaum traveled through the regions that were ruled by the Soviet Union but are not part of Russia, and wrote a book describing the changes in these places she refers to as the "borderlands." The following essay is her description of L'viv in newly independent Ukraine.

Let others go travel where they can, where
    they want,
To Venice, to Paris, to London,
But I, from Lwów, will never leave home,
Mother, may God punish me if I do!

For where do people live, as well as they
    live here?
Only in Lwów!
For where do songs wake you and send you
    to sleep?
Only in Lwów. . . .

              —Polish folk song

On the road going south to L'viv, I stopped in Kovel and bought sweet black grapes from a Georgian[1] trader. His face was darkened by a swarm of bees. Rhythmically, he swatted them away with his purple-stained hand, as if he were keeping time to music.

No guards or gates marked the border between Belarus[2] and Ukraine,[3] but the roads began to improve when we crossed from lands that had been ruled by Russia

---

[1] Georgian—of or from Georgia, a country on the Black Sea that used to be a part of the Soviet Union.

[2] Belarus—an independent country that used to be the Soviet province of Byelorussia, just east of Poland.

[3] Ukraine—an independent country that used to be part of the Soviet Union.

in the nineteenth century into Galicia,[4] which was under Austro-Hungarian rule[5] at the same time. The old border between Russia and Galicia had been out of use since Poland was reconstituted in 1918, and out of memory since the whole region had finally fallen to the Soviet Union in 1945. But it was easier to see than the new border between independent Belarus and independent Ukraine, which was still unmarked. As the bus rumbled on, the trees grew taller, the fields broader, the houses sturdier. Austro-Hungary had managed its land better than Russia, and it still showed.

Austro-Hungary had also left a different architectural legacy. Entering L'viv—Lvov, Lwów, Lemberg, (it meant "lion's mountain")—was like returning to civilization. The concrete grays and muddy browns of Belarus were gone, replaced by the white of marble steps, the bright yellow of churches, the red brick of libraries and museums. Oil street lamps glowed brown in the evening, casting chocolate shadows across the cobbled streets. The opera house ruled over the city like a dowager who has lived in a grander era and tolerates—but just barely—the indignities of the present.

Austro-Hungary: it had been a mixed bag of nations held together by the silken bands of **custom**,[6] the portrait of the emperor, sturdy houses, and squat churches with golden altars. In their time, the Habsburgs were thought oppressive. Yet they are the only rulers of western Ukraine who still inspire nostalgia. The Poles are remembered as petty[7] dictators, the Russians as tyrants, but in L'viv the

Habsburg era is still recalled with fondness. Perhaps that is because the Habsburgs encouraged Ukrainian national ambitions; attempting to weaken Polish influence in the region, they encouraged Ukrainian political parties, Ukrainian parliamentary deputies, Ukrainian newspapers. Perhaps it is also because, in retrospect, the Habsburg empire no longer seems terribly serious. Whatever territorial ambitions the Habsburgs once had no longer matter, whatever cruelties the empire inflicted on its subject nations look mild in the light of what came afterward. Austro-Hungary was never to blame for the horrors of the Second World War or its aftermath. Compared to Soviet rule, the Habsburg legacy in Galicia seems benign.

But there were many other national legacies to be found in L'viv. On my first trip to the city, in the long-ago days of Brezhnev[8] and the stable ruble,[9] time and weather had prevented me from seeing much of L'viv, aside from the cemetery. Now, in the strong autumn sunlight, I could see that the past—the Habsburg past, the Polish past—was still very much in evidence. The past was there in the German names engraved on the sewer lids,

---

[4] Galicia—region in central Europe now divided between Poland and Ukraine.

[5] Austro-Hungarian rule—central European monarchy that ruled over vast territories from 1867–1918. Its capital was Vienna.

[6] **custom**—the usual way of behaving or acting.

[7] petty—mean, small-minded.

[8] Brezhnev—Leonid Brezhnev (1906–1982) leader of the Soviet Union from 1964–1982.

[9] ruble—the currency of Russia.

in the faded-out paint on the old Polish bank, in the cracked windows of the synagogue, in the Italian glaze on the tiles in the courtyards of the big family houses, in the chipped gilt on the altars in the churches. The past was there in the city's central park, where men in brown suits and felt hats sat on benches beneath the tall trees and talked to one another in low voices, sometimes stopping to watch the games of chess that were played in the park all day and all night, too, when the weather was good. The past was there in L'viv's old market square, in the baroque houses, blackened with age, which gazed scornfully at the unimaginative town hall, a nineteenth-century upstart which stood in the center. The lion of St. Mark was carved over the entrance to number fourteen, the old Venetian consulate. Number six had once been the property of King Jan Sobieski, who defeated the Turks at Vienna and saved Christendom from the infidel. Another king, the ineffectual Michal Wisniowiecki, died in number nine.

In the cathedral, plaques and marble vases dedicated themselves to Hoffmans and Tarnowskis. Colored tiles, laid out in the pattern of an Oriental carpet, covered the floor and the walls of the nave. On one tomb, a man dressed as a Polish nobleman (Turkish trousers, blouse, cape, and saber) slept on a stone pillow with a stone hourglass by his side. On another, an armored knight lay with his helmeted head on his hand. *Trompe l'oeil*[10] flowers lined the pillars, light streamed through the windows. Outside and around the corner stood a

private chapel, built in the seventeenth century because the cathedral had already run out of space for all the rich men wanting to erect eternal monuments there. Amber panels lined the walls, and a relief of the Last Supper showed Jesus breaking bread in a L'viv drawing room. The inscription dedicated the building to "George Boym E Pannonia," a wealthy Hungarian merchant. Just nearby, sunlight spilled onto the gravestones in the courtyard of the Armenian church. The spidery script shone dark against the white stone, like a secret code suddenly revealed.

The past was to be found even in my hotel, which was quite different from the Intourist[11] monstrosities I had found in most Soviet cities. Built by an Englishman at the turn of the century and named for St. George, the hotel held traces of his taste. My room had high ceilings, French windows, a threadbare Persian rug, and a wash basin that bore the inscription "Manchester, 1903." Brass signs hung over the doors to the public washrooms: "Gentlemens Toilet" and "Ladies Room." The central staircase was **festooned**[12] with cracked mirrors and Greek columns, and it smelled faintly of sewage. A slovenly maid sat at the top and wrote something down in a little black book whenever anyone came in or out. That was Soviet, but it was Habsburg, too.

---

[10] *Trompe l'oeil*—painted to look real.

[11] Intourist—the official tourist agency of the Soviet Union.

[12] **festooned**—decorated with a chain of flowers, leaves, or ribbons.

It thrilled me at first, this evidence of a lost civilization, the way the evidence of the past had thrilled me in Vilnius and the lands around Nowogródek.[13] But after a while I began to be wary of it. L'viv was part of the borderlands, and the same historical breaks, the same mass murders, the same shuffling of peoples back and forth across borders had affected the city like all other borderland cities. Although the preservation of the old architecture meant that one didn't, at first, feel the lack of continuity so much, the city's lazy grace was deceptive. When a **mollusk**[14] dies, the shell remains, beautiful but empty of life. It can be inhabited only by a different animal, one that knows nothing of the former owner; perhaps L'viv was like that.

While the city's past might have been many things—Polish, Habsburg, or just simply borderland—its present was Ukrainian. There were Ukrainian faces on the buses in the morning, Ukrainian signs on the shops. Ukrainian had not been the city's main language before the war—it fell third, behind Polish and Yiddish—but Ukrainian was the city's main language now. As I walked around the city, half imagining the past, half seeing the present, I tried hard to listen to the sounds that the new Ukraine was making.

"SKANDAL!" screamed the newspapers.

"You've heard about our scandal?" asked my Polish friends Irena and Wladek.

"You ought to be writing about our scandal," a local politician told me, almost proudly. "Our scandal is the biggest in Ukraine."

Over lunch in the restaurant of the Grand Hotel—a few hundred yards and several generations away from the George—Marta told me her side of the story. The restaurant was new: the walls were freshly painted, the tablecloths were clean and white, the cups and saucers were free of cracks and chips. It was also empty, and our waiter tiptoed fearfully up and down the dining hall like a guest who fears himself to be unwelcome. When Marta asked him to recite the wine list he **stuttered,**[15] and forgot which were red and which were white.

"Bulgarian red," she said crisply, not waiting for him to finish, and handed the menu back.

"You cannot imagine," she said, turning to me, "what it took to rebuild this place. To train these people. And see how much farther we have to go!" She shook her head vigorously. Not a strand of blond hair moved out of place. Her hair, like her long red nails, had been lacquered to perfection.

Marta had been born just after the war, in a displaced persons' camp near L'viv.

> *While the city's past might have been many things—Polish, Habsburg, or just simply borderland—its present was Ukrainian.*

---

[13] Vilnius . . . Nowogródek—the capital of Lithuania and city in Russia, respectively.

[14] **mollusk**—an animal with a soft body and usually a hard shell like a snail, an oyster, or a mussel.

[15] **stuttered**—spoke haltingly, often repeating syllables or sounds within words.

Almost immediately afterward, her family had made its way to America, like so many others. Those of the post-war Ukrainian **diaspora**[16] were a special breed: unlike those who crossed the Atlantic earlier, they had more recent memories of an almost-free Ukraine, they had more optimism, they had fought in guerrilla bands against the Red Army.[17] Abroad, in America and Canada, they flourished, speaking their language, building their churches, and publishing little magazines full of nostalgic poetry and angry prose—preserving a version of Ukrainian history different from the one taught in the Soviet Union. Marta had grown up surrounded by the songs and legends of a country she had never known, and she had always dreamed of going back. She had worked, she said, as a Ukrainian-American travel agent, leading tours of Ukrainian-Americans back to places like L'viv. "Small-time stuff," she said, wiping an invisible speck of dust from her impeccable white suit. But in 1989, when things began to change, she began to think of bigger projects, bigger goals. At about that time, a man called Gennady Genschaft drifted into Marta's field of vision.

Genschaft seemed to have connections. He understood the confusing world of hard currency regulations, permission slips, and disappearing telex reservations that riddled the Soviet tourist bureaucracy. He seemed able to procure hotel rooms, to reserve buses, to arrange catered meals. If I can't do it, he told Marta, nobody can. Feeling more confident about Ukraine,

Marta began to make plans. "I said to myself, my children are grown up. I have a nice house. I have a comfortable life. I've achieved most of what I wanted in life. Why not do something for other people now? Why not do something for Ukraine?"

The waiter, his hands shaking ever so slightly, brought us two bowls of bright pink borscht. He laid them carefully on the table, turned, and walked away, clutching the two spoons he had forgotten to give us.

"This hotel," Marta told me, "it was not going to be just any old investment." Western Ukraine might have been defeated, but now the rebuilding could begin. What L'viv needed, Marta told herself, was one hotel, one beautiful hotel, one hotel that businessmen and tourists could stay in, one hotel that would lift the city's profile and make it a place that people would want to visit.

It was important that L'viv recover its glory, Marta said. L'viv had played a special role in the Ukrainian independence movement. Post-Soviet Ukrainian nationalism had not been born in Kiev,[18] after all, but in the West, the lands that were Polish before the war and Austro-Hungarian before that. In the late 1980s, when *glasnost*[19] began, it was western Ukraine that began to encourage a free press, and it was western Ukraine that

---

[16] **diaspora**—people who have been scattered or who have spread geographically.

[17] Red Army—the Soviet army.

[18] Kiev—the capital of the Ukraine.

[19] *glasnost*—a policy of cultural and social openness which was adopted in the Soviet Union in late 1980s.

elected former dissidents as parliamentary deputies and nationalist local governments.

The blue and yellow Ukrainian flag appeared in West Ukrainian villages long before it appeared in the East, and politicians from western Ukraine were always the most fervent advocates of independence. L'viv was the capital of western Ukraine, and it was here, in L'viv, that Marta wanted her hotel to be. Together with Genschaft, she drew up a plan. Marta would be the director; he would be the main partner; and Halych, Inc., their new company, would restore the old Grand Hotel in the center of L'viv, just across from the opera house.

Work began. Marta gave Genschaft a notarized letter permitting him to carry out company transactions in her name. Marta paid Genschaft a salary. Every month she came to examine the hotel's progress, while Genschaft arranged for stonemasons and carpenters, paint and carpets, chandeliers and furniture. Genschaft made sure that the cornices on the ceilings and the plaster around the doorways were completed correctly, that the parquet floors were restored; Genschaft arranged for the roof to be covered with old-fashioned tile. By the time it was finished, the Grand Hotel was a small miracle. Each of its rooms had new furniture, new fixtures, and satellite television. Downstairs, the hotel had a restaurant, a bar, a conference room. It had clear running water, its own generator in case of power cuts. Nothing like it could be found anywhere else in Ukraine, Marta's Ukrainian-American tour groups marveled.

The waiter returned with the spoons. "Sorry, sorry," he kept mumbling. Marta, intent on telling her story, ignored him. He slipped the spoons beneath the soup bowls and **scuttled**[20] away.

"People tell me it is a wonderful thing I have done for Ukraine," she said.

After a few months, Genschaft told Marta that the company really ought to form a joint venture: joint ventures were tax-free for five years. She agreed to write a letter to the mayor of L'viv, asking permission to form the joint venture, but she did not make formal application. Nevertheless, when she next returned, she discovered that the joint venture had been founded: Genschaft had become the majority shareholder.

"My signature appears on the documents," she told me. "My signature appears, and I wasn't even there!"

Marta began eating her borscht. Just then, the waiter appeared with the second course: boiled chicken and rice. "Put it over here," she told him, gesturing toward the next table, which was empty like all the others.

In the meantime, she said, Genschaft had received political asylum in America.

"Political asylum?"

"Yes, yes." Marta pushed her soup bowl to one side. "He is—you know—Jewish. They get permission to **emigrate**.[21] His family are in America."

---

[20] **scuttled**—hurried.
[21] **emigrate**—to leave one's own country and settle in another.

There was no point in arguing with Genschaft in L'viv if he was in America, so Marta took a copy of the joint venture **statute**[22] back to America. There, a Ukrainian-American attorney told her that the document might be invalid. Marta called Genschaft in Philadelphia and arranged to meet him. He failed to appear. Instead, he flew back to L'viv—and Marta followed him.

When she arrived, she found Genschaft sitting in the director's office of the hotel. She tried to lock him out; he broke the lock. She shouted lawsuits. "Go ahead," he told her, "let us see which one of us will win a lawsuit in this city." Marta went to the mayor, screaming corruption, newspapers, the American embassy, the Ukrainian-American community.

The mayor shouted back. Why was she in business with Genschaft anyway? Marta, the mayor said, had told everyone in the city that Halych, Inc., was an American company. And here was this Russian Jew, running everything!

Marta looked up from her chicken. "If everyone thought it was a bad idea to do business with Genschaft, why had no one told me?"

Calming down, the mayor agreed to do what he could to stop Genschaft from taking control of the hotel. He **annulled**[23] the joint venture for thirty days and held an investigation. Genschaft offered Marta $300,000 to leave. She refused. Or, he said, she could pay him $900,000 to leave. She refused again.

"Nobody," said Marta, "nobody can buy me off. I am not here just to make money. I am here to create a legitimate Ukrainian business. I want this hotel to be honest. I want people to do things the right way here, the American way. Ukrainians also want to be honest. They are tired of corruption, tired of being cheated. Ask the staff. The staff are praying that I will not leave. "

Marta grabbed the waiter, who had come back to refill the wine.

"Are you happy working here?"

The waiter looked confused. Marta repeated the question, in Ukrainian. The waiter broke into a confused smile.

"Yes, yes, happy," he said.

She turned back to me. "Then, the final straw: last week, Genschaft was arrested for kidnapping the son of the mayor. He and his friends held him for several hours, trying to force the mayor to change his mind."

She looked up. "The law must triumph. I will see to it. The law must be enforced."

I went to see Genschaft. He was **ensconced**[24] in the director's office in the back of the hotel, and he winced at the sound of Marta's name.

"Crazy lady," he said in Russian. "Crazy lady. She tried to lock me out of my own office."

Genschaft was a handsome man, well coiffed, well fed, and sleek like a prize stallion. He wore a gold watch and a gold

---

[22] **statute**—a written law.

[23] **annulled**—voided or nullified.

[24] **ensconced**—comfortably, safely, or secretly settled.

bracelet, a cashmere sweater, and neat gray flannel trousers. I looked at his feet and saw that he wore fine leather shoes, the first I had seen anyone wear in the former Soviet Union.

"Sit, sit," he said. "What can I get you? Coffee? Tea? Brandy? Whiskey? I have some Armenian cognac, if you would like."

"Tea," I said. He looked disappointed, but he pressed a button under the table. A girl in uniform, one of the waitresses from the hotel restaurant, opened the door and stuck her head around it.

"Two teas," Genschaft commanded, and I heard her scuttle back down the hallway. He turned to me.

"You see," he said, "Marta has put money into this hotel. She helped to start it. But whose idea was this in the first place? Mine. Whose connections got us the lease? Mine. Who found the wood, the tile, the carpets, the furniture? I did. You think you can just walk into a shop and buy things like that in this country? No. You have to barter. You have to know people. You have to know how to get things done."

The girl came back with the tea. Genschaft poured two large spoonsful of sugar into his and waved his arm around the office. "I built this hotel. Without me, this hotel would not exist."

The joint venture was perfectly legal, he claimed: he had done nothing wrong. Marta had given him a notary act, permitting him to sign contracts in her name. Marta had even given him blank sheets of paper with her signature at the bottom. The only reason she was protesting now, said Genschaft, was because Marta had wanted more profits for herself. "She is like a child who has done something wrong and wants to take it all back. She has made a mistake and wants to start all over again. And now she will organize the government against us."

I asked Genschaft about his American citizenship. How had it been possible to emigrate and then to return so quickly? I had thought it was illegal for someone who had been granted political asylum to return to his or her country of origin so quickly without losing the right to return to America.

He waved the question away. "I received permission to emigrate from the Soviet Union, where I was persecuted for being Jewish. Now I have returned to Ukraine, which is a different country— so, you see, I have not come back to the same place. . . ."

His voice trailed off. I looked at him, feeling sorry for all of the authentically oppressed people in the world who are unable to get visas to America. Genschaft must have guessed my thoughts. He leaned forward:

"You realize, of course, that Marta and all of her people have turned on me because I am Jewish and because I speak Russian. They think they can turn popular sentiment against me. Ukraine for the Ukrainians, they say, but it is all nonsense: these Ukrainian nationalists are simply angry that people more clever than themselves are making money in this city, and they want to stop us from doing it."

Marta's nationalism had infected the local government, he said, bringing them around to her side. "The mayor has frozen the bank accounts of my hotel, but the mayor refuses to see me. What can I do? I call him, he refused to speak. I write to him, he fails to write back. Last week, we brought his son, Nazar, in here to help. Nazar works for a friend of mine: Levon Enokyan, a wonderful businessman, by the way, you ought to meet him. Anyway, Levon and I sat Nazar at this table, gave him a little brandy, made a telephone call to his father. Next thing we knew, the police had arrived. Next thing we know, they are accusing us of kidnap!"

Genschaft's eyes narrowed when he spoke of the mayor and his cohorts. "Those little people," he said. "All they can do is shout slogans, they've never run a business, they've never managed companies. They are incompetent. They know nothing. They should leave the conduct of business to those of us who know about business. People who have spent their lives in Siberian camps should not be running governments. And if they break their own laws to give the hotel back to Marta—they will be sorry."

Quite unexpectedly, Genschaft smiled.

"*Miami Vice* that is my dream," sighed Iaroslav.

Iaroslav was a crime reporter for a L'viv newspaper. He knew all of the L'viv mafia, and many of them knew him. Many thought, even, that he was one of them. "They tip me off when they know there is going to be a crime carried out by a rival group, they want me to spill the beans to the police."

Iaroslav knew a different L'viv from the one I knew, and he showed me a new set of sights. He took me first to see a strip of dirty sidewalk near the monument to Adam Mickiewicz.[25] A group of men in windbreakers and imitation Adidas **loitered**[26] there, leaning against street benches. Every so often, one would approach another, whisper something or exchange something, and then drift away. It was the criminal exchange, very different from the commercial exchanges that took place in the park near the opera.

"An assassination can be arranged here for fifty dollars," he explained. "And a theft can be arranged for thirty. But most of these people are just arranging exchanges of goods that are illegal to export." These included quite **mundane**[27] things—wood, for example, and roof tiles—as well as oil, precious metals, and a mysterious substance called red mercury, which was, he claimed, criminal slang for plutonium.[28] Shipments of illegal goods were driven around Ukraine in ten-car convoys protected with automatic weapons.

---

[25] Mickiewicz—Adam Mickiewicz (1798–1855) national poet of Poland.

[26] **loitered**—hung around, lingered.

[27] **mundane**—dull, ordinary.

[28] plutonium—a radioactive element that is the source of energy for nuclear weapons and reactors.

Iaroslav also walked me through what would have been a prewar suburb, a neighborhood filled with squarish, plastered houses, a style the Polish middle classes had once loved; it reminded me of the prewar Warsaw suburbs. We passed one house surrounded by a high wire fence; a German shepherd on a long chain was tethered in front. That, Iaroslav explained, was the home of Levon Enokyan, chairman of LV Holding, L'viv's biggest company.

"You know him?"

"I don't know him yet," I said.

Iaroslav was an admirer. "He is the best businessman in the city, the only Armenian who has really made it here."

We stood outside the gate, listening to the dog bark. After a while, a man in dark glasses appeared on the doorstep and slowly began walking in our direction.

"Let's go," said Iaroslav. "It's a security guard." We walked quickly away, passing a blond woman driving a new Mercedes.

"His second wife," said Iaroslav.

On the way back into town, Iaroslav told me that he had been invited to a party that LV Holding gave to mark its first year in business. The city, he said, had seen nothing like it before. Perhaps people did these sorts of things in Moscow, but not in L'viv.

"They got all of these people from Moscow—oh, rock stars, a famous Russian footballer, an Olympic athlete—and they flew them down here on a *private plane*."

A private plane, in the former Soviet Union, is an almost unheard-of luxury. "Then they brought them from the airport on a *private bus*."

Ownership of a private bus is almost as great a privilege.

"They served caviar, sturgeon, plates of ham and cheese, different kinds of wine—more food than anyone here had ever seen. All of the city government were invited—the mayor, the presidential representative, the city councilors. I could see them sitting there, speaking Ukrainian among themselves, watching the Russian performers from Moscow, growing more and more jealous: it was obvious that LV Holding has more power than all of them put together."

The conversation turned back to crime, criminals, and criminal reporters. "Maybe Sicily," said Iaroslav. "Maybe Sicily would have more interesting stories than those I have to write here."

In his wood-paneled office on the top floor of what used to be the Galician Senate, Ivan Hel, one of L'viv's city councilors, tried to speak first in Polish, then in Russian. He was a stern, strong man, with wide shoulders, a white beard, long white hair, and deathless eyes shaded by white eyebrows. The thick cross he wore around his neck hung all the way down to his large stomach. He was an imposing figure, and yet his face lost something of its granite security as he stumbled and slipped in the languages of Ukraine's former rulers. Finally he gave up.

"You'll just have to listen carefully. It's so close to Polish." And as he switched to Ukrainian—Galician Ukrainian—his voice became clearer and his dignity returned. Every so often, when I failed to understand something, his assistant gently intervened.

Ivan Hel's father had been born blind, but the Virgin Mary of Calvaria restored his sight at age three. The miracle had touched Hel, too: during his term in the Soviet Army, he wore his father's crucifix beneath his uniform. The crucifix could have been discovered in that godless place, but the Virgin preserved him, prevented anyone from noticing.

Afterward, Hel resolved to work for her and for Ukraine, her stepchild, and never to remove the sign of her grace. So the crucifix followed him into basement rooms where the secret printing presses were kept; into the police stations where Russian officers hurled abuse; into the meetings beside Shevchenko's[29] grave, where the Ukrainian national movement was born. The crucifix followed him into Brezhnev's labor camps after a wave of arrests sent most of Ukraine's intelligentsia[30] to Siberia. Finally, the crucifix had followed him into free elections: the Virgin had given Ukraine back to the Ukrainians, and Hel was proud to say that West Ukraine, and L'viv in particular, had led the way from the beginning.

The story of Marta and the Grand Hotel made him sad, very sad, however. It showed how immature Ukraine still was, how she was still not a real nation.

"When Moses took the Israelites out of Egypt, he made them wander for forty years in the desert in order to lose their slave mentality. Generations passed before men felt themselves free again. We also need generations before we will feel ourselves free men," he explained.

For Ukraine to grow up, the nation's leaders had to undertake a program of Ukrainianization, Hel explained. Children needed to be taught Ukrainian history, Ukrainians had to be promoted to high government positions, Ukrainian literature had to be read and celebrated.

It sounded, I said, like the *korenizatsiia*[31] of the 1920s, when the Soviet Union sponsored similar programs.

"No, no," said Hel vigorously, "this is totally different." The new wave of Ukrainianization was also to have an economic component. Institutions had to be created: a central bank, a post office, a diplomatic service, an army. Trade with Russia had to be directed elsewhere. Factories and state enterprises were to be Ukrainianized along with schools and universities. They would have to learn to buy all of their raw materials from Ukraine, not Russia; they would have to learn to sell their products to Ukraine, not Russia.

---

[29] Shevchenko—Taras Shevchenko (1814–1861) Ukrainian poet and nationalist. He is one of the Ukraine's greatest national heroes.

[30] intelligentsia—intellectuals, a class of people thought to have cultural and political initiative.

[31] korenziatsiia—"return to the roots," Soviet policy of encouraging the ethnic cultures of the various regions within the Soviet Union.

I told him that many factories in America buy their raw materials in other countries and sell their products in other countries.

"But that is all very well for America. You have already had your forty years in the desert."

Fighting the mafia was also part of Ukrainianization, Hel explained. A good, clean Ukrainian state could not tolerate these criminals who had sprung up, apparently from nowhere, during the Soviet Union's last few years of life: "When there are new structures and bad laws, these people rise to the surface. This is a very dangerous time for us. We must prevent these kinds of people from gaining power."

But these semicorrupt businessmen were the only businessmen around. I put it to Hel that stopping them meant stopping free enterprise altogether. He disagreed, rather violently.

"Free enterprise? These people do not even have the interests of the Ukrainian state at heart. They were not," he said, lowering his voice, "even Ukrainians. Everyone knew that the mafia were Russians and Jewish."

Hel clasped his hands together.

"The old KGB[32] and the mafia, they are bound together like this . . . And they are all controlled by Moscow. They will sell us to Russia again if we are not careful. They will bind our economy to the Russian economy and corrupt our state if we do not stop them."

As I walked out of Hel's office, a man approached me, very agitated.

"You know the Reuters correspondent?" he asked me.

"What?"

"The Reuters correspondent," and he mentioned a name. "I heard you tell the mayor's secretary that you are a journalist, so I thought you might know him. He is in Moscow, he came here and left a tape recorder. I want to give it back to him."

I looked at the man, and he glanced away from me.

"A tape recorder?"

"Yes," he said quickly, and then changed the subject. "I see you were talking to Mr. Hel."

"I was.

"You are wasting your time. Mr. Hel cannot help you. He knows nothing about this city. If you want to know about this city, you should talk to important people, important businessmen. In fact, you should meet the leader of my company"—his voice dropped to a whisper—"Levon Enokyan. He is the chief Armenian businessman in L'viv."

I said I would be very interested to meet Mr. Enokyan. "But how did you happen to be standing here just now?" I asked him.

Momentarily, he seemed startled by the question, but then he waved it away. "I am trying to get an export

---

[32] KGB—the intelligence service of the Soviet State.

permit," he explained. "These people— these amateurs—they change the rules every week, it is impossible for business. Last week I had an export license, this week they took it away. Now I must reapply."

I thanked him and took down his telephone number. Later I told Iaroslav about it, and he laughed.

"Aha," he said. "They are on to you. They think you might have influence, they think you will write their side of the story. But don't worry—they would never hurt a foreigner. They will never hurt Marta, they will never hurt you. They know it would bring in police from Moscow or Kiev, you see, instead of just the locals whom they can bribe."

I drove to LV Holding in the back of a white Mercedes. The driver, who had picked me up in the city center, kept apologizing for being late.

"We like to treat Levon's friends the right way," he explained.

From the outside, the company head- quarters were not impressive. The offices were on the fourth floor of a shabby office block, on the outskirts of L'viv. But there was a reason: all city property still had to be rented from the city government. Given that LV Holding was not in favor with the city government, this office block was the best they could do.

Inside, one felt immediately how the company differed from a Soviet state enterprise. No less than three clean-shaven thugs in neckties were waiting at the door to search my bag. "Security," one of them mumbled. If they went to the trouble, one had to assume that there was something to protect. A woman wearing what appeared to be a white tennis dress led me down narrow hallways past people running to make their next appointment, and into an anteroom where the telephones never stopped ringing. The bored secretaries, underemployed clerks, and clean desks that marked the offices of a Soviet state enterprise were nowhere to be seen. A man walked in, looked me up and down, and extended his hand.

"Averkov," he said briskly.

"Ania," I replied. He nodded, and walked out again.

After a few minutes, the woman reappeared. "Mr. Enokyan is waiting," she said in English, and led me through the door into a large room lined with Turkish carpets. A large black safe stood against one wall, and an Armenian Bible graced one of the side tables. The chairman sat at a big oak desk, talking on the telephone. He wore an expensive suit, a heavy gold watch, gold bracelets, and yet another pair of fine shoes. As I entered, he put down the telephone.

"Mafia! I hate that word," Enokyan shouted in answer to my first question. "Mafia! Whenever something in this country goes wrong, these nationalists need someone to blame. First they blamed the Communists. Then the Communists left. Now they blame us, new businessmen. Am I responsible for the bread lines?

No. Am I responsible for the cheese shortage? No. Who is responsible? These petty Ukrainians!"

The telephone rang again. He picked up the receiver, barked an order, and put the receiver down again. "What else can I do for you?" he asked, suddenly polite. "Coffee? Tea? Cognac?"

Enokyan had been born in Armenia, and drifted into L'viv sometime in the 1970s, "to study," he said. He had never finished his university course, however. Instead, he said, he had begun to do business in what was then the shadow economy. Back in the days when all private business was banned, he had been involved in "some underground manufacturing and trade." Although people went to jail for it, few Ukrainians really considered such activity to be criminal. Underground entrepreneurs were pillars of the Soviet system, distributing goods where the state failed to do so. And as soon as it became possible—after Gorbachev passed new laws on "cooperative enterprises"—he and a partner opened a restaurant and a shop that sold goods on commission. Business boomed.

But business boomed, in the eyes of some, suspiciously quickly. LV Holding, a group of twelve companies, now claimed a monthly turnover of more than $2 million, a lot of money in a city where the average monthly salary hovered around $10. The sources of the cash also seemed to be peculiarly diverse: LV Holding bought goods abroad and sold them in Ukraine, traded steel and **textiles**[33] across what used to be the Soviet Union, held interests in dollar shops, casinos, and hotels. Enokyan told me that he was also talking to Americans about bottling soft drinks and assembling cars, and to Israelis about making chemicals.

But it was pointless to talk about whether LV Holding was operating legally: laws were so confusing in Ukraine that anyone engaged in business activity on that scale was breaking one of them, and taxes were so high (75 percent of profit for trading companies) that almost anyone who paid them would go bankrupt. The regulations served the purposes of the state, not of the businessmen: every law, every license was an excuse to take a bribe, and every tax prevented businessmen from making too much money. But while it wasn't fair to criticize businessmen for breaking bad laws, that was not quite what Enokyan had been accused of.

"Mafia," Enokyan dismissed the charge. "It is just a slur put about by the Ukrainians. It means that we are competition for them, and they don't like it."

Competition was the right word. Recently, the L'viv district leaders had offered a joint venture deal to a Ukrainian-Canadian, a returning émigré whose interests the city had wanted to promote.

---

[33] **textiles**—fabrics.

LV Holding sent in a counteroffer, which they claimed was far more lucrative for the city. Embarrassed, the city leaders withdrew planning permission for the project altogether—and LV Holding had suddenly encountered unexpected obstacles in its efforts to get export licenses.

The episode with Nazar, the mayor's son, was part of this competition, too, Enokyan explained.

"Nazar—he is a nothing, unimportant."

"Why did you hire him?"

Enokyan shrugged. "I felt sorry for him. Anyway, Genschaft asked me to ask him to help us get in touch with his father, and Genschaft is my friend—I always help my friends. Next thing I know, we are being accused of kidnap. Kidnap! Me! Always law-abiding! I haven't slept for four nights, I've been awake worrying about it."

Enokyan got up from his desk and began to pace around the room. For the first time I saw that he was a rather short man: short with broad shoulders.

"Andrei Sakharov[34] once said that stupidity creates evil. Here, in L'viv, stupidity is creating evil. Here—look," and Enokyan retrieved a newspaper article from his desk. "Look what it says: 'Levon Enokyan put the government to shame, showing off his ability to give to charity.' I gave hundreds, thousands of rubles to orphanages, old people's homes, veterans' homes. What have they ever done for the poor of this city? Nothing."

He threw the newspaper down on the desk.

"You want corruption? I'll tell you about corruption. Every one of those so-called nationalists, every one of those petty governors and mayors and city councilors, every one of them is stealing as much as they can and as fast as they can, because they don't know what the next election will bring. Their salaries are **risible**,[35] their wives want them to bring home food for their children. What can they do except steal? Examples—I could give you hundreds."

Enokyan sat down again.

"Do you mind? I'm not feeling well." He swallowed a pill and waved me out of the room.

The Mercedes took me back into the center of town. On the way, the driver stopped to show me LV Holding's private hotel, used only for clients of the firm. The hotel was in a prewar villa, used until recently as a Communist Party guest house for distinguished visitors—the driver said he didn't know how LV Holding had managed to get hold of it. Inside, the fixtures were in perfect order, and there was satellite television, just like at the Grand Hotel. In fact, the furniture looked just like the furniture at the Grand Hotel, the bathrooms looked like the bathrooms at the Grand Hotel, the floors had the same kind of parquet as those at the Grand Hotel.

---

[34] Sakharov—Andrei Sakharov (1921–1989) Soviet scientist who became one of the country's most famous dissidents. He was awarded the Nobel Peace Prize in 1975.

[35] **risible**—laughable, ridiculous.

It occurred to me that I had never asked Genschaft about the nature of his business with Enokyan.

Before I left, I went to see Marta again, and listened to the latest installment: the case had been further complicated by the possibility of elections. Someone was passing leaflets around the city listing Genschaft, Enokyan, and other local businessmen with Jewish and foreign-sounding names as "anti-Ukrainian elements."

Meanwhile, the Grand Hotel remained empty. Foreign investment into L'viv remained low. From week to week, **inflation**[36] was going up, city services were deteriorating. Energy prices were going up because of Ukraine's conflict with Russia. In central L'viv, the water only ran from six to nine in the morning and from six to nine at night. One afternoon I found my friend Irena at home, weeping: the water had not come on that morning, and she was afraid it would not come on at all that day. Alas, a city official told me, he was unable to increase the supply of water because the peasants in the countryside refused to cooperate with government **edicts**[37] and would not allow a new reservoir to be built on their land. Was that true? Or had someone with commercial interests in the area bribed the official not to increase the supply of water?

When I went to see the mayor the next day, he said that his son Nazar had come home from his famous meeting with Enokyan and Genschaft very upset. I asked the mayor whether the police would be able to prove the charge of kidnapping.

"I don't know," he said simply.

The next day someone said that Nazar was now working for another company, one that had mysteriously been **exempted**[38] from export duties.

Much later I heard that Marta's investment in L'viv had led to at least one tragedy. Marta had returned to America, leaving one of her Ukrainian relatives, an older man, in charge of her business affairs in L'viv.

While she was away, the man was shot in the street. The assailant was never found.

Months afterward, I ran into Marta in a restaurant in Kiev.

"I am still fighting for the Grand Hotel," she told me. "I will not give up on the Ukrainian people."

---

[36] **inflation**—the periodic rise in cost of goods and the decrease of the buying power of money.

[37] **edicts**—laws, official orders.

[38] **exempted**—excused from.

QUESTIONS TO CONSIDER

1. What does Applebaum mean by the "borderlands"?

2. What does Applebaum make of the variety of histories in L'viv? Why does it worry her?

3. Who do you find more sympathetic, Marta or Genschaft? Explain your answer. Why does each seem to want the hotel?

4. Why are westerners safe in L'viv?

5. What is the lesson about the post-Soviet east that Applebaum wants to impart?

Chapter 8

India and Pakistan

Finding a Common Thread

A Place to Call Home

◄ Dating from the late 1700s, this Indian painting, which shows women worshippers of the god Krishna, once formed the backdrop of a household shrine.

A Myth and an Idea

SHASHI THAROOR

Shashi Tharoor (1956–   ) was educated in India and the United States. Since 1978, he has worked as an official at the United Nations. He is a prizewinning author of novels, short stories, a play, and a book about foreign policy. Tharoor's essay "A Myth and an Idea" was written to mark the fiftieth anniversary of Indian independence in 1997.

"India," Winston Churchill once barked, "is merely a geographical expression. It is no more a single country than the **equator.**"[1]

Churchill was rarely right about India, but it is true that no other country in the world embraces the extraordinary mixture of ethnic groups, the profusion of mutually incomprehensible languages, the varieties of **topography**[2] and climate, the diversity of religions and cultural practices, and the range of levels of economic development that India does.

And yet India is more than the sum of its contradictions. It is a country held together, in the words of its first prime minister, Jawaharlal Nehru, "by strong but invisible threads. . . . About her there is the **elusive**[3] quality of a legend of long ago; some enchantment seems to have held her mind. She is a myth and an idea, a dream and a vision, and yet very real and present and pervasive."

How can one approach this land of snow peaks and tropical jungles, with seventeen major languages and twenty-two thousand distinct dialects (including some spoken by more people than speak Danish or Norwegian), inhabited in the last decade of the twentieth century by nearly 940 million individuals of every ethnic extraction known to humanity? How does one come to terms with a country whose population is 51 percent **illiterate,**[4]

---

[1] **equator**—an imaginary line around the earth, centered between the North and South poles.

[2] **topography**—geographic, natural, and artificial features.

[3] **elusive**—difficult to define or understand.

[4] **illiterate**—unable to read or write.

but which has educated the world's second largest pool of trained scientists and engineers, whose teeming[5] cities overflow while four out of five Indians scratch a living from the soil? What is the clue to understanding a country rife with despair and disrepair, which nonetheless moved a Mughal[6] emperor to declaim, "If on earth there be paradise of bliss, it is this, it is this, it is this . . . "? How does one gauge a culture that elevated nonviolence to an effective moral principle, but whose freedom was born in blood and whose independence still soaks in it? How does one explain a land where peasant organizations and suspicious officials attempt to close down Kentucky Fried Chicken as a threat to the nation, where a former prime minister bitterly criticizes the sale of Pepsi-Cola "in a country where villagers don't have clean drinking water," and which yet invents a greater quantity of sophisticated software for U.S. computer manufacturers than any other country in the world? How can one portray the present, let alone the future, of an ageless civilization that was the birthplace of four major religions, a dozen different traditions of classical dance, eighty-five political parties, and three hundred ways of cooking the potato?

The short answer is that it can't be done—at least not to everyone's satisfaction. Any **truism**[7] about India can be immediately contradicted by another truism about India. The country's national motto, emblazoned on its governmental crest, is *Satyameva Jayaté*: "Truth Always Triumphs." The question remains, however: Whose truth? It is a question to which there are at least 940-plus million answers— if the last census hasn't undercounted us again.

But that sort of answer is no answer at all, and so another answer to those questions has to be sought. And this may lie in a single insight: the singular thing about India is that you can only speak of it in the plural. There are, in the **hackneyed**[8] phrase, many Indias. Everything exists in countless variants. There is no single standard, no fixed stereotype, no "one way." This pluralism is acknowledged in the way India arranges its own affairs: all groups, faiths, tastes, and ideologies survive and contend for their place in the sun. At a time when most developing countries opted for authoritarian models of government to promote nation-building and to direct development, India chose to be a multiparty democracy. And despite many stresses and strains, including twenty-two months of autocratic rule during a "state of emergency" declared by Prime Minister Indira Gandhi in 1975, a multiparty democracy—freewheeling, rambunctious, corrupt, and inefficient, perhaps, but nonetheless flourishing—India has remained.

---

[5] teeming—full, overcrowded.

[6] Mughal (also Moghul)—referring to Central Asian tribesmen who conquered India in the mid-sixteenth century and created an empire.

[7] **truism**—a statement which is obviously true.

[8] **hackneyed**—overused and worn out.

One result is that India strikes many as maddening, chaotic, inefficient, and seemingly unpurposeful as it muddles through into the twenty-first century. Another, though, is that India is not just a country but an adventure, one in which all avenues are open and everything is possible. "All the convergent influences of the world," wrote E.P. Thompson, "run through this society: Hindu, Moslem, Christian, secular; Stalinist, liberal, Maoist, democratic socialist, Gandhian. There is not a thought that is being thought in the West or East that is not active in some Indian mind."

That Indian mind has been shaped by remarkably diverse forces: ancient Hindu tradition, myth, and scripture; the impact of Islam and Christianity; and two centuries of British colonial rule. The result is unique, not just because of the variety of contemporary influences available in India, but because of the diversity of its heritage.

Many observers have been astonished by India's survival as a pluralist state. But India could hardly have survived as anything else. Pluralism is a reality that emerges from the very nature of the country; it is a choice made inevitable by India's geography and reaffirmed by its history.

One of the few generalizations that can safely be made about India is that nothing can be taken for granted about the country—not even its name, for the word *India* comes from the river Indus, which flows in Pakistan. That anomaly is easily explained, for what is today Pakistan was part of India until the country was partitioned by the departing British in 1947. (Yet each explanation breeds another anomaly. Pakistan was created as a homeland for India's Muslims, but throughout the 1970s and 1980s there were more Muslims in India than in Pakistan.)

So the Indus is no longer the starting point for a description of India's geography, which underpins the national principle of variety. Instead one might start with the dimensions of the country. India is huge; it is the world's seventh largest country, covering an area of 1,269,419 square miles (3,287,782 square kilometers). It is also the second most populous nation on earth, with an estimated 1996 population of over 940 million against China's estimated 1 billion, but with its population—which grows annually by 13 million, equivalent to a new Australia every year—projected to overtake China's within three decades. Another indication of the immensity of India is the length of its coastline (3,533 miles, or 5,653 kilometers) and its land frontiers with its neighbors (9,425 miles, or 15,168 kilometers).

One figure is particularly revealing. India extends 2,009 miles (3,214 kilometers) from its mountainous northern border with China, in the state of Jammu and Kashmir, to the southernmost tip of the mainland, the rocky beach of Kanniyakumari (formerly Cape Comorin). Indeed, the Andaman and Nicobar Islands, also Indian territory, are hundreds of nautical miles farther to the southeast, in the Bay of Bengal, which flows into the Indian Ocean. India thus stretches from 38 degrees north latitude, well above the Tropic of Cancer and on a line with Atlantic City or Denver, Colorado, to 7 degrees above the equator, the same as Freetown,[9] Sierra Leone, or Addis Ababa.[10] Few countries on earth extend over so many latitudes.

Looked at longitudinally, the distances are only slightly less imposing. From west to east, India's western frontier with Pakistan, in the marshes of the Rann of Kutch, is 1,840 miles (2,944 kilometers) away from the thickly wooded hills of northeastern Assam, on the country's border with Myanmar (Burma). In between, the country of Bangladesh is embraced as an enclave between the Indian state of West Bengal (from which it was partitioned in 1947 as East Pakistan) and the northeastern states of Assam, Meghalaya, Mizoram, and Tripura.

The country's four extremes represent four dramatically different types of ecological systems, but there are still others within the subcontinent they enclose. These range from the Thar Desert of Rajasthan in the northwest, covering about 8 percent of India's land surface, to the lush **alluvial**[11] plain of the Ganga River basin; and India also has the largest area in the world covered by snow and ice, outside the polar regions.

While the Himalaya mountains allowed a distinctive civilization to flourish in their shadows, they are remarkably penetrable. A number of passes, some more difficult than others, have allowed curious scholars, intrepid traders, and ambitious invaders to bring their own influences into India. If the phrase "ethnic melting pot" had been coined two thousand years ago, India would have had a fair claim to the title. The "indigenous people," around 1500 B.C., were probably dark-skinned Dravidians, with aboriginals of Negroid stock in many forests. Then came the great wave of Aryan migration from the Central Asian steppes. The Aryans were pale-skinned and light-eyed nomads whose search for a new homeland branched into three waves, one stopping in Persia, one sweep continuing on to Europe as far as Germany, and the other descending into India. (This common heritage explains why the Nazis in Germany used a variation of the swastika, an Aryan religious symbol still revered by Indian Hindus.) That was not all. Over the centuries, India witnessed the mingling of Greeks, Scythians, and Parthians; Mongols, Huns, and Chinese; and an assortment of mercenary warriors from Central Asia, Iran, Turkey, and even Ethiopia. As they intermarried with each other and with the local population, the Indian melting pot produced a people with a variety of skin colors and every physiognomic feature imaginable, as a look at any Indian cricket, hockey, or soccer team will confirm.

---

[9] Freetown—capital of Sierra Leone, a country in West Africa.

[10] Addis Ababa—capital of Ethiopia, a country in East Africa.

[11] **alluvial**—having very fertile soil.

Immigrants, invaders, and visitors, whether their intentions were warlike or peaceful, usually made for the Gangetic plain, the fertile stretch of land that gave birth to the Indo-Aryan civilization over three thousand years ago. The people of "Aryvrata," the Hindi-speaking national heartland, serve as the stock image of the stereotypical "Indian." But there are dramatically visible differences among those who live within this "cow belt," as urbanized anglophones derisively call it, and further differences between it and the farmlands of what remains of the Indus's **tributaries**[12] in the northwest of India. To the east, the Ganga flows to the sea in Bengal, part of which is now the independent state of Bangladesh. Beyond Bangladesh rise the hills and valleys of India's northeast, most of whose people are physically shorter and have Mongoloid features akin to their neighbors in Southeast Asia. The seven states of the northeast— the "seven sisters"—embrace a wide diversity of cultural strains, from the tribal traditions of the Nagas and the Mizos to the mainstream Hinduism of Manipur, home of a major school of Indian classical dance. The people range from Bengali migrants in Tripura and Assam to the Christian hill folk of Nagaland, whose official state language is English; from anglicized tea planters to aborigines with bones through their noses. Tourist brochures usually call the northeast "picturesque," the kind of **euphemism**[13] that accurately suggests both charm and underdevelopment.

But diversity does not end with the northern latitudes. The aged and weather-beaten peninsula of the Deccan is host to an India of darker shades, hotter food, more rapid speech, and rounded scripts; there is Dravidian pride and a rich overlay of Sanskritic high culture. On both sides of the inverted southern triangle, coastal Indians have for millennia looked beyond their shores for trade and cultural contact with other lands. In the west, traces have been found of contact across the Arabian Sea with Iraq, Yemen, and East Africa going back three thousand years. Jews persecuted in the Babylonian conquest of Judea in the sixth century B.C. and Zoroastrians fleeing Islamic rule in Persia in the eighth century A.D. found refuge and established flourishing communities. Travelers ranged from Saint Thomas the Apostle in the first century A.D., who brought Christianity to the lush southwestern state of Kerala, to the Portuguese sailor Vasco da Gama in 1492, who took away calico[14] (so named for the port of Calicut, where he landed) and spices. The enclave of Goa on the west coast was ruled by Portugal till 1961, and that of Pondicherry in the southeast by France; they still bear a different cultural character from the surrounding states.

Though the Aryans and later the northern rulers never penetrated so far into the south, South Indians cannot be easily

---

[12] **tributaries**—rivers or streams that flow into a larger river or lake.

[13] **euphemism**—a mild expression substituted for one that is viewed as harsh.

[14] calico—cotton cloth.

stereotyped. Kerala hosts the oldest Jewish community in the world outside of the Middle East, and a Christian community going back to the first decades after Christ (and therefore having a faith and rituals much older than those of the European missionaries who arrived centuries later). In the southeast the travel was all in the other direction, with traders and colonists a thousand years ago venturing to Sri Lanka and as far afield as Indonesia, but receiving virtually no visitors themselves from across the seas.

What makes so many people one people? One answer is the physical realities of the subcontinent—mountains to the north and northwest, water surrounding the rest—which have carved out a distinct geographical space for Indians to inhabit. Through the millennia, the peoples of India have moved freely within this space, the political and territorial boundaries within them ever shifting and always fungible;[15] but they have rarely, if ever, ventured beyond these natural confines without being conscious of entering alien lands. A second, equally revealing, answer may be found in the attitude of generations of foreigners, from Alexander the Great to the first of the Great Mughals, Babur, who consistently saw the peoples of the land beyond the Indus—"Hindustan!"—as one. Divided, variegated, richly differentiated, but one.

The history of each of the many peoples of India overlaps with each of the others, but only marginally with those outside the geopolitical space of the subcontinent.

Their **travails**[16] and triumphs, their battles and their blessings, their dreams and defeats, have all been shared with other Indians. History has bound them together as **indissolubly**[17] as geography.

With diversity emerging from its geography and inscribed in its history, India was made for pluralism. It is not surprising, then, that the political life of modern India has been rather like traditional Indian music: the broad basic rules are firmly set, but within them one is free to improvise, unshackled by a written score.

The India that achieved its freedom at midnight on August 14–15, 1947, was the product of several thousand years of history and civilization and, more immediately, of just under two hundred years of British colonial rule. Learned British econometricians have tried to establish that the net result of this experience was neutral—that the British put about as much into India as they took out. The negative side of the **ledger**[18] is easily listed: economic exploitation (often undisguised looting of everything from raw materials to jewels); stunting of indigenous industry (symbolized by the deliberate barbarity with which, on at least two occasions, the British ordered the thumbs of whole communities of Indian weavers chopped

---

[15] fungible—interchangeable.

[16] **travails**—painful labors or efforts.

[17] **indissolubly**—unable to be disintegrated, loosened, or disconnected.

[18] **ledger**—a book used for accounting.

off so that they could not compete with the products of Lancashire); the creation of a landless peasantry (through land settlement acts that vested land ownership in a complaisant squire-archy of *zamindars* created by the British to maintain rural order); and general poverty, hunger, and underdevelopment. The pros to these cons are less obvious. It is true that the British brought in the railways, the post and telegraphs, a national administrative system with a well-planned capital city, libraries, museums, and the English language; but all were instruments of British imperialism, intended in the first place to facilitate and perpetuate British rule, and only secondarily to benefit those among whom these were introduced. It is also true that British rule gave India a political unity it had not enjoyed for centuries; but the British also sowed a variety of political disunity India had never experienced before in its long and tumultuous history, a disunity rooted in **sectarianism.**[19]

Never throughout all the centuries of rule by Hindu, Buddhist, and Muslim kings had any section of the Indian people sought a different political order on the grounds of religion alone; even the most intolerant of Muslim kings, those who razed temples and exacted the jaziya tax on unbelievers, had had Hindu generals and ministers to serve them, including in wars against Muslim rivals. (And the Maratha king Shivaji, idolized by the eponymous but Muslim-hating Shiv Sena party, had Muslim officers in his army, too.) But the idea of dividing Indians by the manner in which they held out their hands to God was born in the wake of the unsuccessful, but multireligious, "mutiny" of 1857, when Hindus and Muslims rose together in revolt against the foreigner. The sight (and the dismaying prospect) of Indians of varying faiths and regions united in a shared struggle against alien rule struck more terror into the hearts of the British than their actual revolt, which was put down by the force of superior arms. Colonial administrators, needing to defend the imperial project, came up with the old Roman maxim *divide et impera*— "divide and rule." What the British euphemistically dubbed "communal feeling" was actively stoked; it became a **tenet**[20] of colonial policy to encourage particularist consciousness among Indians, both religious (so that they would be Muslims or Sikhs first and Indians second, if at all) and regional (so that they would be Bengalis or Dogras rather than Indians). If the structures of British rule tended toward the creation of a united India for the convenience of the rulers, its animating spirit was aimed at fostering division to achieve the same ends. This seeming paradox (but in fact entirely logical construct) of imperial policy culminated

---

[19] **sectarianism**—prejudice or discrimination.

[20] **tenet**—belief or principle.

in the tragic Partition[21] of India upon independence—so that August 15, 1947, was a birth that was also an abortion.

But despite the mourning in many nationalist hearts at the amputation that came with freedom, despite the refusal of Mahatma Gandhi to celebrate an independence he saw primarily as a betrayal, despite the flames of communal hatred and rioting that lit the midnight sky as the new country was born, there was reason for pride, and hope. India's first prime minister, Jawaharlal Nehru, put it in words that still stir the soul:

> Long years ago we made a tryst with destiny, and now the time comes when we shall redeem our pledge, not wholly or in full measure, but very substantially. At the stroke of the midnight hour, when the world sleeps, India will awake to life and freedom. A moment comes, which comes but rarely in history, when we step out from the old to the new, when an age ends and when the soul of a nation, long suppressed, finds utterance. It is fitting that at this solemn moment we take the pledge of dedication to the service of India and her people and to the still larger cause of humanity.

It was typical of Nehru that, at this moment of unprecedented triumph and tragedy for the Indian nation, he should still spare a thought for the "larger cause of humanity." But this was not merely the soaring worldview of an overeducated visionary; India had always seemed, to the more thoughtful of its leaders, a **crucible**[22] of human striving, one that offered, in its mistakes and failings as much as in its successes, lessons for all mankind.

The most striking feature of the first years of Indian independence was an absence. It was the absence of the man whom we all called (though he rejected the phrase) the Father of the Nation, the Mahatma (Great Soul—another term he detested) Gandhi, assassinated by a Hindu fanatic on January 30, 1948. Indian democracy was just five months old, and Gandhi died, with the name of God on his lips, in the capital of the new state he had done more than anyone else on earth to establish. The Mahatma was killed by a young man who thought Gandhi was too pro-Muslim; indeed, he had just come out of a fast he had conducted to coerce his own followers, the ministers of the new Indian Government of India, to transfer a larger share than they had intended of the assets of undivided India to the new state of Pakistan. Gandhi had also announced his intention to **spurn**[23] the country he had failed to keep united and to spend the rest of his years in Pakistan, a prospect that had made the government of Pakistan collectively choke.

---

[21] Partition—When India was granted its independence by Britain in 1947, the colony was divided into two independent countries: India, with a Hindu majority, and Pakistan, with a Muslim majority. This event is known as Partition.

[22] **crucible**—severe test.

[23] **spurn**—to reject.

But that was Gandhi: idealistic, quirky, **quixotic,**[24] and determined, a man who answered to the beat of no other drummer, but got everyone else to march to his tune. Someone once called him a cross between a saint and a Tammany Hall[25] politician; like the best crossbreeds, he managed to distill all the qualities of both and yet transcend their contradictions.

In 1983 the U.S. Academy of Motion Picture Arts and Sciences awarded a rare slew[26] of eight Oscars to Sir Richard Attenborough's film *Gandhi*. Disgruntled supporters of the competition, which included Steven Spielberg's blockbuster *E.T.: The Extra-Terrestrial*, sourly remarked that the Academy was supposed to be rewarding cinematic excellence, not handing out the Nobel Peace Prize. But Gandhi, of course, had never won the Nobel Peace Prize (a distinction the Swedish Academy has since conferred on a series of self-proclaimed Gandhians, from Martin Luther King, Jr., to Adolfo Pérez Esquivel[27]). His prize had been something less **tangible.**[28] Publicity posters for the film proclaimed that "Gandhi's triumph changed the world forever." I saw the posters, enjoyed the film (despite its many historical inaccuracies), and rooted for it when the Oscars were handed out. But I never stopped wondering whether Gandhi had in fact triumphed at all.

Much of the international debate sparked by the film, of course, focused on the man rather than his message. There was the inevitable controversy over the portrayal of the Mahatma and the omission of facts and personalities who might have detracted from the celluloid hagiography.[29] Yet amid both acclaim and accusation, few took Sir Richard Attenborough up on his frequent assertion of the film's contemporary relevance. Gandhi's life was, of course, his lesson. He was unique among the statesmen of the twentieth century in his determination not just to live his beliefs but to reject any separation between beliefs and action; in his life, religion flowed into politics; his public life meshed seamlessly with his private conduct. The claim emblazoned on those publicity posters for the film suggested that the lessons of his life had been learned and widely followed. But even for the man who swept aside the British Raj,[30] Paul Newman, and *Tootsie* in his triumphal progress toward a shelf full of golden statuary, this was a difficult claim to sustain.

Mahatma Gandhi was the kind of person it is more convenient to forget. The principles he stood for and the way in which he asserted them are easier to admire than to follow. While he was alive he was impossible to ignore. Once he had gone he was impossible to imitate.

---

[24] **quixotic**—bold and reckless, extremely impractical.

[25] Tammany Hall—referring to Democratic political machine that dominated New York politics in the late 1880s.

[26] slew—a large number or quantity.

[27] Adolfo Pérez Esquivel—(1931–) Argentine artist and human rights advocate. In 1980, he was awarded the Nobel Peace Prize for his nonviolent protests against the Argentine government.

[28] **tangible**—definite, perceptible by touch.

[29] hagiography—accounts of saints.

[30] Raj—a word used to describe the two centuries during which Britain dominated India.

The screen depicted Gandhi as the extraordinary leader of the world's first successful nonviolent movement for independence from colonial rule. At the same time he was a philosopher who was constantly seeking to live out his own ideas, whether they applied to individual self-improvement or social change: his autobiography was typically subtitled *The Story of My Experiments with Truth.* No dictionary imbues truth with the depth of meaning Gandhi gave it. His truth emerged from his convictions: it meant not only what was accurate, but what was just and therefore right. Truth could not be obtained by "untruthful" or unjust means, which included inflicting violence upon one's opponent.

To describe his method, Gandhi coined the expression *satyagraha*—literally, "holding on to truth" or, as he variously described it, truth-force, love-force, or soul-force. He disliked the English term "passive resistance," because *satyagraha* required activism, not passivity. If you believed in Truth and cared enough to obtain it, Gandhi felt, you could not afford to be passive: you had to be prepared actively to suffer for Truth.

So nonviolence, like many later concepts labeled with a negation, from noncooperation to nonalignment, meant much more than the denial of an opposite; it did not merely imply the absence of violence. Nonviolence was the way to vindicate the truth by the infliction of suffering not on the opponent, but on

oneself. It was essential to accept punishment willingly in order to demonstrate the strength of one's convictions.

This was the approach Gandhi brought to the movement for our independence— and it worked. Where **sporadic**[31] terrorism and moderate constitutionalism had both proved ineffective, Gandhi took the issue of freedom to the masses as one of simple right and wrong, and gave them a technique to which the British had no response. By abstaining from violence, Gandhi **wrested**[32] the moral advantage. By breaking the law nonviolently, he showed up the injustice of the law. By accepting the punishments imposed on him, he confronted his captors with their own brutalization. By voluntarily imposing suffering upon himself in his hunger strikes, he demonstrated the lengths to which he was prepared to go in defense of what he considered to be right. In the end he made the **perpetuation**[33] of British rule an impossibility.

Of course, there was much more to Gandhism—physical self-denial and discipline, spiritual faith, a belief in humanity and in the human capacity for selfless love, the self-reliance symbolized by the spinning wheel, religious ecumenism, idealistic internationalism, and a passionate commitment to human equality and social justice (especially in our caste-ridden country). The improvement of his fellow human beings was arguably

---

[31] **sporadic**—occasional.

[32] **wrested**—took from another.

[33] **perpetuation**—permanent continuation.

more important to him than the political goal of ridding India of the British. But it is his central tenet of nonviolence in the pursuit of these ends that represents his most significant original contribution to the world.

The case for the film's international relevance was typified by the declaration of Coretta Scott King, the widow of Martin Luther King Jr., the most famous of the many who claimed to have been inspired by the teachings of Mahatma Gandhi, that the film "will rekindle worldwide interest in nonviolence. . . . Gandhi's challenge to the world is once again before the public forum and it is up to all of us to translate it into action." One did not have to wait a decade to point to the utter futility of both the prediction and the hope that underlay it. But Mrs. King's comment was particularly interesting because it was her husband, more than anyone else, who had used nonviolence most effectively outside India, in breaking down segregation in the southern United States. King himself had declared that "the Gandhian method of nonviolent resistance . . . became the guiding light of our movement. Christ furnished the spirit and motivation and Gandhi furnished the method."

So Gandhism arguably helped to change the Deep South forever. But it is difficult to find many other instances of its success. India's independence marked the dawn of the era of decolonization, but many nations still came to freedom only after bloody and violent struggles. Other peoples have fallen under the boots of invading armies, been dispossessed of their lands, or been forced to flee in terror from their homes. Nonviolence has offered no solutions to them. It could work only against opponents vulnerable to a loss of moral authority—governments responsive to domestic and international public opinion, capable of being shamed into conceding defeat. In Gandhi's own day, nonviolence could have done nothing for the Jews of Hitler's Germany, who disappeared unprotestingly into gas chambers far from the flashbulbs of a conscience-stricken press.

The power of nonviolence rests in being able to say, "To show you that you are wrong, I punish myself." But that has little effect on those who are not interested in whether they are wrong and are already seeking to punish you whether you disagree with them or not. For them, your willingness to undergo punishment is the most convenient means of victory.

On this subject Gandhi sounds frighteningly unrealistic: "The willing sacrifice of the innocent is the most powerful answer to insolent tyranny that has yet been conceived by God or man. Disobedience to be 'civil' must be sincere, respectful, restrained, never defiant, and it must have no ill will or hatred behind it. Neither should there be excitement in civil disobedience, which is a preparation for mute suffering."

For many smarting under injustice across the world, that would sound like a prescription for sainthood—or for impotence. Mute suffering is all very well as a moral principle, but it had rarely brought about meaningful change. The sad truth is that the staying power of organized violence is almost always greater than that of nonviolence. And when right and wrong are less clear-cut, Gandhism flounders. The Mahatma, at the peak of his influence, was unable to prevent partition, even though, in his terms, he considered it "wrong." Gandhi believed in "weaning an opponent from error by patience, sympathy, and self-suffering"—but if the opponent believes equally in the justice of his cause, he is hardly going to accept that he is in "error." Gandhism is viable at its simplest and most profound in the service of a transcendent principle like independence from foreign rule. But in more complex situations it cannot—and, more to the point, does not—work as well.

Gandhi's ideals had a tremendous intellectual impact on the founding fathers of the new India, who incorporated many of his convictions into the directive principles of state policy. Yet Gandhian solutions have not been found for many of the ills over which he agonized, from persistent interreligious conflict to the ill treatment of Untouchables (whom he renamed Harijans, or "Children of God," as a designation its beneficiaries found patronizing, for were we not all Children of God? Today, they prefer to be know as Dalits, meaning "the Oppressed."). Instead, his methods (particularly the fast, the hartal,[34] and the deliberate courting of arrest) have been abused and debased by far lesser men in the pursuit of petty sectarian ends. Outside India,

too, Gandhian techniques have been perverted by such people as terrorists and bomb-throwers declaring hunger strikes when punished for their crimes. Gandhism without moral authority is like Marxism without a **proletariat**.[35] Yet few who wish to use his methods have his personal integrity or moral stature.

Internationally, Gandhi expressed ideals few can reject: he could virtually have written the United Nations Charter. But the decades after his death have confirmed that there is no escape from the conflicting sovereignties of states. Some 20 million more lives have been lost in wars and insurrections since his passing. In a dismaying number of countries, governments spend more for military purposes than for education and health care combined. The current stockpile of nuclear weapons represents over a million times the explosive power of the atom bomb whose destruction of Hiroshima so grieved him. Universal peace, which Gandhi considered so central to Truth, seems as illusionary as ever.

As governments compete, so religions contend. The **ecumenist**[36] Gandhi, who declared, "I am a Hindu, a Muslim, a Christian, a Zoroastrian, a Jew," might find it difficult to stomach the exclusivist revivalism of so many religions and cults the world over. But perhaps his approach has always been inappropriate for the rest

---

[34] hartal—halting of work; strike.

[35] **proletariat**—member of the working class.

[36] **ecumenist**—one who seeks to promote worldwide religious unity.

of the world. As one of his Muslim critics retorted, to his claim of eclectic belief, "Only a Hindu could say that."

And finally, the world of the spinning wheel, of self-reliant families in contented village republics, is even more remote today than when Gandhi first espoused it. Despite the brief popularity of intermediate technology and the credo "small is beautiful," there does not appear to be much room for such ideas in an interdependent world. Self-reliance is too often a cover for protectionism and a shelter for inefficiency in the Third World. The successful and prosperous countries are those who are able to look beyond spinning *chakras*[37] to silicon chips—and who give their people the benefits of technological developments that free them from menial and repetitive chores and broaden the horizons of their lives.

But if Gandhism has had its limitations exposed in the years after 1947, there is no denying Gandhi's greatness. While the world was disintegrating into fascism, violence, and war, Gandhi taught the virtues of truth, nonviolence, and peace. He destroyed the credibility of colonialism by opposing principle to force. And he set and attained personal standards of conviction and courage that few will ever match. He was that rare kind of leader who was not confined by the inadequacies of his followers.

Yet Gandhi's Truth was essentially his own. He formulated its unique content and determined its application in a specific historical context. Inevitably, few in today's

world can measure up to his greatness or aspire to his credo. No, Gandhi's "triumph" did not change the world forever. It is, sadly, a matter of doubt whether he triumphed at all.

The India of the first fifty years after independence was therefore a post-Gandhian India. It paid lip service to much of its Gandhian patrimony while striking out in directions of which Gandhi could not have approved. But its central challenges remained the ones Gandhi identified: those of overcoming disunity and discrimination, of ensuring the health and well-being of the downtrodden, of developing the capacity to meet the nation's basic needs, of promoting among Indians the integrity and commitment he labeled "Truth." These challenges, modified by the ways in which India has attempted to rise to them in the last fifty years, remain. They will continue to set the defining agenda of the next fifty years.

---

[37] *chakras*—hand spinning wheels used to make cloth. Gandhi advocated them as a way for India to be self-sufficient from Britain.

QUESTIONS TO CONSIDER

1. Why, to Tharoor, is it impossible for India to be anything other than a pluralist state?

2. How does Tharoor feel about the British who dominated India before 1947? What are his reasons?

3. How would you describe Tharoor's attitude toward Gandhi? What does Tharoor define as Gandhi's good points? As his bad points? As the strengths and weaknesses of his position?

Fellow-Feeling

R. K. NARAYAN

R. K. Narayan (1906–   ) was born in Madras in southern India. Though a native speaker of Tamil, the language of much of southern India, Narayan was educated in English and chose this language when he began to write fiction. His first novel was published in 1935, and his novels and stories have regularly appeared up through the 1990s. Narayan's fiction is all set in a city called Malgudi, which he created out of his experiences living in Mysore and Madras. In Malgudi, Narayan has depicted every walk of Indian life, particularly how it changed after independence in 1947. As a portrait of a society, Narayan's writing is an almost unprecedented body of work; Graham Greene wrote that Narayan "wakes in me a special gratitude, for he has offered me a second home. Without him I could never have known what it is like to be an Indian." "Fellow-Feeling" is from An Astrologer's Day and Other Stories (1947). An undercurrent of the story deals with the caste system of the Hindu religion. According to this system, all Hindus fall into one of five groups to which they rigidly belong. Each Hindu would marry within his caste and choose a profession appropriate to his lot. At the top of the system were the Brahmins, the priestly and learned class. In recent decades, caste has lost some of its importance in India, but it is still apparent in all walks of life.

The Madras-Bangalore Express was due to start in a few minutes. Trolleys and barrows piled with trunks and beds rattled their way through the bustle. Fruit-sellers and beedi[1]-and-betel[2]-sellers cried themselves hoarse. Latecomers pushed, shouted and perspired. The engine added to the general noise with the low monotonous hum of its boiler; the first bell rang, the guard looked at his watch. Mr. Rajam Iyer arrived on the platform at a terrific pace, with a small roll of bedding under one arm and an absurd yellow trunk under the other. He ran to the first third-class compartment that caught his eye, peered in and, since the door could not be opened on account of the congestion inside, flung himself in through the window.

Fifteen minutes later Madras flashed past the train in window-framed patches of sun-scorched roofs and fields. At the next halt, Mandhakam, most of the passengers

[1] *beedi*—a small, fragrant cigar.
[2] betel—the leaf of a pepper plant which is wrapped around a betel nut and chewed.

got down. The compartment built to seat "8 passengers; 4 British Troops, or 6 Indian Troops" now carried only nine. Rajam Iyer found a seat and made himself comfortable opposite a **sallow**,[3] meek passenger, who suddenly removed his coat, folded it and placed it under his head and lay down, shrinking himself to the area he had occupied while he was sitting. With his knees drawn up almost to his chin, he rolled himself into a ball. Rajam Iyer threw at him an **indulgent**,[4] compassionate look. He then fumbled for his glasses and pulled out of his pocket a small book, which set forth in clear Tamil[5] the significance of the obscure *Sandhi* rites that every Brahmin[6] worth the name performs thrice daily.

> **"You are a Brahmin, I see. Learn, sir, that your days are over. Don't think you can bully us as you have been bullying us all these years."**

He was startled out of this pleasant languor by a series of growls coming from a passenger who had got in at Katpadi. The newcomer, looking for a seat, had been irritated by the spectacle of the meek passenger asleep and had enforced the law of the third-class. He then **encroached**[7] on most of the meek passenger's legitimate space and began to deliver home-truths which passed by easy stages from impudence to impertinence and finally to **ribaldry**.[8]

Rajam Iyer peered over his spectacles. There was a dangerous look in his eyes. He tried to return to the book, but could not. The bully's speech was gathering momentum.

"What is all this?" Rajam Iyer asked suddenly, in a hard tone.

"What is what?" growled back the newcomer, turning sharply on Rajam Iyer.

"Moderate your style a bit," Rajam Iyer said firmly.

"You moderate yours first," replied the other.

A pause.

"My man," Rajam Iyer began endearingly, "this sort of thing will never do."

The newcomer received this in silence. Rajam Iyer felt encouraged and drove home his moral: "Just try and be more courteous, it is your duty."

"You mind your business," replied the newcomer.

Rajam Iyer shook his head disapprovingly and drawled out a "No." The newcomer stood looking out for some time and, as if expressing a brilliant truth that had just dawned on him, said, "You are a Brahmin, I see. Learn, sir, that your days are over. Don't think you can bully us as you have been bullying us all these years."

Rajam Iyer gave a short laugh and said, "What has it to do with your beastly conduct to this gentleman?" The newcomer

---

[3] **sallow**—sickly and yellowish in color.

[4] **indulgent**—permissive, tolerant.

[5] Tamil—language spoken in southern India and Sri Lanka.

[6] Brahmin—a person of the highest caste among Hindus, whose task is to study the religious texts and to perform the sacred ceremonies.

[7] **encroached**—advanced beyond proper or established limits.

[8] **ribaldry**—vulgar or indecent speech.

assumed a tone of **mock**[9] humility and said, "Shall I take the dust from your feet, O Holy Brahmin? O Brahmin, Brahmin." He continued in a singsong fashion: "Your days are over, my dear sir, learn that. I should like to see you trying a bit of bossing on us."

"Whose master is who?" asked Rajam Iyer philosophically,

The newcomer went on with no obvious relevance: "The cost of mutton[10] has gone up out of all proportion. It is nearly double what it used to be."

"Is it?" asked Rajam Iyer.

"Yes, and why?" continued the other. "Because Brahmins have begun to eat meat and they pay high prices to get it secretly." He then turned to the other passengers and added, "And we non-Brahmins have to pay the same price, though we don't care for the secrecy."

Rajam Iyer leaned back in his seat, reminding himself of a proverb which said that if you threw a stone into a gutter it would only spurt filth in your face.

"And," said the newcomer, "the price of meat used to be five annas per pound. I remember the days quite well. It is nearly twelve annas now. Why? Because the Brahmin is prepared to pay so much, if only he can have it in secret. I have with my own eyes seen Brahmins, pukkah[11] Brahmins with sacred threads[12] on their bodies, carrying fish under their arms, of course all wrapped up in a towel. Ask them what it is, and they will tell you that it is plantain. Plantain that has life, I suppose! I once tickled a fellow under the arm and out came the biggest fish in the market. Hey, Brahmin," he said, turning to Rajam Iyer, "what did you have for your meal this morning?" "Who? I?" asked Rajam Iyer. "Why do you want to know?" "Look, sirs," said the newcomer to the other passengers, "why is he afraid to tell us what he ate this morning?" And turning to Rajam Iyer, "Mayn't a man ask another what he had for his morning meal?"

"Oh, by all means. I had rice, ghee,[13] curds,[14] *brinjal*[15] soup, fried beans."

"Oh, is that all?" asked the newcomer, with an innocent look.

"Yes," replied Rajam Iyer.

"Is that all?"

"Yes, how many times do you want me to repeat it?"

"No offense, no offense," replied the newcomer.

"Do you mean to say I am lying?" asked Rajam Iyer.

"Yes," replied the other, "you have omitted from your list a few things. Didn't I see you this morning going home from the market with a banana, a water banana, wrapped up in a towel, under your arm? Possibly it was somebody very much like you. Possibly I mistook the person. My

---

[9] **mock**—false, pretend.

[10] mutton—sheep flesh used for food.

[11] pukkah—Anglo-Indian slang for good, proper, genuine.

[12] sacred threads—cotton threads of three strands which are constantly worn by Brahmins as an indication of their status.

[13] ghee—a liquid butter clarified by boiling.

[14] curds—dairy product obtained from milk and used as food or to make cheese.

[15] *brinjal*—eggplant.

wife prepares excellent soup with fish. You won't be able to find the difference between *dhall*[16] soup and fish soup. Send your wife, or the wife of the person that was exactly like you, to my wife to learn soup-making. Hundreds of Brahmins have smacked their lips over the *dhall* soup prepared in my house. I am a **leper**[17] if there is a lie in anything I say."

> *Rajam Iyer was seized by a sense of inferiority. The newcomer stood nine clean inches over him.*

"You are," replied Rajam Iyer, grinding his teeth. "You are a **rabid**[18] leper."

"Whom do you call a leper!"

"You!"

"I? You call me a leper?"

"No. I call you a rabid leper."

"You call me rabid?" the newcomer asked, striking his chest to emphasize "me."

"You are a filthy brute," said Rajam Iyer. "You must be handed over to the police."

"Bah!" exclaimed the newcomer. "As if I didn't know what these police were."

"Yes, you must have had countless occasions to know the police. And you will see more of them yet in your miserable life, if you don't get beaten to death like the street mongrel you are," said Rajam Iyer in great passion. "With your foul mouth you are bound to come to that end."

"What do you say?" shouted the newcomer menacingly. "What do you say, you vile **humbug?**"[19]

"Shut up," Rajam Iyer cried.

"You shut up."

"Do you know to whom you are talking?"

"What do I care who the son of a mongrel is?"

"I will thrash you with my slippers," said Rajam Iyer.

"I will pulp you down with an old rotten sandal," came the reply.

"I will kick you," said Rajam Iyer.

"Will you?" howled the newcomer. "Come on, let us see."

Both rose to their feet simultaneously. There they stood facing each other on the floor of the compartment. Rajam Iyer was seized by a sense of inferiority. The newcomer stood nine clean inches over him. He began to feel ridiculous, short and fat, wearing a loose dhoti[20] and a green coat, while the newcomer towered above him in his grease-spotted khaki suit. Out of the corner of his eye he noted that the other passengers were waiting eagerly to see how the issue would be settled and were not in the least disposed to intervene.

"Why do you stand as if your mouth was stopped with mud?" asked the newcomer.

"Shut up," Rajam Iyer snapped, trying not to be impressed by the size of the adversary.

---

[16] *dhall*—an edible yellow split pea.

[17] **leper**—outcast.

[18] **rabid**—extreme in opinion or practice.

[19] **humbug**—a person who is not what they claim to be.

[20] dhoti—the long loincloth worn by Indian men.

"Your honor said that you would kick me," said the newcomer, pretending to offer himself.

"Won't I kick you?" asked Rajam Iyer.

"Try."

"No," said Rajam Iyer, "I will do something worse."

"Do it," said the other, throwing forward his chest and pushing up the sleeves of his coat.

Rajam Iyer removed his coat and rolled up his sleeves. He rubbed his hands and commanded suddenly, "Stand still!" The newcomer was taken aback. He stood for a second baffled. Rajam Iyer gave him no time to think. With great force he swung his right arm and brought it near the other's cheek, but stopped it short without hitting him.

"Wait a minute, I think I had better give you a chance," said Rajam Iyer.

"What chance?" asked the newcomer.

"It would be unfair if I did it without giving you a chance."

"Did what?"

"You stand there and it will be over in a fraction of a second."

"Fraction of a second? What will you do?"

"Oh, nothing very complicated," replied Rajam Iyer, nonchalantly, "nothing very complicated. I will slap your right cheek and at the same time tug your left ear, and your mouth, which is now under your nose, will suddenly find itself under your left ear, and, what is more, stay there. I assure you, you won't feel any pain."

"What do you say?"

"And it will all be over before you say 'Sri Rama.'"

"I don't believe it," said the newcomer.

"Well and good. Don't believe it," said Rajam Iyer carelessly. "I never do it except under extreme provocation."

"Do you think I am an infant?"

"I implore you, my man, not to believe me. Have you heard of a thing called jujitsu? Well, this is a simple trick in jujitsu perhaps known to half a dozen persons in the whole of South India."

"You said you would kick me," said the newcomer.

"Well, isn't this worse?" asked Rajam Iyer. He drew a line on the newcomer's face between his left ear and mouth, muttering, "I must admit you have a tolerably good face and round figure. But imagine yourself going about the streets with your mouth under your left ear . . ." He chuckled at the vision. "I expect at Jalarpet station there will be a huge crowd outside our compartment to see you." The newcomer stroked his chin thoughtfully. Rajam Iyer continued, "I felt it my duty to explain the whole thing to you beforehand. I am not as hot-headed as you are. I have some consideration for your wife and children. It will take some time for the kids to recognize Papa when he returns home with his mouth under . . . How many children have you?"

"Four."

"And then think of it," said Rajam Iyer. "You will have to take your food under your left ear, and you will need the assistance of your wife to drink water. She will have to pour it in."

"I will go to a doctor," said the newcomer.

"Do go," replied Rajam Iyer, "and I will give you a thousand rupees if you find a doctor. You may try even European doctors."

The newcomer stood **ruminating**[21] with knitted brow. "Now prepare," shouted Rajam Iyer, "one blow on the right cheek. I will jerk your left ear, and your mouth . . ."

The newcomer suddenly ran to the window and leaned far out of it. Rajam decided to leave the compartment at Jalarpet.

But the moment the train stopped at Jalarpet station, the newcomer grabbed his bag and jumped out. He moved away at a **furious**[22] pace and almost knocked down a coconut-seller and a person carrying a trayload of colored toys. Rajam Iyer felt it would not be necessary for him to get out now. He leaned through the window and cried, "Look here!" The newcomer turned.

"Shall I keep a seat for you?" asked Rajam Iyer.

"No, my ticket is for Jalarpet," the newcomer answered and quickened his pace.

The train had left Jalarpet at least a mile behind. The meek passenger sat shrunk in a corner of the seat. Rajam Iyer looked over his spectacles and said, "Lie down if you like."

The meek passenger proceeded to roll himself into a ball. Rajam Iyer added, "Did you hear that bully say that his ticket was for Jalarpet?"

"Yes."

"Well," he lied, "he is in the fourth compartment from here. I saw him get into it just as the train started."

Though the meek stranger was too grateful to doubt this statement, one or two other passengers looked at Rajam Iyer skeptically.

---

[21] **ruminating**—pondering, meditating on.

[22] **furious**—of great energy or speed.

QUESTIONS TO CONSIDER

1. What are Rajam Iyer's motivations in speaking to the bully? What motivates the bully to suddenly break off the encounter?

2. Why does Rajam Iyer lie to the meek passenger at the end of the story? What does Narayan want you to think of Rajam Iyer?

3. What role does caste or class seem to play in this story?

A Devoted Son

ANITA DESAI

Anita Desai (1937–   ) was born in Mussorie in northern India. The daughter of an Indian businessman and a German woman, much of Desai's writing has been an examination of how East meets West and also how traditional Indian society has collided with modernity. She began to publish stories in the late 1950s. Despite being married in 1958 and having four children, she has regularly produced novels and stories, with her skill at depicting the difficulties of modern life always increasing. Desai divides her time between India, England, and the United States. "A Devoted Son" is an ironic story about perception: how good things that you wish for have a dark underside, and also how modern life has changed India.

When the results appeared in the morning papers, Rakesh scanned them, barefoot and in his pyjamas, at the garden gate, then went up the steps to the veranda where his father sat sipping his morning tea and bowed down to touch his feet.

"A first division, son?" his father asked, beaming, reaching for the papers.

"At the top of the list, Papa," Rakesh murmured, as if awed. "First in the country."

Bedlam broke loose then. The family whooped and danced. The whole day long visitors streamed into the small yellow house at the end of the road, to congratulate the parents of this *Wunderkind*,[1] to slap Rakesh on the back and fill the house and garden with the sounds and colors of a

festival. There were garlands and *halwa*,[2] party clothes and gifts (enough fountain pens to last years, even a watch or two), nerves and temper and joy, all in a multi-colored whirl of pride and great shining **vistas**[3] newly opened: Rakesh was the first son in the family to receive an education, so much had been sacrificed in order to send him to school and then medical college, and at last the fruits of their sacrifice had arrived, golden and glorious.

To everyone who came to him to say, "*Mubarak*, Varmaji, your son has brought you glory," the father said, "Yes, and do

---

[1] *Wunderkind*—one who achieves great success at a young age.

[2] *halwa*—flaky confections which are served as desserts in India.

[3] **vistas**—views or prospects.

you know what is the first thing he did when he saw the results this morning? He came and touched my feet. He bowed down and touched my feet." This moved many of the women in the crowd so much that they were seen to raise the ends of their saris[4] and dab at their tears while the men reached out for the betel-leaves[5] and sweetmeats[6] that were offered around on trays and shook their heads in wonder and approval of such exemplary filial behavior. "One does not often see such behavior in sons any more," they all agreed, a little enviously perhaps. Leaving the house, some of the women said, sniffing, "At least on such an occasion they might have served pure *ghee*[7] sweets," and some of the men said, "Don't you think old Varma was giving himself airs? He needn't think we don't remember that he comes from the vegetable market himself, his father used to sell vegetables, and he has never seen the inside of a school." But there was more envy than **rancor**[8] in their voices and it was, of course, inevitable—not every son in that shabby little colony at the edge of the city was destined to shine as Rakesh shone, and who knew that better than the parents themselves?

And that was only the beginning, the first step in a great, sweeping ascent to the radiant heights of fame and fortune. The thesis he wrote for his M.D. brought Rakesh still greater glory, if only in select medical circles. He won a scholarship. He went to the USA (that was what his father learnt to call it and taught the whole family to say—not America, which was what the ignorant neighbors called it, but, with a grand familiarity, "the USA") where he pursued his career in the most prestigious of all hospitals and won **encomiums**[9] from his American colleagues which were relayed to his admiring and glowing family. What was more, he came *back*, he actually returned to that small yellow house in the once-new but increasingly shabby colony, right at the end of the road where the rubbish vans tripped out their stinking contents for pigs to nose in and rag-pickers to build their shacks on, all steaming and smoking just outside the neat wire fences and well-tended gardens. To this Rakesh returned and the first thing he did on entering the house was to slip out of the embraces of his sisters and brothers and bow down and touch his father's feet.

As for his mother, she gloated chiefly over the strange fact that he had not married in America, had not brought home a foreign wife as all her neighbors had warned her he would, for wasn't that what all Indian boys went abroad for? Instead he agreed, almost without argument, to marry a girl she had picked out for him in her own village, the daughter of a childhood friend, a plump and uneducated girl, it

---

[4] saris—typical dresses of Indian and Pakistani women, consisting of a long piece of cotton or silk wrapped around the body with one end falling to the feet and the other thrown over the shoulder.

[5] betel-leaves—the leaves of a pepper plant that are wrapped around a betel nut and chewed.

[6] sweetmeats—candied fruits and sugar-covered nuts.

[7] ghee—a liquid butter clarified by boiling.

[8] **rancor**—resentment or ill will.

[9] **encomiums**—expressions of praise.

was true, but so old-fashioned, so placid, so **complaisant**[10] that she slipped into the household and settled in like a charm, seemingly too lazy and too good-natured to even try and make Rakesh leave home and set up independently, as any other girl might have done. What was more, she was pretty—really pretty, in a plump, pudding way that only gave way to fat—soft, spreading fat, like warm wax—after the birth of their first baby, a son, and then what did it matter?

For some years Rakesh worked in the city hospital, quickly rising to the top of the administrative organization, and was made a director before he left to set up his own clinic. He took his parents in his car—a new, sky-blue Ambassador with a rear window full of stickers and charms revolving on strings—to see the clinic when it was built, and the large sign-board over the door on which his name was printed in letters of red, with a row of degrees and qualifications to follow it like so many little black slaves of the **regent**.[11] Thereafter his fame seemed to grow just a little dimmer—or maybe it was only that everyone in town had grown accustomed to it at last—but it was also the beginning of his fortune for he now became known not only as the best but also the richest doctor in town.

However, all this was not accomplished in the wink of an eye. Naturally not. It was the achievement of a lifetime and it took up Rakesh's whole life. At the time he set up his clinic his father had grown into an old man and retired from his post at the kerosene[12] dealer's depot at which he had worked for forty years, and his mother died soon after, giving up the ghost with a sigh that sounded positively happy, for it was her own son who ministered to her in her last illness and who sat pressing her feet at the last moment—such a son as few women had borne.

For it had to be admitted—and the most unsuccessful and most rancorous of neighbors eventually did so—that Rakesh was not only a devoted son and a miraculously good-natured man who contrived somehow to obey his parents and **humor**[13] his wife and show concern equally for his children and his patients, but there was actually a brain inside this beautifully polished and formed body of good manners and kind nature and, in between ministering to his family and playing host to many friends and coaxing them all into feeling happy and grateful and content, he had actually trained his hands as well and emerged an excellent doctor, a really fine surgeon. How one man—and a man born to illiterate parents, his father having worked for a kerosene dealer and his mother having spent her life in a kitchen—had achieved, combined and conducted

---

[10] **complaisant**—agreeable or kindly, eager to please.

[11] **regent**—a person who exercises power in the absence or disability of a kingdom's ruler.

[12] kerosene—distilled petroleum or shale used commonly as a fuel and cleaning solvent.

[13] **humor**—adapt or accommodate.

such a medley of virtues, no one could fathom, but all acknowledged his talent and skill.

It was a strange fact, however, that talent and skill, if displayed for too long, cease to dazzle. It came to pass that the most admiring of all eyes eventually faded and no longer blinked at his glory. Having retired from work and having lost his wife, the old father very quickly went to pieces, as they say. He developed so many complaints and fell ill so frequently and with such mysterious diseases that even his son could no longer make out when it was something of significance and when it was merely a peevish whim.[14] He sat huddled on his string bed most of the day and developed an exasperating habit of stretching out suddenly and lying absolutely still, allowing the whole family to fly around him in a flap, wailing and weeping, and then suddenly sitting up, stiff and gaunt, and spitting out a big gob of betel-juice as if to mock their behavior.

He did this once too often: there had been a big party in the house, a birthday party for the youngest son, and the celebrations had to be suddenly hushed, covered up and hustled out of the way when the daughter-in-law discovered, or thought she discovered, that the old man, stretched out from end to end of his string bed, had lost his pulse; the party broke up, dissolved, even turned into a band of mourners, when the old man sat up and the distraught daughter-in-law received a gob of red spittle right on the hem of her new organza sari. After that no one much cared if he sat up cross-legged on his bed, hawking and spitting, or lay down flat and turned grey as a corpse. Except, of course, for that pearl amongst pearls, his son Rakesh.

It was Rakesh who brought him his morning tea, not in one of the china cups from which the rest of the family drank, but in the old man's favorite brass tumbler, and sat at the edge of his bed, comfortable and relaxed with the string of his pyjamas dangling out from under his fine lawn[15] night-shirt, and discussed or, rather, read out the morning news to his father. It made no difference to him that his father made no response apart from spitting. It was Rakesh, too, who, on returning from the clinic in the evening, persuaded the old man to come out of his room, as bare and desolate as a cell, and take the evening air out in the garden, beautifully arranging the pillows and bolsters on the *divan*[16] in the corner of the open verandah. On summer nights he saw to it that the servants carried out the old man's bed onto the lawn and himself helped his father down the steps and onto the bed, soothing him and settling him down for a night under the stars.

All this was very gratifying for the old man. What was not so gratifying was that he even undertook to supervise his father's diet. One day when the father was really sick, having ordered his daughter-in-law to

---

[14] peevish whim—angry impulse.

[15] lawn—light cotton or linen fabric.

[16] *divan*—a sofa or couch, often usable as a bed.

make him a dish of *soojie halwa* and eaten it with a saucerful of cream, Rakesh marched into the room, not with his usual respectful step but with the confident and rather contemptuous stride of the famous doctor, and declared, "No more *halwa* for you, Papa. We must be sensible, at your age. If you must have something sweet, Veena will cook you a little *kheer*,[17] that's light, just a little rice and milk. But nothing fried, nothing rich. We can't have this happening again."

The old man who had been lying stretched out on his bed, weak and feeble after a day's illness, gave a start at the very sound, the tone of these words. He opened his eyes—rather, they fell open with shock—and he stared at his son with disbelief that darkened quickly to reproach. A son who actually refused his father the food he craved? No, it was unheard of, it was incredible. But Rakesh had turned his back to him and was cleaning up the litter of bottles and packets on the medicine shelf and did not notice while Veena slipped silently out of the room with a little **smirk**[18] that only the old man saw, and hated.

Halwa was only the first item to be crossed off the old man's diet. One delicacy after another went—everything fried to begin with, then everything sweet, and eventually everything, everything that the old man enjoyed. The meals that arrived for him on the shining stainless steel tray twice a day were frugal to say the least— dry bread, boiled lentils, boiled vegetables and, if there were a bit of chicken or fish,

that was boiled too. If he called for another helping—in a cracked voice that quavered theatrically—Rakesh himself would come to the door, gaze at him sadly and shake his head, saying "Now, Papa, we must be careful, we can't risk another illness, you know," and although the daughter-in-law kept tactfully out of the way, the old man could just see her smirk sliding merrily through the air. He tried to bribe his grandchildren into buying him sweets (and how he missed his wife now, that generous, indulgent and illiterate cook), whispering, "Here's fifty *paise*" as he stuffed the coins into a tight, hot fist. "Run down to the shop at the crossroads and buy me thirty *paise* worth of *jalebis*,[19] and you can spend the remaining twenty *paise* on yourself. Eh? Understand? Will you do that?" He got away with it once or twice but then was found out, the conspirator was scolded by his father and smacked by his mother and Rakesh came storming into the room, almost tearing his hair as he shouted through compressed lips, "Now Papa, are you trying to turn my little son into a liar? Quite apart from spoiling your own stomach, you are spoiling him as well—you are encouraging him to lie to his own parents. You should have heard the lies he told his mother when she saw him bringing back those *jalebis* wrapped up in filthy newspaper. I don't allow anyone in my house to buy

---

[17] *kheer*—a milk and rice pudding made with cardamom and nuts.

[18] **smirk**—a smug or pretentious smile.

[19] *jalebis*—pretzel-shaped candy made of deep-fried sugar.

sweets in the bazaar, Papa, surely you know that. There's cholera in the city, typhoid, gastroenteritis—I see these cases daily in the hospital, how can I allow my own family to run such risks?" The old man sighed and lay down in the corpse position. But that worried no one any longer.

There was only one pleasure left the old man now (his son's early morning visits and readings from the newspaper could no longer be called that) and those were visits from elderly neighbors. These were not frequent as his contemporaries were mostly as decrepit and helpless as he and few could walk the length of the road to visit him any more. Old Bhatia, next door, however, who was still spry enough to refuse, adamantly, to bathe in the tiled bathroom indoors and to insist on carrying out his brass mug and towel, in all seasons and usually at impossible hours, into the yard and bathe noisily under the garden tap, would look over the hedge to see if Varma were out on his verandah and would call to him and talk while he wrapped his *dhoti*[20] about him and dried the sparse hair on his head, shivering with enjoyable exaggeration. Of course these conversations, bawled across the hedge by two rather deaf old men conscious of having their entire households overhearing them, were not very satisfactory but Bhatia occasionally came out of his yard, walked down the bit of road and came in at Varma's gate to collapse onto the stone plinth built under

the temple tree. If Rakesh were at home he would help his father down the steps into the garden and arrange him on his night bed under the tree and leave the two old men to chew betel-leaves and discuss the ills of their individual bodies with combined passion.

"At least you have a doctor in the house to look after you," sighed Bhatia, having vividly described his martyrdom to piles.

"Look after me?" cried Varma, his voice cracking like an ancient clay jar. "He—he does not even give me enough to eat."

"What?" said Bhatia, the white hairs in his ears twitching. "Doesn't give you enough to eat? Your own son?"

"My own son. If I ask him for one more piece of bread, he says no, Papa. I weighed out the *ata* myself and I can't allow you to have more than two hundred grams of cereal a day. He *weighs* the food he gives me, Bhatia—he has scales to weigh it on. That is what it has come to."

"Never," murmured Bhatia in disbelief. "Is it possible, even in this evil age, for a son to refuse his father food?"

"Let me tell you," Varma whispered eagerly. "Today the family was having fried fish—I could smell it. I called to my daughter-in-law to bring me a piece. She came to the door and said No . . ."

---

[20] *dhoti*—the traditional long loincloth worn by Indian men.

"Said No?" It was Bhatia's voice that cracked. A *drongo*[21] shot out of the tree and sped away. "*No?*"

"No, she said no, Rakesh has ordered her to give me nothing fried. No butter, he says, no oil—"

"No butter? No oil? How does he expect his father to *live?*"

Old Varma nodded with melancholy triumph. "That is how he treats me—after I have brought him up, given him an education, made him a great doctor. Great doctor! This is the way great doctors treat their fathers, Bhatia," for the son's sterling personality and character now underwent a curious sea change. Outwardly all might be the same but the interpretation had altered: his masterly efficiency was nothing but cold heartlessness, his authority was only tyranny in disguise.

There was cold comfort in complaining to neighbors and, on such a miserable diet, Varma found himself slipping, weakening and soon becoming a genuinely sick man. Powders and pills and mixtures were not only brought in when dealing with a crisis like an upset stomach but became a regular part of his diet—became his diet, complained Varma, supplanting the natural foods he craved. There were pills to regulate his bowel movements, pills to bring down his blood pressure, pills to deal with his arthritis and, eventually, pills to keep his heart beating. In between there were panicky rushes to the hospital, some humiliating experiences with the stomach pump and enema, which left him frightened and helpless. He cried easily, shriveling up on his bed, but if he complained of a pain or even a vague, grey fear in the night, Rakesh would simply open another bottle of pills and force him to take one. "I have my duty to you, Papa," he said when his father begged to be let off.

"Let me be," Varma begged, turning his face away from the pills on the outstretched hand. "Let me die. It would be better. I do not want to live only to eat your medicines."

"Papa, be reasonable."

"I leave that to you," the father cried with sudden spirit. "Let me alone, let me die now, I cannot live like this."

"Lying all day on his pillows, fed every few hours by his daughter-in-law's own hands, visited by every member of his family daily—and then he says he does not want to live 'like this,'" Rakesh was heard to say, laughing, to someone outside the door.

"Deprived of food," screamed the old man on the bed, "his wishes ignored, taunted by his daughter-in-law, laughed at by his grandchildren—*that* is how I live." But he was very old and weak and all anyone heard was an incoherent croak, some

> **"Let me be,"**
> **Varma begged, turning**
> **his face away**
> **from the pills on the**
> **outstretched hand.**
> **"Let me die."**

---

[21] *drongo*—Asian bird.

expressive grunts and cries of genuine pain. Only once, when old Bhatia had come to see him and they sat together under the temple tree, they heard him cry, "God is calling me—and they won't let me go."

The quantities of vitamins and tonics he was made to take were not altogether useless. They kept him alive and even gave him a kind of strength that made him hang on long after he ceased to wish to hang on. It was as though he were straining at a rope, trying to break it, and it would not break, it was still strong. He only hurt himself, trying.

In the evening, that summer, the servants would come into his cell, grip his bed, one at each end, and carry it out to the verandah, there setting it down with a thump that jarred every tooth in his head. In answer to his agonized complaints they said the Doctor Sahib had told them he must take the evening air and the evening air they would make him take—thump. Then Veena, that smiling, hypocritical pudding in a rustling sari, would appear and pile up the pillows under his head till he was propped up stiffly into a sitting position that made his head swim and his back ache.

"Let me lie down," he begged. "I can't sit up any more."

"Try, Papa, Rakesh said you can if you try," she said, and drifted away to the other end of the verandah where her transistor radio vibrated to the lovesick tunes from the cinema that she listened to all day.

So there he sat, like some stiff corpse, terrified, gazing out on the lawn where his grandsons played cricket, in danger of getting one of their hard-spun balls in his eye, and at the gate that opened onto the dusty and rubbish-heaped lane but still bore, proudly, a newly touched-up sign-board that bore his son's name and qualifications, his own name having vanished from the gate long ago.

At last the sky-blue Ambassador arrived, the cricket game broke up in haste, the car drove in smartly and the doctor, the great doctor, all in white, stepped out. Someone ran up to take his bag from him, others to escort him up the steps. "Will you have tea?" his wife called, turning down the transistor set, "or a Coca-Cola? Shall I fry you some samosas?"[22] But he did not reply or even glance in her direction. Ever a devoted son, he went first to the corner where his father sat gazing, stricken, at some undefined spot in the dusty yellow air that swam before him. He did not turn his head to look at his son. But he stopped gobbling air with his uncontrolled lips and set his jaw as hard as a sick and very old man could set it.

"Papa," his son said, tenderly, sitting down on the edge of the bed and reaching out to press his feet.

Old Varma tucked his feet under him, out of the way, and continued to gaze

---

[22] samosas—small fried turnovers filled with seasoned meat or vegetables.

stubbornly into the yellow air of the summer evening.

"Papa, I'm home."

Varma's hand jerked suddenly, in a sharp, derisive movement, but he did not speak.

"How are you feeling, Papa?"

Then Varma turned and looked at his son. His face was so out of control and all in pieces, that the multitude of expressions that crossed it could not make up a whole and convey to the famous man exactly what his father thought of him, his skill, his art.

"I'm dying," he croaked. "Let me die, I tell you."

"Papa, you're joking," his son smiled at him, lovingly. "I've brought you a new tonic to make you feel better. You must take it, it will make you feel stronger again. Here it is. Promise me you will take it regularly, Papa."

Varma's mouth worked as hard as though he still had a gob of betel in it (his supply of betel had been cut off years ago). Then he spat out some words, as sharp and bitter as poison, into his son's face. "Keep your tonic—I want none—I won't take any more of—your medicines. None. Never," and he swept the bottle out of his son's hand with a wave of his own, suddenly grand, suddenly effective.

His son jumped, for the bottle was smashed and thick brown syrup had splashed up, staining his white trousers. His wife let out a cry and came running.

All around the old man was hubbub once again, noise, attention.

He gave one push to the pillows at his back and dislodged them so he could sink down on his back, quite flat again. He closed his eyes and pointed his chin at the ceiling, like some dire prophet, groaning, "God is calling me—now let me go."

QUESTIONS TO CONSIDER

1. Why does Varma's perception of his son change?

2. Who do you find more sympathetic, Varma or Rakesh? Explain why.

3. What do you think is the lesson that Desai is trying to get across in the story? Do you believe conflict is unavoidable?

Facing the Light

TALAT ABBASI

Talat Abbasi was born in Karachi, Pakistan. She finished her education in England and now lives in the United States. Abbasi is a member of a new generation of Indian writers who are as familiar with England and the United States as with their traditional homeland. This group of writers, which includes Arundhati Roy, Jhumpa Lahiri (see page 561), Vikram Chandra, and Romesh Guneskara, will push the boundaries of Indian writing in the years to come.

"I wish to be fair to you," he says and the head goes up as it always does when he wishes to be fair to her. And in sympathy, in **solidarity**,[1] the eyebrows and nose rise to the occasion, positioning themselves upwards. And the mouth tightens into a straight line to underline it all. And together they all say the same thing: And now you may thank us, and now you may thank us. And she, bent over her sewing machine, pricks her finger with its needle which she is pretending to thread and snatches up a tissue, wipes off the drop of blood and tosses it in the direction of the maidservant. The woman springs out of the sea of silk and muslin on the Persian carpet, giggles as she catches it, darts across to the wastepaper basket and still giggling, leaps back into the pile of saris.[2] The room is looking like a smuggler's den with trunks and suitcases spilling out hoards of dazzling material. And there is scarcely room to stand let alone sit for rolls of georgette are billowing on the sofa, brocades are draped over chairs and everything is flowing onto the carpet where a clean bedsheet has been spread.

The seasons are changing. Another few days and summer will be upon Karachi, stretching endlessly like the desert itself from which hot winds are already rising. The brush with cool weather a memory.

So they are right in the midst of sorting out her wardrobe, packing away the heavier silks and satins and unpacking the cool

---

[1] **soldarity**—agreement of attitude or purpose.

[2] sari—typical dress of Indian and Pakistani women, consisting of a long piece of cotton or silk wrapped around the body with one end falling to the feet and the other thrown over the shoulder.

cottons and **frothy**[3] chiffons and she is instructing the little maidservant—these for washing, these for dry cleaning, that black one throw over to me, I have just the magenta and purple border to liven it up. That petticoat for mending. And this whole lot kicked towards her, all that for throwing out. Yes yes of course that is what she meant—that she could have them all. But no, again no, not this midnight blue chiffon sari, most certainly not. Is she in her senses that she can even ask again? A thousand, twelve hundred rupees for the embroidery alone, for these hundreds of silver sequins—real silver, each one of them, sprinkled all over like stars. And she, whenever she'd worn it, so like a goddess who on a summer night stepping out of heaven had hastily snatched a piece of the star-spangled sky to cover herself with. For after all, that had been the whole idea, she'd designed it herself with herself in mind. And now give it away to a servant? Just like that? Throw it down the drain? Preposterous. How did she dare ask again? How did she dare even think? Yes even if the silver was tarnished, even if every single star had blackened and the sari no more than a shabby rag. Which shouldn't have happened because she herself had packed it away at the end of last season, with these hands, trusting no one, wrapped it up in layer upon layer of muslin, buried it like a mummy, deep inside a steel trunk. Safe, airtight. She'd been so certain the Karachi air couldn't possibly get to it and tarnish the silver. But it had and had snuffed out

the stars like candles. And now, on her lap, this veil of darkness, dullness.

And he chooses that precise moment to rap so loudly with his cane on her bedroom door that the midnight blue sari slithers to her feet, an inky shadow. She quickly bends over her sewing machine, pretending to thread the needle. What's he doing here at this time, jamming the doorway of her bedroom? Never home for dinner why here even before tea? "Malik Sahib," announces the woman as though she needs assistance in recognizing her own husband of twenty-two—three—years. And rushes to evict a stack of summer cotton saris which have **usurped**[4] the sofa. But he makes an impatient gesture with his hands and remains standing and immediately begins to be fair to her. So anxious is he to be fair to her.

"Go to your quarter," she says to the woman, for she cannot allow him to be fair to her in front of the servants. Not when he's going out of his way to be fair to her and she can tell that he's going to outdo himself in fairness today. She can tell by that red flower which has blossomed overnight upon his chest and is now blazing out of his button hole. She can tell by that moustache, till yesterday steel grey, stiff as a rod, today henna[5] red, oiled, curled softly, coaxed gently to a fine point at both edges. Like a pair of wings dipped in a rosy sunset!

---

[3] **frothy**—foamy.

[4] **usurped**—seized by force.

[5] henna—a reddish-orange dye made from the leaves of the Asian henna tree.

And as surely as a pair of wings ever did fly she can tell that that moustache will fly tonight.

"But the saris . . ." Such a thrill of excitement has shot through her, lighting up the saucer eyes in the dark face as though car headlights have suddenly flashed in a tunnel. She must stay, she must listen. She mustn't miss a word of this.

"Later."

The woman dares not say another word and hurriedly picks up her slippers at the door.

"Tea in half an hour," she says to the woman so he doesn't spend all evening being fair to her.

The door is closing after her and he is already stretching himself up to his full height—and beyond—in preparation for ultimate fairness to her. Striding over, he will come straight to the point. He will not waste his time blaming her for anything because he realizes that she cannot help herself. And because she will in any case pay for it, regret it all, regrets made more bitter by the remembrance of his own decency throughout, for after all how many men, how many men—but no, straight to the point. Looming over her, smiling, positively beaming down at her in anticipation of her shock at his news, he must tell her that it is too late for regrets. He is leaving. Yes. Leaving and this time it is final. She heard right. She did not imagine it. But in case she thinks she did, he will thump the ground with his cane.

Three times he will thump the ground with his cane. And three times the ground **reverberates.**[6] Final. Final. Final. Yet he will be fair to her. Indeed more than. He will be generous. Large hearted.

And so, his chest is swelling, expanding, the petals on it trembling as it grows larger and larger. In any case, he has a position to maintain and so she will be maintained in the style which she has always been used to and which—stretching himself further up, risking a launch into space in his determination to be fair to her—a man in his position can well afford. Therefore car, house, servants, nothing will change. And looking down at her as at a pebble he has just flung at the bottom of a well he reassures her: car, house, servants . . .

Car, house, servants! Tea in five minutes, she should've said. For—car, house, servants—what more was there? Her fault, her mistake, her stupidity thinking a half hour would be needed, thinking there was so much to say now when not a word had ever been spoken before.

Is she listening? Is she listening?

Noises. Just noises. Two prisoners in neighboring cells and no one on the other side. Hence the tapping noises. One tap for food, two for money. Short taps, sharp taps, clear taps. And please, not too many. Just enough to pull along, I in my cell, you in yours.

Has she heard? Car, house, serv . . .

---

[6] **reverberates**—reechoes or resounds.

The lid crashes down on the sewing machine, the spool of cotton, the thimble, flying to the floor. The other side then! To the far end of the room, to the window, to her big brass bed, there to spread out the sari, all six yards of it, give it another look, every inch of it, one last chance, for surely, surely in the bright light of day, the sun shining directly on it, it would look different. Yes it would, of course it would, everything looks different in the light. So there by the open window, she would see it again, the sparkle of a thousand stars, lost here, in the shadows of the room. It would still be salvaged. Still be saved.

He cannot believe this. Getting up, walking away, right in the middle of his being fair to her. Leaving him talking as though to himself, turning her back to him . . .

Facing the light. The sari laid out on the bed. The curtains drawn aside. The sun streaming through the window, pouring down the skylight onto the bed, warming the brass, setting afire the ruby carpet. Yet here too, that veil of darkness, dullness, will not yield but instead spreads its claim everywhere. For now she sees that same layer of darkness, dullness, on everything. Nothing is safe then, for it is in the air, the very air. Nothing escapes. Nothing remains the same. The toughest metals suffer. Brass blackens. Silver loses its **luster.**[7] Gold dulls. This bed. These bangles. Constantly being polished and repolished. Even these grilles on this window. Painted how long ago?

A month? Two? And already here, there, in patches, the rust is cutting through. Everything is being attacked.

As though an unseen force is snaking its way through the city, choosing its victims, the strongest, the most precious, stalking them, ferreting them out as they lie hidden under paint and polish, shrouded in trunks. Strikes them, robs them of their sparkle, their luster, their very light.

. . . as if he isn't there, as if he doesn't exist. Very well then. Out through that door. This instant.

And some things you simply cannot keep polishing and repolishing no matter how precious they are. Too fragile, the fabric. It will have to be discarded, thrown away on that heap of old clothes. She will have it after all. She will. There is no help for it, for it is in the air, the very air. And so, still facing the light, she begins to fold the sari.

---

[7] **luster**—gloss or shine.

QUESTIONS TO CONSIDER

1. Why is Malik Sahib leaving his wife? From what in the story do you infer this?

2. What purpose does the silver-sequined sari serve in the story?

3. Do you think having two narrators makes the story more effective or more confusing? Explain your answer.

Three Poems

JAYANTA MAHAPATRA

Jayanta Mahapatra (1928–   ) was educated as a scientist and spent thirty-six years teaching physics. Mahapatra began to write poetry in the 1960s and has since become one of the important literary figures in India, publishing poems, stories, essays, translations from his native language Oriya, as well as a literary magazine. As a poet, and a scientist, Mahapatra has struggled with the things in life that are knowable and mysterious. He is fascinated by the different ways a scientist and poet define these things.

30th January 1982: A Story

Another day.[1] Like any other.
The bleating goat on the butcher's block
quickened its last breath and stared wide-eyed.
Its cry bent deeper still over the fringe of its death
while the butcher worried that his knife
was fast losing its sharpness.
At this moment the mobile loudspeaker van
of the Department of Public Relations swept past
pouring out the words of Gandhi's once-favorite hymn.
The rich woman cursed the Government
for waking her up so early when it was not even fully light.
Her five-year-old daughter **cuddled**[2]
the broken doll's head in her arms for she needed
to fill her life. Or so she thought.

---

[1] day—Mohandas Gandhi, whose nonviolent protests led India to independence from the British Empire, was killed by an assassin on January 30, 1948.

[2] **cuddled**—hugged, embraced.

The sunlight stole slowly to the fallow fields
where village women were relieving themselves in the open.
The postman starting out for work
stopped at the garden fence and suddenly clutched his
    hernia;[3]
he gave himself up to those letters
that shut him out for ever.
The empty bedroom sank heavily onto one of the evil
    schemes
which led through the long night into dawn.
No one heard the cry ripening inside himself.
Neighbors both, Amar Babu and Sham Babu smiled
sweetly at one another as they chose
their choice cuts of meat hanging from the hooks
in the marketplace. On a day just like this.
As the scent of new mango blossoms blew in
with the morning breeze, restless
with the heritage of blood.

Taste for Tomorrow

At Puri,[4] the crows.

The one wide street
lolls[5] out like a giant tongue.

---

[3] hernia—the displacement of an organ outside the body cavity that normally contains it, especially the abdomen.

[4] Puri—coastal city in western India. It is famed for the Jaganatha temple that receives hundreds of thousands of pilgrims each year.

[5] **lolls**—to hang or move in a lazy manner.

Five faceless lepers
move aside
as a priest passes by.

And at the street's end
the crowds thronging the temple door:

a huge holy flower
swaying in the wind of greater reasons.

Sanskrit[6]

Awaken them; they are knobs of sound
that seem to melt and crumple up
like some jellyfish of tropical seas,
torn from sleep with a hand lined by prophecies.
Listen hard; their male, **gaunt**[7] world **sprawls**[8] the page
like rows of tree trunks reeking in the smoke
of ages, the branches glazed and dead;
as though longing to make up with the sky,
but having lost touch with themselves
were unable to find themselves, hold meaning.

And yet, down the steps into the water at Varanasi,[9]
where the lifeless bodies seem to grow human,
the shaggy heads of word-buds move back and forth
between the harsh castanets[10] of the rain
and the noiseless feathers of summer—

---

[6] Sanskrit—the ancient language of India, used for literary and religious works.

[7] **gaunt**—grim or desolate in appearance.

[8] **sprawls**—spreads out over or upon.

[9] Varanasi—Hinduism's most holy city, a site for pilgrimage (also known as Benares).

[10] castanets—small pieces of hard material, clicked together for rhythmic accompaniment.

aware that their syllables' overwhelming silence
would not escape the hearers now, and which
must remain that mysterious divine path
guarded by drifts of queer, quivering banyans:[11]
a language of clogs over cobbles, casting
its uncertain spell, trembling sadly into mist.

---

[11] banyans—large Indian trees that can grow to cover several acres.

QUESTIONS TO CONSIDER

1. How does "30th January 1982: A Story" memorialize Gandhi's assassination?

2. What is the contrast in the final couplet of "Taste for Tomorrow"? What does Mahapatra mean by it?

3. What is the "them" of "Sanksrit"? What is the contrast between the first and second stanzas?

4. How would you describe the contrasts in Indian society that Mahapatra presents in his poems? What generalizations about modern Indian society can you make from these contrasts?

Four Poems

FAIZ AHMED FAIZ

Faiz Ahmed Faiz (1911–1984) was born in India when the country was still under British rule. When independence was granted in 1947, the country was divided into two nations: Pakistan and India. Faiz chose to move to Pakistan with its Muslim majority and became the editor of one of the major newspapers. Faiz's political views often brought him into conflict with Pakistan's repressive governments. He was twice imprisoned and eventually forced into exile for some years. Nonetheless, he was recognized as one of the subcontinent's most important writers. Faiz wrote in his native language, Urdu, working in ancient poetic forms. Much of his poetry is about love and longing which puts it in the long tradition of Indian poetry. Faiz wrote that "the true subject of poetry is the loss of the beloved." But his experiences fighting for Indian independence and of imprisonment in Pakistan gave his poems a political dimension not often found in traditional Indian poetics.

Three Quatrains

I

This evening my old friend, loneliness,
has come to drink with me. We wait together
for the moon to rise, for your brilliant face
to appear in the heart of every shadow.

2

These spring nights deepen
      softly as wine being poured.
Mornings arrive like fresh petals opening,
      rose-tinted and **aromatic.**[1]
Why have you abandoned the goblets?
      You must honor the season,
fill your heart to the **brim,**[2] and your eyes
      too,
          with longing and desire.

3

Though they have stolen my paper and
      pen, I don't grieve.
I dip my fingers into my heart's blood.
Though they have gagged me, it hardly
      matters.
I have given my voice to every link in my
      chains.

Elegy

I don't have the courage to look;
      even now when I pass that way
a pain in my heart slows my steps:
      it says the gate is still open,
desire without hope is still sleeping in the
      courtyard
and in some corner, half-hidden, there is
      memory,
a heart-broken child with outstretched
      arms.

---

[1] **aromatic**—having a distinctive odor.
[2] **brim**—the edge of anything hollow.

My heart implores:
    "Let's go someplace far away
where no gate opens on **futility**,[3]
no memory crouches, holding its beggar
    bowl,
where none of the walls knows the ecstasy
    of longing for the beloved face,
and no shadows grieve for flowers that
    once were here."

Prison Meeting

This night is the tree of pain, greater than
    you or me,
greater because in its thicket of branches
a thousand candle-bearing stars have lost
    their way.
In this tree's shadow another thousand
    moons
have wept the last of their light.

This night, the tree of pain, vaster than you
    or me,
lets go of a few pale leaves that fall upon
    your hair;
they bloom there, a spray of pomegranate
    flowers.
From the dew of this same night some
    moments of silence
send rain onto your brow: it forms a pearly
    diadem.[4]

---

[3] **futility**—ineffectiveness, uselessness.

[4] diadem—an ornamental headband worn as a symbol of royalty.

This night is hell's own black yet the
    darkness
flares with your beauty, the golden stream.
A river of blood flows back on its **nether**[5]
    side.
This is my song. The grief whose ashes
    glow
in the circle of your arms, this fruit of the
    tree of pain,
will be the **conflagration**[6] burning
from the furnace of my pain. The branches
of this tree of night shoot arrows into my
    heart.
I pull them out, arrow after arrow.
These will be my weapons.

Be Near Me

Be near me now,
My tormenter, my love, be near me—
At this hour when night comes down,
When, having drunk from the gash of
    sunset, darkness comes
With the balm of musk in its hands, its
    diamond lancets,
When it comes with cries of lamentation,
            with laughter and songs;
Its blue-gray anklets of pain clinking with
    every step.
At this hour when hearts, deep in their
    hiding places,

---

[5] **nether**—lower or under.

[6] **conflagration**—destructive fire.

Have begun to hope once more, when they
    start their vigil
For hands still enfolded in sleeves;
When wine being poured makes the sound
        of inconsolable children
    who, though you try with all your
    heart,
        cannot be soothed.
When whatever you want to do cannot be
    done,
When nothing is of any use;
—At this hour when night comes down,
When night comes, dragging its long face,
        dressed in mourning,
Be with me,
My tormentor, my love, be near me.

QUESTIONS TO CONSIDER

1. What is the tone of these poems?

2. What is being commemorated in "Elegy"?

3. What do you think Faiz meant when he
   observed that "the true subject of poetry is
   the loss of the beloved"? After reading his
   poems, what sort of things do you think Faiz
   meant by "beloved"?

Good Advice Is Rarer Than Rubies

SALMAN RUSHDIE

Salman Rushdie (1947–   ) was born in Bombay in the year that India became an independent nation. He was educated in England and remained there to work. Rushdie became famous in 1988 when his fourth novel, The Satanic Verses, *was condemned by the Iranian government as being defamatory to Islam. A death sentence was pronounced against him, and Rushdie was forced into hiding under police protection. Though he has had more freedom in the last few years, to this day he remains under protection and in fear of his life. Some critics have attacked Rushdie for being insufficiently Indian, but as an international Indian, much of Rushdie's writing examines from the larger view the new nations of India and Pakistan. The following story is set in Pakistan and describes one of the side effects of the large number of Pakistanis who emigrated to England in the 1970s and 1980s. Immigration is heavily restricted, and many Pakistanis try to arrange a visa by claiming to be married to someone who has already emigrated. The government makes these applicants answer detailed questions to prove their relation to the person in England.*

On the last Tuesday of the month, the dawn bus, its headlamps still shining, brought Miss Rehana to the gates of the British Consulate. It arrived pushing a cloud of dust, veiling her beauty from the eyes of strangers until she descended. The bus was brightly painted in multicolored **arabesques**,[1] and on the front it said "MOVE OVER DARLING" in green and gold letters; on the back it added "TATA-BATA" and also "O.K. GOOD-LIFE." Miss Rehana told the driver it was a beautiful bus, and he jumped down and held the door open for her, bowing theatrically as she descended.

Miss Rehana's eyes were large and black and bright enough not to need the help of **antimony**,[2] and when the advice expert Muhammad Ali saw them he felt himself becoming young again. He

---

[1] **arabesques**—ornamental designs in which flowers, plants, fruits, animals, and designs are represented in intricate patterns.

[2] **antimony**—a metallic element used in alloys and medicines.

watched her approaching the Consulate gates as the light strengthened, and asking the bearded lala who guarded them in a gold-buttoned khaki uniform with a cockaded[3] turban when they would open. The lala, usually so rude to the Consulate's Tuesday women, answered Miss Rehana with something like courtesy.

"Half an hour," he said gruffly. "Maybe two hours. Who knows? The sahibs[4] are eating their breakfast."

The dusty compound between the bus stop and the Consulate was already full of Tuesday women, some veiled, a few barefaced like Miss Rehana. They all looked frightened, and leaned heavily on the arms of uncles or brothers, who were trying to look confident. But Miss Rehana had come on her own, and did not seem at all alarmed.

Muhammad Ali, who specialized in advising the most vulnerable-looking of these weekly supplicants, found his feet leading him towards the strange, big-eyed, independent girl.

"Miss," he began. "You have come for permit to London, I think so?"

She was standing at a hot-snack stall in the little shanty-town by the edge of the compound, munching chilli-pakoras[5] contentedly. She turned to look at him, and at close range those eyes did bad things to his digestive tract.

"Yes, I have."

"Then, please, you allow me to give some advice? Small cost only."

Miss Rehana smiled. "Good advice is rarer than rubies," she said. "But alas, I cannot pay. I am an orphan, not one of your wealthy ladies."

"Trust my grey hairs," Muhammad Ali urged her.

"My advice is well tempered by experience. You will certainly find it good."

She shook her head. "I tell you I am a poor potato. There are women here with male family members, all earning good wages. Go to them. Good advice should find good money."

I am going crazy, Muhammad Ali thought, because he heard his voice telling her of its own **volition**,[6] "Miss, I have been drawn to you by Fate. What to do? Our meeting was written. I also am a poor man only, but for you my advice comes free."

She smiled again. "Then I must surely listen. When Fate sends a gift, one receives good fortune."

He led her to the low wooden desk in his own special corner of the shanty-town. She followed, continuing to eat pakoras from a little newspaper packet. She did not offer him any.

Muhammad Ali put a cushion on the dusty ground. "Please to sit." She did as he asked. He sat cross-legged across the desk from her, conscious that two or three dozen pairs of male eyes were watching him

---

[3] cockaded—bearing a rose-shaped ornament or arrangement of ribbon used as a badge of office.

[4] sahibs—masters.

[5] pakoras—pieces of cauliflower, carrot, or other vegetable that are covered in a seasoned batter and deep fried.

[6] **volition**—free will.

enviously, that all the other shanty-town men were ogling the latest young lovely to be charmed by the old grey-hair fraud. He took a deep breath to settle himself.

"Name, please."

"Miss Rehana," she told him. "Fiancée of Mustafa Dar of Bradford, London."

"Bradford, England," he corrected her gently. "London is a town only, like Multan or Bahawalpur. England is a great nation full of the coldest fish in the world."

"I see. Thank you," she responded gravely, so that he was unsure if she was making fun of him.

"You have filled application form? Then let me see, please."

She passed him a neatly folded document in a brown envelope.

"Is it OK?" For the first time there was a note of anxiety in her voice.

He patted the desk quite near the place where her hand rested. "I am certain," he said. "Wait on and I will check."

She finished the pakoras while he scanned her papers.

"Tip-top," he pronounced at length. "All in order."

"Thank you for your advice," she said, making as if to rise. "I'll go now and wait by the gate."

"What are you thinking?" he cried loudly, smiting his forehead. "You consider this is easy business? Just give the form and poof, with a big smile they hand over the permit? Miss Rehana, I tell you, you are entering a worse place than any police station."

"Is it so, truly?" His oratory had done the trick. She was a captive audience now, and he would be able to look at her for a few moments longer.

Drawing another calming breath, he launched into his set speech. He told her that the sahibs thought that all the women who came on Tuesdays, claiming to be dependents of bus drivers in Luton or chartered accountants in Manchester, were crooks and liars and cheats.

She protested, "But then I will simply tell them that I, for one, am no such thing!"

Her innocence made him shiver with fear for her. She was a sparrow, he told her, and they were men with hooded eyes, like hawks. He explained that they would ask her questions, personal questions, questions such as a lady's own brother would be too shy to ask. They would ask if she was virgin, and, if not, what her fiancé's love-making habits were, and what secret nicknames they had invented for one another.

Muhammad Ali spoke brutally, on purpose, to lessen the shock she would feel when it, or something like it, actually happened. Her eyes remained steady, but her hands began to flutter at the edges of the desk.

He went on:

"They will ask you how many rooms are in your family home, and what color

"What are you thinking?" he cried loudly, smiting his forehead. "You consider this is easy business?"

are the walls, and what days do you empty the **rubbish.**[7] They will ask your man's mother's third cousin's aunt's step-daughter's middle name. And all these things they have already asked your Mustafa Dar in his Bradford. And if you make one mistake, you are finished."

"Yes," she said, and he could hear her disciplining her voice. "And what is your advice, old man?"

It was at this point that Muhammad Ali usually began to whisper urgently, to mention that he knew a man, a very good type, who worked in the Consulate, and through him, for a fee, the necessary papers could be delivered, with all the proper authenticating seals. Business was good, because the women would often pay him five hundred rupees or give him a gold bracelet for his pains, and go away happy.

They came from hundreds of miles away—he normally made sure of this before beginning to trick them—so even when they discovered they had been swindled they were unlikely to return. They went away to Sargodha or Lalukhet and began to pack, and who knows at what point they found out they had been **gulled,**[8] but it was at a too-late point, anyway.

Life is hard, and an old man must live by his wits. It was not up to Muhammad Ali to have compassion for these Tuesday women.

But once again his voice betrayed him, and instead of starting his customary speech it began to reveal to her his greatest secret.

"Miss Rehana," his voice said, and he listened to it in amazement, "you are a rare person, a jewel, and for you I will do what I would not do for my own daughter, perhaps. One document has come into my possession that can solve all your worries at one stroke."

"And what is this sorcerer's paper?" she asked, her eyes unquestionably laughing at him now.

His voice fell low-as-low.

"Miss Rehana, it is a British passport. Completely genuine and pukka[9] goods. I have a good friend who will put your name and photo, and then, hey-presto, England there you come!"

He had said it!

Anything was possible now, on this day of his insanity. Probably he would give her the thing free-gratis, and then kick himself for a year afterwards.

Old fool, he berated himself. *The oldest fools are bewitched by the youngest girls.*

"Let me understand you," she was saying. "You are proposing I should commit a crime . . ."

"Not crime," he interposed. "Facilitation."

". . . and go to Bradford, London, illegally, and therefore justify the low

---

[7] **rubbish**—garbage, trash.

[8] **gulled**—deceived, tricked.

[9] pukka—Anglo-Indian slang for good, proper, genuine.

opinion the Consulate sahibs have of us all. Old babuji,[10] this is not good advice."

"Bradford, *England*," he corrected her mournfully. "You should not take my gift in such a spirit."

"Then how?"

"Bibi, I am a poor fellow, and I have offered this prize because you are so beautiful. Do not spit on my generosity. Take the thing. Or else don't take, go home, forget England, only do not go into that building and lose your dignity."

But she was on her feet, turning away from him, walking towards the gates, where the women had begun to cluster and the lala was swearing at them to be patient or none of them would be admitted at all.

"So be a fool," Muhammad Ali shouted after her. "What goes of my father's if you are?" (Meaning, what was it to him.)

She did not turn.

"It is the curse of our people," he yelled. "We are poor, we are ignorant, and we completely refuse to learn."

"Hey, Muhammad Ali," the woman at the betel-nut stall called across to him. "Too bad, she likes them young."

That day Muhammad Ali did nothing but stand around near the Consulate gates. Many times he scolded himself, *Go from here, old goof, lady does not desire to speak with you any further.* But when she came out, she found him waiting.

"Salaam, advice wallah,"[11] she greeted him.

She seemed calm, and at peace with him again, and he thought, *My God, ya Allah, she has pulled it off. The British sahibs also have been drowning in her eyes and she has got her passage to England.*

He smiled at her hopefully. She smiled back with no trouble at all.

"Miss Rehana Begum," he said, "felicitations, daughter, on what is obviously your hour of triumph."

Impulsively, she took his forearm in her hand.

"Come," she said. "Let me buy you a pakora to thank you for your advice and to apologize for my rudeness, too."

They stood in the dust of the afternoon compound near the bus, which was getting ready to leave. Coolies[12] were tying bedding rolls to the roof. A hawker shouted at the passengers, trying to sell them love stories and green medicines, both of which cured unhappiness. Miss Rehana and a happy Muhammad Ali ate their pakoras sitting on the bus's "front mud-guard," that is, the bumper. The old advice expert began softly to hum a tune from a movie soundtrack. The day's heat was gone.

"It was an arranged engagement," Miss Rehana said all at once. "I was nine years old when my parents fixed it.

---

[10] babuji—an honorific title, *babu* for old man, *-ji* for respect.

[11] wallah—Anglo-Indian slang for man of business; for example, a Shakespeare-wallah is an actor.

[12] Coolies—hired workers.

Mustafa Dar was already thirty at that time, but my father wanted someone who could look after me as he had done himself and Mustafa was a man known to Daddyji as a solid type. Then my parents died and Mustafa Dar went to England and said he would send for me. That was many years ago. I have his photo, but he is like a stranger to me. Even his voice, I do not recognize it on the phone."

The confession took Muhammad Ali by surprise, but he nodded with what he hoped looked like wisdom.

"Still and after all," he said, "one's parents act in one's best interests. They found you a good and honest man who has kept his word and sent for you. And now you have a lifetime to get to know him, and to love."

He was puzzled, now, by the bitterness that had infected her smile.

"But, old man," she asked him, "why have you already packed me and posted me off to England?"

He stood up, shocked.

"You looked happy—so I just assumed . . . excuse me, but they turned you down or what?"

"I got all their questions wrong," she replied. "Distinguishing marks I put on the wrong cheeks, bathroom decor I completely redecorated, all absolutely topsy-turvy, you see."

"But what to do? How will you go?"

"Now I will go back to Lahore and my job. I work in a great house, as ayah[13] to three good boys. They would have been sad to see me leave."

"But this is tragedy," Muhammad Ali lamented. "Oh, how I pray that you had taken up my offer! Now, but, it is not possible, I regret to inform. Now they have your form on file, cross-check can be made, even the passport will not **suffice.**[14]

"It is spoilt, all spoilt, and it could have been so easy if advice had been accepted in good time."

"I do not think," she told him, "I truly do not think you should be sad."

Her last smile, which he watched from the compound until the bus concealed it in a dust-cloud, was the happiest thing he had ever seen in his long, hot, hard, unloving life.

---

[13] ayah—a nanny or babysitter.

[14] **suffice**—to be enough or adequate.

QUESTIONS TO CONSIDER

1. How would you describe Miss Rehana? What are her hopes and fears as you can infer them?

2. Why does Muhammad Ali try to help her and later wait for her?

3. In the context of the story what does the title mean? What is its tone?

The Third and Final Continent

JHUMPA LAHIRI

Jhumpa Lahiri is part of a new generation of Indian writers who are deeply westernized. The child of Bengali parents, Lahiri grew up in Rhode Island and was educated in Boston. As American as she is Indian, Lahiri is still recognizably part of the Indian tradition. Many of her stories deal with the experience of the vast numbers of Indians who have moved to Europe and the United States since the 1960s in search of economic opportunity. "The Third and Final Continent" is from Lahiri's first collection of stories, The Interpreter of Maladies.

I left India in 1964 with a certificate in commerce and the equivalent, in those days, of ten dollars to my name. For three weeks I sailed on the S.S. Roma, an Italian cargo vessel, in a cabin next to the ship's engine, across the Arabian Sea, the Red Sea, the Mediterranean, and finally to England. I lived in London, in Finsbury Park, in a house occupied entirely by penniless Bengali bachelors like myself, at least a dozen and sometimes more, all struggling to educate and establish ourselves abroad.

I attended lectures at L.S.E.[1] and worked at the university library to get by. We lived three or four to a room, shared a single, icy toilet, and took turns cooking pots of egg curry, which we ate with our hands on a table covered with newspapers.

Apart from our jobs we had few responsibilities. On weekends we lounged barefoot in drawstring pajamas, drinking tea and smoking Rothmans, or set out to watch cricket at Lord's. Some weekends the house was crammed with still more Bengalis, to whom we had introduced ourselves at the greengrocer, or on the Tube,[2] and we made yet more egg curry, and played Mukesh on a Grundig reel-to-reel, and soaked our dirty dishes in the bathtub. Every now and then someone in the house moved out, to live with a woman whom his family back in Calcutta had determined he was to wed. In 1969, when

---

[1] L.S.E.—the London School of Economics, one of the world's finest academic institutions.

[2] Tube—the subway system in London.

I was thirty-six years old, my own marriage was arranged. Around the same time, I was offered a full-time job in America, in the processing department of a library at M.I.T.[3] The salary was generous enough to support a wife, and I was honored to be hired by a world-famous university, and so I obtained a green card[4] and prepared to travel farther still.

By then I had enough money to go by plane. I flew first to Calcutta, to attend my wedding, and a week later to Boston, to begin my new job. During the flight I read "The Student Guide to North America," for although I was no longer a student, I was on a budget all the same. I learned that Americans drove on the right side of the road, not the left, and that they called a lift an elevator and an engaged phone busy. "The pace of life in North America is different from Britain, as you will soon discover," the guidebook informed me. "Everybody feels he must get to the top. Don't expect an English cup of tea." As the plane began its descent over Boston Harbor, the pilot announced the weather and the time, and that President Nixon had declared a national holiday: two American men had landed on the moon. Several passengers cheered. "God bless America!" one of them hollered. Across the aisle, I saw a woman praying.

I spent my first night at the Y.M.C.A. in Central Square, Cambridge, an inexpensive accommodation recommended by my guidebook which was within walking distance of M.I.T. The room contained a cot,[5] a desk, and a small wooden cross on one wall. A sign on the door said that cooking was strictly forbidden. A bare window overlooked Massachusetts Avenue. Car horns, shrill[6] and prolonged,[7] blared one after another. Sirens and flashing lights heralded endless emergencies, and a succession of buses rumbled past, their doors opening and closing with a powerful hiss, throughout the night. The noise was constantly distracting, at times suffocating. I felt it deep in my ribs, just as I had felt the furious drone of the engine on the S.S. Roma. But there was no ship's deck to escape to, no glittering ocean to thrill my soul, no breeze to cool my face, no one to talk to. I was too tired to pace the gloomy corridors of the Y.M.C.A. in my pajamas. Instead I sat at the desk and stared out the window. In the morning I reported to my job at the Dewey Library, a beige fortlike building by Memorial Drive. I also opened a bank account, rented a post-office box, and bought a plastic bowl and a spoon. I went to a supermarket called Purity Supreme, wandering up and down the aisles, comparing prices with those in England. In the end I bought a carton of milk and a box of cornflakes. This was my first meal in America. Even the simple

---

[3] M.I.T.— the Massachusetts Institute of Technology, the U.S.'s most important university for the study of science and engineering.

[4] green card—a permit for noncitizens to live and work in the U.S.

[5] cot—small bed.

[6] shrill—high-pitched and harsh sounding.

[7] prolonged—drawn out.

chore of buying milk was new to me; in London we'd had bottles delivered each morning to our door.

In a week I had adjusted, more or less. I ate cornflakes and milk morning and night, and bought some bananas for variety, slicing them into the bowl with the edge of my spoon. I left my carton of milk on the shaded part of the windowsill, as I had seen other residents at the Y.M.C.A. do. To pass the time in the evenings I read the Boston *Globe* downstairs, in a spacious room with stained-glass windows. I read every article and advertisement, so that I would grow familiar with things, and when my eyes grew tired I slept. Only I did not sleep well. Each night I had to keep the window wide open; it was the only source of air in the stifling room, and the noise was intolerable. I would lie on the cot with my fingers pressed into my ears, but when I drifted off to sleep my hands fell away, and the noise of the traffic would wake me up again. Pigeon feathers drifted onto the windowsill, and one evening, when I poured milk over my cornflakes, I saw that it had soured. Nevertheless I resolved to stay at the Y.M.C.A. for six weeks, until my wife's passport and green card were ready. Once she arrived I would have to rent a proper apartment, and from time to time I studied the classified section of the newspaper, or stopped in at the housing office at M.I.T. during my lunch break to see what was available. It was in this manner that I discovered a room for immediate occupancy, in a house on a quiet street, the listing said, for eight dollars per week. I dialed the number from a pay telephone, sorting through the coins, with which I was still unfamiliar, smaller and lighter than shillings,[8] heavier and brighter than paisas.[9]

"Who is speaking?" a woman demanded. Her voice was bold and clamorous.

"Yes, good afternoon, Madam. I am calling about the room for rent."

"Harvard or Tech?"'

"I beg your pardon?"

"Are you from Harvard or Tech?"

Gathering that Tech referred to the Massachusetts Institute of Technology, I replied, "I work at Dewey Library," adding tentatively, "at Tech."

"I only rent rooms to boys from Harvard or Tech!"

"Yes, Madam."

I was given an address and an appointment for seven o'clock that evening. Thirty minutes before the hour I set out, my guidebook in my pocket, my breath fresh with Listerine. I turned down a street shaded with trees, perpendicular to Massachusetts Avenue. In spite of the heat I wore a coat and tie, regarding the event as I would any other interview; I had never lived in the home of a person who was not Indian. The house, surrounded by a chain-link fence, was off-white with dark-brown trim, with a tangle of forsythia bushes plastered against its front and sides. When

---

[8] shillings—smallest denomination of coin in England.

[9] paisas—smallest denomination of coin in India.

I pressed the bell, the woman with whom I had spoken on the phone hollered from what seemed to be just the other side of the door, "One minute, please!"

Several minutes later the door was opened by a tiny, extremely old woman. A mass of snowy hair was arranged like a small sack on top of her head. As I stepped into the house she sat down on a wooden bench positioned at the bottom of a narrow carpeted staircase. Once she was settled on the bench, in a small pool of light, she peered up at me, giving me her undivided attention. She wore a long black skirt that spread like a stiff tent to the floor, and a starched[10] white shirt edged with ruffles at the throat and cuffs. Her hands, folded together in her lap, had long **pallid**[11] fingers, with swollen knuckles and tough yellow nails. Age had battered her features so that she almost resembled a man, with sharp, shrunken eyes and prominent creases on either side of her nose. Her lips, chapped and faded, had nearly disappeared, and her eyebrows were missing altogether. Nevertheless she looked fierce.

"Lock up!" she commanded. She shouted even though I stood only a few feet away. "Fasten the chain and firmly press that button on the knob! This is the first thing you shall do when you enter, is that clear?"

I locked the door as directed and examined the house. Next to the bench was a small round table, its legs fully concealed, much like the woman's, by a skirt of lace.

The table held a lamp, a transistor radio, a leather change purse with a silver clasp, and a telephone. A thick wooden cane was propped against one side. There was a parlor to my right, lined with bookcases and filled with shabby claw-footed furniture. In the corner of the parlor I saw a grand piano with its top down, piled with papers. The piano's bench was missing; it seemed to be the one on which the woman was sitting. Somewhere in the house a clock chimed seven times.

"You're **punctual!**"[12] the woman proclaimed "I expect you shall be so with the rent!"

"I have a letter, Madam." In my jacket pocket was a letter from M.I.T. confirming my employment, which I had brought along to prove that I was indeed from Tech.

She stared at the letter, then handed it back to me carefully, gripping it with her fingers as if it were a plate heaped with food. She did not wear glasses, and I wondered if she'd read a word of it. "The last boy was always late! Still owes me eight dollars! Harvard boys aren't what they used to be! Only Harvard and Tech in this house! How's Tech, boy?"

"It is very well."

"You checked the lock?"

"Yes, Madam."

She unclasped her fingers, slapped the space beside her on the bench with one

---

[10] starched—stiffened with starch.

[11] **pallid**—pale and sickly looking.

[12] **punctual**—on time, neither early nor late.

hand, and told me to sit down. For a moment she was silent. Then she **intoned,**[13] as if she alone possessed this knowledge:

"There is an American flag on the moon!"

"Yes, Madam." Until then I had not thought very much about the moon shot. It was in the newspaper, of course, article upon article. The astronauts had landed on the shores of the Sea of Tranquillity, I had read, traveling farther than anyone in the history of civilization. For a few hours they explored the moon's surface. They gathered rocks in their pockets, described their surroundings (a magnificent desolation, according to one astronaut), spoke by phone to the President, and planted a flag in lunar soil. The voyage was hailed as man's most awesome achievement.

The woman **bellowed,**[14] "A flag on the moon, boy! I heard it on the radio! Isn't that splendid?"

"Yes, Madam."

But she was not satisfied with my reply. Instead she commanded, "Say 'Splendid!'"

I was both baffled and somewhat insulted by the request. It reminded me of the way I was taught multiplication tables as a child, repeating after the master, sitting cross-legged on the floor of my one-room Tollygunge school. It also reminded me of my wedding, when I had repeated endless Sanskrit verses after the priest, verses I barely understood, which joined me to my wife. I said nothing.

"Say 'Splendid!'" the woman bellowed once again.

"Splendid," I murmured. I had to repeat the word a second time at the top of my lungs, so she could hear. I was reluctant to raise my voice to an elderly woman, but she did not appear to be offended. If anything the reply pleased her because her next command was:

"Go see the room!"

I rose from the bench and mounted the narrow staircase. There were five doors, two on either side of an equally narrow hallway, and one at the opposite end. Only one door was open. The room contained a twin bed under a sloping ceiling, a brown oval rug, a basin with an exposed pipe, and a chest of drawers. One door led to a closet, another to a toilet and a tub. The window was open; net curtains stirred in the breeze. I lifted them away and inspected the view: a small back yard, with a few fruit trees and an empty clothesline. I was satisfied.

When I returned to the foyer the woman picked up the leather change purse on the table, opened the clasp, fished about with her fingers, and produced a key on a thin wire hoop. She informed me that there was a kitchen at the back of the house, accessible through the parlor. I was welcome to use the stove as long as I left it as I found it. Sheets and towels were provided, but keeping them clean was my own

---

[13] **intoned**—spoke with a particular tone of voice.
[14] **bellowed**—yelled loudly.

responsibility. The rent was due Friday mornings on the ledge above the piano keys. "And no lady visitors!"

"I am a married man, Madam." It was the first time I had announced this fact to anyone.

But she had not heard. "No lady visitors!" she insisted. She introduced herself as Mrs. Croft.

My wife's name was Mala. The marriage had been arranged by my older brother and his wife. I regarded the proposition with neither objection nor enthusiasm. It was a duty expected of me, as it was expected of every man. She was the daughter of a schoolteacher in Beleghata. I was told that she could cook, knit, embroider, sketch landscapes, and recite poems by Tagore,[15] but these talents could not make up for the fact that she did not possess a fair complexion, and so a string of men had rejected her to her face. She was twenty-seven, an age when her parents had begun to fear that she would never marry, and so they were willing to ship their only child halfway across the world in order to save her from **spinsterhood.**[16]

For five nights we shared a bed. Each of those nights, after applying cold cream and braiding her hair, she turned from me and wept; she missed her parents. Although I would be leaving the country in a few days, custom dictated that she was now a part of my household, and for the next six weeks she was to live with my brother and his wife, cooking, cleaning, serving tea and sweets to guests. I did nothing to console her. I lay on my own side of the bed, reading my guidebook by flashlight. At times I thought of the tiny room on the other side of the wall which had belonged to my mother. Now the room was practically empty; the wooden **pallet**[17] on which she'd once slept was piled with trunks and old bedding. Nearly six years ago, before leaving for London, I had watched her die on that bed, had found her playing with her excrement in her final days. Before we cremated her I had cleaned each of her fingernails with a hairpin, and then, because my brother could not bear it, I had assumed the role of eldest son, and had touched the flame to her temple, to release her tormented soul to heaven.

The next morning I moved into Mrs. Croft's house. When I unlocked the door I saw that she was sitting on the piano bench, on the same side as the previous evening. She wore the same black skirt, the same starched white blouse, and had her hands folded together the same way in her lap. She looked so much the same that I wondered if she'd spent the whole night on the bench. I put my suitcase upstairs and then headed off to work. That evening when I came home from the university, she was still there.

---

[15] Tagore—Rabindranath Tagore (1862–1941) Indian poet and novelist, winner of the Nobel Prize in 1913.

[16] **spinsterhood**—the status of being an unmarried woman.

[17] **pallet**—platform.

"Sit down, boy!" She slapped the space beside her.

I perched on the bench. I had a bag of groceries with me—more milk, more cornflakes, and more bananas—for my inspection of the kitchen earlier in the day had revealed no spare pots or pans. There were only two saucepans in the refrigerator, both containing some orange broth, and a copper kettle on the stove.

"Good evening, Madam."

She asked me if I had checked the lock. I told her I had.

For a moment she was silent. Then suddenly she declared, with the equal measures of **disbelief**[18] and delight as the night before, "There's an American flag on the moon, boy!"

"Yes, Madam."

"A flag on the moon! Isn't that splendid?"

I nodded, dreading what I knew was coming. "Yes, Madam."

"Say 'Splendid!'"

This time I paused, looking to either side in case anyone was there to overhear me, though I knew perfectly well that the house was empty. I felt like an idiot. But it was a small enough thing to ask. "Splendid!" I cried out.

Within days it became our routine. In the mornings when I left for the library Mrs. Croft was either hidden away in her bedroom, on the other side of the staircase, or sitting on the bench, oblivious of my presence, listening to the news or classical music on the radio. But each evening when I returned the same thing happened: she slapped the bench, ordered me to sit down, declared that there was a flag on the moon, and declared that it was splendid. I said it was splendid, too, and then we sat in silence. As awkward as it was and as endless as it felt to me then, the nightly encounter lasted only about ten minutes; inevitably she would drift off to sleep, her head falling abruptly toward her chest, leaving me free to retire to my room. By then, of course, there was no flag standing on the moon. The astronauts, I read in the paper, had seen it fall before they flew back to Earth. But I did not have the heart to tell her.

Friday morning, when my first week's rent was due, I went to the piano in the parlor to place my money on the ledge. The piano keys were dull and discolored. When I pressed one, it made no sound at all. I had put eight dollar bills in an envelope and written Mrs. Croft's name on the front of it. I was not in the habit of leaving money unmarked and unattended. From where I stood I could see the profile of her tent-shaped skirt in the hall. It seemed unnecessary to make her get up and walk all the way to the piano. I never saw her walking about, and assumed, from the cane propped against the round table that she did so with difficulty. When I approached the bench she peered up at me and demanded:

"What is your business?"

"The rent, Madam."

---

[18] **disbelief**—the condition of not believing.

"On the ledge above the piano keys!"

"I have it here." I extended the envelope toward her, but her fingers, folded together in her lap, did not budge. I bowed slightly and lowered the envelope, so that it hovered just above her hands. After a moment she accepted it, and nodded her head.

That night when I came home, she did not slap the bench, but out of habit I sat beside her as usual. She asked me if I had checked the lock, but she mentioned nothing about the flag on the moon. Instead she said:

"It was very kind of you!"

"I beg your pardon, Madam?"

"Very kind of you!"

She was still holding the envelope in her hands.

On Sunday there was a knock on my door. An elderly woman introduced herself: she was Mrs. Croft's daughter, Helen. She walked into the room and looked at each of the walls as if for signs of change, glancing at the shirts that hung in the closet, the neckties draped over the doorknob, the box of cornflakes on the chest of drawers, the dirty bowl and spoon in the basin. She was short and thick-waisted, with cropped silver hair and bright pink lipstick. She wore a sleeveless summer dress, a necklace of white plastic beads, and spectacles on a chain that hung like a swing against her chest. The backs of her legs were mapped with dark-blue veins, and her upper arms sagged like the flesh of a roasted eggplant.

She told me she lived in Arlington, a town farther up Massachusetts Avenue. "I come once a week to bring Mother groceries. Has she sent you packing yet?"

"It is very well, Madam."

"Some of the boys run screaming. But I think she likes you. You're the first boarder she's ever referred to as a gentleman."

She looked at me, noticing my bare feet. (I still felt strange wearing shoes indoors, and always removed them before entering my room.) "Are you new to Boston?"

"New to America, Madam."

"From?" She raised her eyebrows.

"I am from Calcutta, India."

"Is that right? We had a Brazilian fellow, about a year ago. You'll find Cambridge a very international city."

I nodded, and began to wonder how long our conversation would last. But at that moment we heard Mrs. Croft's electrifying voice rising up the stairs.

"You are to come downstairs immediately!"

"What is it?" Helen cried back.

"Immediately!"

I put on my shoes. Helen sighed.

I followed Helen down the staircase. She seemed to be in no hurry, and complained at one point that she had a bad knee. "Have you been walking without your cane?" Helen called out. "You know you're not supposed to walk without that cane." She paused, resting her hand on the bannister, and looked back at me. "She slips sometimes."

For the first time Mrs. Croft seemed vulnerable. I pictured her on the floor in front of the bench, flat on her back, staring at the ceiling, her feet pointing in opposite directions. But when we reached the bottom of the staircase she was sitting there as usual, her hands folded together in her lap. Two grocery bags were at her feet. She did not slap the bench, or ask us to sit down. She glared.

"What is it, Mother?"

"It's improper!"

"What's improper?"

"It is improper for a lady and gentleman who are not married to one another to hold a private conversation without a **chaperone**!"[19]

Helen said she was sixty-eight years old, old enough to be my mother, but Mrs. Croft insisted that Helen and I speak to each other downstairs, in the parlor. She added that it was also improper for a lady of Helen's station to reveal her age, and to wear a dress so high above the ankle.

"For your information, Mother, it's 1969. What would you do if you actually left the house one day and saw a girl in a miniskirt?"

Mrs. Croft sniffed. "I'd have her arrested."

Helen shook her head and picked up one of the grocery bags. I picked up the other one, and followed her through the parlor and into the kitchen. The bags were filled with cans of soup, which Helen opened up one by one with a few cranks of a can opener. She tossed the old soup into the sink, rinsed the saucepans under the tap, filled them with soup from the newly opened cans, and put them back in the refrigerator. "A few years ago she could still open the cans herself," Helen said. "She hates that I do it for her now. But the piano killed her hands." She put on her spectacles, glanced at the cupboards, and spotted my tea bags. "Shall we have a cup?"

I filled the kettle on the stove. "I beg your pardon, Madam. The piano?"

"She used to give lessons. For forty years. It was how she raised us after my father died." Helen put her hands on her hips, staring at the open refrigerator. She reached into the back, pulled out a wrapped stick of butter, frowned, and tossed it into the garbage. "That ought to do it," she said, and put the unopened cans of soup in the cupboard. I sat at the table and watched as Helen washed the dirty dishes, tied up the garbage bag, and poured boiling water into two cups. She handed one to me without milk, and sat down at the table.

"Excuse me, Madam, but is it enough?"

Helen took a sip of her tea. Her lipstick left a smiling pink stain on the rim of the cup. "Is what enough?"

"The soup in the pans. Is it enough food for Mrs. Croft?"

"She won't eat anything else. She stopped eating solids after she turned

---

[19] **chaperone**—a person, usually an older woman, who supervises young unmarried women on social occasions.

one hundred. That was, let's see, three years ago."

I was mortified. I had assumed Mrs. Croft was in her eighties, perhaps as old as ninety. I had never known a person who had lived for over a century. That this person was a widow who lived alone mortified me further still. Widowhood had driven my own mother insane. My father, who worked as a clerk at the General Post Office of Calcutta, died of encephalitis when I was sixteen. My mother refused to adjust to life without him; instead she sank deeper into a world of darkness from which neither I, nor my brother, nor concerned relatives, nor psychiatric clinics on Rash Behari Avenue could save her. What pained me most was to see her so unguarded, to hear her burp after meals or expel gas in front of company without the slightest embarrassment. After my father's death my brother abandoned his schooling and began to work in the jute[20] mill he would eventually manage, in order to keep the household running. And so it was my job to sit by my mother's feet and study for my exams as she counted and recounted the bracelets on her arm as if they were the beads of an **abacus**.[21] We tried to keep an eye on her. Once she had wandered half naked to the tram depot before we were able to bring her inside again.

"I am happy to warm Mrs. Croft's soup in the evenings," I suggested. "It is no trouble."

Helen looked at her watch, stood up, and poured the rest of her tea into the sink. "I wouldn't if I were you. That's the sort of thing that would kill her altogether."

That evening, when Helen had gone and Mrs. Croft and I were alone again, I began to worry. Now that I knew how very old she was, I worried that something would happen to her in the middle of the night, or when I was out during the day. As vigorous as her voice was, and **imperious**[22] as she seemed, I knew that even a scratch or a cough could kill a person that old; each day she lived, I knew, was something of a miracle. Helen didn't seem concerned. She came and went, bringing soup for Mrs. Croft, one Sunday after the next.

In this manner the six weeks of that summer passed. I came home each evening, after my hours at the library, and spent a few minutes on the piano bench with Mrs. Croft. Some evenings I sat beside her long after she had drifted off to sleep, still in awe of how many years she had spent on this earth. At times I tried to picture the world she had been born into, in 1866— a world, I imagined, filled with women in long black skirts, and chaste conversations in the parlor. Now, when I looked at her hands with their swollen knuckles folded together in her lap, I imagined them

---

[20] jute—rough fiber from the bark of certain East Indian plants, used for making twine, rope, and fabrics.

[21] **abacus**—simple device used for calculating that is made of beads strung on wire.

[22] **imperious**—bullying, overbearing.

smooth and slim, striking the piano keys. At times I came downstairs before going to sleep, to make sure she was sitting upright on the bench, or was safe in her bedroom. On Fridays I put the rent in her hands. There was nothing I could do for her beyond these simple gestures. I was not her son, and, apart from those eight dollars, I owed her nothing.

At the end of August, Mala's passport and green card were ready. I received a telegram with her flight information; my brother's house in Calcutta had no telephone. Around that time I also received a letter from her, written only a few days after we had parted. There was no salutation; addressing me by name would have assumed an intimacy we had not yet discovered. It contained only a few lines. "I write in English in preparation for the journey. Here I am very much lonely. Is it very cold there. Is there snow. Yours, Mala."

I was not touched by her words. We had spent only a handful of days in each other's company. And yet we were bound together; for six weeks she had worn an iron bangle on her wrist, and applied vermillion powder to the part in her hair, to signify to the world that she was a bride. In those six weeks I regarded her arrival as I would the arrival of a coming month, or season—something inevitable, but meaningless at the time. So little did I know her that, while details of her face sometimes rose to my memory, I could not conjure[23] up the whole of it.

A few days after receiving the letter, as I was walking to work in the morning, I saw an Indian woman on Massachusetts Avenue, wearing a sari[24] with its free end nearly dragging on the footpath, and pushing a child in a stroller. An American woman with a small black dog on a leash was walking to one side of her. Suddenly the dog began barking. I watched as the Indian woman, startled, stopped in her path, at which point the dog leaped up and seized the end of the sari between its teeth. The American woman scolded[25] the dog, appeared to apologize, and walked quickly away, leaving the Indian woman to fix her sari, and quiet her crying child. She did not see me standing there, and eventually she continued on her way. Such a mishap, I realized that morning, would soon be my concern. It was my duty to take care of Mala, to welcome her and protect her. I would have to buy her her first pair of snow boots, her first winter coat. I would have to tell her which streets to avoid, which way the traffic came, tell her to wear her sari so that the free end did not drag on the footpath. A five-mile separation from her parents, I recalled with some irritation, had caused her to weep.

Unlike Mala, I was used to it all by then: used to cornflakes and milk, used to Helen's visits, used to sitting on the bench

---

[23] **conjure**—make to appear.

[24] sari—typical dress of Indian and Pakistani women, consisting of a long piece of cotton or silk wrapped around the body with one end falling to the feet and the other thrown over the shoulder.

[25] **scolded**—criticized for wrongdoing.

with Mrs. Croft. The only thing I was not used to was Mala. Nevertheless I did what I had to do. I went to the housing office at M.I.T. and found a furnished apartment a few blocks away, with a double bed and a private kitchen and bath, for forty dollars a week. One last Friday I handed Mrs. Croft eight dollar bills in an envelope, brought my suitcase downstairs, and informed her that I was moving. She put my key into her change purse. The last thing she asked me to do was hand her the cane propped against the table, so that she could walk to the door and lock it behind me. "Goodbye, then," she said, and retreated back into the house. I did not expect any display of emotion, but I was disappointed all the same. I was only a boarder, a man who paid her a bit of money and passed in and out of her home for six weeks. Compared with a century, it was no time at all.

At the airport I recognized Mala immediately. The free end of her sari did not drag on the floor, but was draped in a sign of bridal modesty over her head, just as it had draped my mother until the day my father died. Her thin brown arms were stacked with gold bracelets, a small red circle was painted on her forehead, and the edges of her feet were tinted with a decorative red dye. I did not embrace her, or kiss her, or take her hand. Instead I asked her, speaking Bengali for the first time in America, if she was hungry.

She hesitated, then nodded yes.

I told her I had prepared some egg curry at home. "What did they give you to eat on the plane?"

"I didn't eat."

"All the way from Calcutta?"

"The menu said oxtail soup."

"But surely there were other items."

"The thought of eating an ox's tail made me lose my appetite."

When we arrived home, Mala opened up one of her suitcases, and presented me with two pullover sweaters, both made with bright-blue wool, which she had knitted in the course of our separation, one with a V neck, the other covered with cables. I tried them on; both were tight under the arms. She had also brought me two new pairs of drawstring pajamas, a letter from my brother, and a packet of loose Darjeeling tea. I had no present for her apart from the egg curry. We sat at a bare table, staring at our plates. We ate with our hands, another thing I had not yet done in America.

"The house is nice," she said. "Also the egg curry." With her left hand she held the end of her sari to her chest, so it would not slip off her head.

"I don't know many recipes."

She nodded, peeling the skin off each of her potatoes before eating them. At one point the sari slipped to her shoulders. She readjusted it at once.

"There is no need to cover your head," I said. "I don't mind. It doesn't matter here."

She kept it covered anyway.

I waited to get used to her, to her presence at my side, at my table and in my bed, but a week later we were still strangers. I still was not used to coming home to an apartment that smelled of steamed rice, and finding that the basin in the bathroom was always wiped clean, our two toothbrushes lying side by side, a cake of Pears soap residing in the soap dish. I was not used to the fragrance of the coconut oil she rubbed every other night into her scalp, or the delicate sound her bracelets made as she moved about the apartment. In the mornings she was always awake before I was. The first morning when I came into the kitchen she had heated up the leftovers and set a plate with a spoonful of salt on its edge, assuming I would eat rice for breakfast, as most Bengali husbands did. I told her cereal would do, and the next morning when I came into the kitchen she had already poured the cornflakes into my bowl. One morning she walked with me to M.I.T., where I gave her a short tour of the campus. The next morning before I left for work she asked me for a few dollars. I parted with them reluctantly, but I knew that this, too, was now normal. When I came home from work there was a potato peeler in the kitchen drawer, and a tablecloth on the table, and chicken curry made with fresh garlic and ginger on the stove. After dinner I read the newspaper, while Mala sat at the kitchen table, working on a cardigan for herself with more of the blue wool, or writing letters home.

On Friday, I suggested going out. Mala set down her knitting and disappeared into the bathroom. When she emerged I regretted the suggestion; she had put on a silk sari and extra bracelets, and coiled her hair with a flattering side part on top of her head. She was prepared as if for a party, or at the very least for the cinema, but I had no such destination in mind. The evening was balmy. We walked several blocks down Massachusetts Avenue, looking into the windows of restaurants and shops. Then, without thinking, I led her down the quiet street where for so many nights I had walked alone.

"This is where I lived before you came," I said, stopping at Mrs. Croft's chain-link fence.

"In such a big house?"

"I had a small room upstairs. At the back."

"Who else lives there?"

"A very old woman."

"With her family?"

"Alone."

"But who takes care of her?"

I opened the gate. "For the most part she takes care of herself."

I wondered if Mrs. Croft would remember me; I wondered if she had a new boarder to sit with her each evening. When I pressed the bell I expected the same long wait as that day of our first meeting, when I did not have a key. But this time, the door was opened almost immediately, by Helen. Mrs. Croft was not sitting on the bench. The bench was gone.

"Hello there," Helen said, smiling with her bright pink lips at Mala. "Mother's in the parlor. Will you be visiting awhile?"

"As you wish, Madam."

"Then I think I'll run to the store, if you don't mind. She had a little accident. We can't leave her alone these days, not even for a minute."

I locked the door after Helen and walked into the parlor. Mrs. Croft was lying flat on her back, her head on a peach-colored cushion, a thin white quilt spread over her body. Her hands were folded together on her chest. When she saw me she pointed at the sofa, and told me to sit down. I took my place as directed, but Mala wandered over to the piano and sat on the bench, which was now positioned where it belonged.

"I broke my hip!" Mrs. Croft announced, as if no time had passed.

"Oh dear, Madam."

"I fell off the bench!"

"I am so sorry, Madam."

"It was the middle of the night! Do you know what I did, boy?"

I shook my head.

"I called the police!"

She stared up at the ceiling and grinned sedately, exposing a crowded row of long gray teeth. "What do you say to that, boy?"

As stunned as I was, I knew what I had to say. With no hesitation at all, I cried out, "Splendid!"

Mala laughed then. Her voice was full of kindness, her eyes bright with amusement. I had never heard her laugh before, and it was loud enough so that Mrs. Croft heard, too. She turned to Mala and glared.

"Who is she, boy?"

"She is my wife, Madam."

Mrs. Croft pressed her head at an angle against the cushion to get a better look. "Can you play the piano?"

"No, Madam," Mala replied.

"Then stand up!"

Mala rose to her feet, adjusting the end of her sari over her head and holding it to her chest, and, for the first time since her arrival, I felt sympathy. I remembered my first days in London, learning how to take the Tube to Russell Square, riding an escalator for the first time, unable to understand that when the man cried "piper" it meant "paper," unable to decipher, for a whole year, that the conductor said "Mind the gap" as the train pulled away from each station. Like me, Mala had traveled far from home, not knowing where she was going, or what she would find, for no reason other than to be my wife. As strange as it seemed, I knew in my heart that one day her death would affect me, and stranger still, that mine would affect her. I wanted somehow to explain this to Mrs. Croft, who was still **scrutinizing**[26] Mala from top to toe with what seemed to be placid disdain. I wondered if Mrs. Croft had ever seen a woman in a sari, with a dot painted on her forehead and bracelets stacked on her wrists. I wondered what she would object to. I wondered if she could see the red dye still vivid on Mala's feet, all but obscured by the bottom edge of

---

[26] **scrutinizing**—carefully or critically examining.

her sari. At last Mrs. Croft declared, with the equal measures of disbelief and delight I knew well:

"She is a perfect lady!"

Now it was I who laughed. I did so quietly, and Mrs. Croft did not hear me. But Mala had heard, and, for the first time, we looked at each other and smiled.

I like to think of that moment in Mrs. Croft's parlor as the moment when the distance between Mala and me began to lessen. Although we were not yet fully in love, I like to think of the months that followed as a honeymoon of sorts. Together we explored the city and met other Bengalis, some of whom are still friends today. We discovered that a man named Bill sold fresh fish on Prospect Street, and that a shop in Harvard Square called Cardullo's sold bay leaves and cloves. In the evenings we walked to the Charles River to watch sailboats drift across the water, or had ice-cream cones in Harvard Yard. We bought a camera with which to document our life together, and I took pictures of her posing in front of the Prudential Building, so that she could send them to her parents. At night we kissed, shy at first but quickly bold, and discovered pleasure and solace in each other's arms. I told her about my voyage on the S.S. Roma, and about Finsbury Park and the Y.M.C.A., and my evenings on the bench with Mrs. Croft. When I told her stories about my mother, she wept. It was Mala who **consoled**[27] me when, reading the *Globe* one evening, I came across Mrs. Croft's obituary. I had not thought of her

in several months—by then those six weeks of the summer were already a remote interlude in my past—but when I learned of her death I was stricken, so much so that when Mala looked up from her knitting she found me staring at the wall, unable to speak. Mrs. Croft's was the first death I mourned in America, for hers was the first life I had admired; she had left this world at last, ancient and alone, never to return.

As for me, I have not strayed much farther. Mala and I live in a town about twenty miles from Boston, on a tree-lined street much like Mrs. Croft's, in a house we own, with room for guests, and a garden that saves us from buying tomatoes in summer. We are American citizens now, so that we can collect Social Security when it is time. Though we visit Calcutta every few years, we have decided to grow old here. I work in a small college library. We have a son who attends Harvard University. Mala no longer drapes the end of her sari over her head, or weeps at night for her parents, but occasionally she weeps for our son. So we drive to Cambridge to visit him, or bring him home for a weekend, so that he can eat rice with us with his hands, and speak in Bengali, things we sometimes worry he will no longer do after we die.

Whenever we make that drive, I always take Massachusetts Avenue, in spite of the traffic. I barely recognize the buildings now, but each time I am there I return instantly to those six weeks as if they were

---

[27] **consoled**—comforted.

only the other day, and I slow down and point to Mrs. Croft's street, saying to my son, Here was my first home in America, where I lived with a woman who was a hundred and three. "Remember?" Mala says, and smiles, amazed, as I am, that there was ever a time that we were strangers. My son always expresses his astonishment, not at Mrs. Croft's age but at how little I paid in rent, a fact nearly as inconceivable to him as a flag on the moon was to a woman born in 1866. In my son's eyes I see the ambition that had first hurled me across the world. In a few years he will graduate and **pave**[28] his own way, alone and unprotected. But I remind myself that he has a father who is still living, a mother who is happy and strong. Whenever he is discouraged, I tell him that if I can survive on three continents, then there is no obstacle he cannot conquer. While the astronauts, heroes forever, spent mere hours on the moon, I have remained in this new world for nearly thirty years. I know that my achievement is quite ordinary. I am not the only man to seek his fortune far from home, and certainly I am not the first.

Still, there are times I am bewildered by each mile I have traveled, each meal I have eaten, each person I have known, each room in which I have slept. As ordinary as it all appears, there are times when it is beyond my imagination.

---

[28] **pave**—make or get ready for use.

QUESTIONS TO CONSIDER

1. Why has the narrator traveled away from India to England and America?

2. What does the narrator and Mala's visit to Mrs. Croft's indicate?

3. How would you compare the world as known to Mrs. Croft with the world as known to the narrator and his son? What is it that seems to create a home for people?

In the Middle of the Journey

V. S. NAIPAUL

V. S. Naipaul (see page 262) is Indian, but he was born on the Caribbean island of Trinidad in 1932. His family had immigrated there in the nineteenth century and are part of a sizable Indian population in the Caribbean. Besides his highly regarded fiction, Naipaul has also written a series of travel books, analyzing cultures around the world. Because of his heritage, India was an early and frequent topic, and Naipaul has written three books on India as well as a series of essays. All of his travel writing is reflective, examining the universal and the specific locality at the same time. The following essay, from the late 1960s, shows Naipaul re-examining his ideas about India.

Coming from a small island—Trinidad[1] is no bigger than Goa[2]—I had always been fascinated by size. To see the wide river, the high mountain, to take the twenty-four-hour train journey: these were some of the delights the outside world offered. But now after six months in India my fascination with the big is **tinged**[3] with **disquiet**.[4] For here is a vastness beyond imagination, a sky so wide and deep that sunsets cannot be taken in at a glance but have to be studied section by section, a landscape made monotonous by its size and frightening by its very simplicity and its special quality of exhaustion: poor choked crops in small crooked fields, undersized people, undernourished animals, crumbling villages and towns which, even while they develop, have an air of decay. Dawn comes, night falls; railway stations, undistinguishable one from the other, their name-boards cunningly concealed, are arrived at and departed from, abrupt and puzzling interludes of populousness and noise; and still the journey goes on, until the vastness, ceasing to have a meaning, becomes insupportable, and from this endless repetition of exhaustion and decay one wishes to escape.

To state this is to state the obvious. But in India the obvious is overwhelming, and

---

[1] Trinidad—island off the coast of Venezuela, which, with Tobago, was a former British colony.

[2] Goa—city on the southwest coast of India, which was founded by the Dutch.

[3] **tinged**—slightly affected or colored.

[4] **disquiet**—uneasiness or anxiety.

often during these past six months I have known moments of near-hysteria, when I have wished to forget India, when I have escaped to the first-class waiting room or sleeper not so much for privacy and comfort as for protection, to shut out the sight of the thin bodies **prostrate**[5] on railway platforms, the starved dogs licking the food-leaves clean, and to shut out the whine of the playfully assaulted dog. Such a moment I knew in Bombay,[6] on the day of my arrival, when I felt India only as an assault on the senses. Such a moment I knew five months later, at Jammu, where the simple, frightening geography of the country becomes plain—to the north the hills, rising in range after ascending range; to the south, beyond the temple spires, the plains whose vastness, already experienced, excited only unease.

Yet between these recurring moments there have been so many others, when fear and impatience have been replaced by enthusiasm and delight, when the town, explored beyond what one sees from the train, reveals that the air of exhaustion is only apparent, that in India, more than in any other country I have visited, things are happening. To hear the sounds of hammer on metal in a small Punjab town, to visit a chemical plant in Hyderabad where much of the equipment is Indian-designed and manufactured, is to realize that one is in the middle of an industrial revolution, in which, perhaps because of faulty publicity, one had never really seriously believed. To see the new housing colonies in towns all over India is to realize that, separate from

the talk of India's ancient culture (which invariably has me reaching for my *lathi*[7]), the Indian **aesthetic**[8] sense has revived and is now capable of creating, out of materials which are international, something which is essentially Indian. (India's ancient culture, defiantly paraded, has made the Ashoka Hotel one of New Delhi's most ridiculous buildings, outmatched in absurdity only by the Pakistan High Commission, which defiantly asserts the Faith.)

I have been to unpublicized villages, semi-developed and undeveloped. And where before I would have sensed only despair, now I feel that the despair lies more with the observer than the people. I have learned to see beyond the dirt and the recumbent figures on string beds, and to look for the signs of improvement and hope, however **faint:**[9] the brick-topped road, covered though it might be with filth; the rice planted in rows and not scattered broadcast; the degree of ease with which the villager faces the official or the visitor. For such small things I have learned to look: over the months my eye has been adjusted.

Yet always the obvious is overwhelming. One is a traveler and as soon as the dread of a particular district has been lessened by familiarity, it is time to

---

[5] **prostrate**—lying submissively.

[6] Bombay—port city in west India. It is the principal city of business in the country.

[7] *lathi*—a staff or stick bound with iron rings.

[8] **aesthetic**—related to the appreciation of beauty.

[9] **faint**—weak, difficult to perceive.

move on again, through vast tracts which will never become familiar, which will sadden; and the urge to escape will return.

Yet in so many ways the size of the country is only a physical fact. For, perhaps because of the very size, Indians appear to feel the need to categorize minutely, **delimit**,[10] to reduce to manageable proportions.

"Where do you come from?" It is the Indian question, and to people who think in terms of the village, the district, the province, the community, the caste, my answer that I am a Trinidadian is only puzzling.

"But you look Indian."

"Well, I am Indian. But we have been living for several generations in Trinidad."

"But you look Indian."

Three or four times a day the **dialogue**[11] occurs, and now I often abandon explanation. "I am a Mexican, really."

"Ah." Great satisfaction. Pause. "What do you do?"

"I write."

"Journalism or books?"

"Books."

"Westerns, crime, romance? How many books do you write a year? How much do you make?"

So now I invent: "I am a teacher."

"What are your qualifications?"

"I am a BA."[12]

"Only a BA? What do you teach?"

"Chemistry. And a little history."

"How interesting!" said the man on the Pathankot-Srinagar bus. "I am a teacher of chemistry too."

He was sitting across the aisle from me, and several hours remained of our journey.

In this vast land of India it is necessary to explain yourself, to define your function and status in the universe. It is very difficult.

If I thought in terms of race or community, this experience of India would surely have dispelled it. An Indian, I have never before been in streets where everyone is Indian, where I blend unremarkably into the crowd. This has been curiously deflating, for all my life I have expected some recognition of my difference; and it is only in India that I have recognized how necessary this **stimulus**[13] is to me, how conditioned I have been by the multiracial society of Trinidad and then by my life as an outsider in England. To be a member of a minority community has always seemed to me attractive. To be one of four hundred and thirty-nine million Indians is terrifying.

A colonial, in the double sense of one who had grown up in a Crown colony

In this vast land of India it is necessary to explain yourself, to define your function and status in the universe. It is very difficult.

[10] **delimit**—to determine limits or boundaries.

[11] **dialogue**—conversation between two or more persons or groups.

[12] BA— bachelor of arts, the lowest form of a university diploma.

[13] **stimulus**—something which causes activity.

and one who had been cut off from the metropolis, be it either England or India, I came to India expecting to find metropolitan attitudes. I had imagined that in some ways the largeness of the land would be reflected in the attitudes of the people. I have found, as I have said, the psychology of the cell and the hive. And I have been surprised by similarities. In India, as in tiny Trinidad, I have found the feeling that the metropolis is elsewhere, in Europe or America. Where I had expected largeness, rootedness and confidence, I have found all the colonial attitudes of self-distrust.

"I am craze phor phoreign," the wife of a too-successful contractor said. And this craze extended from foreign food to German sanitary fittings to a possible European wife for her son, who sought to establish his claim further by announcing at the lunch table, "Oh, by the way, did I tell you we spend three thousand rupees a month?"

"You are a tourist, you don't know," the chemistry teacher on the Srinagar bus said. "But this is a terrible country. Give me a chance and I leave it tomorrow."

For among a certain class of Indians, usually more prosperous than their fellows, there is a passionate urge to explain to the visitor that they must not be considered part of poor, dirty India, that their values and standards are higher, and they live perpetually outraged by the country which gives them their livelihood. For them the second-rate foreign product, either people or manufactures, is preferable to the Indian. They suggest that for them, as

much as for the European "technician," India is only a country to be temporarily exploited. How strange to find, in free India, this attitude of the conqueror, this attitude of **plundering**[14]—a frenzied attitude, as though the opportunity might at any moment be withdrawn—in those very people to whom the developing society has given so many opportunities.

This attitude of plundering is that of the immigrant colonial society. It has bred, as in Trinidad, the pathetic **philistinism**[15] of the renonçant (an excellent French word that describes the native who renounces his own culture and strives towards the French). And in India this philistinism, a blending of the vulgarity of East and West—those sad dance floors, those sad "western" **cabarets,**[16] those transistor radios tuned to Radio Ceylon, those Don Juans with letter jackets or check tweed jackets—is peculiarly frightening. A certain glamour attaches to this philistinism, as glamour attaches to those Indians who, after two or three years in a foreign country, proclaim that they are neither of the East nor of the West.

The observer, it must be confessed, seldom sees the difficulty. The contractor's wife, so anxious to demonstrate her Westernness, regularly consulted her astrologer and made daily trips to the temple to ensure the continuance of her

---

[14] **plundering**—robbing or stealing from the conquered.

[15] **philistinism**—hostility or disbelief in culture.

[16] **cabarets**—nightclubs or restaurants that feature entertainment while guests eat or drink at tables.

good fortune. The schoolteacher, who complained with feeling about the indiscipline and crudity of Indians, proceeded, as soon as we got to the bus station at Srinagar, to change his clothes in public.

The Trinidadian, whatever his race, is a genuine colonial. The Indian, whatever his claim, is rooted in India. But while the Trinidadian, a colonial, strives towards the metropolitan, the Indian of whom I have been speaking, metropolitan by virtue of the uniqueness of his country, its achievements in the past and its **manifold**[17] achievements in the last decade or so, is striving towards the colonial.

Where one had expected pride, then, one finds the spirit of plunder. Where one had expected the metropolitan one finds the colonial. Where one had expected largeness one finds narrowness. Goa, scarcely liberated, is the subject of an unseemly inter-State squabble. Fifteen years after Independence the politician as national leader appears to have been replaced by the politician as village headman (a type I had thought peculiar to the colonial Indian community of Trinidad, for whom politics was a game where little more than PWD[18] contracts was at stake).

To the village headman India is only a multiplicity of villages. So that the vision of India as a great country appears to be something imposed from without and the vastness of the country turns out to be oddly fraudulent.

Yet there remains a concept of India— as what? Something more than the urban middle class, the politicians, the industrialists, the separate villages. Neither this nor that, we are so often told, is the "real" India. And how well one begins to understand why this word is used! Perhaps India is only a word, a mystical idea that embraces all those vast plains and rivers through which the train moves, all those anonymous figures asleep on railway platforms and the footpaths of Bombay, all those poor fields and stunted animals, all this exhausted plundered land. Perhaps it is this, this vastness which no one can ever get to know: India as an ache, for which one has a great tenderness, but from which at length one always wishes to separate oneself.

---

[17] **manifold**—many and various.

[18] PWD—abbreviation for "Public Works Department."

QUESTIONS TO CONSIDER

1. Why is India "overwhelming" to Naipaul?

2. How would you characterize Naipaul's attitude towards the Indians he presents in the essay? Do you think he is fair to them?

3. How does Naipaul view India: as a single entity or a series of disparate parts? What, according to Naipaul, in the end unites the country most?

Literary Atlas

Assia Djebar/Algeria

Leopold Senghar/Senegal

Elephants on an African plain ▶

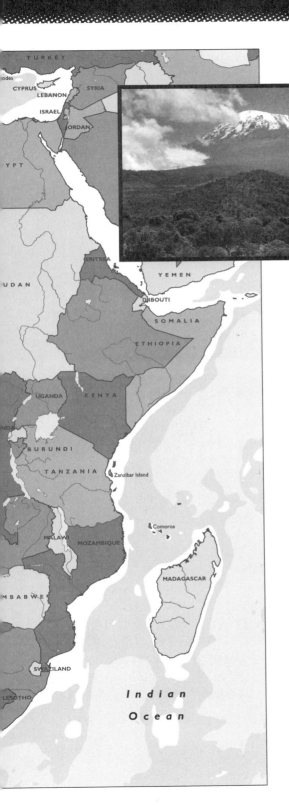

◄ Africa's highest peak, Mt. Kilimanjaro

Chinua Achebe/Nigeria

Nadine Gordimer/South Africa

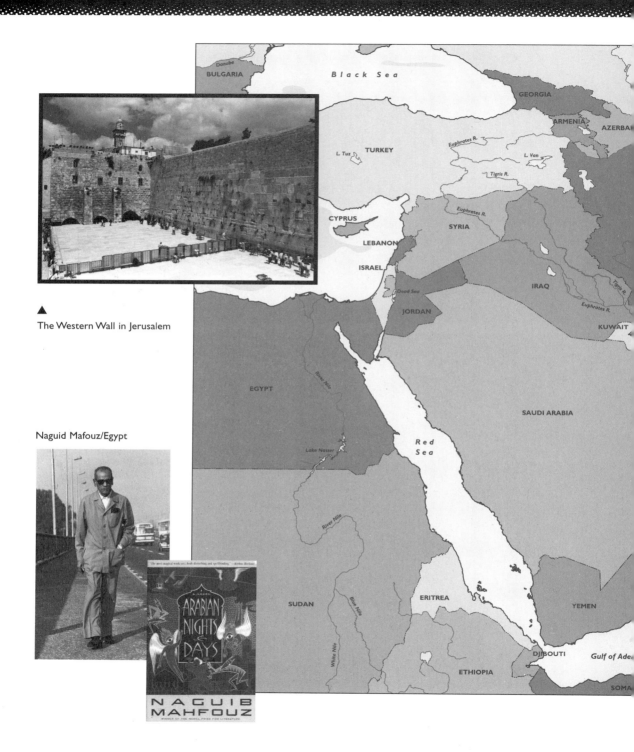

The Western Wall in Jerusalem

Naguid Mafouz/Egypt

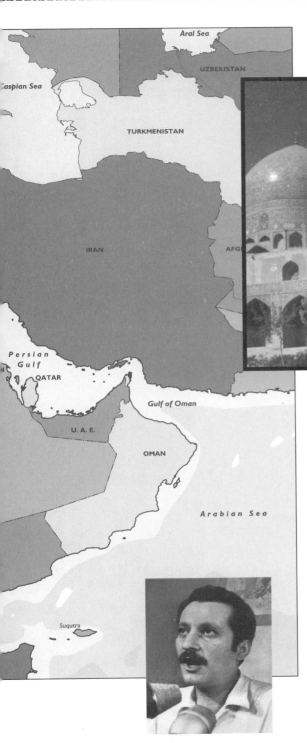

▲
The Masjid-i-Shah mosque in Isfahan

Mahmoud Darwish/Palestine

Ghassan Kanafani/Palestine

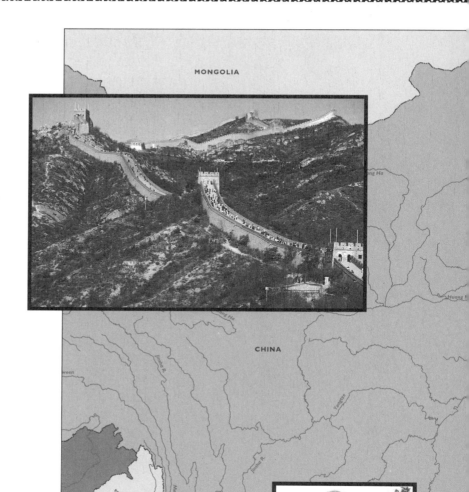

The Great Wall of China ▶

Bei Dao/China

Feng Jicai/China

▲
The Great Buddha of Kamakura

NORTH KOREA

Sea
of
Japan

Huang Ho

SOUTH
KOREA

Yellow
Sea

Honshu

JAPAN

Yangtze

Shikoku

Kyushu

East
China
Sea

Formosa Str.

Pacific
Ocean

Yasunari Kawabata/Japan

KENZABURO OE

JAPAN,
THE   The Nobel Prize Speech and Other Lectures
AMBIGUOUS,
AND
MYSELF

Kenzaburo Oe/Japan

Yukio Mishima/Japan

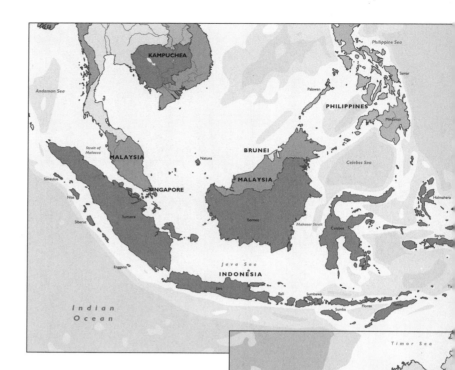

Pramaedya Ananta Toer/Indonesia

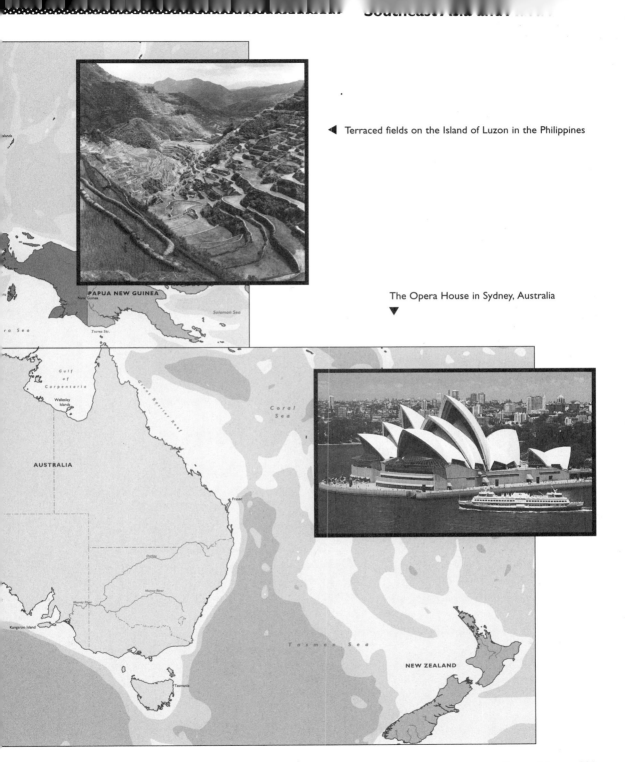

◀ Terraced fields on the Island of Luzon in the Philippines

The Opera House in Sydney, Australia
▼

A wilderness lake in Alberta, Canada.

Margaret Atwood/Canada

A beach on the island of Trinidad ▶

Jamaica Kincaid/Antigua

Aimé Cesaire/Martinique

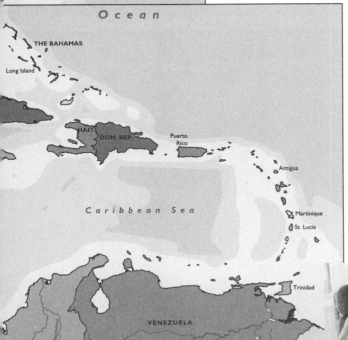

Derek Walcott/St. Lucia

Octavio Paz/ Mexico

▲
A Mayan temple at Palenque, Mexico

Isabel Allende/Chile

Pablo Neruda/Chile

Gabriel García Márquez/Colombia

Clarice Lispector/Brazil

Jorge Luis Borges/Argentina

Wislawa Szymborska/Poland

SEAMUS
HEANEY
SELECTED POEMS
1966–1987

Seamus Heaney/Ireland

▲
The Eiffel Tower in Paris

Italo Calvino/Italy

Danilo Kiš/Yugoslavia

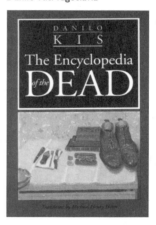

Primo Levi/Italy

The Taj Mahal at Agra, India
▼

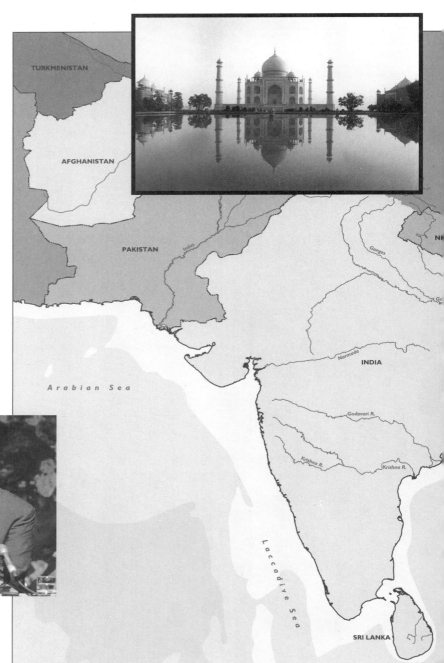

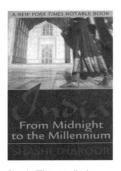

Shashi Tharoor/India

Salman Rushdie/India

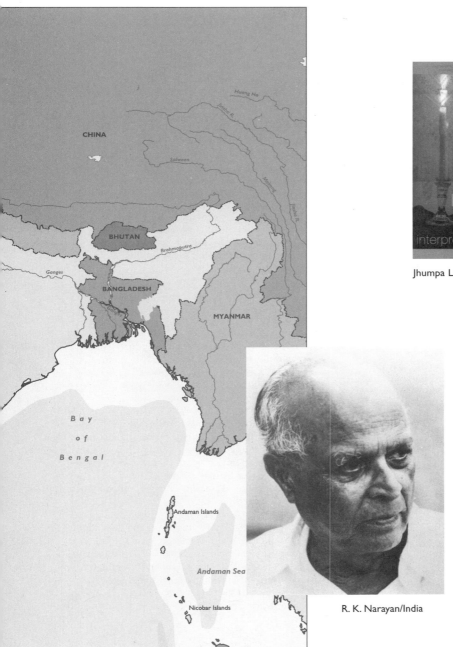

CHINA

BHUTAN

Huang Ho

Yangtze R.

Salween

Mekong

Indus R.

Brahmaputra

Ganges

BANGLADESH

MYANMAR

*Bay
of
Bengal*

Andaman Islands

Andaman Sea

Nicobar Islands

Jhumpa Lahiri/India

R. K. Narayan/India

Texts

2 "The Ultimate Safari" from *Jump and Other Stories* by Nadine Gordimer. Copyright © 1991 by Felix Licensing, B. V. Reprinted by permission of Farrar, Straus and Giroux, LLC. **11** "The Prisoner Who Wore Glasses" from *Tales of Tenderness and Power* by Bessie Head. Published by Heinemann International in the African Writers Series. Copyright © 1989 the Estate of Bessie Head. Reprinted by permission. **17, 19** "The Snow Flakes Sail Gently Down" and "You Laughed and Laughed and Laughed," from *The Fisherman's Invocation*, by Gabriel Okara. Copyright © 1978 by Gabriel Okara. **21** "The Voter" by Chinua Achebe. Copyright © Chinua Achebe. Reprinted by permission of the author. **27** "Your Logic Frightens Me, Mandela" from *Mandela's Earth and Other Poems* by Wole Soyinka. Copyright 1988 by Wole Soyinka. Reprinted by permission of Random House, Inc. **31, 32, 33** "Prayer to the Masks," "Letter to a Poet," and "Black Woman" from *The Collected Poetry of Léopold Senghor* by Léopold Senghor, translated by Melvin Dixon (Charlottesville: Virginia, 1991). Reprinted by permission of the University Press of Virginia. **35, 37** "Song of War" and "The Sea Eats the Land at Home" from *Okyeame* by Kofi Awoonor (Accra, 1961). Reprinted by permission of the author. **38** "At the Gates" by Kofi Awooner, from *Until the Morning After: Collected Poems 1963-1985*. Reprinted by permission of the author. **40** "Taken" by Steve Chimombo. First published in *WASI*. © 1996 by Steve Chimombo. Reprinted by permission of Steve Chimombo. **49** "On African Writing" from *Of Chameleons and Gods* by Jack Mapanje. Reprinted by permission of Heinemann Publishers, Oxford. **51** "There Is No Exile" from *Women of Algiers in Their Apartment* by Assia Djebar, translated by Marjolin de Jager. (Charlottesville: Virginia, 1992). Reprinted by permission of the University Press of Virginia. **61** Chapter 2 from *The Dark Child* by Camara Laye, translated by James Kirkup, Ernest Jones, and Elaine Gottlieb. Copyright © 1954, renewed 1982 by Camara Laye. Reprinted by permission of Hill and Wang, a division of Farrar, Straus and Giroux, LLC. **70** "The Conjuror Made Off with the Dish" by Naguib Mafouz translated from the Arabic by Denys Johnson-Davies. First appeared in the volume, *Egyptian Short Stories*, (Three Continents Press, 1978. Reprinted by permission of the translator. **76, 77** "Of Three or Four in a Room" and "Jerusalem" by Yehuda Amichai, translated by Stephen Mitchell, from *The Selected Poetry of Yehuda Amichai*. Copyright © 1996 Regents of the University of California. Reprinted by permission of the translator and publisher. **78** "An Arab Shepherd is Searching for His Goat on Mount Zion"by Yehuda Amichai, translated by Chana Bloch, from *The Selected Poetry of Yehuda Amichai*. Copyright © 1996 Regents of the University of California. Reprinted by permission of the translator and publisher. **79, 82** "Identity Card" and "On Wishes" from *The Music of Human Flesh* by Mahmond Darwish, translated from the Arabic by Denys Johnson-Davies (Three Continents Press, 1980). Reprinted by permission of the translator. **83, 84** "I Conquer the World With Words," "Equation," "Language," and "Fragments from *Notes on the Book of Defeat*" by Nizar Qabbani is republished with permission of Columbia University Press from *Modern Arabic Poetry*. © Copyright 1987; permission conveyed through Copyright Clearance Center, Inc. **86** "The Butcher" from *The Mullah with No Legs and Other Stories* by Ari Siletz. Reprinted by permission of the author. **94** "The Slave Fort" by Ghassan Kanafani, translated by S. Al-Bazzazz. **98** "From Behind the Veil" by Du' l Nun Ayyoub from *UR Magazine*, Iraqi Center, London, England. **103** "At the Time of the Jasmine" from *Distant View of a Minaret and Other Stories* by Alifia Rifaat, translated by Denys Johnson-Davies (London: Quartet Books Ltd., 1983). Reprinted by permission of the publisher. **112** "The Beginning" from *A Portrait of Egypt: A Journey Through the World of Militant Islam*, by Mary Anne Weaver. Copyright © 1999 by Mary Anne Weaver. Reprinted by permission of Farrar, Straus and Giroux, LLC. **134** "The Pearl" by Yukio Mishima, translated by Geoffrey W. Sargent, from *Death in Midsummer*, copyright © 1966 by New Directions Publishing Corp. Reprinted by permission of New Directions Publishing Corp. **145, 146** "One Step" and "Language" by Bei Dao, from *The August Sleepwalker*, copyright © 1988 by Bei Dao. Reprinted by permission of New Directions Publishing Corp. **147** "A Perpetual Stranger" by Bei Dao, translated by James A. Wilson, from *The August Sleepwalker*, copyright © 1988 by Bei Dao. Reprinted by permission of New Directions Publishing Corp. **148** "The Mao Button" from *Chrysanthemums and Other Stories* by Feng Jicai, English translation copyright © 1985 by Susan Wilf Chen, reprinted by permission of Harcourt, Inc. **157** "The Explosion in the Parlor" by Bai Xiao-Yi. English translation by Ding Zuxin. Reprinted by permission of the author and translator. **159** "The Grasshopper and the Bell Cricket" from *Palm of The Hand Stories*, by Yasunari Kawabata, translated by Lane Dunlop and J. Martin Holman. Translation copyright © 1988 by Lane Dunlop and J. Martin Holman. Reprinted by permission of North Point Press, a division of Farrar, Straus and Giroux, LLC. **163** "The Pan, The Pot, the Burning Fire I Have in Front of Me," by Ishigaki Rin, translated from the Japanese by Hiroaki Sato. Reprinted by permission of Hiroaki Sato. **165** "When My Beauty Was at Its Best" by Ibaragi Noriko, translated by James Kirkup. **167, 168, 169** "Missing You," "Bits of Reminiscence," "Gifts," and "Fairy Tales" by Shu Ting from *A Splintered Mirror: Chinese Poetry From the Democracy Movement*, translated by Donald Finkel. Translation copyright © 1991 by Donald Finkel. Reprinted by permission of North Point Press a division of Farrar, Straus and Giroux, LLC. **171, 172, 173** "Flower-Patterned Snake," "Beside a Chrysanthemum," and "Untitled" by So Chung-Ju from *Winter Sky*, trans. David R. McCann, in *Quarterly Review of Literature, Poetry Series III*, vol. XXII. © 1981 Quarterly Review of Literature. Reprinted by permission of Quarterly Review of Literature. **174** "Speaking on Japanese Culture Before a Scandinavian Audience" from *Japan, the Ambiguous, and Myself: The Nobel Prize Speech and Other Lectures* by Kenzaburo Oe. Published by Kodansha International Ltd. Copyright © 1992 by Kenzaburo Oe. Reprinted by permission. All rights reserved. **186** "Scent of Apples" by Bienvenido Santos. Copyright © 1948 The Manila Chronical, *This Week Magazine*. Permission to publish granted by The Estate of Bienvenido N. Santos, Tomas N. Santos, Personal Representative. **193** "A Gentleman's Agreement" by Elizabeth Jolley from *Five Acre Virgin and Other Stories* (Penguin Books 1976). Reprinted by permission of Jenny Darling & Associates. **199** "Reflections of Spring" ("Hoi Quang Cua Mua Xuan") by Duong Thu Huong. Originally published in the collection *Doi Thoai Sau Buc Tuong* (Hanoi: Nha Xuat Ban Tac Pham Moi, 1987). **206** "The Making of a New Zealander" by Frank Sargeson from *The Stories of Frank Sargeson* (New Zealand: Longman Paul, 1982). Reprinted by permission of Pearson Education New Zealand Limited. **211** "At the River" by Pat Grace from *Wairiki* (New Zealand: Longman Paul, 1975). Reprinted by permission of Pearson Education New Zealand Limited. **215** "Municipal Gum" by Oodgeroo, of the tribe Noonuccal, from *My People, 3e*, The Jacaranda Press, 1990. Reproduced by permission of John Wiley & Sons Australia. **216** "Spiritual Song of the Aborigine" from *Inside Black Australia* by Hyllus Maris, edited by Kevin Gilbert. Published by Penguin Books Australia Ltd. Reprinted by permission of the publisher. **217** Judith Wright: "Bora Ring" from *A Human Pattern: Selected Poems* (Sydney: ETT Imprint, 1996). Reprinted by permission of the publisher. **218** "The Birth" from *A Heap of Ashes* by Pramoedya Ananta Toer, edited and translated from Indonesian by Harry Aveling. Copyright © Harry Aveling 1975. Reprinted by permission of Harry Aveling. **232** "Ah Bah's Money" by Catherine Lim from *Or Else, The Lightning God & Other Stories*. **236** "Cambodia: Back to Sierra Leone?" from *The Ends of the Earth: A Journey at the Dawn of the 21st Century* by Robert D. Kaplan. Copyright © 1996 Robert D. Kaplan. Reprinted by permission of Random House, Inc. **262** "His Chosen Calling" by V.S. Naipaul from *Miguel Street*. Reprinted by permission of the publisher, Penguin Putnam USA. **268, 271** "A Sea-Chantey" and "A City's Death by Fire" from *Collected Poems 1948-1984* by Derek Walcott. Copyright © 1986 by Derek Walcott. Reprinted by permission of Farrar, Straus & Giroux, LLC. **273, 274, 275** "To Know Ourselves," "Merciless Great Blood" and "It Is Myself, Terror, It Is Myself" from *The Collected Poetry: Aime Cesaire*, trans./ed. by Clayton Eshleman and Annette Smith. Copyright © 1983 by The Regents of the University of California. Reprinted by permission of the publisher. **277** "Mother the Great Stones Got to Move" by Lorna Goodison from *To Us, All Flowers Are Roses*. Copyright 1995 by Lorna Goodison. Used with permission of the Poet and the University of Illinois Press. **280** "A Class of New Canadians" from *A North American Education* by Clark Blaise. Copyright © 1973 by Clark Blaise. Reprinted by permission of the author. **288, 289** "True Stories" and "Notes towards a poem that can never be written" from *Selected Poems II 1976-1986* by Margaret Atwood. Copyright © 1987 by Margaret Atwood. Permission to reprint in Canada by Oxford University Press Canada. Permission to reprint in United States by Houghton Mifflin Company. Previously published in *True Stories* (1981). **292** "Dreams of the Animals" from *Procedures for Underground, Selected Poems 1865-1975*. Copyright © 1976 by Margaret Atwood. Reprinted by permission of Oxford University Press Canada and Houghton Mifflin Company. All rights reserved. **295** "Mammie's Form at the Post Office," from *Something Unusual*, by E. A. Markham (Ambit Books, 1986). Reprinted by permission. **299** "The Story" from *Handwriting* by Michael Ondaatje. Copyright © 1998 by Michael Ondaatje. Reprinted by permission of Alfred A. Knopf, a Division of Random House, Inc. **304** "Sweet Like a Crow" from *The Cinnamon Peeler* by Michael Ondaatje. Copyright © 1989 by Michael Ondaatje. Reprinted by permission of Alfred A. Knopf, a Division of Random House, Inc. **306** "Landscapes" from *Legacies: Selected Poems* by Herberto Padillo, translated by Alastair Reid and Andrew Hurley. Translation copyright © 1982 by Alastair Reid and Andrew Hurley. Reprinted by permission of Farrar, Straus & Giroux, LLC. **307, 308** "Man on the Edge" and "A Fountain, a House of Stone" from *A Fountain, A House of Stone: Poems* by Herberto Padillo, translated by Alastair Reid and Alexander Coleman. Translation copyright © 1991 by Alastair Reid and Alexander Coleman. Reprinted by

O'Brien. Copyright © 1957, 1958 by Alfred A. Knopf, Inc. Reprinted by permission of Alfred A. Knopf, a division of Random House Inc. **433** "Black Postcards" by Tomas Tranströmer translated by Joanna Bankier, from Robert Haas, ed., Tomas Tranströmer, *Selected Poems 1954–1986* (Hopewell, New Jersey: Ecco Press, 1987). Reprinted by permission of the translator **434, 436** "Alone" and "To Friends Behind A Frontier" by Tomas Transtömer from *New Selected Poems* translated by Robin Fulton (Bloodaxe Books 1997). Reprinted by permission. **436** "Elegy" by Tomas Transtömer, translated by Robert Bly. Reprinted from *Friends, You Drank Some Darkness: Three Swedish Poets, Martinson, Ekelof, and Transtömer*, chosen and translated by Robert Bly (Beacon Press: Boston, 1975). Copyright © 1975 Robert Bly. Reprinted by permission of the translator. **438** "The Majesty of the Law" from *Collected Stories* by Frank O'Connor. Copyright © 1952 by Frank O'Connor. Reprinted by permission of Alfred A. Knopf, a Division of Random House, Inc., and The Joan Davis Agency. **446, 449, 450** "The Eel," "Little Testament," and "The Prisoner's Dream" from *The Storm and Other Things* by Eugenio Montale, translated by William Arrowsmith. Copyright © Arnoldo Mondodori Editore, Milano. Reprinted by permission. **447** "The Dead" by Eugenio Montale from *Cuttlefish Bones (1920-1927)*, translated with preface and commentary, by William Arrowsmith. Copyright © Arnoldo Mondodori Editore, Milano. Reprinted by permission. **453, 454** "Waiting" and "People" from *Yevtushenko: Selected Poems* translated by Robin Milner-Gulland and Peter Levi, S. J. Translation copyright © Robin Milner-Gulland and Peter Levi, 1962. Reprinted by pemission of Penguin Books, Ltd. **456** "The Encyclopedia of the Dead" from *The Encyclopedia of the Dead: A Whole Life* by Danilo Kiss, translated by Michael Henry Heim. Translation copyright © 1989 by Farrar, Straus & Giroux, Inc. Reprinted by permission of Farrar, Straus & Giroux, Inc. **474, 477, 480** "Whatever You Say, Say Nothing," "'Poet's Chair,'" and "The Nobel Lecture: Crediting Poetry" from *Open Ground: Selected Poems 1966-1996* by Seamus Heaney. Copyright © 1998 by Seamus Heaney. Reprinted by permission of Farrar, Straus and Giroux LLC and Faber and Faber. **482, 483, 485, 486** "Before I Could Call Myself Ángel Gonzalez," "Yesterday," "The Future," and "Diatribe Against the Dead," from *Astonishing World: The Selected Poems of Ángel Gonzalez*, translated from the Spanish by Steven Ford Brown and Gutierrez Revuelta (Milkweed Editions, 1993). Copyright © 1993 by Steven Ford Brown and Gutierrez Revuelta. Reprinted with permission from Milkweed Editions, www.milkweed.org. **488, 489** "Some People Like Poetry" and "A Contribution to Statistics" from *Poems New and Collected 1957-1977* by Wislawa Szymborska, English translation by Stanislaw Baranczak and Clare Cavanagh. Copyright © 1998 by Harcourt, Inc., reprinted by permission of the publisher. **492, 493, 494** "Ars Poetica?," "Return to Kraków in 1880," and "Account" from *The Collected Poems 1931-1987* by Czeslaw Milosz and translated by Robert Hass. Copyright © 1988 by Czeslaw Milosz Royalties, Inc. Reprinted by permission of Harper Collins Publishers, Inc. **496** "L'viv / Lvov / Lwow" from *Between East and West: Across the Borderlands of Europe* by Anne Applebaum (New York: Random House, 1994). Copyright © 1994 Anne Applebaum. Reprinted by permission of Georges Borchardt, Inc., for the author. **514** "A Myth and an Idea" from *India: From Midnight to the Millennium* by Shashi Tharoor. Copyright © 1997 by Shashi Tharoor. Reprinted by permission of Arcade Publishing Inc., New York. **527** "Fellow-Feeling" by R. K. Narayan from *Malgudi Days*. Reprinted by permission of Sheil Land Associates Ltd. **533** "A Devoted Son" from *Games at Twilight and Other Stories* by Anita Desai. Copyright © 1978 by Anita Desai. Reprinted by permission of Harper Collins Publishers, Inc. and the author c/o Rogers, Coleridge & White Ltd., 20 Powis Mews, London W11 1JN. **542** "Facing the Light" by Talat Abbasi. Copyright © 1989 by Talat Abbasi. First published in *Sudden Fiction International*, 1989. Reprinted by permission of the author. **546** "30th January 1982: A Story" by Jayanta Mahapatra from *Indian Literature Journal*. Reprinted by permission of the author and the Sahitya Akademi, New Delhi. **547, 548** "Taste for Tomorrow" and "Sanskrit" by Jayanta Mahapatra from *Selected Poems* (India: Oxford University Press, 1987). Reprinted by permission of Oxford University Press, New Delhi, India. **550, 551, 552, 553** "Three Quatrains," "Elegy," "Prison Meeting," and "Be Near Me" from *Selected Poems of Faiz Ahmed Faiz*, by Faiz Ahmed Faiz. Copyright © 1988 by Princeton University Press. Reprinted by permission of the publisher. **555** "Good Advice Is Rarer Than Rubies" from *East, West Stories* by Salman Rushdie. Copyright © 1994 by Salman Rushdie. Reprinted by permission of Pantheon Books, a division of Random House, Inc. **561** "The Third and Final Continent" from *Interpreter of Maladies* by Jhumpa Lahiri. Copyright © 1999 by Jhumpa Lahiri. Reprinted by permission of Houghton Mifflin Company. All rights reserved. **577** "In the Middle of the Journey" from *The Overcrowded Barracoon* by V.S. Naipaul. Copyright © 1972 by V.S. Naipaul. Reprinted by permission of Alfred A. Knopf, a division of Random House, Inc.

Illustrations

Position of illustration on a page is indicated by these abbreviations: (T)top, (C)center, (B)bottom, (L)left, (R)right.

Index of Authors and Titles